BRITAIN AND THE EUROPEAN COMMUNITY
1955-1963

BRITAIN AND THE EUROPEAN COMMUNITY

1955–1963

BY

MIRIAM CAMPS

PRINCETON, NEW JERSEY
PRINCETON UNIVERSITY PRESS
1964

Published in the United States and Canada
by Princeton University Press, Princeton, New Jersey
Copyright © 1964 by Princeton University Press
London: Oxford University Press
L.C. Card No. 63-23397

Printed in the United States of America

PREFACE

In the last fifteen years European unity has changed from being a distant and imprecise goal meaning many things to many people, commanding widespread but diffuse and disorganized support, to being a dominant issue in the political life of all the countries of Western Europe, including the United Kingdom.

There are deep disagreements about who should belong to a European union, how a European union should be organized, and what policies a European union should pursue, but no one today dismisses a European union as a fanciful or irrelevant goal. Moreover, most people accept the fact that the formation of the European Economic Community was a long step towards the goal of European union, although again views differ on what the next steps should be and who should take them.

This book is about the British search for an accommodation with the European Economic Community. When I began it I thought the search would now be over and the British would have joined the Community. The search continues, but this book necessarily ends on 29 January 1963, with the breakdown of the British negotiations for accession to the Community. For the most part the book is an account of negotiations between governments and the development of official views, although I have attempted to give as well some sense of public attitudes. Democratic governments do not operate in a vacuum, and press and industry played an important part in creating the climate of opinion in the United Kingdom in which it became practical politics to contemplate a radical change in British policy towards Europe. The subject is one which would repay far more study than I have been able to give it. Although I have concentrated on the negotiations in which the British were directly involved, I have also tried to give some account of the negotiations among the Six on the Treaty of Rome, of the development of the Community, and of the discussions among the Six on political union, both to explain what lay behind many of the differences in approach between the Six and the British, and to show the interaction between developments and attitudes in the Six and developments and attitudes in the United Kingdom.

In many ways it would have been desirable to have begun this book with the end of the Second World War, but to have tried to analyse developments during the ten years from 1945 in as much detail as I have done those of the period since the Messina Conference in 1955 would have meant writing two books, not one. Throughout the period about which I have been writing the British Government was contending against difficulties it had done much to create by decisions taken during this earlier period, and it is difficult, as well as misleading, to be too surgical and to have too clean a starting-point. References to earlier developments inevitably occur in the text, I hope with enough explanation to make them understandable. In addition, in Chapter I, I have commented very briefly and superficially on the developments in European institution-building that took place in the first ten post-war years. No one who knows about that period will learn anything new from Chapter I and the book really begins with Chapter II.

In some ways this book is written too late, in other ways too soon: too late, because interest in the detailed issues of negotiations dies quickly and particularly quickly when the points at issue are complicated and technical; too soon, not simply because events are still too close to be seen in perspective but because only a small part of the official record of the negotiations and none of the internal papers of the British Government have been made public. There are a few reasons which may still make a premature history worth while. The historian fifty years from now will have access to the documents but not to the people who wrote them. Moreover, although the contemporary historian may see events out of perspective, he shares the mood, the atmosphere, the disabilities of those whose actions he is recording, and may therefore find it easier to understand and to explain what in the longer perspective of history will seem inexplicable or mad. But the main reason for attempting a book of this kind is that many myths are already taking root, and it may be none too soon to try to disentangle what happened from some of the patterns that are being imposed on the facts.

I have been very fortunate in being able to watch the events covered by this book from a number of desirable vantage-points. From the end of the war until early in 1954 I was in the Department of State and directly concerned with the development of European organizations. Then, for two years, I wrote for *The*

Economist on European institutions. Thereafter I continued to study and to write about the development of European institutions (and the European Economic Community, in particular) and about the development of British policy towards Europe, partly for the Center of International Studies at Princeton University and partly for Political and Economic Planning in London. I am grateful to all these institutions for having enabled me to study these developments at first hand and continuously over such a long period. Although the early years, when I was myself a civil servant, are strictly speaking outside the scope of this book, the experience I gained during that time of the limitations within which all governments inevitably work and, above all, the friendships that I made with officials of other governments and of the European institutions have been invaluable to me. Except for a short period at Princeton, I have lived in England since the spring of 1954 and have therefore been able to visit the Community headquarters easily and have thus had the advantage of being able to talk frequently with those concerned with Community policy as well as with those concerned with the development of British policy. And, living in England, married to an Englishman, I have had the very great advantage of being in a position to absorb osmotically many things which it would otherwise have been difficult to understand about a country not one's own.

Many people have helped me in the writing of this book but my debts to individuals are peculiarly difficult to acknowledge. The list of everyone who has contributed, wittingly or unwittingly, would be unbearably long, and, since some of those to whom I am most grateful are British civil servants who feel strongly that they must remain anonymous, it would be incomplete as well as long. I hope that all those from my own country, from the United Kingdom, from the other countries of the EFTA, from the Six, from the Community institutions, and from other European institutions who have talked to me so long, so often, and so freely over the years will recognize my dilemma and accept my gratitude while forgiving its impersonal character.

I should like to make one exception and to thank Sir Frank Lee for his very great kindness not only in having allowed me to spend many enjoyable hours asking questions but in having read the entire book in draft. It is no secret that his contribution to the development of British policy was unique. I should also like to thank particularly—if anonymously—the others who read and commented on the draft: two British civil servants, an official of the Commission of the European Economic Community, an official of the EFTA, and a journalist, all of whom have been closely concerned with the successive negotiations. Naturally none of these people can be blamed for the shortcomings of this book but all of them helped me enormously in unravelling the technical issues and in understanding what lay behind the differing points of view. My object has been to present as accurate and objective an account as I could of the negotiations, not to prove a thesis or to argue any particular case, and I am very much in debt to all those who read the book in draft for any success I may have had in achieving this aim.

Some parts of this book draw heavily on the shorter studies I have written for the Center of International Studies and for Political and Economic Planning, on whose Common Market study I acted as a consultant. Little of this material has been used without considerable modification, but I am grateful to both institutions for permission to make use of it. I should also like to express my particular thanks to P.E.P. for having provided me with office space and, generally, for having put up with me during the time I was actually writing the book. Mrs. Staples of the P.E.P. staff deserves a special word of thanks for her skill and extraordinary patience in deciphering and typing drafts most people would have refused to touch.

Professor Klaus Knorr, Director of the Center of International Studies at Princeton University, suggested that I write this book, and but for his encouragement I should not have had the temerity to begin it nor the tenacity to finish it.

Cambridge, England   M. C.
  August, 1963

CONTENTS

BRITAIN AND THE EUROPEAN COMMUNITY
1955–1963

I

THE BACKGROUND: 1946–1954

PROPOSALS for European regional action played little part in the planning for the post-war world that was done during the Second World War. The United States Government, in particular, visualized the political and economic organization of the post-war world in 'global' terms. The United Nations in the political field and the three Bretton Woods organizations—the International Bank for Reconstruction and Development, the International Monetary Fund, and the stillborn International Trade Organization—in the economic field formed the institutional skeleton for the new world of the Atlantic Charter.[1] The British Government was always somewhat more sceptical than the United States Government about the possibility of effective co-operation with the Soviet Union, and it was doubtful whether the post-war world would be ready as soon as the United States expected for the non-discriminatory trade and payments systems that had been planned at Bretton Woods. Some adaptations were made to meet British economic arguments; for the most part these took the form of transitional arrangements, permitting temporary departures from the basic rules. And the UN Charter included a provision permitting regional security groups. But these departures from 'universality' were not made with future European institutions in mind.

When the war ended, European regional action was seen by both the United States and the British Governments as a temporary expedient designed to deal with immediate recovery problems, not as a lasting or desirable development. The dimensions of the post-war recovery problem—which had been badly underestimated in the United States, the difficulties of working with the Soviet Union (and, after the *coup* in Czechoslovakia, the clear hostility of the Soviet Union), and the continental pressure for European unity, soon led to a change in attitude towards European organizations

[1] On the Anglo-American planning for the Bretton Woods organizations, see Richard N. Gardner, *Sterling–Dollar Diplomacy* (Oxford, 1956).

on the part of both countries.[2] But although the British Government was quicker than the United States Government to see the need for organizing Western Europe it did not shift position as radically as did the United States, which soon became as strong an advocate of European union as any continental government. The British, in contrast, favoured close co-operation between themselves and the continental countries, but drew the line at integration, or union. And because the British themselves wanted co-operative arrangements, not something more far-reaching, they felt that this prescription was the right one for the continental European countries as well. In the early post-war period this was not because the British thought the formation of a continental European union would pose problems for themselves—they did not believe that a European union was an attainable objective—but because they felt that European regional action could be effective only if they participated, a view that the continental countries fully shared.

The first experiment in European regional action, the Economic Commission for Europe, was a casualty of the cold war.[3] The ECE was set up in Geneva in 1947 as a regional organization of the United Nations 'to initiate and participate in measures for facilitating concerted action for the economic reconstruction of Europe, for raising the level of European economic activity, and for maintaining and strengthening the economic relations of the European countries both among themselves and with other countries of the world'.[4] But soon after its founding the hopes of achieving significant economic co-operation on an all-European basis evaporated. The ECE continued to play a mildly useful role as a bridge between Western and Eastern Europe but it could not become an important organization once the assumptions on which it had been built had been shown to be false.

By 1948, Western Europe was building its own organizations:

[2] See E. F. Penrose, *Economic Planning for the Peace* (Princeton, 1953), for an analysis of the U.S. miscalculation of the dimensions of the post-war economic problem.
[3] The Economic Commission for Europe had been preceded by three temporary organizations: the Emergency Economic Committee for Europe, the European Coal Organization, and the European Central Inland Transport Organization, which had been set up in 1945 at the end of the war in Europe. When the ECE was established the essential functions of these organizations were transferred to the ECE and the three temporary organizations were abolished.
[4] A good straightforward account of the work of the various European organizations commented on in this chapter will be found in Political and Economic Planning, *European Organisations* (London, 1959). Quotation from p. 19.

the Brussels Treaty Organization in March 1948, the Organization for European Economic Co-operation a month later, the Council of Europe in 1949, the European Coal and Steel Community in 1952, Western European Union in 1953, and a few other, less important, or stillborn, organizations as well. Throughout this period of active institution-building there were marked differences of view between the British and the countries that later became the European Community about both objectives and methods. On the Continent the war had not only destroyed industrial plant, transport systems, and economic life generally but it had disrupted the whole process of political life as well. Countries had been occupied, and governments had been discredited or had spent the war in exile. And after the war many of the continental countries and particularly France, Italy, and the three Benelux countries were ready to think and act in European terms. The war had been different for the British and it had left them not with a sense of national failure and a feeling of national inadequacy but with a sense of national achievement and cohesion and an illusion of power. The emotional support for European unity, which was strong on the Continent, was almost entirely lacking in the United Kingdom. And the concept of a 'Third Force' which was attractive to many on the Continent found little support in the United Kingdom. This was largely because the very close wartime partnership with the United States carried over, for a time, into the post-war period, and the preservation of this 'special relationship' was a major object of British policy. But it was also partly because in the 1940's Britain was still the third world power, and the vast distance—in power terms—between the first two and the third had not been fully apprehended. In addition, although the British emerged from the war battered and impoverished, the comparison between the early post-war situation in Britain and the Continent was still striking: British coal production was inadequate, but it was almost as large as that of all the rest of the future OEEC countries combined. And crude steel production in the United Kingdom in 1947 was 12·7 million tons, while in the Continental OEEC countries it was only 17·6 million tons as compared with 1938 figures of 10·6 and 34·9 million tons respectively.[5]

Nevertheless, despite the disparity between Britain and the Continent, the British were operating on a very narrow margin.

[5] ECE, *A Survey of the Economic Situation and Prospects of Europe* (Geneva, 1948).

They needed all their resources and more; for they were trying to combine the immense task of post-war reconstruction with a social revolution at home, and overseas with the rapid transformation of an empire into a commonwealth of self-governing nations. In economic terms the British could not, in fact, do very much to help the Continent in the first post-war years; there was even less that the Continent could do to help the British. Although it was politically short-sighted it is not surprising that in these years the British Government, obsessed with its own problems, looked at its relations with Europe in severely practical and pragmatic terms, and that it felt that much of the continental pressure for political authorities, political assemblies, and customs unions was un-realistic—a sign of political instability rather than of political maturity—that time spent in discussing these ambitious plans was time wasted, and that hard-pressed ministers and civil servants could be more fruitfully employed on a thousand and one more urgent problems.

All British Governments, Labour and Conservative alike, looked at their European relationship as one of a set of three relation-ships: it had no overriding priority. On the contrary, in the first post-war decade most people would have said that it was the least important leg of the tripod on which British foreign policy rested—the relationship with the Commonwealth, the relationship with the United States, the relationship with Continental Europe. Co-operation with Europe was desirable; integration with Europe was not. And no British Government was prepared to undertake an open-ended commitment to Europe, or a commitment which meant giving the European relationship priority over other rela-tionships. Nor was any British Government prepared to transfer control of the British economy, or other aspects of policy, from the British Government to a European body, either through the delegation of power or the acceptance of majority voting. This was partly because the British, with the wartime experience fresh in their minds, felt more confidence in their own skill in handling problems than they did in that of the continental Europeans; partly because they saw no particular advantages and many dis-advantages in terms of their relations with countries in other parts of the world in thus limiting their own freedom of action. The commitment to the North Atlantic Treaty Organization was an exception; but NATO was not a European organization.

Many of the continental countries, and particularly the French,

Benelux, and the Italians, thought of their relationships with each other in quite different terms. They tended to feel that problems that were intractable on the national plane might be soluble on a European plane, and there was none of the British reluctance to set up political bodies or to endorse objectives in the economic field, like customs unions and economic unions which, if realized, would mean not only a more limited role for national governments but a relationship among the European countries that was different, in kind, from their relationship with other countries. However, although Europe had a meaning on the Continent that it lacked in the United Kingdom, the European politicians were better at making plans than they were at carrying them out. This was inevitable, given the political situation on the Continent. In both France and Italy the Communists were the largest single party, and so large that non-Communist governments were, almost by definition, unstable minority governments. And French Governments seldom lasted longer than a few months. Although from 1948 onwards the German Government played an increasing role in European affairs, it did not regain its sovereignty until 1954. Only the Benelux Governments were stable and sovereign. And before the establishment of the European Coal and Steel Community in August 1952 the Benelux Customs and Economic Union was the only one of the various far-reaching proposals that had from time to time been discussed among the continental countries to survive beyond the planning stage. Nevertheless on the Continent in these early post-war years 'Europe' had reality as a political goal, however distant; in the United Kingdom, 'Europe' was simply a geographical expression.

In some contexts the difference of view between the British (and the Scandinavians and Swiss who agreed with them) and the French, the Italians, and Benelux, and later the Germans, about ultimate European objectives was an important bar to progress; in other contexts it was not. The difference of view was obviously of key importance to the work of the Council of Europe which owed its existence to public and political pressure for a European parliamentary political authority.[6] The compromise institutional

---

[6] In May 1948 a vast Congress of Europe was held at The Hague. Although it was non-governmental in character, prominent politicians from all the Western European countries attended, including Winston Churchill, the Leader of the Conservative Party which was then in opposition. The Congress launched the European Movement which brought together in a co-ordinated way the various groups in the United Kingdom and Western Europe working for European

formula of an intergovernmental committee of ministers and a strictly advisory Consultative Assembly of parliamentarians; the irreconcilable differences between 'the federalists' and 'the functionalists' in the Assembly; and the fact that the Statute of the Council of Europe contained no commitments to take specific steps but simply some general objectives (meaning rather different things to different people) collectively condemned the organization to impotence and the Consultative Assembly to frustration.[7]

The difference of view was a much less important obstacle to progress in the Organization for European Economic Co-operation, particularly in the hey-day of the OEEC when the restoration of a viable economy was the clear, accepted, and over-riding priority of every member country. Mr. Ernest Bevin, the British Foreign Secretary, was quick to respond to the suggestion made by General Marshall, the United States Secretary of State, in June 1947, for a recovery programme planned jointly by the European governments, and the British played a leading role in the preparation by sixteen European countries of the four-year programme which formed the basis of the Marshall Plan. However, when it came to establishing a 'continuing organization' to promote co-operation among the European countries in the planning and execution of the recovery programme, the traditional British distaste for strong independent organizations asserted itself, and, despite considerable French pressure (which had American support) for an organization with some direct powers of its own, the British view prevailed and

---

unity. Among other resolutions, the Congress adopted one calling for the establishment of a European Assembly. This proposal was also strongly supported by the French and Belgian Governments. Mr. Churchill's speeches at Zurich on 19 September 1946 and at the Hague Congress on 7 May 1948 are frequently quoted as having done much to stimulate the movement towards European unity. It should be noted, however, that although he called strongly for European unity he did so in lofty but imprecise language and in a way that made it clear that Britain, although working closely with the Continent, would not in any real sense become 'integrated' with the Continent. This was particularly clear in his Zurich speech where he equated Britain—and the British Commonwealth of nations—with the United States and, he hoped, the Soviet Union as 'friends and sponsors of the new Europe'. See R. Churchill (ed.), *Sinews of Peace* (London, 1948), pp. 198–202.

Although there were a few exceptions (e.g. R. W. G. Mackay) the British and the Scandinavian delegates to the Assembly tended to be 'functionalists' and to favour achieving European 'unity' by intergovernmental co-operation on specific projects; the French, Italian, and Benelux delegates tended to be 'federalists' and to favour a more radical approach and the creation of European institutions to which governments would delegate real, if at first limited, powers.

the OEEC was established as an intergovernmental organization on the traditional pattern.

At the time of the founding of the OEEC there were also differences of view about the commitments which the countries of the OEEC should undertake. The American officials who had been working closely with the Preparatory Committee which preceded the OEEC had encouraged the European countries to examine the formation of a customs union as one element of a joint recovery programme. Although many of the continental countries would have been ready enough to endorse this objective the British were not, and the OEEC Convention simply recorded that the members 'will continue the study of Customs Unions or analogous arrangements such as free trade areas. . . . Those Contracting Parties which have already agreed in principle to the creation of Customs Unions will further the establishment of such Unions as rapidly as conditions permit.'[8] The first reference was to the Customs Union Study Group which had been set up by the Preparatory Committee of the OEEC in 1947, but which after a period of study quietly transformed itself into a group for standardizing tariff nomenclatures.[9] The second reference was to the Benelux Customs Union, which materialized, and to the French–Italian Customs Union which reached the point of signature, but which was then allowed to die, partly because of opposition in France, partly because by that time negotiations on the Schuman Plan Treaty had started and the Six-country plan held more promise of accomplishing the political results which had largely motivated both the French and Italian Governments in the first place.

Partly because of British opposition, partly because other problems were more pressing, the OEEC itself did not pursue the question of forming a customs union, but concentrated, in its early days, on three main questions: first, on making recommendations to the United States Administration on how the available aid should be divided among the European countries; second, through its technical committees, on increasing the production of essential commodities; third, on seeking to achieve a higher level of intra-European trade by attacking the two principal and interrelated

[8] The text of the Convention and a useful summary of the OEEC's work during its first ten years are to be found in OEEC, *A Decade of Co-operation* (Paris, April 1958).

[9] Membership in the Customs Co-operation Council which replaced the European Customs Union Study Group is not limited to European countries.

obstacles—quota controls and bilateral payments arrangements. Although the OEEC concentrated on the freeing of trade from quantitative restrictions (quotas) various suggestions were made from time to time for dealing with tariffs as well as quotas and a number of proposals were put forward for freeing particular sectors of trade from both tariffs and quantitative restrictions.[10] The British were cool to these 'sector' schemes and consistently took the position that tariff questions should be left to the GATT (General Agreement on Tariffs and Trade). Although their opposition to the OEEC discussing tariffs was undoubtedly influenced by their desire to damp down pressure for a European customs union, they also felt, probably rightly, that most of the plans that were from time to time proposed would have led to preferential arrangements which would have been in violation of the GATT and that the combined work of the OEEC Trade Committee and of the EPU (European Payments Union) would yield more solid accomplishments.

By the end of the four years (1948–52) which the Marshall Plan had originally been designed to cover, European recovery had been achieved and the OEEC had played a notable part in that recovery. It would be difficult to demonstrate that, within the limits of the programmes the governments had agreed to undertake, the work of the Organization had been seriously hampered by the unanimity rule, or by the fact that no powers had been delegated to an independent commission or secretariat. However, it would also be true to say that the fact that the British (and quite a number of the other OEEC countries and in particular the Scandinavians and the Swiss) were not prepared to go beyond 'co-operation', and to accept arrangements leading to a customs union or an economic union meant that the OEEC did not satisfy those who felt that more far-reaching action among the European countries was required. Moreover, once the post-war reconstruction phase was over, the future of the OEEC itself was somewhat obscure, since the British attitude precluded the OEEC developing

[10] The most important of these proposals was a Dutch plan, the so-called Stikker Plan. This plan foreshadowed the later Common Market proposals of the Benelux countries in a number of respects although it was less ambitious, and partial in the sense that initially, at least, barriers to trade would not have been removed across-the-board but in selected industries only. For a description of this plan and also for an excellent account of the OEEC's work in the field of trade and payments see William Diebold, Jr., *Trade and Payments in Western Europe* (Council on Foreign Relations, New York, 1952).

as the economic base for a European union. Other developments also added to the uncertainty about the future of the organization. After the outbreak of war in Korea in the summer of 1950, substantial amounts of defence support assistance were provided by the United States to the countries of Western Europe and defence-connected aid soon replaced economic aid as the principal form of American assistance. Partly for this reason, partly because the British had always preferred 'Atlantic' to 'European' forums, the British suggested, early in 1952, that some of the OEEC's functions be transferred to the NATO and that the OEEC budget be drastically cut.[11] This proposal met with strong opposition from the continental countries (particularly from the non-members of the NATO of whom Germany was one at this time, but also from the other continental countries as well) and the proposal was modified, with the result that the Organization was pruned down but not emasculated.

About a year later the British took another step which seemed to the continental countries to be further evidence of British loss of interest in the OEEC. This was the discussion during the winter of 1952–3 with the Commonwealth countries and with the United States authorities of plans for progressively restoring convertibility to the pound sterling. Suspicion grew on the Continent that these measures were being planned with little regard for the effect on European currencies and the European payments system. The British sought to dispel these fears and during the spring of 1953 the convertibility plan was fully discussed in the OEEC. The EPU would have disappeared as a by-product of a general return to currency convertibility but the continental countries were strongly in favour of retaining some form of European clearing arrangement largely as insurance against a worsening in the European payments position. Accordingly, during 1954 and the first half of 1955 the major work of the Organization centred on the elaboration of a European Monetary Agreement and certain adaptations in the code of trade liberalization which it was agreed would come into effect at such time as convertibility was restored to currencies accounting for more than 50 per cent. of the EPU quotas.

[11] An important reason for the British preference for the NATO was that they had no difficulty in agreeing to any form of 'common action' to which the United States could agree and they therefore escaped in the NATO the charges of 'foot-dragging' they incurred in the OEEC for their reluctance to become more 'European'.

In the discussions over convertibility, differences of approach were apparent between the British and many of the continental countries, differences which were apparent throughout the history of the OEEC and which frequently led to misunderstandings and sometimes to ill will. Thus when the British were opposing and the continental countries advocating 'a European regional economic system', the views of each side could be looked at in two ways. The British felt they were defending principles that had been accepted by most of the OEEC member countries in the Articles of Agreement of the International Monetary Fund and in the General Agreement on Tariffs and Trade, and that they were trying to live up to those commitments by pushing as quickly as possible towards a world of freer trade and convertible currencies, and they tended to feel that those who resisted these efforts were trying to retain protection for their own industries and to perpetuate a soft currency trading area. Looked at in another light, however, the British seemed to be attacking and the Continentals defending the concept of European unity. Thus, to the British, 'Europeanism' sometimes seemed to be a polite name for 'protectionism', while to the Continentals, the British attachment to the principles of the IMF and the GATT seemed to be a cover for a basic unwillingness to accept the concept of Europe as an economic unit. Motives were mixed on both sides of the Channel.

By 1954 the OEEC had clearly declined in importance and showed every sign of declining further once the pound and other important European currencies were made convertible, and the trade and payments arrangements that had formed the hard core of the OEEC's work became of less significance. The Organization was still strongly supported by those European countries who looked neither to the NATO nor to the new Community of the Six. It still commanded the loyalties of many ministers and officials—from all its member countries—who had played leading roles in its activities during its most productive period. But neither the British nor the leading continental countries saw the OEEC as the basis for a lasting European economic system: the British because they then saw no need for a distinctively European economic system once the post-war problems had been overcome; the Six because they had become preoccupied with their own plans for 'making Europe'.

The treaty establishing the European Coal and Steel Community—the first of the Communities of the Six—came into effect

in the summer of 1952, two years after M. Schuman had made his
dramatic proposal for pooling the coal and iron and steel resources
of France and Germany and of any other European countries
willing to join in putting them under the control of an independent
high authority.[12] It had taken less than a year to draft this precedent-
shattering treaty. The plan had been attacked in France by the
Patronat (the French employers' association), by the Communists,
and by the Gaullists, and it had been looked at askance by some
sections of the civil service. In Germany it had been attacked by
the SPD (the Social Democratic Party) and by the trade unions.
But in both countries the majorities for ratification were substantial
and in the Benelux countries and in Italy there was very little
controversy.

After consultation with the French Government on the terms
of their possible participation, the British Government had decided
not to take part in the conference which drafted the treaty. Both
the National Coal Board and, although less strongly, the steel
industry were opposed to the kind of pooling of resources that the
French had in mind, but the main objection from the British side
was political. The preliminary discussions between the British and
the French centred on the French insistence that countries participating in the treaty negotiations accept as the basis of their work
the main principles outlined in M. Schuman's statement and, in
particular, that they accept the principle of removing their coal,
iron, and steel industries from national control and putting them
under an independent 'supra-national' high authority. A long
exchange of notes brought the British and French views on the
extent and nature of this prior commitment somewhat closer together, and it is conceivable, although not very probable, that with
a little more effort some formula could have been found to enable
the British to participate in the negotiations. The Conservative
Party attacked the Labour Government (which was then in power)
for not having tried rather harder to find a way to participate in the
Conference. But the Front Bench of the Conservative Party was
as opposed as the Government to any yielding of powers to a
'supra-national' organization.[13] It is difficult to disagree with the
conclusion reached by one of the best-informed writers on the

---

[12] An excellent comprehensive account of the European Coal and Steel Community is William Diebold, Jr., *The Schuman Plan, A Study in Economic
Co-operation, 1950-1959* (New York, 1959).

[13] It is worth noting that after the Conservatives came back to power the question
of joining the ECSC was re-considered and rejected.

Schuman Plan that a compromise formula which brought the British into the negotiations would simply have stored up trouble for the future since the British were fundamentally opposed to participation in a European federation which was at the end of the road that M. Schuman and M. Monnet were starting down.[14]

The High Authority of the ECSC took office on 10 August 1952. M. Monnet was the President and in this capacity he was both the driving force of the experiment in creating a common market for coal and steel and, more important, the philosopher and generally accepted leader of the movement for creating unity in Europe by the method of which the Schuman Plan was the prototype. The years 1951, 1952, and 1953 were heady ones for the 'Europeans'.[15] Although the Coal and Steel Community had always been seen by M. Monnet and those who were working with him as a first step in a process, and not as an end in itself, the possibility of an extension of the 'Community method' came sooner than had been expected and before the Schuman Plan treaty had itself been fully drafted.

Shortly after the outbreak of the Korean War in June 1950, the United States Government advocated the rearmament of Germany within the framework of an integrated common defence structure, that is to say within SHAPE, the NATO command structure which was simultaneously proposed by the United States. The French were opposed to the re-establishment of the German army and, in October 1950, the French Prime Minister, M. Pleven, outlined to the French Assembly a proposal for a European army which was

[14] See Diebold, *The Schuman Plan*, p. 59.
[15] Throughout this book 'Europeans' (with quotation marks) refers to those people who are consciously seeking by means of the 'Community method' to go beyond international co-operation and to construct a European federation. The 'Community method' is difficult to characterize in a few words, partly because it is a concept which has changed somewhat over time, partly because it connotes a complex of institutions, procedures, objectives, and attitudes. Perhaps the essential characteristics of the 'Community method' are (1) the *giving of wide powers of initiative to an independent body*, (2) the delegation of real, if, at first, limited, powers to an independent body, (3) legislative and judicial control over the exercise of the delegated powers, (4) majority voting, if, again, only on a limited basis, among the participating governments, and (5) and most important, the progressive replacing of policies which are national in scope and purpose by common policies so that within the participating countries certain national policies are superseded by community policies and for certain purposes the participating countries act externally not as a coalition but as a single entity. See Richard Mayne, *The Community of Europe* (London, 1962) for an account which gives not only a description but the feeling of the Community method.

subsequently submitted by the French Government to the NATO as an alternative to the American proposal. It was clear from M. Pleven's statement that the French plan was not simply a plan for achieving the rearmament of Germany without reconstituting the German army, but was also a military counterpart of the Schuman Plan and was another step in the 'making of Europe'. Thus M. Pleven proposed that there should be a European Minister of Defence responsible to a European Assembly, a European Defence Council of Ministers, and a single European Defence Budget. The participating countries would contribute contingents to the European army, but probably only at brigade level. There would thus be a German contribution to the common defence, but there would be no German army and no German general staff.

The British Government did not like the European army plan and would have much preferred to see the NATO built up as the only organization in the military field, as Mr. Bevin made plain in the House of Commons shortly after M. Pleven made his proposal.[16] However, Mr. Bevin also made it clear that although he thought the proposal misguided, the British would not stand in the way if France and other countries wanted to go ahead. Although only the Six were full participants in the Paris Conference that drafted the EDC treaty, both the United States and the United Kingdom, as well as a number of smaller countries, had observers at the Conference, and after the formation of SHAPE it, too, was formally represented, for it was always a part of the plan that the European Defence Community would be directly tied into the NATO structure. The NATO Council, at its Lisbon meeting in February 1952, heard an account from M. Schuman of the substantial measure of agreement already reached by the Paris Conference and gave its blessing to the Plan. The EDC treaty and protocols covering reciprocal guarantees between the EDC and the NATO were signed on 27 May 1952. Trouble lay ahead, but in the summer of 1952 the 'Europeans' were riding the crest of a wave.

Article 38 of the treaty for the proposed EDC provided that the Assembly of the new Community should examine, within six months of its establishment, the formation of a directly elected

---

[16] See *Hansard*, House of Commons, 29 November 1950, cols. 1170–4. In his comments on the French proposal Mr. Bevin made very clear his own strong attachment to and belief in an 'Atlantic Community', an attachment which strongly coloured his own attitude towards all European proposals.

Assembly which would constitute 'one of the elements in a subsequent federal or confederal structure, based on the principle of the separation of powers and having, in particular, a two-chamber system of representation'. The need to ensure adequate democratic political control of the proposed European army seemed to many people in the Six countries a point of crucial importance and there was considerable pressure for pushing ahead with the planning of a political authority without waiting for the Assembly of the new Community to be formally established. There was also pressure from the Dutch Government to balance the plan for military integration with further economic integration. Accordingly, in September 1952, the Foreign Ministers of the Six requested the Assembly of the Coal and Steel Community, which was then meeting for the first time, to co-opt additional members to bring its membership into line with that foreseen for the EDC Assembly and, thus augmented, to draft a treaty constituting a European Political Authority.[17] Six months later, in March 1953, M. Spaak, who had acted as the president of this *Ad Hoc* Assembly, handed a draft statute for a Political Community to the Six Foreign Ministers.[18] This draft provided for a bicameral parliament, the Peoples' Chamber being elected by direct universal suffrage, the Senate being elected by the national parliaments. Both the Coal and Steel Community and the proposed EDC were to be brought within this new political framework. Thus at the end of a short transitional period there would be a single European Executive responsible to a European Parliament, a single European Court and a Council of Ministers replacing the parallel bodies provided by the ECSC and EDC treaties. Furthermore, the draft treaty expressly provided that the new Community should 'establish

[17] On 30 May 1952 the Consultative Assembly of the Council of Europe had urged the Six Governments to ask either the ECSC Assembly or the Council of Europe Assembly sitting with a membership restricted to the Six countries to define the nature and limits of the powers of a supra-national political authority without waiting for the ratification and entry into force of the EDC. The Council of Europe resolution had also stressed the importance of associating other European countries with these new institutions at all stages of their development. The resolution of the Six Foreign Ministers referred to the Council of Europe resolution and arrangements were made by the *Ad Hoc* Assembly for participation by observers from other European countries and for reports to be made to the Council of Europe.

[18] The German Social Democrats had refused to participate in the work of the *Ad Hoc* Assembly since they were strongly opposed to the EDC and wanted to have nothing to do with it. The Gaullists were of course opposed to the draft treaty.

progressively a common market among the Member States, based on the free movement of goods, capital and persons'.[19]

M. Bidault, the French Foreign Minister, received the report on behalf of the Six Foreign Ministers. Although he was warm in his praise for the efforts of the *Ad Hoc* Assembly it was clear that he did not share the enthusiasm of M. Spaak for the plan itself. Furthermore he made it plain that the governments would now determine how to proceed, thus implicitly rejecting the suggestion that had been made by M. Spaak that the *Ad Hoc* Assembly be continued in being to work with governments in putting the text of the treaty into definitive form.[20] The draft treaty was pigeon-holed and the *Ad Hoc* Assembly disbanded. The following autumn (1953) deputies of the Six Foreign Ministers discussed a European Political Authority—for the problem of political control for the proposed European army was still a real one—and drew up a rather different kind of report which was considered by the Foreign Ministers in The Hague in November.[21] This report indicated, significantly, that 'Europe' would be a 'Community of sovereign states' and that the common institutions would exercise only those supra-national functions that were defined by the treaties in force (i.e. the ECSC treaty, and the EDC treaty when ratified) and any other supra-national functions which might be agreed in later treaties. The Community would have an executive composed of a Council of Ministers and an Executive Council, although the High Authority of the ECSC and the Commissariat of the proposed EDC would also continue to exist as well. There was no agreement on the relationship of these executives to the new Executive Council or on the composition of the new Executive Council. There would be a single bicameral parliament and a single Court, but, again, there was no agreement on the composition of the parliament. The creation of a common market with free circulation of goods, capital, and persons was apparently accepted as a final objective but the French were unwilling to undertake any firm commitments which would give reality to this eventual goal. Although the Ministers appointed a commission to draft a treaty

[19] See Robert R. Bowie and Carl J. Friedrich, editors, *Studies in Federalism*, introduction and appendix (Boston, 1954).
[20] See *L'Année Politique*, 1953, pp. 337-8.
[21] The deputies met with representatives from the *Ad Hoc* Assembly but in the end made little use of the work that had been done by the *Ad Hoc* Assembly. See *L'Année Politique*, 1953, and also Bowie and Friedrich, op. cit., introduction.

along these lines to take the place of the one prepared by the *Ad Hoc* Assembly, no definitive text had emerged before the French Assembly rejected the EDC.

More than two years elapsed between the signing of the EDC treaty and the French Assembly's action on it. During this period a number of new protocols were negotiated and additional commitments sought and obtained from the United Kindom and the United States. But no French Government felt sufficiently confident of success to ask the Assembly for its approval. The treaty aroused strong emotions in France and the controversy has been described by Raymond Aron as 'the greatest ideological and political debate France has known since the Dreyfus affair'.[22] The showdown finally came in the summer of 1954. M. Mendès-France, a Radical, was then Prime Minister, but his Government included Gaullists who were strongly opposed to the EDC and, regardless of his own view of the treaty, which was unsympathetic, it would have been virtually impossible for him to have urged ratification without bringing about the downfall of his own Government. At a meeting of the Six Foreign Ministers in Brussels in August 1954, M. Mendès-France demanded a drastic revision of the treaty which would have shorn it of most of its 'supra-nationality' (at least for an initial period of eight years), would have intensified the discriminatory controls over German rearmament, and would have loosened the French commitments to an integrated force. The rest of the Six refused to emasculate the treaty to obtain the support of the Mendès-France Government. M. Mendès-France was under pressure not only from the other members of the EDC (who had all ratified the treaty) but also from the United Kingdom and the United States to try to obtain the Assembly's approval to the treaty as it stood, not only in order to secure the addition of German troops to the NATO force but, and by this time probably more important, because the return of sovereignty to Germany was contingent on the treaty for the EDC coming into force. Finally, at the end of August 1954, M. Mendès-France put the treaty to the Assembly, which refused to consider it and voted by 319 to 264 to move to other business.

Although there were many diverse strands[23] in the French opposition to the EDC, opposition to the 'supra-national' plans of the 'Europeans' was one of the important strands and the rejection

[22] D. Lerner and R. Aron, *France Defeats the EDC* (New York, 1957).
[23] British aloofness from the plan was another important strand.

of the EDC, and the consequential shelving of the plan for a European Political Community, were widely interpreted as a repudiation by the French Assembly of the European policy for which France had provided the planning, the leadership, and the philosophical content. Throughout the long period of uncertainty over the EDC the drive for a united Europe, on the Community model, had been losing momentum and with the rejection of the EDC the prediction was freely made that, although the Coal and Steel Community would continue to exist, there would be no expansion of the Community methods to new fields.

The first response to the rejection of the EDC was the formation of another organization, Western European Union, which, although it contained some innovations, was much closer to the traditional intergovernmental form of organization than to the proposed EDC. Western European Union was an expedient, rapidly elaborated largely at the initiative of Mr. Anthony Eden, then British Foreign Secretary, to deal with the German problems that the EDC had been supposed to solve, that is, the restoration of sovereignty to Germany and the bringing of Germany into the collective defence arrangements of the West. As a result of two conferences, one in London in September 1954, the second in Paris in October 1954, a series of agreements (known as the Paris Agreements) were reached by the nine participating countries— the United States, the United Kingdom, France, Canada, Italy, the three Benelux countries, and the German Federal Republic. These agreements related to the termination of the occupation régime in West Germany, to the admission of the German Federal Republic to the NATO, and to the transformation of the Brussels Treaty and the Brussels Treaty Organization into a new treaty and a new organization to be known as Western European Union. The Brussels Treaty was a defensive mutual assistance pact which had been signed shortly after the end of the war by Britain, France, and the three Benelux countries, with the possibility of new aggression from Germany in mind as well as the growing danger from the East. Although primarily a defence arrangement, the Brussels Treaty had had economic and cultural clauses as well. The defence aspects of the Brussels Treaty were soon absorbed into the NATO, the economic side was deliberately left to the OEEC, and the cultural work was largely left to the Council of Europe, although the Brussels Treaty Organization performed a few peripheral cultural activities as well. When the

Brussels Treaty Organization was transformed into the WEU, Germany and Italy were added to the organization, the text of the treaty was purged of references to German aggression, and the organization was given a number of new functions directly related to the problem of German rearmament. In particular, under the direction of the Council (the governing body made up of ministers from the participating countries), an Agency for the Control of Armaments and a Standing Armaments Committee were set up; the first was to ensure that commitments made about the levels of stocks and the manufacture of certain types of weapons were observed,[24] the second was to encourage the rationalization of armament production. The WEU was also given a number of other functions stemming from the Paris Agreements, the most important of which were related to the Saar and to the British commitment—which formed part of the Paris Agreements—to maintain four divisions and a tactical air force on the Continent.

The WEU had some of the trappings of a 'Community' organization. For example, the Council could, in certain circumstances, vote by simple majority or by a two-thirds majority, and a Parliamentary Assembly, advisory to the Council, was established. In addition the preamble to the revised treaty stated that it was the object of the Member States 'to promote the unity and to encourage the progressive integration of Europe'. It soon became clear that, despite these indications that the WEU might be the basis for a new relationship among the seven member countries—not wholly unlike the relationship the Six had hoped to achieve among themselves—the WEU had largely justified itself by serving as the means of restoring sovereignty to Germany and of bringing Germany into the NATO. However, at the end of 1954, the WEU was still on the drawing board and its future development obscure.[25]

This, in brief, was the state of European institutional development when the year 1955 opened. The 'Europeans', after a heady period of rapid progress, had suffered a severe, perhaps mortal, setback. The British Government had recently (21 December 1954) signed an 'association' agreement with the Coal and Steel

---

[24] As a part of the general settlement covered by the Paris Agreements the German Government gave a unilateral undertaking not to manufacture A.B.C. weapons, that is atomic, biological, or chemical weapons and also certain types of missiles, warships, and aircraft. See *Documents agreed on by the Conference of Ministers held in Paris, October 20–23, 1954* (Cmd. 9304, H.M.S.O., November 1954).

[25] The first meeting of the WEU Council was held in Paris on 7 May 1955.

Community and had taken the lead in the formation of the WEU. Relations with the Six seemed to be set on a new and mutually acceptable basis of close co-operation and the prospect for further Six-country schemes seemed remote. The OEEC was operating in a fairly low key. The NATO was easily the international organization to which the British Government attached the greatest importance. But even the NATO seemed less important than it had a few years earlier, for Stalin had died and the possibility of a détente in relations with the Soviet Union was very much in the air.

II

THE 'RELAUNCHING' OF EUROPE

The Messina Conference

During the latter half of 1954 negotiations on the WEU (Western European Union) occupied the centre of the diplomatic stage. The 'Europeans' appeared to have been repudiated by the French Government with the rejection of the EDC by the National Assembly, and anyone who had then predicted that the Six would soon be actively engaged in the creation of two new Communities might reasonably have been dismissed as a light-headed visionary. Nevertheless, by the turn of the year plans for 'relaunching Europe' were being laid, and by the end of the year 1955 the negotiations on Euratom and the Common Market were well under way.

In November 1954, M. Monnet, the President of the High Authority of the European Coal and Steel Community, had written to the member governments of the Community stating that he would not stand for re-election when his term of office as president expired on 10 February 1955 and that he would also resign, at the same time, as a member of the High Authority. He gave as his reason for leaving the High Authority his wish to have complete freedom of action to work for the establishment of a United States of Europe.[1]

At this time, M. Mendès-France was Prime Minister of France. M. Monnet had been instrumental in persuading the other countries of the Six to resist making the fundamental changes in the EDC sought by M. Mendès-France and there was therefore little reason to suppose that either as head of the High Authority or as a private citizen he could exert much influence on the French Government, but his views carried great weight elsewhere in the Six. Despite his formal notice of resignation M. Monnet did not, in fact, leave the High Authority in February as he had intended

---

[1] Institut des Relations Internationales (I.R.I.), *Chronique de Politique Étrangère*, Vol. VIII, No. 5, p. 505.

to do, since there was difficulty among the Six Governments in agreeing upon a successor. Thus during the period when the new plans were being formulated M. Monnet was still acting as President of the High Authority. It was, however, an open secret that he was in very close touch with the Benelux Governments and with others within the Six who were working on plans for the *relance*—the 'relaunching' of Europe.

There were at this time several different ideas of how progress could best be made. For some time there had been suggestions for extending the powers of the Coal and Steel Community to new but related economic sectors, such as transport and other conventional forms of energy, like gas and electricity.[2] In addition, atomic energy was then much in the news, and the immense cost of development and exploitation of this new source of power made it an obvious candidate for collective action. Finally, the idea of a European customs union which had been discussed from time to time (and included in the draft treaty for a European Political Community) was still in the air. During the discussions on the *relance* that took place in the winter and spring of 1955 M. Spaak (then the Belgian Foreign Minister) initially, at least, favoured proceeding by extending the powers of the Coal and Steel Community to new sectors; M. Beyen (Foreign Minister of the Netherlands) favoured abandoning the sector approach and proceeding by creating a general customs union; M. Monnet favoured applying the 'Community' method to the new field of atomic energy.

In February 1955 the Mendès-France Government fell and, after a considerable time, a new government was formed by M. Edgar Faure. Although the Faure Government included a number of strong 'Europeans' like M. Robert Schuman and M. Teitgen it also contained intransigent opponents of anything smacking of 'supra-nationalism'. The balance was held by men like M. Edgar Faure himself and M. Pinay, his Foreign Minister, who were in sympathy with the 'Europeans' but were not wedded to the 'supra-national' method and who were convinced that whatever the merits of a more radical approach the most that could be

---

[2] At one time M. Monnet and other 'Europeans' had felt that the centrifugal pressure exerted by the integration of the coal and steel sectors would lead, automatically, to the extension of the Community method to related fields. By the end of 1954, however, it was clear that some new political initiative was required if the process begun in coal and steel was to be carried very much further.

achieved until new French elections were held and a more pro-
'European' Assembly elected was to keep alive the idea of progress
and to keep a certain momentum by means of technical co-operation in a few well-defined fields. This cautious approach was outlined by M. Faure soon after he took office. Answering questions
from journalists on his European policy he indicated that he felt
the *politique européenne* should be pursued, but without dogmat-
ism, and that it might be useful to have some European organization for transport and for energy, and in particular for atomic
energy. Significantly, he also indicated that although he thought
proposals along these lines might well be considered by the Foreign
Ministers of the European Coal and Steel Community this did not
mean that any new organizations would be part of the ECSC.[3]

At the end of April (1955) the Dutch Government announced
that the Benelux Governments would shortly propose the convening of a conference of Western European governments on
European integration. The Dutch announcement came just before
M. Pinay was to meet Dr. Adenauer in Bonn to discuss a number
of interrelated problems: the Saar, the canalization of the Moselle,
the strengthening of economic and cultural ties between France
and Germany, which had been agreed to at a French–German
meeting the previous autumn. The Benelux Governments had
been worried by the emphasis placed on bilateral Franco-German
arrangements by the Mendès-France Government and it seems
probable that the Benelux announcement was meant to have an
impact on the Pinay–Adenauer meeting. In any event, the communiqué issued at the conclusion of the Franco-German talks,
as well as noting the progress made on the Saar problem and the
establishment of a committee for economic co-operation, also
stated that the ministers had agreed that the time had come to give
a new impulse to European co-operation [*sic*] and singled out the
following as the fields in which new steps might be taken: transport,
air navigation, aeronautical construction, and, above all, research
regarding atomic energy and its use for peaceful purposes.[4]

The need for the extension of the Community approach to new
fields figured prominently during the debates of the Common
Assembly of the European Coal and Steel Community in May, and
at the end of the session (14 May) the Assembly unanimously (with
two abstentions) adopted a resolution calling upon the Foreign

[3] See *Le Monde*, 7 April and 15 April 1955.
[4] See *L'Année Politique*, 1955, pp. 375–6.

Ministers of the Six to authorize one (or several) intergovernmental conferences to elaborate—in co-operation with the institutions of the Coal and Steel Community—plans for the next steps
in European integration. A few days later, on 20 May, the Benelux
Governments formally presented a memorandum to the other
member governments of the ECSC for discussion by the Foreign
Ministers who were shortly to meet at Messina.[5] As finally agreed
among the Benelux Governments the memorandum contained
suggestions both for a general Common Market and for new action
in the specific fields of transport and energy, and, in particular,
atomic energy in which the French Government, as well as M.
Monnet, were then known to be particularly interested.[6]

Shortly before the Messina Conference opened, the French
Cabinet met to decide on the position M. Pinay should take on the
successor to M. Monnet and on the substance of the Benelux
memorandum. Its consideration of both problems was complicated
by the fact that M. Monnet had written to the Six Governments
(and had made public his letter just as the French Cabinet was
meeting) informing them of his willingness to remain in office in
the light of the Benelux memorandum.[7] M. Edgar Faure was
unwilling to support M. Monnet at the risk of splitting his Cabinet
but it may well be that the threat of M. Monnet's candidature (and
the support he was known to enjoy from other governments) made
it easier for the Cabinet to agree on M. Mayer (an avowed, if less
active, 'European') and to give M. Pinay rather more latitude at
Messina than might otherwise have been the case.

Although those who were anxious to 'relaunch Europe' anticipated difficulties with the French at Messina, the Germans seem
to have shown themselves to be just as reluctant 'Europeans' as
the French.[8] Dr. Adenauer did not go to Messina but sent the

[5] The Foreign Ministers of the Six were to have met earlier in the year to agree
upon a successor to M. Monnet as president of the High Authority of the
ECSC. The meeting was postponed a number of times, first because of the
change in the French Government, later to give time for the manoeuvring that
was going on behind the scenes about the *relance*.
[6] The text of the Benelux memorandum is contained in I.R.I. (1955), pp. 523–6.
[7] M. Monnet's letter was so worded that, in effect, it linked his willingness to
stay in office with the Governments' agreeing to the *relance* although it
stopped just short of making the condition explicit. For the text of the letter
see I.R.I. (1955), pp. 510–11.
[8] See *Le Monde*, 4 June 1955. '. . . le fait saillant de la conférence est que l'Allemagne a marqué un raidissement assez net et qu'elle a clairement donné à
entendre qu'elle ne serait "européenne" que dans la proportion où la France
le sera.'

State Secretary, Professor Hallstein, a strong 'European'. The German Government was, however, deeply divided on the Benelux proposal and the memorandum the Germans circulated commenting on the Benelux memorandum reflected the somewhat uneasy peace between Dr. Adenauer and the 'Europeans' on the one hand and, on the other, Dr. Erhard and his followers, who made no secret of their antipathy to what they felt to be the 'dirigiste' approach of the ECSC and their preference for the OEEC and the GATT. Although the German memorandum supported the Benelux proposals in general and contained a useful elaboration of the characteristics of a Common Market, it advocated a rather more leisurely procedure and was somewhat more cautious on most points, atomic energy being the exception. And statements supporting the formation of a Common Market were balanced by statements reaffirming the need to work for greater freedom of trade through the OEEC and the GATT.[9]

In the drafting of the Benelux memorandum great care had been taken to present proposals which could be accepted by the French Government without, at the same time, abandoning any of the points of principle to which the 'Europeans' attached real importance. Words and phrases, such as 'supra-nationalism', which in the post-EDC atmosphere were certain to generate unfavourable emotional responses were abandoned in favour of phrases that were neutral emotionally and logically defensible. Thus, on the most difficult aspect of all, that of institutions, the Benelux memorandum side-stepped the acrimonious 'intergovernmental-supra-national' argument but, at the same time, firmly established the central point, that is, that an institution endowed with real power would be required: 'The establishment of a European Economic Community, in the sense meant by the Benelux countries, necessarily presupposes the establishment of a common authority endowed with the powers necessary to the realisation of the agreed objectives.'

The accuracy with which the drafters of the Benelux memorandum had sensed the temper of the others, and in particular the French, was reflected in the resolution adopted by the Six and made public at the end of the Messina meeting. Although, as discussed further below, the resolution was appreciably less explicit than the Benelux memorandum, it not only drew heavily on

---

[9] For the text of the German memorandum and also of a memorandum circulated by the Italians, see I.R.I. (1955), pp. 526–33.

the specific proposals put forward by the Benelux countries but used verbatim a surprising amount of the Benelux memorandum. Thus the general statement of objectives was adopted intact with the single substitution of the word 'construction' for 'integration' of Europe.[10]

After describing in general terms the kind of common action that they believed to be required in the specific fields of transport, energy, and atomic energy, to promote certain social objectives,[11] and to achieve the broad objective of a general Common Market, the Benelux Governments had suggested that a conference be convened and charged with the task not simply of studying the ways and means of accomplishing these objectives but also of preparing the texts of the necessary treaties. Perhaps the most important achievement at Messina was the agreement reached on the *method* to be followed in preparing the next stages in integration. Although the original Benelux proposal was somewhat modified, the essential idea that the intergovernmental conference should prepare the texts of treaties to carry out the objectives that had been agreed (not simply discuss, once again, what was to be done) was retained. The preparation of this conference was to be entrusted to a committee of governmental delegates assisted by experts and presided over by a political personality. Again, the important decision was that this committee was to examine *how* particular ends were to be achieved; it could not call in question the objectives. Finally, by requiring the Committee to report back to the Ministers of Foreign Affairs not later than the beginning of October and, most important, by selecting M. Spaak as the chairman (he was named shortly after the conference closed), a much needed impetus and sense of urgency was given to the Committee's work.

That section of the Messina resolution which dealt with the formation of the Common Market became the text from which the Spaak Committee worked, and it is useful therefore to note how early in the negotiations certain of the key features of the eventual Treaty of Rome were accepted by the Six.[12] The section began by stating that "The six Governments recognise that the establishment

[10] The text of the Messina resolution is reprinted in Appendix A.
[11] The Common Assembly of the ECSC had been particularly vocal on the need to do more in the social field.
[12] As discussed in Chapter I, many of these ideas had been considered earlier in various contexts: the importance of the Messina Conference was that they were then accepted by the Six Governments as a basis of action.

[*constitution*] of a European market, free from all customs duties and all quantitative restrictions, is the objective of their action in the field of economic policy [*politique économique*]. They consider that this market must be achieved by stages and that its entry into force requires the study of the following questions.' Thus, unlike the ECSC treaty which provided that tariffs and quotas were to be abolished on a given date for each of the commodities covered by the treaty, the Common Market was, from the very beginning, thought of as being brought into effect in stages. Eight questions, or topics, were listed as requiring study: (1) The procedure and rhythm of the progressive elimination of the impediments to trade between the participating countries, as well as appropriate measures for the progressive unification of customs régimes with respect to third countries. The first part of this topic was included in the original Benelux proposal, but it is worth noting that the study of means to ensure a common customs régime was not in the original Benelux proposal but was introduced by the French representative. (2) Measures to be taken to harmonize the general policy of the participating countries in the financial, economic, and social fields. This formulation was lifted textually from the Benelux memorandum.[13] (3) The adoption of methods to ensure enough co-ordination of the monetary policies of the member countries to permit the creation and development of the Common Market. (This echoes a provision in the memorandum submitted by the Italian delegation.)[14] (4) A system of escape clauses (*clauses de sauvegarde*); this had been part of the original Benelux proposal. (5) The establishment and operation of a readaptation fund. This proposal was contained in the Benelux memorandum. The Italians in their memorandum had underlined the importance of a re-adaptation fund and had also argued that there should be funds to assist a policy of expansion and investment, particularly in countries poor in capital, as well as funds to facilitate readjustments required by the Common Market.[15] (6) The gradual introduction

---

[13] M. Pinay at a press conference indicated that one of the conditions of French agreement was that there should be harmonization of social regulations and, in particular, those relating to working hours, overtime pay, and the length of paid holidays. This provision had, however, been prominent in the original Benelux memorandum: not simply as something requiring study but as something needing to be done.

[14] The Italians and the French were both anxious that the Six should pursue a co-ordinated policy in moving towards convertibility and, at Messina, the Six agreed to act together. See *Le Monde*, 9 June 1955.

[15] The communiqué recorded the explicit agreement of the Six to the creation

of freedom of movement for workers. The Italian and German memoranda had both included freedom of movement for workers; the original Benelux memorandum had not been very explicit on this point. (7) The elaboration of rules ensuring the play of competition in the Common Market in such a manner as to exclude, in particular, all national discrimination. This point was taken from the German memorandum. And, finally, (8) the appropriate institutional arrangements for the realization and operation of the Common Market. This was a vaguer and weaker formulation than the original Benelux statement on the need for a common authority with powers of decision.

In their memorandum the Benelux countries had proposed that the intergovernmental conference which was to draft the treaties should include, besides the six member countries of the ECSC, 'those countries that have signed a treaty of association with the ECSC' and the ECSC itself. The United Kingdom was the only country that had signed a formal treaty of association with the ECSC, although a number of others, notably the Swiss and the Austrians, had special arrangements with the Community. The Benelux Governments suggested that the advisability of inviting other OEEC members might also be considered, but they were obviously less clear in their own minds about the need for including these countries than they were about the need for inviting the United Kingdom. In their memorandum the Germans assumed that the work of defining what was to be done would be carried on by the Six alone and that the new tasks would be entrusted to the existing institutions of the Six, although they emphasized that the new Community should be open to any state wishing to become a member. The Italians in their memorandum took issue with the German memorandum and argued that the other European countries, and in particular the United Kingdom, should be associated with the new work from the start. The Italian memorandum also suggested that the Treaty of Association with the United

---

of a European investment fund, additional to the readaptation fund, to be used for the development, in common, of the European economic potential and, in particular, for the development of the less favoured regions in the participating countries. This was a point which the Germans had made in their memorandum as well as the Italians in theirs. M. Pinay, at a press conference, also indicated that one of the points on which the French had insisted at Messina was the adoption of means of avoiding the Common Market resulting in the rich regions getting richer and the poor, poorer. See *Le Monde*, 9 June 1955.

Kingdom might form the basis for a future 'plus vaste collaboration avec le Royaume-Uni'.[16]

From contemporary press accounts it seems probable that at Messina the French favoured British participation, in part, at least, as a means of shifting from their own shoulders the onus of being the reluctant 'Europeans'.[17] However, the fact that the French were at this time much more interested in the possibilities of some form of joint action in the development and exploitation of atomic energy than they were in the general Common Market was probably a stronger reason for desiring the participation of, or at least a close relationship with, the United Kingdom. The British were very much further along than were the Continental countries in the development of atomic energy, they had established a close working relationship with the United States on atomic energy questions, and there were obviously considerable technical and material advantages to be gained from British participation.

The Messina resolution recorded the agreement of the Six that the United Kingdom 'as a state belonging to the WEU and associated with the ECSC' would be invited to participate in the work from the start. As in the Benelux memorandum, the position with respect to the other OEEC countries was less clear-cut, and the question of which other states should be invited to participate, and at what stage, was left for later decision by the Foreign Ministers.

In retrospect it is generally recognized that the Messina Conference was a major turning-point in the integration of Europe. The decision reached by the Foreign Ministers as recorded in the published resolution became the text from which the negotiations proceeded, and the resolution contained the seeds of many of the actual provisions of the treaty. At the time, the meeting seemed less momentous. *Le Monde* commented that:

> The programme for a European *relance* which has been adopted by the Messina Conference is a cautious one. It will disappoint the

---

[16] The Treaty of Association between the ECSC and the United Kingdom had recently been ratified by the United Kingdom. When it was debated in the House of Commons speakers from both sides of the House had made the point that it should serve as the basis for a developing relationship with the Continent. See p. 46.

[17] For example, see Harold Callender writing in the *New York Times* of 28 May 1955: '. . . In the heroic days of 1950, M. Schuman laid down the federal doctrine that automatically excluded Britain, and he said France would lead without Britain. But those days are gone. The tendency now is to say "nothing without Britain"—which means nothing, at least for a long time, in the way of the federal programme for which M. Monnet fights.'

partisans of the ambitious plan presented by the Benelux countries which served as the basis for discussion. The six ministers in their final communiqué have used, almost textually, most of the plan. It has been enough for them to modify some phrases and thus to change the character of the plan profoundly. . . . Most important, the governments have implicitly abandoned the idea of 'supra-nationality'.[18]

Although the Messina decisions were not 'heroic' they were ambitious enough to encourage the 'Europeans' in their belief that, provided they moved carefully and were prepared to accept less far-reaching institutional arrangements than they had seen incorporated in the ECSC, and had advocated for the EDC, real progress might yet be made in 'relaunching Europe'. The French position was still the most doubtful. But the French were clearly interested in the possibility of more rapid development of atomic energy through some form of European co-operation. The Belgians had the necessary uranium in the Congo and the Germans could help contribute to the vast financial cost of building a separation plant and the other expensive requisites of the atomic age. There was thus a strong positive attraction to the French in the Messina decisions on atomic energy. There was also the powerful negative fact that the French were anxious to repair the damage to their own prestige and position caused by their rejection of the EDC. Therefore, although they did not much like the Benelux proposal for a Common Market, they joined with the others in 'recognizing that the constitution of a European Common Market, free from all tariffs and quantitative restrictions, is the objective of their action in the field of economic policy'.

The Messina resolution opened the way to action but it did not ensure action and the fact that the opportunity was successfully exploited owed a very great deal to the wisdom and energy of M. Spaak, who presided over the committees which analysed the problems and then prepared the texts of the treaties.

The work of the Spaak Committee, July–December 1955

The Intergovernmental Committee, presided over by M. Spaak, held its first meeting in Brussels on 9 July 1955. British representatives were present at this meeting and for the next five months they played an active part in the discussions. Shortly after the Messina meeting, the Dutch Foreign Minister, Mr. Beyen, had gone to London as emissary of the Six to discuss the terms on which the

[18] *Le Monde*, 5–6 June 1955 (my translation).

British might become associated with the work. In marked contrast to the situation five years earlier, when the French had insisted on a prior acceptance of the concept of the delegation of power to an independent High Authority as a condition for participation in the drafting of the Coal and Steel Community treaty, Mr. Beyen apparently extended to the British an invitation to participate in the Committee's work on any terms it chose.[19]

The basis on which the British agreed to participate was made clear in a letter from Mr. Macmillan, then Foreign Secretary, in answer to a formal letter from the Six written after Mr. Beyen's exploratory talks in London inviting the British to 'participate in the studies to be undertaken by the Committee referred to in paragraph 2, Chapter II, of the Messina resolution'. In his reply, Mr. Macmillan indicated that the British Government was anxious to ensure that the work of the OEEC should not be unnecessarily duplicated and that the views of the other affected countries should be heard, but that 'on this understanding' the Government would be glad to appoint a representative to take part in the studies. The British reply then continued:

> There are, as you are no doubt aware, special difficulties for this country in any proposal for 'a European common market'. They [H.M.G.] will be happy to examine, without prior commitment and on their merits, the many problems which are likely to emerge from the studies and in doing so will be guided by the hope of reaching solutions which are in the best interests of all parties concerned.[20]

At the first meeting of the Spaak Committee it was made clear by the Under-Secretary from the Board of Trade who was participating for the United Kingdom that he was not a delegate (as were the participants from the Six) or an observer but a 'representative'. This designation was apparently intended to indicate that the British were ready to take an active part in the work of the Committee but that they were doing so without the prior commitment to the Messina resolution that the six other countries shared.

The available evidence suggests that at this early stage the United Kingdom Government, and many among the Six as well, were thinking in terms of a British association with whatever new plans

---

[19] See *The Economist*, 25 June 1955, and *Financial Times*, leading article, 23 June 1955.

[20] White Paper, *Correspondence arising out of the Meeting of the Foreign Ministers of the Governments of Belgium, France, the Federal Republic of Germany, Italy, Luxembourg and the Netherlands held at Messina on 1–2 June 1955*. (Cmd 9525, July 1955, H.M.S.O.)

emerged from Messina similar to the association that had recently been established between the United Kingdom and the Coal and Steel Community. This seemed to be the concept implicit in the Italian and German memoranda circulated at Messina. It would have been a logical arrangement had the new plans taken the form of an extension of the powers of the existing community, as M. Monnet and some of the other 'Europeans' at first believed they should. And, earlier in the year, in opening the debate in the House of Commons on the motion approving the association agreement with the Coal and Steel Community, Mr. Duncan Sandys, speaking for the Government, had seemed to suggest that a new relationship between the United Kingdom and the Six might develop from the association agreement.[21]

As discussed further below, interest in the United Kingdom and on the Continent centred initially on the British relationship to whatever was agreed in the field of atomic energy. From the very first, British reservations about a Common Market were made clear and the French coolness to a Common Market was well known. Previous attempts to create a European customs union had proved abortive and there was considerable scepticism everywhere about the chances of success in this field. Most of the 'Europeans' felt that progress was more probable in the new field of atomic energy, where there were as yet no vested interests and where the French, in particular, could see positive advantages in some form of joint action. Not only were there economic and technical advantages in pooling efforts, but common action seemed to many Frenchmen a means of reinforcing the WEU guarantees by further controls over the development of atomic energy in Germany. In atomic energy both the British and the Continentals felt the British had more to give than to receive. And it seems probable that the fact that the British were, initially at least, so clearly 'wanted' in the atomic energy field contributed to the miscalculations they later made about their bargaining strength on the free trade area.

The first meeting of the Spaak Committee (le *comité directeur*) was largely procedural; four committees of experts were established and the general plan of work agreed.[22] The committees were

---

[21] See below, p. 46.

[22] The *comité directeur* was composed of the heads of the six national delegations and the British representative. It was presided over by M. Spaak, and its function was to 'animate, direct, co-ordinate, and follow in a regular way'

to meet every week, except for an unusually short holiday break in August. M. Spaak was losing no time and clearly intended to meet, if it was at all possible to do so, the 2 October deadline agreed at Messina.

At the first meeting of the Spaak Committee, the German delegate, again Prof. Hallstein, affirmed with considerable vigour the support of the Federal Government for the policy of European integration. It was clear he was seeking to counteract the impression that the German Government was as reluctant as the French to embark on further 'supra-national' experiments, and that he was trying to reassure the other countries that the opposition of German industry and of Dr. Erhard to the further development of the Community and their obvious preference for looser, broader economic arrangements did not correspond to the views of the Chancellor. This statement and one made to the Council of Europe by the Foreign Minister, Herr von Brentano, at about the same time underlined the political importance of European integration and reflected the Chancellor's willingness to override the economic and technical preferences of men like Dr. Erhard and Herr Strauss when they appeared to conflict with the goal of a united Europe.[23]

Not surprisingly, the October deadline was not met. This was partly because the task that M. Spaak had set himself and his

---

the work of the four committees on: (1) the Common Market, investments and social problems; (2) conventional energy; (3) atomic energy; (4) transport and public works. (I.R.I. (1955), p. 549.)

[23] Prof. Hallstein said in part: '. . . the Federal Chancellor has sent me here to make clear once again the broad lines of German policy. This policy does not consist only in accepting without reservation the resolution adopted at Messina but also in the firm wish to give, within the limits of possibility, a preference to the European solution rather than to other alternatives. . . . Two things are necessary, on the one hand the establishment of free economic relations in a free Western world and on the other the creation of a Europe united on the political level and which must become an integral part of the system of the free Western world. The two complement and underline one another . . . it is not only necessary to know whether this or that solution would be preferable from the economic and technical point of view but also and above all whether the solution would contribute to the unification of Europe. . . . It is in consequence frankly absurd to suppose that the Federal Government has taken a position in principle against a supra-national solution in such or such a field . . . if on occasion the idea of integration in certain specialized fields has been considered less desirable that is not because such a partial integration has appeared too "European" but because the solutions envisaged were disadvantageous, possibly harmful. . . .' See also statement by Herr von Brentano at the Council of Europe on 6 July 1955 in *Official Report of Debates* (1955), Vol. I, pp. 45-47.

committees was a big one but it seems probable that it was also part of a deliberate strategy. There were some signs that a more positive French policy with respect to the *relance* was developing and there was much to be said for trying to keep a sense of momentum while avoiding bringing the work to a point where political decisions had to be taken.[24] Early in September, the Foreign Ministers of the Six met at the Dutch North Sea resort, Nordwijk, to review progress.[25] The rather meagre press accounts suggest that the French seemed slightly more favourable to the Common Market than they had been earlier in the summer, although it was clear that they viewed the plan as a price that might have to be paid to obtain German and Benelux agreement to Euratom rather than as a development which they favoured on its own merits.

By early October, it was clear that the expert discussions had gone about as far as they could usefully go without political guidance. Although the experts had been working as experts and were not committing their governments, most of the differences of view which their discussions revealed, although formally based on technical grounds, were clearly traceable to important differences of view among the governments concerned. M. Spaak therefore decided to take the work out of the hands of the experts and to sharpen up the issues so that as soon as the political situation in France appeared suitable he could present a report on which the Foreign Ministers could take decisions of principle. Accordingly, the work of the committee on the Common Market was brought to a conclusion about mid-October and the results incorporated in a report to the heads of delegations, that is the Intergovernmental Committee presided over by M. Spaak. This report was an exploratory document rather than a definitive one. Where the experts were in agreement their common view was given; where they were in disagreement the conflicting views were outlined. Sometimes the line along which a compromise might be sought was adumbrated; in other cases the different points of view were simply set out. In most cases of disagreement there were two principal points of view, but occasionally there were several and, in one case, that of institutions, seven separate proposals were

[24] The fall of the French Government in November 1955 and the decision to hold new elections meant that there was an even longer delay than was at this time anticipated before a report was made to the Foreign Ministers.

[25] The British Foreign Minister was apparently invited as well but he did not attend, for reasons that are not clear.

recorded. Most aspects of the Common Market as it eventually took shape in the Treaty of Rome were at least mentioned in this first report. However, one of the most controversial questions in the negotiations on the treaty (and one that was troublesome in the search for an agreement between the Six and the British)— that is, whether the treaty should cover only European territories of the member countries or extend to their overseas territories— was simply recorded as a question the committee had not been ready to examine. A second troublemaker, agriculture, was recognized as presenting special problems but was not discussed in much detail. And, as noted above, on a third, institutions, opinions varied widely and no attempt was made to put forward an agreed proposal.

Some of the differences of view that preoccupied the experts in these early discussions became relatively unimportant at later stages, others continued to bedevil the Six throughout their negotiations on the Treaty of Rome. Moreover, many of the main points of difference between the British and the Six show an unbroken descent from this first document.

Two fundamental differences between the United Kingdom experts and the experts from the Six were apparent from the start; first, the British preference for a free trade area rather than a customs union; and second, the British desire to make maximum use of the OEEC and to continue the OEEC method rather than to establish new institutions or to embark on new activities outside the OEEC framework. These questions and a few subsidiary differences of view between the United Kingdom and the others are discussed further below. On other points, the odd man out tended to be the French expert. And, as was later to be the case in some phases of the free trade area negotiations, the others were never sure whether the French objections were substantive or tactical, that is whether the French experts were trying to find a formula that would meet legitimate French worries or whether they were simply seeking to weaken and perhaps invalidate the commitment to free trade.

Potentially the most serious difference between the French and the rest was over the length and the precision of the transitional period. Most of the experts (including the British) were convinced that it was important to include in the treaty a date by which all barriers to trade must be abolished, and the French reluctance to agree to the fixing of a *delai final* gave rise to considerable doubt as to whether the French really accepted the ultimate objective of a genuine Common Market. There was general agreement among the experts that there must be a transitional period—indeed the Messina resolution had said as much—and that it would not be wise to remove all barriers on a given date as had been done in the case of Benelux and the Coal and Steel Community.[26]

But although they differed on the method they favoured for removing barriers, most of the experts, save the French, felt that the period should be short enough to give industry a sense of urgency in adapting to the new situation (ten years appeared to be generally acceptable), that the process should be clearly irreversible, that any escape clauses should be temporary in character, and that the timetable for the removal of barriers should be laid down in the treaty together with the firm date by which the process should be completed. The French agreed on the irreversibility of the scheme but favoured a long transitional period and a less explicit, less automatic scheme of tariff reduction. They appeared willing to agree in advance on the first stage but wanted to let governments decide later, as the transitional period proceeded, on the timing and extent of further tariff cuts in the light of the economic conditions existing at the time. M. Spaak, speaking to the Assembly of the Council of Europe on the status of the *relance* at about the time the experts reported, reflected the uneasiness of many of the other countries at the French introduction of the concept of stages. As he made clear, the others were not against dividing the transitional period into stages but they felt the French reluctance to commit themselves to precise undertakings beyond the first stage put the final objective in doubt.

Of course we proceed by stages. But let this be clear: there exists a theory which merits outright rejection, based as it is on a false conception of the word 'stage'. In my view a stage constitutes a part of an entity. The first lap of the 'Tour de France' is the first stage of the course competitors must cover in order to win the race—not a first race they must run only to stop at the end of the first lap. Let us therefore be careful to make proper use of this word 'stage'. A stage is the part of a whole. If, as I trust, we finally agree on the whole, then we can easily

---

[26] In the ECSC there was a short transition period but the removal of tariffs was not phased: thus, on 10 February 1953, the common markets for coal, iron ore, and scrap were established. The common market for steel was established on 1 May 1953 (it should have been established on 10 April 1953), and that for special steels on 1 August 1954.

accept the idea of stages. The main thing when one embarks on the first stage is completely and definitely to agree on the goal.[27]

A closely-related question was, of course, the nature and method of resort to escape clauses. The experts recognized the key importance of this question, and it is worth noting here that the provisions finally incorporated in the Treaty of Rome bear a close resemblance to the views expressed in this first report. The committee as a whole was in agreement that resort to escape clauses should be strictly limited and exceptional; that they should be temporary in character and considered as a measure of last resort to be invoked only if other measures (mutual aid, harmonization) were inadequate; that the procedures to be followed in invoking escape clauses should be spelled out in the treaty; and finally, that some kind of organization would be needed to authorize the use of the escape clauses.[28] The majority of the committee felt that the tests for invoking the escape clauses should become progressively more stringent during the transitional period and that after the end of the transitional period there should be no possibility of reimposing restrictions on intra-community trade. Here the French differed and were not ready to forgo the possibility of reimposing restrictions after the end of the transitional period. The French and some of the others (including the British) were also unwilling to accept a binding commitment to obtain a prior authorization from the organization but argued that in times of sudden crisis a country must be able first to take action and then to obtain an authorization for the maintenance of the emergency measures.

Another difference between the French and the rest, and one which tended to become rather more prominent and more clearly defined in later stages of the negotiations, was the relationship between the timetable for the reduction of trade barriers and the progress made in harmonizing legislation and regulations of an economic, social, or fiscal nature which might otherwise give rise to 'distortions'. Here the problem was twofold: first, there were differences of view on the extent to which it was necessary to have harmonization, and second, there were differences of view

[27] Council of Europe, Consultative Assembly, *Official Report of Debates*, 1955, Vol. III, p. 615, 21 October 1955.
[28] The experts considered that resort to escape clauses should be permitted in case of a serious disequilibrium in a country's balance of payments or serious trouble in one sector or one region of the economy. Escape clauses might take the form of a temporary suspension of the obligations to reduce tariffs and to enlarge or remove quotas, or of a temporary re-establishment of quotas.

on the extent to which harmonization was a *precondition* of trade liberalization. The experts appear to have made considerable progress in distinguishing between those differences which could not be said to hamper the functioning of a Common Market but, rather, to provide the basis of a sensible specialization, and those which might introduce an element of 'unfairness' or 'distortion'. But there appears to have been little agreement between the French and the rest on how much 'harmonization' was needed *before* trade could be freed, or on how progress on the two fronts should be related. Again, M. Spaak was quite outspoken in his report to the Consultative Assembly:

Next comes the problem of so-called harmonization. . . . Now what does it all amount to? Some countries rightly claim that their present-day economy is overladen with certain social burdens. The French, for instance, quite truly tell us that in their country men and women receive equal pay and that overtime is paid for at extra rates after 40 hours of work. They add that this special situation unduly burdens their economy since it constitutes what experts call a 'distortion' and that the first step is to remedy this state of affairs.

Let us be clear about one thing: is this a 'preliminary' problem or does it merely imply a series of concomitant measures? If it is a precondition, then we may just as well wash our hands of the whole business. Does it really mean that we cannot set up a common market until we have completely co-ordinated our social, economic, and financial policies? This task would take many years and would doom all our present chances of success. . . . Though I am quite opposed to the idea of setting any preliminary condition, I, nevertheless, realize that the idea of setting up a common market compels us to try to harmonize our social, economic, and financial policies.[29]

Finally there were differences between the French and the others on the height of the external tariff. The French wanted a high tariff; the others, moderate or low tariffs. The Benelux experts were the principal advocates of a low external tariff, partly because they felt that any raising of their own low tariffs would increase prices and lower their standards of living. They also argued that a low tariff would encourage industry throughout the Common Market to modernize and thus to strengthen its competitive position in third markets. They also feared that a high tariff might invite reprisals from third countries and that it might make it more difficult for certain third countries to join the Common

[29] Council of Europe, *Debates*, loc. cit., p. 616.

Market. The French argued that a high tariff would make the adaptation to the Common Market easier and would thus help countries to establish and to maintain the Common Market. They also felt that a high tariff would be an important bargaining weapon with third countries for a general lowering of tariffs, and in particular for bargaining with the United States and the British Commonwealth. They also produced the rather typically French argument that a certain equality of sacrifice on the part of the various countries in modifying their national tariffs might be psychologically important.[30] The committee was aware of the GATT provision that a common tariff must not be higher or more restrictive than the tariffs it replaces and several experts advocated taking an average of existing tariffs for this reason.[31] The French felt that as a Common Market implied a more far-reaching commitment than that implicit in a customs union the GATT provision was not necessarily strictly applicable. The question of the height of the tariff was not resolved, but the low tariff countries were ready to examine an average tariff, and it was generally agreed that the applicability of the GATT provisions should be further studied.

The most important difference of view on the external tariff was, however, the fundamental difference between the United Kingdom and the Six on the need for a common external tariff. In the light of the later negotiations on a free trade area it is worth examining the positions taken at this early stage. The United Kingdom expert pointed out that there were advantages in a free trade area arising from the fact that it did not require drastic modifications in the tariff policy of each state with respect to the rest of the world and that this fact was particularly important where a country's tariff included preferential treatment for certain goods. Furthermore, he argued that a free trade area would result in fewer disturbances for the industries in the member countries and less change in the cost of living than would the establishment of a common tariff. He recognized, of course, that a free trade area implied origin controls but pointed out that these would in any case be needed during the transition period of a customs union. Although he was speaking as an expert and not on instructions, it is of interest in the light of later history that he went quite far in

---

[30] The French raised a somewhat similar political–psychological point at the time of the acceleration discussion in May 1960. See Chapter VIII.
[31] See Article XXIV of the General Agreement on Tariffs and Trade.

recognizing that there would be pressures towards harmonization of the external tariffs and even appeared to contemplate that at some time in the future substantial harmonization of tariffs might be necessary. He suggested, however, that even though a date for the abolition of barriers within the Common Market were fixed, it would be wise to leave open both the timing and the nature of the final tariff régime towards third countries.

The experts from the Six were agreed among themselves that the Common Market should have the form of a customs union rather than a free trade area. They felt that the Messina resolution had implied a customs union since it had listed the 'gradual unification of their tariffs against third countries' as a topic to be studied. The Six wanted to avoid retaining internal frontier controls for psychological and political as well as for practical and economic reasons; the unifying effect of a common tariff was, of course, recognized. The experts from the Six were also impressed by the fact that a common tariff would be useful in GATT negotiations, although the feeling of most of the experts from the Six that it was important for the Common Market, as a matter of principle, to act externally as a single unit was apparently made rather clearer in the discussions on the need for a common commercial policy than it was during the discussion on tariffs. It is significant that in M. Spaak's address to the Council of Europe on 21 October 1955 he assumed that the Common Market would take the form of a customs union, rather than a free trade area, and also, by implication, assumed that the United Kingdom would not be a member but a country with which the Community might negotiate some arrangement, even though, at this stage, the British representative was still participating in the Intergovernmental Committee.[32]

It is also interesting to note that these early discussions clearly foreshadowed another problem, namely the compatibility of the quota provisions of the Treaty of Rome with those in the OEEC's Code of Trade Liberalization. The British representative (with a certain amount of support) argued that the task of completing the removal of quantitative restrictions (quotas) should be left to the

[32] Council of Europe, *Debates*, loc. cit., p. 616: 'In fixing the customs tariffs of the Community *vis-à-vis* third parties one must open some channel of negotiation with those who do not propose to enter the Community. We have no desire to create a protectionist area. Once we have become a Community of 150 million inhabitants, we shall be able to negotiate with those who do not belong to our organization, with a view to obtaining increasingly large-scale reductions in return for similar reductions in our own tariffs.'

OEEC, which had had much experience with this problem and covered a wider area of trade. He argued that given the progress already made it was reasonable to hope that the OEEC would have succeeded in removing all quotas by the end of the transition period. Others felt it important to have a special system for the Common Market although at this stage there was no consensus on the plan to be followed. There were several technical arguments for a separate system, apart from the obvious political–psychological reasons. It would enable the Common Market countries to move faster than the OEEC as a whole might be prepared to go. It would also make it easier to maintain a close parallelism between quota removal, tariff reduction, and harmonization.[33] Most important, it would enable the Common Market countries to agree on a tighter system of escape clauses than that embodied in the OEEC Code. Even at this very early date there was controversy on a related point which became a principal bone of contention some years later, that is, whether or not the states participating in the formation of a Common Market could legally, having regard to the OEEC Code, extend to each other more favourable treatment than they did to the other OEEC countries.[34]

Finally there was the disputed question of institutions. The British preference for a free trade area rather than a customs union appears, at this early stage at least, to have been regarded by the rest as a reasonable British position, although one they did not share. What struck them as unreasonable, and what was perhaps particularly annoying to M. Spaak, was the unfailing British tendency to argue that little new machinery outside the OEEC framework was required and that most of the objectives sought at Messina might be better pursued by strengthening the OEEC. The Six were by no means in agreement on what kind of institutions they wanted, and the French position, in particular, was one of considerable uncertainty, but all of them, including the French, were clear that the OEEC formula, although still useful in certain contexts, was not appropriate for these new tasks. The experts from the Six differed among themselves about the kind of institutional arrangements the new communities should have but they

[33] The Benelux countries, and other low tariff countries, had for some time been trying (unsuccessfully) in the OEEC and the GATT to make quota removals contingent on some tariff reduction by the countries with relatively high tariffs.

[34] See below, Chapters V and VI.

appear to have been in agreement that new institutions of some kind would, at some point, be required.

After the French rejection of the EDC, 'supra-nationalism' had become a dirty word and M. Spaak and the other leaders of the *relance* expunged it from their vocabularies. Wisely, in order to avoid fruitless debate and in order to try to make progress without arousing passions or precipitating prematurely the taking of firm positions, M. Spaak made it clear to the experts that they should begin their work by deciding how the substantive problems of forming a Common Market could be solved. Only after they were clear about the tasks to be performed should they consider the kind of institutional arrangements required. He exhorted them not to start from the premise that a surrender of national sovereignty was necessary, or from the opposite premise that no surrender of sovereignty could be contemplated, but to cast aside preconceptions and to see where the logic of the situation led. He, himself, avoided speaking of relinquishing national sovereignty and talked instead of the need for independent or statutory authorities which would not take the place of concerted action by governments, where that was adequate, but which would come into play when inter-governmental action proved insufficient to accomplish the agreed tasks.[35] The approach, as M. Spaak explained to the Council of Europe, was different from that followed at the time of the negotiations on the Schuman Plan:

> At that time the principle of a supranational authority had been decided and in order to participate in the activities to be engaged upon by the European Coal and Steel Community it was necessary, *a priori*, to accept the concept of a supranational authority. The line we are now following is rather more diplomatic—to some minds it may perhaps appear rather more Machiavellian—somewhat more subtle: it aims at making people face up more fully to their responsibilities, asking them not dogmatically to prejudge issues, but rather to be willing to draw logical conclusions from certain facts.[36]

No effort was made at this stage to resolve the institutional differences, and the experts' report simply recorded widely differing opinions. Ever since the Schuman Plan negotiations it had been an article of faith among the Six that the unanimity rule of the OEEC tended to be stultifying and would be unacceptable in their

[35] See, for example, M. Spaak's statement to the Council of Europe, *Debates*, loc. cit., p. 617.
[36] Ibid., p. 654.

own more far-reaching arrangements. But the Benelux countries, in particular, were strongly opposed to any system of majority decision that would leave them at the mercy of the larger powers; they insisted on having some institution with powers of its own, which would be able to act, in certain circumstances, independently of national governments and which would view problems from a common, rather than a national, standpoint. The 'Europeans' in all the Six countries also believed in the importance of an institution that was independent of governments. But at this time many of the 'Europeans', particularly in France, were inclined to feel that the case for a strong independent institution was more apparent and less easily contested in the case of Euratom: in the Common Market discussions, therefore, the Benelux countries were normally the strongest advocates for independent institutions. The clearest need for an independent institution in the context of the Common Market arose in connexion with the granting of escape clauses, and it is worth noting that this point was made by a number of the experts during their discussion of the escape clause problem.[37] Nevertheless in all of the proposals for institutional arrangements discussed at this early stage, even in the Benelux proposals, the role to be played by national governments was much more prominent than it had been in any of the previous Six-country plans: the Schuman Plan, the EDC, the EPC. Moreover the whole question of the role of an independent institution was being approached in a much less gingerly way in the parallel discussions on Euratom.

The French coolness to the whole idea of a Common Market and the desire of the others to avoid giving the French any emotional or other reasons for opposing it were probably the principal reasons for this excessive caution. There was, too, a certain amount of disenchantment with the institutional arrangements of the ECSC born of experience and of the realization on the part of those who had been the strongest supporters of 'supra-nationalism' that the High Authority had, in fact, not lived up to their expectations but had been more dependent on national governments than the language of the treaty would suggest. There is nothing to indicate that the shying away from the institutional question was prompted

[37] Under the Treaty of Rome the Commission's power to authorize escape clause action is one of its few direct powers. It is worth noting that during the free trade area negotiations the British came round to the view that decisions on escape clauses should be taken by an 'independent' body; see Chapter V.

by a desire to make participation easier for the British and equally
little to suggest that the British exploited the opportunity afforded
by the undoctrinaire attitude of the Spaak Committee to try to
see whether new institutional arrangements which they might
accept could be devised. On the contrary, as noted above, in the
discussions on institutions the British primarily sought to protect
the position of the OEEC, much to the annoyance of some of the
others.

On 7 November 1955 M. Spaak presided at a meeting of the
heads of delegations (*le comité directeur*) which he had called to
review the report of the expert committees and to wind up that
phase of the work. Although it was at first supposed that all delegations would comment at this time, M. Spaak later decided to ask
for comments only from those who had not accepted the principles
of the Messina resolution, that is from the British representative,
and from the representatives of the OEEC, the Council of Europe,
the European Coal and Steel Community, and the Committee
of Ministers of European Transport who had also been sitting on
the committees.[38] Presumably this change in tactics was in part,
at least, to give time for a more favourable situation to develop
in France and to avoid forcing the French to take a position prematurely.

When asked for his comments on the reports of the committees,
the British representative indicated, on instructions from London,
that the British Government could not take a definite position on
the Common Market report until it knew all the details of the plan
(as indicated above, the experts had left numerous important
points unsettled), but that the difficulties the United Kingdom
would have in participating in a Common Market were well
known and had been discussed in detail in the committee. He
added that these difficulties still seemed to be real and did not
appear to be diminishing. Although he reiterated that his Government had reached no final decision and wanted to study further
the questions involved, the tone of the comments and the repeated
emphasis on the need to avoid any duplication with the work of
the OEEC were interpreted by his hearers as a clear indication of

---

[38] The Messina resolution had envisaged further integration in the fields of conventional energy and transport. Although these questions were examined by
the experts and reports filed, they attracted little notice. The experts' conclusions on these subjects were later incorporated, to the extent they were
relevant, in the work on Euratom and the Common Market.

British unwillingness to take part in the kind of scheme that was taking shape.[39]

M. Spaak undoubtedly expressed the general view of the Six when he commented that the statement by the British representative showed a tendency to admit only one form of co-operation and one which, although it represented progress in 1947, did not respond to the needs of the present situation. He then announced that the work of the experts was finished and that the heads of delegations would now prepare a final report for the Foreign Ministers. M. Spaak made it clear that, as this next stage of the work involved a political willingness to proceed on the basis of the Messina resolution, participation would be confined to the Six countries and that the only results to be made public would be the final report from the Intergovernmental Committee to the Foreign Ministers. He indicated that his original plan of completing the report by 1 December would probably be revised if, as seemed probable, elections in France were shortly to be held.[40]

It had apparently always been assumed that the final work of drafting the report for the ministers would be confined to those countries that accepted the Messina objectives, so that the departure of the British representative at the end of the expert discussions was not unexpected either in London or in Brussels. Nevertheless, there had been considerable hope that the British would give their blessing to the efforts of the Six and that they would express their interest in establishing some form of far-reaching association with the Common Market and Euratom.[41] Some people

[39] The statement made by the British representative on the report on atomic energy was slightly different in tone. He noted that the kind of institutions envisaged in this case involved so appreciable a delegation of power to a common organ that it would be very difficult for the United Kingdom to envisage *full* participation (my italics). However he reiterated that no decision had been taken and that before reaching a final decision the United Kingdom Government wanted to see not only the final report of the committee on atomic energy but also the report of the OEEC working party which was also engaged in studying the possibilities for European action in this field.

[40] The French political situation had become increasingly uncertain during the autumn. Finally, at the end of November, the Government of Edgar Faure fell. The National Assembly was dissolved at the beginning of December and new elections were held in January 1956.

[41] Because of the uncertainty in the French position, there was considerable feeling among the Six that British support for their projects might be crucial and there was some tendency to feel that the British were not simply deciding on their own role but prejudicing the chances of success among the Six. This, not surprisingly, was much resented. For the reaction in Brussels to the British statement see 'Britain and Europe's "Third Chance"' in *The Economist*, 19 November 1955.

within the Six had even hoped for a substantial shift in the British position and their hopes were apparently given something to feed on in a discussion between Mr. Butler (then Chancellor of the Exchequer) and Mr. Beyen, the Netherlands Foreign Minister, shortly before the 7 November meeting of the heads of delegations. It is far from clear what, precisely, occurred during this discussion, but Mr. Beyen left London under the impression that there was a real possibility that the United Kingdom might join with the Six in the plans that were emerging. The flat and unimaginative tone of the British statement, the repetition of the familiar British preference for entrusting all possible work to the OEEC rather than establishing new institutions, and the emphasis on their concern at the degree of 'supra-nationalism' envisaged for Euratom, combined with the total absence of any words of encouragement, would at best have been disappointing to the Six. Coming as it did on top of the false optimism aroused by the Beyen–Butler talk, the statement sounded in Brussels even more negative and un-helpful than was the intention when it was being drafted in London. No steps were apparently taken to try to improve the atmosphere, rather the contrary, for the British seem to have gone out of their way to underline their criticism of the plans of the Six to M. Spaak and in the capitals of the Six.[42]

The reasons for the British withdrawal

Although it was realized by very few people at the time, the British withdrawal from the Spaak Committee in November 1955 was a critical turning-point in the development of relations between the Six and the United Kingdom and the beginning of a long period of tension between the two. Why did it happen?

After the French rejection of the EDC it seems probable that the British Government, consciously or subconsciously, wrote off the possibility that the Six would again try to go farther and faster than the British were prepared to go, at least in any way that mattered. The British initiative for converting the Brussels Treaty Organization into Western European Union had been accepted by the Six with surprising celerity and, in February 1955, the Treaty of Association between the United Kingdom and the European Coal and Steel Community had been ratified. Mr. Duncan Sandys, in introducing the motion approving the Association Agreement with the Coal and Steel Community, had seemed to suggest that

[42] See below, p. 44 ff.

a new relationship between the United Kingdom and the Six might develop from the Association Agreement:

> In conclusion, let me say that we do not regard this Agreement as an end in itself. It provides the machinery to facilitate consultation and co-operation. It creates a framework within which we sincerely hope a closer association between Britain and the Community will progressively develop. I have spoken mainly of the economic aspects of the Agreement, but it also has considerable importance from the political standpoint, for it will rightly be interpreted as further evidence of Britain's determination at all times to play her part in promoting the unity and stability of Europe, and, by so doing, to contribute to the strength and peace of the free world.[43]

The debate in the House of Commons on the motion approving the association, as well as being full of good will for the Six, reflected the feeling, on both sides of the House, that a satisfactory basis for a new and evolving relationship between the United Kingdom and the Six was being laid.[44] This debate and Mr. Macmillan's speech to the Assembly of the Council of Europe just after the Messina meeting both convey a similar impression of satisfaction with the kind of relationship established with the Six.[45] They also contain self-congratulatory pats on the back for the part being played by the United Kingdom 'in promoting the unity and the stability of Europe'. It seems clear that in 1955 the dominant impression in the United Kingdom was that European unity was developing fast enough and in a way in which the United Kingdom could comfortably assist. The prevailing attitude was that, with the establishment of the WEU and the approval of the Agreement of Association between the United Kingdom and the ECSC, European developments were once again under control and attention could be given to other, more important, matters: in the economic field, creating the conditions for convertibility; in the

[43] *Hansard*, House of Commons, 21 February 1955, Cols. 881–7.

[44] Similar views about the future of the Association Agreement were also held on the Continent. It seems clear that, although the leaders of the *relance* were encouraged by the British willingness to participate in the work of the Spaak Committee, they hoped for a close association and did not anticipate full participation; no one, on either side of the Channel, appears to have thought very hard about how, in fact, a close association with a customs union could be organized. It is worth noting that M. Monnet, in the letter setting forth the aims and objectives of his Action Committee for a United States of Europe, spoke of the need for assuring the 'close association of Great Britain with these new accomplishments'.

[45] Council of Europe, *Official Report of Debates*, 6 July 1955, Vol. I, pp. 33–38.

political field, trying to find a basis for an accommodation with the Soviet bloc.

Although British enthusiasm for a rapid move to convertibility—which had worried the other OEEC countries early in 1954—had become considerably cooler by 1955, it is significant that the principal subject discussed at the OEEC Council meeting in June 1955 (just after the Messina meeting of the Six) was the change in the European system of trade and payments that should be made when the principal European currencies became convertible. At this meeting, as indeed during the previous year, the British appeared to want to go farther and faster than most of the other OEEC countries felt was prudent in dismantling the EPU and moving forward from the OEEC trade liberalization rules to those of the GATT. It is not without irony that six months later the British concern lest action by the Six detract from the role of the OEEC caused intense annoyance in the Spaak Committee in Brussels.

There were other reasons—apart from their feeling that European relationships had just been firmly re-established and their preoccupation with other matters—that made the British slow to appreciate the meaning of Messina. There had never been much real understanding in the United Kingdom of the depth of the drive towards real unity, as distinct from intergovernmental co-operation, on the Continent. Except for a handful of people, no one really accepted or believed in the feasibility or in the desirability of the 'Monnet approach' to a united Europe. The *Financial Times* probably put it quite accurately when it said that the unsympathetic in the United Kingdom had regarded the Coal and Steel Community as 'a cross between a frustrated cartel and a pipe-dream'.[46] In contrast to the situation on the Continent, there was at this time little or no feeling in the United Kingdom that the war had created a new situation and that only by coming together could the nation states of Western Europe hope to exert influence on the two super-powers and to regain their past 'great power' status. Furthermore the United Kingdom shared neither the sense of inferiority nor the readiness to make a new and radical break with the past which the common experience of defeat had bred among the Six.

On a wholly different level—it seems probable that the way responsibility for the Brussels discussions was assigned also contributed to the British Government's misjudgement of the situation.

[46] *Financial Times*, leading article, 6 February 1956.

The question was regarded within the Government as economic and commercial, not political, and the principal British representative was therefore from the Board of Trade. In contrast, among the Six, the Messina resolution had been framed by Foreign Ministers, the chairmanship of the intergovernmental committees entrusted to a Foreign Minister, M. Spaak, and the delegations even at the expert level normally contained officials from the Foreign Ministries. At the very end of the year 1955, M. Spaak reported to a meeting of the Council of Ministers of the Western European Union at which Mr. Macmillan, then Foreign Secretary, represented the United Kingdom. This seems to have been the first time that the essentially political nature of the Common Market question was really brought home to the United Kingdom. And it is perhaps not without significance that it was Mr. Macmillan who represented the United Kingdom at this meeting and bore the brunt of M. Spaak's indignation at British policy with respect to the Six.

There is little to suggest that at any time during 1955 any real consideration was given by the British to joining some form of Common Market. It was generally accepted uncritically and as an article of faith that the United Kingdom should not join a supranational organization and could not join a customs union, partly because of its arrangements with the Commonwealth and partly because the British, like the Six, were always very conscious of the pressures towards political union inherent in a customs union. As indicated above, the merits of the alternative of a free trade area were pointed out by the British representative during the expert discussions, but this was on his own initiative; he had no mandate to seek to interest the Six in forming a free trade area with the United Kingdom.

It seems probable that the British Government looked somewhat more closely at the problems which Euratom would pose for them than at those which a Common Market would pose, partly because the French position made Euratom seem more real, partly because the British hoped to sell reactors and other atomic energy equipment to the Continent, and partly because the formulation of the plan for Euratom coincided with a tremendous burst of interest in the use of atomic energy, arising from a preoccupation with the increasing cost of conventional forms of energy and the 'energy gap' that both British and Continental experts were then predicting. There seem to have been three objections to participation in Euratom, in addition to the dislike for the institutional arrangements. First, the United Kingdom was clearly ahead of the Continent in the development of atomic energy, and the British felt they not only had little to gain from a general pooling of experience but that participation in Euratom might drain away some of their own much-needed scientific manpower. Second, by virtue of its contract with Canada, the United Kingdom had an assured source of uranium. At this time uranium was thought to be in short supply, and acceding to Euratom seemed to involve giving up a sure source of uranium and becoming dependent for supplies on the decisions of a 'supra-national' authority. Third, there were various complications arising from the fact that the United Kingdom had developed atomic energy for military as well as for peaceful purposes and in this connexion had certain agreements with the United States.

The British opposition to the 'supra-nationalism' planned for the new institutions appears to have owed rather more to reflex reaction than to an objective study of the documents. It is true that some of the leaders of the Six were hoping for the delegation of far-reaching powers to independent institutions and that these ideas were being discussed outside the conference room. However, the actual documents that emerged from the Spaak Committee in the autumn of 1955 were cautious and circumspect. It is worth noting that at the same time as the British representative was being instructed to comment unfavourably on the amount of power to be delegated to the proposed new institutions, Pierre Drouin was writing in Le Monde: 'On a pris soin en effet de vider les solutions envisagées de toute charge explosive d'ordre politique. L'Europe n'apparaît plus comme une construction tirée au cordeau dans laquelle on invite les peuples à pénétrer pour leur plus grand bien, mais comme la résultante d'une série d'efforts patients pour aboutir à un marché commun. Entre cette Europe et celle de la C.E.D. il y a un abîme.'[47]

Towards the end of the year (1955) the British attitude to the Common Market appeared to change from one of indifference to one of opposition and it seems clear that for a comparatively brief period some attempt was made to discourage the Six from forming a Common Market among themselves. The principal British delegate to the OEEC outlined the British views on the proposed Common Market to the other OEEC delegates at a

[47] Le Monde, 10 November 1955.

special unofficial meeting which he had called for that purpose. Both the substance of what he had to say and the procedure the British adopted to make their views known incensed the Six. With considerable justification, the Six felt that if the British now had views on the plans which they had been invited to join with the Six in formulating (and on which they had given only preliminary comments in November) the correct procedure was for them to make their definitive views known to the Spaak Committee, not to another, rival, group. No official account of the statement made by the British representative to the OEEC delegates has been made public but from comments current at the time and from press accounts that appeared a few weeks later he seems to have gone rather beyond the position taken by the British representative at the Spaak Committee and not only to have made clear Britain's own inability to participate but also to have warned the Six that if they continued with their Common Market plans they might well come into conflict with the OEEC with unfortunate results. The British position on Euratom appears to have been somewhat less uncompromising. It seems clear that the British indicated that they foresaw difficult relations with the other OEEC countries if the Six created a general common market for nuclear materials but that, so far as the other aspects of the plan were concerned, they simply stressed the need to integrate the Euratom plan and the atomic energy work in the OEEC.[48]

It is rather easier to understand why during the summer and autumn of 1955 the United Kingdom did not take the *relance* as seriously as it should have done than it is to understand why for a time during the winter of 1955–6 this difference was allowed to turn into opposition. The change from apathy to apparent hostility seems to have been based on a serious under-estimation of the strength that the *relance* had gathered during the autumn and on the assumption that an unequivocal statement of British views might be enough to cause the Six to abandon the plan for the Common Market or at least to transfer the discussions to the OEEC. There appears to have been a serious misjudgement by the British of the French position and very little appreciation of the extent to which French views had changed during the autumn

[48] The meeting of OEEC delegates is referred to at some length in articles in the *New York Times* from its correspondent in Paris, Harold Callender. See issues of 1 and 5 February 1956. Mr. Callender was himself an enthusiastic supporter of M. Monnet's plans for the Six. See also the report from London in the *New York Times*, 2 February 1956.

and winter.[49] In fact, the various rather unvarnished statements of
the British view that were made at about this time (both in the
OEEC and through diplomatic channels) had results diametrically
opposite to those intended and strengthened the determination
of the Six to go ahead on their own. The seeds of mistrust that
were sowed in these few weeks undoubtedly complicated later
British efforts to find an accommodation with the Six. Moreover,
and of considerable importance for the future, British attitudes
at the end of 1955 seemed to have convinced some of the influential
'Europeans' that time spent trying to find ways to bring Britain
along was time wasted.

However, although the ill will and mistrust created at this time
was not easily or quickly dispelled, this essentially negative
British attitude to the plan of the Six was, in fact, short-lived. By
the end of February (1956) a kind of truce had been reached on
Euratom and the British had, at last, begun to think seriously
about ways of coming to terms with the Common Market. A
number of factors contributed to the development of this more
positive British policy. It had become clear that the Six were
unlikely to be deterred by British coolness or even by outright
opposition. The fact that the new French Government formed
soon after the January elections was headed by M. Mollet, a
strong 'European', and included as Foreign Minister M. Pineau,
a less ardent but still sympathetic 'European', had greatly encouraged M. Spaak and his colleagues and had given a new impetus
to their work. The position of the United Kingdom clearly counted
for less than it had when the French position was in doubt. Moreover, the United States had once again entered the picture and
this, too, not only made British support less important to the Six
but made the British take more seriously the prospect of a successful conclusion of the Spaak Committee negotiations.

Mr. Dulles, the United States Secretary of State, was an ardent
supporter of M. Monnet's ideas and of the federalist approach to
European unity and from the first there was strong, if latent, support in the United States for the new plans, particularly for
Euratom. The United States administration had gone very far in

---

[49] During the summer and early autumn many people on the Continent as well
as in England had felt that an encouraging attitude by the United Kingdom
might be a determining factor in the French willingness to go ahead with the
Messina plans—and vice versa. By the winter, the situation in France had
begun to change and the British attitude was much less important for either
success or failure.

seeking to encourage the acceptance of the EDC and the French rejection of that plan was, in part at least, a rebuff to the United States. Both European and American leaders were anxious to avoid repeating any of the mistakes that had contributed to the rejection of the EDC. Nevertheless the advantages the United States could confer on Euratom in the form of 'know-how' and of supplies of fissionable material were so important that any scruples the 'Europeans' may have had about American assistance seem to have been swallowed without much difficulty. The progress being made, particularly in atomic energy, was discussed at some length by Mr. Dulles with M. Monnet when the Secretary of State was in Paris for the NATO meeting in mid-December 1955, and from that time onwards the prospect that the United States might give support in the form of technical 'know-how' and enriched uranium was a formidable asset to M. Monnet and others who were arguing for the establishment of a European atomic energy institution with real powers.[50] The prospect of direct dealing between the Six and the United States also, of course, removed one of the main reasons for the continental interest in British participation and thus drastically weakened the British bargaining position with the Six.

It is perhaps worth noting that when the Prime Minister (Mr. Eden) and the Foreign Secretary (Mr. Selwyn Lloyd) visited Washington in the latter part of January 1956—primarily for discussions on the Middle Eastern situation—the United States administration made it clear that they felt the British were being ill-advisedly hostile to the plans of the Six. Mr. Eden barely touched on this point in his report to the House of Commons, which was, understandably enough, mainly concerned with the Middle East, but he later made it plain that the British and the

---

[50] See *Financial Times*, 15 December 1955. Earlier, James Reston in the *New York Times*, 6 December 1955, had written from Washington: 'The United States Government is taking a marked and sympathetic interest in the efforts to create an international federal-type authority for the development of nuclear energy in West Europe. . . . Secretary of State Dulles is taking the lead here in urging the West European nations not to be downhearted about the failure to unify Germany but to concentrate on working for European unity while they are working for German unity. He said at his news conference last week . . . that the West "shouldn't just sit around waiting" for the unification of Germany. "They should go ahead with the plans for the increasing of integration and unity of Europe," he added. "I am not thinking primarily in terms of the military unification, although that is important. I am thinking more in terms of the general development of the 'European idea' and moving toward a United States of Europe in terms of economic and political unity. . . ."'

United States differed about the Common Market and Euratom proposals.[51]

Presumably recognition of the fact that the Six could now count on United States support contributed to the British conclusion that continued coolness to the plans of the Six would simply antagonize the Six and perhaps the United States as well and that the time had come to think (and to think with some urgency) about the kind of arrangements that might be made if the plans came to fruition. In any case, on the eve of the meeting of the Foreign Ministers of the Six held in February 1956, soon after the formation of the new French Government, the British Ambassador (Sir Gladwyn Jebb) apparently informed the French Government that the British wished Euratom well and hoped to find some means of co-operating closely with it once it was formed.[52]

The direction of the new British thinking on the Common Market question had not yet become apparent. But, in January 1956, Mr. Macmillan had become Chancellor of the Exchequer and as one of his first acts he had injected a sense of urgency into the rather desultory consideration of possible courses of action that had already been started in Whitehall. Early in the spring, ideas of a free trade area comprising the United Kingdom and the Six began to be floated.

[51] In his statement to the House of Commons, Mr. Eden said simply: 'We discussed various projects for closer association in Western Europe, and I indicated our desire to press ahead, in particular, with the arms control programme within the W.E.U.' *Hansard*, House of Commons, 13 February 1956, cols. 2082–3. In his Memoirs, Mr. Eden (later Lord Avon) commented on his Washington talks: 'We were not so completely in agreement in our attitude towards two new schemes for economic integration in Europe. . . . The United States Government entertained for these proposals the same enthusiasm as they had shown towards the ill-fated European Defence Community.' *Full Circle* (London, 1960), p. 337.

[52] No official account is available of what Sir Gladwyn Jebb was authorized to say. For press accounts, see *New York Herald Tribune* (Paris edition), 12 February 1956, and *Financial Times*, 13 February 1956.

III

DRAFTING THE TREATY OF ROME

The Spaak Report

Most of the important questions that had to be settled before a common market could be formed had been discussed by the experts before the British withdrew from the Spaak Committee, although no definitive answers had been given to some of the most difficult problems and others, such as agriculture, had been touched upon in only the most perfunctory way. During the winter of 1955–6 M. Spaak and a committee restricted to representatives from the Six, assisted by experts from the High Authority of the ECSC, developed further the plans for the Common Market and for Euratom. After the formation of the new French Government, at the end of January 1956, M. Spaak presented an oral report on the winter's work to the Foreign Ministers of the Six. The communiqué issued at the end of this meeting was exceptionally sterile but from press accounts it appears that the principal points discussed were whether or not the member countries of Euratom should forswear the use of atomic energy for military purposes, the question of the ownership of fissile materials, the position the Six would take in the OEEC meeting later the same month when the question of OEEC action on atomic energy was to be considered, and the relationship between the Euratom and the Common Market treaties and, in particular, whether the two plans should be formally linked together and governmental and parliamentary approval of the two projects sought simultaneously. The Benelux countries, with considerable support from the Italians and Germans, were determined to tie the Common Market to Euratom, fearing that unless this were done the French Government would agree to Euratom but turn down the Common Market. The French 'Europeans' wanted, above all, to obtain approval of Euratom and feared that if the two were tied together too closely neither plan would succeed. They therefore argued that each plan 'had its own rhythm', that the Common Market plan needed much more study, and that before proceeding very far with the Common Market it would in any case be necessary for the French Government to consult with French agricultural and industrial organizations if a débâcle like the rejection of the EDC were to be avoided.[1]

At this time Euratom was much more in the news than was the Common Market. The controversial question of whether or not Euratom should be the sole owner of fissile material and the related question of whether or not the member countries of Euratom would agree to forswear the use of fissile material for military purposes were hotly debated, particularly in France. Although Euratom is outside the scope of this book, it should be noted that M. Monnet's position, which received considerable support from the United States Government, was that the member countries should commit themselves to use atomic energy for peaceful purposes only, and that Euratom should be the sole owner of fissile material.[2] However, when it became clear that a commitment to peaceful use was likely to raise many of the same French arguments that had sunk the EDC, this point was not pushed either by M. Monnet or by the United States. The ownership problem took longer to solve and the final agreement was a compromise which, in practice, has been even further watered down.

M. Spaak and M. Monnet disagreed about the relative importance of Euratom and the Common Market. M. Spaak, rightly as things turned out, was more interested in the Common Market. M. Monnet, on the other hand, wanted to give priority to the Euratom treaty, which he felt could be negotiated and ratified more quickly, thus maintaining momentum in 'making Europe'. He had a number of reasons for this view. Atomic energy was a new field, so that there were, as yet, no vested interests to be overcome. The French were clearly interested in some kind of European atomic energy organization. Atoms were news and could be dramatized in a way that quotas and tariffs could not. Moreover, like others at this time, he was impressed by forecasts of an impending 'energy gap' and felt this lent an

[1] See *Le Monde*, 13, 14, and 25 February 1956.
[2] One of the strong arguments for this position was that it would eliminate any feeling of 'discrimination' on the part of the Germans, who, in the context of the WEU agreement, had unilaterally given up the right to make atomic weapons. Another, of course, was that it would limit the spread of atomic weapons and make the problem of international control easier.

urgency to the Euratom proposal which the Common Market plan lacked.[3]

Shortly after the February meeting of Foreign Ministers, the task of distilling out of ten lengthy reports a single, comprehensive, yet easily comprehended document was entrusted to a small committee composed of M. Pierre Uri, at that time the principal economist of the High Authority of the Coal and Steel Community, assisted by a German, Herr von der Groeben (later to become a member of the EEC Commission) and a Belgian, M. Hupperts. At about the same time, M. Spaak addressed a special meeting of the Assembly of the Coal and Steel Community and gave a fairly detailed account of the two plans as they had then taken shape.[4] This speech was in large measure a preview of the 'Spaak Report' which is discussed at some length below. But three points are perhaps worth noting here. First, M. Spaak dealt in far greater detail with the plan for a Common Market than he did with Euratom and it was clear enough from his presentation that in his mind the Common Market was by far the more important of the two plans. Second, he made it clear that if the Six Governments approved the main lines of the report from his committee, the next step would be the drafting of a treaty à la fois on the Common Market and atomic energy; he thus linked the two plans as closely together as possible—despite the efforts of M. Monnet to give prominence and priority to Euratom and the obvious and much stronger interest of the United States in the Euratom plan. Finally, in this speech, in contrast to the one he had made a few months earlier to the Council of Europe, he made no mention of the United Kingdom and made no suggestion that arrangements between the new institutions and the United Kingdom might be necessary and desirable. This omission may, in part, be attributable to the fact that his audience this time was drawn entirely from the Six, but it seems probable that it also reflected a change in his own feeling.

M. Uri and his colleagues performed their task brilliantly and the Spaak Report, as the final report from the heads of delegations to the Six Foreign Ministers is generally called, is not only an

---

[3] At this time the future European energy position was miscalculated by almost everyone: by M. Monnet, by a group of experts appointed by the Six, and by another appointed by the OEEC, and by the British Atomic Energy Authority.

[4] The text of M. Spaak's speech is in the *Debates* of the Common Assembly of the European Coal and Steel Community for 14 March 1956. My quotations are from the provisional text.

important document, it is also readable and intellectually impressive. As Baron Snoy has commented: 'It is a model of its kind from the literary point of view; it is easier to understand than the Treaty of Rome itself, where the legal approach sometimes makes for heavy going.'[5]

The heads of delegations considered the draft report in April. Some 150 amendments were apparently discussed but few fundamental changes were made, which in itself testified to the success with which the authors had welded conflicting views into a coherent structure. The Report bears signs of compromises and of the addition of last-minute caveats, and lies somewhere between an objective blue-print and a negotiated plan. It was formally a report to the Foreign Ministers and not a document already accepted by governments. But although it did not fully meet the desires of any of them, the delegates unanimously recommended it to their governments as the basis of negotiations on the formal treaty.

The Spaak Report is both a plan for a Common Market and a statement of the motivation and the philosophy that underlie the Treaty of Rome. Although a few of the most ingenious and carefully elaborated formulae were modified or abandoned in the course of the treaty negotiations, many of the suggestions in the Report found their counterparts almost unchanged in the provisions of the Treaty of Rome. But it is primarily as a statement of the economic philosophy on which the Treaties of Rome were based that the Report remains of interest. The full understanding, and general acceptance, of the main objectives and of certain basic ideas set out in the Spaak Report provided a solid basis of common understanding and of common agreement on terms and on ideas. This was an invaluable asset in the actual treaty negotiations. In contrast, the lack of common agreement on a number of the central concepts contributed importantly to the failure of the free trade area negotiations.

One of the most enduring dogmas of the Six (and in particular of the French and of the European Commission) appeared in the foreword of the Report, that is the concept of a rounded, balanced

---

[5] Baron Snoy was the Belgian representative on the Intergovernmental Committee presided over by M. Spaak. His interesting account of the free trade area negotiations in Institut Royal des Relations Internationales (I.R.R.I.), *Chronique de Politique Ètrangères*, Vol. XII, nos. 5–6, September–November 1959, contains a number of illuminating comments on the genesis of the Treaty of Rome. The quotation above is from p. 592 (my free translation).

plan which is internally consistent: 'It is not claimed that the answers given are the only possible ones, but it must be emphasized that they constitute a coherent whole, in which the solutions given for the various problems reinforce and help one another.'[6] Pre-occupation with internal balance characterized the subsequent negotiations on the treaty and, later, the development of Community policies, and one of the chief complaints made by the Six about the free trade area proposals was that they lacked balance and coherence. Similar charges were made about some of the proposals put forward by the British during the accession negotiations.[7]

The Report made it plain at the very outset that the creation of a new economic unit was the fundamental purpose of the Common Market; the freeing of trade was simply an aspect of this more radical objective: 'The object of a European Common Market must be to create a large area with a common economic policy, constituting a powerful production unit and permitting continuous expansion, increased stability, an accelerated rise in living standards, and the development of harmonious relations among the States thus joined together.'[8] The Report also stressed in the opening paragraphs that the advantages of free trade could not be garnered unless collective means were available to facilitate adaptation to the new situation, unless practices limiting competition among producers were terminated, and unless there was co-operation among states to ensure monetary stability, economic expansion, and social progress. Because the influence of governments on production is today so pervasive, a Common Market was only conceivable if there were common rules, common action, and a system of institutions supervising the development of the market. A Common Market could thus only be established between states which felt themselves close enough to one another to make the necessary adjustments in their legislation and to achieve the necessary solidarity in their policies. However,

[6] Comité Intergouvernemental créé par la Conférence de Messine, *Rapport des Chefs de Délégation aux Ministres des Affaires Ètrangères* (Brussels, 21 April 1956), p. 10 (my free translation). The report is hereafter cited as Spaak Report.

[7] The Treaty of Rome as it emerged from the negotiations was, of course, the product of much hard bargaining and some of its provisions were clear concessions to national interest. In consequence, the British sometimes found the arguments put forward about the coherence of the treaty and the sanctity of all of its parts a little strained.

[8] Spaak Report, p. 13. (My free translation, here and in subsequent extracts.)

although a true Common Market could, by its nature, only be established among a limited number of countries the authors were quick to add that this exclusiveness should not be regarded as working against the interests of others. On the contrary, they argued that the Common Market, by strengthening the economies of the member countries, would reduce their need for protection and would put them in a position to contribute to a general lowering of tariffs. Furthermore the Report held out the prospect that the new group would be able to establish with countries which did not feel able to join it 'relations that are closer than those they previously had with each of these States individually'.[9] Although no countries were named, it seems probable that this sentence was written with the British, among others, in mind.[10]

The prospect of special relations with certain third countries was referred to again later in the Report when the reasons why the Six should base their own Common Market on a customs union rather than a free trade area were elaborated. And here the United Kingdom was clearly uppermost in the minds of the authors. The first objection to a free trade area among the Six had already been brought out in the experts' discussions, that is the fact that a free trade area would require the maintenance of controls along the interior boundaries of the Common Market to guard against trade deflection. The authors of the Spaak Report put forward a new argument against a free trade area and one which was to colour the views of the Six in the later discussions on a wider free trade area:

The other objection is of an economic order. By allowing different commercial policies and different tariff levels *vis-à-vis* third countries, the formula of a free trade area makes it possible to maintain exchange rates which are not tied to a common policy towards third countries. This affects the conditions of equilibrium and the character of the trade in the Common Market itself; this is an obstacle to the establishment

---

[9] Spaak Report, p. 15.

[10] Austria, Denmark, and Switzerland also seem to have been in the minds of the drafters. Somewhat surprisingly in view of its later position that joining the Common Market was inconsistent with her neutrality, Austria was apparently felt by some to be a potential member of the Community. M. Spaak was reported to have felt at one time that if the French were unable, in the end, to join the Common Market the other five should go ahead and that in this event Austria would be a useful 'land-bridge' between Italy and the rest. At about this same time, the possible accession of Austria to the ECSC was under consideration.

of conditions which will ultimately ensure the stability and prosperity of the internal market.[11]

Despite this second objection, the Report nevertheless stated that although there were decisive economic and technical reasons for choosing a customs union among the countries on the Continent, these did not exclude the possibility of superimposing upon it a free trade area with another country (*tel autre pays*), which because of distance and the costs of transport and of loading and unloading could maintain a separate tariff with respect to third countries without risk of deflexion of trade.[12]

All the important provisions in the Treaty of Rome save those relating to the association of the overseas territories were foreshadowed in the Spaak Report, and on most points the provisions in the Treaty of Rome simply developed further or refined principles and procedures discussed in the Report. The Spaak Report dealt in considerable detail with the method and timetable for removing tariffs and quotas and for establishing a common external tariff, but for many other aspects of the Common Market it outlined the objective to be sought and the considerations to be borne in mind in pursuing the objective but did not give a detailed blue-print. To some extent this unevenness in the Report was a reflection of the fact that there was substantial agreement among the Six on some points but only uneasy compromise on others; to some extent it resulted from the fact that the authors realized that it was impossible to see the end of the interplay in forces that the process of forming a Common Market would set in motion and therefore felt it was unrealistic to try to legislate in great detail too far in advance. However, because the play of the market and a developing situation required flexibility, the authors felt it doubly necessary to be able to rely on institutions with clearly defined powers and on a wide variety of procedural arrangements to deal

[11] Spaak Report, p. 21.
[12] Spaak Report, p. 22. M. Uri later wrote that the concept here was much more limited than that in the later British plan and that all that was envisaged in the Spaak Report was that British tariffs might differ from the common tariffs by the amount of the transport costs: 'On n'avait pas envisagé autre chose que des tarifs harmonisés, sans contrôle de l'origine, l'écart maximum correspondant aux coûts de transport, avec un pays tel que la Grande-Bretagne dont la situation insulaire leur donnait une incidence substantielle.' See 'Europeus', *La Crise de la zone de libre-échange* (Librairie Plon, Paris, 1959), pp. 5–6. This may have been all M. Uri had in mind but it was certainly not what the British representative at the Spaak Committee had in mind when he argued the advantages of a free trade area.

with problems as they arose. The close interrelationship between the powers of the institutions and the detail with which the measures required in the later stages of the formation of the Common Market needed to be agreed in advance, is another theme that recurred throughout the negotiations on the Treaty of Rome and again in the negotiations in the OEEC on a free trade area.

As noted above, little effort had been made in the expert discussions during the autumn of 1955 to find agreement on the institutional arrangements for the new Community and M. Spaak had at all times dealt with this question most circumspectly. But the report to the Foreign Ministers, if it were to be the basis of a definitive treaty, had to grasp the nettle. It did so and, in effect, outlined the institutional arrangements found in the Treaty of Rome. There was little obvious trace of any doctrinaire commitment to supra-nationalism. Although one can be confident that M. Spaak and other leading figures in the *relance* had from the start a reasonably clear idea of the kind of institutions they wanted, the Report here as elsewhere was carefully reasoned and the institutional arrangements were put forward as the logical consequence of certain largely non-controversial principles, rather than as principles in themselves. The parentege of the ECSC was clear but the balance between the national and the supra-national elements was somewhat altered. The Council of Ministers emerged as the principal decision-making body and the Commission as an objective initiator of proposals and as the executive body charged with ensuring the carrying-out of the treaty and with the administration of the escape clauses. The Spaak Report introduced a number of useful new ideas into the institutional discussions. First, as noted above, by emphasizing the importance of establishing procedures and the institutional means for arriving at later decisions and by ensuring that these procedures safeguarded both objectivity and national interest, it made it possible for the treaty to be, in certain important respects, an outline treaty. Second, it introduced the idea that the Council could logically act by some form of qualified majority, rather than by unanimity, where it was acting on the proposal of an objective body, the Commission, and within the general framework of action agreed in the treaty. Third, it suggested that the voting system might become more liberal in the later stages of the transitional period—that is, that unanimity might in many cases give way to

some form of qualified majority voting after the second stage.
The Spaak Report left substantially more of the details of action
for later formulation by the Commission than does the Treaty of
Rome. The greater precision of the treaty thus inevitably somewhat reduced the role foreseen for the Commission, but, in
general, the interrelationship between Council and Commission
in the treaty is that of the Spaak Report. The 'logic' of the relationship and of the voting arrangements are clearly the same.

The experts had dealt even more perfunctorily with agriculture
than with institutions, but there was no disagreement among the
Six, at any time, on the principle of including agriculture, and the
Spaak Report stated flatly that it was impossible to conceive of the
establishment of a general common market in Europe without the
inclusion of agriculture. This, it pointed out, was not simply
because agriculture was one of the sectors which could profit
most from a greater specialization of production and broadening
of markets but because the inclusion of agriculture in the Common
Market 'is a condition of equilibrium in the trade between the
different economies of the member states'.[13] Once again, a controversial point in the later free trade area negotiations with the
British was put forward—and accepted—as axiomatic. However,
although its inclusion was never in doubt, agriculture clearly gave
the Spaak Committee great difficulty and this section of the Report,
like the Treaty of Rome itself, set forth the general objectives to
be attained by the end of the transitional period but left most of
the details to be formulated by the Community institutions. The
general principle was clearly established that, as in other sectors,
obstacles to trade in agricultural products must be eliminated,
but it was recognized that the problems that had led to the
organization and control of national agricultural markets would not
disappear just because barriers to trade were removed. For some
products stabilization measures would continue to be necessary in
the Common Market, but all national measures would have
gradually to be replaced by Community regulations. Although
these could not be 'national' in design or effect, they did not need
to be the same for all products, or, indeed, for all regions.[14] As in

---

[13] Spaak Report, p. 44.

[14] Spaak Report, p. 48. 'L'unité de conception dans une politique pour la Communauté n'exclut pas la diversification des choix et des méthodes en fonction
des positions et des vocations des diverses régions; bien au contraire, cette
diversité répond à l'exigence d'une spécialisation interne à la Communauté
que facilitera le marché commun.'

other sections, the fundamental rule was that at the end of the transition period and in relations both with member states and with third countries there must be no regulations which were separate and different, state by state: these must either have disappeared or have been replaced by a common system.

The Spaak Report recognized rather more explicitly than does the Treaty of Rome the problems that the organization of agriculture on a Community basis might create for third countries and pointed out that 'without doubt it is necessary to guard against the danger that the measures for organizing the market as a whole, when substituted for national regulations, will tend to create a large area protected against the outside world and aligning its own prices on those of the marginal producers'.[15] On the other hand, the Report was quick to add that competition with third countries raised a number of problems and that it was appropriate for a preference to be given to Community products when the price of production compared favourably with the *internal* price in other countries, that is in contrast to the price at which third countries might be disposed to sell their surpluses. The Report emphasized that it was particularly necessary to take a long-term view of agricultural questions and suggested that 'certain partners will have to renounce short-term advantages that they might derive from the pricing practices of third countries'. Here and elsewhere, the authors of the Report were obviously trying to reconcile in a logical and plausible way the desire of the French for a 'Community preference' for their agricultural exports with the desires of other countries, in particular Germany, to continue to import from the cheapest source. This basic difference in outlook was not resolved and emerged very clearly during the Community's discussions of the details of the common agricultural policy in the winter of 1961–2 and also during the negotiations on British accession.

The Foreign Ministers of the Six formally considered the Spaak Report at a meeting in Venice at the end of May 1956. In the weeks before the meeting the points left open by the Report—these were mostly points relating to Euratom—were the subject of considerable public controversy. This was particularly violent in France where the argument over the question of whether or not the members of Euratom should give up the right to make nuclear weapons threatened to rake the embers of the EDC controversy

[15] Spaak Report, p. 51.

into another destroying blaze. The Common Market plan was, by contrast, almost ignored by the French, not because it was acceptable but because unlike Euratom it had no strong advocates in France and at this stage, at least, the opponents were reasonably confident that it had little chance of being accepted. The situation in the other countries of the Six was quite different. Both in Germany and in the Benelux countries, and to some extent even in Italy, there was strong governmental and industrial support for the Common Market, little positive enthusiasm for Euratom, and some strong opposition to it. In Germany, the Chancellor (Dr. Adenauer) was having a running fight with the industrialists who disliked Euratom, and in Belgium there were many who felt that, given their uranium resources in the Congo, they would be in a strong enough position in the new age of atomic energy without Euratom. As indicated above, both in Germany and in the Benelux countries there was great insistence on keeping the Common Market and Euratom plans so closely linked together that the French could not accept Euratom and then reject the Common Market.

At this time the United Kingdom was maintaining an aloof silence. There were beginning to be signs of new thinking in government circles and of greater awareness generally that the Six were embarked upon plans which if they came to fruition would have important implications for the United Kingdom.[16] However, there was probably a greater tendency to feel that the opposition to Euratom in Germany and the opposition to the Common Market in France and the insistence of the Benelux countries on tying the two plans tightly together would result in the foundering of both plans, than there was to reason, more optimistically, that the considerable support for Euratom in France and for the Common Market in Germany and the Benelux countries would result in both plans succeeding.

The Venice meeting of the Foreign Ministers of the Six was very short and there was little discussion of the substantive points at issue. Presumably the Foreign Ministers intentionally avoided discussing the controversial points to accommodate the French, who would have been reluctant to take a final position before the debate on Euratom in the National Assembly. (See below, p. 66.) Contrary to the fears of the other countries, M. Pineau, the French

---

[16] See, for example, the leading article in *The Times*, 29 May 1956, 'Ambiguity is not Enough'.

Foreign Minister, indicated that the French Government was prepared to accept the Spaak Report as the basis for the drafting of treaties on the Common Market as well as Euratom. However, as all the French delegates throughout the discussions in the Spaak Committee had done, M. Pineau emphasized the French view that there must be a link between the harmonizing of social charges within the Community and the freeing of trade.[17] In this connexion, he proposed that before proceeding to the second stage of the transition period the member countries should agree that the measures laid down for the first stage had been taken and that the necessary harmonization had been achieved on the three subjects to which the French attached particular importance: overtime pay, length of paid holidays, and equal pay for men and women.[18] To the surprise of the other delegates, M. Pineau also proposed that the overseas territories of the countries forming the Common Market be included within the scope of the treaty. This seems to have been interpreted by the other delegates as a sign that the French were, at last, taking the Common Market seriously rather than as a sign that they were looking for new difficulties to put in its path, and it was agreed that this question would be examined by a special committee of those countries with overseas possessions—France, Belgium, and the Netherlands—and discussed again by the Foreign Ministers in the autumn.

A compromise was found for the controversial question of the link, if any, to be made between Euratom and the Common Market: it was agreed that there would be only one diplomatic treaty-drafting conference but that it would be organized in two sections, one on Euratom, the other on the Common Market. Although work in the two sections would proceed simultaneously the French succeeded in getting the others to agree that each

[17] The Spaak Report contained an interesting section distinguishing situations in which differences in legislation, fiscal systems, etc., led to distortions that must be corrected if the Common Market was to function satisfactorily from situations in which these differences were simply the comparative advantage that makes trade economically profitable (see pp. 60–61). This analysis clearly conditioned the thinking of the Six not only during the Treaty of Rome negotiations but also during the free trade area negotiations.

[18] Although rejecting, on economic grounds, much of the French argument about the need for a prior harmonization of social charges, the Spaak Report conceded that, even if the existing disparities did not imply distortions, it would be necessary for the governments to make a special effort to harmonize progressively the regulations in force concerning the principle of equal pay for men and women, the length of the working week and overtime pay, and the length of paid holidays. See Spaak Report, pp. 65–66.

section 'should have its own rhythm', and the question of whether one treaty might in the end be ratified before the other was left open.

The Venice Conference authorized M. Spaak to invite any other OEEC country that was now prepared to accept the Spaak Report as the basis of future work to participate in the drafting of the treaties; it was also agreed that the treaties should contain provisions for the adhesion or association of third countries. Shortly after the conference the British apparently suggested to M. Spaak that a British official should again sit with the group, but since the United Kingdom was not prepared to accept the Spaak Report this proposal was rejected.[19]

The Venice Conference settled none of the outstanding substantive questions but the agreement to begin drafting treaties on the basis of the Spaak Report was an important step forward. Although work on the treaties was started in Brussels at the end of June, little was accomplished before the break in August for summer holidays and the conference really began in earnest in September 1956. From then on, it met in almost continuous session until the drafting of the two treaties was completed in March of the following year (1957).

Early in July 1956 the French Assembly had a long and crucial debate on the *relance* in general, and on Euratom in particular. The French Government was very conscious of the need to avoid a repetition of the mistakes and bitterness of the EDC débâcle and it had deliberately sought a debate both to strengthen its own position when it came to ratification and to give its representatives in Brussels a firmer position from which to negotiate.

Despite the importance of the subject and the obvious political interest in Euratom, the debate itself was poorly attended. Nevertheless the Government treated the debate as a matter of first importance and the press covered it very fully. Although the Government had decided not to ask for a vote of confidence, on the eve of the debate M. Mollet let it be known that he would resign if the final vote went against the Government. This implied threat aroused considerable resentment, and the two Gaullist members of the Cabinet added to a confused situation by indicating that if the final vote were for Euratom (i.e. supported

[19] There was some confusion about Turkey. Apparently the Turks indicated a desire to participate but were eventually persuaded by the Six that their problems could be examined better at a later date.

M. Mollet) they would resign. In his final speech before the Assembly, M. Mollet withdrew his threat and made an eloquent plea, with no strings attached, for support for the motion requesting the Government to continue negotiations. He used as his strongest argument not the economic advantages to be derived from a pooling of efforts but the fact that the unification of Western Europe was a 'political imperative' for France: first, because only a United Europe would carry weight with the two colossi—the U.S.A. and the U.S.S.R.—and second, because the only sure guarantee against an eventual German–Soviet alignment lay in integrating Western Germany into a European system.[20] He also made the subsidiary, and somewhat contradictory, point that unless Euratom were created Germany and the United States might be expected to collaborate closely in atomic matters, a prospect that was known to be attractive to the German industrialists.

The principal points attacked in the Assembly debate, as in the press discussion that preceded it, were, first, the fact that only the Six countries were participating in Euratom; second, the powers and particularly the 'supra-nationalism' of Euratom; and finally, and by far the most important, the possibility that Euratom might preclude France from becoming the fourth nuclear power. Other subsidiary points, such as the linking of the Common Market and Euratom, also came in for criticism. M. Mendès-France and those of the Radicals that followed him were the principal critics of the fact that Euratom was limited to the Six. The Government was on strong ground in pointing out that many efforts had been made to interest the United Kingdom without success but once again gave assurances that it wanted other countries to join and that in any case Euratom would work in conjunction with the OEEC.[21]

The attack on the powers and supra-nationality of Euratom came

---

[20] 'Ma conviction profonde, inchangée depuis des années, est que seule l'integration de l'Allemagne à un ensemble européen qui lui soit supérieur, qui ait autorité sur elle comme sur les autres États participants, fournira une solution durable du problème allemand.' See Assemblée Nationale, *Débats*, 11 July 1956, pp. 3382–5.

[21] See *Le Monde*, 8–9 July 1956. It is worth noting that Maurice Faure, in answering those who were critical of the fact that the Six were going ahead without the United Kingdom, said that the United Kingdom could only be led to re-examine the question of participating by the organization of a European Community. He added that the British attitude was beginning to evolve favourably and that if this evolution was speeded up, the principal 'hypothèque politique qui pèse sur les projets en cause serait levée'.

principally from the Gaullists. The French Government was at pains to play down the powers of Euratom and, in addition, made a specific concession to the Gaullists by indicating that the French negotiators would be instructed to oppose any institutional links between Euratom and the Coal and Steel Community.[22] The onslaught on the idea of committing France through its participation in Euratom to forgo developing atomic energy for military purposes came from all sides, but particularly from the Gaullists. Here the Government offered a compromise: France would commit itself not to explode an atomic bomb before 1 January 1961, but thereafter would regain complete freedom of action. In the meantime there would be no bar to the research and development of the atomic bomb. This 'compromise' was, in effect, the end of any real hope that Euratom might play a part in stopping the spread of nuclear weapons. As the French Ministers who supported Euratom were at pains to point out to their critics during the debate, the very limited French commitment had little meaning, for no one supposed that France would, in any case, be in a position to test an atomic bomb before 1961.

The Socialist motion in support of continuing the negotiations was in the end approved by the surprisingly large majority of 332 to 181 with 70 abstentions. Reluctance to run the risk of another governmental crisis undoubtedly helped to secure the sizeable favourable vote, and much of the debate could not have been cheerful reading for France's partners in the Six. Nevertheless the simple fact of a favourable vote, even though important concessions were made to achieve it, helped to dispel some of the doubts as to the ability of the French Government to obtain eventual ratification of the new treaties and thus helped to put the negotiations on firmer ground when they began in earnest in September 1956.

Negotiating the Treaty

Several factors gave a sense of urgency to the drafting of the treaties when the Brussels conference was resumed in September 1956. The 'Europeans' were anxious to get the treaties signed before the German election campaign began in 1957. They

---

[22] The Spaak Report had recommended that the new Communities share with the Coal and Steel Community the Assembly and the Court of Justice. The French were not successful in persuading the other countries to give up this link.

also wanted to make all possible progress while the pro-European Mollet Government remained in power in France; because of the controversy over Algeria, its days were clearly numbered. The British interest in a free trade area (see Chapter IV) also contributed—in two rather contradictory ways—to a speeding-up of the work of the Six. On the one hand it reassured those in the Six countries who had been reluctant to proceed very far without British participation; on the other hand, it increased the zeal of those who feared it would be difficult to reach agreement on a full-blooded Common Market once negotiations on the free trade area began in earnest. The July debate on Euratom in the French Assembly, unsatisfactory as it had been in many respects, had at least helped to clear the air. And although the French confronted their partners in the Six with a number of difficult and unpalatable demands during the autumn negotiations, the other five felt that the French now meant business on the Common Market scheme as well as on Euratom. Finally, the Suez episode, by underlining Europe's diminished role in world affairs, gave a strong new impetus to the drive for unity.

The French demands that were pressed during this last phase of the negotiations can be divided into three groups. First, there were demands for certain exceptional arrangements for France. For example the French wanted to be permitted to retain after the entry into force of the treaty the special taxes on imports and special aids to exports that had been introduced in 1954, largely to compensate for the over-valuation of the French franc. Secondly, there were demands relating to 'harmonization', and the closely-related French demand that passage from the first to the second stage of the Treaty of Rome should not be automatic, as the Spaak Report had proposed, but subject to the unanimous agreement of the member governments. Finally, there was the French demand for the inclusion of the overseas territories of the member countries within the scope of the treaty. In addition, of course, the French, like the others, had strongly-held views on the way the outstanding unresolved questions should be settled: of these the most important were the arrangements for agriculture, the height of the external tariff, and the institutional arrangements.[23]

French demands for a 'special position' were not new and at

---

[23] The French also insisted on the unilateral right of a member country to re-impose import restrictions not only in the event of balance of payments difficulties but also in the case of a serious threat to a particular industry.

various times in the past a number of possible 'empty chair' arrangements for France had been considered. For example, it had at one time been suggested that the French should participate in the negotiations and sign the treaty but that the treaty should not become immediately applicable to France. During the autumn discussions, the idea of a later starting date for France and other sweeping forms of 'special position' were abandoned and the French concentrated, instead, on the particular points mentioned above. It was agreed that France's special import charges and export subsidies could be maintained subject to an annual review by the Commission and the Council, but that the Council, acting by majority vote on the proposal of the Commission, could decide that they should be abolished if the balance of current payments of the franc area remained in equilibrium for a period of more than one year and if monetary reserves were also at a satisfactory level.[24]

The method of passing from the first to the second stage, 'harmonization', and the inclusion of the overseas territories all raised much more important difficulties, and difficulties of a conceptual as well as of a practical character. From the earliest days of the discussions in the Spaak Committee, the representatives of most countries (including the United Kingdom in the days when the British were participating in the discussions) had been convinced that the commitment to the abolition of trade barriers must be reasonably limited in time, largely automatic in execution, and irreversible. The experts felt that the temptation to become stuck half-way and to end up as a preference area with tariffs reduced but not completely eliminated would be very great and should be guarded against by the treaty.[25] They were also impressed by the need to give industry a firm basis for planning. During the experts' discussions and later during the negotiations on the treaty, the French sought various ways of loosening the

---

[24] See Protocol relating to certain provisions of concern to France, Treaty of Rome. The provisions relating to the French right to maintain import charges and export subsidies were, in effect, rendered obsolete by the French decision to devalue the franc at the end of 1958 and the French economic reforms which, *inter alia*, abolished these charges.

[25] It is worth noting that experience to date has shown that this fear (like many of the others that occupied the negotiators) has not materialized. Industry (even French industry) has pressed for a faster formation of the customs union than the treaty stipulates rather than for any slowing down of the timetable. However, the picture might have been different had Europe experienced a sharp recession during this period.

commitment. They argued for a long transitional period; for stages; for a trial period of four years and a subsequent decision on further action at the end of the trial period; for a less automatic procedure for passing from one stage to the next; and for the unilateral right to resort to escape clauses.[26]

The final agreement on a twelve- to fifteen-year transitional period was a concession to the French; the other countries would have been content with ten years and some of them would have preferred as short a period as five years. The decision to divide the transitional period into stages and to phase the achievement of other aspects of the treaty with the progressive reduction of trade barriers was also accepted largely in response to French arguments. The others, however, from the start adamantly opposed French suggestions for a trial period with only the most general commitment beyond the first four years and, by the time the serious negotiations began, the French had abandoned this extreme request. During the autumn the argument centred on two issues: first, the relationship to be established between the stages of trade liberalization and the progress made in 'harmonization'; and second, the procedure by which the decision to move to the second stage was to be made. Earlier in the year the French had argued that a substantial measure of 'harmonization' was a condition 'préalable' to the freeing of trade but by the autumn they were ready to agree that during the first period trade liberalization and 'harmonization' could take place simultaneously. They insisted however that certain measures of harmonization must be achieved during the first four-year period. The French sticking-points were those named by M. Pineau at Venice: equal pay for men and women; the standardization at French levels of the length of paid holidays; and agreement on arrangements for over-time pay comparable to those that existed in France. The first two conditions—equal pay for men and women and standardization of paid holidays—in the end caused no very great difficulties. All of the Six had already subscribed to the ILO convention on equal pay for men and women, and they therefore regarded the acceptance of the commitment to 'ensure and subsequently maintain the application' of this principle as, at most, a slight acceleration of an

---

[26] Since escape clause action usually took the form of a reimposition of restrictions—or of a release from an obligation to remove a restriction or to reduce a tariff—easy resort to escape clauses could vitiate the automaticity and irreversibility of the plan.

inevitable development.[27] An examination of the existing arrangements for paid holidays revealed a surprising degree of similarity among the Six, and the French were therefore satisfied with the simple stipulation that member states should 'endeavour to maintain the existing equivalence of paid holiday schemes'.[28] But the third French demand—harmonization of overtime pay—was much more difficult to meet.

The Germans, and in particular the Minister of Economics, Dr. Erhard, were greatly worried by the possibility of inflation and feared the effect on wages of agreeing to accept the more generous French level of overtime as the norm to be reached by the end of the first stage. At this time the French had a standard working week of 40 hours, the Belgians one of 45 hours, the others, 48 hours. The question was discussed at a meeting of the ministers of the Six in Paris in the latter part of October. According to an account in *Le Figaro*, Dr. Erhard maintained 'in the face of general scepticism' that the German economy could not stand an increase in wages of about 4 per cent. in four years. One of the novelties of this meeting of the Six, according to the same account, was that France tended to be in agreement with the other four on a number of issues while the Germans tended to be the odd man out.[29] After further discussion by the heads of delegations in Brussels in November a compromise was finally reached. Thus, in the special Protocol for France it was stated that the member states considered that by the end of the first stage of the transitional period the basic levels for overtime pay and the average rates for overtime would correspond to those existing in France in 1956. If they did not, the Commission was, in certain circumstances, to authorize France to take safeguard measures for those branches of industry that were adversely affected.[30]

[27] See Treaty, Article 119. The fact that equal pay for men and women had not been achieved by the end of the first stage was pointed out by the French during the discussion in the autumn of 1961 on the move to the second stage and an agreement was reached on how the objective should be achieved.

[28] Ibid., Article 120.

[29] See *Le Figaro*, 22 October 1956. The other principal issue on which France and the other four were lined up against the Germans concerned Euratom. The Bonn correspondent of the *New York Times*, in an article on 4 November 1956, reported that the German authorities refused to agree to the French request on overtime pay because they did not want to cut the ground from under German industry which was about to open wage negotiations with organized labour. The report added that the West German authorities nevertheless thought the 40-hour week 'inevitable'.

[30] See *Le Monde*, 18–19 November 1956. The provision incorporated in the

The French, as well as insisting that these three conditions must be fulfilled during the first stage, argued that before moving to the second stage the Six Governments must find *unanimously* that these and all other measures that had been agreed for the first stage had, in fact, been implemented. The others felt that a unanimous decision held too great a risk of a French veto and that they might well find themselves indefinitely held up by the French. Again, a compromise was eventually found, although not a very happy one. At the end of the fourth and at the end of the fifth year a unanimous decision would be required to move to the second stage. But as insurance against an indefinite delay the French agreed that, if the first stage had not previously been terminated, at the end of the sixth year the Council would act by a qualified majority vote, rather than by unanimity. However, this concession was qualified and a member finding itself out-voted (or any member if there was no qualified majority for moving to the second stage) could require the Council to refer the matter to an Arbitration Board whose decision would be binding.[31] As in the case of a number of the other hard-fought compromises, the anticipated difficulties did not materialize.

The final demand—the inclusion of the overseas territories—was the most difficult of all the French requests and by the end of the year very little progress had been made on this question. When the French first seriously proposed the inclusion of the overseas territories, they apparently had no very clear idea of the detailed arrangements they wanted to see made, nor were they even sure to which of their territories they wanted the special arrangements to apply. During the autumn the French sought to

---

special Protocol, although advantageous for France, in fact reflects the general thesis of the Spaak Report on harmonization, namely that harmonization is not a precondition for, but will tend to be a consequence of, the establishment of a Common Market. The account in *Le Monde* suggests that a brief meeting between M. Mollet and Dr. Adenauer early in November helped to open the way to the final compromise on harmonization. On the compromises on 'harmonization' see also the account by Baron Snoy in I.R.R.I. (1959), pp. 594–5.

[31] Treaty, Article 8. The Treaty does not make clear what would happen if the Arbitration Board supported the view that the conditions for a move to the second stage had not been fulfilled. However, it should be noted that sub-paragraph 6 of Article 8 reads as follows: 'The provisions of the preceding paragraphs shall not have the effect of extending the transitional period beyond a total duration of fifteen years after the date of the entry into force of this Treaty.' Here, and elsewhere, the quotations are from the English text published by the Secretariat of the Interim Committee for the Common Market and Euratom, Brussels.

clarify their own views and to concert them with the Belgians. Negotiations with the rest of the Six on the overseas territories did not really begin until after the turn of the year and, as discussed further below, the differences in view could in the end only be resolved by the Heads of Government.

Somewhat more progress was made during the autumn on agriculture, the external tariff, and the institutional question, but hard bargaining on these questions continued during January at the heads of delegation and Foreign Ministers level and a few key points had to be reserved for the meeting of the Heads of Governments in February 1957.

Several points are worth noting about the discussions on agriculture. Contrary to the impressions that became current later, and also in contrast to the situation that developed when the details of the common agricultural policy were being thrashed out, the protagonists at this time were the Dutch and the French, not the Germans and the French.[32] The principal differences of view were over the extent to which the development of agricultural trade within the Community should be controlled or should be left free, with the Dutch favouring as free a system as possible and the French arguing for specific measures both to guard against disruption of the internal market by imports and to stimulate intra-Community trade.[33] During the negotiations the French advocated the use of two principal mechanisms: minimum prices to guard against market disruption and the negotiation of long-term contracts to encourage the expansion of intra-Community trade. The Dutch were suspicious of both: minimum prices if set high enough could be as effective a protective device as quotas and tariffs, and long-term contracts could

[32] In the latter part of 1961, Walter Lippman wrote a series of illuminating articles on the EEC. In one of them he characterized the Treaty of Rome as a deal between French agriculture and German industry, and this observation was picked up by numerous commentators. It is undoubtedly true that the French always saw more opportunity for themselves in exporting agricultural products than industrial products, and this has become an increasingly important French interest. But at the time the treaties were being negotiated the Franco-German 'deal' was really between the Common Market treaty and Euratom, as explained above.

[33] The French, with some justification, felt the Dutch were so strongly in favour of Community free trade because their own agriculture was so well organized that they had a competitive advantage over the others. The Dutch, also with justification, felt the French looked to Community organizations to do the job of organizing domestic agriculture which the French Government had not been able to do.

result in France arrogating to itself the lion's share of certain markets, particularly the German market, to which the Dutch also wanted access.

Although the Spaak Report had laid down the general principles that quotas and tariffs should be removed from trade in agricultural as well as industrial products and that, in the final period, market intervention must be on a Community, not a national basis, it had not specified in any detail what form the final common organization of the market should take. The Treaty of Rome follows the Spaak Report both in foreseeing a common organization of the market and in deferring for later determination by the Community institutions which of a number of forms the common organization should take. But it is worth noting here that the key feature of the eventual common policy, the common price policy, is referred to in the treaty in a rather perfunctory way.[34]

Thus, partly because the Treaty of Rome postponed the most difficult aspects of the agricultural policy for later determination by the Community institutions, and partly because the argument at this time was primarily concerned with the principle of how free a market should be established (and here German interests were closer to the French than to the Dutch), agriculture was not an important issue between the Germans and the French. Moreover to the extent that the question of prices came into the discussions, German agricultural interests saw no cause for alarm, since at that time French and German prices for the main farm products were roughly in line with one another. It is important to note that the Treaty of Rome negotiations took place before the devaluations of the French franc in mid-1957 and at the end of 1958, and the German revaluation of the mark in early 1961; the difficult Franco-German argument on prices took place in the latter part of 1961 and in 1962 and 1963 after these three exchange adjustments had taken place.[35]

The main points of controversy on agriculture during the Treaty of Rome negotiations were the criteria and method for determining minimum prices, the conditions governing the use of long-term contracts, and the list of products to be considered to be 'agricultural products'. Apart from some language intended to

---

[34] See Treaty, Article 40 (3): 'A common price policy, if any, shall be based on common criteria and on uniform methods of calculation.'
[35] See P. J. Lardinois, 'The United Kingdom and the European Economic Community', in *Journal of Agricultural Economics*, December 1961, pp. 534-5.

guard against minimum prices being used in too restrictive a manner, the chief concession made to the Dutch was the French agreement that at the end of the transition period the minimum price system (to the extent it was still operative) would be determined by a qualified majority vote of the Council rather than by a unanimous vote.[36]

In January 1957, during the final stages of the negotiations on these fundamental aspects of the treaty, the French Assembly held a long and important debate on the Common Market. As in the case of the debate on Euratom in July, the Mollet Government had taken the initiative in requesting a debate. Except for the provisions on the overseas territories, the main outlines of the treaty on the Common Market were clear, and the Mollet Government hoped for an endorsement of the progress already made. It wanted general support in the last phases of the negotiations, not detailed instructions, for its area of manoeuvre was very small. Major concessions had been made to the French negotiators by the other countries and any new demands from the Assembly would have been extremely awkward for the Government. Despite the danger of a debate at the eleventh hour, the French Government appears to have been confident of support, and the press was reassuringly predicting a fairly comfortable majority. Throughout the autumn the Government, through the Economic Council, had kept in close touch with the industrial and farm organizations and many of their most important demands for safeguards and special arrangements had already been largely satisfied in the negotiations. French industry was beginning to realize that France alone was too small and that its highly protected economy was a source of weakness. The Patronat was becoming impressed with the advantages of a Common Market, although it had an almost inexhaustible appetite for safeguards.[37] The farm organizations also tended to favour a

---

[36] Certain guiding principles on minimum prices are laid down in Article 44 of the Treaty but 'objective criteria' were to be determined by the Council acting unanimously on a proposal of the Commission during the first three years. Article 44(2) is worth noting because it contains the only reference in the agricultural articles of the Treaty to the principle of Community preference, a principle which was to figure so prominently in the British accession negotiations. 'The minimum prices shall not be such as to lead to a reduction of exchanges existing between Member States at the date of the entry into force of this Treaty and shall not be an obstacle to a progressive expansion of such exchanges. The minimum prices shall not be applied in such a manner as to be an obstacle to the development of a natural preference between the Member States.'

[37] See *Le Monde*, 17 January 1957.

Common Market—on conditions. The Force Ouvrière and the CFTC (the two non-Communist labour federations) were also favourable, again on conditions.[38] The Suez fiasco had generated a new wave of 'Europeanism' and had visibly strengthened the feeling in France that only through European unity could France regain a position of power and independence in the world.

Although the motion favoured by the Government was adopted by 322 to 207 votes, the debate in the National Assembly was not without its hazards. Opposition had been expected from the extreme right and the extreme left and criticisms from these quarters were not too difficult to deal with.[39] The criticism of M. Mendès-France was of more concern to the Government, as was a motion proposed mid-way in the debate by four former Prime Ministers (MM. Pinay, Reynaud, Edgar Faure, and Laniel).

M. Mendès-France's attack on the Common Market plan was two-pronged. First he made a number of what he described as technical criticisms of the Common Market, although these criticisms, in fact, tended to strike at the roots of the plan. He deplored what he felt to be serious imprecisions and lacunae in the treaty and he attacked the extent of supra-nationality. Somewhat curiously, given his apparent preference for the free trade area, he criticized the Common Market for being based on the 'classical liberalism of the nineteenth century'. His strongest point was that the Government, bemused by the advantages of a larger market, was not dealing with the fundamental problem, i.e. the need for France to put its own economic house in order. He accused the Government of trying to cure the economic weakness of France by exposing it to external pressures (with unforeseen and perhaps disastrous consequences) rather than by dealing with France's economic problems directly. He warned that a democracy could abdicate in two ways: either by giving all power to a man of destiny or by the delegation of powers to an external authority which, in the name of technical efficiency, in effect exercised political power.[40] His second main line of attack was to question the need for haste and in this connexion to deplore the apparent desire of the Government to proceed with the Common Market

[38] See *Le Monde*, 18 January 1957. The CGT, the Communist-controlled labour federation, was, of course, strongly opposed.

[39] It is strikingly easy to find parallels between the French and British parliamentary reactions to the Treaty of Rome.

[40] Assemblée Nationale, *Débats*, 18 January 1957, p. 166.

rather than responding to British initiatives and trying to find a way of proceeding in company with the United Kingdom.[41]

M. Mendès-France was only one of many speakers to question the wisdom of proceeding with the Common Market without the British. Some of those who appeared to prefer the free trade area to the Common Market were obviously adopting this position for tactical reasons and, having successfully disposed of the Common Market, would then have opposed the free trade area.[42] But there was, as well, a clear desire on the part of many speakers to be reassured that agreement on the Common Market would in no way prejudice the conclusion of a subsequent agreement with the British and the other OEEC countries. The Government was at great pains to emphasize that it was a mistake to believe that the two plans were alternatives. Repeatedly the point was made that it was only because the Six had gone ahead with the Common Market that the British had become interested in a free trade area. And M. Mollet went further and expressed his own fear that if the Brussels plan fell through, the free trade area would be no more than a memory.[43] It is also worth noting that the Government spokesmen were at pains to underline that there was a curious contradiction running through much of the debate: on the one hand there was criticism of the Government for not having obtained more safeguards, more guarantees, and more advantageous treatment for French agriculture; on the other hand, there was praise for the free trade area plan which, in the form then being discussed in the OEEC committee, envisaged very few of the arrangements that practically all speakers believed to be necessary to cushion the effects of free trade. Moreover the British had made it clear in the OEEC discussion that they wished to exclude agriculture from the free trade area. Maurice Faure, the Minister of State and leader of the French delegation at Brussels and the minister most fully imbued with the ideas current in Brussels, also clearly already had considerable technical reservations about the free trade area.[44] However, although the Government spokesmen emphasized that completion of the Common Market treaty must come first, they repeatedly reassured the Assembly that it was their intention to supplement the Common

[41] Assemblée Nationale, *Débats*, 18 January 1957, pp. 197–8.
[42] For example, M. Pierre Cot.
[43] *Débats*, loc. cit., p. 214.
[44] Ibid., p. 212.

Market of the Six by a free trade area. Moreover the motion that received their support expressly stated that the negotiations on a free trade area 'which would in particular include the United Kingdom' should be pursued with determination. In the light of future developments it should, however, be noted that the motion also included the important qualification that the free trade area should have guarantees equivalent to those contained in the Common Market.[45]

The motion introduced during the debate by the four Prime Ministers (and others) was apparently more hostile to the Common Market than some, at least, of its signatories intended and would have required the Government to seek additional and probably unobtainable concessions from its partners.[46] After some discussion behind the scenes this motion was withdrawn, as was a pro-Common Market motion that had been introduced by M. Teitgen. And a new motion supported by M. Teitgen, M. Reynaud, M. Pleven (and others) was put forward with the Government's approval. This was the motion adopted. In addition to urging early progress on the free trade area it requested the Government to obtain three points before signing the treaty: first, express confirmation of the agreements already reached by the experts on 'harmonization'; second, in so far as agriculture was concerned, the conclusion before the end of the first stage of the transition period of long-term contracts at guaranteed prices and the progressive replacement of nationally organized markets by a European organization, which would give the same security to producers; and third, the association of the overseas territories on the basis of the principles the Government had outlined in the course of the debate.[47]

Although much of the emphasis in the debate was on the dangers of free trade and the need for adequate safeguards, more positive themes were also apparent. All three Government spokesmen—the principal negotiator M. Maurice Faure, the Foreign Minister M. Pineau, and the Prime Minister M. Guy Mollet—stressed the positive economic and political advantages. The Suez episode was very present in their minds and in the minds of their audience, and the argument that only by joining together could the countries of Europe hope to arrest, and then to reverse, the decline in their

---

[45] *Débats*, loc. cit., p. 217.
[46] See *The Economist*, 26 January 1957.
[47] *Débats*, loc. cit., p. 217.

influence on world events was a prominent theme and one which had a strong appeal. On a different level, it is worth noting that not only the strongest advocates of the Common Market but also its most persuasive critic, M. Mendès-France, were agreed in condemning the protectionism, both internal and external, that was strangling the French economy. On the institutional question the Government was careful to disown any doctrinaire attachment to 'supra-nationalism' and to play down the role proposed for the Commission, emphasizing that the amount of 'supra-nationality' which would be accepted would be only the minimum needed to make the Common Market function effectively. Nevertheless the Government was outspoken on the need for allowing the Council of Ministers to take operating decisions (as opposed to decisions establishing broad lines of policy) by majority votes. It also made it very clear that, over time, common, European policies would replace national, French policies in many fields.

Soon after the Assembly debate, the Foreign Ministers of the Six met in Brussels to try to resolve the points on which the heads of delegations were still not agreed. Throughout the negotiations it had been the French to whom the most concessions had been made, first on the special arrangements for France and on harmonization, later on agriculture, finally on the overseas territories. In the closing days of the negotiations the Dutch, who had borne the brunt of many of the arguments with the French, felt that the others, and perhaps M. Spaak in particular, were being unduly influenced by the need for bringing the negotiations to an early conclusion and that they were acceding too easily and too often to French demands. At this meeting of the Foreign Ministers the Dutch dug in their heels, and what was to have been a short meeting designed to put the finishing touches to the treaty (save for the arrangements on the overseas territories) was adjourned, in deadlock, while M. Spaak paid a hurried visit to The Hague, partly to seek compromises, partly to try to restore Benelux harmony, which he had himself badly strained by openly criticizing the Dutch for obstructionism.[48] His visit to The Hague coincided with the publication of a statement drawn up by eight prominent Dutchmen (among whom were three former cabinet ministers, Dr. Hirschfeld, an economic adviser to the Government, and Mr. Rijkens, a former head of the Dutch side of Unilever) warning that the treaty which seemed to be emerging from the

[48] See *Le Monde*, 29 January 1957.

Brussels discussions appeared likely to be a very protectionist document and putting forward the view that unless modifications were made it might be wise for the Netherlands to join the free trade area but not the Common Market.[49] The authors of the statement feared that the common external tariff would be fixed at too high a level, particularly for raw materials and semi-manufactures, and that this, together with the commitments to harmonize social charges, would push up Dutch costs to the point where Dutch industry would find it difficult to remain competitive. These fears tended to be shared by much of Dutch industry. The authors of the statement were also critical of the restrictionist character of the arrangements under discussion for agriculture. Here again Dutch official and private views largely coincided.

At the resumed session of the Foreign Ministers' meeting early in February, compromises were finally found on most points (except for the overseas territories). However, some of the thorniest questions were settled by finding ways to postpone decisions until after the coming into effect of the treaty rather than by resolving the difficulties. Thus although the principles by which the external tariff was to be settled were agreed, the most difficult rates were relegated to a special list, List G, on which it was agreed that negotiations would be held during the first stage of the transition period.[50] Similarly in the agricultural field the highly controversial question of the criteria to govern minimum prices, which were to be permitted as a control device on intra-Community trade during the transition period, were left for later formulation by the Council of Ministers.

The disputed tariff rates were in fact settled relatively painlessly and much more quickly than was foreseen; agriculture has continued to be a difficult and contentious problem.

Another controversial question that had to be resolved in this last phase of the negotiations was the voting arrangement. Although the general outlines of the Community's institutional arrangements had been agreed, the matters on which the Council could

---

[49] See *New York Times*, 2 February 1957, and *Le Monde*, 3–4 February 1957.

[50] See Treaty, Article 20. It should also be noted that Article 25, permitting the authorization of tariff quotas for certain goods, was a concession to the low tariff countries who were particularly opposed to French demands for tariffs or raw materials. For a discussion of the principles underlying the common external tariff see Isaiah Frank, *The European Common Market; An Analysis of Commercial Policy* (London, Stevens, 1961), pp. 102–7.

act by a qualified majority vote rather than by unanimity had still to be settled, the way in which votes were to be weighted had to be decided,[51] and the cases in which the Commission could act on its own initiative (principally in connexion with escape clauses) had to be precisely defined. It was not difficult to agree that unanimity should be the general rule where the decision to be taken broke new ground and, in effect, extended the scope of the treaty. In other cases the Spaak Report had rather timidly suggested that unanimity might, in certain circumstances, give way to majority voting. Somewhat surprisingly the negotiators were prepared to be a little bolder and to agree that progressively during the transition period, and generally after the end of the transition period, decisions which implemented the broad lines of policy already established by the treaty might be taken by a qualified majority vote. The hottest arguments came over how the principle of majority voting was to be applied. The Benelux countries, although anxious on the one hand to find a way round the veto, feared that in any system of majority voting they would be systematically outvoted by the three big countries. Three safeguards were eventually agreed upon. First, it was agreed that in most cases the Council could only act by means of a qualified majority when it was acting on a proposal put forward by the Commission, that is on an objective, independent proposal. Second, in the few cases where qualified majority voting was permitted when the Council was *not* acting on a Commission proposal, it was agreed that the qualifying majority must include the votes of at least four members, that is, at least one Benelux country must be in favour of the proposal. Third, it was decided that the Council could not amend a Commission proposal except by unanimous action.[52]

Far and away the most difficult problem before the Six was, however, the régime to be applied to the overseas territories. And here differences of political objective reinforced differences in economic doctrine. The French had a number of motives in proposing the association of the overseas territories. In the first place

[51] For most purposes, votes are weighted as follows: France, Germany, Italy— four votes each; Belgium and the Netherlands—two votes each; Luxembourg —one vote. Twelve votes are, normally, a qualifying majority.

[52] For an interesting account of the theory behind the Treaty of Rome voting arrangements see the article by M. Pierre Uri in *Le Monde*, 18 January 1962. In this article M. Uri was describing how the voting arrangements might be adapted if the United Kingdom acceded to the treaty.

there was the straight technical problem that arose from the fact that imports from the overseas possessions entered the mother country tariff-free. The French, like the British, were not prepared to see their ties with their overseas territories strained and perhaps broken by the imposition of the common external tariff of the Six, but they chose to solve the problem not by rejecting the idea of a common tariff, as the British did in proposing a free trade area, but by arguing that the right of free entry into the Community as a whole should be extended to their overseas territories. They realized that a one-sided arrangement of this kind would have small appeal to the rest of the Six, but the overseas territories were just beginning the process of industrialization and could hardly be expected to grant tariff-free entry to the highly industrialized countries of Europe. The French therefore proposed that the associated overseas countries and territories should benefit from all the tariff reductions and quota enlargements made among the Six but that the associates should be allowed to follow a somewhat different régime. Essentially, the associates were required to put all of the Six on the same footing. Thus the *differences* between the tariff treatment given the mother country on the one hand and the rest of the Six on the other would be progressively reduced. At the end of the transition period the overseas territories might still have tariffs on their trade with the Six, but France (or any other mother country) would receive no preferential treatment from its former or present possessions.

The French were concerned with a larger question than simply marrying their existing trading arrangements with the new commitments of the Common Market. In Africa the acceleration of the trend towards independence was all too plain and the French were seeking, and with some success, to evolve from the old colonial relationship a new pattern, that of the French Community, in which their colonies would move progressively to self-government but would continue to be closely linked with France. The crying need in Africa as in other developing areas was, of course, for funds for development. The French were spending in Africa at a very impressive rate, but it was not enough. Because of their overriding desire to maintain the closest possible economic and political ties with their former possessions as they moved towards independence, and thereafter, the French were reluctant to open up their colonies to outside investment. But the formation of a European Economic Community of which they were a leading member opened up a new perspective. Logically, a French economic responsibility could become a Community economic responsibility. Economically (although not politically) French Africa could become Eurafrica, having preferential trading arrangements with the Common Market and receiving substantial investments from the Germans and others of the Six.

The flaw in this conception was that it was not attractive to most of the rest of the Six and, in particular, to the Germans, who were to be the principal contributors. The Germans had lost their African colonies at the end of the First World War and were in consequence largely free from the taint of 'colonialism'. They had no desire to become too closely identified in the minds of the African and the other underdeveloped countries with French (or Dutch or Belgian) policies. Nor were they happy with the trading arrangements proposed by the French. In particular they were reluctant to give a substantial preference to certain tropical products from French Africa at the expense of their traditional suppliers elsewhere. Coffee was a case in point. Here the 16 per cent. common external tariff would give the producer in French Africa a marked advantage over his competitor in Brazil, and Brazil was a far more important market than French Africa for German industrial goods. The Dutch and Italians shared many of the German misgivings. The Belgians were in a somewhat different position: they were, in any case, already a 'colonial power' to the Africans and they had worked with the French in formulating the proposals made to the others.[53]

In addition to these difficulties, the settlement of the overseas territories question was complicated by the problems the inclusion of overseas territories in the Common Market raised for the wider free trade area proposal. As discussed further below (Chapter IV), the OEEC committee that had been investigating the possibility of a free trade area had reported that such an arrangement would be feasible, and it was clear that the British Government was ready to go ahead with the plan. However, the British colonies

[53] On the eve of the signing of the Treaty the Belgians apparently had second thoughts about the inclusion of the Congo in the list of associated overseas territories. Because of its rich resources of uranium and copper the Belgians felt they could raise any capital needed in the normal way and saw little point in gaining access to the development funds of the Community if the price was the dilution of their own position in the Congo. In the end, the Congo was technically an associated country but the proposed amounts of the Belgian contributions to, and Congo receipts from, the overseas territories fund were scaled down. See *Le Monde*, 6 March 1957, and *Combat*, 9–10 March 1957.

and former colonies in Africa, like other parts of the Commonwealth, were not to come within the scope of the proposed free
trade area. A decision to include French and Belgian Africa in the
Common Market would create difficulties for the free trade area, as
both the British and the Portuguese made very plain to the Six.
And any step that diminished the chances of a free trade area
was a step which the Germans and the Dutch were very loath to
take. At this time, there was strong industrial (and some governmental) criticism of the height of the proposed common external
tariff and in both countries the prospect that a large share of their
external trade would be unaffected by the common tariff, once the
free trade area came into effect, was a very important factor in
gaining acceptance of the common external tariff.

The overseas territories question was finally only resolved at the
Heads of Government level. It was probably only resolved because
M. Mollet put his appeal to the rest, and particularly to the
Germans, in terms of political necessity, and made it clear that
without a satisfactory arrangement for the overseas territories he
could not hope to get the treaty through the National Assembly.
But the French had to accept far smaller commitments to financial
aid than they had hoped for and more Community control over
the expenditure than they liked.[54] They also had, in the end, to
propose that the Convention on the Overseas Territories should be
contracted for a trial period of five years only. Before the Convention expired the Council would, by unanimous action, determine
the detailed arrangements to be made for a further period.

During the last few weeks of the negotiations, misgivings about
the shape the treaty was assuming under pressure from the French
were heard in Germany, in the Netherlands, and also but to a lesser
extent in Italy and Belgium. Industrial circles in Germany were
already arguing that the proposed free trade area offered a better
means than did the Common Market of achieving the industrialists' principal objective, a wider market. They were critical
of the common external tariff and particularly of the fact that it
would mean raising some German tariffs; they were opposed to
the harmonization of social charges, which would tend to raise
costs; and they disliked the arrangements for the overseas territories, particularly the creation of new preferences for French and
Belgian tropical produce. Generally speaking, those arrangements
which in French eyes provided necessary safeguards, or ensured

[54] See *The Times*, 20 and 22 February 1957.

equity, or would lead to balanced development of the economy of the Community appeared to German eyes as imprudent concessions to French protectionism and unnecessary impediments to healthy competition, or thinly disguised 'dirigisme'. The truth was somewhere in between. These critical views of German industry were openly supported, and nourished, by Dr. Erhard, then the German Minister of Economics. He also undoubtedly shared the opinion of some sections of the German press that the drafting of the treaty had been handled too much by diplomats from the Foreign Ministry and too little by hard-headed realists from the Economics Ministry, with the result that the treaty was an 'abstract construction' built 'with great mystery'.[55] A debate, without a vote, was held in the Bundestag a few days before Dr. Adenauer left for the signing ceremony in Rome. The Social Democrats, like practically everyone else in Germany, were critical of the arrangements for the overseas territories, and they were also worried lest German participation in the Community accentuate the problems of German reunification. Nevertheless, the Social Democrats gave the treaty their qualified support on condition that trade with East Germany would not be affected and that the free trade area should be achieved as soon as possible. Dr. Erhard, despite the fact that he had described the Common Market as 'economic nonsense' and 'European incest' only a few days before, toed the Government line in the Bundestag, although he criticized the lack of dynamism and the excessive caution of the treaty.[56] The Government's case was put by Prof. Hallstein, the State Secretary and the principal German negotiator. He defended the economic arrangements set out in the treaty on their merits, but his main argument was clearly political: 'It may be the last chance for the nations of Europe to maintain their old positions in the world or even for them to survive at all.'[57]

The signing of the two Treaties of Rome, one establishing the European Economic Community and the other the European Atomic Energy Community, took place on 25 March 1957. Only two years had intervened since the Benelux countries had first begun actively to agitate for the *relance*, but a rather curious reversal of roles had occurred in the attitudes of the Six to the two plans. At Messina and for the following year, the Common Market

[55] See *Le Monde*, 26 January 1957.
[56] See *Manchester Guardian*, 22 March 1957, and *Financial Times*, 22 March 1957.
[57] *Manchester Guardian*, 22 March 1957.

proposal had been the cherished hope of the Benelux countries, particularly of the Netherlands, and of Germany; Euratom the only aspect of the *relance* of interest to France. By the final stages of the negotiations, many in Germany and the Netherlands had doubts about the Common Market, and it was the French who, in effect, pushed the plan through the last stages of the negotiation. In part the changes in attitudes were a tribute to the success of the French negotiators (Maurice Faure and Robert Marjolin), in part the consequence of the prospect of the wider free trade area. There was also a certain shift in the attitude of many of the most convinced 'Europeans'. Euratom had initially been the plan which M. Monnet, and many others, had expected would provide the dramatic new step on the road to unity. And they had assumed it would be ready for signature before the end of 1956, while the Common Market might be bogged down in controversy for several years. Not only were the two treaties signed simultaneously, but by this time it was apparent that it was the Economic Community, not Euratom, that contained the seeds of a major revolution in European economic life. Furthermore, it was clear that it was the Common Market, not Euratom, that had set in train a re-examination of British assumptions about relationships with the Continent.

Ratifying the Treaty

The Mollet Socialist–Radical Government fell in May (1957), ostensibly over a finance bill, in reality because of the dissatisfaction with policy in Algeria. After a confused interval, M. Mollet was succeeded by a member of his own Government and one of his close associates, M. Bourgès-Maunoury (a Radical). Like his predecessor, M. Bourgès-Maunoury was anxious to move ahead as rapidly as possible with the ratification of the treaties. The imminence of the German elections made early French action important, for, with the memory of the EDC still vivid, none of the Six countries was prepared to complete the ratification process until after the French Assembly had acted.

The Germans began their ratification process soon after the treaties were signed. The debate and vote in the Bundestag came while the French Assembly was actually debating the two treaties, but the formal ratification of the treaties was made conditional on favourable action by the other member countries. The Social Democrats who had opposed both the ECSC and the EDC supported both the new treaties, although as mentioned above they were critical of certain features of both treaties.[58] They extracted confirmation from the Government that German interzonal trade would not be affected and also a statement to the effect that a reunified Germany would not be bound by the treaty. And Herr von Brentano, the Foreign Secretary, sought once more to reassure both those in his own party (the CDU) and the Social Democrats who were critical of the relatively high tariff proposed for the Common Market, by promising to work for an early conclusion of the wider free trade area. The vote in the Bundestag—on 5 July 1957—was overwhelmingly favourable.

The ratification debates in the Bundestag and in the French National Assembly took place in early July and coincided with an intense heat-wave. This, combined with the technical complexities of the treaties, perhaps accounted in part for the fact that there was little emotion and few moments of drama in either debate. In addition, in France many deputies appear to have felt that the issue had really been settled in January. The early days of the debate in particular were notoriously poorly attended. Maurice Faure again carried the main burden of the debate for the French Government; he again spoke with complete control of the facts, and a clear conviction that, despite the uncertainties and the risks, there was no other course that offered France and Western Europe the same eventual prospect of economic strength and the hope of regaining a position of political importance in the world.[59] As in January, M. Mendès-France was the most important critic of the Common Market, but his interventions made less impression and clearly caused the Government less concern than had his rather more forceful onslaught in January.[60] Supporters as well as critics of the treaty were merciless in their condemnation of the economic weakness of France and insistent on the need to use the eighteen

---

[58] M. Monnet played an important part in persuading the German Social Democrats to support the Treaties of Rome.

[59] Assemblée Nationale, *Débats*, 5 July 1957, pp. 3298 ff. M. Faure ended his opening presentation on the theme which had also been prominent in the Government case in January: 'Voyez-vous, mes chers amis, nous vivons encore aujourd'hui sur une fiction qui consiste à dire: il y a quatre "Grands" dans le monde. Eh bien, il n'y a pas quatres Grands, il y en a deux; l'Amérique et la Russie. Il y en aura un troisième à la fin du siècle: la Chine. Il dépend de vous qu'il y en ait un quatrième: l'Europe.' *Débats*, p. 3305.

[60] The principal critic of Euratom was M. Pierre André, who argued that France had the resources and the technical 'know-how' to become a significant atomic power on its own.

months of grace before the first tariffs cuts required by the treaty to put their financial house in order. It is worth noting here that the debate coincided with a sweeping reimposition of French import controls which lent considerable force to M. Mendès-France's arguments that the first task before France was to reform her domestic economy, and that talk of a Common Market could wait. As in the January debate, there was impressive agreement on the fact that protectionism in all its forms was strangling the French economy, and there was much preoccupation with the slow rate of growth of the French economy. As in the case of the United Kingdom four years later, there was also the realization and the fear that unless France decided to participate others would act without her. As M. Savary, the rapporteur of the Commission on Foreign Affairs, put it, the choice before France was not a choice between the Community and the *status quo* but a choice between the EEC and 'solitude'.[61]

The 'European' case was made by M. Schuman and M. Pleven on the final day, but they like the Government spokesmen—the Prime Minister, M. Pineau, and M. Maurice Faure—repudiated any suggestion of a doctrinaire attachment to 'supra-nationalism' or to a special 'European' mystique. As in the January debate many speakers emphasized their hope that the free trade area would soon supplement the Common Market. However, both M. Pineau and M. Maurice Faure appear to have been even more cautious about the free trade area in July than they had been in January. Both of them emphasized the fact that substantial technical difficulties still had to be overcome and indicated that the omission of many of the safeguards of the Treaty of Rome from the British scheme made the latter unattractive in its present form, and M. Pineau was categoric on the need to include agriculture.[62] M. Faure, perhaps more clearly than any of the other speakers, made it quite plain that the French concept of the Community was not that of a simple customs union but of a kind of economic union in which freeing of trade was a part, but only a part, of the construction, and he was at pains to emphasize the difference between this concept and that underlying the proposed free trade area. Not enough notice seems to have been paid by the United Kingdom and some of the other OEEC countries to these warning signals of difficulties ahead. But even in the French

[61] *Débats*, July 1957, p. 3140.
[62] See M. Pineau's statement on 6 July (*Débats*, p. 3370).

Assembly, attitudes were still curiously ambivalent; many of the speakers appeared to want the free trade area yet at the same time to feel that the much more attenuated risks of the Common Market were almost too great to be borne.

At no time during the debate was the final ratification of the two treaties in doubt. It was clear that with one exception the Government had substantially met the conditions laid down by the Assembly in its June 1956 vote on Euratom and its January 1957 vote on the Common Market. The exception was the French failure to obtain the agreement of the other countries to the establishment of a new Parliamentary Assembly for Euratom and the Common Market which would be entirely separate from the Assembly of the Coal and Steel Community. However, M. Pineau's explanation of the pressure for a single assembly that had come from the rest of the Six, and also from the existing European parliamentary assemblies (ECSC, WEU, and the Council of Europe), was accepted. And the final vote gave a comfortable majority for the ratification of the two treaties. Somewhat surprisingly there was a slightly higher favourable vote for the Common Market than for Euratom.[63] Two weeks later the French Council of the Republic approved the treaty by a large majority.[64]

The debate in the Italian Chamber of Deputies followed immediately after the debate in the French Assembly. As in France, the large Communist Party was strongly opposed to both treaties. Nevertheless the treaties received widespread support, as much for political as for economic reasons, from the Communist-ridden CGIL, the largest trade union organization. Furthermore, for the first time the Nenni Socialists openly broke with the Communists and in the final vote abstained on the Common Market and voted for the Euratom Treaty. Views in Italy on the economic consequences of the Common Market were somewhat mixed. The prospect of wider employment opportunities in the other countries

[63] The votes in the French National Assembly were: 341–235 for the Common Market treaty; 337–243 for Euratom; and 342–239 for the single instrument of ratification covering the two together. Débats, 9 July 1957, pp. 3485–6.

[64] Two motions adopted by the Council of the Republic at the same time are worth noting. The first called on the Government to secure increased protection and increased investment in the French overseas territories within five years, presumably in connexion with the negotiations for a renewal of the Convention on the Overseas Territories. The second motion stated that the Council would always reject any proposal that sought to alter or diminish the prerogatives that constituted the sovereign power of France. The Times, 25 July 1957.

of the Community was welcomed on all sides, but as in the other countries, the views of farmers' groups and industrialists were coloured by their estimates of their competitive position. The Italian Government in presenting the treaties to the Parliament made no bones of the fact that initially the benefits of the Common Market might be outweighed by the drawbacks. However, the Italian economy had clearly benefited by the very high level of trade liberalization achieved by Italy in the OEEC framework (over 99 per cent.) and the 'European' policy followed by the various Italian Governments since the war had no real critics in Italy, save the Communists. Only the Communists voted against the treaties, which were ratified by large majorities in the Chamber of Deputies and, later, in the Senate.[65]

The Dutch Lower House was the next to act. Although the outcome was never in doubt, there were probably more genuine misgivings in the Government and in influential circles in the Netherlands at the time of the signing and the ratification of the Common Market treaty than in any of the other countries. There was a pervasive feeling that too many concessions had been made to the French in the course of the negotiations and that the Dutch would be the main sufferers. Dutch costs would tend to rise as a result of the obligation to harmonize social charges and as a result of raising the low Benelux rates to the generally higher common tariff. The Dutch also felt with considerable justification that the agricultural arrangements had been tailored to meet French needs, and that the commitments to liberalization in the transport field (of particular interest to Dutch carriers) were too vague and uncertain. Like the Germans, they felt the treaty as a whole was too *dirigiste* in approach and they disliked the concessions made to the French on the overseas territories, particularly the preferential arrangements envisaged for tropical products. Finally the Dutch, more strongly than the others, felt that the compromise on the institutional arrangements gave too much power to the Council of Ministers and too little to the independent, 'supra-national' Commission.[66] The Benelux countries, and perhaps particularly the Dutch, looked to the Commission and to 'supra-nationalism' generally as the chief guarantee

---

[65] See *New York Times*, 31 July 1957. The Senate ratified the treaties early in October 1957.
[66] See *Netherlands News*, 14 August 1957, *The Times*, 10 September 1957. The Dutch Lower House voted on 5 October. See *Le Monde*, 6–7 October 1957.

that the interests of the small countries in the Community would be given appropriate weight. As in Germany, the Dutch Government in commending the treaties to the Parliament sought to reassure those who were worried by the effects of raising tariffs by emphasizing their hope that the wider free trade area would soon be agreed and that in consequence a large part of Dutch imports would enter duty-free. The Lower House approved the Common Market treaty by 114 to 12 but with a fairly large number of abstentions (24). Action in the Upper House was not taken until December, thus making the Netherlands, who had at first been the strongest advocates of the Common Market, the last to complete the ratification process. The same doubts as had been expressed in the Lower House were repeated during the debates in the Upper House but it was clear from the start that on political grounds alone Dutch ratification was assured. As in the other countries of the Community, the Communists (only two in the Upper House) voted against both treaties; in the vote on the Common Market three Liberals also voted against ratification.

The debate in the Belgian Parliament was rather less critical of the Common Market treaty than that in the Dutch Parliament, partly because the Belgians did not share the Dutch concern over agriculture, or have a special interest in transport. Furthermore, they were, for historic reasons, rather less opposed to the 'protectionism' which the Dutch felt the French had succeeded in building into the treaty. There was some concern at the height of the proposed common external tariff and some criticism of the fact that in relation to the financial contributions made by the mother country the French territories stood to do much better than the Belgian territories from the fund for the overseas territories, but the vote in both chambers of the Belgian Parliament was virtually unanimous, except for the tiny Communist vote. Luxembourg, like Belgium, ratified the treaties, practically unanimously, at the end of November.[67] And, on 1 January 1958, the European Economic Community was born.

[67] The vote in the Belgian Chamber of Deputies was 174–4 with 2 abstentions (*The Times*, 20 November 1957). The vote in the Belgian Senate was 134–2 (*The Times*, 29 November 1957). The vote in the Luxembourg single-chamber Parliament was 46–3 (*New York Times*, 27 November 1957).

IV

THE PROPOSAL FOR A FREE
TRADE AREA

The beginning of a new policy

The period of open British hostility to the plans of the Six was
short-lived, and fairly early in 1956 there were signs that the
British Government was beginning to think in terms of the kind
of arrangements that it might make with the Six if the latter
succeeded in establishing Euratom and the Common Market.
Signs of a more co-operative attitude towards Euratom came first;
the earlier British position that Euratom was unnecessary and
that joint European action for the development of atomic energy
should take place only in the OEEC[1] was modified and emphasis
was placed, instead, on the need to make the Euratom and OEEC
programmes complementary. The arrangement to be made in
Europe for the exploitation of atomic energy dominated the OEEC
ministerial meeting held at the end of February 1956. The United
Kingdom, the Six, and the United States were all anxious to avoid
any clash of views and at pains to emphasize the compatibility
between the two plans. Open controversy was averted but substantive decisions were, in effect, put off until the summer. Meanwhile a special committee was established to examine not only
what should be done within the OEEC but the relationship
between any new OEEC machinery and Euratom.[2]

During the spring and early summer of 1956 the Six apparently
still hoped for something more positive from the United Kingdom
than co-operation within the OEEC on atomic energy. Early in

[1] On 10 June 1955 the Ministerial Council of the OEEC had set up a working
party of three members to examine the 'scope, form and methods' of co-
operation in the development of nuclear energy. The working party brought
out its report in January 1956. See OEEC, *Possibility of Action in the Field of
Nuclear Energy* (Paris, 1956). The Six felt, with some justification, that the
OEEC group were working with unaccustomed speed in order to get their own
plans accepted in preference to those of Euratom.
[2] See *The Economist,* 10 March 1956.

June, M. Monnet went out of his way in a talk to the Anglo-American Press Association in Paris to emphasize the need for the United Kingdom to participate in Euratom. According to the report in *The Times*, M. Monnet said he had changed his mind about the need first to create a European Community, such as the Coal and Steel Community, and then to seek Britain's participation or association. Neither Britain nor the Six could solve their problems independently of one another and, in his view, it was neither 'natural or wise' that Britain should not participate in the efforts on the Continent.[3] In addition, M. Maurice Faure (who was the head of the French delegation in the negotiations on the Treaties of Rome) and M. Marjolin (his deputy) visited London in mid-June for informal talks with the United Kingdom on the status of the *relance* and, in particular, of Euratom. Efforts were made on both sides of the Channel to play down the importance of these discussions, perhaps because they yielded so little. Early press reports that the French had once again sought British participation and had, once again, been turned down were officially denied. French–British agreement on the need for close co-operation between Euratom and the OEEC and the reiteration of the United Kingdom view that its own co-operation with Euratom could best be worked out in the context of the OEEC were said to be the chief fruits of the meeting.[4] At about the same time a similar comment was made by Mr. Nutting (then Minister of State in the Foreign Office) in the House of Commons in reply to a question on the possibility of the United Kingdom participating in Euratom:

Notwithstanding what has been said by M. Monnet, for whom I have the greatest respect, the Euratom plan as it stands is incompatible with the interests of the United Kingdom because Euratom is to have a monopoly of the ownership and distribution of raw materials and will fix prices and control the use of those materials which it sells to outside countries. That is not compatible with United Kingdom interests, but, nevertheless, we hope that the Euratom project will develop complementary-wise with that of OEEC in which we are already playing a full part.[5]

[3] See *The Times*, 6 June 1956.
[4] See *The Times*, 16 and 18 June 1956.
[5] *Hansard*, House of Commons, 13 June 1956, col. 559, oral answers. At this time one of the important reasons for British reluctance to join Euratom was the fact that a recently concluded long-term contract with Canada gave them a guaranteed supply of uranium.

The Common Market proposals attracted much less public comment than the Euratom plan during the first half of the year 1956. Nevertheless a good deal of fresh thinking was taking place about the problems a Common Market of the Six might pose for the United Kingdom, and the possibility of linking the United Kingdom to the Common Market by means of a free trade area was already being given serious consideration in Whitehall. It will be recalled that the British representative who participated in the discussions during the early days of the Spaak Committee had outlined the advantages of a free trade area to his colleagues from the Six. Although the Six were unanimous in preferring a customs union among themselves, the idea of some kind of a free trade area link between the Six and the United Kingdom had never been ruled out by any of them. And the Spaak Report had appeared to suggest that it would be a feasible and perhaps even a desirable arrangement. The possibility of a free trade area was referred to intermittently in the press during the spring and the advantages of such a scheme were set out in some detail by James Meade in two articles in the *Manchester Guardian* in mid-March.[6] By the early summer it was reasonably clear that something was brewing and replies to probing in the House of Commons strengthened this impression. Finally, in the debate on the adjournment on 5 July, Sir Edward Boyle, the Economic Secretary to the Treasury, confirmed that the Government was in fact engaged on a major reappraisal of its policy with respect to the Common Market. After reviewing briefly the progress that the Six had made in their own negotiations, Sir Edward Boyle pointed out that there were special difficulties for the United Kingdom in a Common Market because of Britain's other commitments and that

the changes of policy which we should have to adopt to take part in the project in its present form would certainly not be easy to reconcile with our existing policies and our obligations to the Commonwealth. . . . The House should realise that there are many weighty questions still unresolved, and many difficult features of the Common Market as at present envisaged. We cannot, at this stage, be sure that the venture will succeed. Some of these features may yet be discarded, but at present it has been suggested that not only should there be a single external tariff . . . but freedom of movement of labour and of capital . . . and supporters . . . believe that it will be necessary also to harmonise

[6] *Manchester Guardian*, 14 and 15 March 1956. It seems probable that Professor Meade was given some official encouragement and that the articles were, in part at least, intended as a trial balloon to test British reactions.

economic policies, and indeed social policies as well, with the prospect
of great pressure towards ever closer integration. . . . I cannot, tonight,
go any further in stating the policy of the United Kingdom, but what I
should like to say to the House, and indeed to the country generally, is
this—because I think it is important on this point to be quite explicit.
In making this speech tonight I am quite deliberately—and my right
honourable Friend has authorised me to say this—not ruling out any
possibilities at all for the future.

There is no question at all of the Government having closed their
mind on the subject. I am not putting up, as it were, a smoke screen to
conceal the fact that the Government have made up their mind in a negative direction . . . we do not want to associate ourselves too closely at
this stage and then to be open later to a charge of bad faith. We must,
first, make the basic political decision. . . . I know that I am absolutely
safe in saying that there is no subject which will more attract the attention of the Government during the months ahead than this. We fully
realise that there is a major policy decision to be made here. We are
completely open-minded and will be guided solely by what we conceive
to be the proper harmony of the interests of the Commonwealth, the
interests of Europe and of the free world as a whole.[7]

Although Sir Edward Boyle's statement might be read to imply
that consideration was being given not only to links between the
United Kingdom and the Six but to British participation in the
Common Market, it seems clear enough from other statements
that the British did not, at this early stage, seriously consider the
major break with past traditions that participation in a full customs
union would have implied. Rather, it appears that they were then
considering either full membership in a 'common market' based
on a free trade area and excluding agriculture if, in the end, the
Six failed in the attempt to form their own common market and
were prepared to go ahead with the British on this basis; or, if
the Six succeeded, as by this time seemed more probable, a free
trade area link between themselves and the customs union of the
Six. As Sir Edward Boyle pointed out, the scheme outlined in
the Spaak Report was still far from being fully worked out in a
number of crucial matters (e.g. agriculture) and the success of
the whole enterprise was by no means assured. Nevertheless the
British seem to have somewhat overestimated the fluidity of
the situation and to have underestimated the importance of the
Venice decisions. They also seem not to have appreciated how
much suspicion they had earlier stirred up among the Six and

[7] *Hansard*, House of Commons, vol. 555, cols. 1667–80, 5 July 1956.

not to have foreseen that their genuine attempts to find an arrangement which could be reconciled with their own commitments
would tend to be discounted in some European quarters as destruc-
tive manoeuvres.

In the spring of 1956, certain developments in the OEEC, as
well as the progress being made among the Six, contributed to the
British decision to review their European trade policy and led,
probably unfortunately, to the decision to negotiate the free trade
area in the framework of the OEEC rather than directly with the
Six. As indicated in Chapter I, despite some early pressure from
the United States and some European countries, the OEEC had
not pursued the question of a European customs union but had
concentrated instead on the important, if less drastic, task of freeing intra-European trade from the strait-jacket of the bilateral
trading pattern of the immediate post-war years. Quantitative
import restrictions were progressively removed from intra-
European trade and, through the European Payments Union,
European currencies were made convertible with one another.
However, almost from the beginning of the OEEC's trade
liberalization effort the low tariff countries (i.e. the Benelux
countries, Switzerland, Sweden, and Denmark) had argued that
it was unreasonable to expect them to go very far in freeing trade
from quotas unless the European countries who had high tariffs
were prepared to cut their tariffs. When the quota liberalization
goal was pushed to 90 per cent. in 1955 the low tariff countries
made it plain that their agreement was conditional on some action
being taken on tariffs. The low tariff countries recognized that
preferential reductions of tariffs would be in conflict with the
GATT and therefore proposed a plan for cutting tariffs (automatically and progressively) on only those products that were of
particular importance in intra-European trade. Reductions in the
tariffs on these products would be generalized to the other members
of the GATT in accordance with the most-favoured-nation
(m.f.n.) commitment, but the criteria used in selecting the items
would ensure that the members of the OEEC in fact received the
major benefit from the reductions. Although this plan would have
been consistent with the GATT, it was not acceptable to the
United Kingdom, which did a much smaller proportion of its total
trade than most of the OEEC countries with its European partners.
Furthermore, at this time the United Kingdom was particularly
interested in reductions in the United States tariff and a 'European

list' of any real importance would have involved giving some uncovenanted benefits to the United States. After considerable discussion, the OEEC countries agreed that the 'European Commodity list' would be used as a guide in the GATT negotiations that were to begin early in 1956 and that the position would be reviewed at the conclusion of the negotiations. In fact little progress was made in reducing tariffs during that round of GATT negotiations; partly because the United States had little leeway under its existing legislation to make significant concessions; partly because the United Kingdom was reluctant to make concessions on the 'European Commodities' which would give unrequited benefits to the United States and other third countries; partly because the French, who were at this time arguing in the Treaty of Rome negotiations for a fairly high common external tariff, were also hostile to the 'European list' proposals.

By the time the Council of the OEEC met in July 1956, it was clear that there was little prospect of further tariff reductions on a GATT basis in the near future and that the low tariff countries would certainly not agree to 'consolidate' the 90 per cent. decision, let alone agree to any further quota liberalization measures, unless something was done to reduce the high European tariffs. Pressure from the low tariff countries for some action on tariffs thus gave added urgency to the re-examination of British policy.[8] Had it not been for this pressure from the low tariff countries in the OEEC for action on their own tariff-cutting plan, it seems probable that the British would have pursued the question of a free trade area, initially at least, directly with the Six rather than in the OEEC. However, by the time of the OEEC Council meeting, the British Government had got far enough with its own examination of a free trade area to find it attractive, and an OEEC investigation of this possibility offered a way out of the impasse with the low tariff countries.

The OEEC Council of Ministers at its July 1956 meeting took two interlocking decisions on trade questions. On a proposal formally made by the Secretary-General, but strongly supported by and generally assumed to have been inspired by the British, it decided to establish a special OEEC working party to study the possible forms and methods of association between the customs

---

[8] The German and Benelux Governments were strongly in favour of the low tariff club plan as a way of counteracting French pressure for a relatively high external tariff for the Common Market.

union of the Six and the other OEEC countries and, specifically, the possibility of a free trade area which would include the customs union of the Six as one element. Although the British representatives made plain, once again, their objections to the low tariff club plan, the low tariff countries were not yet sure enough that the British meant business on a free trade area to agree to shelve their plan. Accordingly it was remitted to the OEEC's Steering Board for Trade. And it was agreed that, early in 1957, the OEEC Council would determine whether the study of a free trade area by the special working group held out 'a prospect of substantial progress being achieved before the end of 1957'; if it did not, the Council would instruct the Steering Board to complete the alternative plan, which would then be considered by the Council.[9]

At the time they were made, neither the statement by Sir Edward Boyle in the House of Commons early in July nor the decision of the OEEC Council of Ministers at the end of that month attracted the attention they deserved in the United Kingdom, perhaps because of the customary sleepiness of the press during the summer or perhaps because the Government was not yet ready to see the launching of a full-scale debate. Early in September (1956), however, the press woke up with such a concerted bang to the fact that a free trade area was under serious consideration that some official prodding seems probable. The Government had already begun to sound out industry through the Federation of British Industries, and at the end of the month Mr. Thorneycroft (then President of the Board of Trade) joined Mr. Macmillan (then Chancellor of the Exchequer) in Washington for discussions of the plan with the Commonwealth Finance Ministers following the annual meetings of the International Bank and the International Monetary Fund. Reasonably well-informed accounts of these discussions found their way into the papers and on their return to London from Washington, the two ministers held a press conference at which the Government's ideas were outlined in considerable detail.[10]

In their statement to the press on the free trade area the two British ministers emphasized that food, drink, and tobacco would

---

[9] For text of decisions see OEEC Information Division, Press Release A (56) 32 and A (56) 33.

[10] The early reports from Washington indicated—inaccurately—that the United Kingdom was discussing a plan to link not just the United Kingdom but other Commonwealth countries as well with the Common Market.

be excluded from the scope of the proposed free trade area, but that exceptional treatment for special groups of industrial products could not be expected. They also made it clear that the scheme would not limit the right of the United Kingdom (or of other member countries) to impose import restrictions if these became necessary on balance of payments grounds.[11] For all industrial goods, tariffs and quotas would be progressively eliminated over a ten- to fifteen-year period.

At this stage nothing was said about institutions, rules of competition, and various other aspects of the plan as it was later presented to the OEEC and to the House of Commons. Many important details of the plan of the Six had still to be settled, and the relationship to be established between the two plans was, on many important points, still obscure. However, the adoption of free trade in industrial products with important competitors like the Six would mean a major change in British trade policy, which for nearly twenty-five years had been highly protectionist; this was the central question on which the Government was anxious to test public opinion. In their presentation to the press, Mr. Macmillan and Mr. Thorneycroft made it plain that no Cabinet decision had yet been taken, that the initial response of the Commonwealth Finance Ministers had been sympathetic, but that no decision could be taken until the British Government had received the 'considered views' of the Commonwealth countries, and that both sides of industry would be fully consulted. Both ministers were themselves clearly in favour of the plan and both stressed the positive advantages to the United Kingdom of a larger market, rather than basing themselves on the strong but negative case, that 'we can not afford to stay out'—an argument which became the prominent feature in the great debate on the free trade area which was touched off by the press conference.

The immediate reactions in the United Kingdom to the press conference were surprisingly favourable for a country which for so long had been accustomed to protection. Except for the Beaverbrook papers, the press was strongly in favour of the new approach, and there was substantial backing from industry. On the Continent, reactions appear to have been somewhat more guarded. *The Times* correspondent, writing from Paris two days after the Macmillan–Thorneycroft press conference, pointed out that things were likely

---

[11] Note the similarity to the French emphasis in the Treaty of Rome negotiations on the retention of the unilateral right to reimpose restrictions.

to move rather more slowly than the publicity in the United Kingdom might lead one to expect. He also drew attention to the fact that the British exclusion of raw and manufactured foodstuffs had already been made plain by the British representative at the OEEC special working party and that this had had a 'somewhat chilling effect' on some of the other delegates, the Danes in particular.[12] Apart from the resentment at the British unwillingness to open their own markets, there was fear lest a British request for an exception of such magnitude would prompt others, and in particular the French, to press for exceptions of comparable scope. There was also a feeling in some 'European' quarters that the British initiative, rather than making it easier for the Six to come to an agreement on the Common Market, would, at best, delay agreement by introducing an important new factor, and, at worst, might prejudice agreement by offering an alternative. There was also some suspicion of British motives.[13]

M. Monnet's Committee for a United States of Europe, although welcoming the OEEC studies on a free trade area, made it plain in a declaration on 20 September that they attached primary importance to quick agreement by the Six Governments on the Common Market and particularly on Euratom.[14] M. Spaak appears to have had a similar reaction. He visited London early in September (1956) at the request of the United Kingdom Government to discuss how the examination of the free trade area proposal might best be linked with the work of the Six on the Common Market. Although the release to the press following the meeting was non-committal, it seems clear that the British had proposed that the two schemes should be worked out together, but that M. Spaak preferred to push ahead separately with the drafting of the Common Market treaty. M. Spaak looked at the free

[12] *The Times*, 5 October 1956.
[13] See, for example, the comments made by the Financial Editor in the *Manchester Guardian* of 16 October 1956: '. . . . very few people on the Continent seem to believe so far that Britain is in earnest. Everybody I asked during the past week, in France, in Germany and elsewhere, expressed either complete disbelief or strong suspicion. At best, the British suggestion . . . is distrusted as a clever move to induce France to stop short of the full integration process. At worst, it is seen simply as a mischievous move to torpedo the Continental efforts by raising false hopes of an even larger plan.'
[14] The Action Committee was concerned, above all, with the early establishment of Euratom: they urged that the Euratom treaty be concluded and submitted for ratification before the end of the year (1956). See 'Action Committee for the United States of Europe', *Resolution*, Third Session, Paris, 19–20 September 1956.

trade area as a supplementary scheme which could best be worked out after agreement had been reached on the Common Market. The British thought of it as a plan which should be developed simultaneously with the Common Market so that the two plans could have as many features as possible in common and could enter into effect simultaneously. The Spaak view prevailed among the Six and not only were OEEC investigations of the feasibility of a free trade area carried on separately from the Brussels negotiations but, as discussed further in Chapter V, the OEEC negotiations were later deliberately held up to avoid the danger that the French Assembly might use the prospect of the free trade area as an excuse for delaying or refusing to ratify the Treaty of Rome. This attitude by M. Spaak and M. Monnet reflected the very real fear on the part of the 'Europeans' that the looser arrangement proposed by the British would prove more attractive to many within the Six, and to many in Germany and France in particular, than the tighter, more far-reaching Common Market proposals.[15] If the two schemes were discussed together, or if progress on the free trade area plan were as rapid as that on the Common Market plan, the free trade area scheme might prove, in the event, to be not a supplement to but a substitute for the Common Market scheme. After the Treaty of Rome had been safely ratified, fear on the part of the 'Europeans' that the broader, looser arrangement would tend to supplant the tighter, more far-reaching plan contributed importantly to the failure of the free trade area negotiations. But at this early stage, it seems clear that the leading 'Europeans' felt the British plan might be a helpful *supplement* to the plan of the Six; they were concerned at the timing of the discussions but were not yet, as many of them later became, opposed to the free trade area plan in principle.

Notwithstanding some doubts about British motives and some concern at the timing of the new initiative, the prospect of a close

[15] The reaction of the 'Erhard group' in Germany to the British proposal was particularly enthusiastic and this, in turn, gave rise to some of the apprehensions of the 'Europeans'. The Bonn correspondent of the *Financial Times* wrote: 'As far as the European free trade zone is concerned, German Governmental support will be marked and unanimous. Minister Erhard is one of the fervent supporters of the plan which he described to me a few days ago as "one of the many brilliant economic concepts of our time and the best way to draw Britain closer to the Continent".' The article in the *Financial Times* also quoted *Die Welt* as saying 'Without Britain there is no Europe. It is better to give up the idea of supra-national authority than to give up the idea of British participation.' See *Financial Times*, 27 September 1956.

link with the United Kingdom clearly gave welcome reassurance
to those within the Six who feared the growing strength of
Germany. Furthermore, as indicated in Chapter III, the prospect
of a wider European trading arrangement made the relatively
high external tariff and other potentially restrictive features
of the Treaty of Rome more palatable to the economic liberals
within the Community, particularly in the Netherlands and in
Germany, than would otherwise have been the case. Thus,
positively, by giving political and economic reassurance to those
among the Six who felt the Common Market was too limited
an arrangement, and negatively, by implicitly threatening to
supplant the Common Market, the British initiative undoubtedly
contributed to the success of the negotiations on the Treaty of
Rome.

On a somewhat different plane, in the early autumn of 1956,
before the Anglo-French landings at Suez took over the centre
of the stage, the political leaders in France, Germany, and the
United Kingdom appeared to be coming closer together and
moving towards a rather similar conception of the role of Europe.
Moreover, some aspects of American policy—in particular the attitude of Mr. Dulles, then Secretary of State, at discussions during
the summer and early autumn on the problem of the Suez Canal,
and the rumours that the United States administration might be
seriously thinking of revising its military commitments in Europe
in accordance with the so-called Radford Plan—caused a certain
disenchantment with the United States and contributed to the
growing feeling among the principal European countries that they
must work more closely together and with less dependence on
the United States. Perhaps the change in attitude was most
marked in the case of Dr. Adenauer, who had hitherto been
worried by the French tendency to base the case for European
unity in part, at least, on the need for the European countries to
constitute an effective 'third force' capable of making its views
felt in Washington as well as in Moscow. Dr. Adenauer throughout
most of the period under review was overwhelmingly conscious
of West Germany's dependence on the commitment of United
States forces to Europe and very reluctant to take any action that
might lead to any reduction in the United States commitment.
However, for a brief period during the autumn of 1956 he apparently feared that the United States might adopt a 'Fortress
America' strategy and his response was to seek to tighten the ties

between France, Germany, and the United Kingdom.[16] On
25 September 1956, in Brussels, and again a few days later in
Hamburg, Dr. Adenauer spoke publicly of the need for strengthening the seven-nation Western European Union and transforming
it into a confederation or federation (he used both terms). He
said that the federation 'must not suffer from the disease of our
time—perfectionism' and that 'its institutions need not always be
supranational in nature. We want to choose ways so that nobody is
scared off.' In both speeches he made it abundantly clear that he
wanted a European system that included the United Kingdom.[17]

A few days later, Dr. Adenauer and M. Mollet met together
primarily to put the final touches on the Saar agreement. Other
problems were discussed as well, and the two leaders called for the
'active participation' of the United Kingdom in the building of a
united Europe. To this end they announced their intention of
striving to give new meaning to such organizations as the OEEC,
the Council of Europe, and, in particular, the WEU.[18]

In the light of all that had been said by the Six since the Messina
meeting about the importance of some form of British participation
and against the immediate background of an apparently new
political emphasis by France and Germany on the need for
European unity including the United Kingdom, it is not surprising
that the British Government had the impression that its willingness to contemplate a free trade area with the Six would be interpreted on the Continent, as it was in the United Kingdom, as a
major reorientation of British policy and the beginning of a new
and more durable relationship with its continental partners. The
unwillingness of M. Spaak and M. Monnet to see the efforts of the
Six merged with those of the larger group and the new sense of
urgency that the British move inspired in the drafters of the
treaties were unwelcome straws in the wind, but the British
Government unquestionably felt that in agreeing to the OEEC
examination of a free trade area it was making a move that was
very much desired on the Continent. The Government assumed

[16] It is worth noting here that Dr. Adenauer's *rapprochement* with Mr. Macmillan
in the autumn of 1960 likewise owed something to disenchantment with the
United States; in the latter case the German Chancellor felt that the United
States on the eve of a national election was not providing adequate leadership
to the West. See below, Chapter IX.
[17] See *New York Times*, 26 September and 2 October 1956. See also *L'Année
Politique*, 1956, p. 359.
[18] See *New York Times*, 30 September 1956, and *L'Année Politique*, loc. cit.

that its problem was not to persuade the Six of the advantages of a free trade area link but to make the prospect of free trade with the Continent acceptable at home, and in particular to industry and to the trade unions. In this estimate of the situation they were to be proved wrong. But because the Government (and the many influential newspapers and private groups who were interested in encouraging the new European policy on the part of the Government) were primarily preoccupied with heading off strong protectionist pressures (pressures which, in fact, largely failed to materialize) the arguments in favour of the new proposals that tended to be used the most were not reassuring to the French, already worried by the prospect of competition from Germany, nor were they music to the ears of the 'Europeans'. Too often the heart of the argument in favour of the free trade area was reduced to double negatives—'We can't afford to stay out.' Too frequently the advantage of the particular arrangement proposed by the Government was praised as one which would enable the British to have the best of both worlds: free trade with the Continent and preferential trade with the Commonwealth. And fears of competition from the Continent were assuaged by calculations demonstrating that British industries could be counted on to expand at the expense of their less efficient European counterparts. These themes, which were prominent throughout the long internal debate in the United Kingdom about the free trade area proposals, tended to dwarf the very genuine positive political motivation that, together with strong economic and commercial considerations, clearly lay behind the Government's proposals.

The formal British Cabinet decision to seek to negotiate a free trade area which would include the Six, the United Kingdom, and any other OEEC countries wishing to participate was taken during the autumn of 1956 after the Government had heard the views of the principal domestic groups affected by the scheme and after a fairly intensive public discussion in the press. At the end of November a full debate was held in the House of Commons on the Government's decision to proceed with negotiations.[19] No vote was taken; the Labour Party welcomed the decision but outlined various points which it felt should be safeguarded.

[19] The Government's timetable was upset by the Suez crisis. The Opposition had been pressing for a White Paper on which a debate and a vote could be held. In the end, the debate was held on a motion for the adjournment and the White Paper was presented to the House of Commons in February 1957.

Mr. Macmillan, then Chancellor of the Exchequer, opened the debate for the Government. He outlined at some length the reasons for the Government's decision to seek to negotiate a free trade area, and he and Mr. Thorneycroft (then President of the Board of Trade) described the kind of arrangements the British had in mind. The plan described was essentially that later formulated more precisely and in somewhat greater detail in the White Paper. Mr. Macmillan rejected categorically the possibility of the United Kingdom ever being able to join a customs union with the Six, largely on the grounds that it would mean an end to the preferential treatment given to Commonwealth goods in the United Kingdom market:

> I do not believe that this House would ever agree to our entering arrangements which, as a matter of principle, would prevent our treating the great range of imports from the Commonwealth at least as favourably as those from the European countries. So this objection, even if there were no other, would be quite fatal to any proposal that the United Kingdom should seek to take part in a European Common Market by joining a Customs union. I think we are all agreed there. I feel sure that the Governments of the countries who are negotiating their Customs union in Brussels understand and appreciate our position in this matter. So that is out.[20]

Earlier in the debate, Mr. Macmillan had referred to the fact that the United Kingdom could not hope to retain its preferences in Commonwealth markets if it imposed the common tariff on Commonwealth goods and he pointed out that it would be disadvantageous to lose the preference. However, although the two points were obviously closely related, it is clear that the fact that joining a customs union would mean subjecting Commonwealth goods to a 'reverse preference' and treating them less favourably than similar goods from Europe was a more important consideration, since this, it was felt, would weaken, if not destroy, the whole economic-political fabric of the Commonwealth. This point was not fully grasped either in the United Kingdom or abroad; instead, attention was too frequently centred on the fact that the United Kingdom would doubtless lose its own preferences in the other Commonwealth countries if it joined a European customs union. Although the conflict with the Commonwealth arrangements was the main 'technical' reason for the British unwillingness to consider joining a European customs union, there was, of course,

---

[20] *Hansard*, House of Commons, 26 November 1956, cols. 37–38.

a more fundamental objection, as well. The British felt that by joining a customs union and, particularly, by accepting a common commercial policy, they would be taking a long step towards federation with the Continent. And the British Government was very far from being ready to contemplate steps leading in that direction.

Since a customs union was 'out', the Government had thought in terms of a free trade area in order to be able to 'associate with Europe without injury, and indeed with benefit, to Commonwealth relationships. After all, a strong and expanding Europe is the best guarantee of Commonwealth prosperity.'[21] In the light of developments during the negotiations, a number of points made by Mr. Macmillan in his opening statement are worth noting. First, he made it clear that he envisaged that the customs union of the Six would join the free trade area 'as one unit', and he added that the British proposals were 'not in any way intended to replace or to lessen the importance of the Customs union itself'.[22] Although he categorically excluded agriculture (food for man or beast, drink, and tobacco) from the scope of the free trade area and even went so far as to say that unless this exclusion were accepted the Government could not proceed with the negotiations, he made it plain that this did not exclude 'practical measures for promoting greater trade in agricultural products'.[23] And again, although the welfare of British farmers and the need to maintain the British system of support were given as important reasons for this position, it is clear that the need to maintain Commonwealth free entry was the controlling consideration. Like other speakers later in the debate, he emphasized that the Six were not, in fact, advocating free trade for agriculture and that, in trading terms, the United Kingdom had a much freer market for agricultural imports than most countries.

In his review of the advantages of a free trade area Mr. Macmillan, like practically all the other advocates of the free trade area, began with the 'negative advantage', that is, that only in this way could British goods avoid being discriminated against in the rapidly growing markets of Western Europe. However, he did not labour this negative theme but went on to emphasize the positive advantages to Britain of participation in a large market: the opportunities for greater specialization, the stimulus to growth, the

[21] *Hansard*, House of Commons, 26 November 1956, col. 39.
[22] Ibid.   [23] Ibid., col. 42.

incentive to more economic forms of production, the benefits to the consumer of wider variety and lower prices. Like other speakers from both sides of the House he emphasized the need for the United Kingdom to become more competitive, to achieve a higher rate of investment, to grow more rapidly. And like other speakers he emphasized that whatever the problems that had to be faced in the free trade area, they were, for the most part, problems that had to be faced in any case and would be harder to face if the United Kingdom were outside the European market. Although Mr. Macmillan's presentation was predominantly in economic terms, the political implications of action, and of inaction, were not ignored. As in all the British statements on Europe that had been made since the war, the dilemma of reconciling the 'three great forces working upon us', the Commonwealth, Europe, and the Atlantic relationship, was the starting-point. But the importance of finding a way of associating with the new move in Europe to strengthen the 'old world' without weakening or running counter to other interests was his dominant theme. There was a shift of emphasis, at least, away from the need to maintain perfect balance, and a new stress was put on the need to 'play our part in strengthening Europe as an integral part of the whole free world'. The strong interest in avoiding a further division in Europe (a theme that became increasingly prominent after the breakdown of the free trade area negotiations) was present as well.[24] As has been noted above, there was at this time some suspicion on the Continent that the free trade area was a British attempt to torpedo the drive towards further unity among the Six. In an obvious effort to still these rumours and to emphasize the positive nature of the free trade area proposal, Mr. Macmillan set out in clear, almost brutal terms the three courses of action before the British Government: first, to do nothing; second, 'to use all our efforts to upset this plan . . . and thus avoid having to make up our minds on the matter'; and third, to proceed with the free trade area. The second course of action he rejected out of hand as 'a very wrong decision'.[25]

[24] 'This desire [to find a way to associate with the Six] is based not only on limited trade interests, important and vital as they are to us, but on the fact that we must be concerned with another interest. We want to feel sure that such arrangements as those of the Messina Powers, which are intended to unite Europe, do not have the effect of actually dividing it still further. That is the tremendous reason for some association of other countries with the Six.' *Hansard*, loc. cit. col. 38.

[25] Ibid., col. 54.

Mr. Harold Wilson opened for the Labour Party and supported the Government's decisions, although he spelled out numerous safeguards and conditions which the Labour Party felt it essential to have written in to any agreement. He was more sceptical than Mr. Macmillan of the positive economic advantages to be gained from the free trade area and based himself on the safe and generally accepted but not very inspired argument that 'we cannot afford to stay out'.[26] A more 'European' speech was made by the late John Edwards in winding up for the Opposition. Not only was he well aware of the political implications of what the Six were creating, but he was also one of the few speakers on either side of the House who drew attention, and with approval, to the fact that the plan of the Six was not a plan for free trade among themselves on classical lines, which was what he felt the British plan amounted to, but something which he personally preferred: 'a system in which the forces involved in the free play of the market are helped sometimes by planned intervention and the social consequences are mitigated by common services and individual and special aid'.[27]

The debate was remarkable for the absence of controversy and the unanimity of view on both sides of the House that the course of action outlined by the Government was, broadly, the right one. There was general acceptance of the need to do something, wide support for the Government's view that a customs union was 'out' and that agriculture must be excluded, and almost no questioning of the negotiability of the Government's proposals.[28] The negative theme 'we cannot afford to stay out' was somewhat more prominent than the positive, but positive arguments, both political and

[26] Among the additional safeguards and conditions advocated by the Opposition the following were the most prominent: the need to reserve all powers to protect the balance of payments; the re-negotiation of the gold payment clause in the EPU to permit larger credit swings; the need for domestic full employment policies, a development area policy, international commitments to full employment; positive action to improve labour standards; specific anti-cartel provisions; retention of freedom to 'double price' steel and coal.

[27] *Hansard*, loc. cit., col. 149.

[28] Although no one advocated treating agriculture in the same way as industrial products, some of the 'European-minded' back-benchers in both parties expressed doubts about the wisdom of the blanket exclusion of agriculture. For example, Roy Jenkins (Labour) commented: 'I do not think anyone in the House will dispute that agriculture in this country and agricultural trade within the Commonwealth must have a great degree of special protection . . . at the same time I am not convinced that the Government's policy of a straightforward blanket exclusion of agriculture is the best way of going about it. This will be a pretty difficult thing for some of our partners . . . to swallow.' Ibid., cols. 106–7.

economic, were made on both sides of the House. Probably Mr. Thorneycroft's peroration reflected fairly accurately the diverse strands which lay behind both the Government's decision to proceed with the free trade area plan and the Opposition's acceptance of that decision:

We are not at the end, but at the beginning. We are taking the first step along a road which may lead to great opportunities in the future. Dangers lie ahead. No doubt when this scheme comes into effect, as I believe it will, much will be blamed upon it. But if there are dangers for the weak, let us not under-estimate the prizes for the strong, the chances which a market of 250 million will give to our exporters and the fine opportunity which will lie ahead for our traders, our merchants, our financiers and our bankers.

On the negative side, do not let us forget the dangers of staying out of a European bloc dominated by our principal competitor, Western Germany. I would make my own position clear. I would defend these policies not on the negative, but on the positive approach. I would defend them not for the dangers they avoid, but for the hopes which they give. Here, in Europe, we have the cultural centre of the free world. We should not leave it Balkanised, divided and weak, but growing closer together, stronger, more compact and linked through us with a great Commonwealth and Empire.

Here is a chance of achieving something which matches the scale of present events. Do not let us be so obsessed by the problems of action that we forget the dangers of doing nothing. I believe that in the months ahead we have a chance to lay solid foundations for the future and of giving to our descendants a chance at least of building something worth while.[29]

The OEEC Report and the British White Paper

The OEEC working party that had been examining the feasibility of a free trade area that would include the Common Market as one element completed its work in December 1956. The OEEC group had been handicapped in its work by the fact that the Six were just reaching the most critical phase in their own negotiations, so that on a number of crucial questions they could not yet give firm indications to the wider group on the details of their own plan. Moreover, as indicated above, the Six were not prepared to merge their negotiations with the OEEC discussions in order to work out together solutions to those problems that the Common Market and the free trade area would both face. The OEEC report

[29] *Hansard*, loc. cit., cols. 163-4.

had, in consequence, to be a somewhat theoretical analysis of the problems inherent in establishing a free trade area rather than a specific plan for 'completing' the Common Market of the Six with a free trade area of the other OEEC members.

The report of the special working party was published in January 1957,[30] and the action to be taken in the light of the report was the subject of a meeting of the OEEC Council at ministerial level in mid-February. A few days before the Council meeting the British Government circulated to the other members of the OEEC a memorandum in which it set out its own views on the working party's report and proposed that the Council should approve the creation of a European Industrial Free Trade Area and should establish machinery for negotiating the detailed arrangements. This document was also published as a White Paper.[31]

In retrospect it is clear that it was a mistake for the British to have combined in a single public document what was, in effect, both an outline scheme for a European free trade area and a statement of the British negotiating position. This method of presentation tended to label the free trade area once and for all as a 'British', rather than a European, plan. It also tended to make for a rigidity in the British position in the subsequent negotiations which might have been avoided had the British position been in the pockets of the negotiators rather than circulated in advance, and in such unequivocal terms, to the other members of the OEEC, to Members of Parliament, and to the world at large. Two factors presumably contributed to this initial tactical mistake. First, there was a commendable desire to avoid generating false hopes on the Continent and false fears at home about what the British Government was prepared to do. Second, there was the same miscalculation of bargaining strength that seems to have been at the root of many of the tactical mistakes made by the British during the Maudling Committee negotiations, a miscalculation based on the belief that the Europeans were so anxious for British participation that the United Kingdom could lay down terms.

The general organization and method of presentation of the material in the OEEC report clearly reflected the strong British influence in the working party: for example, the points the British

[30] OEEC, *Report on the Possibility of Creating a Free Trade Area in Europe* (January 1957).
[31] *A European Free Trade Area, United Kingdom Memorandum to the Organisation for European Economic Co-operation* (Cmnd. 72. February 1957, H.M.S.O.).

regarded as the essentials of a free trade area were separated out
from the numerous other questions which the British wanted to see
soft-pedalled. Thus Part I of the report first concentrated on the
essential question of whether or not it was technically possible to
operate a free trade area in Europe. Having answered this question
in the affirmative, the remainder of Part I addressed itself to two
further questions: the specifically commercial problems that had
to be solved, and the problems common to a free trade area and a
customs union that must be solved in an identical manner. Not
very surprisingly—for this was an 'expert' report—the working
party was in fairly general agreement on the main points made in
Part I. Thus the report was clear on the need for origin controls
and on the ways they might be operated, on the desirability of
having the same method, and the same timing, for tariff removal
among the Six and among the larger group of countries, and on
the 'paramount importance' of the adoption of common methods
of quota liberalization.[32] There was also much common ground
in the section on escape clauses although here evidence of diverse
views began to appear, particularly over the question of whether
resort to escape clauses should or should not be limited to balance
of payments difficulties and over the need for prior authorization.[33]
In this section, again, the need for common or parallel rules and
procedures between the customs union and the free trade area was
stressed, and again, as in the sections dealing with tariff reductions
and quota removals, the working party had to confess its inability
to give precision to its work because of its ignorance of the régime
finally adopted by the Six. The first part of the report concluded
with a section on the rules of competition. Here there was agreement on the general principle that action by governments (e.g.
subsidies) and by private arrangements (e.g. cartels) could frustrate
the development of a free trade area and a general recognition that

[32] This statement should be noted because of the heated controversy over 'non-
discrimination' at the end of 1958. See below, Chapters V and VI. It should
also be noted that three essentials of a free trade area were repeatedly stressed
in this first part of the report: 'reciprocity, equilibrium, and non-discrimination'.

[33] The British, and to some extent other countries, were fearful that the French
would tend to make excessive use of the escape clauses, and they were therefore
anxious to draft these provisions as strictly as possible. As indicated in the
White Paper and in the Government statements to the House of Commons,
the United Kingdom was never prepared to go so far as to forgo the right to
unilateral resort to escape clauses in the event of a balance of payments crisis,
but the British, unlike the French in the Treaty of Rome negotiations, were
prepared to restrict resort to escape clauses to balance of payments difficulties.

some rules and some procedure for dealing with these questions would be needed. But the report did not go very deeply into either the problems or the remedies.

The second part of the report dealt with more controversial questions: the disputed question of how much harmonization of economic, financial, and social policies would be required and, in particular, the question of whether harmonization should be assumed to result from trade liberalization or should be a precondition of trade liberalization; the status of the OEEC countries in the process of development; and the position of agriculture. The first and third questions had been a source of considerable difference of view between the French and the rest of the Six in the course of the Treaty of Rome negotiations, and both questions were to prove contentious during the free trade area negotiations. The nature of the arrangements that might be made for the less developed OEEC countries was a less 'doctrinal' question and not particularly contentious. Some countries felt that it would be better to associate the underdeveloped countries with the free trade area only when they were able to undertake commitments in the same way as the developed countries; other countries, and in particular the underdeveloped countries themselves, wanted to participate from the start but with special provisions. The second half of the report made no pretence at unanimity. The general form was to indicate that some countries thought this while other countries thought that. And the section dealing with agriculture was quite categoric on the difference of view between the United Kingdom and most of the rest of the OEEC countries.

The third part of the report dealt with institutions. Here blatant differences of view were avoided since there was general agreement that little progress could be made on the institutional problem until the functions of the free trade area had been agreed. It was nevertheless clear that there were reservations on the part of other countries about the British view that a somewhat strengthened OEEC would be adequate for the job.

The White Paper setting out the British views on the OEEC report and proposing the establishment of a 'European industrial free trade area' in effect endorsed Part I of the OEEC report and gave somewhat more explicitly than had been possible in an OEEC report the British views on the controversial sections of that report. The categoric way in which the British drew distinctions between their own concept and the concept of the Six tended to overshadow the passages in the White Paper that indicated that the United Kingdom nevertheless believed that the free trade area would be the beginning of an evolutionary process which might, over time, result in arrangements that were not very dissimilar to those the Six were prepared to embrace at once. The following passage illustrates both the British insistence on a different concept and their intellectual acceptance of the fact that they might, in fact, be led by the operation of a free trade area to do in the future many of the things they were not yet ready to agree to, now, in 1957.

Her Majesty's Government's concept of the Free Trade Area differs in some important respects from that of the Customs and Economic Union now contemplated by the Messina Powers. The arrangements proposed for the Customs and Economic Union involve far-reaching provisions for economic integration and harmonisation of financial and social policies, and for mutual assistance in the financing of investment. These arrangements are to be effected within an appropriate institutional framework. Her Majesty's Government envisage the Free Trade Area, on the other hand, as a concept related primarily to the removal of restrictions on trade such as tariffs and quotas. Nevertheless, Her Majesty's Government recognise that co-operation in the field of economic policy is of great and continuing importance. In practice an appreciable movement towards closer economic co-operation may be expected to take place among the members of a Free Trade Area over a period of years, either as a matter of deliberate policy or as a spontaneous development.[34]

It is small wonder that the Europeans tended to focus on the flat statement that the British concept was related primarily to the removal of trade restrictions and to ignore, or to discount, the less forthright hints of things to come. But many of those in the United Kingdom most closely concerned with the negotiations were themselves firm believers in the inevitability of the evolutionary process and therefore tended to read the White Paper in a wholly different light. In consequence they were not as sensitive as they should have been to the negative impact it made on the Continent.

In particular, the British position on agriculture was phrased far too negatively. A simple statement that special arrangements would be needed would have raised no hackles, but the unimaginative reiteration of the extreme British position that agriculture

[34] White Paper, Paragraph 11.

'must be excluded' was bound to give rise to strong objections almost everywhere on the Continent and not simply among the Six. The United Kingdom was far and away the largest single importer of agricultural products and discussions within the working party had already made it plain that on this issue the United Kingdom was isolated. The flat statement on agriculture was, apparently, a condition of Cabinet agreement to the plan and indicates the strength of the opposition—both within the Government and from the Commonwealth countries—to any modification in the existing arrangements for British agriculture and for imports from the Commonwealth. But the fact that agriculture was dealt with not only so categorically but so unimaginatively suggests a British overestimation of bargaining strength as well. It is also curious, purely from a tactical viewpoint, that the British thought it wise to include in a document of this kind a warning to the Six about the nature of their own arrangements on agriculture.[35]

The dangers of writing simultaneously for foreign and domestic consumption were also painfully well illustrated by the flat statement on preferences: 'It is essential that the United Kingdom should be able to continue the preferential arrangements which have been built up over the last twenty-five years.' This proposition may have been self-evident to the House of Commons but the continental countries were bound to ask 'why'? And, from the nature of the presentation in the White Paper, they were also bound to assume that the reason was the desire to retain for exports from the United Kingdom the preferential arrangements they enjoyed in Commonwealth markets. This was one reason; but not the strongest one.[36]

The discussions at the OEEC Council meeting in February

[35] See Paragraph 15 of the White Paper: 'Indeed it appears to be the intention of the Messina Powers to institute a regulated market for agricultural produce, rather than a free market as is proposed for industrial products. Any special arrangements for agricultural produce, if restrictive in character, might clearly give rise to difficulty in securing international agreement.' Presumably the 'international agreement' referred to was approval by the GATT.

[36] See Paragraph 14 of the White Paper. To the British reader it might have been clear from this paragraph that the United Kingdom was mainly concerned about the effect on the Commonwealth countries and the colonial territories of the loss of their preferential position on the United Kingdom market. It was not clear to the continental countries. Moreover, one of the reasons why it was not clear was that until very late in the day the Government hoped to be able to retain the British preferential position in Commonwealth markets as well, and was therefore not prepared to be very explicit on this point.

(1957) did not go smoothly.[37] The British position that agriculture should be excluded from the proposed free trade area was strongly contested, and the United Kingdom again found itself in a minority of one as it had in the working party.[38] The uncompromising British line on this issue tended to make the other OEEC countries less sympathetic than they might otherwise have been to British arguments for the need for speedy negotiations on a free trade area. At this Council meeting, as in the ensuing negotiations, the British delegates stressed repeatedly the importance of the free trade area and the Common Market coming into operation simultaneously, and with the same timetable for trade liberalization, so that discrimination among the OEEC countries would be avoided. M. Spaak, speaking for the Six, resisted all suggestions which implied any slowing-down of the Treaty of Rome negotiations or any changes in the draft treaty in order to accommodate the needs of the free trade area. At the Council meeting he reaffirmed the view he had expressed privately to the British earlier in the year, that an overriding priority must be given to pushing ahead with the Treaty of Rome.[39] M. Spaak's unwillingness to compromise provoked objections from Dr. Erhard, the German

[37] For accounts of the OEEC Council meeting see *Financial Times*, *Manchester Guardian*, and *The Times*, 13 and 14 February 1957.

[38] Annoyance at the British on this score was undoubtedly aggravated by the fact that at about this time the Danes and the Dutch, in particular, were suffering from the export of British eggs to Germany—an unnatural British export that had been stimulated by the high domestic subsidy.

[39] Early in January, while the French Assembly was debating the Common Market, M. Spaak visited London for discussions on the relationship between the Common Market and the free trade area. The British Government had just been reorganized, following the resignation of Sir Anthony Eden. Mr. Macmillan had become Prime Minister and Mr. Thorneycroft, Chancellor of the Exchequer. These two ministers had taken the lead in formulating and pressing for the free trade area, and they were clearly determined to push ahead as rapidly as possible. The discussions with M. Spaak were widely covered in the British press. It seems clear from these accounts that the British had three main objectives in these discussions. First, to make it clear to M. Spaak that the exclusion of agriculture was of key importance to the economic structure of the Commonwealth and, in consequence, was an essential and non-negotiable aspect of the British plan. Secondly, since the British were convinced that the free trade area and the Common Market must have the same rules, procedures, and timing for trade liberalization and tariff reduction, they wanted M. Spaak to agree to keep the Treaty of Rome sufficiently flexible so that any necessary modifications could be made to bring the two systems into line without having formally to amend the Treaty of Rome. Finally, they were greatly alarmed at the prospect that the overseas territories of the Six might be brought within the scope of the Treaty of Rome. The British made very little headway with M. Spaak on any of these points.

Minister of Economics, who was already displaying his personal preference for a free trade area rather than the tighter and more far-reaching Common Market.[40] The French, in contrast, were already sceptical about the free trade area. At the time the working party report was completed in December 1956, a revealing article appeared in *Le Monde*, written by M. Pierre Drouin, who throughout the negotiations reflected official French views with remarkable accuracy. He made it clear that the French both feared and, even more important, rejeced intellectually the British concept of a system essentially limited to the removal of barriers to trade.

The British were unable to obtain the firm commitment to proceed with an industrial free trade area that they sought from their OEEC partners. Instead the Council decided, rather cumbersomely, 'to enter into negotiations in order to determine ways and means on the basis of which there could be brought into being a European Free Trade Area, which would, on a multilateral basis, associate the European Common Market with other Member countries of the Organisation, and to prepare the necessary instruments'.[41]

The British were also forced to abandon hope of achieving any clear exclusion of agriculture. The Council decision was formally 'neutral' with respect to the inclusion or exclusion of agriculture but, in the same paragraph as that quoted above, the Council drew 'special attention to the objective of finding ways to ensure the expansion of trade in agricultural products on a non-discriminatory basis between all Member countries of the Organisation'. Attention was also drawn to the need to deal with the special situation of member countries in the course of economic development. The Chairman of the Council (Mr. Thorneycroft) was given the task of organizing the necessary working parties, and he was requested to make a report to the Council so that it would be in a position to take further decisions before 31 July 1957. In accordance with this resolution Mr. Thorneycroft proposed, and the Council approved, in mid-March, the establishment of three working parties. The first, and most important, Working Party No. 21, was to undertake *negotiations* 'to determine the conditions

[40] See *Manchester Guardian*, 13 February 1957.
[41] For the full text of the Council decision see *Negotiations for a European Free Trade Area*, Documents Relating to the Negotiations from July 1956 to December 1958 (Cmnd. 641, H.M.S.O., January 1959), p. 8. Hereafter cited as Blue Book.

under which a European Free Trade Area associating, on a multi-lateral basis, the European Common Market with the other Member countries, could be brought into being'. Agriculture and the arrangements that might be made for the less developed countries were excluded from the purview of Working Party 21 but were to be examined by two other working parties established simultaneously.[42]

Although uneasy compromises had thus been found by the OEEC Council it was clear that the Six were so preoccupied with completing their own negotiations that progress on the free trade area would be slow. It proved to be even slower than the pessimists predicted.

During the early months of 1957, while the British were striving to breathe a sense of urgency into the free trade area negotiations, mistrust and suspicion of British motives flared up on the Continent, particularly in France. The suspicion that a strong, if not the primary, motive behind the British proposals for a free trade area was the desire to undermine the Six took root very early in the negotiations, particularly among the 'Europeans' and particularly in France, and this suspicion persisted—with periods of comparative dormancy and periods of great virulence—until the negotiations finally collapsed. The wave of suspicion in the early months of 1957 was nourished by the British attempts to persuade M. Spaak, and others, to keep the Six from agreeing on a system of tariff reduction and quota removal and on procedures for invoking escape clauses before they could be discussed within the wider group, and by the insistence with which the British argued the need for concerting the arrangements on these matters between the two groups. Similarly, the strong British opposition to the inclusion of the overseas territories appeared to some on the Continent as another attempt to side-track the Treaty of Rome. Early in the year, when the British realized, somewhat belatedly, that the French were pressing for the extension of common market treatment to their overseas territories, they had made strong representations to the Six, pointing out, among other things, the difficulties this would raise for everyone in the free trade area negotiations. The British protests were continued in various places and at various levels until the final decisions were taken by the Six, but they were unavailing.

[42] Blue Book, pp. 8 and 9.

The British motives on both issues were considerably purer than they were given credit for being, although it is undoubtedly true that the result of acceding to some of the British suggestions for discussion of common problems would have been a delay in the signing of the Treaty of Rome and an increase in the likelihood that the free trade area system would, in the end, supersede that of the Common Market. Moreover, although the British were undoubtedly on very firm ground in emphasizing the difficulties that the preferential arrangement for the overseas territories would raise for other countries (and not simply for their own colonies), it is hard to quarrel with the judgement of the French negotiators that an arrangement for the French overseas territories was a necessary price for French ratification of the Treaty of Rome. It was eventually privately agreed between the British and the French that despite the provisions for the associated overseas territories in the Treaty of Rome, exports from the Community's overseas territories and from British overseas territories would be excluded from the scope of the free trade area. But in the GATT discussions of the Treaty of Rome and elsewhere the British continued to point out the very real difficulties that the arrangements in the treaty presented to their own colonies and former colonies—by giving substantial new preferences to their competitors—and to question the compatibility of those arrangements with the rules of the General Agreement.[43]

Related developments in the spring of 1957

At about this time, two actions by the British Government, although not in the main stream of the Common Market–free trade area discussions, increased the suspicion and intensified the latent mistrust on the Continent, and considerably confused and perplexed many Europeans who were disposed to be friendly to British overtures. The first was the so-called 'Grand Design' proposal of Mr. Selwyn Lloyd, then Foreign Secretary. The second was the decision of the United Kingdom to reshape its defence policies to give greater priority to its own nuclear deterrent and to reduce the numbers of troops that had been stationed in Germany

---

[43] Strictly speaking, the association arrangement was neither a free trade area nor a customs union, since although the Six would eventually admit goods from their associates free from tariffs and quotas, the associates remained free to impose tariffs on imports from the Common Market countries provided they did so on a non-discriminatory basis.

pursuant to Britain's undertaking to its partners in Western European Union.[44]

The 'Grand Design' was the name rather ill-advisedly given to a Foreign Office plan for regrouping and reorganizing the various European parliamentary assemblies. These ideas were sketched out by Mr. Selwyn Lloyd at the NATO Council meeting in December 1956, leaked, probably intentionally, to the press during the spring, and described in some detail by Mr. Ormsby-Gore (then Minister of State, Foreign Office) to the Consultative Assembly of the Council of Europe in May 1957. The proposals had by that time already provoked considerable suspicion and mistrust, so that the British spokesman was rather on the defensive at the Council of Europe meeting and it seems probable that the form in which the ideas were there outlined had been tailored in an attempt to meet some of the apprehensions of the critics.

The central idea of the 'Grand Design' was the replacing of the existing, and proposed, European and Atlantic parliamentary bodies by a single parliamentary assembly which through the device of semi-autonomous commissions (with membership varying with the subject matter) would cover all aspects of 'Western co-operation'. The British were not alone in feeling that the proliferation of parliamentary assemblies was getting out of hand. Already there were the Consultative Assembly of the Council of Europe, the Assembly of Western European Union, and the Common Assembly of the Coal and Steel Community. It was not yet entirely clear whether the Assembly proposed for the two new Communities would be that of the ECSC or a new body, as the French were advocating, and, in addition, parliamentarians from the NATO countries, although not formally organized into a NATO Assembly, had begun to hold annual meetings. However, although the existence of a problem was generally recognized, the solution proposed by the British found very little favour with anyone. Those neutrals who participated in the Council of Europe disliked the suggestion that NATO questions should come within the scope of the new Assembly even though, under the British plan, discussion of defence questions would take place in a commission on which only the NATO countries would be represented. In addition, those who had fought for many years to strengthen the role of the Consultative Assembly of the Council of Europe

[44] See Chapter I.

and to increase its power to influence governments felt the British proposal would be a step backward and would widen the gap between the parliamentarians and the ministers they were seeking to influence. There was also opposition from those who felt that the inclusion of parliamentarians from the United States and Canada would weaken the impetus for European unity: 'We must not drown Europe in the Atlantic', became a favourite warning.[45] The strongest opposition of all came from the 'Europeans' within the Six who saw in the proposal further evidence of the British tendency to ignore, or to seek to diminish, the underlying difference in concept between the cautious intergovernmental approach of the OEEC and the bolder 'federal' approach of the Communities. They saw in this proposal, as they saw in the free trade area, a calculated British move to undermine the plans of the Six by merging the Community institutions with other more inclusive but less powerful institutions. At Strasbourg, Mr. Ormsby-Gore sought to reassure the 'Europeans': 'We all recognize that the Assembly of the Six has an executive task to carry out; and except, perhaps, for sharing administrative facilities, and perhaps participating in joint sessions, it is not our wish to encroach upon its activities in any way.'[46] But the damage had been done and his hearers at Strasbourg were not convinced by Mr. Ormsby-Gore's explanations.[47] Eventually a non-committal resolution was adopted recognizing the need for rationalization, noting that the British plan among others was being studied by the WEU Assembly, and expressing the Consultative Assembly's wish to be consulted before any decision was taken.

The British decision to seek WEU agreement to the withdrawal of certain British troops from the Continent also cast doubt on the genuineness of the 'Europeanism' of the United Kingdom and disturbed the French in particular. The French had no economic interest in a wider area of free trade (rather the opposite) and the only appeal of the British plan for a free trade area lay in the political advantages of a closer relationship with the British. Although it was diminishing with surprising rapidity, there was

[45] See A. H. Robertson, *The Council of Europe* (2nd ed., London, 1961), pp. 102–5.

[46] For the text of Mr. Ormsby-Gore's speech see Consultative Assembly of the Council of Europe, *Official Report of Debates*, First Part, Ninth Ordinary Session, 1 May 1957, pp. 73 ff.

[47] For a 'European' view of the British proposals, see remarks by M. Teitgen (France) in *Official Report of Debates*, 2 May 1957, pp. 170 ff.

still a substantial residuum of distrust of the Germans and the continued presence of British troops in Germany had been a large part of the price paid for French agreement to German re-armament. The British Government's wish to reduce its forces in Germany was intimately bound up with the decision to recast its defence policy and to put more emphasis on its own nuclear deterrent and less on conventional forces.[48] To many on the Continent the new British defence policy seemed further evidence of a British determination to try to play the role of a great power and of a stubborn unwillingness to recognize, as the continental countries had done, that the countries of Western Europe could regain and effectively exercise power only by pooling their strength.

During the spring of 1957 the British Prime Minister saw M. Mollet (the French Prime Minister) and, later, Dr. Adenauer (the German Chancellor) to try to dispel the fears and suspicions that had arisen.[49] In these and a number of other high level talks during the spring the British also sought to gain more positive French and German support for the free trade area. There was a particularly important meeting in London early in May, between M. Maurice Faure (the principal French negotiator on the Treaty of Rome and the French delegate to the OEEC Council), Mr. Thorneycroft (Chancellor of the Exchequer), and Sir David Eccles (President of the Board of Trade). This meeting took place against a background of rumour on the Continent that the United Kingdom was seeking to torpedo the Common Market and of suspicion in England that France, having got what it wanted in the Treaty of Rome, had lost interest in the free trade area. As evidence of the genuineness of their repeated statements that they wished the Community well, the British agreed to the French request for a postponement of the OEEC Council meeting originally planned for July, at which the British had hoped to make definitive progress on the free trade area. The French wanted the meeting postponed because the ratification debate in the

---

[48] WEU and NATO were consulted on the reduction of forces in Germany during the winter of 1956–7 and the spring of 1957. For details of the reduction see *Defence, Outline of Future Policy* (Cmnd. 124, April 1957, H.M.S.O.).

[49] Mr. Macmillan met M. Mollet on 9 March in Paris and Dr. Adenauer in Bonn on 8 May. The Chancellor of the Exchequer and the President of the Board of Trade had discussed the free trade area negotiations with Dr. Erhard in London on 28 March 1957.

National Assembly on the Treaties of Rome was planned for July and there was considerable fear that if the free trade area were attracting attention at the same time the chances of ratification might be prejudiced. The French Government was probably less worried about the tiny minority who might genuinely have preferred the free trade area to the Common Market than they were about the prospect of the free trade area being used simply as a pretext for turning down the Common Market by the much larger group who were basically opposed to any move towards freer trade. In return for their agreement to this slowing down of the negotiations on a free trade area, the British received assurances from both the French and the Germans (who supported the French request for a postponement of the OEEC Council Meeting) that once French ratification had been completed the two Governments would be ready for serious negotiations on a free trade area.[50]

An article in *Le Monde* commenting on the visit made it plain that although the *communiqué* recorded apparent agreement on the creation of a free trade area, the British and French ideas of

---

[50] The communiqué issued after the talks with M. Maurice Faure stated: 'The meeting discussed the stage now reached in the negotiations for the European Common Market and the Free Trade Area. The United Kingdom representatives welcomed the signature of the Treaty of Rome and emphasised the importance which they attached to its ratification. The French representatives on their side emphasised their support for the association in a Free Trade Area of the United Kingdom and other countries of the O.E.E.C. with the European Economic Community.

'There was a satisfactory exchange of views and it was agreed that the two Governments would do what they could to ensure that the negotiations in the O.E.E.C. for the creation of the Free Trade Area should be carried forward to a satisfactory conclusion.' Text given in White Paper, Cmnd. 648, *Negotiations for a European Free Trade Area* (H.M.S.O., January 1959).

This White Paper also contains the following paragraph: 'At the meeting on 6th May a request was made by the French Government for a delay in the free trade area negotiations until there had been substantial progress with the ratification of the Treaties of Rome. This request was supported by the German Government at the meeting on 8th May. Her Majesty's Government agreed to the proposed delay, while reiterating the importance they attached to bringing the free trade area negotiations to an early and successful conclusion.' The White Paper also contains the text of the relevant section of the communiqué issued after the Macmillan–Adenauer talks: 'Both Heads of Government agreed that the interests of Europe would best be served by the early ratification of the Rome Treaties. They further agreed that it was necessary to establish as soon as possible a Free Trade Area as a complement to the Common Market. They therefore resolved to do all in their power to ensure that the negotiations to this end are carried forward with a view to their successful conclusion at the appropriate time.' (Op. cit., p. 4.)

what constituted a satisfactory arrangement were very far apart.
M. Drouin, with his usual accuracy, pointed out that the French
feared that the safeguard and other clauses of the Treaty of Rome
would be 'emptied of their contents' by the free trade area convention, for Dr. Erhard would not be unhappy to take back with the
other hand what he had given up in the Common Market negotiations. It is not clear whether, as M. Drouin supposed, M. Maurice
Faure made it clear to the British during these discussions that
France could not accept fewer guarantees in the free trade area
than she had done in the Common Market; but in any case the
British should by this time have had few illusions about the French
attiude towards the free trade area.[51]

The improvement in relations that followed the talks with
Maurice Faure was soured a few days later by some unhappy
comments made by Sir David Eccles in a speech to the Congress
of the Federation of Commonwealth and British Empire Chambers
of Commerce. Foreshadowing the even more unhappy comments
by Mr. Macmillan three years later in Washington, the President
of the Board of Trade, in explaining why the political reasons for
the free trade area were even more important than the economic,
remarked that 'although it is not military or hostile in its intent—
six countries in Europe have signed a treaty to do exactly what, for
hundreds of years, we have always said we could not see done with
safety to our own country. . . . If, when the common market of the
Six comes about, we were left outside and made no effort to join
it and liberalize it and make it look outwards instead of inwards,
the Germans would run it . . . the present German Government
under Dr. Adenauer knows it and fears it and does not want to
do it'.[52] These remarks alarmed the French on several counts:
they seemed to confirm a basic British distrust of the Six and to
reaffirm that the British Government still thought in terms of
holding the balance of power on the Continent; in addition, the
French feared they would stimulate fears of Germany in France
and thus increase the danger that the Treaties of Rome would not
win the necessary majorities in the French Assembly.

In June, Sir David Eccles held talks and gave a number of
speeches in Paris and Rome to try to clear up misunderstandings
about the British position. In a speech to the British Chamber
of Commerce in Paris he gave perhaps the strongest and

[51] See *Le Monde*, 7 May 1957.
[52] *The Times*, 28 May 1957.

warmest support yet given to the Treaty of Rome by a British minister:

My Government welcomes the initiative of France and the other five Powers who have agreed upon a revolutionary change in their commercial and financial policies. . . . This is one of the masterpieces of history—something above and beyond the ordinary scope of international arrangements. It is a pact which owes its origin to the European tradition of universality and its execution to the humanity, patience and idealism of great Frenchmen and great Europeans. . . . When the experts explain to us the Treaty of Rome in terms of economics we see beyond the tariffs and the quotas, for we know that Europe is feeling its way to something much more fundamental than the exchange of goods and money.

However, he coupled a warning with his support:

But, gentlemen, granted that European solidarity and peace is the purpose of the Treaty of Rome, how illusory might this be if the result were to divide Europe. . . . If the Common Market came into existence without the Free Trade Area then Western Europe, which over the centuries has suffered so often the agonies of division, and has all the time dreamed the same dreams of unity might again fly apart.[53]

This warning of the dangers of 'dividing Europe' was to become a prominent British theme in the months and years to come.

In accordance with the French request, the July OEEC Council meeting was postponed until the autumn. Mr. Thorneycroft, who as chairman of the Council had been entrusted with the co-ordination of the work on the free trade area, nevertheless called for reports from the chairmen of the three working parties and circulated these together with a note of his own to the other members of the OEEC Council during the summer. The most interesting report was that of Mr. Melander (Norway), the chairman of Working Party 21. This working party, in effect, began its work where the working party (No. 17) that had made the basic study of a free trade area had left off. The Treaty of Rome was now available and the new working party took the provisions of the treaty as its starting-point. The working party identified the key

[53] Quotation from press release of Sir David Eccles' speech to British Chamber of Commerce, Paris, 7 June 1957. In this and other speeches at about the same time Sir David Eccles also sought to make it clear that although the British Government had not altered its view that the general rules for trade liberalization and tariff reduction could not be applied to agriculture they were ready to explore ways of co-operating more closely with the continental countries and of expanding trade in agricultural products.

problems and foreshadowed most of the areas of controversy that developed later on; but little progress was made in reaching agreement, for, as Mr. Melander frankly pointed out, there was no commonly-held conception of the free trade area.[54] The report of the chairman of the working party on agriculture (No. 22) was also frank enough to say that negotiations had not yet really started. Some progress had been made in the sense that the sterile argument about 'inclusion' or 'exclusion' of agriculture had given way to agreement that something had to be done about agriculture. But there was no agreement on what kind of action should be taken and the chairman of the working party (M. Sergent, the Secretary-General of the OEEC) concluded his report with the flat statement that 'I am satisfied that Group 22 cannot usefully pursue its discussions . . . unless substantially different instructions are given to its members'. In a detailed Annex to his report, M. Sergent pointed out that since Denmark, the Six, and to a lesser degree a number of other countries considered that a provision for the increase of quotas and progressive abolition of tariffs on agricultural products was essential for a free trade area, this had been taken as a working assumption in order to open the way for the discussion of other questions, e.g. the effectiveness of minimum prices as an alternative system of control. But, he added, 'The value of this assumption, even as a working hypothesis, is however to some extent reduced because the principal purchaser of agricultural produce [i.e. the United Kingdom] has been unable to accept it.'

[54] Mr. Melander's report was extremely good in that it did not seek to gloss over but, in fact, dramatized the conceptual difference: 'When the discussions . . . began, it seemed to me that the Six considered that the institution of a Free Trade Area necessarily involved the settlement of a large number of general economic problems and that fundamentally (if I may perhaps exaggerate a little) they visualised the Free Trade Area Convention as a facsimile of the Rome Treaty. As against this, a number of other Member countries saw the Convention as a kind of trade agreement containing nothing more than a number of rules, as strictly drawn as possible, setting out the timing and method of removing barriers and stating a number of general principles applicable to competition between Member States. These countries did not deny that the economics of the Member countries of the area would become increasingly interdependent as the trade barriers between them disappeared, and that it would be necessary to co-ordinate their economic and financial policies more closely, but they relied on the O.E.E.C., and a gradual development of its consultation procedures, to achieve this. These differences of approach go to the root of the problems before us.' Blue Book, pp. 11 and 12. Mr. Melander also pointed with great sureness to the fundamental difficulty of how to achieve co-ordination between the institutions of the free trade area and Common Market, particularly with respect to escape clauses. See para. 13.

Working Party 23 on the arrangements for the less developed OEEC countries had made even less progress.[55] Four countries—Iceland, Ireland, Greece, and Turkey—had made preliminary submissions about the kind of arrangements they might like but these tended to be vague and unrealistic. It was generally conceded, however, that little real progress could be made on this problem until the basic nature of the free trade area was clearer.

In the light of these reports, Mr. Thorneycroft concluded that there was little point in asking the officials to do much further work until the ministers had made another attempt to find some agreement on the fundamental differences of view that had been expressed in the working groups. And he urged the negotiating governments to use the interval before the ministers met again, in October, to reconsider their positions to see what changes each might make to meet the views of others.[56]

The proposal for a free trade area with Canada

At this ministerial meeting in October, the British proposed new procedural arrangements for the negotiations but, before turning to the work of the Maudling Committee, it is necessary to make an apparent digression to Canada—to Mont Tremblant (near Montreal) and to Ottawa. As indicated above, the British had consulted the Commonwealth countries in the autumn of 1956 before proposing a free trade area and the progress made in the negotiations continued to be a regular item on the agenda of subsequent Commonwealth discussions. At a meeting of Commonwealth Prime Ministers in London early in the summer of 1957, Mr. Diefenbaker, who had recently become Canadian Prime Minister, urged that a new Commonwealth trade conference be held to examine the possibilities of expanding Commonwealth trade. Mr. Diefenbaker made no secret of his concern at the increasing Canadian economic dependence on the United States and, at about this time, he also suggested to the United Kingdom that an attempt be made to change the direction of Canadian trade and, specifically, that the United Kingdom and Canada should seek to achieve a 15 per cent. increase in their trade with one another.

[55] The reports of Working Groups Nos. 22 and 23 are in the Blue Book. See pp. 22–38.

[56] See ibid., pp. 42–44, for the text of Mr. Thorneycroft's note.

Although there was considerable scepticism in the United Kingdom and elsewhere in the Commonwealth about the scope for a 'new Ottawa', it was agreed that Mr. Diefenbaker's proposal for a trade conference would be examined further by the Commonwealth Finance Ministers who normally met each year in the early autumn at the time of the annual meetings of the IBRD and IMF. Shortly before this meeting of the Finance Ministers at Mont Tremblant the British countered the Canadian proposal for an expansion of United Kingdom–Canadian trade by privately suggesting to the Canadians the formation of a free trade area between the United Kingdom and Canada. This proposal, which soon leaked to the press, was further discussed by Mr. Thorneycroft, Sir David Eccles and Mr. Maudling with their Canadian counterparts immediately after the Mont Tremblant meeting.

Although it may well have been true that an increase in trade of the size desired by the Canadians could only have been achieved by a drastic step of this kind, the proposal was too strong medicine for the Canadians. Presumably there were few illusions in London that the Canadian Government would be pleased by the proposal, and the reasons for making the suggestion seem to have been primarily tactical. It served to indicate that the British were not, in principle, against an expansion of British–Canadian trade, but it transferred the onus for lack of action to the shoulders of the Canadians. In addition it demonstrated once again for the benefit of doubters within the United Kingdom that a Commonwealth free trade area was not a possible alternative to a European free trade area, since even the most developed country of the Commonwealth was not ready for free trade.[57] However, although the

[57] The Commonwealth Finance Ministers approved the proposal of the Canadian Government for the Commonwealth Trade and Economic Conference in 1958, but it was already clear that the development needs of the Commonwealth would play a larger part in the discussions than would measures for expanding Commonwealth trade. It should be noted that this meeting of Commonwealth Finance Ministers gave perhaps the most explicit endorsement that had yet been given to the formation of a free trade area in Europe. The relevant passage of the final communiqué read as follows: 'United Kingdom Ministers reported on the progress made following the United Kingdom initiative for the establishment of a Free Trade Area in Europe. The Commonwealth Ministers recognised that the establishment of an outward-looking Free Trade Area in Europe would broaden the advantages to be derived from economic integration in Europe not only by the United Kingdom but by all the other participants. This was regarded as important as it could contribute to agreed Commonwealth policies of expanding world trade.' (Press Release, U.K. Treasury.)

proposal may have served a useful domestic political purpose, it made the British task in Europe more difficult. It nourished the doubts about British motives and strengthened the feeling in France, in particular, that free trade with the United Kingdom would be an open door to the rest of the world.

V

THE FREE TRADE AREA
NEGOTIATIONS

The first phase

Once the French had ratified the Treaty of Rome, in July 1957, the British hoped to make rapid progress in the free trade area negotiations so that the freeing of trade under the two plans could begin simultaneously on 1 January 1959. In August 1957, Mr. Maudling was named Paymaster-General and given the full-time task of co-ordinating the work on the negotiations within the British Government. A small staff of officials from the Foreign Office and other departments was assigned to him. Soon after his appointment Mr. Maudling visited most of the other OEEC countries to try to find the basis of an agreement and to try to instil in others some of the urgency felt by the British. There were still wide differences of view within the Six about the free trade area proposal and there was much apprehension that the British would try to exploit these differences, apprehensions that Mr. Maudling's bilateral discussions did little to allay.

In view of the specific commitments made to the British by the German and French Governments in the spring of 1957 it was inevitable that the free trade area negotiations would be resumed once French ratification was out of the way, although the French Government would have been happy to see the project quietly dropped, and many of the 'Europeans' in all the six countries would have preferred to have organized the Community institutions and to have made some progress in formulating their own policies and in evolving their own methods of working together before trying to graft a free trade area on to the Common Market.[1] The French Government made no secret of the fact that

---

[1] After the signing of the Treaty of Rome, but before its formal entry into effect, ministers (or their representatives) from the six countries met together from time to time as the 'Interim Committee' to discuss questions of concern to the new Community, such as the position to be taken by the six countries

it saw serious technical difficulties in surrounding a common market with a free trade area, or of the fact that it felt that origin controls adequate to deal with the threat of deflections of trade would need to be so comprehensive that the scope of the free trade area would be severely restricted. There was strong (and vocal) opposition to the free trade area proposal from the Patronat and from other influential industrial groups in France, which contrasted sharply with the strong support given to the plan by the Federation of British Industries and other industrial organizations in the United Kingdom. The Government and the industrial, agricultural, and labour organizations in France were alike in feeling that the free trade area was an 'unbalanced' arrangement which would expose the French economy to the risks of free trade without providing either the safeguards or the compensatory advantages of the Treaty of Rome. They feared that French industry could not stand the added competition of the free trade area, and they also worried about the effect the free trade area might have on the attitudes of their partners in the Common Market: if the British succeeded in getting the trade advantages without giving comparable commitments, might not Germany and the Benelux countries be tempted to renege on some of the concessions made to the French during the negotiations on the Treaty of Rome? In addition, the feeling was widespread in France that the arrangement under discussion was far more advantageous for the United Kingdom than it was for France. The British would gain free access to the continental market for their industrial goods but would not, in return, give comparable freedom of access to the United Kingdom market to the continental exporters of agricultural products. Furthermore the British manufacturer would have a cost advantage arising from 'cheap food' and from the low (or nil) tariffs charged on most Commonwealth raw materials. Moreover, in contrast to the situation with respect to the French overseas territories under the Treaty of Rome, the free trade area proposal would leave intact the British preferential position in Commonwealth markets, thus enabling the United Kingdom 'de jouer gagnante sur deux tables'. And this, so the

---

when the Rome Treaty was discussed by the contracting parties to the GATT in the autumn of 1957 and the position to be taken in the free trade area negotiations. Prof. Hallstein and M. Marjolin, who were later to become President and Vice-President of the Commission, both played a prominent part in the work of the Interim Committee.

argument ran, would make the United Kingdom a stronger magnet for United States investment than those countries having access to only one preferential market.

The Italians tended to share many of the French reservations but the Germans and the Dutch (and to a lesser extent the other two Benelux countries) were genuinely anxious for the eventual 'completion' of the Common Market by the free trade area in order to increase the area of free trade and to weaken the 'protectionist' colouration of the Common Market. And many people in all the Six countries, but particularly in the Benelux countries, wanted an arrangement with the British for political reasons. However, despite the differences among the Six, there was by the autumn of 1957 a sense of commitment to the Treaty of Rome which ran very deep and which enabled them to find a measure of common agreement. Although the treaty was not yet fully ratified it was already exerting a restraining influence on the freedom of action of the member countries. Even the Dutch, who during the last days of the Treaty of Rome negotiations had been the most outspoken in asserting that too many concessions had been made to the French, attached such strong political importance to the proposed Economic Community that they were as unwilling as the rest to contemplate arrangements for the free trade area which would make the working of the Common Market difficult or which would prejudice its evolution into an economic union.

The very fact of having successfully completed two years of intensive negotiation in itself tended to give the Six a sense of cohesion and of common purpose. And even where they disagreed, there was a willingness to go to considerable lengths to preserve a common front in the negotiations with other countries. Furthermore, there was widespread feeling among the Six that the problems arising from the differences in external tariffs (differences that are, of course, inherent in a free trade area) and from the United Kingdom's participation in the Commonwealth preference system, were more difficult problems than the British were prepared to acknowledge. Many among the Six were also impressed by the conclusions reached during the two years of negotiation on the Treaty of Rome, and they felt that the United Kingdom underestimated the degree to which policies would have to be co-ordinated, institutions strengthened, and common rules accepted, if a free trade area were to achieve its purpose without creating excessive dislocation or hardship. The feeling that the

British proposal was a throwback to 'nineteenth-century liberal-ism' and was inadequate in the second half of the twentieth century was quite general. The Six were also in agreement that the British position on agriculture was untenable, although they differed among themselves about the appropriate arrangements for agri-culture. Above all, the Six Governments were agreed that a clear priority should be given to maintaining the integrity of the Treaty of Rome. Their agreement on this point was to be of crucial importance. There was room for argument among the Six about whether various arrangements did or did not threaten the Treaty of Rome, and the arguments were numerous and heated. But once satisfied that the threat was real, the Six always stuck together.

By the summer of 1957 it was clear that the British stood no chance of obtaining agreement on the simplified plan outlined in the White Paper, and during the summer and early autumn various compromises were discussed behind the scenes by the interested governments, by the OEEC secretariat, and by well-wishers on the sidelines. But none of the various schemes that were floated could be reconciled with both the British and the French positions. The French case was essentially that free trade was tolerable in the context of the Treaty of Rome only because the commitments to free trade were accompanied by agreements on other arrangements—common rules, harmonization of social policies, a common tariff and a common commercial policy, a common agricultural policy, mutual aid commitments, the right of establishment, freedom of movement for labour and capital, strong institutions. If, after two years' study, it had been concluded that this complex of interrelated arrangements and commitments was needed to ensure equity and balance, why should free trade with the British and other countries be acceptable without comparable arrangements?

Since the British, and other OEEC countries, had made it clear that they would not accept all the Treaty of Rome arrangements the French concluded that the provisions for freeing trade in the free trade area would have to be different from those agreed for the Common Market. Although the Benelux and German Govern-ments were anxious for a free trade area, they were, at the same time, impressed by the logic of the French position (as well as by the political difficulties in France), and various ways of achieving a 'difference' which would make the plan acceptable to the French were examined within the Six. At one time or another there were suggestions for a slower rate of tariff reduction, for limiting tariff reductions and quota removal to certain categories of goods rather than applying them across-the-board, or for a *décalage*, that is, for starting the freeing of trade in the free trade area later than in the Common Market. The *décalage* proposal, in turn, took numerous forms: the rate of reduction might be the same after a later starting date; there might be both a later starting point and a slower rate of reduction; there might be a delayed start but a later acceleration by the free trade area so that the two groups would achieve complete free trade at the same time.

All these schemes for introducing 'differences' between the trade liberalization in the Common Market and in the free trade area clearly involved introducing a measure of 'discrimination' between the Six and the rest of the OEEC countries, and this the British were determined to resist. Outside the Six, ideas for compromises therefore took a different form. The possibility of offering the French various kinds of special position with special safeguards within the free trade area was considered; so too was the possibility of an 'empty chair' arrangement, a possibility the Six themselves had discussed during the Treaty of Rome negotiations. But arrangements of this kind conflicted with the basic principle of the Six, that nothing should be done to weaken the cohesiveness of the Six or the integrity of the Treaty of Rome.

Perhaps the most promising basis for a compromise discussed during the autumn of 1957 was some kind of interim undertaking for the first four years during which more detailed arrangements for the longer term could be negotiated. However, attempts to find compromise solutions along this line also broke down: the French were unwilling to give a precise enough commitment on the situation that would exist after the initial period to satisfy the British that the end result would not be simply a partial tariff reduction on an OEEC basis—and discrimination by the Six against the rest at the end of four years.[2]

The OEEC ministerial meeting which had been postponed from July was finally held in Paris on 16 and 17 October 1957. It was already clear to everyone that the British and the French were the protagonists. If they had been able to agree on the essential features of an arrangement between the Six and the other OEEC countries the rest of the negotiation would have been

---

[2] The idea of an interim arrangement was revived again in the spring of 1958. See below p. 150.

comparatively easy. But neither an agreement on fundamentals nor a basis for a compromise was in sight. Once again, the OEEC Council adopted a general resolution on the formation of a free trade area and once again an agreement on procedural arrangements gave an illusion of progress. Somewhat surprisingly, since the positions of the principal countries had, in fact, moved rather further apart in the intervening months, the October resolution was in somewhat stronger terms than the resolution adopted the preceding February.[3] Thus the Council declared its determination

to secure the establishment of a European Free Trade Area which would comprise all Member countries of the Organisation; which would associate, on a multi-lateral basis, the European Economic Community with the other Member countries; and which, taking fully into consideration the objectives of the European Economic Community, would in practice take effect parallel with the Treaty of Rome.

The Council also declared its determination to reach agreement at the same time on methods of further co-operation between all member countries in agricultural matters with a view to ensuring an expansion of trade in agricultural products. This formulation gave rather greater prominence to agriculture than had the February resolution. Similarly, the Council was more explicit about the need to take account of the interests of the economically less developed member countries of the OEEC.[4]

Although the Council decision made it clear that *all* the member countries of the OEEC intended to participate in the free trade area, it was resoundingly silent on the central, disputed question, that is, how many of the commitments and functions of the Economic Community should have parallels in the free trade area. And it shed no light on the difficult problem of how the 'scope' of the free trade area was to be determined, that is, what rules of origin should be applied. Furthermore, the decision was somewhat ambiguous on the controversial question of whether the liberalization measures and their timing would be identical in the Common Market and in the free trade area. The statement that the free trade area would 'in practice take effect parallel with the Treaty of Rome', while a partial victory for the British, did not

---

[3] It should be noted that at the time of the OEEC meeting the French had a caretaker government. The Bourgès-Maunoury Government had fallen on 30 September 1957 and the Gaillard Government was not invested until 5 November 1957.

[4] The text of the Council resolution is contained in the Blue Book, pp. 48–49.

rule out the possibility of tariff reductions which, while parallel to those in the Common Market, were not identical.

The OEEC Council agreed to establish an Intergovernmental Committee at ministerial level to give effect to its new resolve to form a free trade area. The Intergovernmental Committee held its first meeting the following day and elected Mr. Maudling as its chairman; shortly thereafter Mr. Maudling circulated an annotated agenda to serve as a basis for the work of the Committee. The problems that needed to be resolved were by then well known and the document was an orderly listing and grouping of topics, most of which had received considerable attention from the experts. Although impartial in tone, the structure of the agenda reflected the British approach to the problem. Thus, what the British regarded as first things were put first; what they regarded as subsidiary points were included, but placed later on the agenda. Agriculture was on the agenda, but it was treated as a separate issue. Nevertheless the document was a useful guide to the subjects requiring discussion, and the points of concern to other countries were fairly presented even when the British themselves regarded them as largely irrelevant.[5]

The first substantive discussions in the Intergovernmental Committee were held early in November 1957. At the start of the Committee's work the French delegate, M. Maurice Faure, was very explicit about the reservations the French Government had about the whole proposal.[6] The Gaillard Government had now taken office and M. Faure's statement was an important one: it confirmed the French position on the importance of having a 'difference' between the trade arrangements in the free trade area and the Common Market and clearly foreshadowed the difficulties to come.

After summarizing the reasons why the French felt that the free trade area agreement should not simply deal with the dismantling of tariffs and quotas but should be virtually a replica of the Treaty of Rome, M. Faure discussed the crucial problem arising from the fact that the countries of the free trade area would have different external tariffs. He indicated that the French felt that a free trade area would not be fully satisfactory unless it entailed, as a general

---

[5] The annotated agenda is contained in the Blue Book, pp. 51–59.

[6] At the ministerial meeting in October, the ministers from most OEEC countries had outlined their countries' views on the substance of the arrangement under consideration. Because of the governmental crisis in France, the French spokesman had, however, confined himself to procedural comments.

rule, a common external tariff with as small as possible a number of derogations from this rule. Otherwise, the French felt, competitive conditions would be distorted for reasons that had nothing to do with the relative productivity of firms. M. Faure considered that the work done by the experts on the problem of the definition of origin had not led to any satisfactory solution but had simply emphasized the complexity of the problem of trade deflexion. He also felt it was inconceivable that the members of a free trade area could retain full autonomy in trade policy. He was driven by the force of his own logic to conclude that there was no alternative to the substantial harmonization of tariffs and trade policies save a drastic limitation of the scope of the free trade area, to the point where it lost much of its meaning. He suggested that in some cases where the harmonization of the external tariffs might be neither possible nor desirable, member countries might be allowed to levy compensatory charges on trade in these goods within the area—an idea which was to appear again, under Sr. Carli's auspices, the following spring (see below, p. 142). In conclusion, M. Faure stated quite baldly that unless the Treaty of Association (the term he used in preference to free trade area treaty) between the Six and the other OEEC countries was roughly similar to the Treaty of Rome and like that treaty ensured an adequate 'balance' between commitments of different kinds, the trade advantages would have to be different and more limited than those enjoyed by the members of the Community. Otherwise it would be difficult to explain to the French people why the 'advantages' of the Treaty of Rome should be made available to those who would not accept the 'obligations'. M. Faure suggested that one way of demonstrating the 'difference' would be by having a somewhat slower timetable, at least initially, in the free trade area.[7]

M. Faure did not disguise the fact that the free trade area lacked —for him and for the French people—the political appeal of the Common Market and that this in turn made the disadvantages stand out more starkly. Although the French Assembly, when it ratified the Treaty of Rome, had asked the Government to continue negotiations on a free trade area, it had indicated that the free

[7] Another possibility, he said, would be to require a unanimous decision before passing from one stage of the transitional period to the next, i.e. to give the French a veto. M. Faure had also made the point earlier in his speech that 'in view of the inadequate guarantees offered by the Free Trade Area' resort to escape clauses should be easier than it would be in the Common Market.

trade area should include the same guarantees as the Treaty of Rome. M. Faure was acutely aware of the contradiction in this position, and he was undoubtedly right when he pointed out that if the Treaty of Association were to be ratified by the French Assembly there was very little room for manoeuvre.

Notwithstanding the fundamental nature of these French reservations, a certain amount of progress was made by the Maudling Committee and the various sub-committees and groups working under its direction during the winter of 1957–8. On many questions—although not on the central issue of tariff autonomy—the British were prepared to depart substantially from the simplified approach of the White Paper of February 1957. During the winter and spring of 1958 their general approach was to work from the text of the Treaty of Rome, accepting provisions comparable to those in the Rome Treaty wherever they felt able to do so. Where they were not prepared to accept similar provisions, they were usually ready to recognize the right of a country to bring a complaint if the absence of such a provision in fact resulted in trade deflexion, hardship, or a demonstrably unfair situation. If the complaint was found to be justified and the offending country was not prepared to alter its policy, the usual remedy would be to permit the injured country to have recourse to an escape clause to protect itself. Consistent with this approach of advocating extensive reliance on a complaints procedure, the British modified their views about the institutional arrangements that would be required. To guard against too easy a recourse to the escape clauses, they not only accepted, but advocated, the need for majority voting in the institutions that would hear complaints and would authorize safeguard measures and exceptions.[8]

In January 1958, the British circulated a paper setting forth their views on the arrangements that might be made for agriculture. This paper, which took the form of a draft agreement, was a somewhat more precise formulation of ideas which Mr. Maudling had already outlined orally to the OEEC Committee and to the Council of Europe.[9] The proposed agreement opened with a statement of unexceptionable objectives: increased productivity and low unit costs of production, adequate standards of living for those engaged in agriculture and fisheries, reasonable

[8] See White Paper, Cmnd. 648, January 1959, and Blue Book, p. 94.
[9] See Council of Europe, *Official Report of Debate*, Ninth Ordinary Session, Second Part, pp. 530–1, 23 October 1957.

market stability, and adequate supplies to the consumer at reasonable prices. These objectives were to be 'furthered' by co-operation among the contracting parties to bring about 'freer and increased trade' although, at the same time (and deliberately given equal importance), 'traditional channels of trade including trade with third countries' were to be taken into consideration. Protective policies or practices were to be applied in such a way as to make domestic production more economic and to reduce distortion of competition. The contracting parties were also to co-operate to seek to avoid excessive fluctuations in the production of and trade in agricultural and fisheries products. The principal means suggested for working towards these objectives were annual reviews of production, consumption, trade, and prices; systematic confrontations of the policies of member countries; and a complaints procedure. In addition, the British proposed commodity reviews to see what possibilities might exist for freeing and expanding trade in particular commodities (again 'consistent with the obligations to third countries') and that a plan for the eventual elimination of quotas should be drawn up, although no timetable was suggested. The British paper also proposed rules governing the use of subsidies and procedures for modifying various forms of internal restrictions having a protective effect. The draft agreement also contained a section on commodity arrangements which was apparently designed to make it possible for the Six to conclude certain kinds of marketing arrangements among themselves, provided these arrangements were open to the other contracting parties, provided they did not conflict with existing obligations, and provided they had regard to the legitimate interests of third countries.[10] Although these proposals were an advance on the initial British position, agricultural products were still to be excluded from the key commitment of the free trade area—the obligation to abolish tariffs.

The British paper was coolly received by most of the other countries and, later in the year, the Swiss, the Six, and the Scandinavian countries all circulated papers on agriculture.[11] These revealed some common ground, but the agricultural issue had not

[10] One of the difficulties, of course, in making much progress on agriculture was the fact that the Six were still very far from agreement on their own common agricultural policy. At this time marketing agreements seemed likely to be a prominent feature of their policy.
[11] These papers are reprinted in the Blue Book. They were remitted to a working party just before the collapse of the negotiations.

really been joined by the time the negotiations broke down.[12] After the initial rather futile argument over whether agriculture should be 'in' or 'out' had been settled by the decision to have an agreement on agriculture, there was considerable feeling that a compromise on agriculture might well be easier to find than would the answers to some of the other key problems, since no country, except Denmark, wanted free trade in agriculture. This might have proved illusory had the negotiations ever reached the point of discussing in detail the provisions of a special agricultural agreement. But that point was never reached and the Maudling Committee was principally concerned with three other clusters of problems: problems arising from the lack of harmonization of internal social and economic policies; institutional questions; and, above all, problems arising from the fact that in the free trade area there would not be a common external tariff and a common commercial policy.[13]

There was never any disagreement that, if a free trade area were to be established, origin controls would be needed to ensure that deflexion of trade and of economic activity did not result from freeing trade among a group of countries while leaving their external tariffs unharmonized. The argument arose rather on the technical feasibility of operating controls and, more particularly, over the 'scope' of the controls, that is how liberally the goods to be considered entitled for free trade area treatment were to be

[12] There was a good deal of superficial similarity. See chart in PEP, *Agricultural Policies in Western Europe*, Occasional Paper No. 3, May 1959, p. 25. But it is difficult to believe that the view of the Six that nothing in the agreement of the Seventeen should in any way 'prejudice either the content or the implementation of the Rome Treaty' could have been easily reconciled with the views of the other countries.

[13] The escape clause–institutional arrangements complex of questions was potentially almost as controversial as the cluster of questions arising from the existence of different external tariffs. However, since the procedure followed in the Maudling Committee, as in the Spaak Committee, was to seek to gain agreement on the substantive aspects of the free trade area before getting down to the details of organization, rather less time and effort had been expended on this group of questions by the time the negotiations broke down. They could not be avoided entirely, if only because of the increasing importance the British placed on the recourse to a complaints procedure, partly as an alternative to tariff harmonization and a common commercial policy, and partly as an alternative to various commitments to harmonize internal economic and social policies. Although the complaints procedure formula advocated by the British to meet the cluster of problems relating to 'harmonization' was recognized by most of the Six as going far to meet these problems, it might not, in the end, have proved satisfactory to the French. See *Negotiations for a European Free Trade Area*, Cmnd. 648, January 1959, pp. 10–11.

defined. If the 'area' tariff reductions were to apply only to those goods that were wholly produced in the area the amount of trade liberalized would have been very restricted. The resulting arrangement would have met many of the French points but it would not have met the British objective of equality of treatment with the principal competitors on the Continent, nor would it have met the GATT test that a free trade area must cover 'substantially all trade' between the countries concerned. Throughout the negotiations the British, the Scandinavians, and the Swiss, with considerable support from the Germans and Dutch, argued for liberal rules of origin; the French, the Italians, and frequently the Belgians, for far more restrictive rules. The first group of countries felt that important deflexions of trade could be prevented by origin rules and they were in general agreement on the use of three criteria of origin. They felt that as a general rule a product should qualify for 'area' treatment if 50 per cent. of the value of the goods was of 'area' origin. In addition, these countries favoured the adoption of a 'basic materials list' to supplement the percentage test. Goods on this basic materials list would be deemed to be of 'area origin' wherever they, in fact, originated. Thus the effect of the basic materials list would be partly to simplify the operation of the origin controls and partly, and more important, to bring more trade within the agreement.[14] Thirdly, this group of countries (although with little enthusiasm on the part of the British) was ready to agree on a list of processes which if performed in the area would entitle the goods thus processed to area treatment. However, they tended to regard the 'process test' as an optional alternative to the percentage test suitable for certain types of cases, rather than as a general substitute for the percentage test.

Although 'origin problems' had been exhaustively examined by OEEC working parties, a special group of trade experts was asked

---

[14] Use of a 'basic materials list' would extend the 'scope' of the free trade area not only by defining some goods as entitled to area treatment, regardless of where they, in fact, originated, but also by making it easier for many 'mixed' products to meet the 50 per cent. added value test. The Scandinavian countries were the most active supporters of a basic materials list. Their argument for an extensive basic materials list was in a sense a 'deflexion of trade' argument based not on the usual grounds of the advantage gained by a low-tariff country, but on the advantage enjoyed by countries with indigenous production in comparison with countries, like the Scandinavians, who were highly dependent on imports. See Blue Book, p. 116, para. 9. A basic materials list was, not surprisingly, a feature of the EFTA 'origin control' system. See Chapter VII.

by the Maudling Committee to make a further, even more detailed, study of the origin problem, and the group sought to identify the problems that might actually arise in the most important sectors of trade and to suggest ways of meeting them. However, very little common ground could be found between the British, Scandinavians, and others, who advocated the 'liberal' rules outlined above, and the French, Belgians, and Italians, who felt the percentage criterion would not only be difficult to administer, but would not, in actual fact, prevent certain kinds of deflexion of trade and of economic activity from taking place. The French, Belgians, and Italians also opposed the inclusion of many of the items the others wanted to see added to a basic materials list, not infrequently because this would tend to undermine the protection they wanted to continue to give to their own production. For a few sectors these countries were prepared to accept the percentage added-value test of origin (although they tended to advocate a higher qualifying percentage than did the British and their even more 'liberal' followers) but more frequently they advocated processing tests of a fairly restrictive character. And, for some sectors, they felt the only answer lay in tariff harmonization. Generally speaking, throughout the long discussions on 'origin' problems the French, normally supported by the Italians and Belgians, argued for measures which dealt with the problem of different external tariffs either by restricting the scope of the free trade area, or by counteracting the effects of differential tariffs, or by eliminating the differences by harmonizing the tariffs.[15]

The group of trade experts also discussed briefly the possibility of dealing with some of the problems posed by tariff disparities by permitting compensating charges on intra-European trade when external tariffs were far apart. A comprehensive plan based on the use of compensatory charges was formally proposed by Signor Carli, the Italian Minister of Foreign Trade, at a meeting of the

---

[15] The examination of the basic materials list, and to a lesser extent other aspects of the problem, was hampered by the fact that the Six had not yet reached agreement among themselves on the tariffs to be applied to the items on List G, many of which were basic materials. If the tariffs on these goods were set low, the problem of deflexion would be of much less importance than if they were set high. Positions taken in the group of trade experts naturally enough corresponded to the positions taken in the List G negotiations within the Six; thus the Germans and Dutch tended to argue for low List G tariffs and liberal rules of origin, the French, Italians, and Belgians for higher List G tariffs and more limiting definitions of origin.

Maudling Committee in mid-March (1958) at which the experts' report, and the origin problem generally, was being considered. Under the 'Carli plan', goods would be allowed to move freely within the area so long as the external tariffs applied by the area countries were within a specified margin on either side of an agreed norm. Countries could retain external tariffs which were outside these margins but, in that event, compensatory taxes could be levied on like products when they were traded within the area. This plan had the great merit of administrative simplicity, once the norms and the width of the bands around them had been agreed. But it also had drawbacks from the standpoint of the British and the countries that shared their general approach to the problem. Apart from a number of technical difficulties their big objection to the scheme was that it really only permitted free trade within the area for those goods for which the external tariffs were, if not the same, at least quite close together. It would, therefore, have exerted strong pressure for tariff harmonization. In short, like most of the other devices favoured by the French and the Italians, it dealt with the problems of a free trade area by restricting the freedom of trade to those sectors where the differences in external tariffs were not significant and set up strong pressures to turn the free trade area into a customs union.[16] Their overriding determination to preserve tariff autonomy (and effective preferences for certain Commonwealth products) led the British to oppose the plan rather brusquely when it was proposed in the spring of 1958. There was some feeling among the British

[16] Shortly after the breakdown in the free trade area negotiations the Swedish Ministry for Foreign Affairs published an account of the negotiations which gives many useful insights into the positions of the various countries and particularly, of course, of the group which later became the EFTA. For example: 'The main objection to the Carli plan, at least in its original form, is that it implies an actual, if not an explicit, restriction on the freedom of member countries to determine autonomously their tariffs in relation to third countries, a freedom which is in fact the basic feature of a free trade area. This objection stems from the fact that the Carli plan encourages member countries to place their tariffs within the band in order that they may enjoy tariff exemption within the area—i.e. that the plan contains an incentive to level out or harmonize tariffs. In that regard the further objection is made that the tendency of harmonization would be an increase of tariff levels in the low-tariff countries.' (*Negotiations for a European Free Trade Area 1956–1958*. Documents published by the Royal Ministry for Foreign Affairs, Stockholm, 1959, p. 29.) It should be noted that the Swedes later proposed a modified Carli scheme; in contrast to the British, they were less opposed to the principle of harmonization than to the pressure to harmonize at a level appreciably above that of their existing tariffs. Op. cit., pp. 29–31.

experts that this was unwise, and the Government must later have regretted that it had not accepted the Carli formula, in principle, and then tried to improve it. Although any statement about what might have been is hazardous, it seems probable that had the British been willing in the spring to accept the Carli formula as the main solution to the origin problem they might well have achieved an agreement similar to the one they would have been ready to accept by the autumn.

The Carli plan, in a slightly different form, was to reappear again in the report the Six presented to the Maudling Committee in October. But for the time being it was relegated to the experts for further examination. After one further brief meeting at the end of March the Maudling Committee itself went into recess while the Six discussed among themselves some much-heralded new French proposals. Reports of a French plan had been current for several weeks and further discussions in the Maudling Committee were obviously pointless until the French proposals had been agreed to, modified, or rejected by the Six as a group.

In the middle of February (1958) the French Economic Council (an influential advisory body) unanimously rejected the kind of free trade area then under discussion in the Maudling Committee and recommended that the Community negotiate arrangements with other countries, product by product and country by country. About the same time the French Government circulated to the rest of the Six a memorandum containing its ideas. Shortly thereafter fairly full accounts of the French memorandum appeared in the press. In this memorandum the French reverted to the idea of a *décalage* and proposed that the freeing of trade within the Community start three years before that in the wider group—which they renamed the Union for European Economic Co-operation. The idea of a longer transitional period for the free trade area also reappeared. Moreover, the French now advocated a sector by sector approach and proposed that a series of industrial agreements be negotiated between the Community and the other members of the OEEC. These agreements would be multilateral, not bilateral, in form, but the nature of the arrangements would vary from industrial sector to industrial sector.[17] The freeing of

[17] The 'sector approach' to trade liberalization had frequently been advocated by the French in various contexts, e.g. in the OEEC and in the Treaty of Rome negotiations. The Coal and Steel Community was, of course, an experiment in sector integration; the abortive Green Pool would have been another had it materialized.

trade in any sector would be tied to the harmonization of the conditions of competition in that sector. Thus trade might be freed in some sectors more rapidly than in others. In addition, for the first time in the negotiations, the French formally proposed that the continental countries share, to some extent, in the Commonwealth preferential system. The French accepted the British position that agriculture should be treated separately, but argued that some improvement in continental access to Commonwealth markets was needed to balance the fact that the continental countries were opening their markets to British industrial goods while the United Kingdom was not opening its markets to agricultural exports from Europe to the same extent. Apparently the French memorandum suggested that a certain quota of continental goods might, when sold in the Commonwealth, attract the British preference rate of duty rather than the m.f.n. rate; the goods to be given the preferential rate and the size of the quota would be matters for negotiation.[18]

There had been some cautious optimism earlier in the year that when the French had formulated their counter-proposals the shadow boxing in the Maudling Committee could give way to hard bargaining. But when the contents of the French memorandum became known, the prospects for any kind of agreement looked bleaker than ever. It would have been difficult to construct a plan that was more unpalatable to the other OEEC countries, and particularly to the British. The sector approach opened the way to the worst kind of protectionist log-rolling. It would have meant long and very complicated seventeen-country negotiations and it offered no guarantee that the end result would be a free trade area. The eventual series of arrangements would almost certainly have been in conflict with the GATT, as would the extension of Commonwealth preferences to the Six.

M. Maurice Faure travelled round the capitals of the Common Market countries in late February and early March explaining the French proposals. But the rest of the Six, like the other OEEC countries, felt that the proposals were a step backward and he made little headway. Even the Italians, who had heretofore been the closest to the French in outlook, felt the new French approach was far too negative, and it is significant that Signor Carli formally

---

[18] See *Financial Times*, 28 February 1958, and *The Economist*, 1 March 1958, p. 767. Also see Baron Snoy, op. cit., pp. 614–15, and *L'Année Politique* (1958), p. 309.

made his proposal in the Maudling Committee shortly after
M. Maurice Faure had held talks on the French proposals in
Rome.[19] Elsewhere in the Six, the reactions to the plan were even
sharper. The principal motivation behind the plan seemed to be
protectionism of the most blatant kind, rather than an attempt to
meet the technical difficulties and inadequacies of the free trade
area plan which all the Six agreed existed. Even in France itself
little effort was made by the press or by independent commentators
to defend the plan.[20]

As details of the plan became available in the United Kingdom
the press began to speculate on the consequences of a failure of
negotiations and there were frequent hints of counter-measures.
The 'division of Europe' theme was played very hard, officially as
well as unofficially, and some warnings were given about the
repercussions that a failure to agree might have on the whole
military-political-economic structure that had been built up in
Europe since the war, and some suggestions were put forward for
retaliation by the OEEC countries outside the Six.[21] The industrial
federations of the 'Other Six' were, in fact, already busy on plans
for a limited free trade area if the larger negotiations failed.[22]
Accurately, but rather unfortunately for relations between the two

---

[19] See *Financial Times*, 7 March 1958. The Italians apparently made some
impact on the French, for M. Maurice Faure was quick to endorse the Carli
plan when it was proposed during the Maudling Committee discussions.

[20] See *Le Monde*, 28 February 1958. The comment on the French plan by M.
Uri in his book, *La Crise de la zone de libre-échange* (p. 22), is also revealing:
'Il avait davantage pour objectif de passer sans difficulté un Comité inter-
ministériel français, en satisfaisant aux préoccupations particulières de chaque
ministre, que de constituer une base nouvelle pour la négociation à pour-
suivre.'

[21] See, for example, the leaders in the *Financial Times* of 3 and 20 March 1958.
On 28 March 1958 Mr. Maudling, in the course of a debate on the negotiations
in the House of Commons, pointed out that: 'People in Europe must not
assume that if there is a Common Market but no Free Trade Area, everything
else—E.P.U., O.E.E.C., and so on—will go on as before. It certainly will not.'
Hansard, House of Commons, 28 March 1958, col. 797.

[22] During the early spring of 1958, representatives of the industrial federations
and of the employers' organizations of the 'Other Six' (United Kingdom,
Sweden, Denmark, Norway, Switzerland, and Austria) met together a number
of times, and on 14 April 1958 they issued a detailed statement of the kind of
trade arrangement they felt should be established among the OEEC countries.
Although the principal motive behind these discussions and the purpose of
the joint statement was to strengthen the negotiating position of their governments *vis-à-vis* the Six (and perhaps to toughen their resistance to further concessions), they were also already considering the possibilities of some arrangement among the 'outer countries' if the negotiations among the larger group
failed.

countries, the British press concentrated on the French as the obstacle to agreement and the comment was frequently rather bitter. And, increasingly, British hopes were too ostentatiously pinned on the Germans bringing the French around.

A little comfort was drawn from the fact that the French had not formally circulated their proposals outside the Six and that they had made it clear that their memorandum was to be a basis for discussion with their Common Market partners. A committee of representatives from the Six under the chairmanship of the Belgian permanent delegate to the OEEC, M. Ockrent, was given the thankless task of trying to find a common position acceptable to all the Six which also stood a chance of being negotiable with the British and the other OEEC countries. But in April 1958 the French Government fell. For the next six weeks France hovered on the brink of civil war. Although a certain amount of technical work continued, no decision of any importance affecting France was possible, and negotiations among the Six, as well as within the OEEC, were suspended until after the assumption of power by General de Gaulle.

Developments outside the Maudling Committee

In January 1958, the Treaty of Rome entered into effect and later that month the Commission of the Community formally took office. In February, Prof. Hallstein began attending the meetings of the Maudling Committee in his position as president of the Commission although the role of the Commission in the negotiations was rather unclear. Had the negotiations been initiated after the entry into force of the Treaty of Rome, it seems probable that the Commission would have borne the main responsibility for negotiating with the other OEEC countries on behalf of the Community.[23] However, when the negotiations began the Treaty of Rome had not yet been signed and, inevitably, once the ministers and officials of the Six Governments had become deeply involved in the negotiations, there was little disposition to transfer

[23] This procedure would seem to be in accordance with Article 228 of the Treaty of Rome which reads: 'Where this Treaty provides for the conclusion of agreements between the Community and one or more States or an international organisation, such agreements shall be negotiated by the Commission. Subject to the powers conferred upon the Commission in this field, such agreements shall be concluded by the Council after the Assembly has been consulted in the cases provided for by this Treaty.' Article 238 of the treaty provides that the Community may conclude agreements creating an association with a third country, a union of states or an international organization.

responsibility. Behind the scenes M. Monnet argued forcefully, but without success, for a drastic change in procedure and for the transformation of the negotiation into one essentially between the Commission and the British.[24] He had a number of motives: to strengthen the position of the Commission; to change the nature of the problem from a French problem to a Community problem; to take out of the central negotiation the particular claims of the smaller countries (in his view these could be patched up later); and to reduce the number of participants in the negotiation to a manageable number.[25]

The Commission was never given the responsibility for the negotiations, but it soon began to formulate and to expound a 'Community' philosophy on the negotiations which helped to keep the Six together, and, in the final judgement, it must bear a large measure of the blame, or praise, for the failure to form a free trade area.

At the first session of the European Parliamentary Assembly, held at Strasbourg in March 1958, Prof. Hallstein spoke at considerable length on the external relations of the Community. It was clear from his remarks on the free trade area negotiations that the Commission had only begun to study the problem and had, as yet, no new substantive contribution to make, although it obviously shared the view of those in the Six who had serious doubts about the validity of the basic concept of a free trade area.[26] The most

---

[24] Later in the year M. Monnet's Action Committee formally resolved that it was urgent 'to arrange for the Commission to negotiate in the name of the Six for the association of Great Britain and the other European countries with the Common Market'. *Joint Declaration*, Action Committee for the United States of Europe, Paris, 16, 17 October 1958.

[25] The Maudling Committee discussions were, in fact, attended by far too many people. The seventeen delegations, many of them large, the United States and Canadian observers, and experts from the OEEC secretariat brought the number of people in the room to about 200.

[26] See European Economic Community, Commission, Statement by Dr. Walter Hallstein, President of the Commission, to the European Parliamentary Assembly, 20 March 1958, pp. 22–24. Dr. Hallstein questioned the validity of a free trade area both on the grounds that the lack of a common external tariff would lead to serious shifts in economic activity and on the grounds that 'in view of the intimate connection between all State measures in economic matters, the elimination of tariffs cannot lead to economically reasonable results or be maintained in the long run unless it is supplemented by a series of economico-political measures'. Dr. Hallstein also pointed out that the association of the other OEEC countries with the existing Common Market of the Six raised a number of problems and he emphasized that 'the six-country community can only accept measures which leave that community itself inviolate'.

interesting section of Prof. Hallstein's speech was that in which he flatly rejected the charge which was then being made with some fervour by the British, the Scandinavians, and the Swiss that unless the free trade area was formed the Six would have split Western Europe and would be 'discriminating' against the other members of the OEEC.

> We should state clearly that we reject this charge of discrimination and that therefore the argument about division which has been built up on it is invalid . . . it is indeed true that the consequence of setting up the Community is that transactions within the Community are treated differently from transactions between the Community or its Members and the outside world. There is therefore differentiation. But differentiation is not always discrimination. . . . Discrimination may be said to exist only when the same situation is handled differently without justification. This, however, is not the case. The situations are not the same.
>
> The European Economic Community represents one situation. That, we all know, does not mean only the abolition of customs barriers and of innumerable restrictions on trade between the six Member States; nor is it only a Customs union with a uniform external tariff. It is the harmonization, co-ordination, even unification, of major aspects of economic policy and profoundly modifies the economic policy of the six States. . . . Thus there can only be discrimination, in other words an unwarranted differentiation in the treatment of other European States, if the Six deny to other European States the treatment which they accord one another, that is, if they refuse admission to a State which is willing to pay the same price as the Six for the advantages of membership of the customs union. Obviously that has not happened. Quite the opposite: the Treaty embodies the principle of the open door.[27]

Professor Hallstein's remarks have been quoted at considerable length because argument between the Six and the rest of the Seventeen on what constituted discrimination assumed increasing importance as the year wore on. Both sides put forward some rather dubious arguments and much of the rancour that marked the discussions at the end of the year stemmed from differences of view on this point.

By the time the European Parliamentary Assembly met in June 1958, the Commission had been actively seeking to make its views felt in the negotiations and had addressed several memoranda on the subject to the member governments of the Community. M. Rey, the member of the Commission responsible for the

[27] Op. cit., pp. 11-13.

Community's external relations, outlined the Commission's views to the parliamentarians in considerable detail; his general approach to the problems was very similar to that contained in the report eventually submitted by the Six to the Maudling Committee —the so-called Ockrent Report.[28] M. Rey also sought the Assembly's endorsement for the idea of an interim agreement, a proposal the Commission had made to the Council of Ministers of the Community in March and which had been discussed by the Ministers of the Six but on which no decision had yet been taken. In the Commission's view there was no chance that negotiations on the free trade area (or the European Economic Association, as they preferred to call it) could be completed and the treaty ratified by the end of the year. They therefore proposed that when the first tariff cut among the Six was made on 1 January 1959 not only the Six but all the OEEC countries should cut their tariffs with respect to one another by the 10 per cent. required by the Treaty of Rome. This cut would be a provisional one, for eighteen months. During this time the definitive arrangement between the Community and the other OEEC countries should be worked out, and later tariff cuts could then be made in parallel. If the negotiations on the definitive arrangement foundered, all countries would regain their freedom of action, the Six continuing to reduce tariffs among themselves on the schedule laid down in the Treaty of Rome.[29]

The idea of a provisional arrangement found favour with the Assembly and for a time the Commission's proposal (and variations of it) were quite actively explored, although no formal proposal for a provisional agreement was made by the Six to the others until after the collapse of the negotiations. The British were, however, very cool to the idea for they felt that a provisional

[28] See below, p. 157. Unlike the British, who, at best, would have been ready to have the 'Carli formula' used in a few cases (but not as a general rule), the Commission, and later the Six, in the Ockrent Report, advocated adoption of the 'Carli formula' as the general rule, with a few exceptions to be agreed. The Commission also followed the French proposals and anticipated the Ockrent Report in indicating that the Commonwealth preference system could not be left inviolate.

[29] A tariff cut on an OEEC basis would have been contrary to the GATT, in the absence of a firm commitment to form a free trade area, or a customs union. Because of this, the Commission suggested that the Seventeen should express their willingness to cut their tariffs by 10 per cent. on a most-favoured-nation basis provided the other GATT countries would reciprocate. If the other countries refused, the Commission felt the GATT should be tolerant if the Seventeen then took action among themselves.

arrangement would tend to reduce the pressure to find agreement on the long-term arrangement.[30] Furthermore, in the form proposed by the Commission, there was no commitment that there would ever be a free trade area; and any attempt to stiffen the terms of the provisional arrangement to include a commitment on an eventual free trade area would not have been acceptable to the French, who refused to commit themselves to free trade at some date in the future until they knew what the other arrangements were to be. Moreover, the Commission's proposal left the problem of quotas untouched and it was the discrimination arising from the enlargement in quotas scheduled to take place on 1 January 1959, rather than from the 10 per cent. reduction in tariffs, that, at this time, was of the greatest concern to the other OEEC countries.[31]

In the early months of 1958, negotiations involving the French—on a Six- as well as a Seventeen-country basis—had been difficult and unproductive, since the French were preoccupied with formulating their own proposals; later, during the six weeks of government crisis, negotiations with the French became impossible. Almost inevitably, therefore, the British resorted to bilateral discussions with others in the Six. Just as inevitably, this procedure bred suspicion in France and gave rise to not wholly unjustified fears that the British were seeking to isolate the French. During April, the British Ambassador in Rome (Sir Ashley Clarke) was particularly active in trying to bring about a change in Italian opinion, and he was reported to be making a certain amount of headway.[32] Also during April, important three-day meetings were held in London between Mr. Macmillan and Dr. Adenauer, and between other British and German ministers, including Mr. Maudling, Dr. Erhard, and high officials on both sides concerned with the free trade area questions. The communiqué issued at the

---

[30] One of the Commission's motives was precisely to reduce this pressure and to enable the Community to get some of its basic policies worked out, e.g. the List G tariff rates and the main lines of its agricultural policy, before determining its relations with the other OEEC countries.

[31] At this time quotas were still a much more serious barrier to intra-European trade than tariffs. This was particularly true in the case of France, which had 'deliberalized' its trade in June 1957. For further discussion of the quota problem, see Chapter VI. The British felt that a tariff cut on an OEEC basis could not legitimately be reconciled with the provisions of the GATT; on the other hand they were loath to diminish their future bargaining power by generalizing the tariff cut and giving unrequited benefits to the other GATT members.

[32] See *Financial Times*, 23 and 24 April 1958.

conclusion of the talks reported that Mr. Macmillan and Chancellor Adenauer agreed upon 'the cardinal political and economic
importance in the interest of European unity of complementing
the European Economic Community of the six States by the
European Free Trade Area'. Both Dr. Adenauer and Professor
Erhard spoke optimistically to the British press about the chances
of success, and the impression was created that Dr. Adenauer was
now ready to use his good offices with the French to secure an
agreement.[33]

Presumably the promise of help received from the Germans at
this meeting encouraged the British to resist suggestions for interim
arrangements and contributed to the decision to continue pressing
hard for a definitive agreement, even though by the summer of
1958 the chances of a successful conclusion to the negotiation
appeared to be minuscule—at least to this outside observer.

General de Gaulle assumed power in France on 1 June, and
soon afterwards the ministers from the Six Governments renewed
their efforts to find agreement on the basis of a report which had
been prepared by the Ockrent Committee. At the end of the
month, Mr. Macmillan and Mr. Selwyn Lloyd visited Paris for
discussions with General de Gaulle. The free trade area came
high on the British list of problems, but it was clear that it was
not given a similar priority by the French leader. And, although
it was agreed that Mr. Maudling should discuss the matter further
with the French Foreign Minister, M. Couve de Murville, the
Paymaster-General returned from Paris empty-handed a few days
later. It would have been very surprising if the French had been
ready to compromise on the free trade area, or, indeed, if General
de Gaulle had yet given any appreciable amount of thought to the
question. Even had it not been for the fact that the Algerian
problem dominated all French political life, General de Gaulle
was by temperament far more interested in political questions than
in economic matters, which he tended to leave to the 'technicians'.
And the technicians were against the British plan. Moreover, it
was almost unthinkable that such an accomplished politician
would have taken the political risk of supporting the free trade
area in the face of solid, and vociferous, opposition from French
industry and agriculture, on the morning after a civil war had
been narrowly averted, and just before the holding of a referendum

[33] See *Financial Times*, 19 April 1958.

on a new constitution and of the elections that would follow the approval of the constitution.

During July, the rest of the Six applied considerable pressure on the French and urged them to come to some kind of a compromise on the free trade area. For, although there was a good deal of sympathy within the Six for the substantive aspects of the French position, there was less sympathy for the delays which now seemed a part of the French tactic; there was a strong feeling that the British and others were, at the least, entitled to a clear statement from the Six of what they would, and what they would not, accept. The Germans, in particular, seem to have taken a much stronger line during the summer of 1958 than they had done earlier. The Macmillan–Adenauer discussions presumably had some effect on German policy but it seems probable that two other factors also counted heavily. Dr. Erhard and the great bulk of German business and financial interests had always favoured the free trade area and their interest in it and pressure for it grew stronger as doubts increased about the ability of the French to implement the Treaty of Rome on schedule. Within the Six, the French market was the most attractive to the Germans: the Benelux countries already had comparatively low tariffs and the potential of the Italian market was generally underestimated. The United Kingdom and the Scandinavian markets appeared to offer rich prospects and these would become particularly attractive if, as seemed very probable in the summer of 1958, the French were going to have to make full use of the escape clauses provided in the Treaty of Rome when tariff cutting and the enlarging of quotas began on 1 January 1959. Finally, and probably of most importance, there was little reason to suppose that General de Gaulle would support the kind of economic and political unity in Europe to which Dr. Adenauer gave overriding importance. General de Gaulle had been an outspoken opponent of the EDC and a scornful critic of the Treaties of Rome. In the circumstances Dr. Adenauer could be expected to wonder whether attachment to the Treaty of Rome really played any significant part in the French Government's opposition to the free trade area.

The last phase

The rest of the Six apparently felt they had made some progress with the French during the ministerial discussion they held among themselves just before the Maudling Committee eventually met again at the end of July 1958. Encouraging rumours that General de Gaulle had now considered the free trade area proposal and that the French were at last really ready to negotiate circulated in Paris. However, although the atmosphere at the meeting appears to have been good, the Six were not yet in a position to make agreed proposals to the Maudling Committee on any issue save agriculture,[34] and once again the Maudling Committee made progress by agreeing to adopt a new procedure rather than by taking substantive decisions.

On the central issue of 'origin' the Maudling Committee in effect accepted the inevitable, and agreed that no single solution to the problems arising from the existence of differing external tariffs would fit all cases. Accordingly, the OEEC Steering Board for Trade was asked to propose the rules to be used for determining origin for each of the main sectors of trade. This was a considerable step in the direction of meeting the French position that what was required was not a few exceptions from the general rules to take care of intractable cases, but a sector by sector appraisal, with rules tailored to the needs of each sector. Moreover the Steering Board was also asked to examine, 'at the request of any interested country, any other specific questions (such as differences in export regimes, or problems of internal competition) which may, in particular sectors, create difficulties . . . and to make appropriate proposals'.[35] This agreement to examine any sector in which difficulties were anticipated, not simply sectors that would experience difficulties because of differences in external tariffs, was an even more important concession to the French. The wording adopted opened the way both to special arrangements for the pulp and paper industry (although the French difficulty here arose simply from the fact that the Scandinavian countries had a comparative advantage arising from natural resources) and also to special arrangements to satisfy French claims that the United Kingdom derived unfair advantages from the Commonwealth preference system. The Steering Board for Trade was also asked

[34] See Blue Book, pp. 199–204. On the disputed tariff question the Community paper proposed a 'standstill' on agricultural tariffs, the reduction of certain very high rates, and the granting of tariff quotas—within the area. During the first stage of the transitional period the rules for the abolition of customs duties and the parallel introduction of a 'concerted agricultural policy' would be drawn up.
[35] The resolution adopted by the Maudling Committee is reprinted in the Blue Book, p. 178.

to draw up a 'Code of Good Conduct' committing the member countries to avoid causing deflexions of trade within the area when making changes in their own tariffs. Such a code had been suggested by the British earlier in the year to meet some of the dangers the French saw in a system which permitted tariff autonomy and which lacked a common commercial policy.

The British were prepared to go this far to meet the French largely because they felt that the French were now, at last, ready to bargain. This judgement seems to have been based partly on statements made by M. Wormser, the principal French negotiator, and partly on impressions of the French position received from other members of the Six after the intra-Six discussions. Both the Germans and the Dutch apparently encouraged the British to persevere. The reliance placed on the German ability (and willingness) to bring the French round was one of the basic British miscalculations in the negotiation and stemmed from an overestimation of Dr. Erhard's power and an underestimation of the depth of Dr. Adenauer's conviction that the construction of unity in Europe rested, in the first instance, on the Franco-German *rapprochement* and his readiness, in consequence, to give an overriding priority to relations with France.

The willingness of the British to proceed on a sector basis—which they had earlier strongly resisted—was also a symptom of their desperation and of the fact that during the summer and autumn of 1958 they were ready to accept almost unworkably cumbersome arrangements in order to meet their self-imposed deadline of an agreement by 1 January 1959. At this time it seemed to many observers that the British were greatly overemphasizing the necessity for reaching an agreement by the end of the year and that it would have been better to adjourn the negotiations than to continue to bring pressure on the Six for an immediate agreement. The deadline of 1 January became a bone of contention, in itself. Both sides were concerned with the effect on trade but both sides also wanted to establish a principle. The Six, and particularly the French, wanted to make it clear that the Treaty of Rome created a new situation and to force the other OEEC countries to accept a 'difference' in treatment; the British, and others, wanted to keep the 'difference' from ever being created and to gain more solid recognition for the principle of nondiscrimination on an OEEC basis.

The OEEC committees set up to examine particular sectors were unable to make progress, for the French took the logical but time-consuming position that the Six should agree among themselves on the treatment to be given to particular sectors before information was made available by any of the Six to the OEEC committees. Sector studies were put in hand among the Six during September, but work in the OEEC was, once again, effectively stalled and the flush of optimism in which the July meetings had ended quickly faded.

During the summer and early autumn the Six were also still trying to reach agreement among themselves on the 'Ockrent Report'—their promised, and long-awaited, agreed plan. The Council of Ministers of the Six held an important meeting in Venice towards the end of September at which some of the thorniest points still at issue were finally agreed. In particular the rest of the Six reluctantly accepted the French view that all decisions in the free trade area should be taken unanimously (it was agreed that this decision might later be reviewed but it was, in any case, to be binding for the first stage of the transitional period). Inasmuch as the Six also agreed that they would act together within the free trade area institutions, most of them felt that the French insistence on unanimity was unnecessary and that they could have accepted a two-thirds majority rule without any appreciable risk since the Six, acting together, could have blocked any action they disliked.[36] As had happened so frequently during the Treaty of Rome negotiations, the Germans supported the French when the point of real decision came, although it was widely known before the meeting that they were in favour of majority voting. And it is significant that the first meeting between General de Gaulle and Dr. Adenauer had been held at Colombey-les-deux-Églises a few days before the Venice meeting, and had been a considerable success.

Finally, after a further meeting of the Council of Ministers in October, agreement was reached on the Ockrent Report, and it was given to the other OEEC countries on 17 October. It was still an incomplete document, since it did not cover all the points at issue in the negotiations. Moreover, in the course of a lengthy meeting of the Maudling Committee that was held a few days after the circulation

---

[36] The French insisted on unanimity presumably to plug the hole that might exist if it were agreed that certain actions, e.g. measures of safeguard, could be taken unless disallowed by a two-thirds majority.

of the Report the French representative went well beyond the common position as set forth in that document.

There were many signs of the strong disagreements that still existed among the Six in the Ockrent Report and it was not a coherent plan of association but a collection of the conditions which the Six felt any association arrangement must meet. Nevertheless the document is worth commenting on in some detail as it was the most comprehensive exposition of the 'Community' point of view made during the negotiations. The concessions made to the French point of view were more impressive than the concessions made by the French to the views of others—particularly as subsequent events cast doubts on the reality of some of the apparent French concessions. The Report revealed the same ambivalence that characterized the French (and to a considerable extent the Commission's) approach throughout the free trade area negotiations; that is, an uncertainty whether the interests of France (or, *pari passu*, of the Community) would be better served by making the free trade area as like or as unlike the Community as possible. The tendency in the Ockrent Report was to advocate substantive arrangements that were as similar as possible, but to argue for very dissimilar institutional and procedural arrangements. This combination would clearly put the Six in the strongest position *vis-à-vis* the other countries and would, at one and the same time, satisfy the fears of both the protectionists and the 'Europeans'.

The Report from the Six[37] began by indicating that it should not be considered an exhaustive statement of the Community's position and that the Six reserved the right to supplement it later. This general reserve was followed by a point of considerable importance, namely that the common positions set out in the memorandum were dependent on the 'success of the current negotiations, particularly those referred to in this memorandum'. The negotiations still going on within the Six (and yet to begin in the OEEC) on the precise trade arrangements to be made for each sector were the heart of the whole matter; this apparently innocent caveat was therefore a reservation of controlling importance, and the presence of this statement may well account for the fact that the French were ready to accept the Report.

[37] *The Memorandum from the European Economic Community* (called variously the Ockrent Report or Ockrent Memorandum) is contained in the Blue Book, pp. 96–104.

The Report then solemnly reaffirmed the Community's determination 'both for economic and political reasons, to arrive at an
agreement which will make it possible to associate with the Community on a multilateral basis the other Member States of the
OEEC'. Again a little reading between the lines is required, for this
solemn reaffirmation loses much of its meaning in the light of the
clear and well-recognized differences of view that existed as to the
nature of the 'multilateral arrangements' to be sought. Furthermore, the immediately following sentence foreshadowed the view
that was to become the explicit position of the Commission the
following spring, that is, that continued and somewhat intensified
co-operation with the rest of Europe through the GATT and the
OEEC might be sufficient.[38] The Report then stated that the
Association Agreement with the other OEEC countries must not
in any way prejudice either the content *or the implementation* of the
Treaty of Rome (my italics). Given the statements made repeatedly by the French, and heard increasingly from members of
the Commission, that a free trade area would inevitably hinder the
development of the Community, these words were also not very
comforting to those who still hoped for a free trade area. Furthermore, the Six took the position that not only should the sanctity
and precedence of the Treaty of Rome be written into the new
agreement but that the other members of the OEEC should
explicitly recognize the validity of the Treaty of Rome 'from the
point of view of the principles of international trade' and should
accept the fact that the differences in treatment inherent in the
functioning of the Community did not constitute 'discrimination'.
Since the Six, and to an increasing extent the Maudling Committee, were now discussing an arrangement that was very
different from the original free trade area plan, the Community
also proposed that the arrangement under discussion be renamed
the 'European Economic Association'.

As indicated above, the Report in effect left to the groups
already engaged in 'sector studies' the crucial question of the
solutions to be agreed to the problems arising from tariff disparities and from 'other problems of competition'. Nevertheless it
confirmed what had been apparent for some months, that the Six
would advocate an extensive use of the Carli formula and of a
particular version of the Carli formula which, if adopted, would
act as a strong inducement to the harmonization of external

[38] See Chapter VI.

tariffs at approximately the level of the common external tariff agreed for the Community.[39]

Three points are worth noting in the section of the Report that dealt with the co-ordination of trade policies. First, the general position of the Six on this question is worth quoting because it was on this crucial point that the French representatives took a more extreme position during discussions in the Maudling Committee:

The Community considers that although a common trade policy should not be regarded as one of the objectives of the Association, it is nonetheless essential that Member States of the Community should proceed to co-ordinate their trade policies in regard to third countries. The Community attaches the same importance to solving this problem as it attaches to solving problems due to disparities between external tariffs.

Second, the Community advocated that the institutions examine members' trade policies and be informed of proposed changes. In the event of a country considering that the import system applied by another resulted in distortion of competition, the institutions might make recommendations and the member state affected might have recourse to an escape clause. This procedure was roughly that already discussed in the Maudling Committee, although the Community clearly intended that the institutions should play a more minor role than the British now envisaged. However, the importance of this passage lies not so much in what it said as that it was said at all, for the need for a procedure rests on the assumption that there would not only be different external tariffs initially but that the member countries would retain freedom to alter them, a point the French representative later contested.

Third, the Report included a somewhat curious paragraph permitting the other member countries to be released (after consultation) from the obligations of the agreement if one of the members concluded an agreement with one or more third countries which 'by the scope of its clauses, the broadness of its aims and its

---

[39] The kind of Carli formula advocated by the Community was described in a special annex. In brief, it was suggested that the norm should be the common external tariff of the Community and that the limits either side of the norm should be settled by negotiation, sector by sector. Unless specifically excepted, compensating charges would be levied, automatically and compulsorily, on products whose tariffs fell outside these limits. If the tariff of the product in question fell within the band but the product was made from a raw material or a semi-manufacture whose tariff fell outside the band, the product might also be liable to compensating charges, although the details of how this latter arrangement might work were not spelled out. See Blue Book, pp. 103-4.

duration, would impede the attainment of the objectives of the Association'. Presumably the Community had in mind the still-born British proposal to the Canadians for a free trade area. The fact that this problem was even mentioned revealed a rather surprising lack of knowledge on the part of the Six about the state of affairs within the Commonwealth. It also reflected their fears that the British wanted the free trade area not, primarily, as a way 'into Europe' for themselves so much as a way of starting the process of breaking down trade barriers, which, indeed, was one of the objectives of British ministers.[40] ·

The Community also recorded its view that the United Kingdom gained certain advantages from its position in the sterling area and the Commonwealth, and the Six specifically reserved the right to raise problems arising from the existence of the imperial pre-ference system in the coming discussions on the arrangements to be made for each sector. In addition the Six, in effect, adopted the French view on the need for harmonization of social conditions and the Report stated that the Treaty of Rome provisions on equal pay for men and women, overtime pay, and paid holidays, as well as the more general provisions on harmonization of legisla-tion, should be simply taken over into the Treaty of Association. As noted above, the Six also accepted the French view that the institutional arrangements in the Association should be analogous to those already existing in the OEEC, the Council, at the outset, acting only by unanimity.

In the course of agreeing on the Ockrent Memorandum the French had made two concessions of some apparent importance to their partners: first they had agreed that the Association should come into force on 1 January 1959, that is at the time the Com-munity was to take the first steps in dismantling tariffs and quotas. They also agreed that the Treaty of Association should contain a fixed limit to the length of the transitional period, which, in principle, should correspond to that of the EEC, and, in any case, should not exceed it by more than three years. Although the same starting-point and a fixed terminal date for the transitional period had heretofore been points on which the French had been un-willing to agree, the concessions now made looked rather more

---

[40] The complications arising from the fact that the British had several objectives rather than one clear, overriding, objective is commented on below, p. 170. The Commission later had similar fears about the 'mondialization' of the Community as a result of British membership.

substantial than they were, for there had, as yet, been no agreement on how much trade would, in fact, be freed. That was to be decided sector by sector. Furthermore, the fact that the Association was to come into force on 1 January 1959 did not necessarily mean that trade liberalization measures comparable to those in the Treaty of Rome would begin on that date.

All in all, the Ockrent Report, although it was the product of six months' argument and much hard bargaining among the Six, was a disappointing document to those who still hoped for a seventeen-country agreement. And during the discussion of the Report in the Maudling Committee the few loop-holes for compromise that the Report had left open were effectively plugged by M. Wormser, the French spokesman. Although, as indicated above, the Memorandum from the Six had appeared to recognize that members of the free trade area would retain their right to make autonomous tariff changes and that there would not be a common commercial policy in the free trade area as there was to be in the EEC, the French representative at the Maudling Committee challenged both points.[41] He accepted the fact that at the time the free trade area was established, tariffs might be different as among the member countries, but he pointed out that these differences, to the extent they were important, would have been compensated for in the basic arrangements agreed for the Association. Unilateral freedom to modify tariffs at some later time would not only raise new possibilities of trade deflexion but, and of more importance, it would upset the balance of advantage built into the arrangement. M. Wormser made it unmistakably clear that in French eyes the Six, in the Common Market, were granting each other reciprocal and permanent tariff advantages and that what the OEEC should be trying to construct was an arrangement for exchanging permanent mutual tariff advantages among Seventeen countries. Two elements lay at the heart of the French position: first, that member countries of the Association should enjoy a certain level of protection against third countries and second, that

---

[41] This was not the first time that French representatives had questioned the principle of tariff autonomy. As described above (pp. 136–7), M. Maurice Faure had indicated that he saw difficulties in the principle very early on. And, just before the meeting of the Maudling Committee discussed above, the French representative at the OEEC Steering Board for Trade had argued for a 'standstill' on external tariffs, subsequent changes to be made only with the approval of a majority of the member states. See the Swedish report on the free trade area negotiations, op. cit., p. 35.

the preferred position in each other's market should not be altered except by agreement. Both were points the British Government would not accept.

The British were prepared to recognize that once a free trade area was created a country had an obligation to consider the impact on the other members of any changes it proposed to make in its tariffs or in other aspects of its trade policy. They, and those other members of the OEEC who supported their general approach, were ready to agree to a code of good conduct that would specify in some detail the kind of matters that must be discussed and the kind of action a country might take if another member violated this code. They were ready enough to agree that problems of trade deflexion would have to be dealt with and that policies would have to be 'co-ordinated', but they would not agree that free trade between the Six and the other OEEC countries required the adoption of a common commercial policy or the abandonment of the right to make unilateral changes in their own tariff. Mr. Maudling, in his capacity as British representative, took particularly sharp exception to the French view that members of the Association should have the right to a particular level of preference against third countries. Mr. Maudling made it plain that in the British view the Seventeen were exchanging free access to each other's markets, not establishing preferred positions within each other's markets.[42]

The Ockrent Report had left just enough room for a compromise between the Six and the rest: it had proposed that tariff changes be notified to the institutions of the Association but had not gone so far as to suggest that prior approval would be required. The French interpretation left no room, for it in effect asked the British to accept an arrangement that was tantamount to a customs union.[43] And the British were at this time very far from being ready to cross that bridge. It is not altogether clear whether the French Government deliberately pushed its demand to a point which it knew to be beyond the British reach or whether it thought

---

[42] Mr. Maudling also made it clear that he thought the Association's rules on quotas must not operate to put a brake on the dismantling of quantitative restrictions in accordance with the prior commitments in the GATT and the IMF, that is, that quotas should not be used to perpetuate a preferred position when the balance of payments position permitted their removal.

[43] M. Wormser had also pointed out that under his concept the Seventeen would participate in future GATT tariff negotiations 'with a single point of view discussed between them beforehand'.

it possible that the British might in effect accept the French view, but subsequent French actions strongly suggest the first conclusion. In any case, the fact that the French, after insisting on the need for prior agreement among the Six, now felt free to go beyond that agreement was seen by the British negotiators as evidence that the French Government had decided to try to block an agreement.

The difference of view on institutional questions was also given an airing at this session of the Maudling Committee. An institutional pattern similar to that which had existed in the OEEC was generally acceptable but there was no agreement on voting procedures or on how escape clauses were to be invoked. The Six stuck to the positions they had taken in the Ockrent Report: that all voting should be by unanimity and that escape clauses could be invoked unilaterally without the prior approval of the organization. The British, who had changed their position markedly during the course of the negotiations, submitted a new paper in which they came out strongly for voting by a qualified majority on most kinds of escape clause action and on complaints.[44] Except for a few specifically defined cases, they proposed that there should be no unilateral right to invoke an escape clause; the general rule would be that a country would require prior positive authorization granted by a qualified majority of the Council. On the assumption that all the seventeen members of the OEEC became members of the Association, the United Kingdom proposed that the qualifying majority should be twelve. They pointed out that the Six, acting together, could thus veto any decision, although they could not impose a decision.[45]

On these controversial aspects of the institutional question and on the questions relating to tariffs and trade policy discussed above, the Maudling Committee could make no progress. And the general atmosphere of the meeting had not been helped by the fact that although the Committee was supposed to be meeting at ministerial level, the French treated it as another technical session and were represented by an official rather than a minister.[46] It was now clear to everyone that only political decisions at the highest

---

[44] The British document is contained in the Blue Book, pp. 236-7.

[45] As the British pointed out, it would, therefore, be very important to make absolutely clear in each case where majority voting was to be permitted, whether the vote would be on a positive or a negative resolution.

[46] Too much should not be made of this point since the official, M. Wormser, had as much power as most ministers in the de Gaulle Government.

level could save the negotiations, but once again a procedural device was found to keep the negotiations limping along. It was agreed that from 19 November a 'second Maudling Committee' would sit in permanent session to receive the sector reports on which the Six were working. This second Maudling Committee would be empowered to take decisions binding on governments, so that if the reports from the Six offered room for agreement some real progress by the end of the year was still barely possible. The decision to establish this second Maudling Committee was a concession to the British; Mr. Maudling had first urged that his main committee continue in session to try to thrash out, then and there, the main unsolved problems.[47] The explanation of the unwillingness of the Six (led by France) either to accede to this suggestion, on the one hand, or to call off the negotiations, on the other, appears to have been that the French Government had not yet reached a final decision on its own position. The British had been pushed so far that an agreement on the lines of the Ockrent Report, liberally interpreted, might well have been possible: a compromise on the lines of the Ockrent Report, stiffened by the French remarks in the Maudling Committee, clearly was not possible.

The end of the negotiations was not far off. Early in November, M. Couve de Murville, the French Foreign Minister, visited London for a day's discussion with British ministers. No communiqué was issued but from the press reports it seems clear that the British and French found themselves once more in irreconcilable positions: the French wanted more harmonization of tariffs and of commercial policies than the British were prepared to accept and an institutional system which would have meant not only a dominant position for the Community but the possibility of considerable discrimination in quota treatment arising from the implementation of the escape clause procedures.[48]

In mid-November the main Maudling Committee met to continue its discussion of the Ockrent Report. As the fruitless but apparently amicable two-day meeting was concluding, the French Minister of Information, then M. Soustelle, announced to the press that 'it was not possible to form a free trade area as had been wished by the British, that is to say by having free trade between the six countries of the Common Market and the eleven other

[47] See *Manchester Guardian*, 30 October 1958.
[48] See *Manchester Guardian*, 7 November 1958, and *Financial Times*, same date.

countries of the OEEC, without a common external tariff and without harmonization in the economic and social spheres'.[49] No notice was given to the other members of the OEEC before this statement was made. Nor, apparently, were the other members of the EEC consulted on the announcement, although it was, in effect, a partial repudiation of their agreed memorandum.

Although the announcement was abrupt and undiplomatic, it seems unlikely that the French expected this statement to be interpreted as the bombshell it was taken to be across the Channel. The French press had been full of reports that the French Council of Ministers was about to take a position on the free trade area and the speculation about the probable outcome of their consideration gave no grounds for any British optimism.[50] The Patronat had recently launched a new all-out attack on the plan. The comments M. Wormser, the French delegate, had made at the Maudling Committee were clear enough signs of a hardening of position. And it seems probable that the Soustelle statement simply confirmed in rather more brutal terms what the British Government had already been led to expect by M. Couve de Murville. The announcement received comparatively little notice in the French press and the French were at some pains to point out that they were not slamming the door but were, on the contrary, actively searching for another solution. The British press, however, tended to dramatize the statement.[51] Mr. Maudling, expressing surprise as well as dismay, postponed the meeting of his second committee pending clarification of the confused situation. It seems probable that Mr. Maudling hoped that the rest of the Six, if confronted with the stark prospect of failure, would bring some

[49] The text of the statement made by M. Soustelle after the meeting of the French Council of Ministers was as follows: 'Il est apparu à la France qu'il n'était pas possible de créer la zone de libre-échange, comme l'avaient souhaité les Britanniques, c'est-à-dire par l'établissement du libre-échange entre les six pays du Marché commun et les onze autres pays de l'O.E.C.E., et cela faute d'un tarif douanier unique à la lisière des dix-sept pays et faute d'harmonisation dans les domaines économique et social.

'Cela ne signifie pas qu'il n'y ait pas une solution donnant satisfaction aux six pays du Marché commun et aux autres pays de l'Europe occidentale dans leurs rapports mutuels sur le plan économique. Le gouvernement français, pour sa part, s'emploie activement à en chercher une. Aussi ne faut-il pas interpréter la position actuelle comme une porte fermée. Si la solution que propose la Grande-Bretagne ne paraît pas acceptable telle quelle, l'étude du problème doit être poursuivie.' *L'Année Politique*, 1958, p. 482.

[50] See, for example, the articles by Pierre Drouin in *Le Monde*, 23 October 1958 and 6 November 1958.

[51] See Chapter VI.

last-minute pressure to bear on the French. However, although neither the French nor the British may have foreseen the result of their actions, the negotiations for a free trade area were over.

The reasons for the failure

The central issue throughout the negotiations was the complex of problems that arose from the fact that the British (and others) were proposing not a customs union but a free trade area. Discussion of a complex of closely interrelated questions stemming from this fact—the 'scope' of the area (i.e. the goods to be entitled to 'area' treatment), the nature of the origin controls, the degree of co-ordination of commercial policy, and, in particular, the extent of tariff autonomy—consumed the lion's share of the time, energy, and ingenuity of the negotiators from the time of the first OEEC studies in the autumn of 1956 until the negotiations finally broke down two years later. These problems could not be solved because, as M. Faure had pointed out, key groups in France, and to some extent in the rest of the Six countries, were fundamentally opposed to linking the Common Market with another arrangement that gave comparable trade benefits but had less far-reaching commitments to common tariffs, common policies, and common action. The objections to so doing were of two kinds. At one level they were economic and sometimes frankly 'protectionist' in spirit; at another level they were political and 'European'. During the course of the negotiations confusion and misunderstandings arose from the interplay of these two, quite different, kinds of opposition to the concept of surrounding the Common Market of the Six with a free trade area of the Eleven. Thus the first type of opposition to the fact of the difference of tariffs and to the absence of commitments to harmonize policies in the free trade area arose from the feeling that the low tariff countries in the free trade area and the British, by virtue of their preferential arrangements with the Commonwealth,[52] would have certain advantages over the countries of the Common Market: to the extent that origin controls were not fool-proof there might be trade diversion and even where this was not the case the fact of lower tariffs would carry with it a cost advantage and the risk of a deflexion of economic activity.

[52] Although the British most-favoured-nation tariff was comparable to that of the 'high tariff' countries, the fact that goods from the Commonwealth (mostly foodstuffs and raw materials) entered duty free or at low preferential rates gave the United Kingdom many of the competitive advantages of the low tariff countries. i.e. Denmark, Sweden, and Switzerland.

The absence of commitments to level up social charges and of commitments to adopt common agricultural policies would also yield cost advantages and thus add to the competitive advantage of those countries that were in the free trade area, but not the Common Market.

The other type of opposition—the 'European' and political—became rather more explicit during the unsuccessful attempts at 'bridge-building' that followed the collapse of the free trade area negotiations, but it was a fundamental conceptual difficulty during the later stages of the negotiations on a free trade area. The 'European' case against the free trade area was that, regardless of intent, the existence of the free trade area would tend to undermine the tighter construction of the Six. With considerable reason the 'Europeans' feared that if the free trade area offered comparable commercial advantages with fewer obligations, those who supported the Common Market principally to gain the benefits of a larger market (and there were many, particularly in Germany, who did so) would lose interest in giving content to those provisions of the treaty which were designed not simply to bring about a customs union but to go further and to open the way to a far-reaching economic union. The 'European' opposition to the free trade area was to some extent born of the recognition of their own weakness. Had the 'Europeans' been more confident of strong and continuing support in France and Germany, there would have been fewer fears that the Community would fail to develop or would 'dissolve' if it were part of a wider grouping. However, there would still have been some concern on this score, for in addition to increasing the temptation to leave parts of the Treaty of Rome unimplemented, there were a number of technical reasons why the free trade area might well have become the dominant organization if the two had been linked in the way that the British proposed. For example, if one traces through the possible procedures that might be followed in invoking escape clauses it is clear that either the Six had to be bound by decisions taken in the wider group, or the wider group had, in fact, to accept discrimination within the area—a principle that is clearly inconsistent with the basic concept of a free trade area as the British, rightly and endlessly, pointed out.[53]

[53] In this context it is worth remembering that in the Treaty of Rome one of the few direct powers given to the European Commission was the power to grant or withhold the right of resort to escape clauses.

In the course of the negotiations the British made substantial concessions to counter the charge that they stood to gain 'unfair' advantages and to meet the fears of those who opposed the free trade area on commercial and economic grounds. But there were only two ways in which the free trade area could be made acceptable to the 'Europeans'. Either it could be transformed into an arrangement as far-reaching as the Treaty of Rome, with the same promise of eventual economic union so that the prospect of the wider group superseding the narrower group became irrelevant, or it could be so 'different' that there would be no temptation to opt for it in preference to the Treaty of Rome and no danger of an automatic undercutting of the tighter, more far-reaching arrangement. The only kind of 'difference' that could make it safely unattractive was a substantial difference in the amount of trade to be freed. As indicated above, M. Faure had posed these alternatives in October 1957. During the course of the Maudling Committee negotiations, the French tactics sometimes appeared to be based on one of these approaches to this problem, sometimes on the other. But neither approach was acceptable to the British, who, on the one hand, were determined to avoid any significant difference in commercial treatment and, on the other hand, were unwilling, at this stage, even to contemplate an arrangement that involved accepting any of three crucial characteristics of the Treaty of Rome: a common external tariff, a common commercial policy, or a common agricultural policy.

Throughout the free trade area negotiations the British laboured under the handicap of having misjudged the strength of the movement towards greater unity among the Six in the autumn of 1955 and the depth of the suspicion aroused by their brief but ill-advised hostility towards the Common Market during the winter of 1955–6. They continued to underestimate the cohesiveness of the Six and to underrate the extent to which the Treaty of Rome created a new situation which even the least enthusiastic among the Six accepted. Mr. Maudling, himself, was clearly out of sympathy with the objective—and the methods—of the 'Europeans', and this undoubtedly heightened 'European' suspicions of British motives. So, too, did the rather disdainful British attitude towards the European Commission.

British tactics throughout the negotiations were easy to fault: in particular at times they seemed designed to drive into each other's arms the 'Europeans' and the 'protectionists'—two groups who should never have been allowed to make common cause. The British also badly and repeatedly overestimated their own bargaining power. Had they initially put forward the kind of scheme they were ready to accept by the summer of 1958 the negotiations would almost certainly have succeeded. If, in the spring of 1958, they had been prepared to accept the 'Carli formula' as the general solution to the origin problem, there might still have been an agreement. And had the British at any time been prepared to accept a customs union it seems clear enough that they would have had little difficulty, at this period, in negotiating the kind of sweeping exceptions for agriculture and the Commonwealth that, later, it became impossible for them to do. A valuable year at the start of the negotiations was lost arguing about an unrealistically simple plan, and by the time the British were ready to make concessions both the growing cohesion of the Six and the political situation in France had created a new situation. Given all the difficulties that beset the negotiations, it is less surprising that they failed than that they came so close to succeeding. Although in retrospect the failure has seemed to many people to have been inevitable, it was touch and go, even at the end, whether the Six would, in fact, hold together and back up the French.

During the whole of the second year of the negotiations, there was an air of unreality about the proceedings. This arose in part from the French reluctance (and at times obvious inability) to come to grips with the problem and really to begin to bargain, in part from the British tactics of turning a blind eye to certain fundamental differences and of exaggerating the importance of self-imposed deadlines. But mostly it arose from the fact that there was never any clear understanding or real agreement among the negotiating governments about underlying objectives. Moreover, the confusion was compounded by the tendency—on the part of both the British and the Six—to find ways of skirting fundamental issues and to avoid looking under the stones.

The Six harboured such a wide diversity of views—ranging from those of Dr. Erhard, who would have been happy to accept the plan outlined in the British White Paper, to those who would have been satisfied only by a replica of the Treaty of Rome— that a distillation of a common view was extremely difficult. Until the spring of 1958, when the Commission began to play a co-ordinating role behind the scenes, there was little real attempt on the part of the Six to speak with one voice. Although they were not acting completely independently, they were not, as in the later negotiations on British accession, acting as one. And the fact that they could act neither as six nor as one added to the difficulties of the negotiations. So too did the fact that the Six had not really thought through the problems of linking the Common Market with a wider group before the Six Governments had committed themselves, repeatedly, to the formation of a free trade area. As the negotiations proceeded the very real problems inherent in an association between the Common Market and a looser, broader arrangement became clearer, particularly to the Commission and to the French, but governments were by then so committed to the negotiations that it was difficult to see a respectable way out. The result was repeated delays and a tendency on the part of the French to bring up new difficulties as soon as the British overcame any particular objection, and these tactics in turn gave rise to real doubts about whether the French were negotiating in good faith.

The lack of clarity was not all on the side of the Six. The 'lowest common denominator' of what the British sought was an arrangement that would keep British exports from being put at a disadvantage in the markets of Western Europe without at the same time significantly affecting existing Commonwealth trade arrangements. But, in addition, some people in the British Government were seeking a way of preserving and strengthening the co-operation that had developed in the OEEC; others were seeking a way to go further and to share in the more radical process of economic integration that the Six had begun among themselves; others were primarily looking for a way to make a frontal attack on trade barriers and not least on the tariffs that were protecting inefficiency in the United Kingdom. These were all laudable objectives and, up to a point, the original free trade area plan was a step towards all of them. But the contradictions latent in these various objectives became clearer and harder to ignore as the negotiations proceeded. And, at the end, the British were being asked by M. Wormser whether they were more interested in creating unity in Europe or in encouraging the freeing of trade on a world-wide basis. The French saw a conflict between these goals; the British argued that a conflict was unnecessary. In a sense, both of them were right.

During the negotiations the words 'inward-looking' and 'outward-looking' were much used, and misused, and they acquired strong pejorative overtones. The British were clearly right in calling the French position 'inward-looking' but they were wrong in equating 'inwardness' with 'protectionism'. Protectionism played a large part in the French position at this time but what was called 'inward-looking' also had a more positive aspect. The common tariff, the common commercial policy, and the common agricultural policy may well be more restrictive of trade between the Six and third countries than the arrangements proposed for the free trade area, but they are all essential elements of the new entity the Six are seeking to construct. The principle that those who belong to the Community are entitled to treatment that is different from the treatment given to third countries, in short the concept of 'Community preference', can, in one sense, be called 'inward-looking' but it need not be protectionist.[54] A distinction should be made between the *right* of members of the Community to treat each other *differently* from third countries and an *obligation* to give each other *better* treatment than they give third countries. The first is a valid principle; the second is not a principle at all but simply a matter of choice. But both the 'Europeans' and the French 'protectionists', for different reasons, attached importance not only to having the right to a difference recognized but also to maintaining a significant difference. And much confusion of principle with expediency resulted.

Political developments outside the scope of the free trade area negotiations also clearly complicated the search for an agreement. It was a time of acute political crisis and near civil war in France. Moreover, during this period there were important British–French differences of view on military-political matters, particularly after the de Gaulle Government came to power. Until the record becomes available it is difficult to know how much weight to attach to these differences, but British coolness to General de Gaulle's plans for a three-power directorate of the NATO and to his desire to make France the fourth atomic power doubtless had some effect on his willingness to make concessions to them on the free trade area. As he made clear in his memoirs and underlined by his later veto on British membership of the EEC, the United Kingdom has no real place in General de Gaulle's concept of Europe. Nevertheless it seems probable that at the time of the free trade area negotiations the possible long-term political implications of the formation of a free trade area were of much less importance—if indeed they were of any

---

[54] Much confusion of thought on this question also characterized the negotiations on British accession. See Chapter XIV.

importance—in General de Gaulle's attitude towards the plan than the fact that the free trade area was very unpopular in France and he needed domestic support in the forthcoming elections and in the referendum on the constitution.

Whatever the weight given to the political crisis in France and to General de Gaulle's aspirations for France, it is highly doubtful that the French Government would have held out in the end had they had to do so alone. General de Gaulle's position in France and France's position in the world were far weaker in the autumn of 1958 than they were in January 1963. The decisive factor in determining the outcome of the negotiations was that the Six, despite their deep differences of view, first compromised with one another and then stuck together. The free trade area was defeated by loyalty to the Treaty of Rome. But it was a very narrow defeat.

VI

THE AFTERMATH OF THE BREAK-
DOWN OF THE FREE TRADE AREA
NEGOTIATIONS

The argument over discrimination

Towards the end of the free trade area negotiations there was considerable speculation in the British press about the forms of retaliation that might be in order on 1 January 1959 if no agreement had been reached by then and if the Six began 'discriminating'[1] by implementing the tariff and quota provisions of the Treaty of Rome.

During the autumn, representatives of the industrial federations from the 'Other Six'[2] were already more or less openly discussing the possibility of establishing a limited free trade area if the

---

[1] Discrimination was a word that was much used, and misused, during the latter part of the free trade area negotiations and particularly just after the collapse of the negotiations. A problem arises because some discrimination is legal (i.e. permitted) and some discrimination is illegal. Because of the pejorative overtones the word has acquired, it would be desirable if it were only used to describe cases of illegal discrimination. Unfortunately only a very few people stick to this rule and government statements as well as press comments all too often use the word discrimination to mean any difference in treatment whether legal or illegal and whether in the use of quotas or of tariffs. Since the Six were in the process of forming a customs union they were, under the rules of the GATT, legally 'discriminating' against other countries when they cut their tariffs with respect to one another but did not generalize these cuts to any or all of the other members of the GATT. It would therefore have been clearer if, in the context of the European trade dispute, the word discrimination had never been used with respect to tariffs. As far as quotas were concerned the situation was rather different, since OEEC rules as well as GATT rules applied and, as further described in the footnotes on pp. 178–9, there was a real prospect of illegal discrimination on the part of the Six in the use of quotas. I have tried to put 'discrimination' (in quotation marks) when the word is being used simply to describe a difference in treatment and to use it without quotation marks only when I am referring to illegal discrimination. But I obviously cannot follow my own rule when I am directly quoting others who have used the word simply to mean a difference in treatment.

[2] The United Kingdom, Austria, Denmark, Norway, Sweden, and Switzerland.

Maudling Committee negotiations failed. The possibility of a trade war in Western Europe was frequently discussed in the press, although official statements tended to discount this possibility. Official British statements were carefully worded, but the charge of 'dividing Europe' was repeatedly levelled at the Six and warnings were given by more than one minister that unless the negotiations succeeded, economic, political, and even military co-operation in Western Europe might be strained to the breaking-point. Following the Soustelle announcement, rather blunter warnings, a good deal of angry recrimination, and some ill-considered overstatements found their way into print. On 18 November *The Times* ran a first leader called 'France the Wrecker', which on the other side of the Channel was assumed, incorrectly, to have been officially inspired. It did nothing to improve relations and somewhat overshadowed the far more restrained statement made by Mr. Maudling in the House of Commons.[3]

The reaction generally in the Six to the open breakdown in negotiations was less alarmist than in the United Kingdom (and in Scandinavia and Switzerland), although economic circles in Germany gave free rein to their indignation at the French.[4] However, everywhere in the Six there was the conviction that for political as much as for economic reasons some action must be taken on 1 January to soften the impact on the other OEEC countries of the steps the Six proposed to take among themselves. Soon after the cancellation of the meeting of the Maudling Committee the Benelux countries proposed to the rest of the Six a plan for extending to the rest of the OEEC countries most of the

[3] The last paragraph of *The Times* leader read as follows: 'It is not too much to say that France has wrecked the negotiations single-handed after wasting many precious months in sheer prevarication. Neither Britain nor any of the other non-Community countries has ever refused to consider concessions, and a willingness to negotiate remains. It is now up to the other members of the Community to see that the negotiations are put back on course.' For Mr. Maudling's statement see *Hansard*, House of Commons, 17 November 1958, cols. 845–50. Mr. Maudling was much more understanding of the French position, although he somewhat disingenuously implied that this was the first time that the French had called into question the basis on which the negotiations had been proceeding.

[4] German industrial circles and representatives of the Economic Ministry (Dr. Erhard and Herr Mueller-Armack) had never hidden the fact that they preferred the free trade area to the Common Market, and they did not seek to disguise their annoyance at the French position during the latter days of the negotiations. See, e.g., the article by their Bonn correspondent in *Le Monde*, 5 November 1958.

changes in tariffs and quotas that the Six would be making among themselves on 1 January. Prof. Hallstein, the President of the European Commission, toured the capitals of the Six to explore this and other possible types of provisional arrangements. His tour was, at least in part, a tactical move. In October, M. Monnet's Action Committee for a United States of Europe had adopted a resolution calling for the Commission to be given the task of negotiating with the British and the other OEEC countries, on behalf of the Six. The Commission also felt that it should play a more prominent role and the suspension of the Maudling Committee seemed to offer an opportunity to put the negotiations on a new basis when, or rather if, they were renewed. However, the Commission, as well as the Benelux initiative, was soon overshadowed by the announcement from Paris that, at General de Gaulle's suggestion, he and Dr. Adenauer were to meet on 26 November to discuss the situation.

The Bad Kreuznach meeting between General de Gaulle and Chancellor Adenauer was an important landmark in the development of Franco-German relations and in the history of the European Community. The fact that General de Gaulle was willing to leave France between two rounds of the French elections to meet the German Chancellor on German soil was in itself impressive evidence of the success of Dr. Adenauer's policy of putting political relations with France above the commercial interests of Germany. And the agreements and understandings reached at Bad Kreuznach provided an auspicious beginning to the opening of the Common Market. Here, as at other times, French firmness on Berlin was an important ingredient in the new relationship between France and Germany.

General de Gaulle was reported to have toasted Dr. Adenauer as 'a great man, a great European, and a great German'. Certainly he appears to have done much to still the remaining doubts the Chancellor may have had about his readiness to continue the policy of close Franco-German co-operation and to have reassured the Chancellor that France would not only honour its commitments under the Treaty of Rome but would not invoke the escape clauses on 1 January as had been widely feared. Dr. Erhard had accompanied the Chancellor to the meeting and there had been some press speculation that the Germans would bring strong pressure on the French to adopt a more helpful attitude towards the free trade area negotiations. In the end, however, the French view on the central question prevailed, although the task of convincing the Germans was not, apparently, an easy one. The two Heads of State agreed that the free trade area negotiations should not now be reopened within the OEEC, but the President of the Commission of the Community should be asked to elaborate a plan for a 'multilateral association' between the Community and the other OEEC countries. General de Gaulle's agreement to entrust this task of formulating a new proposal to Prof. Hallstein was presumably a concession to Dr. Adenauer, since the General's coolness to 'supra-national' bodies was well known. And press accounts suggest that it was only with difficulty that the French accepted the word 'multilateral' before association.[5] Although the decision that there should be no immediate reopening of negotiations was a very considerable victory for the French, it was in accord with the views of many of the strongest 'Europeans', and of the European Commission. It seems probable that Dr. Adenauer was influenced by arguments put forward by Prof. Hallstein as well as by the views of the French Government.[6]

Agreement was also reached at Bad Kreuznach on the measures that the Six might take to mitigate but not to eliminate the difference in tariff and quota treatment between the Six and the other OEEC countries that would arise on 1 January 1959. Although these were based on the Benelux proposals they did not go as far as those proposals in eliminating discrimination in the application of quotas.

The communiqué issued after the Bad Kreuznach meeting did not give any details of the agreement reached between the Germans and the French since the measures to be taken on 1 January and the procedure of asking Prof. Hallstein to make a proposal for the longer-term arrangement had yet to be discussed with and accepted by the rest of the Six. The Council of Ministers of the Community met in Brussels on 3 and 4 December and apparently reached agreement on the substantive points without much difficulty. At French insistence, it was agreed that the British and the other OEEC countries would simply be informed that these actions would be taken by the Six on 1 January, and it would be made clear that this was not a preliminary offer

---

[5] *Financial Times*, 28 November 1958.
[6] It seems clear from contemporary accounts that the Commission had a considerable hand in the formulation of the trade and procedural arrangements agreed to at Bad Kreuznach.

susceptible to improvement by bargaining but a firm decision on the action the Community countries would take.

The measures the Six agreed to take with respect to the other OEEC countries on 1 January were as follows:[7] The external tariffs of the Six countries would be reduced 10 per cent. on a most-favoured-nation basis except that, where a 10 per cent. reduction would bring a country's tariff below the level of the eventual Common Market tariff, rates with respect to countries outside the Community would only be reduced to the level of the common tariff. Agricultural tariffs would be reduced only if the products were controlled by some other means. In so far as quotas were concerned, the Six would put the Treaty of Rome provisions into force among themselves, that is, they would globalize (on a six-country basis) existing bilateral quotas and increase the resulting total by an overall amount of 20 per cent. by value, the global quota for each product being increased by at least 10 per cent. In cases where the resulting quotas would be less than 3 per cent. of national production (and where nil quotas had previously been in effect) quotas equivalent to 3 per cent. of national production would be established for the Community countries as a group. For the rest of the OEEC countries, the Six proposed—on a basis of reciprocity—to increase existing quotas by a total of 20 per cent. by value, the quota for each product that was already liberalized being increased at least 10 per cent. The determination of which quotas would be increased by more than 10 per cent. would be arrived at by bilateral bargaining. This same procedure would also apply to nil and tiny quotas: that is, there would be no obligation to establish quotas for all products at at least 3 per cent. of national production as the Treaty of Rome countries would do among themselves, but increases in tiny quotas—and presumably the opening of quotas where none existed—would form part of the bilateral negotiations on how the overall increase of 20 per cent. was to be achieved.

These arrangements would not have eliminated discrimination within the OEEC on 1 January—they were deliberately designed to maintain a clear difference of treatment—and they were accordingly considered inadequate by the United Kingdom and the other OEEC countries. Two aspects of the proposed arrangement

---

[7] The text of the decision of the Six on the action to be taken on 1 January 1959 is contained in Institut Royal des Relations Internationales, *Chronique de Politique Étrangère*, vol. XII, no. 5–6, pp. 747–8.

were particularly strongly criticized: first, the fact that the
3 per cent. quotas would be available—as a matter of right—
only to Treaty of Rome countries; and, second, the fact that
France still seemed to be proposing to implement fully her
Treaty of Rome commitments while doing little to reliberalize
trade in accordance with her OEEC commitments. A French reliberalization of her OEEC trade of the order of about 40 per cent.
was at this time being freely predicted.[8] The United Kingdom and
the others also objected to the idea that negotiation on the size of
quotas should be carried on bilaterally rather than, as in the past,
multilaterally in the OEEC.

Shortly after the cancellation of the meeting of the Maudling
Committee the Swiss had suggested that the 'Other Six' meet to
take stock of the situation, and on 1 December (after Bad Kreuznach but before the meeting of the Six) high-ranking officials from
these countries met together in Geneva.[9] By this time the general
line the Six would take was becoming clear, and the others sought
to concert their response. The principles of sticking together, of
continuing to insist on a multilateral solution to the European
trading problem, and of continuing the fight for a non-discriminatory quota régime among the OEEC countries were reaffirmed.
The available evidence suggests that the possibility of retaliation
by restricting imports from the Six—if, as seemed probable, the
proposals from the Six did not eliminate discrimination—was also
discussed but that no agreement was reached on the steps that
might be taken.

With great difficulty the British persuaded the Six to agree to a
meeting of the OEEC Ministerial Council to take stock of the

---

[8] In June 1957 the French Government had reimposed quotas for balance of
payments reasons. Under the OEEC Code of Liberalization, France was committed to 'do its best' to reliberalize at least 60 per cent. of its trade by June
1958 and at least 75 per cent. by December 1958. In June 1958, France had
felt unable to restore any measure of liberalization. The other Treaty of Rome
countries and most of the other OEEC countries had liberalized 90 per cent.
or more of their private intra-OEEC trade pursuant to OEEC resolutions.
Until the French also regained their former liberalization level it was clear
that if they removed quotas on trade with the Six without extending the same
treatment to the other OEEC countries, they would be violating the OEEC
Code which stipulated that when any country reimposed restrictions it must
do so in a non-discriminatory way.

[9] The original intention was to limit the meeting to officials from the 'other Six'.
Portugal, however, wished to be present and was welcomed. So too was the
Chairman of the OEEC Committee that had been examining the problems of
the 'peripheral countries': Greece, Turkey, Ireland, and Iceland.

situation. This meeting, held on 15 December 1958, was the stormiest in the history of the Organization. It opened peacefully enough with a brief, straightforward report by Mr. Maudling on the work of his Committee and its inability to reach agreement.[10] Once again there were many general expressions of the desire to find some way of associating the rest of the OEEC with the Six, but no specific proposals were put forward. The Council then turned to consider the paper from the Six outlining the action they intended to take on 1 January. The discussion centred on what constituted discrimination and soon became acrimonious. Although for many months the British and other OEEC countries had been claiming that what the Six proposed to do on 1 January was tantamount to discrimination, this point had always been resisted by the Six, and the counter-thesis along the lines of the Hallstein statement to the European Parliamentary Assembly advanced (see p. 149). If the French had been on a par with the other Treaty of Rome countries in respect of their OEEC obligations, it would have been difficult to sustain the argument that what the Six were proposing to do was discriminatory. However, as things stood, the weak point in the argument of the Six was the fact that the French were far below the liberalization level agreed by the OEEC and showed every intention of fulfilling their Treaty of Rome commitments while defaulting on their prior commitment to OEEC.[11]

Although it did nothing to sweeten Anglo-French relations it was logically correct for the British spokesmen to concentrate, as they did, remorselessly, on the French situation. However, as the discussion proceeded it was clear that there was a more fundamental point at issue. The British were determined to establish and to gain acceptance for the principle of non-discrimination in all trade among OEEC countries—liberalized and non-liberalized; the French were equally determined to preserve a clear 'difference'

[10] Mr. Maudling's report was reproduced in the Blue Book, pp. 1 ff.

[11] The OEEC tradition of non-discrimination was much more clearly established with respect to trade that had been 'liberalized' than it was with respect to trade in the 'non-liberalized' sector. The OEEC Code of Liberalization contained a general provision indicating that the rule of non-discrimination should apply to non-liberalized trade, but details of how this should be done were never agreed by the Organization. Furthermore, the OEEC Code had a 'customs union clause' recognizing the right of countries forming a customs union to extend additional measures of trade liberalization to each other without extending them to other members of the Organization. In contrast, the principle that 'deliberalization' of trade must be made on a non-discriminatory basis was well established, as was the corollary that reliberalization to the agreed OEEC level must be accomplished in a non-discriminatory way.

between the treatment the countries of the Economic Community would accord to one another and the treatment they would accord other OEEC countries, and to obtain recognition from the other OEEC countries for the legality of this difference. These conflicting goals complicated the consideration of the proposal made in the course of the session by the British delegate, Sir David Eccles. This proposal was, in brief, that the Treaty of Rome quota arrangements should be put into effect on an OEEC-wide basis by all the OEEC countries that wished to do so on a basis of full reciprocity. In one sense this was an ingenious proposal, since it would not have 'cost' the Six anything; they would not have been freeing any greater volume of goods but would simply have been letting more countries compete for the same quotas, and, in return, they would have received the right to compete for new 3 per cent. quotas established by the other OEEC countries. However, by accepting the British proposal the most obvious and important difference in treatment between a Treaty of Rome country and an OEEC country would have been eliminated, no appreciable 'Community preference' would have been established on 1 January, and a firm precedent of OEEC-wide non-discrimination would have been created.[12] The French wanted to put off consideration of the British proposal until some time in the New Year, by which time the very difference in treatment that the British were fighting to avoid would have come into effect. Sir David Eccles indicated that in that event 'defensive measures' might be in order, whereupon the French delegate, M. Couve de Murville, refused to negotiate further 'under threats', and for a time it seemed probable that the French would withdraw their agreement to the concessions earlier agreed upon among the Six. The most that could eventually be retrieved from an explosive situation was agreement to adjourn the meeting until 15 January. Meanwhile the British proposal and the plans of the Six were to be studied by the OEEC to see what the effects of each would be.

On 1 January (1959) the tariff cuts and increases in quotas provided for by the Treaty of Rome came into effect. The Six generalized to all countries with which they had m.f.n. commitments those tariff cuts that did not result in any reductions below

---

[12] The fact that, in some cases, countries with low tariffs would be lowering their tariffs with respect to their Treaty of Rome partners, and not to the others was, of course, another 'difference' although a small one, and a legal one. This was mentioned but received much less emphasis from British quarters than from some others, e.g. from the Swiss.

the eventual level of the common external tariff and they extended
to the other OEEC countries half of the 20 per cent. increase in
quotas that they made with respect to each other. No agreement
had been reached within the Six on whether to extend the other
10 per cent. to the rest of the OEEC countries or on the nil quota
problem. The Eccles proposals were extremely attractive to some
in the Six, particularly to Germany and to the Benelux countries,
and the French had a hard time persuading their partners not to
accept them. But there was both a practical consideration and an
important point of principle at stake—the need to bring home to
industrialists the tangible advantages of belonging to the Common
Market and the need to establish the 'right' to different treatment
—and the French views prevailed in the end. Moreover, both the
substantive and the legal aspects of the quota problem appeared
in a rather different light in January from what they had at the
time of the stormy OEEC Council meeting in mid-December.
As indicated above, the weakest aspect of the position of the Six on
quotas was the fact that the French were in default of their OEEC
obligations. As 1958 ended, the French decided on a radical programme of economic and financial reform. As part of this programme, the franc was devalued by $17\frac{1}{2}$ per cent. and made
convertible on current account, and trade with the other OEEC
countries was liberalized to the agreed level of 90 per cent. The
most solidly based argument of the other OEEC countries that
the action of the Six was discriminatory was thereby eliminated.

The decisions by the leading European countries to make their
currencies convertible on current account[13] were taken after
apparently amicable consultation in the corridors at the NATO
meetings in mid-December, only a few days after the free exchange
of insults at the OEEC, and the replacing of the EPU by the
European Monetary Agreement was accomplished smoothly. Since
the annual meetings of the International Bank and the International Monetary Fund at New Delhi in October 1958, there had
been persistent rumours that sterling would shortly be made
convertible. As the free trade area negotiations became more
difficult, there was speculation in the British press that a return to
convertibility might be one of the measures of retaliation that
would be taken if the negotiations broke down, for restoring

---

[13] The degree of convertibility varied somewhat from country to country: sterling, the French franc, and the German mark were made convertible for non-
residents and for current account transactions only.

convertibility to sterling would almost certainly mean the end of the European Payments Union and the French were major debtors to the Union at this time. In 1955, alarmed by an earlier British flirtation with convertibility, the OEEC countries had agreed upon the terms of a European Monetary Agreement to replace the European Payments Union when countries whose quotas in the EPU totalled 50 per cent. made their currencies convertible.[14] For some time, the German Federal Republic had made it clear that the mark would be made convertible 'five minutes after sterling' and enough other countries were certain to follow suit to bring about the transfer from the EPU to the EMA once the British moved. However, despite the collapse of the free trade area negotiations, the timing of the general move towards convertibility was, in the event, governed by the French decision to devalue the franc, not by British pique.

The move towards convertibility and the termination of the automatic credit facilities of the EPU removed much of the justification for continued resort to the control of imports by quotas—by the Six and by the other OEEC countries—since the accepted rationale for the retention of quotas against countries outside the OEEC while relaxing them on trade within the area was that the EPU eliminated, or at least substantially mitigated, balance of payments problems within the area and thus made it possible for members to remove quotas on trade with one another at a faster rate than on trade with countries outside the system. Differences in quota treatment continued to be an irritant in relations between the Six and the other OEEC countries for a year or two, but from the time of these convertibility moves at the end of 1958, attention shifted increasingly to the tariff problem.

The OEEC, at official levels, continued to examine the quota problem during the early months of 1959, but the main discussion on ways of mitigating the difficulties arising from the decision of the Six to reject the Eccles proposals (or, more accurately, their failure to agree to accept them) occurred outside the Organization. The three countries with the largest amount of important industrial goods in the 'non-liberalized' sector were France, Italy, and the United Kingdom and it was eventually agreed that the possibility of some expansion of trade in the 'non-liberalized' products should be examined bilaterally and on a purely pragmatic

---

[14] See Chapter I. The principal difference between the EPU and the EMA is that the latter has no automatic credit facilities.

basis. Bilateral talks were begun between the British and the French in January and were continued until the end of March. Bilateral talks were also held between Britain and Italy, between Britain and the Benelux countries, and between France and most of the 'Other Six'. The result was the opening of some new quotas but not the complete removal of the difference in treatment.

Throughout the winter and the spring of 1959 British ministers continued to emphasize the dangers of a division in Europe and to reiterate that a long-term arrangement was essential. Furthermore, although British spokesmen frequently expressed their willingness to consider any proposals, they usually added that they continued to believe a free trade area was the best, and probably the only, satisfactory arrangement.

In February 1959, the House of Commons held an extended debate on the free trade area problem.[15] This was the first real debate on the question in the House since that of November 1956, when the free trade area proposal was first outlined by Mr. Macmillan. Mr. Maudling opened for the Government and, since the President of the Board of Trade, Sir David Eccles, had been smitten with 'flu', he wound up the debate as well. The Liberal Party had already begun to advocate joining the Common Market,[16] but there was little difference of view between the front benches of the two principal parties. Already there were signs, which were to become much more prominent later, that greater differences of view existed within each party than between the leaders of the two major parties. The debate was notable for the deliberate effort made by all the principal spokesmen to avoid recrimination and to concentrate on exploring the possibilities for the future rather than raking over the coals of the past. Although it suited party politics, it is perhaps worth noting that, on the whole, the President of the Board of Trade, Sir David Eccles, came in for more acrimonious comment for his conduct at the OEEC ministerial meeting in December (1958) than did the French for their tactics during the negotiations. The clear feeling on both sides of the House was that a close association with the Common Market was still an objective that must be vigorously pursued, although there were very few new ideas about how this might be done. One of the few came from the late John Edwards,

---

[15] *Hansard*, House of Commons, 12 February 1959.
[16] The Liberals did not divide the House on this question, as they were to do in the summer of 1960 (see below, Chapter IX, p. 301).

who opened the debate for the Labour Party and pointed out that tariff harmonization with the Six might be a much less formidable operation than most people appeared to believe. Speakers from the front benches of both parties mentioned the possibility of forming some kind of arrangement with the three Scandinavian countries, Switzerland, and Austria—the 'Other Six' as this group was called—although this possibility engendered little real enthusiasm. Mr. Maudling referred to the fact that the industrial organizations from the 'Other Six' were examining this possibility but he forbore to mention that Government officials were doing so as well. It was clear enough that Mr. Maudling had doubts about the scheme, although he did not elaborate them, and that he, for his part, still felt that the right solution, and probably the one that would ultimately be found, would approximate closely to that under discussion in his committee when the negotiations broke down.

The views of the Six on relations with other countries

From the side of the Six, the Council of Ministers of the Community had, at its meeting on 3 December 1958, expressed its desire 'to continue the efforts to establish a multilateral association between the European Economic Community and the other states of the Organization for European Economic Co-operation' and had asked the Commission to make 'a detailed examination of the problems and of the possibilities of resolving them' and to submit a report by 1 March 1959 'on the joint position which could be taken up by the Member States'.[17]

Although they had stuck together at all the decisive points during the free trade area negotiations, fundamental differences of view on the question of a wider association existed among the Six Governments. The de Gaulle Government, which was now formally and constitutionally in power, was openly opposed to the free trade area plan. Moreover, the French Government and important elements in the Commission were opposed to the early resumption of negotiations on any long-term plan. In consequence, the memorandum from the Commission (produced in February 1959) did not suggest how negotiations might be resumed, but proposed, instead, a course of action to mitigate the effects of the

[17] The text of the resolution is contained in European Economic Community, *First Memorandum from the Commission of the European Economic Community to the Council of Ministers of the Community* (Brussels, 26 February 1959).

failure to reach a Europe-wide agreement. In this memorandum, the Commission outlined the argument—an argument that it developed more fully as the year proceeded—that the European problem was not a special question requiring a special solution, but simply one facet of the general problem of the Community's external relations. In place of a purely European settlement the Commission sketched out ideas that were later elaborated and made more precise in the *Second Memorandum* on association: the need for closer co-operation on economic policy between the Community, the United States, and the United Kingdom; the need for more, and better co-ordinated, assistance to the under-developed countries; the need for a general reduction of trade barriers by all the highly industrialized countries.

It was clear from the memorandum that, in the Commission's view, the total elimination of trade barriers among a group of countries would be acceptable only within a framework that, like the Treaty of Rome, also provided for most of the other attributes of an economic union.[18] In an interesting echo of the Spaak Report the Commission concluded that there were only two entirely satisfactory systems of multilateral free trade: 'the customs union (or, more exactly, the economic union) which secures for all participants the same conditions of supply, and world free trade, which ensures this same equality'. The Commission then made the further point that a free trade area was an acceptable arrangement 'only to the extent that it is fitted into a setting of increasing liberalization of world trade and abandons any idea of strengthening European economic solidarity in the strict sense of the word, or approximates to the type of the customs union'.[19] This description of a free trade area as reasonable only if conceived as a step towards world-wide free trade was in keeping with French views, and French fears, of the British motives in pressing for the free trade area.[20]

It would have been unacceptable to all but the French Government if the Commission had written off the possibility of a wider European agreement. And here and there in the analysis that

[18] See criteria enumerated in para. 33, pp. 17 and 18.

[19] *First Memorandum*, p. 19. The English version of the Memorandum was a poor translation.

[20] It was difficult for the British to realize during the free trade area negotiations how damning in French eyes was any suggestion that the free trade area might be transitional to world-wide free trade, for 'world-wide free trade' seemed to the British to be a worthy, if unobtainable, objective. Many of Sir David Eccles' pronouncements were like red rags to a bull.

otherwise supported the Commission's central thesis—that the European problem was simply one aspect of a wider problem and should be tackled in that framework—there were numerous statements emphasizing the importance of a broader European arrangement and the need for maintaining and developing the work of the OEEC. However, despite these statements of encouragement to those who wanted a European arrangement, the *First Memorandum* always stopped short of endorsing the objective of complete free trade among the OEEC countries, although it also forbore to rule it out as an eventual possibility. The basic issue of the nature of an association between the Six and the other OEEC countries was deliberately side-stepped. Instead, the Commission advocated a number of measures which could be taken to ease the tension without prejudice to the question of a long-term agreement. The principal suggestions made by the Commission in this *First Memorandum* were that the OEEC countries should increase their quotas to each other by 20 per cent. annually, and that differences in tariff treatment should be reduced to the extent possible in the course of the GATT negotiations (the so-called 'Dillon round') which the United States had suggested be held in the winter of 1960–1. The Commission suggested that the position of the OEEC countries might be co-ordinated before the GATT negotiations, so that the special interests of those European countries with which the Common Market had extensive trade could be taken into account. It was also suggested that the Community might open tariff quotas where other European countries experienced hardship and that there might be some scope for European tariff reductions even before the GATT negotiations.[21]

The Commission drew attention to the availability of Article 237 (membership) and Article 238 (association) of the Treaty of Rome and made a slightly unseemly bid for Danish membership.[22] In

---

[21] It was recognized by the Commission that, in the absence of any commitment to form a free trade area, or customs union, any tariff reductions made by OEEC countries would have to be generalized to the other members of GATT. The idea behind the 'European tariff reductions' was that there might be a number of goods which were primarily traded on a European basis and perhaps some goods for which European prices were substantially below those of potential competitors. The generalization of reductions in tariffs on these goods would be relatively painless. The OEEC had examined a similar scheme in 1955 and had concluded that there were few important items solely, or preponderantly, traded among the European countries, but the idea of a 'European list' persisted. See Chapter VIII.

[22] Paragraph 84 of the *First Memorandum*, a paragraph which was obviously written for Danish consumption, read as follows: 'The will of the Com-

the light of subsequent controversies over the intentions and meaning of the treaty provision for association, this first pronouncement by the Commission on Article 238 is of considerable interest and worth quoting in full:

> Association does not create such close links. The essential advantage of this system is its very great flexibility. Firstly, it allows of both multilateral and bilateral association. Secondly, it allows of all solutions: those which adopt only certain provisions of the Treaty of Rome, and those which take over that instrument almost in its entirety. Furthermore, the system makes it easier both for the country applying for association and for the Community to draft special clauses exactly adapted to the situation of the country in question and to the relations which it already has with the Community. Finally—and this is perhaps the essential difference—the associate country retains its full individuality on the political plane. The pledges which such a country would give in return for certain facilities, like any other commitment to which it subscribed, would be of a contractual nature and it would put them into operation by its own independent action.[23]

As discussed further below, the Commission soon came to question the whole concept of association and its later interpretations of this article were very different and very much more restrictive.

In conclusion, the Commission explained that its memorandum was a preliminary reply to the Ministers and suggested that it be asked to continue its work in close contact with the representatives of the member states. The Commission commented that 'in the course of these exchanges of views it would doubtless be possible to work out in detail the common position of the Member States of the Community on the basis of the various suggestions contained in this Report, both in the matter of long-term solutions and in that of the measures to be undertaken immediately'. This suggestion, like some of the other references to the desirability of a 'wider arrangement', shows signs of having been added at the last moment to make the memorandum more palatable to those within

---

munity to reach a multi-lateral settlement for agriculture in the framework of the Association in no way prevents it from taking a positive attitude towards requests which might be submitted by certain countries wishing to adhere to the joint agricultural policy of the Community. This attitude is nevertheless conditional on the countries in question accepting membership of the EEC for the whole of their economy.'

[23] *First Memorandum*, p. 38.

the Community who were pressing for a broader arrangement, as well as to the other European countries.[24]

The Commission's review of the reasons why no agreement appeared possible was unexceptionable, and its statements on the need for the Community to accept its responsibilities as a powerful new economic unit—particularly with respect to the underdeveloped countries—and to pursue liberal and constructive economic policies, although not very elegantly formulated, were encouraging signs that the new Community would be responsible and 'outward'-looking. Nevertheless, the general reaction on the part of all those who wanted a wider agreement (those within the Community as well as outside) was that the report was negative and inadequate, and the European countries outside the Six tended to discount its espousal of 'liberalism' as an evasive tactic. Within the Community there was considerable annoyance with the Commission for its failure to carry out its mandate to define the basis on which negotiations could be reopened. When the report was discussed by the Council of Ministers in March 1959, all the governments, save the French, who rather opportunistically supported the Commission's line, reiterated their conviction that a European 'free market' must be established and made it clear that they felt the Commission's proposals for reliance on GATT in the tariff field were particularly inadequate.[25] Although there was little agreement on how it could be attained, the feeling in favour of a wider European arrangement was so strong that the Council of Ministers simply took note of the report, rather than accepting it, and unanimously reaffirmed its determination to try to establish a multilateral association between the EEC and the other countries of the OEEC.[26] The member

[24] The Memorandum had been discussed in draft form with the member governments, and various internal inconsistencies can doubtless be attributed to the strongly conflicting views held by the member governments.

[25] Most of the Commission's statements about the need for the Community to pursue liberal policies were more in line with German and Benelux sentiments than with French views and it is open to question whether the French were, at this time, really endorsing much of the Memorandum save the Commission's view that new negotiations would be unprofitable.

[26] The Germans were the most critical of the Commission's report and were apparently not convinced that the kind of arrangement being discussed by the Maudling Committee need be abandoned. The Benelux representatives thought a large measure of tariff harmonization should be an ingredient of a new plan and that this would be acceptable to the other OEEC countries. The Italians seem to have favoured a form of customs union. See Heinrich Siegler, *Dokumentation der Europäischen Integration 1946–1961, unter besonderer Beachtung des Verhältnisses EWG–EFTA* (Bonn, Vienna, Zurich, 1961), p. 280.

governments of the Community were requested to inform the Commission before 15 April of their comments on the memorandum and a Special Committee, composed of representatives of the Governments as well as of members of the Commission, was established to make a further report to the Council.

The fact that representatives of member governments were to work with the Commission in the Special Committee was a sign of the general dissatisfaction with the Commission's first effort and a step backward from the suggestion in the original decision of the Council of Ministers that the Commission might be given a larger role in the negotiations, as M. Monnet and other strong 'Europeans' had urged.[27]

The Special Committee appointed by the Council of Ministers of the Six and chaired by M. Rey, the member of the Commission responsible for the external relations of the Community, met at the end of April and again in May. The position of the French Government had hardened even further during the six weeks that had elapsed since the Council of Ministers had discussed the *First Memorandum* from the Commission. Although the French had concurred in the ministerial resolution, the French representative at the Rey Committee openly questioned the objective of ever seeking any form of wider European association. It was clear that the differences of view among the Six no longer revolved around the nature of the wider association or the timing of the negotiations, but centred on the fundamental question of whether or not a tariff-free area of the OEEC countries was a desirable objective. The French and some members of the Commission felt that, with the recovery from the war and the return to *de facto* convertibility, the 'Europe of the Seventeen' had little validity. They saw no satisfactory middle position: the other European countries could either join the Community in accordance with Article 237 (or perhaps negotiate an association agreement with it as foreseen by Article 238) or they could accept a relationship similar to that of other third countries, such as the United States.[28] The Dutch

[27] The relevant section of the 3 December 1958 resolution by the Council of Ministers read as follows: 'The Council, when it has approved this report, will decide on the procedure to be followed. One possibility that may be considered is that the Commission should make official contact with other Governments in order to discuss the problem with these Governments.'

[28] 'Association' was really a middle position. It is clear that the implications of 'Association' under Article 238 had not been thought through by the Commission before they began advocating it as an alternative to a multilateral arrangement.

were the furthest removed from this position, and took very strong exception to it. The Belgians, the Germans, and some within the Commission were also still trying hard to find a European solution.[29] The Italians appeared to favour a European solution in principle but they tended to share most of the French objections to the particular European solutions that were put forward.

Towards the end of April the question of relations between the Six and the other Eleven was a major theme of the discussions at the Consultative Assembly of the Council of Europe and a resolution calling for the re-opening of negotiations with a view to an agreement on a declaration of intent by the end of the year was adopted by an overwhelming majority. It is worth noting, however, that the pressure for action came largely from the Benelux, Scandinavian, and British delegates and that the French delegates abstained from voting.[30]

The kind of thinking that underlay the Commission's *First Memorandum* was directly challenged by Mr. Maudling in his speech to the Consultative Assembly. Part of his statement is worth quoting, not only because it was the most direct and explicit British criticism of the Commission's views that was made publicly but also because his defence of 'European discrimination' was, rather surprisingly, strikingly similar to the Hallstein argument for 'Community discrimination' quoted in Chapter V:

[29] In April 1959, the Benelux countries put forward a proposal which was discussed in Community circles and then outlined by the Benelux representatives to the Council of Europe. The Benelux countries argued that it should be possible for the Six and the other European countries to declare, immediately, that their end objective was the establishment of a 'free market' within which there would be no barriers to trade, and that this 'free market' would be achieved at the end of a fixed period which would also be agreed and announced. The decision whether the final arrangement would be a free trade area, or a customs union, or some combination of the two, and other aspects of the arrangement, could be studied further and negotiations carried on during the first stage of the transition period provided by the Treaty of Rome. During this period, all the OEEC countries would liberalize trade as provided by the Treaty of Rome but on an OEEC basis. However, the Benelux proposal—and other similar ideas which had been examined within the Commission—came up against the refusal of the French to subscribe to any commitment for complete free trade until they knew all the other features of the arrangement. The GATT provisions, and the attitude of other European countries, ruled out the opposite approach of starting with the disarmament of tariffs and quotas, but leaving for later decision the question of whether the removal of barriers would be complete or partial.

[30] Council of Europe, *Official Report of Debates*, Eleventh Session, Vol. I, Appendix II (Strasbourg, 1959).

The first question we must ask ourselves is whether there is a need for a European solution. I am myself confident that the answer of the Assembly will be 'Yes'. I say 'a' European solution meaning to emphasise that it must be one solution for all the seventeen members of the OEEC, a multilateral solution and not a bilateral agreement. . . . There must be one solution, and it must be a European solution, in the sense that it is a system for Europe whereby we do not discriminate against one another but we do discriminate against the rest of the world; we treat one another, as Europeans, differently from the way in which we treat other countries, but we treat one another as Europeans in the same way as we treat all other Europeans.

There are some people who say the opposite of that. They say that the Community must find its place in the world as a whole and not merely in Europe. They say that while it is true that the Community has problems in its relations with Scandinavia and Switzerland, it equally has problems of relations with the United States, Japan and Costa Rica. I do not accept that point of view, and I do not think that any of us who support the ideal of Europe as a unity can support that idea. If we have before us this ideal of Europe as the home of our civilisation and as a cultural, social and political entity, surely we must believe in Europe as an economic entity. Unless we all regard ourselves as Europeans and as members of a European system in solving our economic problems, we shall soon find it impossible to do so in solving some of the great political problems. I conclude that we must seek a single multilateral system for Europe, meaning by Europe all seventeen members of the OEEC.[31]

Any hopes of a resumption of negotiations that may have been aroused by the coolness shown by the Council of Ministers to the Commission's memorandum, by the Benelux proposals, or by the debates in the Council of Europe were short-lived. By the time the summer holidays interrupted the discussions in the Rey Committee no progress had been made in finding a common position among the Six. And when the discussions were resumed at the end of the summer it was clear that the general thesis of the Commission had not only become more generally accepted in Community circles but had attracted the support of a powerful ally—the United States.

A number of factors combined to convince the Commission that the main lines of its diagnosis and the main elements of its prescription were correct and that the right course was to stop the search for a long-term, Europe-wide arrangement and to

---

[31] Council of Europe, *Official Report of Debates*, 27 April 1959, pp. 273–4.

concentrate instead on steps which would minimize the difficulties for all of the trading partners of the Six, not simply its European partners. In addition to the strong French opposition to a wider agreement, the three developments that probably contributed most to the Commission's conviction that the emphasis should now be placed on 'globalism' were, first, the decision taken by a number of the leading 'Europeans' during the summer to try to speed up the establishment of the Community; second, the increasing United States emphasis on 'non-discrimination'; and third, the decision taken by the British, and others, to form the EFTA.

In a number of respects the early months of 1959 were not very cheerful ones for the 'Europeans'. Although the French financial and economic reforms had made it possible for the first tariff cuts and increases in quotas to be made on time and without the wholesale resort to escape clauses that had been feared, the attitude of the de Gaulle Government to the concepts and aspirations of the 'Europeans' was far from reassuring. M. Debré, in his first address as Prime Minister to the French National Assembly, made it very clear that by European unity the Government of General de Gaulle meant co-operation among strong national governments—'l'Europe des patries'. Gaullist scorn for and opposition to 'supra-nationalism' inevitably had its repercussions on the institutions of the new Communities. The Commission walked on eggs, implementing those sections of the treaty that were clear and inescapable but playing for time and a better atmosphere before seeking decisions on controversial issues. During the spring the prestige of the European institutions also suffered from the open rebuff given to the High Authority of the Coal and Steel Community by both the French and the German Governments.[32] And the general sense of uncertainty and insecurity was nourished by a spate of rumours that the French Government was considering proposing amendments to the Schuman Plan Treaty to cut down the powers of the High

---

[32] The coal controversy is too long and complex a story to be told here. In brief, the High Authority was inept and dilatory in recommending action to deal with the rapidly mounting coal stocks but when it finally proposed measures to deal with the situation, both the German and the French Governments (for rather different reasons) flatly refused to accept the 'Community nature' of the coal problem and flagrantly impeded the High Authority in its attempts to work out a solution. For further details see the *Eighth General Report* of the European Coal and Steel Community.

Authority and to bring them into line with the powers of the Commission of the EEC. In April, the news that Dr. Adenauer was planning to stand for the largely titular position of President of the Federal Republic added a new dimension to the worries of the 'Europeans'. It was generally assumed that his successor as Chancellor (the controlling position in German political life) would be Dr. Erhard, the Minister of Economics, who had been a strong advocate of the free trade area and who was still pressing for an arrangement on those lines.

However, during the summer, 'European' developments took a turn for the better and the mood changed. In June, Dr. Adenauer reversed his earlier decision to stand for President and declared his intention of retaining his position as Chancellor. Earlier fears that General de Gaulle's attitude towards NATO might put the German Government in the position of having to choose between NATO (and the United States) and the new alliance with France had somewhat abated. Despite various rumours, the French Government had, as yet, made no specific proposals for amending the Schuman Plan Treaty. Moreover, France was visibly profiting from the combined effects of the Pinay–Rueff economic policy and of the Common Market, and, although most of French industry had originally opposed the Common Market and had freely predicted disaster if the Treaty of Rome came into effect, the Patronat was now encouraging a faster reduction in barriers than that called for by the treaty. This constellation of favourable economic and political factors encouraged the 'Europeans' to decide to give an overriding priority to the development of the Common Market and to try to reach the 'point of no return' as soon as possible so that the knitting together of the economies of the Six countries could not be unravelled if the economic or the political climate deteriorated.[33]

Numerous ideas for strengthening Six-country action and for speeding up the timetable laid down in the Treaty of Rome began to be considered. To many of the 'Europeans' the reopening of negotiations on a wider European arrangement would, at best, have been a distraction and, at worst, a threat to the success of their own plans. The argument made during the free trade area negotiations that the identity of the Community would 'dissolve'

[33] At this time it was generally assumed that by the time tariffs within the Community had been cut by 50 per cent. the process of integration would have gone far enough to be irreversible.

if surrounded by a larger group was again much heard and further developed. The most obvious sign of the 'reality' of the new Community was that industries within the Common Market (and outside) were planning on the assumption that the Common Market, and only the Common Market, would come into being. This industrial interest was the strongest cement then binding together the new Community. And, once industries had a vested interest in the realization of the Common Market they could be counted on to bring pressure on their governments to see that the process continued and was, perhaps, accelerated. The 'Europeans', understandably enough, did not want to see this precious support dissipated as would have been inevitable had the 'difference' in trading opportunities between the Six and the rest been obliterated. Naturally enough at a time when the support of some of the principal governments for the creation of a real Community was uncertain, the strongest possible industrial support seemed indispensable. Not all the 'Europeans' shared these apprehensions about the effects of a wider arrangement and during the autumn, as is discussed further below, the Benelux Governments tried, although without success, to tie the decision to speed up the timetable of the Common Market to a commitment to make progress on a wider European trading arrangement.

The second development which tended to strengthen the Commission's attachment to 'globalism' and to harden the opposition to an arrangement with the other European countries was the attitude of the United States. In 1958 and 1959 the deficit in the United States balance of payments increased very sharply— to 3·5 billion dollars in 1958 and 3·8 billion dollars in 1959. Moreover, the unusual size of the deficit appeared to result, mainly, from rising imports and falling exports, and it was accompanied by a substantial outflow of gold. The Western European countries were the principal gainers: in 1958 and 1959 exports to the United States from the OEEC countries were at an all-time high and European reserves rose from 15·4 billion dollars in 1957 to 20·5 billion dollars in 1959.[34]

For a number of years United States representatives in the OEEC and the GATT had been arguing, with some success, for the removal of quotas on dollar goods. After the principal European countries had restored a large measure of convertibility to their currencies at the end of 1958, American pressure for the

[34] See OEEC, *Europe and the World Economy* (1960).

removal of discriminatory quotas was stepped up. The United States Administration, confronted with a deteriorating balance of payments position, substantial unemployment, and signs of rising protectionism in the United States, was understandably loath to encourage any developments that added to American trading difficulties in Europe. The Communities of the Six had from the earliest days of the Schuman Plan enjoyed strong political support in the United States, and the 'discrimination' the Common Market implied was generally accepted as a cheap price for the political advantages of a united Europe. A Europe-wide free trade area (and also the EFTA—see next chapter) seemed to many people in the United States to lack the political advantages of the Common Market. Given its domestic preoccupations and its predisposition to back the 'Europeans' on political grounds, it is not surprising that the United States Administration actively encouraged the Commission to feel that the right answer to the European problem lay not in an OEEC-wide arrangement but in the adoption of liberal trade policies by the Community and in handling on an *ad hoc* basis any specific difficulties that, in fact, materialized in the Community's trade relations with the other European countries.

The Commission's desire to avoid intensifying, or even appearing to intensify, American difficulties was motivated in part by an appreciation of the willingness of the United States to accept and even to encourage discrimination against itself in the post-war period and in part by the recognition that it was to the interest of the rest of the world that the United States should be helped to meet its difficulties through expanding its exports rather than by cutting its foreign aid programmes or restricting its imports. But it is clear enough that political expediency played its part in the Commission's position as well, and one element in the Commission's solicitude was the hope that the United States would support the Commission (and the French) in withstanding the pressure for a Europe-wide arrangement.

Finally, the decision of the Seven to form a free trade area among themselves (which is discussed in the next chapter) contributed to the Commission's decision to try to call off the search for a Europe-wide arrangement. Reactions within the Community countries to the preliminary talks about the formation of the EFTA were mixed. Some of those in the Benelux countries who were most anxious to see an OEEC-wide agreement encouraged the Seven because they felt that the resulting economic pressure on the

Six would increase interest within the Community in a wider arrangement. The early reactions of those who had come to oppose a broader arrangement seems to have been a combination of relief —the fact that the Seven were busy negotiating among themselves took some of the steam out of the pressure for a wider arrangement —and scepticism that the discussions would in the end bear fruit. When the draft plan for the association was published at the end of July 1959 it was realized that the Seven were in earnest and that later in the year there would certainly be renewed pressure for a settlement. But the draft plan, and later the Stockholm Convention, seemed to many on the Continent to be not a step forward but a move back, and fresh evidence that the Seven were interested only in a commercial agreement, and that only in a form which the Six had already rejected—the purest form of free trade area. As had been made clear in the Spaak Report, in the Treaty of Rome negotiations, in the abortive free trade area negotiations, and, most recently, in the *First Memorandum* from the Commission, some of the most influential 'Europeans', both within the Commission and outside, were convinced that free trade in the twentieth century only made economic sense in two situations: as one aspect of economic union (or an arrangement going very far in that direction) or in the context of free trade on a world basis.

The formation of the EFTA also seemed a backward step even to many of those who were not convinced that the way of the Community was the only way to integrate the Continent economically, for it appeared to confirm the views of those who had argued that the British were only interested in a commercial arrangement and that they were not prepared to join in the process of economic integration or to undertake the kind of political commitment which for many within the Six would have been the real justification for a wider arrangement. Moreover, during the Maudling Committee negotiations, and after they had broken down, many people—on both sides of the Channel—had felt that direct negotiations between the United Kingdom and the Six offered the best chance of finding an acceptable arrangement, and that once the central relationship had been established the problems of the other countries would be relatively easy to handle. The decision to form the EFTA limited the freedom of action of the United Kingdom and made a United Kingdom–Six negotiation seem unlikely, although, as later events proved, it did not in the end rule out direct negotiations.

It is worth noting here that in the spring of 1959 M. Monnet had been among those who felt that the Commission was taking rather too negative an attitude towards the resumption of negotiations. At its sixth session on 11 May 1959 the Action Committee (of which he was the moving spirit) had proposed 'that the Commission of the Common Market and the British Government should meet in a round-table conference to define the bases of a multilateral negotiation on the European Economic Association'. This reflected his own view at that time that an arrangement with the United Kingdom, in particular, was desirable and that the main requirement was to change the 'method' by which the negotiations were being pursued. During the summer, however, he changed his views. When the Action Committee met again in November (1959) it, like the Commission, emphasized the need to look at the European trade problem not as a primarily European problem but in a wider setting. In effect, the Committee withdrew its earlier proposal and suggested the convening of a round-table meeting to be attended not only by the Community (represented by the Commission) and the United Kingdom but by the United States and a non-Community member of the OEEC to seek 'a joint solution to what are from now on joint problems'.[35]

A *Second Memorandum* on association was produced by the Commission in September (1959). This Memorandum was, technically, a memorandum from the Commission to the Special Committee on association—the Rey Committee—which had been set up by the Council of Ministers in the spring. However, in an attempt to try to generate support for the Commission's point of view, Prof. Hallstein outlined the report to the European Parliamentary Assembly during its September session, and the memorandum itself was then released to the press.

In the introductory section, the Commission quite candidly admitted that the Special Committee was no nearer agreement than when it began its work 'despite redoubled efforts'. It also pointed out that the uncertainty about relations with the other European countries was disliked by industry and that discord and tensions within the Community as well as between the Community and its European neighbours were resulting from the prolonged uncertainty and the differences of view. The Commission clearly

[35] See *Joint Declaration* of the Action Committee for the United States of Europe, Sixth Session, 11 May 1959, and the same, Seventh Session, 19 and 20 November 1959. Also see Chapter VIII below.

agreed with those who were opposed to a revival of any form of free trade area, but it was well aware that the pressure for a renewal of negotiations within the Six countries was so strong that the only hope of avoiding a negotiation lay in putting forward an alternative line of action which would not only alleviate any real hardship caused by the formation of the Community but would also appeal to the liberal elements in the Community who tended to coincide with the groups most in favour of a wider European agreement.

In its *Second Memorandum* the Commission advocated action on three levels: measures to be taken (some unilaterally, others on conditions of reciprocity) to narrow the difference between the quota and tariff arrangements operating on trade within the Community and those affecting trade with other countries (not simply other European countries); measures to be taken to mitigate particular difficulties that were experienced by other European countries as a consequence of the formation of the Common Market; and measures to strengthen and extend the co-operation on economic questions between the Community, the United Kingdom, and the United States. In the first category, the Commission proposed that the Community should declare itself ready to extend to the other European countries, on conditions of reciprocity, the next (1 January 1960) 20 per cent. increases in quotas called for by the Treaty of Rome. The Commission went beyond the somewhat similar proposal made for the first year in two ways: first, by indicating that action on quotas should be taken in such a way as to reduce rather than to increase the difference in treatment between the other European countries, on the one hand, and the rest of the world, on the other; second, by indicating that third countries (both in Europe and outside) should also share 'to an appreciable extent' in the increases made in the nil and tiny quotas. How these objectives were to be achieved was not spelled out.

So far as tariffs were concerned, the Commission proposed that the Community should reaffirm its intention of pursuing a liberal policy with respect to the rest of the world and reiterated its willingness to participate in the GATT tariff negotiations proposed for the latter part of 1960.[36] In addition, it suggested that the Community should declare that it would propose (on

---

[36] The Commission had in mind a tariff cut of the order of 20 per cent., but, after some discussion, no precise figure was mentioned.

conditions of reciprocity) a further substantial reduction in the Common Market tariff, over and above whatever reductions were achieved in the 'Dillon round'. Finally, the Commission recommended that the Community countries should extend to third countries those reductions in tariff made internally on 1 July 1960 that did not result in rates below the eventual level of the common external tariff. This was the procedure followed at the time of the first tariff cut in January 1959: since the high tariffs have, in any case, eventually to be reduced to the Common Market level, the effect of adopting this procedure would simply be to give third countries a tariff reduction somewhat earlier than they would get it otherwise.

On the purely European level, the Commission proposed that a 'contact committee' should be established between the Community and other European countries (or groups of countries) to see what difficulties in trade arose and to propose means of remedying them. In this context, the Commission suggested that the Community declare itself ready to open tariff quotas, on conditions of reciprocity and in accordance with the rules of GATT.[37] The Commission also reiterated its earlier suggestion that the Community should declare its willingness to consult with its European partners to see whether some of the 'neuralgic' points in the trade between them could be alleviated by reducing the tariffs causing particular difficulties during the forthcoming GATT negotiations.

In its *Second Memorandum* the Commission reiterated its view that it would become much easier for the Community to follow a liberal external policy once it became more firmly established. Accordingly, it proposed that the Community should declare that it would accelerate the pace of integration 'in this spirit and to this end', and, specifically, that it should shorten the transitional stages provided by the treaty, speed up the formulation of a common commercial policy, and reinforce the 'monetary solidarity' of the Six countries.

There was even less in the *Second Memorandum* than in the Commission's *First Memorandum* to comfort those who wanted a European settlement, although the Commission emphasized that its suggestions did not prejudge any eventual solution to the problem of association—'*la porte reste ouverte à cet égard*'. Like the

---

[37] The Commission later became very hostile to the use of tariff quotas since tariff quotas in effect breached the common external tariff.

earlier memorandum, the *Second Memorandum* met with a mixed reaction among the Six. The German and Benelux representatives at the Special Committee felt there should be a renewed commitment to the ultimate objective of an OEEC-wide free trade arrangement. The French and the Commission were opposed to any such statement. The German and the Benelux representatives also felt that the proposals would be more likely to be acceptable to the other European countries if, instead of suggesting the establishment of a contact committee in Brussels, the new committee were to be established in Paris under the aegis of the OEEC. The French Government had, however, become strongly opposed to any use of the OEEC: they felt that the British controlled the OEEC and they feared (and not without reason) that any discussions on trade relations between the Six and the other European countries that was undertaken in that forum would soon be turned into new negotiations on a free trade area.

The German position deserves special comment for, as had been the case during the whole course of the free trade area negotiations, it was full of contradictions which worried the 'Europeans' and misled the British and others. During the summer, Dr. Erhard had tried to persuade M. Pinay, then the French Minister of Finance, to agree to resume negotiations on a free trade area, but he had failed to make any progress. Nevertheless he continued to be the spearhead of the considerable drive in Germany for a resumption of negotiations and his position was undoubtedly strengthened by fears in industrial circles that the formation of the EFTA would result in an appreciable diversion of trade. Before the meeting of the Consultative Assembly of the Council of Europe in September 1959 there were rumours that at that session Dr. Erhard would put forward new German proposals for a compromise between the two groups. In the event, Dr. Erhard did not go to Strasbourg and it was generally assumed that Dr. Adenauer had once again intervened, perhaps at the initiative of Prof. Hallstein, and reasserted German support for the general approach advocated by the Commission and acceptable to France.[38] However, the silencing of Dr. Erhard, if that is what it was, was short-lived. On 5 October, large advertisements freely acknowledged to have been paid for by Dr. Erhard appeared in the German press. These were dramatically headlined '6 + 7 + 5 = 1', and appealed for a European-wide trade arrangement, bringing together in a

[38] See *The Times*, 22 September 1959.

single market the Six of the Common Market, the Seven of the EFTA and the five peripheral countries. This outburst was quickly followed by a meeting of the German Cabinet (at which Prof. Hallstein was also present), after which a short communiqué was issued reaffirming Germany's existing policy on European questions, but 'with the maximum possible liberalism towards the outside world'.[39]

Reactions at the September session of the European Parliamentary Assembly were similar to those expressed by the representatives of the Six Governments in the Special Committee. The discussions in the Assembly opened on a rather sour note. The rapporteur (Mr. Blaisse of the Netherlands) of the parliamentary committee that had been examining the problem of external relations had apparently held discussions with the Commission in Brussels a few weeks before the Assembly was to meet but had received no inkling of the new proposals and his report had, accordingly, been drawn up with no reference to them. He, and other speakers from the Netherlands, strongly criticized the Commission for ignoring the formation of the EFTA, for ducking the problem of relations between the Six and the Seven, and for allowing the French to dictate Community policy. The Dutch tended to be echoed by the Belgians and by some, although not all, of the Germans. In contrast, M. Pleven (France) strongly supported the Commission's line but emphasized that in his view it was a 'maximum' position, not a negotiating position. He also objected to any connexion between the proposed contact committee and the OEEC. Both Prof. Hallstein and M. Rey were at pains to soothe the sensibilities of the rapporteur and to reassure the Assembly that they were not being kept in the dark, explaining that the Commission's *Second Memorandum* had only just been drafted and that, far from withholding information from the Assembly, they were outlining the Commission's proposals to them at the very earliest opportunity, despite the fact that, technically, the Memorandum was one from the Commission to the Special Committee. The Commission spokesmen met the charge that they were avoiding the issue of European trade by frankly admitting that the Six Governments were in fundamental disagreement. Their current proposals were a way out of the immobility in which the problem was now fixed, a way which would not prejudice later developments, and a way which would not

[39] See *Financial Times*, 16 October 1959.

require any of the member governments to abandon its views. This display of frankness largely won over the Assembly. Moreover most of the speakers, regardless of their views on the European trade question, attached importance to the speeding up of the formation of the Common Market and welcomed the Commission's proposals in that connexion.

The Six Governments continued to discuss the Commission's proposals throughout the autumn of 1959 and the question of the relations to be established with the other European countries became intertwined with the consideration being given to steps that might be taken to speed up the introduction of the Common Market and to strengthen Community action in other fields. As explained above, the excessive caution and the policy of deliberately marking time that had been characteristic of Community circles during the first part of 1959 had given way during the summer to a new burst of confidence and to a rush of new ideas for quickening the pace of integration. In mid-July, the first of what were to become regular quarterly meetings of the Finance Ministers of the Six was held in Bonn. At about the same time the French, after discussion with the Italians, put forward suggestions for regular meetings of the Foreign Ministers of the Six.[40]

Shortly after the summer holidays, the Belgian Foreign Minister, M. Wigny, circulated to the rest of the Six a memorandum containing various ideas for extending Six-country action to other fields, for speeding up the establishment of the Common Market, for strengthening the Community institutionally, and for making it more responsive to the needs of the underdeveloped countries. Many of these ideas had been in the air for some time and a start had already been made on some of them. For example, he reviewed the case for direct elections of the Assembly, a question already under examination by the parliamentarians; as others had done, he advocated better co-ordination between the three communities (although not necessarily the merger of the Executives); and he underlined the need for an early decision on a single seat for all the Six-country institutions.[41] M. Wigny also made suggestions for further action in the political and monetary fields,

[40] In addition to regular meetings of Foreign Ministers the French proposed the establishment of a permanent secretariat in Paris, but they did not press this suggestion when it met with a cool reception from the others.
[41] The EEC and Euratom Commissions were (and still are) in Brussels, the High Authority of the ECSC and the Court of Justice in Luxembourg, the European Parliament in Strasbourg.

although here again his suggestions were mostly variants of existing ideas and proposals. Perhaps the aspect of M. Wigny's memorandum that attracted the most attention was the suggestion that the transition period for the establishment of the Common Market should be cut to eight years. He proposed that the first period of four years should be left unchanged but that the second and third stages should each be cut from four to two years and that the transition period should definitely end on 1 January 1966.

M. Wigny made it clear that it was the view of the Benelux countries that the strengthening of the Community and the shortening of the transition period must go hand-in-hand with progress in establishing a free market with the other OEEC countries. He put forward once again the earlier Benelux suggestion that the Six should accept, forthwith, the goal of a free market, working out the details (such as the amount of tariff harmonization) during the first stage of the transition period while the Six themselves were also a free trade area.[42] Like many others at this time, he felt that inspection would show that, for a wide range of products, tariffs were already near enough together so that the risk of deflexion of trade was minimal, that some of the other rates could be harmonized without much difficulty, and that special arrangements could be made for the rest. This approach to the trade problem had considerable support in Germany and Italy but the French and the Commission were by this time even more firmly opposed to it than they had been in the spring when the idea was first put forward by the Benelux countries. In contrast, the idea of accelerating the formation of the Common Market met with fairly general approval, although views differed on how it should be done. The Commission, the French, and the Italians were inclined to favour a faster reduction of trade barriers during the first stage, while economic conditions were favourable, but were reluctant to commit themselves beyond the first stage.[43]

In November, while the Rey Committee was still trying to thrash out some kind of agreement on the Commission's proposals, the French considerably embarrassed their Benelux partners by endorsing the idea of an acceleration in the reduction of

---

[42] Under the Treaty of Rome the first *rapprochement* in the external tariffs was not to be made until the end of the first stage of the transition period. It was in fact made in January 1961, a year earlier than the treaty required.

[43] The Benelux countries were anxious not to complicate negotiations with the other European countries, which changing the arrangements for the first four years seemed likely to do.

tariffs on trade among the Six, but coupling with it a proposal for simultaneous action on the introduction of the external tariff. In brief, the French proposed that on 1 July 1960 the internal tariffs should be cut by 20 per cent. instead of the 10 per cent. required on that date and that the first *rapprochement* of national tariffs to the common tariff should be made on the same date.[44] There was irrefutable logic in the French argument that if internal tariffs were to be reduced on 1 July 1960 to the level the treaty had stipulated for the end of December 1961, the action on the external tariff required on that date should also be taken and the first move made towards the common tariff. But in the eyes of the Benelux countries this was even worse than the plan the Commission had been advocating, since it would mean creating (on 1 July 1960) an even greater difference between the tariffs the Six applied on trade with one another and the tariffs they applied on trade with the other OEEC countries.[45] Furthermore, adoption of the French proposal would mean that the Benelux countries would have to increase, not simply to refrain from decreasing, certain of the tariffs they levied on goods coming from outside the Community.

Shortly thereafter the Dutch countered the French proposals with the so-called Luns Plan. Briefly, the Netherlands Foreign Minister suggested that both European groups should generalize (i.e. extend not only to one another but to all the members of the GATT) the first 20 per cent. cuts in tariffs made within each group, and that the common external tariff of the Six should also be cut by 20 per cent. One reason for linking a reduction in the common external tariff to the suggestion that each group generalize its internal tariff cuts was to make the proposal more attractive to the Seven. The Seven, and the other countries in the GATT, were bound to receive the benefits of the reductions that the high tariff countries made when aligning their rates with the common tariff and, therefore, if no reduction was made in the level of the common external tariff the Seven would be 'paying' for something they would eventually receive, in large measure, in any case.[46] The Dutch proposal 'expressed the wish' that the main trading

[44] See Treaty, Article 23.
[45] The Dutch had been opposed even to the Commission's position that no tariff reductions that resulted in tariffs lower than the common tariff should be extended to the other European countries.
[46] The Dutch, of course, were very anxious to have a lower external tariff even apart from the need to make the arrangement more attractive to the Seven.

partners in the GATT, and particularly the United States and Canada, would make cuts in their own tariffs in the course of the forthcoming GATT negotiations (the 'Dillon round') which 'without necessarily being identical' would nevertheless 'constitute a satisfactory concession'.[47]

The Commission's proposals, the French proposals, the Luns proposals, and numerous variations on them were much discussed in Europe during November and December 1959. Within the Six, the Luns Plan was generally felt to go too far in weakening the commitment to the central discipline of the Common Market—the common external tariff—since it would permit the low tariff countries not simply to refrain from starting the process of aligning their tariffs, as desired by the French and the Commission, but to cut further their external tariffs and thus to widen the difference between their national rates and the agreed common rates. There was also little enthusiasm—either in the Six or in the United Kingdom—for handing a 20 per cent. unrequited tariff cut to the other GATT countries and, in particular, to the United States, on the eve of new negotiations. Nevertheless, although there were differences of view about how it should be done, the general idea of some kind of mutual tariff-cutting by the two groups was very much in the air, on both sides of the Channel, as the year ended.

In many ways the discussion among the Six on the tariff question at the end of 1959 paralleled that on quotas the year before. At the end of 1959, as a year earlier, the French were the strongest proponents of the need for some 'Community preference', and in 1959 as in 1958 the Dutch were the most ardent advocates of extending to the other European countries (and if need be to the other members of the GATT) the action taken by the Six with respect to one another. By the end of 1959, however, there was greater confidence than there had been a year earlier that the French were in earnest about the Common Market. Moreover, protectionism now played a smaller part in the French argument. Although it was clear that one element in the French position was a desire for a stronger position *vis-à-vis* potential competitors from third countries there was a greater disposition on the part of the other countries to accept at face value the 'Community' aspect of the French case, and there was considerable agreement with the

---

[47] It is worth noting that Mr. Luns visited London for discussions with British ministers on 20 November 1959, a few days before he put forward his plan.

French argument that adoption of the Luns proposal would, in fact, represent a threat to the integrity of the Community.

Late in November, the Foreign Ministers of the Six met in Strasbourg for three purposes: first, in their capacity as Foreign Ministers, to discuss how to give content to the general feeling that the Six should have more, and more organized, exchanges of view on foreign policy questions; second, in their capacity as the Council of Ministers of the Community, to discuss Community questions, and finally, also in their capacity as the Council of Ministers, to take part in a general exchange of views with the Parliamentary Assembly. In all three sets of meetings the main topics for discussion were the interrelated questions raised by the Wigny Memorandum, by the French and Italian ideas on political co-ordination, by the Commission's proposals, and by the French and Dutch ideas on acceleration.

The Foreign Ministers' discussion on the question of political co-ordination anticipated the lines taken by the Six Governments a year later in response to the somewhat more ambitious proposals made by General de Gaulle (see Chapter IX). The Benelux countries and Germany were worried that, under French leadership, the political consultations would spill over into the defence field and would detract from the primacy of the NATO. The Benelux countries also felt that if the consultations were institutionalized—as the French had suggested, with a Secretary-General and staff in Paris—they would tend to undercut the existing Communities. They saw in this suggestion further evidence of a French desire to enhance national, and particularly French, influence within the Six at the expense of the 'supra-national' concept which for them was the essence of the European endeavour. There was also apprehension, again mainly among the Benelux countries, that the kind of closer co-ordination the French appeared to have in mind would widen the chasm between the Six and the United Kingdom. There was considerable feeling—a feeling which at this time was being actively encouraged by the British—that the WEU (Western European Union) should play a more active role in the relations between the Six and the United Kingdom.[48]

The upshot of the November discussions was an agreement that the Foreign Ministers would meet quarterly, that their discussions would be primarily on problems which grew out of membership

[48] See below, p. 234.

in the European Communities and would not prejudice discussions in the WEU or the NATO, that no formal secretariat would be established but that the meetings of Foreign Ministers would be prepared by officials, and that when discussion bore directly on the work of the Communities, the Commissions would be informed and might be invited to participate in the consultations.[49]

Sr. Pella, in his capacity as Chairman of the Council of Ministers, outlined to the November session of the European Parliamentary Assembly the conclusions the Ministers had finally reached on the controversial question of economic relations with third countries, and with the other European countries in particular. In general these followed the main lines of the Commission's proposals. The decision on quotas clearly reflected the changed balance of payments situations both in Europe and in the United States and the increasing pressure by the United States (and Canada) for an end to discrimination against dollar goods. Sr. Pella announced that the Community would extend to all GATT members increases in quotas for industrial products 'analogous' to those they were to give one another on 1 January 1960. Unlike the Commission's proposal, the Council did not ask for reciprocity on the part of the other European countries, although Sr. Pella pointed out that it would 'appear normal' for the other member countries of the OEEC to take similar measures.

The Council's decision on tariffs was less forthcoming, and did not touch the main point at issue. The next reduction in tariffs under the Treaty of Rome was not called for until 1 July 1960 and the Six were not yet in agreement on the interrelated questions of the speed at which the internal tariffs should be cut and the common external tariff brought into effect. Benelux and the Germans were still resisting any proposal which accentuated the differences between the Six and the other countries or meant an increase in their own low tariffs. The French, supported by the Italians, and with encouragement from the Commission, were advocating accelerating the tariff cuts within the Community but only on condition that the low tariff countries began simultaneously the process of aligning their tariffs with the common external tariff. Given this wide divergence of views, the most that

[49] The text of the Communiqué is contained in the *Bulletin of the European Economic Community*, No. 5, 1959, pp. 77 and 78. For further information see also Sr. Pella's statement to the European Parliamentary Assembly, session of November 1959, *Débats*, pp. 232 ff.

could be agreed was a reaffirmation of the intention of participating in the 'Dillon round' of GATT negotiations with a view to making them as fruitful as possible and a general undertaking that, thereafter, the Six would propose some further reduction of the external tariff provided that reciprocal action was taken by other countries. Sr. Pella also reported that the Six were now in agreement that countries could (permissive not obligatory) extend to third countries the reductions they made among themselves the following July where doing so would *not* result in tariffs below the proposed common external tariff.

The Council of Ministers accepted the Commission's suggestion for a contact committee to study and seek to mitigate any commercial difficulties that arose between the Six and the other OEEC countries. The committee might also see what steps could be taken so that the tariff reductions negotiated in the GATT relieved the worst strains in European trade. The Council also endorsed the Commission's suggestion for regular consultations with the United States and the United Kingdom, but broadened the proposal to include Canada and the other European countries as well. Like the Commission, the Council felt that aid to underdeveloped countries and 'conjuncture' policy might well be the two main subjects for discussion by this group of countries.[50]

Although Sr. Pella assured the Assembly that the Council had not given up the search for closer forms of co-operation with its European partners, he made it clear enough that for the time being the approach he had outlined was the most that could be expected, given the divergent views of the member governments, the obligation to be consistent with international commitments such as the GATT, and the need to be responsive to the changed balance of payments situation of the United States. Although most of the Benelux speakers and some of the Germans pressed for a more forthcoming attitude on trade relations with the Seven, the debate did not focus on the European trade problem as intensively as it had in September but ranged more widely: the proposals for political co-ordination and for strengthening the Communities,

---

[50] At this time there was considerable Community interest in working with the British on aid to the underdeveloped countries. Co-operation on this problem seemed to offer a number of advantages: it would re-establish close contacts, but not on the controversial subject of trade, and it would appeal to the United States, which was trying to get others to take on more of the burden of aiding the developing countries. Moreover, General de Gaulle was known to feel that Europe should be doing more about the underdeveloped countries.

and the need for more and better co-ordinated assistance for the underdeveloped countries were the prominent themes.

At the end of the year the Commission and the Rey Committee were continuing their search for some way of reconciling the sharply conflicting views about the action to be taken on the external tariffs when the next reduction in internal tariffs was made on 1 July 1960. Until a way out of this impasse could be found, the acceleration in the establishment of the Common Market which everyone wanted could not be achieved.

VII

THE EUROPEAN FREE TRADE ASSOCIATION

The decision to form the EFTA

Just as the six countries of the Common Market frequently found themselves taking similar positions in European organizations, such as the Council of Europe and the OEEC, well before the formation of the European Economic Community, so the United Kingdom and the three Scandinavian countries (Denmark, Norway, and Sweden) had a tradition of thinking alike and acting together well before the formation of the EFTA. The split in the Council of Europe between 'federalists' and 'functionalists' was in the main a split between these two groups of countries. And in 1949 the British and Scandinavians had formed UNISCAN, at a time when the Benelux countries, France, and Italy were discussing among themselves the more ambitious, but in the end abortive FINEBEL plan.[1]

During the course of the Maudling Committee negotiations the United Kingdom, the three Scandinavian countries, and frequently Switzerland and Austria as well were generally fairly close together on the key issues, and as the negotiations proceeded a habit of close

---

[1] In the autumn of 1949 Paul Hoffman, the administrator of the Marshall Plan, made a major speech to the OEEC in which he emphasized the importance that the American Administration, and the Congress, attached to progress towards European integration. Partly in response to this speech, a proposal —the so-called FINEBEL plan—for linking the Benelux customs union with the proposed Franco-Italian customs union was revived and some new features added, e.g. suggestions for a high degree of convertibility as between the currencies of the member countries. The British, at about the same time, proposed to the Scandinavian countries an arrangement for freeing certain types of financial transactions and for consultation on certain types of economic questions. Although UNISCAN was, in origin, largely a riposte to FINEBEL and a defensive move to forestall renewed American pressure for further 'integration', the British and the Scandinavians went ahead with UNISCAN even after it was clear that the proposed FINEBEL plan would be still-born and that the OEEC would not pursue the question of a customs union.

consultation developed among these countries, who became known as the 'Other Six'.[2] In particular all these countries wanted the arrangements between the Common Market and the rest of the OEEC countries to take the form of a free trade area, rather than a customs union, although the reasons for their preference differed somewhat from country to country.

A customs union, requiring as it does a common tariff and a common commercial policy, would have raised problems for the neutrals which a free trade area did not. The exact nature of the conflict between a policy of neutrality and membership in a customs union was exhaustively examined by the three neutrals when they came to apply for association with the Community.[3] During the negotiations in the OEEC the strong position taken by the United Kingdom against a customs union and in favour of a free trade area was one the neutrals found congenial, for a free trade area was obviously much easier to reconcile with a policy of neutrality and was an arrangement which, on other grounds as well, they strongly preferred. Two of the neutrals, Sweden and Switzerland, had relatively low tariffs. The industrial structure of these countries had been built up on the assumption that they could import tariff-free, or at very low tariffs, most basic materials and semi-manufactured products, and they were strongly opposed to any raising of their own tariffs, which harmonization with the common tariff of the Six would have meant. The other relatively low tariff countries in the 'outer' group, Denmark and, to a lesser extent, Norway, also were opposed to any arrangement which would have meant an increase in their tariffs. The Austrians, in contrast, had relatively high tariffs and were not particularly troubled by the economic consequences of harmonization. However, they not only shared the doubts of the Swedes and Swiss about the possibility of reconciling a policy of neutrality with participation in a customs union, but were disturbed as well by the political implications of a close economic arrangement with Germany. Moreover, even apart from the implications for their policy of neutrality, the three neutrals, and also Norway, did not want to become caught up politically in the integration movement.

[2] Portugal's problems were rather different in character, and the 'Other Six' did not become the Seven until the free trade area negotiations had broken down. During the life of the Maudling Committee, Portugal was usually grouped with the other less-developed countries—Greece, Turkey, Iceland, and Ireland. This grouping was sometimes called the 'Forgotten Five'.
[3] See Chapter XIV.

And, like the United Kingdom, they did not want to lose any significant measure of control over their own domestic economic policies or their external commercial policies. Switzerland was the extreme case. From the earliest days of the OEEC, the Swiss had been quick to see, and to object to, any infringement of sovereignty, and they continued to be the most reluctant of any of the Seven to undertake commitments that might impinge on their own freedom of action.[4] But all of the Seven strongly preferred a pragmatic, co-operative, evolutionary approach to 'European unity', and they all fundamentally disliked the formal, legalistic, and much more far-reaching approach of the Six.

Denmark tended to be the odd man out. As a low tariff country Denmark preferred a free trade area and was opposed to an upward harmonization of tariffs, but the Danes had fewer objections than the others to the close ties of the Common Market, and they had a very strong agricultural interest in securing and expanding their markets within the Six, particularly in Germany. Denmark's links with the other Scandinavian countries, her economic ties with the United Kingdom (the United Kingdom market was slightly more important than the German market), and a general preference for the looser pragmatic system advocated by the United Kingdom kept her in the 'outer' group. But Denmark was the least enthusiastic advocate of the free trade area of any of the Seven and has always been a rather restless member of the EFTA.

The industrial federations in the 'Other Six' played an active part in encouraging their governments to take some form of collective action. During the early spring of 1958, representatives from the industrial federations and from the employers' organizations had met together a number of times and, in April 1958, they had issued a detailed statement of the kind of trade arrangement they felt should be established on an OEEC-wide basis.[5] Although the principal purpose of the joint statement was to strengthen the negotiating position of their governments *vis-à-vis* the Six, the idea of establishing a free trade area among themselves, if the OEEC negotiations eventually failed, was also discussed, and this possibility was further examined during the autumn as the odds

---

[4] The way power is divided between the Swiss Federal Government and the cantonal governments also made it difficult, and sometimes impossible, for the Swiss to undertake certain kinds of commitments.

[5] *Free Trade in Western Europe*, a joint statement by the Industrial Federations and Employers' Organizations of Austria, Denmark, Norway, Sweden, Switzerland, and the United Kingdom (Paris, 14 April 1958).

lengthened against an OEEC-wide agreement. Although the Federation of British Industries (FBI) appears to have played an important part in the early discussions of a free trade area among the more limited group of countries, the Swedish Federation soon became the most active promoter of the scheme. It was logical that the Swedes, both on the industrial level and later on the governmental level, should have shown the most interest in the plan, for it probably offered them clearer economic advantages than it did any of the other countries. Moreover, for some years the Swedes had been the chief advocates of a Nordic Customs Union, and the problems inherent in freeing trade in that context had been under almost continuous study by Swedish industrial organizations, as well as by government experts.[6]

On 17 December 1958, after informal discussions between representatives of the Federation of British Industries and of the Swedish Federation, a statement was issued calling for the immediate establishment of a trading association among the 'Other Six', using as the starting point the report of the six federations that had been issued the preceding April.[7] During the winter of 1958–9 discussions among the industrial federations continued with the knowledge and tacit approval, if not open support, of the governments.

The possibility of an arrangement among the 'outer' group of countries was apparently first considered by the British Government during the summer of 1958 but, as it was so clearly a 'second-best' arrangement, no very serious consideration was given to the plan at that time. During the early months of 1959, however, there were various exchanges of view among the 'outer' group through normal diplomatic channels and on 21 February high officials from the Seven (Portugal had joined the group) met together in Oslo. Consideration was obviously being given to a plan, but the discussions were well shrouded in secrecy. Mr. Maudling was open-minded, but extremely circumspect, on the wisdom of proceeding with the development of an association

---

[6] The Scandinavian interest in the establishment of a Nordic Customs Union tended to fluctuate with the prospects for wider arrangements. There was some feeling in Sweden, and in the other Scandinavian countries, that a Nordic Customs Union should be pursued, regardless of other developments, in order to strengthen the position of the Nordic countries within a free trade area. But, in the end, negotiations on broader arrangements were given priority and plans for a Nordic Customs Union held in abeyance.

[7] See The Times, 18 December 1958.

among the 'outer' countries during the debate on the failure of the free trade area negotiations, which was held in the House of Commons on 12 February, and it seems clear enough that at this time no decision, in principle, had been taken.[8]

Experts from the 'Outer Seven' met again in Stockholm on 17 and 18 March. By this time it was apparent that there was no prospect of an early, fruitful resumption of negotiations with the Six. Prof. Hallstein, the President of the European Commission, had visited London on 16 February 1959 to discuss the problem of association with British ministers. Thus, although the Commission's *First Memorandum* was not officially considered by the ministers of the Six until mid-March, the general approach which the Commission would recommend was already known in London. Furthermore, the increasingly negative attitude of the French Government to any resumption of negotiations on a free trade area had become clear enough during the bilateral discussions on the quota problem which Sir Paul Gore-Booth, of the Foreign Office, and M. Olivier Wormser, of the Quai d'Orsay, held during the early months of 1959. The Stockholm meeting was less clandestine than the earlier meeting in Oslo, but secrecy as to the details of the discussion was still maintained and efforts in the House of Commons to probe the Government's intentions met with little success. The farthest Mr. Maudling would go in reply to a question about the Stockholm meeting was to confirm that there had been several meetings of a confidential nature.

Following the March meeting in Stockholm, Mr. de Besche, the Swedish Foreign Office official who was acting as the co-ordinator during this phase of the negotiations, visited the capitals of the Seven countries and, on the basis of these discussions, plans for the EFTA were more fully developed. Sometime during May the British Government appears to have taken a decision, in principle, that, provided the remaining technical problems could be satisfactorily solved, the United Kingdom should proceed with the plan for a free trade area among the 'Outer Seven'. By the time officials of the Seven countries met again on 1 June at Saltsjöbaden

[8] 'Finally, it is suggested that we might discuss a getting closer together with some other countries in Europe outside the Six. This idea is being canvassed a good deal in public, and a number of industrial organizations are studying it at some length. . . . There are attractions in this idea, but I think that there might also be disadvantages. All I would say about it now is that it is a matter on which the Government will certainly keep an open mind, and all suggestions of this kind we shall be very glad to examine.' *Hansard*, House of Commons, 12 February 1959, col. 1386.

near Stockholm all attempts to disguise the fact that they were working on a free trade area of the Seven had been abandoned, and the product of their fortnight's work was a draft plan for consideration by their Governments.

The decision to go ahead with the formation of the EFTA was not an easy one for the British Government and the available evidence suggests that it was taken with many misgivings. At the time the decision was made the prospect of an early resumption of fruitful negotiations with the Six was bleak, the British Government was under considerable pressure from the Swedish and the Swiss Governments to agree to the plan, and the British press and British industry were demanding action of some kind.

The press was far from clear what action should be taken but was almost unanimous in feeling that the one thing that the Government should not do was to sit still. British industry was also calling for action, although like the press it was calling rather more loudly than clearly. During the winter of 1958-9 the Federation of British Industries had pursued the project of an 'outer group' with more obvious zeal than had British government officials but there was a reversal of roles as the spring wore on and some feeling on the part of British industry that events were moving unnecessarily quickly. In particular, there was strong industrial opposition to a proposal for a very rapid reduction in tariffs which was at one time considered by government officials. Shortly before the June meetings in Stockholm, the FBI sent an extensive questionnaire to all sections of British industry seeking their views on the project. The detailed answers to this inquiry were not released, but a carefully worded statement, based on the replies to the questionnaire, was issued by the Grand Council of the FBI. From this and other industrial comments it seems clear that there was little real industrial enthusiasm for the plan. The overriding interest of British industry was in finding an acceptable arrangement with the Common Market, and the plan of the Seven was supported, with some misgivings, 'on the basis that every effort should be made to give it a form which will as far as possible assist the negotiation of an acceptable association with the Six'.[9]

However, although by the summer of 1959 industrial enthusiasm for the 'Outer Seven' had somewhat abated, there continued to be industrial pressure on the Government to take action

[9] Federation of British Industries, *European Trade* (mimeographed statement, 17 June 1959).

of some kind. Businessmen inside and outside the Community had accepted the fact that a customs union among the Six would be realized and they were beginning to plan, and to act, accordingly. British industrialists feared not only that there would be a diversion of foreign investment—particularly United States investment—from the United Kingdom to the Six, but also that industrial patterns on the Continent would 'freeze' and thus make their own eventual entry into the market more difficult.[10]

Had the British Government reached the point of seriously considering joining the Six, or even forming a customs union with the Six, the decision to proceed with the EFTA would presumably never have been taken, for by tying itself to a group of low tariff countries and to a number of neutral countries, the United Kingdom was obviously adding to the problems which would have to be settled in a future negotiation in these terms. The major premise of British government thinking was still that a negotiation with the Six in terms of membership, or in terms of a full customs union, would never be undertaken. If one accepted this major premise, but only if one accepted this major premise, the formation of the EFTA was understandable. Proceeding with the EFTA was easier to defend politically than was a policy of simply sitting tight. Moreover it was a way of keeping the 'Other Seven' together, by reducing the pressure some of the smaller countries were under to join the Community or to make a bilateral agreement with the Six. Of the 'outer countries', only Denmark had, by this time, seriously considered joining the Common Market, but it was reasonable to suppose that some of the others would have come to some arrangement with the Six had no alternative been in sight.

There were a number of reasons why the British wanted to keep other countries from being drawn into the orbit of the Six. The Scandinavian countries and Switzerland, although small countries, were fairly important to the British in trade terms, and there was an understandable reluctance to see any worsening in the British export position. In addition, the countries that would be under the most domestic pressure to reach agreement with the Six were, by definition, those whose trade with the Common Market was particularly important. Much of the pressure on the Six that the Seven together might exert, by discriminating

[10] This was a well-founded fear. The newspapers were full of reports of new industrial link-ups between industries in the Six countries.

collectively against the Six, would be lost if these countries made separate deals. Furthermore, once some countries began making bilateral agreements with the Six, others would be tempted to follow suit and, if that happened, a multilateral association would soon become impossible. Instead of a broad free trade area in which each country maintained similar relations with every other country within the group, a new pattern of trading would be established based on an inner group of countries (the Six) at the centre of the web, with ties radiating out to the surrounding countries. The resulting network of bilateral agreements would not only discriminate against the United Kingdom, but would tend to increase trade with the Six at the expense of the considerable trade carried on by the 'outer' countries with one another. The political implications of such an arrangement were also unwelcome to the British, for the tightening of the economic links between the Six and the other countries of Western Europe would inevitably have tended to increase the political magnetism of the Six, largely at the expense of the United Kingdom.[11]

A number of other arguments were also put forward in favour of the EFTA plan. It was argued—and by some of the Six as well as by the Seven—that the economic pressure it would bring to bear on the Six would increase their interest in a settlement. This was a somewhat doubtful argument, since the economic pressure was exerted, for the most part, on the wrong people: on the Germans, the Belgians, and the Dutch, who were anxious for a broader agreement, rather than on the French who were not. Moreover the line between the desire to induce the Six to negotiate by bringing economic pressure to bear upon them and the urge to retaliate is an almost impossible line to draw. After the collapse of the Maudling Committee negotiations the air was thick with talk of retaliation and when the discussions among the Seven began there was undoubtedly a strong element of reprisal in the scheme. The human urge to hit back was suppressed at a fairly early stage by those in the United Kingdom who were concerned with the EFTA negotiations, but seems to have been a rather stronger and more long-lived motive on the part of some of the Swedes and the Swiss. This is not surprising, for a much higher percentage of the trade of these two countries was carried on with the Six and the problem of the creation of a large free

[11] About this time both Greece and Turkey were showing interest in becoming associated with the Six.

trade area was regarded in more purely commercial terms by them than it was, by this time, by the British. The Danish Government was, if anything, even more anxious than the British Government to eradicate any smell of economic warfare from the plan. But the retaliatory aura of the plan could not be entirely dispelled.

Another argument of rather doubtful value that was sometimes advanced for proceeding with the plan was that it would demonstrate to the Six that a free trade area—as well as a customs union—was a workable arrangement. The desire to prove they were right undoubtedly influenced the British, but it probably had rather more effect on the nature of the EFTA convention than on the decision to go ahead with the plan. Moreover it should have been plain that the demonstration was not apt to make much dent on the thinking of the Six. The composition of the Seven and the preponderant position of the United Kingdom within the group seriously limited the validity of the example. In addition, and of more importance, it was clear that the Six were by this time far less troubled by the technical difficulties of a free trade area than they were by other aspects of the plan. To those who, in effect, wanted a Treaty of Rome on a seventeen-country basis, the technical feasibility of a free trade area was irrelevant.

There was another, rather more plausible, argument put forward in support of the view that the formation of the EFTA would improve the prospects for an agreement with the Six. One of the strongest objections of the 'Europeans' to the original free trade area scheme was that, regardless of intention, it would tend to undercut the Common Market and to 'dissolve' it in the larger, looser arrangement. By the formation of a second group the way would be opened to a free trade area between the Common Market of the Six on the one hand, and the free trade area of the Seven on the other. Such an arrangement, it was argued, would be less of a threat to the integrity of the Treaty of Rome than the original plan. The Six could agree among themselves and the Seven among themselves, according to their own methods, on those matters that concerned only trade within each group and on such other economic activities as each group chose to undertake. Rules and procedures to govern the trade between the two groups would have to be agreed between them. The fact that the Seven were a free trade area with liberal rules of origin would raise familiar problems, and the result might well be that less trade was freed between the two groups than was freed within each group. But the 'discrimination' that would result might be easier to accept because it would be mutual, and the very fact that it was mutual would, in itself, create a pressure tending towards eventual parity of treatment. Similarly, it would be easier to adopt one of the early French proposals, that of a *décalage*, in this new framework: although trade within each of the two groups could be liberalized at the same rate, trade between the two groups could be liberalized at a somewhat slower rate.

There were a number of difficulties with this idea of an agreement between two dissimilar groups, as the abortive efforts at 'bridge-building' subsequently revealed. In particular, so long as the United Kingdom was a member of the EFTA the fear of the 'Europeans' that some of their members would be attracted to the looser arrangement remained valid. Nevertheless, as discussed further below, the idea of a link between two groups continued to find favour in some of the smaller EFTA countries long after it had been abandoned (as inadequate as well as non-negotiable) by the British Government.

The EFTA plan was also defended on its economic merits, but the conviction with which this argument was made varied greatly from country to country. In the United Kingdom the economic argument was put forward half-heartedly and somewhat defensively, for reasons that were all too plain. The advantages to be gained by countries like Sweden and Switzerland from a reduction in the relatively high British tariff were far greater than those the British could expect from reductions in the already low tariffs of their much smaller partners. The Austrians were frankly worried by the economic aspects of the plan: their exports went overwhelmingly to the Six rather than to the Seven and their tariffs were high. The EFTA promised competition for industries that might well need protection without the same prospect for expansion of their traditional exports as had the OEEC-wide free trade arrangement. The Norwegians were also worried about the ability of their industries to withstand the competition and were, at best, circumspect about where the net economic advantage lay. The Danes were perhaps the most doubtful about the economic advantages of the plan: the scales were finally tipped in favour of the plan by British tariff concessions on bacon and cheese and by the assurances the Danes received from the Germans that traditional Danish agricultural exports to Germany would not suffer if they joined the EFTA. (See p. 221 below.) The economic advantages were clearest in the case of Sweden. Freer access to the large British market was also attractive to Switzerland, although geography and traditional ties made Swiss trade relations with the Six relatively more important.

Although the Swedes might have been prepared to go ahead with the EFTA plan simply for the economic gains it promised, it seems clear that none of the others would have done so unless they had persuaded themselves that by so doing they were strengthening their individual bargaining power and increasing the chances of getting the kind of accommodation with the Six that they all wanted. Despite the mounting evidence to the contrary, the British and their partners still hoped that, in time, the Six would be prepared to negotiate in terms that were not substantially different from those under discussion when the Maudling Committee negotiations broke down.

Once the decision to go ahead with the formation of the EFTA had been taken by the British Government, the negotiations proceeded very rapidly. In these negotiations, the British consistently took the position that the plan should be as simple and as automatic as possible and to many on the Continent they seemed not to be beginning where the Maudling Committee negotiations had left off but to be reverting to the approach typified by their original White Paper. There were a number of reasons why the British favoured a simple plan. 'Integration' was not the goal of any of the EFTA countries. Moreover, at least for the British, there was much less to be gained (and freedom of action to be lost) from co-ordinating policies with the small EFTA countries than there would have been from co-ordinating policy and action with a group that included the large European countries. Finally, of course, there was the desire to demonstrate the validity of the free trade area concept.

The most difficult aspect of the negotiation was that of finding a way of making the plan attractive to the Danes. Having insisted on a separate arrangement for agriculture in the Maudling Committee, the British were clearly not going to agree to include agriculture on the same basis as industry in the EFTA; nor, for that matter, would others of the Seven, e.g. the Swiss, have been willing to do so. On the other hand, it soon became apparent that the general undertakings on agricultural policies and objectives that the British were ready to write into the Stockholm Convention were not considered adequate by the Danish Government, which was under considerable pressure from its farmers to join the Six. To make the EFTA arrangement more attractive, the British (and some of the other EFTA countries) made bilateral agreements with the Danes. Briefly, the United Kingdom agreed to eliminate its 10 per cent. *ad valorem* tariff on bacon imports from Denmark (and from the other countries in the area) in two stages: a 50 per cent. reduction in the tariffs to be made on 1 July 1960 and the tariff to be completely eliminated a year later. The British also agreed to eliminate a few other less important tariffs.[12] In addition, the British Government assured the Danes that it would not nullify the effect of the tariff cut on bacon by changes in subsidies and that, more generally, it 'did not intend to adopt policies likely to deny to Danish producers the opportunity to maintain their market in the United Kingdom for commodities of concern to them, or to share in any increase in the United Kingdom market for those products".[13]

Before finally deciding to join the EFTA, the Danes also satisfied themselves that the Germans would not regard Denmark's participation in the free trade association as an unfriendly act but would continue to implement the understanding reached earlier in the year to the effect that for the next three years, at least, the Danes could expect to receive their fair share of any increases in German agricultural quotas.

Ministers from the Seven countries met at Saltsjöbaden near Stockholm on 21–22 July 1959 and—after some strenuous arguments—approved with a few minor alterations the plan that government officials had elaborated during their lengthy conference early in June. This draft plan, together with the communiqué issued at the end of the ministerial meeting, contained the main principles of the final Convention.[14] A considerable amount of hard bargaining on the precise formulation of the detailed provisions, and in particular on the rules of origin, took place during the autumn when the officials met again to cast the general principles into formal treaty provisions.[15] But the disagreements

[12] It was agreed that the tariff on canned pork luncheon meat (5 per cent. on some types; 10 per cent. on others) would be abolished in two steps and that the 10 per cent. tariffs on canned cream and blue-veined cheese would be eliminated in one step on 1 July 1960.

[13] *Financial Times*, 9 July 1959.

[14] The Draft Plan and communiqué were issued as a White Paper, *Stockholm Draft Plan for a European Free Trade Association* (Cmnd. 823, July 1959, H.M.S.O.).

[15] The negotiations on the origin rules were difficult and time-consuming and

and the bargaining were, for the most part, on details, not on principles.

The most controversial question that arose during the autumn was the treatment to be given to frozen fish fillets. Although the principle of applying the basic provisions for freeing trade to industrial products alone had been accepted by the other members of the Seven, the Danes had agreed only because of the British tariff concessions on bacon, blue-veined cheese, and canned cream, and the Norwegians and, to a lesser extent, the other Scandinavians and the Portuguese, felt strongly that the British should make some concessions on fish as well. In the case of Norway, in particular, a good argument could be made that the arrangement would be badly unbalanced if the Norwegians opened their markets to industrial goods from Britain and the other countries, without obtaining some improvement in trading arrangements for their principal export—fish. The British apparently agreed at a fairly early stage that processed and tinned fish should be treated as industrial products, and the Norwegians recognized at a fairly early date that they stood no chance of having fresh fish treated as an industrial product. The controversy centred on frozen fish and more particularly on frozen fish fillets. Ultimately the British largely conceded this point, although not until the final meeting of the ministers in Stockholm in November.[16]

A seemingly disproportionate amount of time and energy is always consumed—in any negotiation—on questions like the treatment to be given frozen fish fillets. However, the fact that problems related to agriculture and fish were so troublesome and were only settled because the British made concessions was of some general importance, for it underlined the need for the British to

---

were not completely finished until after the signature of the Convention. Despite the fact that the basic criteria could be simply and briefly described in the Convention, the document setting forth the definitions, process tests etc. is a brochure of 133 pages, *European Free Trade Association. Text of Schedules to Annex B to Convention approved at Stockholm on 20th November 1959* (Cmnd. 906–1, H.M.S.O.).

[16] The British finally agreed to regard frozen fish fillets as industrial products but retained the right to have the question reconsidered if at any time it appeared that imports from Scandinavia would exceed 24,000 tons a year or if there were a change in the competitive conditions of the industry, by which was meant, presumably, any extension in fishing limits by the Norwegians. See *The Times*, 21 November 1959. British imports of frozen fish fillets from Scandinavia in 1958 were about 6,500 tons.

re-examine the assumption that agriculture could be treated as a special case in any future negotiation on European trading arrangements.[17]

The Stockholm Convention

The Stockholm Convention is readily available and there is, therefore, no need to summarize it here in any detail. The schedule of tariff reductions was designed to enable the Seven to catch up with the Six by 1 July 1960 and thereafter to keep in step with the Six.[18] In part to ensure parallelism with the Six and in part so that the Seven could, at some later stage, increase their economic pressure on the Six, provision was also made for accelerating tariff cuts, either across-the-board, or by categories, or by particular countries. Unlike the Treaty of Rome (but like what has, in fact, proved to be the practice of the Six), the Stockholm Convention provided for flat cuts in each tariff position rather than permitting a measure of flexibility. Not surprisingly, the origin rules followed the general lines advocated by the British (and others of the Seven) in the Maudling Committee negotiations: a 50 per cent. value added test, processing tests, and a basic materials list. The only notable backsliding from a fairly 'liberal' approach was in the case of textiles, where a more restrictive cumulative processing test was agreed.

Examination of the likelihood of deflexions of trade and discussion of the means of averting deflexions of trade had consumed many thousands of man-hours during the Maudling Committee negotiations with little to show for the effort. The Stockholm Convention, rather ostentatiously, put its faith in the adequacy of the origin controls to prevent trade deflexions and in the goodwill of the member countries to meet any difficulties that might arise. The Council was to keep the general operation of the origin control system under surveillance and if any state believed that deflexion of trade had occurred and was causing injury to one of its industries it had a right of recourse to the Council.[19] The

---

[17] The British also made a concession to the Portuguese on wine: in the next Budget the duty on port was reduced.

[18] A special, slower, timetable was agreed for Portugal, which was given until 1980 to eliminate all tariffs. The arrangements applying to Portuguese tariffs and quotas are set out in Annex 9 of the Convention.

[19] The Council may amend the rules of origin or deal with the cause of deflexion 'by such other means as it may consider appropriate'. This language was presumably meant to include the possibility of tariff harmonization. When considering a complaint from a member state that trade deflexion is occurring,

closely allied problem of tariff autonomy which gave rise to so much acrimony in the Maudling Committee negotiations was also dealt with in a deliberately simple, pragmatic manner. The EFTA countries agreed that, 'in so far as practicable' they would notify the Council thirty days in advance of any tariff changes and would consider any comments made by their partners. They affirmed their desire not to cause difficulty for one another and provided a right of recourse to the Council in the event of difficulties nevertheless arising. It is worth noting that by the end of 1962, no case of trade deflexion had been referred to the Council. Although minor improvements and simplifications in the system had been made, no situation had arisen requiring the Council either to modify the origin rules to an important extent or to propose a harmonization of tariffs.

The Convention provided for the total elimination of quotas as well as of tariffs by the end of the transition period and followed the example of the Six in adopting a system for annual increases in quotas. It is worth noting, however, that, under the control of the Council acting by a majority vote, the temporary retention or the temporary re-imposition of quotas was clearly envisaged as a means of giving protection to vulnerable industries during the transition period. It is also worth pointing out that the EFTA countries recognized that the 'legality' of quotas had been altered by the greater convertibility of currencies and that the pressure that had already begun to build up in the GATT for the complete elimination of quotas was bound to be intensified. Accordingly the Convention provided that the Council should review the quota provisions not later than 31 December 1961.[20]

In view of the arguments in the Maudling Committee, the EFTA provisions on exceptions and the arrangements for consultations and complaints are also worthy of comment. One of the broad generalizations on which there was universal agreement in the Maudling Committee was that the simpler and more auto-

---

the Council by majority decision may authorize the member state to take safeguard measures for not more than two months; these can be exceptionally extended by the Council for a second two months.

[20] The provisions on global quotas appear to permit, but not to require, that global quotas may be open to third states as well as to member countries, provided the member countries obtained the general increase in their own trade provided by the basic rules. See Article 10, paragraph 5. Quotas, although not yet entirely abolished, have been eliminated (or their restrictive effect has been reduced) more quickly than the Convention required.

matic the plan for freeing trade, the greater the need for the possibility of resort to escape clauses. Put another way, countries forming a free trade area or a customs union can either attempt to foresee the difficulties that will arise when trade is freed and include provisions in the basic agreement to forestall, or compensate for, these developments; or they can keep the basic rules simple and provide a procedure for making adjustments if difficulties, in fact, arise. The Stockholm Convention relied heavily on dealing with difficulties when they arose rather than on anticipating them. The difficulties that may be expected to arise can, very broadly, be classed in two groups. First, there are difficulties that a country may experience as a result of its own action in reducing tariffs or enlarging quotas. In this case the Convention provided for recourse to 'an escape clause' permitting a country to derogate from its obligations. Second, there are difficulties, or what might be called 'unfair disadvantages' (or the frustration of anticipated benefits), that may arise not from a country's own removal of tariffs and quotas, but from action, or lack of action, on the part of other members. In this case the recourse was to the 'complaints procedure' and the remedy usually consisted in action by the country complained against, coupled, in urgent cases, with safeguarding action (i.e. resort to escape clauses) by the country bringing the complaint.

The Stockholm Convention also distinguished between balance of payments difficulties and the difficulties for particular sectors or regions that might arise from the freeing of trade. In the case of balance of payments difficulties, countries retained the unilateral right to reimpose quantitative restrictions 'consistently with its other international obligations', although the Council by majority vote might 'make recommendations designed to moderate any damaging effect of these restrictions or to assist the Member State concerned to overcome its difficulties'.[21] There was a somewhat tighter control over the resort to escape clauses in the event of difficulties in a particular region or sector of an industry, although the provisions finally agreed appear to be rather looser than the principles laid down in the draft plan. It is clear that the British desire for a simple, clean, automatic system with very limited and

[21] See Article 19. This article also provided that if the balance of payments difficulty persisted for more than eighteen months and seriously disturbed the operation of the Association, the Council acting by majority decision might 'devise special procedures to attenuate or compensate for the effect of such measures'.

tightly controlled resort to escape clauses was not fully shared by the other countries and that some of the 'purity' of the draft plan was lost in the negotiations on the Convention.[22] Although it was assumed that in most cases there would be prior consultation before action was taken, the Convention permitted member states to take unilateral action and to cut back imports to the level of the previous year if there were an appreciable rise in unemployment in a particular industrial sector or geographic region, provided the unemployment had been caused by increased imports arising from trade liberalization. These restrictions could not, however, be continued for more than eighteen months without the authorization of the Council. As in other places in the Convention, the Council was given wide powers to suggest modifications in the form of the restrictions or the adoption of other measures to achieve the same end. Somewhat surprisingly, the Council by majority vote could authorize a member state to reduce tariffs at a rate different from the basic rates laid down in the Convention if it found that difficulties of the kind described were liable to result from the country's adhering to the schedule of tariff reduction in the Convention. This is analogous to the power given to the Council to authorize a member state to depart from the annual 20 per cent. increases in quotas. Together, these two provisions represented a substantial departure from the British ideal of a completely automatic, irreversible system of trade liberalization.

As indicated above, where any state felt that it was being denied a benefit conferred by the Convention or that any of the objectives of the Association were being frustrated (by trade deflexion, by cartel action, by subsidy, etc.), recourse to the 'complaints procedure' was provided. The Council was to be informed of the difficulty and it could either itself examine the complaint or refer it to an independent examining committee. In the light of the evidence produced, the Council might make to any member state, by majority vote, 'such recommendations as it considers appropriate', and if these recommendations were not adopted it could authorize a member state to suspend measures of trade liberalization *vis-à-vis* the recalcitrant state.

From these brief comments on the main features of the Convention it is clear that in the EFTA the role of the Council is all-

---

[22] For example, in defining the kind of situations justifying resort to an escape clause, the draft plan spoke of 'a spectacular decrease in internal demand', the Convention refers to a 'substantial decrease'.

THE EUROPEAN FREE TRADE ASSOCIATION 227

important.[23] Practically all the features of the Convention, except the commitment to abolish all tariffs and quotas by the end of the transition period, can be modified by the Council acting unanimously, and many of the details concerning escape-clause action and the action to be taken on complaints are left to the Council to determine, by majority vote, as the need arises and in the light of circumstances prevailing at the time.

One final provision of the Convention should be mentioned, that is, the right of any member to withdraw on twelve months' notice. This provision, perhaps more than any other, underlined the fact that the EFTA was, for all its members, an arrangement that was thought to be transitional to another arrangement—an agreement with the Six—and not, as in the case of the Treaty of Rome, the beginning of a process of economic integration from which, logically as well as contractually, there could be no withdrawal.

Largely at Swiss initiative, the ministers from the Seven countries adopted a resolution on relations with the Six at the same time as they initialled the text of the EFTA Convention. Although only a page long, this resolution was in a sense the reply of the Seven to the two reports on association produced by the Commission of the Community. The resolution began by pointedly underlining the more than ten years of successful cooperation in the OEEC and drawing attention to the fact that the OEEC had not only played a large part in Europe's post-war expansion but had had 'beneficial effects far beyond Europe' by creating the conditions for the progressive elimination of restrictions on trade with third countries.

The Seven then declared their determination 'to do all in their power to avoid a new division in Europe' and stated that they regarded their Association 'as a step towards an agreement between all member countries of OEEC'. They concluded by indicating their readiness to negotiate as soon as the Six were prepared to do so. They also gave a fairly broad hint about the kind of arrangement they had in mind. Although not explicitly described, this would appear to have been the idea that was then current in British official circles of a free trade area link between the Common Market of the Six and the free trade area of the

---

[23] Each member state is represented on the Council and each has one vote. A majority vote requires four affirmative votes. The Council can meet either at the ministerial or at the official level.

Seven with, perhaps, a measure of tariff harmonization between the two groups.[24]

The Seven, understandably enough, were clearly not disposed to allow Prof. Hallstein to pre-empt for the Common Market the role of apostle of freer world trade and of champion of the under-developed countries. And the 'liberalism' of the Seven was emphasized even more strongly in a communiqué which was issued, at the same time as the Resolution, at the end of the November ministerial meeting. This read in part:

As world trading nations, the countries of the European Free Trade Association are particularly conscious of Europe's links with the rest of the world. They have therefore chosen a form of economic co-opera-tion which, while strengthening Europe, enables them to take full account of the interests of other trading countries throughout the world, in-cluding those facing special problems of development. The Association is a further expression of the post-war drive towards lower trade barriers, and reflects the principles which have been established by the General Agreement on Tariffs and Trade (GATT). The individual freedom of action of EFTA members in their external tariffs will allow each of them to participate actively in GATT negotiations for tariff reductions.[25]

Like the Six, the Seven obviously had one eye on the United States.

By the time the Stockholm Convention was actually signed, some of the support the plan had commanded earlier in the year in the United Kingdom had evaporated. There was surprisingly little criticism of the Government's decision to go ahead with the EFTA (apart from criticism from the paper industry[26] and from a

---

[24] The Resolution read in part: 'Such an agreement, based on the principle of reciprocity, should not cause any damage to the measures taken by the European Free Trade Association and the European Economic Community. More-over, it should allow member States of either organisation to eliminate in common the obstacles to trade between them, and more generally, to seek to solve the problems they share. Among those, there is the problem of aiding the less developed countries in Europe and in other continents, which is one of the foremost tasks of the more advanced countries.

'Common action in these fields would strengthen the already existing bonds between the European countries as well as the solidarity arising from their common destiny, even if their views on the way in which European integration should be achieved are not always identical.'

[25] The White Paper (Cmnd. 906, November 1959) which gives the text of the Stockholm Convention also contains the communiqué and the Resolution.

[26] The paper industry had not liked the original OEEC free trade area plan but it had been restrained in its criticisms because it felt the plan was in the

few other industries that were particularly likely to be affected) but there was also very little positive enthusiasm for the arrangement, and increasingly the EFTA was looked upon in the United Kingdom, at least, as a holding operation.

The debate in the House of Commons on the motion to approve the Government's action in establishing the EFTA was rather poorly attended and all the speakers were much more interested in debating the prospects for an agreement with the Six (most of the speakers were not very sanguine) than they were in discussing the EFTA.[27] The Labour Party, having urged the Government to consider action with the rest of the Seven earlier in the year, was in no position to attack the Government. However, Labour speakers expressed considerable scepticism about the pure free trade area form given to the Convention, both on economic grounds and because they felt it would not improve the chances of negotiations with the Six, and they abstained in the final vote.[28] The Chancellor of the Exchequer (Mr. Heathcoat Amory), opening the debate for the Government, gave four reasons for the belief that the EFTA would facilitate agreement with the Six: the Seven, by acting as a group, should dispose of the fear that the non-members of the Common Market were anxious to sink the identity of the Common Market in a wider association; the Convention was written so that the Seven could keep pace with the Six and this would make an agreement technically easy; the EFTA would demonstrate that a free trade area, as contrasted with a customs union, was a practicable proposition; and it would demonstrate that the Seven, like the Six, were not afraid of free trade. None of these arguments seemed to impress the House and the doubts expressed by Roy Jenkins, who opened for the Opposition, were well founded: 'I have a feeling that in negotiating the EFTA we have been too much concerned with showing the Six that what they rejected is a perfectly workable arrangement. I think that the EFTA will be perfectly workable, but I do not believe that in the last resort the Six rejected the Free Trade Area

---

national interest, despite the fact that the paper industry might suffer. The paper industry felt the general benefits of the EFTA were not important enough to warrant restraint.

[27] See *Hansard*, House of Commons, 14 December 1959, cols. 1055–1180.

[28] The Liberals divided the House; they felt the Government should have gone further in trying 'to associate' with the Common Market. The vote was 185–3 in favour of the Government motion approving the EFTA.

because they thought it would not work. They rejected it because, whether it worked or not, it was not what they wanted.' He, Mr. Thorneycroft (whose comment presumably had more impact on the Government), and a number of other speakers argued that the free trade area idea was dead and that the Government should be thinking in new terms, and specifically in terms of a considerable measure of tariff harmonization.[29]

Although there were considerable doubts about the contribution that the EFTA would make to 'bridge-building', it is worth noting that there was very little feeling in the United Kingdom that by joining the EFTA the Government was needlessly complicating its own future negotiations with the Six. This, in itself, was evidence of the fact that few people were yet ready to contemplate any very far-reaching arrangements with the Six, for it was not hard to see that the United Kingdom was limiting its own freedom of action in any subsequent negotiation with the Community by undertaking new contractual obligations and by substantially increasing its moral commitment to negotiate—if not necessarily collectively—at least in very close co-operation with its EFTA partners.[30]

The ways in which the existence of the EFTA affected the search for a settlement with the Six are discussed in later chapters. Although there is room for disagreement about whether the formation of the EFTA was a move towards or a move away from the goal of an agreement with the Six, it is clear that the EFTA, as an organization, has worked satisfactorily within the limits it set for itself. Quotas and tariffs have been removed somewhat more quickly than the Convention required; the origin controls have operated smoothly; the few problems that have arisen in connexion with the implementation of the Convention have been settled amicably; the modest institutional arrangements have functioned efficiently and unobtrusively. In March 1961 an agreement creating an Association between the member states of the European Free Trade Association and Finland was signed in Helsinki, the product of many months of ticklish negoti-

---

[29] Mr. Thorneycroft was at this time a Conservative back-bencher. It is worth noting that he pointed out that the problem was essentially a political one and that he urged the Government not to be afraid of common institutions.

[30] The author was one of the very few people to make this point at the time, although, later, it became a commonplace. See, for example, *The Listener*, 'Stockholm: Bridge or Barrier?', 31 December 1959.

ation.[31] However, although the member countries have been well satisfied with the functioning of EFTA as an institution it is fair to say that the EFTA has not captured the imaginations of the public in the member countries and that the EFTA 'concept', unlike the Community concept, has had little emotional appeal. In the United Kingdom spasmodic attempts were made by the Government and by private groups to generate greater popular support for and industrial interest in the EFTA, but they met with little success.[32] Attempts to encourage British businessmen to exploit the opportunities opened up by the EFTA were also rather disappointing. It is not without significance that during the three years 1960, 1961, and 1962, when the United Kingdom was competing at a tariff disadvantage in the markets of the Six and with a tariff advantage in the markets of the Seven (for two and a half of the three years), exports to the EEC rose by 55 per cent. while exports to the EFTA went up by only 33 per cent.[33]

[31] The agreement in effect established a free trade area between Finland and the EFTA, supervised by a Joint Council. The schedule of tariff reductions was similar to that in the EFTA convention, although for some items Finland was allowed a slower rate of tariff reduction. Finland was also permitted to maintain certain quotas on balance of payments grounds. For the texts of the agreement see *Agreement creating an Association between the Member States of the European Free Trade Association and the Republic of Finland* (Cmnd. 1335, H.M.S.O., April 1961).

The agreement can be terminated by Finland or by the member states of the EFTA (acting by a decision of the Council) at three months' notice.

[32] For example, in the autumn of 1960 the United Kingdom Council of the European Movement organized a three-day conference of government and business leaders from the Seven. The Conference was well attended but it did not succeed in creating more than a passing public interest in the EFTA.

[33] During the latter part of this period the expectation that the United Kingdom would join the Six presumably strongly affected the direction of trade.

VIII

'BRIDGE-BUILDING' AND THE
REORGANIZATION OF THE OEEC

In the late autumn of 1959, one year after the breakdown in the OEEC negotiations, the relationship between the Six and the other European countries could be described as follows. There were now two groups: the six Common Market countries on the one hand, the seven EFTA countries on the other. The remaining OEEC countries were not formally aligned with either group although Greece and Turkey had indicated their desire to become associated with the Six, and Finland (not an OEEC country) had been in close touch with the EFTA developments. The OEEC itself was in the doldrums. The Council had not met at ministerial level since the stormy meeting on 15 December 1958. Work on a technical level on problems unrelated to the central issue of the relationship between the two groups was continuing but there was little real feeling of purpose or importance left in the Organization.

Within the Community the first cuts in tariffs and increases in quotas required by the Treaty of Rome had been implemented uneventfully. The fear that the Government of General de Gaulle would emasculate the treaties had yielded to a cautious optimism that a way could be found to work with the de Gaulle Government. French industry had clearly come to accept the Common Market and General de Gaulle was obviously ready to continue the policy of solidarity with Germany laid down by his predecessors. Furthermore, although the French were proving to be difficult partners in the NATO, the welcome given to President Eisenhower by the Government as well as the people of France during his visit to Paris in September 1959 had somewhat allayed fears that the de Gaulle Government would put an unbearable strain on the NATO alliance. Although General de Gaulle appeared to see in the Community of the Six an opportunity for establishing France as the leader of the Continent—which was not the concept of the 'Europeans'—the predominant feeling at this time in

'European' circles was that it might nevertheless be possible to take advantage of the favourable economic climate and to move ahead more quickly than the treaty had stipulated, at least with the formation of the customs union. Part of the price of French co-operation in building the Community was, however, a stronger opposition to 'bridge-building' with the Seven than many in the Benelux countries and in Germany were ready to accept. And by the end of the year (1959) the differences of view among the Six on the question of relations with the British and the other European countries threatened the plans of the 'Europeans' for speeding up the formation of the Common Market.

Once the Seven had completed their own plan, the smaller EFTA countries were anxious to begin 'bridge-building'. The British were more circumspect. They were in no mood to begin another round of negotiations until the prospects for success were good. And, at the end of 1959, the attitude of the French Government, the attitude of the Commission, and the support being given by the United States to the Commission's advocacy of 'globalism' made success very unlikely.

In a number of respects the principal countries were further apart by the end of 1959 than they had been a year earlier when the negotiations in the Maudling Committee broke down. Not only were they now formally organized into two groups, but the differences in approach that had been latent throughout the free trade area negotiations had been sharpened by the developments during the intervening year. The fact that for almost a year both European groups had been primarily concerned with furthering their own plans and contact between them had been spasmodic also contributed to the divergent ways in which they tended to view the problem of an accommodation.

Within the Six, even the strongest advocates of a wider arrangement felt that the argument that the creation of the Seven would demonstrate the feasibility of a free trade area was utterly irrelevant. Moreover, even the least 'European'-minded among the Six felt that the Community and the EFTA were different kinds of organization, and the tendency of the Seven to equate the two was resented and dismissed as fresh evidence of a lack of understanding of the basic purpose of the Six. The Commission and many other 'Europeans' had already begun to question the validity of *any* form of association (short of full membership in the Community), particularly with respect to the United Kingdom. And the de Gaulle Government appeared to be opposed to any arrangement that would increase the British presence on the Continent and thus diminish the role that General de Gaulle felt belonged to France.

However, despite the differences in outlook between the two groups, much of the bitterness and animosity that had existed at the time of the breakdown in the OEEC negotiation had been dissipated. This was partly the effect of time and partly the result of a deliberate attempt on the part of the British Government— after the Conservatives were returned to power in the General Election in October 1959—to improve relations and to strengthen political ties with the Six and with General de Gaulle and Dr. Adenauer in particular. On 11 and 12 November (1959) the Foreign Secretary (then Mr. Selwyn Lloyd) visited Paris and a week later Dr. Adenauer visited London. Ministers from the Benelux countries and Italy also visited London towards the end of the year. The fact that the Six had begun, however tentatively, to explore closer political ties among themselves clearly contributed to the British desire to draw closer to the Six politically, and the discussions in the autumn yielded not only a better political atmosphere but, at British initiative, an understanding that more use would be made of the Western European Union (WEU) as a way of keeping the British and the Six in closer touch politically. The British suggested that the WEU headquarters be moved from London to Paris and tried to extract a firm commitment from the Six that when political discussions among the Six strayed beyond the strict confines of the Treaty of Rome, the discussions would be held in the WEU (or, in some instances, in the NATO Council) rather than on the narrower Six-country basis.[1] Although the

---

[1] Mr. Profumo, then Minister of State at the Foreign Office, confirmed to the Assembly of the WEU in November 1959 that since the election the British Government had been 'examining each facet of our relations with the Governments of the Six-power Communities to see where they can be improved' and that Britain was 'determined to draw closer to Europe'. Commenting on the plans of the Six for closer political consultation, he told the Assembly: 'Although we do not think it is in the interests of the alliance as a whole to form a WEU block within the NATO Council, we consider WEU . . . has a distinctive part to play. . . . To be frank, the reasons our minds have been particularly directed to this now is because of the talk of political consultations among the Six. Let me emphasize we are in no way opposed to these provided they are not exclusive. But we think it would be a mistake for the Six, as much as for WEU, so to order their affairs that they would form themselves into a block within NATO. . . .' He confirmed that the British Government had proposed that political consultations of the Six 'might immediately be followed

Benelux countries were sympathetic to this approach, the French and Germans were more reticent and the final decision of the Foreign Ministers of the Six taken at their Strasbourg meeting in November (see above, pp. 206–7) clearly did not go as far as the British would have liked.[2]

In these autumn talks between ministers of the United Kingdom and of the Six, the British also found far greater acceptance of the need for a European settlement to the trade problem on the part of the Benelux ministers than on the part of French ministers or Dr. Adenauer. The French and Germans assured the British that they wanted a close working relationship with them on many economic problems and indicated that the Community would adopt 'liberal' trade relations with third countries, but they seem to have held out little hope of a single market between the Six and the Seven. And it is probable that one result of the autumn talks with the French and the Germans was to encourage British consideration of a new, more drastic approach to the Six by convincing a number of key people in the United Kingdom that the possibilities of renewing negotiations in the near future on anything like the old basis were very slim indeed.

United States views on 'bridge-building'

At the very end of 1959 a new perspective was given to the problem of relations between the Six and the United Kingdom (and the other OEEC countries) by the intervention of the United States. As has already been noted in Chapter VI, the Commission, in its *First Memorandum* on Association, and even more directly in its *Second Memorandum*, had emphasized that any European arrangement should not be at the expense of the United States. The argument that a coming together of the two European groups would mean added, and unwarranted, 'discrimination' against the United States conveniently strengthened the other arguments of those who were opposed to a wider European arrangement, and it

by a meeting of the WEU Council at ministerial level. In this way, we would be able to prevent a gap from growing between the Six and Great Britain.' *Official Record* of the WEU Assembly, 30 November 1959, pp. 60–62.
[2] On this point the communiqué stated: 'These consultations [i.e. among the Six Foreign Ministers] will be held without prejudice to those which take place in NATO and WEU. Wherever necessary these organisations will be kept informed on matters of interest to them.' The text of the communiqué is given in *The Bulletin of the European Economic Community* (Brussels, December 1959).

was used a great deal, and sometimes rather disingenuously, during the summer and autumn of 1959.[3] It was an argument that was bound to meet with a sympathetic response from a United States faced with a mounting balance of payments deficit, and it is worth noting that while the Rey Committee was discussing the *Second Memorandum* from the Commission, and before the Six had taken any action upon it, the United States in effect endorsed the approach advocated by the Commission. In October 1959, in the course of his principal speech to the Tokyo meeting of the Contracting Parties to the GATT, Mr. Dillon, then Under-Secretary of State, commented: 'We have noted the recent proposals of the Commission of the European Economic Community designed to emphasize the liberal orientation of the Community's relations with the rest of the world. We welcome these proposals. We believe they should be supported by the Governments of the six countries. And we urge that they be reinforced by further actions making evident beyond any doubt the intention of the Community to remove any cause for concern that the creation of the Community may be harmful to international trade.'[4] Although Mr. Dillon had simply applauded the liberal orientation of the Commission's report and had not commented on the report in detail, his statement was widely, and rightly, interpreted as indicating the Administration's support for the Commission's thesis that the European trading problem should be resolved primarily in the context of liberal, global trade policies rather than on a purely regional basis.

There were a number of reasons why the United States was sympathetic to the Commission's position.[5] The Administration attached importance to the rapid consolidation of the European Community and accepted the thesis that negotiations at that time between the two groups—whatever their outcome—would interfere with that process. The argument was a double-barrelled one. If the negotiations succeeded there was the risk that the looser, more general, commitments acceptable to the British and the

---

[3] See for example Prof. Hallstein's statement to the Conference of NATO parliamentarians in Washington, 18 November 1959.

[4] The text of Mr. Dillon's statement was put out as a press release by the United States Information Service.

[5] The general approach adopted by the Commission in its *Second Memorandum* was commonly assumed to have been discussed with officials in the United States Administration by M. Marjolin when he was in Washington in September for the annual meetings of the IMF and the IBRD.

others would supplant the more far-reaching commitments of the Community. On the other hand, if, in the end, the negotiations were once again unsuccessful, the development of the Community would, at best, have been impeded and perhaps damaged beyond repair by the internal strains which another prolonged period of fruitless negotiation would inevitably have caused. The United States was also obviously anxious to see no action taken which would worsen its own deteriorating balance of payments position. The Common Market of the Six, the Free Trade Area of the Seven, and any coming together of the two groups in a Europe-wide trading system all meant increased difficulties for United States exports. But the European Economic Community had from the start enjoyed strong support from the United States Administration, from the Congress, and from the public generally. The boldness of the conception of a United Europe (which many of the important Community figures were now much less reluctant than they had been earlier to proclaim as their ultimate goal) and the promise the Community held of a lasting *rapprochement* between France and Germany captured imaginations and seemed to be strong reasons for accepting additional commercial 'discrimination'. The Commission, by advocating an acceleration of the Common Market on the one hand and by displaying a willingness to cut the external tariff on the other, thus both appealed to the United States' desire to see the Community more firmly established and responded as well to American concern at the inevitable trade 'discrimination'.

In contrast, the formation of the European Free Trade Association of the Seven, although it in fact offered a less important obstacle to American exports than did the Common Market, was greeted by the United States Administration with a coolness that for a time verged on hostility. It was seen as a largely defensive move with no long-term political purpose to offset its economic disadvantages for the United States. Furthermore the formation of the EFTA had the avowed object of keeping the problem of relationship between the two groups very much alive, and almost any arrangement that brought the two groups together into a single trading area would have increased the area of 'discrimination' against the United States. The arrangement that appeared to be emerging at the end of the OEEC Maudling Committee negotiations was one which would have had neither the tariff flexibility towards third countries of a true free trade area, nor the advantages of economic union. Some of the compromise suggestions that had been made in the intervening twelve months had been in terms of special sector arrangements, or vague and qualified commitments to a 'free market'. It seemed not unlikely that the best that could be achieved from a new negotiation would have been worse, from the standpoint of third countries, than the plan under discussion when the earlier negotiations failed. Moreover, regardless of the actual disadvantage to American exporters that might result from an arrangement between the two groups, the Administration feared pressure from protectionist forces within the United States, if, at a time when exporters were already experiencing difficulty, new measures were taken by the European countries which seemed to intensify their difficulties. As Mr. Dillon later pointed out, 'United States commercial policy is not formed in a vacuum'.[6]

The United States' concern at a coming together of the two groups also undoubtedly owed something to the deep-seated dislike of economic regionalism that characterized much of the Administration's post-war approach to international economic problems. In the immediate post-war period, the European countries had no effective choice between 'globalism' and 'regionalism': had the United States insisted on a non-discriminatory system of quota liberalization, the result would have been a continuation of bilateral trading arrangements and a desperately low level of trade. However, once the major European countries had become prosperous and their currencies largely convertible, the case for regional rather than global action became less obvious. The Six, by endorsing the ultimate objective of economic and political unity, could be considered a federation in embryo and, in these terms, the Community was acceptable even to those in the United States Administration who opposed 'regionalism'. But the Seven, and—even more—a wider arrangement which lacked the goal of eventual union, encountered the traditional opposition to the development of regional action, particularly on those matters that came within the competence of global organizations like the International Monetary Fund and the GATT.

In contrast to the Administration's position, there was some support in business circles in the United States for a coming together of the two groups, perhaps largely because the con-

[6] In his speech to the Special Economic Conference in January 1960. See below, p. 244.

tinuing uncertainty about European trade arrangements made investment decisions difficult. And there was some concern, particularly in academic circles, that the split between the Six and the Seven might, in fact, have the political repercussions which the British were forecasting. The Administration was disposed to discount the inevitability of a political drifting apart and to feel that the British—by going ahead with the formation of the EFTA and by constantly giving warning of the political repercussions if no European trade arrangement were found—were accentuating the division rather than helping to heal it. Nevertheless, it was clear enough that—inevitably or not—the European trade dispute was placing strains both on the internal cohesion of the Community and on relations between the Six and the other European members of the NATO. And a positive desire to try to improve relations between the European countries—albeit in a way that preserved the integrity of the Six—as well as a negative, but understandable, desire to forestall new 'discrimination' against American exports contributed to the United States decision to play a more active role in the search for a way out of the deadlock.

A separate, but closely allied, range of developments also encouraged the United States Administration to inject itself into the European argument. During the summer and autumn of 1959 there had been considerable pressure from a number of leading figures for strengthening 'Atlantic' economic co-operation, partly to give a more positive, less purely military flavour to the alliance and thus to encourage greater cohesiveness, and partly as a way of responding more effectively to the needs of the underdeveloped countries. In London, in June 1959, a special Atlantic Congress of public leaders from the NATO countries had recommended that governments should consider transforming the OEEC into an Organization for Atlantic Economic Co-operation.[7] In October, Mr. Dean Acheson had made a somewhat similar suggestion in Bonn which had attracted enthusiastic support in Germany. In the late autumn, Lord Franks (then Sir Oliver), addressing the trustees of the CED (Committee for Economic Development) in New York, had emphasized the key importance of what he called the North-South problem: 'I mean the problems of the relationship of the industrialized nations of the North to the underdeveloped and

[7] See the Report of the Atlantic Economic Committee reproduced in the *Atlantic Congress Report* (International Secretariat of the NATO Parliamentarians' Conference, London, 1959).

developing countries that lie to the south of them, whether in
Central or South America, in Africa or the Middle East, in South
Asia or in the great island archipelagoes of the Pacific. If twelve
years ago the balance of the world turned on the recovery of
Western Europe, now it turns on a right relationship of the
industrial North of the globe to the developing South.'[8] He
suggested that some new official group, perhaps simply an
informal one, might be required both to co-ordinate and make
more effective the assistance the industrialized countries should be
extending to their less fortunate southern neighbours and to ensure
the growth and economic stability in the industrialized countries
themselves which was the precondition of effective help. Although
Lord Franks was inclined to favour establishing a new group, he
recognized that there was also a case for modifying the OEEC so
that it could perform these tasks.

M. Monnet had also been urging that more attention be given
to the twin problems of effective assistance to the underdeveloped
countries and adequate rates of economic growth at home and had
begun to advocate an 'Atlantic' approach to many problems. And,
as noted in Chapter VI above, the Action Committee for the
United States of Europe had proposed in November 1959 that the
European Community call a round-table meeting composed of
representatives from the United States, from the United Kingdom, from the Commission acting for European Community, and
from a non-Community member country of the OEEC, to consider
how best to approach the interlocking economic problems of the
free world: tariff arrangements, monetary stability, economic
expansion, and aid to underdeveloped countries.[9]

The idea of some kind of new organized effort by the United
States and the other highly industrialized countries, particularly

[8] Reprinted in the *Saturday Review*, 16 January 1960.
[9] The coincidence of M. Monnet's views with those of the Commission was not,
of course, accidental. Although both M. Monnet and the Commission undoubtedly had tactical reasons for wishing to bring the United States into
any new economic machinery established between the Six and the other
European countries, this should not detract from the fact that M. Monnet
has always envisaged the consolidation of the Six as a step towards a better
organization of the free world and not as an end in itself. In this connexion
see also the statement by M. Monnet in the *Financial Times*, 11 January 1960.
In this he outlined the thesis that the existence of the European Community
introduced a 'new dynamic element on this side of the Atlantic, both economically and politically', which would lead to Atlantic co-operation. He felt
that Britain would ultimately join the Community; meanwhile any trade
arrangements would have to include the United States.

those in Western Europe, was therefore very much in the air during the latter half of 1959. Even had there been no European trade problem to give urgency to the question of relations between the two groups, it seems probable that some reform of the OEEC would have been undertaken. In many ways it would have been better if the question of a reorganization of the OEEC could have been considered apart from the trade question, for the identification of the OEEC with the trade problem and with the unsuccessful attempt to form an OEEC-wide free trade area complicated and made much more difficult an objective assessment of the reforms that were needed.

Early in December 1959, Mr. Dillon spent a week in Europe informing himself at first hand of current thinking in London, Paris, Bonn, and Brussels on three major economic questions: European trade, discrimination against dollar trade, aid to underdeveloped countries. The impression in official circles in the United Kingdom after Mr. Dillon's visit to London appears to have been that the United States, although cool to an OEEC-wide free trade area (or modified free trade area), was becoming increasingly concerned at the prospect of friction between the two European groups and was interested in encouraging (and itself participating in) the search for palliatives, and particularly palliatives such as the Luns Plan (see above, p. 204), which envisaged generalizing intra-European tariff reductions to third countries. Mr. Dillon was himself planning to attend the OEEC ministerial meeting to be held on 14 January 1960; this, in itself, was an indication of the fact that the United States intended to play a more active role in that organization. And Mr. Dillon seemed to share the British view that the OEEC was the right forum for discussions on the European trade question as well as an organization which might be used with more effect on other problems, particularly in encouraging larger, and better co-ordinated, programmes of aid for the developing countries.

Whatever Mr. Dillon's view on the institutional question may have been when he left London, it seems clear that the Commission of the Community, M. Monnet, and the French Government all made it plain during his subsequent discussions with them that they disliked the OEEC as a forum, particularly as a forum for the discussion of European trade questions. Their dislike arose in part from the OEEC's connexion with the ill-fated

Maudling Committee negotiations and the fear that almost any discussions on trade in that forum would soon be turned into a new multilateral negotiation on something very like the old free trade area plan. It was also felt, and with some justification, that the British controlled the OEEC.[10] Moreover, in the eyes of M. Monnet and of the European Commission, the OEEC had the added disadvantage that its composition tended to detract from the collective character of the Community rather than to strengthen it as would their own proposals for some new mechanism built essentially on the three major economic groups of the free world: the European Community, the United Kingdom (and Commonwealth), and the United States. Mr. Dillon appears to have been impressed by the arguments against seeking to breathe new life into the OEEC, and by the time he left Paris on 15 December his thoughts were turning in the direction of some special group not formally under the OEEC auspices, although almost inevitably composed of most of the same countries.[11] However, the Six were not yet cohesive enough or supra-national enough to be represented by the Commission, and the United Kingdom could not, in fact, really have represented either the Seven or the Commonwealth, so that the kinds of arrangement advocated by the Commission and by M. Monnet were not feasible.

In mid-December 1959 Paris was the scene of several sets of overlapping meetings and there were abundant opportunities for formal and informal bilateral and multilateral discussions among Cabinet Ministers from all the European and North Atlantic countries. The Ministerial Council of the WEU, the Ministerial Council of the Council of Europe, the NATO Council with a full array of Foreign, Finance, and Defence Ministers, all met within a few days of each other. To crown it all, a Western 'Summit' of the Heads of State or Government of the United States, the United Kingdom, France, and Germany was held on 19–21 December.[12]

[10] Since 1952, a British minister had been the chairman of the OEEC Council.
[11] In the press release issued on 11 December 1959, after Mr. Dillon's discussion with the Commission in Brussels, it was stated that 'Mr. Dillon made it known that the United States Government is following closely the problems posed by European trade from the point of view of GATT. It was agreed that the United States and Canada should take part in the examination of these problems which would have to take place soon. The framework for these discussions has still to be decided.'
[12] The Western 'Summit' had originally been planned to co-ordinate views before an East–West Summit meeting, but the latter had been postponed and

At the initiative of the United States three economic questions were rather unexpectedly much discussed at the Paris meetings, particularly in the corridors: the general problem of achieving better co-ordination on economic questions among the Western powers, the possibility of some redistribution of the costs of defence and development assistance, and the trade problem. A special communiqué on 'new economic proposals' was issued at the conclusion of the three-day Summit meeting. The communiqué had all the marks of a highly negotiated document and, particularly in its references to the European trade problem, of being a somewhat uneasy compromise between sharply differing points of view. The Heads of State and Government recorded their view that 'virtually all of the industrialised part of the free world is now in a position to devote its energies in increased measure to new and important tasks of co-operative endeavour with the object of: (a) furthering the development of the less developed countries, and (b) pursuing trade policies directed to the sound use of economic resources and the maintenance of harmonious international relations, thus contributing to growth and stability in the world economy and to a general improvement in the standard of living'. They then expressed the view that 'these co-operative principles' should govern the 'discussions on commercial problems arising from the existence of European economic regional organisations, which are or will be constituted within the framework of the G.A.T.T., such as the European Economic Community and the European Free Trade Association', and that 'relations both with other countries and with each other should be discussed in this spirit'. These sentiments could obviously not be opposed by any country, for they did little more than underline what everyone had always agreed—that a European settlement must be consistent with the GATT. The 'little more' was the emphasis given to the interest of third countries, an emphasis that the British, who had always argued the need for an 'outward looking' arrangement, could hardly object to, although in this context it was clearly a concession to the United States–French view that difficulties for third countries were implicit in any coming together of the Six and the Seven.

some of the urgency had therefore gone out of the December discussions on Berlin and disarmament. The NATO Council met before and after the Western 'Summit' so that the other NATO countries could be kept fully informed.

It was also agreed that an informal meeting should be held in Paris in the near future to consider 'the method of furthering' these 'principles'. There was disagreement among the Four over which countries should attend the meeting; the French favoured a very restricted group, the British argued that since all OEEC countries were concerned, they should all be represented. Eventually a compromise was reached, and in the communiqué[13] it was proposed that the 'members and participants of the Executive Committee of the OEEC and the Governments whose nationals are members of the Steering Board for Trade of the OEEC' should be represented at the Paris meeting. The Commission of the EEC as well as the United States and Canada were included by this rather awkward formula as they were 'participants' in the Executive Committee. The OEEC member countries excluded from the Paris meeting by this formula were Austria, Iceland, Ireland, Luxembourg, Norway, Spain, and Turkey. It is difficult to believe that a meeting of twenty would have been very much more cumbersome than one of thirteen and the compromise seems hardly worth the bother it must have been to negotiate and to implement.

The Special Economic Conference—January 1960

The Special Economic Conference of the Thirteen met in Paris on 12 and 13 January 1960. Because the seven OEEC countries that had been omitted from this group naturally refused to be bound by decisions in which they had no part, the Thirteen reported to a Conference of the Twenty. This, in turn, was followed by a meeting of the Council of the OEEC, in which the same twenty countries participated, although on this occasion the United States and Canada were present in their role as 'associate members' rather than as full members.

Before these mid-January meetings took place there was a rather elaborate press build-up and much speculation that the beginning of a new era in Western economic relations was at hand. The guarded and somewhat evasive language of the four-power communiqué was, however, a reflection of the fact that the preconditions for bold new initiatives did not, in fact, then exist. The United States in an election year, and faced with its own

---

[13] The text of the communiqué is contained in the report *A Remodelled Economic Organisation* (Paris, April 1960), pp. 7–8. The introductory reference to industrial countries rather than European or Atlantic countries presumably reflected the United States' interest in 'de-regionalizing' OEEC and opening the way to Japanese participation.

balance of payments difficulties, was in no position to take important substantive steps either in the trade or in the aid field and there was little real agreement among the principal governments about the purposes of the Special Economic Conference. In the trade field, in particular, it was clear that the views of the principals were very far apart. The British wanted to gain acceptance of, and support for, a European trading arrangement embracing both the Six and the Seven; the French wanted to rule out such an arrangement, finally and clearly. The United States hoped that European differences would be composed by reducing barriers globally rather than on a regional basis. And some people, particularly in Germany, dreamed of an Atlantic free trade area. Despite the fact that the United States Administration had never held out any hope of an Atlantic free trade area, or customs union, there was so much press speculation about this possibility during the latter part of 1959, and particularly after the 'Summit' communiqué, that the Administration went out of its way to make it plain before the January meeting that it had no intention of proposing, or subscribing to, any such plan.

The December discussions in Paris, and the exploratory talks carried on between the principal countries before the January conference opened, made it abundantly clear that the United States, although interested in improving political relations between the two European groups and willing to examine ways of meeting particular difficulties that might arise, was just as opposed as were the French and the Commission to a multilateral European trading arrangement and was strongly in favour of resolving the commercial side of the problem by a general lowering of tariffs in the GATT. It was indicative of the United States view that Mr. Dillon in a statement to the press on his departure from Washington did not even mention the Six–Seven question.[14] In contrast, the British and the other EFTA countries, in the exchanges that took place before the meeting and during the meetings, acknowledged the importance of greater co-operation on aid, trade, and economic policy on an 'Atlantic' basis, but doggedly refused to be diverted from what they considered to be the crucial prior issue,

---

[14] 'It will be our purpose on January 12 and 13 to consider the need for, and possible methods of, continuing consultation on the important problems of expanding liberal multilateral world trade and stimulating aid to the less developed countries of the free world.' *Press Release* dated 11 January 1960, issued by United States Embassy, London.

namely the bringing together of the Six and the Seven into a single trading area.[15]

The Special Economic Conference of the Thirteen and the subsequent Conference of the Twenty (the Commission of the EEC was also represented at both meetings) were held not at the Château de la Muette, although that would have been easier to arrange, but in conference quarters which had been made available by the French Government, in order to dramatize the break with the OEEC and to underline the fact that the conference was the beginning of a new relationship between Europe and North America and not a continuation of the post-war OEEC pattern of intra-European co-operation. The United States having suggested the Special Conference, it was logical that throughout the meeting the initiative should have been taken by Mr. Dillon. Since his views, in the main, were similar to the agreed position of the Six they were happy to let him take the lead. The British were in an awkward position. They were annoyed at Mr. Dillon's obvious support for the French but they did not want to accentuate their own differences of view with the United States and they were anxious to avoid a repetition of the highly-charged encounter with the French in December 1958. They therefore tended to let the Swedes and the Swiss defend the interests of the EFTA countries —which they did with vigour, tinged with some bitterness at the way the United States was backing the Six.

At the opening session Mr. Dillon outlined the United States' views and formally introduced resolutions embodying his specific proposals on the three main subjects the Conference had been convened to discuss: trade, aid, and organizational arrangements. The United States' ideas had been informally discussed with the British, French, and others beforehand and Mr. Dillon's specific suggestions—which were in any case largely procedural—came as no surprise. The least controversial of the United States proposals was that on aid. The United States suggested that a small committee of capital exporting countries be set up immediately— without waiting for decisions to be taken on other organizational questions—to co-ordinate Western policies towards the under-developed countries. It was clear from the terms of the resolution that the new group was not itself to provide or distribute aid. It was also clear that the United States felt that membership of the group

---

[15] See the first leader in *The Times*, 12 January 1960, which appears to have been a fairly accurate reflection of official views.

should not be limited to the Atlantic countries and, in particular, wanted Japan to become a member of the group. The United Kingdom, and others, were rather reluctant to broaden the membership since they felt this might prejudice the consideration of the larger question of the future of the OEEC. However, a resolution along the lines proposed by the United States was agreed without much difficulty, although Portugal—hardly a major capital exporting country—was added to the group in response to its own wish, supported by the British in a gesture of EFTA solidarity.[16]

The United States' proposal on organizational questions ran into rather more difficulty. Mr. Dillon suggested that the twenty governments who were members or associates of the OEEC should examine the question of whether there should be a 'successor' organization to the OEEC which would continue those functions of the OEEC that still seemed important, take on appropriate new functions, and be so constructed that the United States and Canada could become full members. He felt that these discussions on a successor organization should be carried on outside the institutional framework of the OEEC and on the basis of a report to be prepared by a group of three experts: one to be chosen from the EFTA countries, one from the EEC countries, and one from the other countries who were members of, or associated with, the OEEC. Because of the strong similarity of views between the Community and the United States, particularly on the trade question, the Seven felt that this group of three would be un-balanced. The Seven were also anxious that neither the resolution nor the terms of reference given to the 'Wise Men' should imply that the OEEC had completed its task and had ceased to be a useful institution. The resolution, as finally adopted, reflected concessions to the Seven on both points.[17]

It was agreed that a meeting of senior officials of the twenty governments that were members or associates of the OEEC, to which the European Communities would also be invited, should be convened in Paris on 19 April 1960 to consider the question of organizational arrangements on the basis of a report to be pre-pared by four 'Wise Men'. The original expectation of the United

---

[16] The members of the Development Assistance Group were: Belgium, Canada, France, Germany, Italy, Portugal, the United Kingdom, the United States, and the EEC Commission. At its first meeting, Japan was invited to become a member. Other countries joined later.

[17] The text of the resolution is contained in the Report by the Group of Four, *A Remodelled Economic Organisation* (Paris, April 1960), pp. 8–9.

States—and of most of the Six—was that a member of the Commission would represent the Six on this group. However, the French Government opposed this suggestion and, in the end, it was agreed that the committee would be composed of a Frenchman, an Englishman, an American, and a Greek. Although they were appointed to act in their individual capacities they were broadly representative of the four main groups—the Six, the Seven, the North American associates, and the 'forgotten Europeans'—and, with the exception of the Greek, they were all government officials.

The argument on the wording of the resolution on organizational questions was essentially an argument about the validity and importance of the 'larger Europe'. To the more ardent 'Europeans' the OEEC was the embodiment of the British concept of European unity: co-operation without political commitment. This kind of unity they believed to be inadequate and they feared that if it were allowed to flourish it would undermine the European Community by attracting those people within the Community who were, at best, uncertain 'Europeans'. The French, the Commission, and some others within the Six also wanted to make a definite break with the past and to approach the re-establishment of relations with the other European countries in a context that held no precedents of 'non-discrimination' as between European countries. The United Kingdom and the rest of the Seven were, in contrast, determined to have the existence of a European loyalty and sense of mutual interest that ran beyond the Six—the 'larger Europe'—fortified and acknowledged. It was not without a certain irony that the United Kingdom, which at various times in the past had sought to turn the OEEC into a less European, more Atlantic organization, and the French, who had, in the past, strongly resisted these attempts, now found their roles reversed.

The United States shared the view of the Six that the purpose of reforming the OEEC was to establish a new relationship, not to strengthen an old one, but they were thinking in somewhat different terms from the Six. As their insistence on the inclusion of Japan in the work of the Development Assistance Group made clear, they were, at this time, thinking less in 'Atlantic' terms than in the 'North–South' terms outlined by Sir Oliver Franks. Moreover, although they and the Six arrived at much the same conclusion on the trade question their objectives were slightly different. The Six, particularly the Commission and the French, wanted to be rid of any obligation, however tenuous, to be 'non-discriminatory' within the Europe of the OEEC; the United States wanted to obtain recognition of the fact that the circumstances which had led to American acceptance of 'discrimination' on an OEEC basis no longer existed. The final resolution contained some verbal concessions to the Seven but the basic differences of view remained unreconciled, as the subsequent difficulties in agreeing on the scope of the new organization made all too clear.

Although the difference of view between the Six and the Seven on the solution to the European trade problem had been implicit in the argument on organizational questions, the controversy flared into the open during the discussion of the resolution dealing directly with the trade problem. In his introductory remarks, Mr. Dillon had suggested that the Special Economic Committee might itself continue to discuss trade problems but he had not elaborated on this suggestion. The resolution subsequently introduced by the United States delegation gave little comfort to those who had hoped that the conference, and in particular the United States Government, would explicitly recognize the urgency of the trade problem and would endorse the need for a European settlement. The resolution proposed that the Special Economic Committee should meet from time to time to consider commercial problems, not simply European problems, arising from the existence of the two European groups and ways of meeting any difficulties that might arise, consistent with the obligations of the GATT, and that the Executive Secretary of the GATT should participate in these discussions. There was no suggestion that the Committee should seek ways of bringing together the two European groups, nor any implication that this was a desirable objective.

The Seven were determined that the problem of relations between the two groups should be given priority, and they were strongly opposed to having the European problem swamped in verbiage about the need for everyone to pursue constructive trade policies consistent with the GATT. They wanted the need for a European arrangement accepted as a positive goal, and they felt the United States was simply proposing machinery for the settlement of disputes similar to the 'contact committee' recommended by the Commission in its *Second Memorandum*, a proposal which had been made again by the Commission's representative at the Special Economic Conference.

The United Kingdom therefore introduced an alternative resolution; this emphasized the need to solve the Six–Seven split and proposed that a nine-man group composed of three representatives from the EEC, three from the EFTA, one from the United States, one from Canada, and one from the small countries in neither European group be established to examine the problem.[18] After prolonged argument, during which it was again clear that the United States position was very close to that of the Six and sharply at variance with that of the Seven, a cumbersome compromise was adopted which fully satisfied no one. Like the resolution on organizational arrangements it reflected no real meeting of minds and could be interpreted in different ways by different groups. Although individual words and phrases in the resolution went some way to meet the points emphasized by the Seven, the operative clauses suggested that these concessions were of little importance. It was agreed that the Special Committee would propose to all twenty governments (the eighteen OEEC members and the United States and Canada) that they, 'together with the EEC', constitute themselves into a new committee (in which the Executive Secretary of the GATT would be invited to participate) for the consideration of trade problems. The resolution was unavoidably vague when it came to defining the problems coming within the competence of this new committee and simply referred back to the problems mentioned in the preamble of the resolution.[19] A phrase in the preamble referring to 'the need to

[18] See *Le Monde*, 15 January 1960, and *New York Herald Tribune* (Paris edition), 14 January 1960.
[19] The resolution read as follows:

'Recognizing that there are problems of commercial policy of particular concern to the twenty Governments who are members of, or associated with, the OEEC;

'Taking note of the existence of the EEC and of the convention for an EFTA;

'Bearing in mind the relationship between the provisions of these agreements and general international commercial policy;

'Considering the need to examine, as a matter of priority, the relationship between the EEC and the EFTA with due regard to the commercial interests of third countries and the principles and obligations of the GATT;

'Decides to propose to the twenty Governments that they constitute themselves, together with the EEC, a committee with power to:

(1) establish one or more informal working groups for the consideration of these problems without infringing the competence of the existing international institutions such as the GATT or the OEEC; these groups should report back to the Committee;

(2) transmit an invitation to the Executive Secretary of the GATT to participate in these discussions.'

examine, as a matter of priority, the relationship between the EEC and the EFTA' was the principal concession made to the Seven. However, subsequent attempts on the part of the Seven to construe this phrase as recognition of the need for a European settlement, or even as a commitment to give serious consideration to the terms of a settlement, proved unavailing.

The resolutions adopted by the Special Economic Committee of Thirteen were endorsed by the Twenty Governments (i.e. the Thirteen and the remaining OEEC countries) who met as a special conference for this purpose before meeting immediately thereafter at the Château de la Muette as the Council of the OEEC. The important discussions having already taken place in the Special Committee, the OEEC Council had little to do and the meeting was short and uneventful.

The reactions in the United Kingdom to the Paris conference were, understandably enough, somewhat mixed. On the one hand, there was satisfaction that the trade problem was once again to be discussed in a forum which contained both the Six and the Seven. On the other hand, there was wider recognition and some resentment of the fact that the United States was no longer the sleeping partner it had been during the earlier free trade area negotiations.[20] It was clear that the more active United States interest in the problem, although it might well be helpful in making the Six more energetic in their search for palliatives and more liberal in their policies, would add to the difficulties of negotiating an agreement between the two groups. The impression gained from various official statements at this time is that the British Government would have been sympathetic to a United States argument—based on the deterioration in its balance of payments position—that there should be an initial m.f.n. tariff reduction and a delay in 'discriminatory' bridge-building, provided the United States had openly recognized the desirability, in the long term, of a single European trading arrangement. It was the United States'

[20] See, for example, the criticism of the United States position in the House of Commons on 15 February 1960, by Sir John Vaughan-Morgan. This debate was ostensibly on the second reading of the Bill on the EFTA. In fact, most of the debate was given over to trying to pry out of the Government some indication of the lines of action it was now considering in the light of the evidence that 'bridge-building' was plainly not possible. It should be noted that in public statements Government spokesmen were always very careful to avoid attaching blame to the United States, and in fact showed considerable understanding for at least those aspects of the United States position that were based on its concern with its balance of payments.

unwillingness to accept the British thesis that, over the long term, economic division would lead to political division and be undesirable for the free world generally that particularly troubled the British.[21]

British reactions to the proposed reorganization of the OEEC were also somewhat mixed. An Atlantic rather than a European economic organization had a strong appeal to many people and, in the past, the British had themselves felt that it would be desirable for the United States and Canada to play a more active role in the OEEC and for the organization to be given an 'Atlantic' rather than a purely European outlook. However, since the United Kingdom was now seeking to persuade the United States and the Six of the importance and validity of the 'larger Europe', it was an awkward time to reorient the organization that had given the most substance to that concept. Partly for this reason, partly because the United States had made it fairly plain that it was thinking not of a powerful new organization but of a consultative body, the Atlantic approach, which might have been expected to attract strong British support, was treated with considerable circumspection. Since the United States representatives had made it clear that, because of the imminence of the presidential election, a new organization could not come into being for, say, eighteen months, it was fairly easy for the United Kingdom to find ways of reconciling the diverse strands in its own position and to welcome the prospect of closer co-ordination of policy on an Atlantic basis while insisting that the OEEC was performing certain invaluable functions which must be preserved while institutional 'improvements' were under consideration.

The Paris Conference had agreed that senior officials from the Twenty Governments and a representative of the Commission of the European Economic Community would meet in the near future to discuss matters arising from the resolution on trade and that the Committee of Twenty-one (as it was usually called)[22] would itself reconvene shortly after Easter to receive the report on organizational questions from the four 'Wise Men'. In the event

[21] For a comprehensive official statement of British views just after the Paris meetings, see the speech made by the President of the Board of Trade, Mr. Maudling, to the Economic Club of New York entitled 'Trade Policies for a Free World'. (Press release, 18 January 1960.)

[22] After the opening conference the Committee was sometimes called the Committee of Twenty but more often the Committee of Twenty-one: the representative from the EEC, as an entity, was the twenty-first member.

both meetings were postponed. The first trade meeting was not held until the end of March and the Wise Men were unable to produce a final report until mid-May.

It was clear that neither the Six nor the United States shared the sense of urgency of the Seven about the trade problem and that the United States, in particular, wanted time to explore informally the possibility of an interim accommodation between the two groups. Rather ironically, they felt that this could be done better by bilateral discussions than by the trade committee they had taken the initiative in establishing. At this time, the United States was principally interested in the short-term problem of finding a way to keep to manageable proportions the tariff 'discrimination' between the two groups—and against United States exports—which would arise on 1 July 1960, when the Six were to make their second cut of 10 per cent. in the tariffs on intra-Community trade and the Seven their first cut of 20 per cent. in the tariffs on intra-EFTA trade. The United States' hope was that each group would extend to the other group, and generalize to the United States and to the other members of the GATT, most of the tariff reductions that were to be made on 1 July. But the United States shared the view of the French, the Commission, and many others in the Community, that no cuts in the tariffs of the Community countries should be generalized where the rates were already below the rates of the eventual common tariff or where the result of the cut would be to bring the rates below those of the eventual common tariff. The Commission, and others, felt that the difficulties of bringing the Common Market tariff into effect would be increased if these low tariffs were further reduced, and also that if all the tariff cuts were generalized the Seven might claim that this interim arrangement constituted another precedent for a policy of 'non-discrimination' in intra-European trade.

The 'acceleration' proposals

As described in Chapter VI, in November 1959 the Council of Ministers of the Six had been unable to agree either on the details of an acceleration of the Common Market timetable or on the related question of the action to be taken with respect to third countries at the time of the 1 July 1960 reduction of tariffs on trade among the Six, and these interrelated problems had been remitted to the Commission for further study. The Commission's new proposals were made public early in March 1960, although they had, as yet, received no endorsement from the member governments and were to be the subject of much discussion and considerable controversy during the spring and early summer. The main features of the Commission's proposals were obviously attractive to the United States, and the Administration officially welcomed them the day after they had been made public by Prof. Hallstein.[23]

The Commission introduced its specific proposals—they took the form of a report to the Ministers[24]—by reviewing the reasons for believing that an acceleration of the rhythm of the treaty would be desirable. The Commission pointed out that the economic situation of the Six countries was now quite different from that prevailing at the time the treaty was drafted: the level of reserves was more satisfactory, the rates of exchange better adjusted, the financial situation more stable, the differences in economic and commercial policies of the Six much less pronounced than they had been two years earlier. Furthermore, economic relations within the Community had developed so rapidly that formal acceleration of the customs union would simply conform the trading arrangements to a situation which in some respects already existed. The Commission also reiterated the view it had expressed in its *Second Memorandum* on association, that 'the sooner economic integration is achieved, the more surely will the commercial policy of the Community be dynamic, outward-looking, and liberal'.

The Commission emphasized that an acceleration in the customs union provisions of the treaty should be matched by action in other fields to preserve the balance of the treaty, but its recommendations in these other fields were more general in character, for, as the Commission pointed out, in many cases faster co-ordination of policies depended on the will of governments, not on any action the Commission could take.

The specific recommendations made by the Commission to speed up the implementation of the customs union were as

[23] See Press Statement released by the Department of State, Washington, 4 March 1960. It was generally assumed that the proposals had been discussed in detail with the United States officials who, at Mr. Dillon's initiative, had gone to Europe following the January meetings to try to find a basis for an interim tariff arrangement between the two European groups that would be consistent with United States' interests.

[24] Communauté Économique Européenne, Commission, *Recommandations de la Commission en vue de l'Accélération du Rythme du Traité* (Brussels, 26 February 1960).

follows: (1) quotas on trade in industrial products within the Common Market and (on conditions of reciprocity) on trade with third countries (at a comparable stage of development) should be eliminated by the end of 1961; (2) tariffs on intra-Community trade should be reduced by 50 per cent. by the end of 1961, the reduction on 1 July 1960 to be by 20 per cent. rather than by 10 per cent. as stipulated in the treaty, and the reduction on 31 December 1961 also to be by 20 per cent. rather than by 10 per cent.; (3) the first steps towards the common external tariff should be taken on 1 July 1960 instead of on 31 December 1961, but for the purpose of this alignment the common external tariff should be reduced by 20 per cent. This reduction in the external tariff should be 'provisional' until the 1960-1 GATT negotiations were completed and a decision should then be taken, in the light of the concessions received from other countries, on whether all or part of this 20 per cent. reduction in the common tariff would be maintained. The tariff reductions the Six made to one another could be generalized provided no reductions below the level of the common tariff were made. A measure of immediate reciprocity should be sought from most of the industrialized GATT countries benefiting from these concessions, but because of its domestic procedural requirements the United States should not be expected to make its concessions until the GATT negotiations.

Within the Community, there were conflicting reactions to these proposals. The French were pleased by the suggestion that the date for making a start on the common tariff be brought forward to July 1960, but less happy with the proposal that the common tariff level less 20 per cent. be used as the basis for this first step in the approximation of tariffs. They felt this was giving away too much bargaining power in advance of the GATT negotiations. The Dutch, on the other hand, were only prepared to agree to the proposed acceleration in the timetable because of the 20 per cent. reduction in the Common Market tariff, and they argued that the reduction should be adopted unconditionally and not made subject to review after the GATT negotiations. The Germans were divided. The Foreign Office and Herr Etzel, the Minister of Finance, supported the Commission's proposals; Dr. Erhard, the Minister of Economics, and Dr. Schwarz, the Minister of Agriculture, opposed them, as did much of German industry. There were several reasons for concern in Germany.

The Economics Ministry was worried by signs of inflation and feared that the increase in tariffs resulting from the introduction of the first step towards the common tariff would raise costs and thus contribute to inflationary pressure. Opinions differed between the Commission and the German Government, and within the German Government, about the effect on costs of the Commission's proposals, the Commission taking the view that the net effect would be slight since the increase in external tariff rates would tend to be offset by the greater reductions made in the tariffs on intra-Community trade. There was also some concern in Germany—although this was of less importance—that the acceleration in the reduction of tariffs within the Common Market would give another boost to German exports and thus further increase the already large credit surplus.[25] Finally, for much of German industry, markets in the Seven were as important as, or more important than, markets within the Six. They were therefore reluctant to take a step that seemed likely to precipitate a parallel acceleration of the timetable of the Seven, and to make more difficult negotiations on an accommodation with the Seven.

The Council of Ministers of the Six discussed the Commission's proposals on 10 March. Although the Ministers declared themselves to be in favour of acceleration, in principle, they were unable to reach agreement on the details and they agreed to discuss the plan further in May. Meanwhile the plan was referred to the Permanent Representatives for further study and the Rey Committee was asked to examine its effect on the Community's relations with third countries.

The effects on third countries were rather mixed. On the one hand, the Commission's proposal to use the Common Market tariff less 20 per cent., rather than the legal common tariff, as the basis for the first *rapprochement* in Community tariffs benefited third countries. Where tariffs were to be raised as the first step towards the establishment of the common tariff, the increase

[25] The situation was complicated by the fact that the German Government had made a 25 per cent. 'business cycle' reduction in their tariffs in 1957, just before the entry into force of the Treaty of Rome. The Common Market tariff had, however, been calculated on the legal German rates, not those actually in force. Therefore, if the first steps towards the common tariff were to be taken on 1 July, the Germans would have had first to raise their tariffs to the legal level and then to apply the treaty provision that the gap between those rates and the Common Market rates be reduced by 30 per cent. (or the rates aligned on the common rate where the difference was less than 15 per cent.).

required would be smaller. Moreover the cuts to be made in the high tariffs would be larger than they would be if the legal common tariff were to be used as the basis for the *rapprochement*. On the other hand, despite these gains from the 20 per cent. concession, third countries stood to lose from the fact that some low tariffs would be raised against them eighteen months sooner than the treaty required, and, in these cases, there would also be—for that eighteen months—a greater disparity in treatment between the Common Market countries and other countries than there would be if the Treaty of Rome provisions were carried out without modification.

The Commission's proposals were an ingenious attempt to achieve an acceleration in the timetable of the Common Market while satisfying conflicting interests among the Six, appealing to the United States, and offering a basis for an interim accommodation with the Seven. But, although the plan won American support, it was greeted by the Seven not as an accommodating step but as a 'hostile act', which would needlessly intensify 'discrimination' and make a European settlement more difficult. In particular the United Kingdom and the rest of the EFTA countries made no bones about the fact that they would regard a decision to bring forward the first steps towards aligning external tariffs as an unfriendly move. As explained above, the Seven attached importance to the fact that during the January discussions in Paris they had succeeded in obtaining recognition from the Six, and from the United States, of the need to discuss relations between the Six and the Seven as 'a matter of priority'. Although an acceleration had been under consideration within the Community since the previous summer, the Seven felt that the Commission's proposals were deliberately timed to create a new situation before the Committee of Twenty-one could begin considering the trade question. The Seven were less opposed to the proposal to cut internal tariffs by 20 per cent. (rather than 10 per cent.) than they were to the suggestion that the first steps in aligning the external tariffs should be taken eighteen months ahead of the schedule laid down in the treaty. The opposition of the EFTA countries was based partly on the economic effects of the raising of the low tariffs and partly on negotiating considerations. The Six, for their part, were determined to have the fact that they were to be a customs union accepted. Moreover, as in the dispute over quotas in December 1958, the Six were determined to have a 'difference' in tariff treatment between the Six and the other European countries recognized and accepted, although they were ready—as they had been in the case of quotas—to negotiate with the others to reduce the size of the difference.[26]

It seems clear that in the spring of 1960 the British Government recognized that the prospects for an early, fruitful negotiation with the Six on a long-term settlement were not bright. Their main hope during the spring was that a way could be found to keep 'discrimination' from increasing and the economic gap from widening on 1 July when the Six and Seven both cut their tariffs. There were frequent references in official statements and in the press to the desirability of an interim arrangement to give a 'breathing-space' of eighteen months before the next internal tariff cuts were due to be made within each group, and before the Six were required by the treaty to take the first step in transforming themselves from a free trade area to a customs union. Many things could change in eighteen months: the United States balance of payments difficulties might diminish; changes in the French or German Governments might occur; the Six, either because they were stronger and more confident or because they were weaker and less confident, might come to look with more favour on a wider arrangement; and, as discussed further in the next chapter, the British Government themselves might be more ready for a far-reaching arrangement than they were in the spring of 1960.

In mid-February, senior officials of the Seven, meeting together in London, had discussed a scheme, similar to the Luns Plan, whereby each European group would extend to the other (and generalize to the other members of the GATT) the tariff cuts they were to make internally on 1 July.[27] The proposal was to be considered further by the Council of Ministers of the EFTA in Vienna early in March, shortly before the first meeting of the Trade Committee (of the twenty governments and the EEC) in Paris. It seems clear that by the time of the Vienna meeting the British, at least, were reasonably convinced that the scheme the Seven had been discussing stood almost no chance of success and that some version of the Commission's proposals was almost certain to be accepted by the Six. Nevertheless they made a

---

[26] A small tariff difference already existed, since tariff cuts resulting in levels below the Common Market level had not been generalized at the time the first 10 per cent. tariff reduction was made by the Common Market countries on 1 January 1959.

[27] See *Financial Times*, 15 February 1960.

considerable effort to persuade the Six to reject, or at least to modify, the Commission's proposals. As a first step, the Seven agreed at their Vienna meeting that they would not negotiate with the Six on the basis of the Commission's proposals and that they would put forward their own proposal for mutual tariff cutting.[28]

At this time the position among the Six appeared to be that the Dutch would only agree to the acceleration if the 20 per cent. reduction in the external tariff were made, whether or not any reciprocity was received from other countries. The French disliked the 20 per cent. cut on any basis and appeared very unlikely to accept it if there were no reciprocity from the Seven. The attitude of the Seven therefore seemed likely to have some effect on the ability of the Six to reach agreement. It was recognized by the Seven that their unwillingness to negotiate on the basis of the Commission's plan might mean that no interim accommodation could be found before 1 July. Nevertheless, the Seven, and the British in particular, felt they would be rather better off tactically if the Treaty of Rome were to be implemented in the way originally foreseen than if the timetable were accelerated. The British also felt they would probably be at least as well off economically. Given their relatively high tariffs, the British were in a strong position to bargain with the Six for tariff reductions during the forthcoming GATT negotiations, and they thought they could probably obtain concessions that would be more important from their own standpoint in that way than by negotiating on the basis proposed by the Commission.[29] Moreover, they saw no reason for 'paying' for the reduction of those national tariffs that were above the common external tariff, since these were reductions which they would get in the course of time in any case.

At this time the British were also in no mood to give unrequited tariff concessions to the United States. They felt, with some reason, that the United States Administration was hindering rather than helping their attempts to find an accommodation with the Six and that despite protestations of neutrality the United States was in fact supporting those elements within the Six who wanted to rule

[28] British agreement to the putting forward of the EFTA scheme was unenthusiastic and a concession to some of the other EFTA countries who, because of their low tariffs, were not as well placed as the British to negotiate tariff reductions in the GATT.

[29] The 20 per cent. reduction in the eventual common external tariff was not as immediately important to the United Kingdom as a reduction in the national tariffs.

out the possibility of a Europe-wide free trade area. This feeling
was strengthened when, just at the end of the Vienna meeting of
the EFTA ministers and shortly before the Twenty-one were to
convene for their first trade discussion, the Commission's proposals were endorsed in the communiqué issued at the conclusion
of discussions between Dr. Adenauer and President Eisenhower
in Washington.[30] The Seven had seen in the German uncertainty
the best hope of a postponement of acceleration and they strongly
resented this action by the United States Administration.

At the end of March (1960), the Trade Committee of the
Twenty-one met in Paris for its first discussion. It was generally
agreed that the immediate task was to see whether there were
acceptable ways of narrowing the differences in tariff treatment
that would arise when both groups cut their tariffs internally on
1 July. The EFTA countries put forward their suggestion which,
as anticipated, was coolly received. However, in the absence of a
decision among the Six on the details of their own proposals there
was little disposition to begin bargaining and the only progress
was procedural. The Secretariat was asked to make a factual study
of the effects of the Commission's proposals, of the EFTA proposals, and of the simple application on 1 July of the provisions
of the Treaty of Rome and of the Stockholm Convention. It was
also agreed that the chairman of the Committee, Mr. Luns,
would arrange consultations with countries, or groups of countries,
that might wish to exchange views on an informal basis. This was a
small concession to the EFTA countries, who were anxious to keep
alive the question of a long-term settlement.

Some decision by the Six on the acceleration proposals was
clearly needed before the Trade Committee could get down to
business, for the British had not yet abandoned hope that the Six
could be prevailed upon to drop at least those aspects of the
acceleration proposals that related to the external tariffs. The
strength of the British opposition to the Commission's proposals
for acceleration is difficult to explain. Moreover, some of the tactics

[30] Joint Statement on Eisenhower–Adenauer meeting issued in Washington,
15 March 1960. The communiqué simply stated: '. . . they discussed the
recent trade proposals of the European Economic Commission. They noted
that, should proposals along these lines be adopted, the result would be a
major contribution to a general lowering of world trade barriers.' However,
as reported in the *Financial Times*, 21 March 1960, 'officials have since told
the *New York Times* that this was intended to be a "full-fledged endorsement
of the proposals" '.

used in trying to influence the decision tended to be counter-productive and to hark back to the tactics that the free trade area negotiations had shown to be not only unsuccessful but likely to feed the almost pathological fear among the Six that the real objective of the United Kingdom was to blight their incipient unity. Thus, Mr. Macmillan's discussions in Washington at the end of March, which are discussed in more detail in the following chapter, although presumably intended to induce the United States Administration to think again about some of the implications of its strong support for the Commission's proposals, had the effect in Europe of lining up the waverers behind those who wanted to speed up the formation of the Common Market. At a dramatic session, the European Parliamentary Assembly, which was then debating the Commission's proposals, dropped its criticisms and endorsed the plan, almost unanimously, as news reports were received of the Prime Minister's warnings in Washington of the political consequences of the continued economic split in Europe.

In addition, although very little was officially revealed, or leaked, about the discussions between General de Gaulle and Mr. Macmillan at Rambouillet in March (1960) and in London early in April, it seems probable that the British view that acceleration would accentuate the difficulties of finding a reasonable settlement in Europe were put to General de Gaulle at both meetings, albeit with little effect. If anything, opposition to acceleration (and, perhaps, indications that the British might be prepared to make far-reaching concessions to achieve a settlement) appears to have strengthened the French view that it was important to move ahead and to consolidate the position of the Six by taking the first definite step towards a customs union before negotiations with the United Kingdom were reopened.[31]

British views were listened to rather more sympathetically elsewhere in the Six, particularly in the Netherlands and in Germany. As indicated above, the Germans had internal domestic reasons for wanting to postpone the first move towards the common external tariff, and they were also much more interested commercially than were the French in a settlement with the Seven. They were, therefore, more impressed by the argument that acceleration would deliberately and unnecessarily create a situation which would make it more difficult to find both an interim arrangement and a

[31] See article by Nora Beloff in the *Observer*, 3 April 1960.

long-term settlement. As usual, the German Cabinet was divided and, also as usual, Dr. Adenauer prevailed over Dr. Erhard on the main issue and the principle of acceleration was accepted. However, the position finally agreed upon by the German Cabinet went some way to meet the views of the Seven. As outlined to the Bundestag by Dr. Erhard, the German delegate to the ministerial meeting of the Six (Herr von Brentano) would be instructed to urge that the first steps in aligning the external tariffs should not be taken until the end of the year, rather than in July as proposed by the Commission, thus giving a short 'breathing-space' for talks with the Seven.[32]

The Council of Ministers of the Six finally acted on the Commission's acceleration proposals in mid-May. The principal problems that had to be settled by the ministers at this long and difficult session were: the timing of the acceleration; the extent to which other aspects of the treaty, not simply the customs union features, should be accelerated; the arrangements to be applied to agriculture; and the extent to which the proposed 20 per cent. reduction in the common external tariff would be conditional on the reciprocity received from other countries. Compromises were eventually found on all points, although the agreement on agriculture—which had by this time become the main stumbling-block—postponed rather than settled many of the difficulties.

At this time the Germans and the Dutch were the protagonists in the discussion on the arrangements to be applied to agriculture, with the French and Italians supporting the Dutch. The Germans wanted the acceleration of the cuts in the internal tariffs and in the elimination of other restrictions on internal trade to be limited to industrial products. This would have accentuated the difference in treatment between agricultural and industrial goods that already existed, to the annoyance of the Dutch, and the Dutch were determined to obtain some improvement in the treatment of their agricultural exports within the Community and, in particular, in Germany. The compromise which was finally found made a few, rather meagre, concessions to the Dutch viewpoint. The most substantial point was that the Commission and the Council of Ministers agreed to a specific timetable for the consideration of the Community's common agricultural policies. In addition, the Council stated that the liberalization measures laid down by the treaty—and only partially carried out in the case of

[32] *The Times*, 5 May 1960.

agriculture—were to be implemented before the end of the year. This was a polite way of asking the Germans to stop violating the treaty and to increase their quotas on agricultural products. On the other hand, it was agreed that the acceleration of the first step towards the common tariff would not apply to agricultural products, and that the increase in the rate of reduction of internal tariffs would have only a limited application to agricultural products.

The basic decision on acceleration retained the principle of an acceleration as from 1 July but in reality permitted countries to delay taking the actual tariff actions, i.e. the additional internal 10 per cent. tariff cut and the first steps towards the common external tariff, until the end of the year 1960. It was agreed that in making this first *rapprochement* the common tariff less 20 per cent. would normally be used as the base for tariff alignment. A number of exceptions were, however, to be permitted: first, for any product on List G a member might be permitted by the Commission to use as the base the full rate rather than the rate less 20 per cent.; second, in any case where the use of the rate less 20 per cent. would result in a tariff being reduced below the level of the eventual common tariff, the rate would be reduced only to the common tariff level; finally, a specific concession was made to the Germans. It was agreed that they should be allowed to rescind only half of the earlier 'balance of payments' reductions (see footnote above, p. 256) before making the first *rapprochement* in external tariffs.

It was also agreed that member countries could extend to third countries, against reciprocal concessions, any reductions in national tariffs which did not result in cuts below the common tariff. The Community itself would negotiate for reciprocity for the provisional cut in the Common Market tariff and, in order to preserve the Community's bargaining-power, the question of whether all, or only part, of the 20 per cent. reduction in the common external tariff would be consolidated was to be left open to be determined in the context of the forthcoming GATT negotiations. The Council accepted the Commission's proposals on quotas in so far as intra-Community trade was concerned, that is, that all quotas on industrial goods should be abolished by 31 December 1961. The Council also affirmed that quotas on imports of industrial goods from third countries would be removed as soon as possible.

Looking to the future, it was agreed that, at the least, the 10 per cent. tariff cut on internal trade required by the treaty at the end of December 1961 would be made on that date, and that a decision would be reached before 30 June 1961 on whether the 31 December cut could be doubled. Thus, the Community would have reduced its internal tariffs by 40 per cent., rather than by the 30 per cent. required by the treaty, at the end of the first stage and might have reduced them by 50 per cent.[33]

The Ministers confirmed their intention of accelerating other aspects of the treaty, not simply the customs union features, and requested the Commission to make specific proposals within three months on a number of subjects.

Finally, the Ministers adopted a 'declaration of intention' with regard to relations with third countries. This reaffirmed the Community's determination to pursue a liberal policy with regard to third countries (and notably the other European countries) which would take account of the principal interests of these countries. The Community also indicated its willingness—within the framework of the Trade Committee established by the Paris conference —to undertake negotiations with the members of EFTA. It indicated that these negotiations should be designed to maintain traditional trade between the Community and the member countries of EFTA and, if possible, to increase that trade. It was made clear, however, that any reciprocal reduction of tariffs must respect the principles of the GATT, and it was also made clear that the fact that the Community was a customs union must be accepted as a starting-point. The declaration also recalled that the Community had proposed a contact committee to watch the evolution of trade and to seek means of dealing with any particular difficulties that might arise. The tone of the declaration was noticeably friendlier to the other European countries than that of many recent Community statements, including the *Second Memorandum* from the Commission on association. However, the Community's declaration made it clear that the Council of Ministers were thinking in terms of finding ways of mitigating the effects on trade of the existence of the two European groups, rather

[33] In fact, tariffs on intra-Community trade had been reduced by 40 per cent. by the end of the first stage. However, the cuts foreseen for the second stage were accelerated and internal duties on industrial goods had been reduced by 50 per cent. by 1 July 1962. According to the schedule set out in the Treaty of Rome, tariffs would not have been cut by 50 per cent. until the end of 1964.

than of new negotiations on a comprehensive European agreement.[34]

EFTA reactions

The Council of the EFTA met at Lisbon a week after these decisions had been taken by the Council of the Community. This was the first formal meeting of the EFTA Council since the entry into force of the Stockholm Convention and a number of housekeeping matters required attention. The principal substantive questions before the group were the arrangement to be made with Finland; the position to be taken by the Seven on the report of the Wise Men on the remodelling of OEEC; a possible acceleration within the Seven; and the attitude to be adopted in the forthcoming meeting of the Trade Committee of the Twenty-one in the light of the 'declaration of intent' by the ministers of the Six.

In the communiqué issued at the end of their two-day meeting the ministers of the seven EFTA countries made it clear that although they were ready to talk about short-term arrangements they had not abandoned hope of a long-term settlement with the Six. They warmly welcomed the 'declaration of intent' and deliberately interpreted it in the broadest possible way, reading into it not only a willingness to negotiate on an interim arrangement but also a willingness to renew discussions on a long-term settlement. The communiqué reaffirmed that the Seven still considered a 'Europe-wide market' the best solution to the economic problems created by the existence of EEC and EFTA, but did not specify what form this should take. The communiqué appeared to be intended to encourage the Six to specify their requirements for a long-term settlement while, at the same time, leaving the door wide open to an interim accommodation if—as appeared to be the case—that was the most that the Six were prepared to discuss. Although the Seven discussed the question of speeding up their own tariff cuts, the communiqué simply referred to this as a problem that would be considered.

The wording of the communiqué[35] and statements made following the meeting by Mr. Maudling, and others, strengthened the impression that had been growing for some time that the United

---

[34] The text of Council of Ministers' decisions and the declaration of intent was set out in a Press Release of 13 May 1960.

[35] The text of the Lisbon communiqué is contained in the EFTA *Bulletin* of October 1960.

Kingdom and others among the Seven were now ready to negotiate in terms of a customs union (with some special arrangements) rather than in terms of a free trade area, although the arrangement envisaged appeared to be an agreement between the two European groups.[36] The development of public opinion in the United Kingdom and the evolution in the Government's thinking about the European problem that had taken place since the General Election in the autumn of 1959 are discussed in more detail in the next chapter. Here it is worth noting that shortly before the Lisbon meeting there had been a spate of rumours that the United Kingdom was reconsidering its position *vis-à-vis* the European Communities. There was enough suspicion among the other members of EFTA that the United Kingdom might be preparing to negotiate a separate settlement with the Six to call for a categorical denial by the British spokesman at that meeting. A few days later, the Prime Minister also made it clear in a statement to the House of Commons that Britain had no intention of running out on its EFTA partners. In other respects his statement was tantalizingly ambiguous and contributed to the growing impression that the Government was approaching the problem of relationship with the Communities in a new way and might soon make some dramatic approach to the Six.

Despite numerous indications of British willingness to negotiate in rather different terms than heretofore and some speculation that the forthcoming meeting of the Trade Committee of the Twenty-one might be the occasion for a new initiative, neither the Six nor the United Kingdom were yet ready for bold new initiatives. It seems probable that the United Kingdom would have responded in a forthright way if any suggestion for a resumption of long-term negotiations had come from the side of the Six but that none was seriously expected. The British Government had decided that, for the near future, its best course was to adopt a reasonably co-operative attitude in the Trade Committee of the Twenty-one (despite reservations about its real usefulness); to seek to make the

[36] Thus the communiqué referred to 'preserving the integrity of EFTA' as well as that of the EEC: 'With a willingness to compromise on both sides, these negotiations should make it possible to settle in the common interest the economic problems created by the existence of the EEC and the EFTA.

'Such a settlement, while preserving the integrity of the EEC and the EFTA, should provide for a partnership of the two in a common system of European trade consistent with the GATT and contributing to the development of liberal policies and the expansion of trade throughout the world. . . .'

forthcoming GATT tariff negotiations as productive as possible; and, as described in the next chapter, to explore informally and without publicity various new possibilities with government leaders in the Six countries. Sensibly enough, the British were determined to see their way clear to some kind of a settlement before taking any new public initiative.

The discussions at the 10 June meeting of the Committee on Trade Problems (the Twenty-one) centred on the problem of how to mitigate the economic difficulties arising from the existence of the two European groups and the meeting was friendly and non-controversial. It was quickly agreed that a Study Group would be established with three main tasks: to examine the possibility of the Six and the Seven extending to each other (and generalizing to other countries) at least some part of the tariff reductions that each group would make internally; to analyse the factual trade situation and to prepare the ground so that the forthcoming tariff negotiations in the GATT would result in reductions which would contribute as much as possible to removing difficulties and to expanding trade generally; to watch over the development of trade and to seek means consistent with the GATT for dealing with any particular difficulties that might arise. The Study Group, in effect, took the place of the contact committee which had been proposed by the Six, but with the difference that membership in the Group was open to any member of the Committee on Trade Problems. And rather more emphasis was placed on organizing for the GATT negotiations than on seeking *ad hoc* solutions to particular trade difficulties. Although there was little discussion of the long-term problem, the Seven at least obtained recognition of the fact that it remained unsolved, for the committee agreed 'to continue its discussions of the long-term aspects of the trade relations between the European Economic Community and the European Free Trade Association with full regard to the commercial interests of third countries and the principles and obligations of the GATT'.[37]

Although the Study Group held several meetings and prepared voluminous studies of the effects of the two groups on European trade, the value of its work was primarily negative. It disposed of the case for dealing with the European trade problem as a series of hardship cases by showing that no real hardship cases had yet arisen. It also showed, once again, that the pattern of European

[37] Committee on Trade Problems, Press Release No. 3 (Paris, 10 June 1960).

trade was such that it was difficult to construct a meaningful list of 'European' commodities, that is, of commodities which were traded only (or preponderantly) among the European countries so that mutually advantageous tariff cuts could, in fact, be made on a 'European' basis even though to be consistent with the GATT the tariff cuts were formally generalized to third countries.

The reorganization of the OEEC

During the spring and summer of 1960 differences of view on the solutions to the European trade problem, and, more fundamentally, differences of view about the kind of European unity which should be sought considerably complicated the discussions on the reorganization of the OEEC. The Group of Four (the Wise Men), which had been instructed by the Paris conference in January 1960 to prepare a report on the organizational question, held discussions with representatives of the twenty governments, and with representatives of the European Communities, of the OEEC, and of various other international organizations, and early in April the group produced a report and a draft convention for an 'Organization for Economic Co-operation and Development'.[38]

It had not been easy for the Four to find a common view about the kind of organization that was required and their report reflected the confusion and the conflicting objectives of the principal countries. The Four claimed to have been 'encouraged' to find substantial agreement on three major points: (1) that the post-war co-operation by the Western European countries and the two associated countries (the United States and Canada) had been successful and should be continued and strengthened; (2) that a turning-point had been reached and new types of problem had arisen; and (3) that countries with economic power had great responsibilities towards the less developed countries. This was a rather meagre list of agreed points on which to base a bold new initiative and a new organization. The views of the twenty governments varied widely on key questions, such as the powers to be given to the new organization and the extent to which the commitments entered into within the OEEC should remain valid, and, more fundamentally, on whether what was needed was a

[38] *A Remodelled Economic Organisation.* A Report by the Group of Four (Paris, April 1960). The four were: W. Randolph Burgess (U.S.), Bernard Clappier (France), Sir Paul Gore-Booth (U.K.), and Xenophon Zolotas (Greece).

'regional' economic organization (and, if so, whether the primary emphasis should be on its 'European' or its 'Atlantic' character), or whether what was required was an organization of developed countries co-operating principally to ensure a more rapid rate of growth not only in their own countries but in the less developed countries of the world.

Although at the time of the founding of the OEEC, and during the early years of that organization, the United States had encouraged those who argued for a strong institution capable of exerting a real influence on national governments, American spokesmen—who were very alive to Congressional sensibilities—now led those who wanted a purely consultative organization. The Swiss were the most vociferous advocates of a relatively strong organization and they were supported not only by the Swedes and by the representatives from some of the other smaller EFTA countries but also by representatives from the Benelux countries and, to some extent, by the Germans. The British were fully aware of the legislative problem in the United States. Moreover, the reasons for the reluctance of the United States to limit its own freedom of action by commitments to combined action in an 'Atlantic' group were not unlike the reasons that led to the United Kingdom's own reluctance to commit itself fully to combined action on a 'European' basis, and the British were undoubtedly rather embarrassed by the persistence with which their EFTA partners (and in particular the Swiss) opposed some of the American suggestions.

In recognition of the strength of the small countries' feelings, the Wise Men had gone considerably beyond the purely consultative organization that the United States had originally advocated, and the institutional arrangements and the voting provisions outlined in their report generally followed the OEEC pattern. Nevertheless, the Swiss, and others, felt that the convention which the Wise Men proposed for the new organization was still too weak. They felt that it failed to endow the organization with any effective powers of decisions and they felt the way the convention was drafted (which was cumbersome) left it open to a country not only to count itself out of an undertaking (as the OEEC Convention permitted) but to block other countries from going ahead among themselves.

The most controversial question that arose during the discussions both with the Wise Men and later in the full group was, not surprisingly, the competence to be given to the new organization in the trade field. This issue not only raised the whole complex of questions involved in the Six–Seven controversy but the further question of whether any trade matters should come within the purview of the new organization or whether, given the changed payments situations, they should now be left to the GATT.

Anyone reading the Wise Men's report 'cold' would have the greatest difficulty making head or tail of the section dealing with trade. The tortuous drafting accurately reflected the fact that the Wise Men had not been able to distil any real agreement from the wide range of views that prevailed on a number of controversial points. However, it was clear that the initial American and French view that all trade questions could now be left to the GATT was not generally acceptable. In any case, it was obvious that if the new organization was to deal broadly with economic policy questions and with problems of economic development, the trade aspects of these matters could not be ignored. The Wise Men also recognized that it would be unrealistic to suppose that the new organization could remain totally unaware of the Six–Seven dispute, although the paragraph on this question is one of the star examples of deliberately ambiguous drafting.[39]

On one important aspect of the trade question the report of the Wise Men was clear: that was that the OEEC's Code of Trade Liberalization should expire, given the substantial measure of external convertibility of the principal European currencies. The French, for familiar reasons, were determined to bury the Code and all that had gone with it, once and for all. The United States and Canada were understandably anxious to bring to an end the remaining quota discrimination against themselves and they were eager to remove the temptation the European countries would have, if their balance of payments deteriorated, to reimpose restrictions against the dollar while giving different, more liberal treatment to their trade with one another. However, the smaller countries and Germany felt that the Code was an important piece of insurance, and they were strongly in favour of keeping it on the

[39] The paragraph read: 'Since the future Organisation will from the beginning have to deal with more or less integrated economic groups, it will certainly have to be alert that their existence does not impede the work of international solidarity which is its main justification. Here again it should therefore be permissible, if necessary, to call upon its competence in trade questions.' Report of the Group of Four, p. 29.

books as a stand-by measure. There was also hope, in some quarters, that the United States and Canada might themselves accept the Code. This would, of course, have removed the discriminatory element to which these countries were opposed, but it would have raised problems of conflict with the GATT and the IMF, and it would have posed difficult, probably insuperable, legislative problems for the United States.

Senior officials from the twenty countries met in Paris in May 1960 to discuss the Wise Men's report and the proposed draft convention. The Swiss had circulated an alternative draft which not only gave greater prominence to the decision-making role of the new organization but in effect reversed the proposal of the Wise Men and provided that the acts of the OEEC (including the Code) should continue to be binding until repealed by the new organization. (In the draft convention proposed by the Wise Men all decisions were to lapse unless specifically approved by the Council of the new organization.) The Swiss draft also placed much emphasis on the role of the new organization in dealing with European trade questions and, generally, in promoting economic co-operation on the OEEC pattern. The emphasis the Wise Men had given to the role the new organization could and should play in assisting economic development was, in contrast, missing from the Swiss proposal.

The upshot of the May meeting was the appointment of an *ad hoc* group to try to reconcile the two drafts in preparation for a ministerial meeting in July. At the July ministerial meeting a number of important concessions were made to the countries, principally the smaller OEEC countries, who stuck fast to the position that they were being asked to buy a pig in a poke and that before they could agree to a new organization they must know much more precisely how it was to be constituted, what it would do in certain fields, and, in particular, how much of the work of the OEEC would be continued. It was agreed that the Preparatory Committee which was to be presided over by the Secretary-General designate of the new organization (Mr. Thorkil Kristensen, a Dane) would forthwith review all the acts of the OEEC to decide which should be terminated and which should be kept in force. The Preparatory Committee was also to complete the draft convention and to recommend what committees should be established, their composition, and their terms of reference. The United States was not prepared to see the continuation or the

extension of the Code of Trade Liberalization but, somewhat to
the dismay of the French, it was ready to agree that the new
organization should have a trade committee in which the trade
policies of the member countries could be discussed, specific
trade problems examined, and problems arising from the Six–
Seven split considered, provided always that the action taken in
the new organization was consistent with the rules of the GATT
and that it supplemented, rather than duplicated, the work of the
GATT.[40] A resolution in this sense was agreed by the ministers,
although for some it did not go far enough and for others it went
rather too far in opening the door to Six–Seven discussions.

The Preparatory Committee completed its work in the autumn
of 1960 and the Convention of the Organization for Economic
Co-operation and Development was finally signed in Paris on
14 December 1960. At the same time the ministers approved the
report of the Preparatory Committee, thus meeting the desires of
those who wanted to know in detail how the existing functions
and commitments of the OEEC would be affected. Given the
position from which the United States, the French, and the other
EEC countries had started, a surprising amount of the work and
method of the OEEC was, in fact, carried over into the new
organization. However, the major United States objective, an
objective that was fully shared by the French and to a considerable extent by the rest of the Six, had been achieved. The
focus of the organization had been shifted: it was no longer an
organization for European co-operation on European problems
but an organization for co-operation on economic problems
affecting not only relations between Europe and North America
but their relations with the developing countries as well.

The British Government would undoubtedly have been happy
to see the reorganization of the OEEC provide the opportunity for

[40] One of the reasons why the United States became readier to see a trade committee established was its desire that any discussions between the Six and
Seven should take place in a forum in which the United States was represented. It is worth noting that during the Senate hearings in connexion with
the ratification of the OECD, Mr. George Ball, Under-Secretary of State, in
reply to questions about the trade provisions of the Convention, said: 'The
major interest of the United States in this, as Secretary Dillon has said, is in
relation to the resolution of the existing problems between the Six and
Seven. Our concern there is to see that in the consideration of this problem
the interests of the United States are represented.' U.S. Senate, Committee on
Foreign Relations, *Organization for Economic Co-operation and Development*
Exec. Report No. 1, 87th Congress, 1st Session.

bringing the Six and Seven together and for re-establishing European co-operation on the basis of a free trade area or of a modified customs union. Alternatively, it would undoubtedly have welcomed the establishment of an organization designed to promote real integration on an 'Atlantic' basis. But after the Special Economic Conference in Paris in January 1960, it realized, and accepted the fact, that neither outcome was on the cards and that the main promise of the new organization lay in promoting closer co-ordination on economic policies between the United States and the European countries. In these circumstances, British views on the kind of organization that should be established were not very different from those of the United States. Moreover, on some of the questions that arose they probably found it rather easier to agree with the French than they did with their EFTA partners.

IX

THE SHIFT IN BRITISH POLICY: REAPPRAISAL

First signs of a new policy

The decision to negotiate with the Six in terms of joining the European Economic Community represented a radical change in British policy. The conclusion that participation in the Community was the right course of action was not reached suddenly nor was it reached simultaneously by all those who share the main responsibility for decision-making. The case for joining the Community had many strands—technical, commercial, economic, political. Some of the arguments for joining were always more important than others, but different people weighted the various arguments differently; they also weighted the same argument differently at different times. To most people, the political reasons for joining were more important than the economic reasons and, as time went on, the political case seemed to most people to grow stronger and the economic case rather weaker. It is clear that in the British Government's decision political considerations were the controlling ones. Mr. Macmillan's announcement in the House of Commons of the Government's decision to open negotiations in terms of joining the Community was not made until 31 July 1961. The year 1960 and the first six months of 1961 was the crucial period during which the Government came, gradually, to this decision. This chapter and the next deal with that period and that process.

After the final breakdown in the free trade area negotiations in December 1958 there had been some rethinking of British policy towards Europe but the time was not propitious for a fundamental reappraisal of policy. The Prime Minister was preoccupied with the problem of East–West negotiations and his impending trip to Moscow. It was clear that a General Election was not far off. The de Gaulle Government was clearly opposed to the free trade area and to variations on that theme, but the prospects for the de Gaulle Government in France and the implications of the de Gaulle

Government for the future development of the European Community were far from clear. British industry, and particularly the powerful FBI, were urging the Government to do something immediately to keep the commercial position in Western Europe from deteriorating further. The Government, albeit with some misgivings, went forward in the only way that then seemed open to it—without a reversal of policy—and consolidated its position with the other OEEC countries by the formation of the EFTA. As indicated in Chapter VII, the EFTA implied no fundamental change in policy; it seemed to be a way of buying time without prejudicing the later reopening of negotiations. The dominant assumption was still that, in time, some kind of free trade area link between the Six and the other European countries would be negotiable and that such a link corresponded with the long-term needs of the United Kingdom. But even before the negotiations on the Stockholm Convention were completed many influential people had come to question the first part of this assumption, that is, the negotiability of a free trade area.[1] And, gradually, there began to be questioning of the second, much more important part of this assumption, that is, that a 'bridge' or an association with the Six, as opposed to membership in the Community, was the right relationship for the United Kingdom.

By the spring of 1960 it was generally accepted that a pure free trade area would not be negotiable and that any arrangement with the Six would, at the least, involve a large measure of tariff harmonization, and a considerable number of responsible people felt that a new negotiation would have to be in terms of a fully-fledged customs union. A few people felt that only a willingness to join the Community would suffice. But the argument about whether the United Kingdom's real interest lay in joining the Six or in a looser

[1] As indicated above, pp. 183–4, during the debate in the House of Commons after the collapse of the free trade area negotiations, Mr. John Edwards had suggested that in a new negotiation the possibility of offering a large measure of harmonization should be considered. See also two very interesting articles in the *Manchester Guardian* of 4 and 5 May 1959 by Mr. Peter Thorneycroft, at that time not in the Cabinet but a Conservative M.P. He proposed an approach compounded of the following ingredients: a harmonized tariff with the Six for manufactures and for raw materials (with a few exceptions), continued free entry for food (which he, mistakenly as later events proved, thought would present no problem), and the gradual elimination of the preferential treatment given to British goods in Commonwealth markets. As part of this plan, the Commonwealth countries would use their elimination of the preference rate for British goods to negotiate for better access to the Six for Commonwealth products.

arrangement had only just begun. On one level the decision as to whether joining or association was the right answer was related to the judgement as to whether or not the Six would insist—as a basic condition—on a full customs union; some people felt the Six would not go that far and that if the United Kingdom agreed to align its m.f.n. tariffs with the common external tariff of the Six it might be allowed to continue to give preferential rates, or at least free entry, to all, or most, of the imports from the Commonwealth.[2] On a more fundamental level the judgement on whether association or membership was the right answer turned on the assumptions made about Britain's position in the world over the long term.

Soon after the General Election in October 1959, at which the Conservative Government was returned with an increased majority, the problem of the British relationship to Europe began to be examined in a more fundamental way than had occurred at any time since the end of the war. It was obvious that although there were certain advantages to be gained from membership in the EFTA, the EFTA was, essentially, of peripheral importance. The core of the problem had always been, and would continue to be, until settled in one way or another, the relationship to be established between the United Kingdom and the Six. The first and most obvious task after the General Election was to rebuild cross-channel communications, particularly with the French and German

---

[2] One of the big difficulties in accepting a common external tariff (which would be necessary if the United Kingdom joined either a customs union or the Common Market) was the fact that the United Kingdom would have to establish a 'reverse preference' against the Commonwealth, that is, to take away an existing preference and to treat the trade of the Commonwealth countries not simply on a par with that of the Six but worse than that of the Six. The British felt that it should be possible to find some way of avoiding this. One possibility was to retain tariff freedom for certain items. Other possibilities, consistent with accepting a common external tariff, were the granting of tariff-free quotas or the reduction to nil of the common external tariff on the goods affected. If some such arrangement could be made, the Commonwealth countries would not have had a 'reverse preference' established against them, although they would have lost their own preference in the British market. Members of the Government at various times emphasized that it would be a step backwards to put on tariffs where none existed before. For example, Mr. Erroll (Minister of State, Board of Trade), in a speech at Hamburg on 22 June 1960, said: 'Our trade policy and arrangements, in particular our system of free entry for Commonwealth goods, and of Commonwealth preferences, is designed for a world outside Europe. To assume the tariffs of the Common Market, and to place tariffs on imports where no tariffs have been, seems to us a curious step to have to take in order to obtain greater freedom of trade. We hope that we shall never have to do this. We hope too that the will to compromise on these matters will develop.' Board of Trade Press Release.

Governments. Mr. Macmillan's efforts at summitry early in 1959 had profoundly annoyed both the German and the French Governments and had led to a coolness on the diplomatic front. Moreover, during 1959 a period of mutual back-turning had more or less inevitably resulted from the Community's preoccupation with the coming into force of the substantive provisions of the Treaty of Rome and from the Seven's preoccupation with the formation of EFTA. This drifting apart was accentuated by the inactivity of the OEEC and the drying-up of the daily encounters at working level that had been the rule since the formation of the OEEC in 1948. In the summer of 1959 the gulf between the British, on the one hand, and the French and Germans on the other hand threatened to become wider and deeper, partly as a result of the deliberate policy of close *rapprochement* pursued by Dr. Adenauer and General de Gaulle, and partly as a result of the efforts of the 'Europeans' to push ahead even more rapidly than the Treaty of Rome provided and to extend Six-country co-operation to new fields.

Accordingly, in the autumn of 1959 a several-pronged attack on the problem was mounted by the British Government. First there was a considerable effort to improve political relations. Mr. Selwyn Lloyd visited Paris in mid-November (1959) and Dr. Adenauer was invited to London later in the month. Before both sets of visits the press of the two countries indulged in an orgy of introspection on the reasons for the obvious lack of warmth in Anglo-French and then Anglo-German relations, and after each of the visits there was considerable comment to the effect that the worst was now over and that a new period of greater mutual understanding of each other's problems and intentions had begun. The British also made use of forums such as the Assembly of the WEU and the Consultative Assembly of the Council of Europe to try to dispel the widespread suspicion of British motives that existed on the Continent and to make it clear not only that they were genuinely in favour of the Common Market (as an arrangement for the Six, that is) but also that they were genuinely anxious to find a way to co-operate closely with the Common Market without undermining it. This was the period, too, when (as described in Chapter VIII) the British sought to breathe new life into the WEU and to persuade the Six that any steps taken to tighten political arrangements among themselves should be accompanied by a tightening of relations on a WEU basis and that any closer co-operation in the political or defence field should be within the framework of the

WEU and NATO. This dual approach of seeking, on the one hand, to emphasize their support for the Six and their own 'Europeanism', and, on the other, of trying to dissuade the Six from developing an independent line on political and defence questions was very prominent in Mr. Selwyn Lloyd's address to the Consultative Assembly of the Council of Europe on 21 January 1960. This speech was obviously a considered statement of the British Government's views as they existed at the turn of the year and it is therefore worth quoting at some length from the section of the speech relating to the European problem.

I want to put to you as simply but as definitely as I can the British position. We regard ourselves as part of Europe, for reasons of sentiment, of history and geography. The fact that the Alps and the Pyrenees have been more easily crossed in war than the Channel does not disqualify the United Kingdom from European status. It is true that we have also another association, but it is one not incompatible with our European status. Our Queen is the head of the Commonwealth, and that fact of the Commonwealth, with its widely differing peoples, has certain constitutional and economic consequences which must be taken into account. But that does not disqualify us from European status. We are also members of the Atlantic Community, but again, this is not inconsistent with European status, because we share that position with many other European countries. A larger 'Atlantic Community' does not preclude a European association.

I shall be told: 'It is all very well for you to say that you are part of Europe, but you have done nothing to promote European unity since the war. You did not come into the Coal and Steel Community. You did not come into E.D.C. You are opposed to the Six. You prefer a Europe which is divided and in which you can play one group off against another. What is more, when you are being your nicest you are most to be suspected.'

My answer to that sort of statement would be along these lines. On the first point, I believe we made a mistake in not taking part in the negotiations which led to the formation of the Coal and Steel Community. I know that we ended up by making a Treaty of Association with the Community,[3] but I fully appreciate that that is not the same thing as joining. Moreover, I am not certain that the arrangements for the Association are working out in practice as well as they might have been hoped to.

So far as E.D.C. was concerned, I say frankly that I always doubted whether it was a practicable proposition. I think that recent events have served to sustain that doubt.

[3] Treaty Series No. 51 (1956), Cmnd. 13.

But the matter with which you are concerned in your debate, the topical matter, is the suggestion that we in Britain are opposed to the Community of the Six. This I categorically deny. We welcomed the Rome Agreements at the time. It is true that we were assured by all concerned that they would lead to a Free Trade Area, but we welcomed the Rome Treaties for their own sakes, because a strong political unity of the Six is good for Western Europe and for Britain. We welcome it, and we will support it. There is one proviso about which I have found no difference of opinion, a proviso which is generally accepted. I could detect no difference of opinion about it in the speeches yesterday. It is that this new entity should not develop as an inward-looking political or economic group. It should not be in opposition to a bigger Europe. I will say exactly what I mean by that.

In the field of economics, if the Community has high tariffs, and is rigidly protectionist, then there will be a trade war in Western Europe, and political cohesion will not survive. The last 12 months have given us some experience from which we must profit. After the failure of the Free Trade Area negotiations just over a year ago, there was an unpleasant undercurrent. There was a definite deterioration in relations between London and Paris and London and Bonn. There was a feeling of division, almost of distrust. I am not talking so much of the relations between Governments, the relations between Foreign Offices, but of something more general.

It was because of that feeling that immediately after the Election I decided to go to Paris to speak frankly to my French colleagues along these lines, and to see whether we could not make a fresh start. I told the French Ministers exactly what I have said to you to-day about our attitude to the European Community. I also spoke on these lines to the other Foreign Ministers. I received in return assurances that it was not intended to be a highly protectionist rigid Community, and that liberal trade policies were to be put into force. My French and other colleagues said that they realised the need to prevent this gap opening in Europe. I was therefore very glad to hear Professor Hallstein confirm that view yesterday.

So far as political matters are concerned, if the Six become an exclusive Community, it will mean a change in European relationships. For example, if the Six were to decide to discuss and form a common policy about matters outside the internal affairs of the Community, if they were, for example, without consultation with their other allies, to formulate their policy with regard to disarmament, or Africa, or East–West relations, to give three examples—they have a perfect right to see things develop in that way, but, if it were to happen—I do not see how Western European Union could survive, and the obligations which we have undertaken thereunder. I think also that it would profoundly affect NATO. On that matter also, however, I have been told

definitely by all my colleagues of the Six that there is no wish or intention to develop political consultation among the Six in the way
which I have described above.[4]

In addition to using ministerial meetings, normal diplomatic
channels, and various European forums to try to create a better
political atmosphere and to draw closer to the Six, the British also
undertook, early in 1960, a profound re-examination of their
relations towards Europe and of the assumptions that had governed
their European policy since the end of the war. In particular, there
seems to have been a searching re-examination of the validity of
the Churchillian doctrine of the three interlocking circles, that is,
of the assumption that the United Kingdom had a unique role to
play as the common factor in three sets of relationships—the
relationship with Europe, the relationship with the Commonwealth, and the relationship with the United States—and also of
the validity of the assumption that too close a relationship with
Europe would necessarily weaken the other two relationships.
This process of review and re-examination took place on various
levels and continued throughout the spring and early summer.
Mr. Selwyn Lloyd's speech to the Council of Europe was evidence
that the Foreign Office was now taking a new interest in the problem of Britain's relations with the Six. Foreign Office interest had
been conspicuously lacking during the long negotiations on a free
trade area but seems to have been aroused by the deterioration in
relations after the breakdown in those negotiations and to have
increased markedly as the signs grew that the Six were seriously
discussing new forms of political co-operation.

Early in the New Year, the Economic Steering Committee, an
interdepartmental committee of senior civil servants concerned
with questions of broad economic policy, with Sir Frank Lee as
Chairman, re-examined the courses of action open to the Government in their relationship with the Six.[5] This review, which was
highly confidential, seems to have covered a wide range of policy
questions—political as well as economic—and the whole spectrum
of possibilities from abandoning the attempt to find any accommodation with the Six to joining the Community. The short-term
and the long-term implications of various courses of action were

---

[4] Council of Europe, *Official Report of Debates*, Eleventh Ordinary Session of
the Consultative Assembly, Strasbourg, January 1960, pp. 760–4.
[5] On 1 January 1960 Sir Frank Lee had moved from the Board of Trade to
become Permanent Secretary at the Treasury.

considered in the light of probable developments in Europe, in the Commonwealth, and in relations with the United States. The conclusion reached by Sir Frank Lee and his group was that the United Kingdom should seek to join the Six. The reasons for their conclusion were primarily, although not exclusively, political.

Most of the considerations that played a part in the eventual decision to seek to join the Six seemed to have been present in the discussions in the Economic Steering Committee, although some of the arguments for joining the Six tended to gain in force and others to become less important as time went on. The fear of political instability on the Continent apparently loomed very large at this time; there was great uncertainty about what would happen in France after de Gaulle (this was the period of maximum anxiety over Algeria when General de Gaulle was under constant threat of assassination) and in Germany after Dr. Adenauer ceased to be Chancellor. There seems to have been very real concern that the European Community might not be strong enough to weather the strains of political upheaval in France or to restrain a less 'Atlantic' minded Chancellor than Dr. Adenauer. And it was recognized that the disintegration of the Community would be a set-back for the Western world. Coupled with this feeling that the United Kingdom would be profoundly affected by political upheaval on the Continent and must in its own interest see that the Community was a success, there was a rather contradictory concern: if the Community prospered and became a strong, closely knit power-complex of 170 million people to which inevitably as the years went by the United States looked as its main partner in the free world, the United Kingdom was bound to lose in relative power, with all that implied for its own relations not only with the United States but with the Commonwealth as well. The judgement that the shortest way to a real Atlantic partnership probably lay through the United Kingdom's joining the European Community also played a part in these early discussions, although this consideration assumed more importance later on. The economic case for joining was secondary; however, the Steering Committee felt that participation in the Community would be likely to stimulate economic growth by giving British industry the opportunity to exploit the advantages of scale offered by a large domestic market and by exposing the British economy to the forced draught of competition. It seems clear enough that Sir Frank Lee and his colleagues came to the conclusion that both the political and the economic advantages they sought would be more surely obtained by joining the Community than by some form of 'association' and that, in any case, 'association' was unlikely to be negotiable.

The Prime Minister appears to have been very much in agreement with the conclusions reached by the Economic Steering Committee but many members of the Cabinet felt there was no need for such a radical shift in policy, and that an arrangement short of membership was preferable and, in time, negotiable. Nevertheless, during the spring the government departments concerned were asked to examine the Treaty of Rome, article by article, and to report on the implications of accepting the main provisions of the treaty, both in terms of the cost in pounds, shillings, and pence and in terms of the modifications in British policy that would have to be made. This detailed examination of the problems inherent in joining the Community took place during the spring and seems to have been finished late in May or early in June.

Mr. Dillon's initiatives at the end of 1959 and early in 1960 thus came at a time when the British were in the process of rethinking their position but well before they had come to any conclusion. It was nevertheless a symptom of the change that had, in fact, already taken place in Britain's view of its relationship with Europe that the American proposals made during the winter of 1959-60 were greeted with reserve and a measure of scepticism rather than being enthusiastically welcomed. Had the United States been prepared to accept commitments with respect to the OEEC countries that went as far as those the United Kingdom was then ready to accept, the response might well have been different. But it was clear that for a number of reasons—some good, some less persuasive—the United States was not then ready to go nearly as far as was the United Kingdom in freeing trade, in co-ordinating policies, or in accepting institutional arrangements that impinged materially on sovereignty. In addition, the linking of the discussion on the reorganization of the OEEC with the European trade dispute raised doubts about whether the primary motive behind the American proposals was to launch a new form of Atlantic co-operation or whether the primary motive was to help those in the Six who were seeking to divert pressures for a European settlement. Thus, because opinion in the United Kingdom about the kind of relationship it wanted, and felt it needed, with the Continent had developed to the point where only a much more far-reaching American proposal would have been considered to be a substitute for a

European arrangement, the British response was to welcome the United States' initiative for the promise it held of somewhat closer 'Atlantic' relations and as another means of re-establishing and maintaining contacts with the Six until the time came for real negotiations, but to welcome it as a supplement to, not as a substitute for, a European settlement.

It seems clear that United States policy at this time, far from diverting the United Kingdom from pursuing the goal of a European settlement, tended to strengthen the position of those who argued that the right course of action lay in seeking the closest possible relationship with the Six. The limited character of the obligations the United States was prepared to undertake in the reorganized OEEC helped to disillusion those who had hoped that an Atlantic framework would be created soon enough to obviate the need for a prior decision on the British relationship with the Six. In addition the obvious United States backing for the Six in the Paris meetings annoyed the British and added to the feeling that the 'special relationship' between the United Kingdom and the United States was in danger of being supplanted by a 'special relationship' between the Six and the United States, and that this danger would grow as the Six became more cohesive. During the spring the strong United States support for the acceleration of the Common Market seemed to be further evidence that the 'special relationship' with the United States was more apparent and more real to the United Kingdom than it was to the United States. So, too, did the American reactions to Mr. Macmillan's discussions in Washington in March (1960). These also underlined the fact that the United States Administration did not, at this time, share the British estimate of the dangers implicit in a form of European unity that did not include the United Kingdom.

Very little has been officially revealed about the Macmillan 'incident'. The British Prime Minister had gone to Washington, ostensibly, at least, to discuss questions relating to negotiations with the Soviet Union and, in particular, the latest Russian suggestion on the control of nuclear explosions. While in Washington he also talked about the European trade problem with the Secretary of State and with Mr. Dillon and he emphasized—in very strong terms—the dangers he saw arising from a continuation of the split in Europe. The exact language he used to express his fears and the precise steps he indicated that the United Kingdom might feel it necessary to adopt if no accommodation with the Six were found have never been made entirely clear. A report that appeared in the *Washington Post* was widely quoted in the British and continental press. This seemed to confirm the worst suspicions of those who had always maintained that the British objective was to break up the Six and to keep continental Europe divided. According to this report, Mr. Macmillan had indicated that, if the split continued, Britain would have no alternative but to lead another peripheral coalition, much as it had done in the days of Napoleon. He was also reported to have said that the economic results of the division might be severe enough to cause the British to reimpose dollar import restrictions and further to reduce British troops in Germany.

The continental reaction to the Washington press report was immediate and violent, and the Foreign Office took the unusual step of issuing a statement denying certain aspects of the report. This was followed by a statement by the Prime Minister himself in the House of Commons on his return from Washington. Both the Foreign Office statement and Mr. Macmillan's statement sought to make it plain that the Prime Minister's object had been not to destroy or weaken the Six, nor to disparage the new friendship between Germany and France, which, as Mr. Macmillan told the House of Commons, was 'absolutely vital to the future peace in Europe', but to keep the economic gap in Europe from growing:

> What I have pleaded for—and I pray that I have said it strongly, because I feel it so deeply—is that we should not allow an economic gap, a sort of division, to grow up which, gradually—I do not say in the short run, but in the long run, as all history has proved—will make another division in Europe. We have seen over and over again how fatal that is: in my own lifetime I have seen it twice. It is not the particular groupings of Powers, but a division, and I have made the plea, and I make the plea again, that, somehow or other, we should, in the next period, try to make that gap so small that it is wearable and does not have these effects.[6]

At this time, the British Government felt that the United States, the European Commission, and others in the Six were deliberately going out of their way to deepen and harden the gap between the United Kingdom and the Six, and emotions and resentment ran high. The immediate question on which the Prime Minister sought a change in American policy was the acceleration of the Common Market. But it seems clear that his main concern was with the

[6] *Hansard*, House of Commons, 1 April 1960, cols. 1671–2.

larger and more fundamental question of whether Europe was to be organized into a tight but limited grouping or on a more inclusive but less far-reaching basis; regardless of his exact words, Mr. Macmillan was essentially seeking United States support for, or at least acceptance of, a looser, larger European grouping which would include the United Kingdom.

The Prime Minister's statement and the Foreign Office statement unequivocally denied that the United Kingdom wanted to weaken or destroy the Six and reiterated that the British concern was not with the unity of the Six, as such, but with the signs of a deepening of the gap between themselves and the Six. Nevertheless it was also clear that the British were deeply concerned at the political implication of a new independent power on the Continent. Significantly, the Prime Minister used the phrase 'this commercial treaty' to describe the arrangement among the Six that he was welcoming, and the Foreign Office statement endorsed the statement made by the Foreign Secretary to the Council of Europe in January, quoted above, in which he welcomed the economic and political unity of the Six but with the proviso that 'this new unity should not develop as an inward-looking political or economic group. It should not be in opposition to a bigger Europe.'

In the short term the Prime Minister's plea in Washington was counter-productive: rather than encouraging second thoughts it strengthened the support in Washington and on the Continent for the acceleration of the Common Market. One of the most disturbing aspects of the incident for the British was the readiness with which even the most flamboyant versions of what Mr. Macmillan was reported to have said were accepted without question on the Continent. In the longer term, the incident and the emotional explosion that followed probably helped to clear the air. The continental reactions certainly brought home to the British in a dramatic way the widespread mistrust and suspicion of their intentions that still had to be dispelled. Moreover, the episode contributed to the growing conviction that the next British approach to the Six—if it were to be well received on the Continent and in Washington—would have to be one that took full account of 'European' hopes and fears.

During the late spring and early summer of 1960 speculation and press comment on Britain's relations with the Six came in torrents. In mid-May the Commonwealth Prime Ministers met in London, and this meeting gave rise to various rumours that new

British proposals were being considered. The communiqué issued at the end of the meeting was studiously uninformative.[7] And questions in Parliament elicited only a meagre additional crumb from Mr. Butler: 'I think I can quote the words of the Prime Minister of Australia. Speaking in London on 28 April he said: "We want to see the highest possible measure of unity. We do not want to see it at the sacrifice of matters that are important to you and are important to us." Provided we agree on that and do not do away with Commonwealth free entry, which might otherwise be in danger, certainly we shall do our best to get constructive unity in Europe.'[8]

It seems clear that at this Commonwealth meeting the European economic problem was discussed, but only perfunctorily and in the most general terms. British ministers apparently indicated that they thought negotiations with the Six were unlikely to be resumed for some time. They also appear to have indicated that in a new negotiation they might decide to give up their right to preferential treatment in the Commonwealth, doubtless pointing out that this would give the Commonwealth countries a useful counter for bargaining for better access for their own goods in the markets of the Community. And, as Mr. Maudling later made plain, the British once again reaffirmed the promise they had previously given the Commonwealth countries that in any negotiation with the Six they would safeguard existing entry arrangements into the United Kingdom market for food, drink, and tobacco from the Commonwealth.[9] The serious discussion with the Commonwealth countries

[7] The relevant paragraph of the communiqué read as follows: 'The Ministers discussed European trade problems. They expressed concern at the prospect of any economic division in Europe and its possible political implications. The countries of Europe form an important market for Commonwealth exports. The Ministers expressed their hope that these countries would follow trade policies in accordance with the principles of the General Agreement on Tariffs and Trade, and thus avoid damage to the economies of the primary producing countries and those that are also developing exports of manufactured goods. In addition, European countries have an important contribution to make in assisting the economic development of the less advanced countries. The Ministers hoped that these problems could be speedily and satisfactorily resolved, with due regard to the interests of countries outside Europe.' Press Release, Commonwealth Relations Office, 13 May 1960.

[8] *Hansard*, House of Commons, 19 May 1960, col. 1483.

[9] In winding up the debate in the House of Commons on 25 July (see below, p. 298) Mr. Maudling, then President of the Board of Trade, said: 'I was asked about the position of the Commonwealth countries. I can say that they have always recognised the importance of a united Europe and the difficulties and dangers involved for the United Kingdom, and, indeed, for them as well in a

on the implications of a British decision to join the customs union of the Six did not begin until the autumn.

Although *The Economist* and some other papers had edged fairly close to advocating joining the Common Market during the brief period after the collapse of the free trade area negotiations and before the formation of the EFTA, the temper of the debate in the United Kingdom in the late spring and early summer of 1960 was different in kind as well as degree from the much more tentative and short-lived flirtation with the idea of joining the Six that had taken place the year before. Except for the Beaverbrook papers, led by the *Daily Express* and, at the other end of the political spectrum, the *Daily Worker*, which were adamantly against involvement with the Six, the British press was united in feeling that the Government must work for the closest possible relationship with the Continent and, by the summer of 1960, some papers had begun to advocate joining the Common Market.

The Government's decision to abandon Blue Streak (which was made public in April) was seen by several commentators as a turning-point in government policy and a turning-point which made inevitable, sooner or later, a decision to join the European Community. For example, Harold Wincott, writing in the *Financial Times* of 26 April 1960, commented: 'A Britain which aimed at less of the old kind of prestige but which was more willing to get into the European complex—right in, if necessary—would be more viable and ironically enough, would end up with greater prestige.'[10]

On 11 June, *The Economist* announced that its mind was made up: 'With due flourish, and after appropriate consultations with fellow members of EFTA, we believe that Britain would be wise to make an offer of full-scale participation in the European common market and community.' The *Observer* also advocated joining,

---

division of Western Europe. Also, they have always relied on the promise that we have given them time and time again that we would maintain their position in our market for their foodstuffs, drink and tobacco. Of course, signing the Treaty of Rome would involve putting that policy of preference completely on its head and giving preference to Europe instead. Therefore, although the Commonwealth countries have been and remain extremely helpful, sympathetic and understanding of our difficulties, they have always felt that they could rely on the undertaking that we have given them.' *Hansard*, House of Commons, 25 July 1960, cols. 1209–10.

[10] During the winter of 1960–1 the *Financial Times* became one of the most ardent advocates of full membership, but at this time, during the spring and summer of 1960, its preferred prescription appeared to be a European customs union.

although throughout the long debate this paper revealed an ambivalence that was characteristic of much of the liberal support for joining the Community. On the one hand it deplored the timidity of the Government's approach to Europe and, initially at any rate, it tended to minimize the difficulties in Britain's joining the Community; on the other hand, it repeatedly voiced its concern lest a stronger organization of the Western European community would make permanent the division of Germany and prejudice the adoption of various schemes for *détente* in central Europe. Moreover, the *Observer*, like a number of other British papers, took a somewhat jaundiced view of the 'fanaticism' of the 'technocrats' in Brussels, a line of comment that did little to reassure the 'Europeans'.[11]

The *Guardian*, although somewhat more circumspect than *The Economist* and the *Observer*, was also an early champion of joining. Its position was summed up in a leader on 27 May: 'The choice is exceedingly difficult; once the initial shift towards Europe is made, radical changes in defence and foreign policy must follow. But the choice is between swimming in the main stream and vegetating in a backwater.'

The pressure for a Government decision to join the Community did not come only from professional journalists. Various Members of Parliament, Conservative and Labour as well as Liberal, advocated this course of action, as did some business leaders, although the main pressure from industrial circles did not come until the following spring. On 18 July a closely reasoned article by Aubrey Jones (a former Conservative minister) appeared in the *Guardian*. He argued that the United Kingdom should join the Common Market and 'the mainstream of the whole process of European integration' and should do so now rather than hoping that the terms would become easier if the decision were postponed. Many influential people came to share, and to voice, this view during the next twelve months, but in the summer of 1960 the prevailing view in Government and business circles was that time would make a settlement easier.

Although the number of voices calling for a more radical policy was impressive, there was a hectic, over-heated aspect to much of the public argument during the spring and summer of 1960. 'Shut your eyes, hold your nose, and jump!' was too frequently the brief prescription. Moreover the strongest 'join Europe now' arguments

[11] See, for example, the leader in the *Observer*, 3 July 1960.

were disconcertingly often coupled with reassurances that once in the Community, the British could ensure that the 'federalist' water did not become too deep. This line of argument, like the enthusiasm shown by *The Times*,[12] among others, for General de Gaulle's disparaging comments on federalism, simply renewed apprehensions in many quarters of the Continent about the motives behind any appearance of British enthusiasm for Europe. Then too, much of the argument was in terms not of the positive advantages to be gained from becoming 'European' but was simply a counsel of despair; that joining was the only way to achieve the limited objective of free trade with the Six. On the other hand, some advocates of joining went to the other extreme and argued as Alan Day did: 'In the simplest terms, if we do not get involved in Europe, we shall find ourselves in twenty years' time remarkably like those tourist advertisements for Britain in the *New Yorker*— quaint, charming, pleasantly prosperous, and rather ineffectual.'[13] Most of the advocates of joining minimized the difficulties of doing so, or supported the approach then being advocated by M. Monnet, and some other European leaders as well, namely that the United Kingdom should first sign the Treaty of Rome and then arrange, from within the Community, any necessary safeguards for the Commonwealth and for British agriculture.[14]

In addition to the clarion calls for taking the plunge and joining the Community there was also a good deal of discussion, in the press and elsewhere, of the feasibility of Britain's participating in a European customs union, for the assumption now generally accepted by the Government, by industry, and by informed public opinion was that any new negotiation with the Six, if it were to stand any chance of success, would—as a minimum—have to be in terms of a customs union rather than a free trade area.[15] At this time there were also numerous suggestions that the United Kingdom should, as a first step, join the European Coal and Steel Community and Euratom. As indicated above, the Foreign Secretary, Mr. Selwyn Lloyd, had indicated in his speech to the Consultative Assembly of the Council of Europe in January that he felt it had been a mistake for the United Kingdom to have held aloof from the Schuman Plan. And, early in June, a statement made

[12] See leading article, 2 June 1960.
[13] See *Listener*, 7 July, 1960, 'Get In or Keep Out?'
[14] See, e.g., Alan Day in the *Listener*, loc. cit.
[15] See the feature article 'What European Customs Union would mean', *Financial Times*, 10 June 1960.

to the WEU Assembly in Paris by Mr. Profumo (then Minister of State, Foreign Office) gave substance to the rumours that the possibility of joining the ECSC or Euratom, or both, was now under consideration, although, as Mr. Profumo made clear enough in his statement, it was only under consideration as part of a general settlement.

The WEU consideration of British membership in one or two of the Communities was short-lived and came to nothing in the end, but the episode is worth describing because it presumably contributed to the official British view that the time was not yet ripe for new negotiations. The problem of the United Kingdom relationship to the Six was debated at the WEU Assembly meeting early in June (1960) on the basis of a report prepared by the chairman of the General Affairs Committee, M. Conte, a French socialist. The report included a recommendation to the Council of the WEU asking it to use its good offices to 'facilitate the successful conclusion of the negotiations at present being conducted in the Committee on Trade Questions of the Twenty-one with a view to achieving a practical agreement between the European Economic Community and the European Free Trade Association'. It also included a recommendation, to which M. Conte said he attached much more importance, namely: 'That the governments of the seven member States which form the Council examine together the possibility of the United Kingdom acceding as a full member of the European ·Atomic Energy Community (Euratom).'[16] Mr. Profumo, in commenting on M. Conte's report, was circumspect but encouraging:

I cannot, of course, say what will be the view of the Council of Western European Union to these recommendations. I can say, however, that the British Government, without regard to all that has happened in the last few years, will certainly be ready to consider anew the proposal that Britain should join Euratom, and indeed, the European Coal and Steel Community as well. But I do not want to be misunderstood. This is not, at this particular moment, a simple question. First, we have to know whether we would be welcome. I am encouraged by what M. Conte has said. Then, since this has not only technical, but political, significance, we have to know what the effect would be upon the immediate situation. Any decision that we would take, if we were given the opportunity, must be taken with full regard to the loyalties that we have towards our partners in the European Free Trade As-

[16] Recommendation No. 48, adopted by the WEU Assembly at their Sixth Sitting, June 1960.

sociation. I would feel that the best way to look at this would be from the point of view of what makes a real contribution to the purpose that we all have in mind—the unity of Western Europe.[17]

Mr. Profumo was reacting to a specific suggestion put forward in the Assembly, and by a Frenchman at that, and was not therefore necessarily deliberately flying a kite, although he may well have been happy to grasp the opportunity to do so. Reaction in the WEU Assembly was encouraging and the recommendation was adopted unanimously. Reactions elsewhere in the Six were less encouraging, however, and there were those among the 'Europeans' who felt that, far from being a helpful move, this was simply a British attempt to forestall the consolidation of the Communities. For some time the merging of the Executives of the three Communities had been under active consideration among the Six, and presumably recognition that an unflattering construction might therefore be put on a move to join one or two Communities was one reason for the tentative nature of the British statement.

M. Monnet took the opportunity of an interview on television in London, two days later, to make it clear that he did not think much of the suggestion: 'Now, the institutions—Coal and Steel, Euratom, Common Market—they are all steps towards that goal. They are nothing in themselves, and therefore I think as far as Great Britain is concerned the main question is whether she will decide to join the whole procession, if I may say so, and not a piece of it, leaving the rest aside.' During the same interview M. Monnet also stressed the point that he, for his part, felt that the difference between a free trade area link between the Six and the Seven and a link by means of a customs union was not significant: 'In both of them a preferential agreement will be created between the nations that will form that zone, and it will discriminate against the United States. And it will not provide what the Common Market provides, which is the creation of an economic unit. What you are talking about is a trading arrangement. What I am talking about is getting the nations and the individuals together, to form a vast market of production, which will change, we think, not only the conditions of production but the attitude of people towards one another. This is entirely different from a trading agreement'.[18] And, on 11 July 1960, the Action Committee for the United States of Europe, of

[17] WEU, *Debates*, Sixth Ordinary Session, First Part, June 1960, p. 137.
[18] See *Guardian*, 4 June 1960.

which M. Monnet was the founder, president, and moving spirit, adopted the following resolution:

> The European Community has always been open, and remains so. Now that the Common Market is becoming irreversible and profitable in the eyes of all, the conditions exist for the creation of new links between the European Community and the United Kingdom and the other European countries.
>
> Today, it is possible to envisage the participation of all in the common task of unifying Europe.
>
> Accordingly the Action Committee, echoing the wishes of the vast majority of citizens in our countries, earnestly hopes that the United Kingdom and the other European countries will simultaneously become members of the Coal and Steel Community, Euratom and the Common Market which are three facets of a single reality. This reality is the emerging European economic union, that is paving the way for a political unity, the exact nature of which cannot now be foreseen.[19]

The recommendation from the WEU Assembly was before the WEU Council when the Ministers met at The Hague later in the month. It would have been difficult to take no action and it may well have been that Mr. Selwyn Lloyd welcomed this opportunity to renew Mr. Profumo's offer and to test ministerial reactions among the Six to the possibility of beginning the process of *rapprochement* in this way. The upshot of the discussion by the WEU Council was the decision to request an *ad hoc* group (not a formal WEU sub-committee but the Ambassadors in London of the Six and a representative from the Foreign Office) to examine the problem. This was about the least that could decently have been done and it is rather surprising that, at first, the decision was played up by the British press as a dramatic new development; comments soon became more realistic. Little was officially revealed about the ministerial talks but it seems probable that Mr. Selwyn Lloyd was more concerned to test reactions and to create the right atmosphere for future negotiations on the larger problem of the British relationship with the Common Market than he was to begin active negotiations looking towards British membership in the ECSC and Euratom. It also seems probable that reactions at this meeting and at the subsequent discussion in the *ad hoc* group, as well as at the Trade Committee meeting in Paris (see Chapter VIII), led the Foreign Secretary and Mr. Maudling to say quite categorically in

---

[19] *Joint Declaration*, adopted unanimously by the Action Committee at its Eighth Session, 11 July 1960, Paris.

the July debate in the House of Commons that the Six had recently shown that they were not ready for negotiations.

The committee set up by the WEU Council met in London on 22 June. It was plain that the representatives from the Six were in some disarray and that none of them were very much interested in discussing the Euratom and the ECSC problem until the British Cabinet took a decision, in principle, on the broader question of joining the Economic Community. The furthest the Cabinet was then prepared to go was not to decide not to join; this left the problem too vague for definitive work by an intergovernmental group, and it is hardly surprising that after a few more meetings the *ad hoc* committee quietly petered out.

The British interdepartmental examination of the implications of joining the Community was completed in the late spring and the question was considered by the Cabinet during the early summer.[20] The report prepared for the Cabinet has not, of course, been made public, but the broad conclusions of the policy review can be deduced from press comment and from Government statements during the debate in the House of Commons at the end of July. The main conclusions appear to have been (1) that, in the long term, the interests of the United Kingdom lay in giving a higher priority than heretofore to its European relationship, (2) that joining the Treaty of Rome might in fact be the only way to achieve as close a relationship with the Six as was now felt to be desirable, (3) that joining was technically feasible provided, but only provided, certain modifications in the Community's arrangements could be negotiated, and (4) that the political case for 'close association' or for joining was stronger than the economic case.

Mr. Macmillan, a few other members of the Cabinet, and a few key people in the upper reaches of the civil service had come to feel that, at the right time, it might well be desirable to negotiate with the Six in terms of joining the Treaty of Rome, but this was still very far from being Government policy. Broadly speaking, there appears to have been general agreement on the objective of free trade and close political relations with the Six but considerable disagreement over whether the way to achieve this

[20] On 14 July 1960 the *Daily Express* carried banner headlines and a short summary account of a 'sensational secret report' prepared in Whitehall 'on the personal instructions of Mr. Macmillan'. The *Daily Express* also commented editorially that the report was a 'blueprint for disaster' and that it meant 'soaring prices for the housewife', 'ruin for the small farmer', and 'betrayal of Empire producers'.

end was by a negotiation in terms of joining the Community or in terms of forming a modified customs union with the Six and strengthening political links, perhaps through WEU. However, the Government was in full agreement that no negotiations should be formally opened until there had been careful informal preparation and until a successful outcome seemed reasonably assured. The prevailing view was that the time was not yet ripe for a negotiation, and the Government was determined not to be panicked into making a premature move by the mounting pressure to take the plunge and join the Common Market.

The Common Market campaign carried on by the press and by 'European' groups in the United Kingdom during the spring and summer of 1960 was both useful and confusing. On the one hand it undoubtedly encouraged the Government to feel that public opinion might well support a shift of policy in favour of a more complete commitment to the Continent than any that had previously been contemplated. On the other hand even the most sophisticated journals and newspapers grossly oversimplified the very real problems inherent in joining the Community, generally taking the position that once the decision in principle to join had been made the difficulties would be seen to be readily soluble. Although the emphasis on the need for a decision in principle was undoubtedly right, the underplaying of real difficulties complicated the Government's negotiating position with the Six. In addition, the calls for immediate action and the suggestions that dramatic moves were imminent pushed the Government into a defensive position and made it necessary for official spokesmen to say publicly and categorically that the British Government was not planning either to 'rat' on the Seven or to walk out on the Commonwealth. And these denials, in turn, added to the confusion. Finally, the campaign tended to obscure how far the Government's position had, in fact, changed. Against the background of demands for ringing declarations, Mr. Selwyn Lloyd's major statement of policy to the House of Commons at the end of July came as an anti-climax, and many people in the United Kingdom and, perhaps more important, on the Continent were therefore slow to appreciate the full significance of what he was saying.

The British Parliament held two notable debates on the European problem during the summer of 1960. The first was held in the House of Lords on 29 and 30 June, the second in the House of Commons at the end of July. The debate in the House of Lords was a wide-ranging debate on international affairs generally in which the U-2 incident and the East–West summit fiasco shared honours with the European problem as matters of particular concern. Of the numerous speeches primarily on the European problem, Lord Boothby's speech, not surprisingly, attracted the most comment from the press. He made a long, passionate, in parts well documented, in parts somewhat emotional, attack on British policy towards Europe since the war, dwelling on the host of lost opportunities. The Conservative Party, to which he belongs, was castigated more thoroughly than the Labour Party, largely because it was Conservative leaders, and not least Winston Churchill, who at various times had roused hopes on the Continent that Britain was ready to give real leadership in creating real unity, and had then let the Continent down by half measures and divided loyalties. He felt it very understandable that, in the light of the record, the 'Europeans' were still deeply suspicious of the intentions of the British Government. He had no doubts about what should be done: 'The choice . . . which now confronts us is a naked one. This is, as I believe, full participation in the Common Market or active estrangement . . . the time has come to jump.'[21]

Although Lord Boothby's speech was an impressive *tour de force*, perhaps the most interesting and most significant speech, although one of a very different character, was that made by Lord Strang, for five critical years (from 1949 to 1953) Permanent Under-Secretary of State (i.e. top civil servant) in the Foreign Office. He felt British policy towards Europe had been both consistent and wise, although he candidly admitted that many people would not agree with him. He described it in the following terms: 'on the one hand, the widest, closest and most intimate co-operation with Continental Western Europe on an inter-governmental basis; on the other, hesitation, except in specified cases and within defined limits, to agree to subject themselves to majority decisions'. He felt it would be dishonest to seek to join the European Economic Community unless the United Kingdom was prepared to face ultimate political integration with the Six and he felt that that was the fundamental difficulty. Short of that, the problems that arose simply from joining the Common Market (the external tariff, agriculture, repercussions on the Commonwealth, harmonization of social policies, and free movement of labour) all raised difficulties but not, he thought, insurmountable ones. 'No . . . it is the

[21] *Hansard*, House of Lords, 30 June 1960, cols. 855–67.

proposed political integration, the creation of common sovereign political institutions, the surrender of sovereignty in important spheres in national life which is the real obstacle, and it is a formidable one.' But having said that, he then indicated quite clearly that there might, in fact, be no real alternative but to join the Six: 'It may become clear that the disadvantages of not accepting the Treaty of Rome will far exceed the disadvantages of going in— that is to say, if the others will have us. This is a point which will demand the most anxious thought. But until that time comes, if it ever does, there are possible middle courses to explore.' And later, in reply to a prodding question from Lord Boothby, he went a little further: 'What I have been trying to say is that, if we want to go ahead, we have to contemplate the possibility of joining the Six. It may be that there is no middle way. But what I am saying, in addition, is that if we do contemplate joining the Six, we ought to be pretty clear in our own minds what the effect on our internal life will be; and my view is that it is much more serious than most people imagine.'[22]

The Government's main statement of policy came a month later in the debate in the House of Commons on the European problem which was opened by Mr. Selwyn Lloyd, then Foreign Secretary but shortly to become Chancellor of the Exchequer.[23] His speech made it clear beyond doubt that the United Kingdom was determined to go very far to reach an agreement with the Six and that a negotiation in terms of full British membership in the Common Market was certainly a possibility. It was clear both from his statement and from that of Mr. Maudling, then President of the Board of Trade and the other Government spokesman in the debate, that the time was not considered ripe for a renewal of negotiations. It was also clear from the general tenor of the two statements that there was not yet full agreement in the Cabinet about how far 'into Europe' the United Kingdom would be prepared to go. Mr. Selwyn Lloyd's statement clearly went as far as Cabinet consensus would then permit. Mr. Maudling in his speech, consciously or unconsciously, revealed the fact that he, at least, still had some reservations about even that highest common factor of agreement.

[22] *Hansard*, House of Lords, 30 June 1960, cols. 753–6. Lord Strang spoke before Lord Boothby made his main speech.
[23] For the debate see *Hansard*, House of Commons, 25 July 1960, cols. 1099–1218.

The Foreign Secretary moved the Government motion which was positive enough about the general objective but intentionally ambiguous as to method: 'That this House recognises the need for political and economic unity in Europe and would welcome the conclusion of suitable arrangements to that end, satisfactory to all the Governments concerned.' He made it clear that when he spoke of Europe he included the United Kingdom:

My first point is that if Britain were to be regarded as outside Europe we could not fulfil our complete role in the world. Nor do I believe that Europe would be complete without us. . . . I state categorically our wish for a united Europe, politically, economically, and commercially. But there are different ways of attaining this. Some people talk of integration, others of federation, others of confederation, and others, again, of association. One is not any the less a good European because one prefers one method rather than another. Our purpose is a united Europe, and we accept the need for some political organisation as an element in this unity.

He then, without defining more precisely how unity was to be achieved, reviewed the problems. Significantly, the problems outlined were those that would have to be solved if the United Kingdom were to join the Community.

First, the Commonwealth. . . . The strength and cohesion of the Commonwealth is, in part, buttressed by its economic pattern, and we have a duty to see that no action of ours in the economic field endangers the immense political potential of this association . . . acceptance of a common tariff of the Six, as laid down in the Treaty of Rome, would be the end of the principle of Commonwealth duty-free entry of goods and commodities. It would mean not only putting a tariff on the Commonwealth, but giving free entry to European producers and so a preference to them over the Commonwealth producers except for items on which the common tariff is nil. . . . If, in addition, we adopted the common agricultural policy of the Six . . . this would be a further blow to one of the most important parts of Commonwealth trade.

He then remarked, and, in many ways, this was the most important sentence in the whole speech: 'I do not for a moment say that it [the Commonwealth problem] is insoluble, but it is a formidable problem.' The second problem was agriculture, that is, the problem of changing from the British methods of supporting farm incomes to the continental method, with the consequent increase in the cost of food to the consumer. Again, although he pointed out the advantages of the British system and the difficulties in changing to

the continental system, he certainly did not imply the impossibility of change, rather the contrary: 'This is a problem which we
shall have to consider very carefully before we make changes.' The
third point made by Mr. Selwyn Lloyd was that, under the Treaty
of Rome, members would have to abandon their direct commercial relations with third countries by 1970. He pointed out that this
would include United Kingdom relations with the Commonwealth
and that 'the political consequences of such a development would
be far-reaching', but he gave the impression of being far less
troubled by this prospect than was Mr. Maudling.[24] The Foreign
Secretary then referred to the EFTA: 'We attach great importance
to our membership of that Association and we shall always act in
the closest consultation with our EFTA partners. In loyalty to
them we must ensure that any plan to secure political and economic unity in Europe takes care of their interests and their preoccupations and is formulated after full discussion with them.'
Finally, he referred to institutions: 'It is no use trying to burke this
issue and to say that there is not a problem, because there is. What
is not yet clear is how the institutions of the Six are to work out.
For us, with our traditions in this Parliament, with the contribution it has made to Parliamentary democracy, if the plan is to make
this Parliament subordinate to some higher Parliament, it is no
light matter.' Again, however, he made it clear that he was outlining a problem, not taking a position: 'I have not pronounced
against us going into some form of European institution, but we
have to be careful what these institutions are, what they are to do
and what would be our responsibilities in the matter.'

   From the way the Foreign Secretary reviewed the problems it
was clear that serious thought had, in fact, been given by the
Cabinet to the possibility of joining. An unconditional signing of
the Treaty of Rome—the 'join now, negotiate afterwards' course
of action—had obviously been ruled out, but a negotiation with a
view to joining, if suitable arrangements for the Commonwealth,
and other interests, could be made, was clearly now one possible
course of action, although no decision to go that far had yet been
taken. And, from Mr. Maudling's winding-up speech, it seems clear
that he, and probably some of the other members of the Cabinet,
although prepared to *consider* the possibility of joining, still felt
that there might be a less drastic course of action open to them.
The President of the Board of Trade still seemed to envisage a

[24] See *Hansard*, House of Commons, loc. cit., col. 1210.

negotiation between the Six and the Seven, as groups, and he seemed clearly to prefer some form of 'close association' with the Community to membership in the Community. Although virtually all the speakers in the debate agreed that the United Kingdom, having taken a leading part in the formation of the EFTA, could not now abandon its partners in that organization, Mr. Maudling went much further than had the Foreign Secretary (or other speakers) in stressing the advantages of the EFTA and in urging its further development pending new negotiations with the Six.[25]

Although both Mr. Selwyn Lloyd and Mr. Maudling emphasized that the Six had recently made it abundantly clear that they were not yet ready for negotiations, it was apparent from the differences in emphasis between the two Government speakers that the United Kingdom had not yet resolved its own internal differences of view on the arrangement to be sought. The immediate opening of formal negotiations—in contrast to informal talks and some indication from the Six about the real sticking-points—might well have come as something of an embarrassment.[26]

The general course of action the Government proposed to follow was outlined to the House by the Foreign Secretary in the following terms:

First, we have to develop in every way we can our trade and other relations with EFTA. . . . Secondly, there is no reason why EFTA trade with the Six should not expand. . . . I am not at all sure that there is not a little too much defeatism in some quarters about the future of our trade with the Six. Next, it is in our interest from every point of view to try to reduce so far as possible the discrimination between the two groups and to play a full part in the GATT conference this winter

[25] Unlike Mr. Selwyn Lloyd, Mr. Maudling also clearly revealed a strong preference for the method of the Seven: 'We must make more use of the trade opportunities that are opening there [i.e. in the EFTA]. We must think of the EFTA not merely in terms of trade, but in terms of collaboration over the whole range of economic and social interests, collaboration between independent States who work together because they want to work together and not because they are forced into any particular federal mould.' *Hansard*, loc. cit., col. 1215.

[26] The Government clearly hoped for informal exploratory talks with the Six on the ways of meeting the problems outlined by Mr. Selwyn Lloyd: 'I say this quite frankly, I think that it would help if we could be given some indication of the attitude of the Six towards the special problems which I have mentioned—particularly the problems of Commonwealth free entry, support for United Kingdom agriculture and the possibilities of meeting the special needs of our associates in EFTA. I repeat that we are anxious to discuss these matters.' Ibid., cols. 1108-9.

in order to bring about a useful reduction in the level of world tariffs. In addition, and perhaps the most important of all, we have to do all in our power to strengthen the political will in Western Europe directly towards achieving satisfactory and suitable arrangements.

It is worth noting that at the end of his speech Mr. Selwyn Lloyd reverted to the theme on which he had opened, that is, that the 'suitable arrangement' he was seeking was as much a political relationship as it was an economic relationship, and he went out of his way to add that 'when we talk of suitable arrangements, I certainly would not exclude participation in common institutions'.

Mr. Harold Wilson and Mr. Denis Healey were the principal Opposition speakers in the debate. Although they inevitably condemned the Government for bungling the earlier negotiations, they agreed with the general course of action now proposed by the Government. They were somewhat cooler than was the Foreign Secretary to the prospect of as intimate a relationship with the Six as joining the Community implied, but they also tended to be rather clearer than was Mr. Maudling that middle courses, close associations, and so forth were unlikely to be negotiable.[27] Mr. Denis Healey outlined the political reservations he had about joining the Six, views which he developed more fully at various times during the next two years.[28] Mr. Healey's main worry was that joining the Common Market would almost inevitably mean adjustments in British policy towards the Soviet Union and towards the developing countries of Africa and Asia. He disliked many features of French and German foreign policy and he did not want British policy brought more closely into line with them. He felt the situation might be better in a few years, either because the Six might themselves opt for a loose form of unity or because 'the policies of the Six towards Russia, Afro-Asia and the Commonwealth may become more compatible with ours'. Mr. Healey felt that the issue needed to be considered in the light of the *most* that might be involved in joining the Community: 'The people who are now dominating policy in the Commission in Brussels and in most of the countries in the Common Market want

[27] See, for example, Mr. Wilson: '. . . the original seventeen-nation Free Trade Area, as originally conceived, is dead, damned and past hope of resurrection. . . . I cannot help feeling that the President of the Board of Trade . . . still acts as though he thinks that it has all been a bad dream and that one sunny morning he will wake up and find all Europe ready to sign on the dotted line.' *Hansard*, loc. cit., col. 1112.

[28] See for example his article in the *Observer*, 22 April 1962.

a total economic union as the end result of their efforts, and they want a total economic union, as laid down in the Treaty of Rome, mainly because they believe that it will lead to a total political union. We should be deceiving ourselves if we did not accept this as a starting point in deciding our policy.'[29] He made the strong point that 'it would be disastrous if any British Government committed the British people to joining the Common Market without first coming clean with them about what it would mean', and he rightly felt that there was a tremendous job of education still to be done.

The Liberals divided the House, not because they wished to defeat the Government's motion but because they felt it did not go far enough and that the Government should have said they were prepared to enter the Common Market. There were quite a number of abstentions both by those who agreed with the Liberals that the Government had not been sufficiently forthcoming and by those on the extreme left and extreme right who felt that, given any encouragement, the Government was apt to go too far. The Government motion was carried by 215 to 4.

As Mr. Denis Healey in winding up for the Opposition pointed out, 'two points of extreme importance have emerged from this debate. The first is that there is no longer anybody in this House who believes it inconceivable that we should join the Common Market.' He usefully elaborated this point: 'I hope that our Continental friends will take note of the fact that the sort of Pharisaism towards the Continent which governed the attitude of both parties —I admit this—towards European unity for so many years immediately after the war, is completely dead.' The second point 'is that no one in this debate thinks we can join the Common Market as it now stands, and no one thinks we can join the Common Market alone or without the agreement of our partners in the European Free Trade Area'.

It is rather surprising that the debate did not attract more attention, proving, once again, that it is almost impossible to make news in Europe at the end of July or in August, short of declaring war. But the lack of response seems also to have been the result of the fact that most people in Britain, on the Continent, and in the United States had become so accustomed to British arguments about the difficulties of joining the Six that they were slow to appreciate the fact that the emphasis had now been decisively

[29] *Hansard*, loc. cit., col. 1203.

shifted, and these difficulties, although still important, were no longer being described as insuperable but in double negatives, as not insuperable, and that the problems were listed not as excuses for inaction but, quite literally, as problems, and problems for which solutions could probably be found.

Discussions on the political construction of Europe

The British Government's views of the relationship it should seek with the Six were affected by the progress made by the Six in their discussions on political union. Similarly, the ideas of the Six about the way Europe should be 'organized' coloured their views about the relationship with the United Kingdom. Before continuing with the account of the development of opinion in the United Kingdom it is therefore necessary to digress and to give a short account of the suggestions for political co-operation put forward by General de Gaulle during the summer of 1960 and the reactions of the rest of the Six to these suggestions.

On 31 May 1960, General de Gaulle spoke on the radio about the principles governing French foreign policy. The major part of his speech was devoted to an analysis of the reasons for the failure of the Summit meeting and of the implications of the breakdown. In the context of this broad review of foreign policy he spoke of the Common Market and of the wider problem of the organization of Western Europe in the following terms:[30]

To help to build Western Europe into a political, economic, cultural and human group, organised for action, progress and defence is the aim of the French Government. Already West Germany, Italy, the Netherlands, Belgium and Luxembourg are co-operating directly with her in several fields. In particular the Common Market of the Six will, on 31 December, become a practical reality. Of course, the participants do not want this organisation to injure the other countries of Europe, and we must expect a way to be found of accommodating their interests. Also, of course, the nations which are becoming associated must not cease to be themselves, and the path to be followed must be that of organised co-operation between states, while waiting to achieve, perhaps, an imposing confederation. But France, as far as she is concerned, has recognised the necessity of the organisation of Western Europe, which in former times was the dream of the wise and the ambition of the

[30] Quoted from *France and the European Community* (Occasional Paper No. 11, 30 January 1961, Political and Economic Planning), pp. 8–9. The full French text of General de Gaulle's broadcast is reprinted on pp. 647–9 of *L'Année Politique*, 1960.

powerful and which appears today as an indispensable condition of world equilibrium.

In the last analysis, always, it is only in equilibrium that the world will find peace. On our old continent the organisation of a Western group, at the very least equivalent to that which exists in the East, may one day, without risk to the independence and freedom of each nation and taking into account the probable evolution of political regimes, establish a European Entente from the Atlantic to the Urals. Then Europe, no longer split in two by outdated ambitions and ideologies, would once again be the heart of civilisation.

Inevitably these words were read differently in different places. In the United Kingdom, General de Gaulle's reference to 'accommodating' the interest of the other countries was read as a good omen for the Trade Committee of the Twenty-one which was to meet in Paris the following week (see Chapter VIII), and his description of the kind of unity he favoured (organized co-operation among states)[31] appeared to be so similar to traditional British views that hopes were aroused that it might be much less difficult than had been feared to reach an agreement.[32] Within the Six the speech was read rather differently and was generally seen as the most far-reaching endorsement yet given by General de Gaulle to the European Community. Although his emphasis on the national state was not particularly welcome to the 'Europeans', this unfortunate lapse tended to be played down and greater notice taken of his description of the Common Market as a 'practical reality', of his apparent endorsement of the Commission's pragmatic approach to the trade problems of the other European countries, and, above all, of his endorsement of an 'imposing confederation' as the ultimate objective.

During June, the Prime Minister, M. Debré, and the Foreign Secretary, M. Couve de Murville, both gave a little more precision to some of the ideas touched on by General de Gaulle. Speaking in the foreign policy debate in the French Assembly on 14 June, M. Couve de Murville said: 'Europe must also organize and unite in

[31] It should be noted that General de Gaulle used the phrase 'une co-operation organisée des États'. It was M. Debré, not de Gaulle, who used the expression 'l'Europe des patries'. General de Gaulle in a press conference in May 1962 pointed out that he had never used the phrase 'l'Europe des patries', although it was commonly attributed to him.

[32] See, for example, the leader in The Times of 2 June 1960, 'A New Opening'. See also Mr. Thorneycroft's question in the House of Commons and Mr. Heathcoat Amory's reply on 23 June 1960. Hansard, House of Commons, col. 654.

the monetary field, in the cultural field, perhaps in the field of defence, lastly and certainly in the political field. In certain respects things are already moving. But, the main thing is the political problem. A beginning was made last year when we agreed with our partners to organize regular meetings of our foreign ministers to discuss international problems. . . . If one wishes to be realistic, and, in consequence, effective, the basis of our action must be an active co-operation among States, that is, Governments. Thus we will arrive one day at that imposing confederation of which General de Gaulle spoke in his speech of May 31.'[33] Later in the same debate M. Debré reaffirmed that: 'It is co-operation—and not fusion—which will make it possible to create among the European countries the confederal type of link to which the President of the Republic clearly alluded.'[34]

At the end of July (1960) M. Debré, in a statement on foreign policy to the National Assembly, announced that some initiatives would shortly be taken to bring about greater organized co-operation among the European states.[35] The new French initiatives were discussed a few days later (on 29 July) by General de Gaulle with Dr. Adenauer at Rambouillet.

Relations between General de Gaulle and Dr. Adenauer appear to have been rather strained before the Rambouillet meeting and Dr. Adenauer had become increasingly apprehensive about certain aspects of the French Government's policy. The German Chancellor had never shared General de Gaulle's rather contemptuous views of NATO, and he was strongly opposed to the suggestions General de Gaulle was known to have made for an American–British–French directorate of NATO. Moreover Dr. Adenauer believed in 'supra-nationalism', resented the scorn the Gaullists poured on this concept, and mistrusted, not least for its effects in Germany, the Gaullist emphasis on the national state. Matters had not been improved by some remarks made by M. Debré in the French National Assembly shortly before the Rambouillet meeting: he had argued the need for the French *force de frappe* and had implied that Germany, because of her lack of atomic weapons, would inevitably become a 'satellite'.[36]

Most of the discussion at Rambouillet took place between the

---

[33] *L'Année Politique* (1960), p. 505 (my translation).
[34] Ibid., p. 507 (my translation).
[35] See Assemblée Nationale, *Débats*, 25 July 1960, p. 2205.
[36] See reports from Bonn and Paris in *New York Times*, 28 July 1960.

two principals, attended only by their interpreters, and the exact form of the proposals made by General de Gaulle and of the replies or counter-proposals made by Dr. Adenauer are far from clear. The fact that Herr van Scherpenberg (State Secretary in the German Ministry of Foreign Affairs) went to Paris shortly after Dr. Adenauer's return to Bonn seeking enlightenment on a long list of points suggests that General de Gaulle and Dr. Adenauer parted with rather different ideas of what had been agreed. It seems probable that at Rambouillet General de Gaulle and Dr. Adenauer were in greater agreement when they were diagnosing the problems confronting their two countries than they were when discussing prescriptions. They had similar views about the failure of the Summit and about the probability of new diplomatic offensives by the Russians, and they both apparently felt that the imminence of the presidential elections in the United States created a dangerous political vacuum. However, although they doubtless agreed that it was up to Western Europe to organize itself to fill the vacuum, it seems probable that they did not see eye to eye on the specific steps that should be taken. General de Gaulle appears to have been thinking primarily in terms of how to increase the power, prestige, and influence of the continental countries, and particularly of France, and it seems unlikely that he felt any need for closer ties with Britain. Dr. Adenauer, on the other hand, although he undoubtedly agreed with General de Gaulle that the Six should extend their collaboration to new fields, was clearly not in sympathy with the way General de Gaulle wished to set about it. And at this time, he seems to have felt that a closer relationship with the United Kingdom might be desirable, as well as a tightening of the links among the Six. In short it seems probable that General de Gaulle looked at the political vacuum as an opportunity to assert leadership, whereas Dr. Adenauer saw it as a warning that the West should close ranks.

Although both French and German official spokesmen were very reticent after the Rambouillet meetings, the main features of the French proposals and the main criticisms made of them by the Germans, and later by others of the Six, became common knowledge before long. At the end of August, General de Gaulle outlined his ideas to the Dutch Prime Minister and Foreign Minister (Mr. de Quay and Mr. Luns). Early in September he talked with the Italian Prime Minister and Foreign Secretary (Signor Fanfani and Signor Segni) and later in that month with the Belgian Prime Minister and Foreign Minister (M. Eyskens and M. Wigny) and with the Luxembourg Prime Minister and Foreign Minister (M. Werner and M. Schaus). These frequent ministerial encounters naturally gave rise to statements to the press and to considerable press comment on the ideas under discussion. Moreover, on 5 September, General de Gaulle devoted a large section of his press conference to setting forth the ideas he was then in the process of discussing with the rest of the Six.

Briefly, the kind of structure envisaged by General de Gaulle was as follows. The principal organ of co-operation among the Six would be a Council of the Heads of Governments. This would be served by a permanent secretariat to be located in Paris. In addition there would be four specialized commissions to ensure regular co-operation among the states in the political, economic, cultural, and defence fields. There would also be an Assembly composed of delegates from the national parliaments. This new European construction would receive popular endorsement by means of a referendum to be held in the member countries. The role of the existing communities in this construction was not clear, nor was the relationship between the proposed Six-power co-operation in the political and defence fields and the co-operation already taking place on a wider basis in the WEU and the NATO. And on both points the reaction to probings from the rest of the Six tended to be alarming rather than reassuring.

At this time the 'European' analysis and the 'Gaullist' analysis of the need for unity in Europe appeared to be very similar. Moreover, although de Gaulle might talk of 'an imposing confederation' and the federalists of 'a United States of Europe', everyone agreed that the ultimate goal could not yet be foreseen with any precision. The sharpest difference of view came, therefore, not over the reasons for greater unity nor over the ultimate form of the union but over the means, over the steps by which progress should be made. And the differences of view between the French Government and the rest of the Six (and also between the Gaullists and the 'Europeans' in France) were particularly pronounced because General de Gaulle's proposals could not be considered in a vacuum but took colour from his other policies and statements. Thus suggestions that might well have been acceptable to the rest of the Six if his other policies or even his phraseology had been different became suspect. In particular General de Gaulle's insistence that defence was a necessary and logical subject for action among the Six aroused strong opposition because, in other contexts, he was opposing various measures for bringing about greater integration of defence on an Atlantic basis, because he was advocating a three-power directorate of NATO that was anathema to the rest of the Six, because he was insisting on the need for a French (not European) *'force de frappe'*, and generally because his policy for Western Europe seemed to assume independence, if not deliberate estrangement, from the 'Anglo-Saxon' powers, a kind of independence that the rest of the Six disliked and feared. There was general agreement within the Six that Europe united could exercise a power and influence in the world that a divided Europe could not, but there was also fear that the Europe envisaged by General de Gaulle was not a Europe working in close and equal alliance with the United States but a 'Third Force' Europe playing a dangerous power game between East and West.[37] This concern about the basic orientation of French policy coloured the reactions of the rest of the Six to de Gaulle's proposal for political co-ordination as well as to his proposal for extending Six-country action to defence questions.

Similarly, the rest of the Six viewed his proposal for a new organization in the economic field against the background of earlier rumours that General de Gaulle was planning to propose emasculating revisions in the Treaties of Paris and Rome and in the light of his continued emphasis on the merely 'technical' value of the Community institutions. They therefore suspected that the creation of a new economic council or commission might simply be another way of bringing about the down-grading of the European Commission and the elimination of the few attributes of real supra-nationality in the existing Communities.

There would obviously have been much less suspicion and a much greater willingness to take at face value General de Gaulle's statements that his proposals were genuinely designed to 'build

[37] In the third volume of his *War Memoirs*, General de Gaulle wrote of his postwar plan for France as follows: 'I intended to guarantee France primacy in Western Europe by preventing the rise of a new Reich that might again threaten its safety; to co-operate with East and West and if need be contract the necessary alliances on one side or the other without ever accepting any kind of dependency; to transform the French Union into a free association in order to avoid the as yet unspecified dangers of upheaval; to persuade the states along the Rhine, the Alps and the Pyrenees to form a political, economic and strategic bloc; to establish this organization as one of the three world powers and, should it become necessary, as the arbiter between the Soviet and Anglo-American camps.' Charles de Gaulle, *Salvation, 1944–1946* (Eng. trans. London, 1960), p. 178.

Europe' had he not habitually poured scorn on the 'federalists', and dismissed their concepts as dreams and myths, and their method as an illusion.[38] Although many of the strongest 'Europeans' had their own doubts about whether the time was ripe for a directly elected European Parliament (and for much the same reasons as those given by a Gaullist, M. Peyrefitte[39]), General de Gaulle's obvious contempt for the French National Assembly increased their concern at the relatively minor role he apparently envisaged for a European Assembly. Similarly, his use of the referendum to strengthen his own position intensified the distaste with which most of the other European leaders viewed his suggestion that a referendum be held to give popular endorsement to the goal of a confederated Europe.[40] And again, although no one would have denied that General de Gaulle was right when he argued that the nation state was still the effective unit in European life, the 'Europeans' believed profoundly that effective collaboration among states was only possible if a way could be found to prevent national vetoes from stultifying progress. The only way around national vetoes that was acceptable to small powers involved bringing independent authorities, like the Commission, into the decision-making process. M. Peyrefitte's articles suggested that the Gaullists also recognized that the national veto must, eventually, be superseded by some kind of qualified majority voting.[41] But the small

---

[38] For example, in his press conference of 5 September at which he outlined his new proposals General de Gaulle said: 'To construct Europe, that is to say to unite it, is obviously essential. It is banal to say so. Why should this great centre of civilization, of strength, of reason, of prosperity be smothered by its own ashes? But, at the same time, it is necessary to proceed not by following dreams but realities. Now, what are the realities of Europe? What are the pillars on which one could build? In fact they are the national states. It is an illusion to imagine that one could build something capable of effective action, which would be approved by the people, above and beyond the national state.' (My translation from the text given in L'Année Politique, 1960, p. 657.)

[39] M. Alain Peyrefitte, a young but influential Gaullist deputy (later (1962) Minister of Information), wrote a series of articles entitled 'The Future of Europe' that appeared in Le Monde on 15, 16, 17, and 18 September 1960. These were reported to correspond very closely to the thinking of General de Gaulle and M. Debré. In his second article M. Peyrefitte analysed the weaknesses of a directly elected Assembly in a situation where the work of the Executives was technical and extremely limited, and the framework of political unity still unclear.

[40] The referendum, as well as being associated in the minds of the Six with its use in France by de Gaulle, was also associated with Hitler's rise to power in Germany.

[41] See the third of M. Peyrefitte's articles. Even in his analysis, this was a very long-term development and, as discussed further below, General de Gaulle's

countries feared that the veto the French might eventually want to find a way round would be a small power veto and that General de Gaulle's real objective was to create a situation in which France, or perhaps a French–German diarchy, became the controlling power in Western Europe.

Finally, General de Gaulle's attitude towards the United Kingdom was ambiguous, to say the least. His emphasis on confederation as the goal and an organized co-operation among states as the method was in tune with British attitudes towards European unity, but there was nothing to suggest that he regarded the United Kingdom as a necessary part of an 'organized Europe'.[42]

There was a good deal of truth in General de Gaulle's analysis of the causes of weakness in the existing Communities, although his criticisms were put in an infuriatingly patronizing way. Moreover, in the hands of a skilful advocate like M. Peyrefitte the Gaullist doctrine could be presented as a coherent, logical scheme for building a confederation.[43] These considerations, together with

unwillingness to accept a commitment to move, at a later stage, to majority voting was one of the points at issue between the French and the rest of the Six in the discussions on political unity in 1962.

[42] Shortly after the meeting between General de Gaulle and Dr. Adenauer there were press comments that Mr. Macmillan had written a letter to General de Gaulle and it was assumed that he had indicated his interest in discussing de Gaulle's ideas with him. Although there were numerous meetings between the British ministers and other members of the Six during this period, it is worth noting that there were no discussions between French and British ministers until Mr. Heath's visit to Paris early in October.

[43] At the end of his second article M. Peyrefitte wrote: 'Faced by recent developments in French policy the "Europeans" both in France and elsewhere have tended to fall into two groups. The first of these groups, which despairs of winning over the French Government to orthodox federalism, has decided that nothing can be done while General de Gaulle remains President. When the President's mission is accomplished, and when perhaps his regime has come to an end, they will be able to resume their work for the self-evidently desirable end of integration. While they wait they will be content, first, to denounce the General's "desire for hegemony" and, also, his "ulterior purpose of creating a third force". Secondly, they will reject as treachery any policy which, by failing to fit in with classic federalist doctrine, might endanger the move of the Six to integration. Their attitude is just like that of the Foreign Ministers who, at the time of their historic meeting at Brussels in August 1954, encouraged by certain French groups, rejected the modifications which M. Mendès-France had proposed in order to make the EDC Treaty acceptable to the French Parliament.

'The second group, determined to make the best of the situation, has decided to fit in as well as it can with the European policies of General de Gaulle, if only because it might succeed in altering these policies to accord more with its own views.

'Whether the second group will prevail over the first will depend on how

the fact that so many articulate Frenchmen clearly did not agree
with the extremes of the Gaullist position, kept the rest of the Six
from rejecting the proposals outright, and led them to try to work
them into something which would represent some further progress
towards the kind of European unity they could accept. In the discussions on political unity during the summer of 1960, and in the
discussions which were carried on intermittently and at various
levels until the spring of 1962 the rest of the Six concentrated on
three important points: first, they sought reassurance that the
Europe which was being created would operate within the framework of the NATO and not as a separate and potentially incompatible 'third force'; second, they sought to preserve the independence of the existing Communities and to safeguard their
potential for further development; finally, they tried to keep the
door open for later development on a federal pattern and, in this
connexion, to gain acceptance of the eventual need for majority
voting and its corollary, independent institutions.

After this first round of discussions on General de Gaulle's
proposals the prevailing reaction among the rest of the Six was a
mixture of hope and fear: hope that a way to work with de Gaulle
could be found and fear that his real objective and theirs might be
totally irreconcilable. This uncertainty about whether to be encouraged or alarmed was reflected in the statement the Belgian
Foreign Minister, M. Wigny, made to the press after his talks with
General de Gaulle in mid-September:

> We are in favour of a new, supplementary structure, but anxious as
> regards any reconstruction or modification of what exists. We must not
> take one step forward in order to take two steps backward. We are in
> favour of everything which reinforces European cooperation and con-
> cerned about anything which would retard it. More concrete proposals
> will emerge from this exchange of views. We hope they will be con-
> structive.[44]

Before his meeting at Rambouillet with General de Gaulle, Dr.
Adenauer had taken the initiative in seeking an early meeting with
Mr. Macmillan. A number of factors seemed to have prompted
Dr. Adenauer to display a warmer attitude towards the British at

---

the General's basic proposals to our partners in the Six are developed and
worked out.' Mr. Peyrefitte's articles were clearly addressed to the second
group. Quotation taken from P.E.P. paper, cited above, p. 302, pp. 30–31.
[44] Quotation taken from account in P.E.P. paper, p. 6.

this time. As discussed above, he felt that the breakdown of the Summit meeting might be a prelude to an intensified Russian diplomatic offensive over Berlin and he felt that the imminence of the United States election added to the danger by creating a political vacuum. Although Mr. Macmillan's trip to Moscow early in 1959 had seemed ill-advised and somewhat presumptuous to Dr. Adenauer, as well as to General de Gaulle, the British Prime Minister's firmness after the collapse of the Summit meeting had gone some way to dispel the Chancellor's fears that the British might be 'soft' on Berlin. Dr. Adenauer was alarmed by some of General de Gaulle's ideas about the role of France and of Europe and in particular he was afraid that de Gaulle's policies would encourage a weakening of the United States' commitment to Europe. Moreover, since progress towards a 'supra-national' Europe was in any case now blocked by the de Gaulle Government, one of Dr. Adenauer's important reservations about too close a relationship with the United Kingdom had lost some of its substance. There were also strong domestic political reasons why Dr. Adenauer should have become more inclined to try to work something out with the British, even at the price of some slowing down in the establishment of the Common Market. The German federal elections were imminent and the German farmers were hotly opposing the early institution of the Community's agricultural policy, which was, at French and Dutch insistence, an integral part of the acceleration plan. Moreover, the powerful BDI (Bundesverband der Deutschen Industrie) and other industrial groups were pressing hard for a settlement between the Six and the Seven.

Whatever the relative importance of the various factors influencing Dr. Adenauer, a new mood appears to have prevailed during his talks with Mr. Macmillan on 10 and 11 August. Although official statements after the meeting made it clear that the kind of arrangement that might be made was not discussed in any detail, Mr. Macmillan appears to have felt satisfied that the Chancellor was now genuinely interested in finding a way to help the United Kingdom back into the mainstream of European developments. According to press accounts, the two Foreign Secretaries (Lord Home and Herr von Brentano) drew up a list of problems that would have to be solved if the Six and Seven were to come together, and it was agreed that discussions on these problems would be continued between officials of the two Governments. The communiqué indicated that the officials would concentrate, initially, on the key problem of Commonwealth free entry. The singling out of this problem for immediate attention was, of course, in line with Mr. Selwyn Lloyd's statement in the House of Commons. This was the crucial problem for which answers had to be found, whether the final settlement was to take the form of a customs union link between the Six and Seven, or of an all-European customs union into which the Six would fit as a unit, or of Britain's (and perhaps others') joining the Six. Moreover, the answers found to the problem of Commonwealth free entry, as well as being necessary ingredients of any of these solutions, might also affect the choice of solution.

The British and the Germans both made it clear that they were in no sense negotiating for their respective partners but were simply studying problems and exchanging views and that their partners would be kept fully informed at every stage of their talks.

Although Mr. Macmillan's comment that the meeting was an 'historic' one seemed rather extravagant at the time, since the only 'hard' agreement was a procedural one, the meeting marked the opening of a new chapter in the British search for a long-term settlement with the Six.

X

THE SHIFT IN BRITISH POLICY: CHANGING COURSE

From 'close association' to 'membership'

By the summer of 1960 the British Government was agreed that a 'close association' with the Six was needed. Mr. Macmillan, a few other ministers, and a few top civil servants had already begun thinking in terms of ultimately joining the Community, but the prevailing view within the Government was that an arrangement short of full membership in the Common Market should be sought. The main problems that joining the European Community posed for the United Kingdom had been examined by the civil servants and some preliminary possible ways of meeting (or avoiding) these difficulties had been sketched out, but there was still much to be done before the Government was ready to reach a decision either on the type of arrangement it would seek to negotiate with the Six or on the timing of new negotiations. It was necessary to have much more thorough discussions with the Commonwealth countries about the implications for them of the various arrangements then under consideration, ranging from a customs union for industrial goods to full British membership in the Common Market. It was necessary to have more discussion with the EFTA partners about their views both as to the kind of arrangement that they felt should be sought and about the timing and the strategy of any new negotiations with the Six. It was necessary, as Mr. Selwyn Lloyd had said in his speech in July, to have some indications from the Six about the kinds of modification in the Treaty of Rome (or the scope for interpretation in its application) that they would be prepared to countenance. It was also necessary to sound out the United States, for events since the breakdown in the free trade area negotiations had plainly indicated that benevolent neutrality, at the least, on the part of the United States would be a condition of the success of a new negotiation. Finally, but most important, there was need both within the

Government, and in the country generally, for the choice before them, and the implications of that choice, to be more thoroughly examined and understood.

Before the decision to negotiate could be taken, the Government, and enough other people (in the Conservative Party and in influential circles generally) to make the decision politically viable, had to be convinced, first, that a 'close association' was not negotiable, and second, and of more importance, that full membership would be, in any case, more advantageous for the United Kingdom than a looser connexion with the Six. Moreover, before the decision to open negotiations could be taken, the Government had to become convinced that time was not apt to make the negotiation easier. If the United Kingdom was to join the Community there were strong reasons for doing so as soon as possible, while the policies that would govern the Common Market were still being formulated and before the Six had consolidated themselves politically.

At the end of the summer (1960), a number of changes were made in the Government and certain dispositions were made in the Civil Service to ensure that 'European' questions received priority and sympathetic attention. Mr. Sandys, who in the early post-war period had been very active in the European movement and was one of the most 'European-minded' members of the Cabinet, was moved from the Ministry of Aviation to the Commonwealth Relations Office. Mr. Soames, another strong pro-European, was moved from the War Office to the Ministry of Agriculture. The attitudes of the Ministers heading these two departments would be crucial when the time came for a final Cabinet decision and these shifts made by Mr. Macmillan in the summer of 1960 were astute strategic moves. Mr. Heath, previously the Government Chief Whip and thereafter Minister of Labour, was named Lord Privy Seal and given special responsibility for European affairs. He was to be, as well, a Foreign Office Minister and the Foreign Office spokesman in the House of Commons. The concentration of responsibility for European questions, political as well as economic, in the hands of one minister was important. Moreover, the fact that Mr. Heath was to be in the Foreign Office (rather than functioning in a kind of limbo outside the established departments as Mr. Maudling had done during the free tread area negotiations) was evidence that Britain's relationship with the Six had now become a key foreign policy question and was no longer looked at primarily as a commerical problem. There were other advantages in the designation of Mr. Heath as the responsible minister. As Chief Whip he had been well liked and had shown skill in handling the parliamentary party. As a newcomer to the Cabinet he was untainted by the previous abortive free trade area negotiations. He was a new face to the 'Europeans', and, although none of them probably knew it, his maiden speech in the House of Commons had been a 'European' speech, urging the Labour Government, which was then in office, to participate in the discussions on the Schuman Plan.[1]

Within the Civil Service, a committee of senior civil servants from the various departments concerned, with Sir Frank Lee as chairman, was responsible for the necessary interdepartmental co-ordination and for providing the impetus to ensure that the new ideas then circulating at the upper levels in the Civil Service were translated into effective proposals.

Towards the end of September (1960), Mr. Heath described the Government's new approach to the Consultative Assembly of the Council of Europe:

> Then why, you may ask, cannot the United Kingdom join the Community as it stands? We have devoted much time in London in recent weeks to the examination of this question and to a review of the whole range of European economic problems. We have been looking at the practical effects of the Common Market on our economy and on our international links, and at the difficulties which have to be met if this problem is to be solved. When we have isolated these, we want to see how far it is possible to go, and we shall then be ready to discuss with others the results of our researches. But we shall only be able to reach the stage of a negotiation when they, too, have looked at the problem from their point of view. We fully realise that this problem raises difficulties which are just as serious for them as they are for us.

And he reiterated, as Mr. Selwyn Lloyd had done in the House of Commons, that 'in our studies we have maintained an open and flexible attitude to all possible solutions'.[2]

It was, perhaps, indicative of the new and more far-reaching way in which some, at least, of the Cabinet were now thinking

---

[1] See *Hansard*, House of Commons, 26 June 1950, cols. 1959–64. Mr. Heath was speaking in support of the motion by the Conservative Party, then in opposition, which urged the Government to join the talks, subject to the same condition as the Netherlands Government, 'namely, that if discussions show the plan not to be practicable, freedom of action is reserved'.

[2] Council of Europe, Twelfth Ordinary Session, September 1960, *Official Report of Debates*, pp. 565–6.

that Mr. Heath, although welcoming the Consultative Assembly's positive approach to the problem of European economic unity, was careful not to endorse the specific recommendation for a modified customs union link between the Six as a group and the Seven as a group which was contained in the report then being debated by the Assembly (the Vos Report), although this solution was in line with the kind of solution the British Government had itself been advocating a year earlier. And it is worth noting that Mr. George Brown, a leading member of the Labour Party, welcomed the Vos recommendation more warmly than did Mr. Heath.

The first task after the summer holidays was to hold more detailed consultations with the Commonwealth countries than had yet been done. The Commonwealth Finance Ministers met in London towards the end of September for their usual discussions before the annual meetings of the International Bank and International Monetary Fund. At these meetings, and during the preparatory discussions among officials which were held shortly before the ministerial meetings, the process of exploring with the Commonwealth countries the problems that would arise from British participation in a customs union with the Six, or, conceivably, from British membership in the European Community, was begun in earnest. However, unlike some of the later Commonwealth discussions on the Common Market, very little was made public about these early talks and the exact terms in which the British sought to elicit reactions from the Commonwealth countries can only be guessed at. From Mr. Heath's later statement to the WEU (see below, p. 331), it seems probable that the discussions centred on the problems that would be raised by the acceptance of a common external tariff with the Six. At this time the British seem to have been assuming that although Commonwealth goods would have to lose the preference they enjoyed in the United Kingdom market, willingness on the part of the United Kingdom to give up its own preference in the Commonwealth markets would give the Commonwealth countries a useful counter with which to bargain for better access to the markets of the Six. Of more importance, they also appear to have been hoping that arrangements could be made which would ensure that the Commonwealth exports to the United Kingdom were not put at any disadvantage as compared with those from the Six: that is, although the Commonwealth countries might lose their preference in the United Kingdom market they would not be confronted with a 'reverse' preference. There were various ways in which this result might be achieved and presumably some or all of them were discussed: the common external tariff might in some cases be reduced to nil; tariff-free quotas might be negotiated for some goods or, more simply and more sweepingly, an arrangement similar to the 'Morocco Protocol' in the Treaty of Rome might be made.[3] The problem of agriculture was not, apparently, discussed in any detail at this meeting, partly, at least, because the system the Six would apply among themselves had not yet taken shape. Whatever the precise scope of the discussions, a number of Commonwealth countries, New Zealand and Canada in particular, made it clear that they foresaw severe dangers for their own economies unless considerable changes in the system envisaged by the Treaty of Rome could be negotiated.[4] Nevertheless, the communiqué issued at the conclusion of the ministerial meeting indicated that no final position had been taken and that the British felt they had enough room for manoeuvre to continue with their exploratory talks with the Six: 'The Council [of Commonwealth Ministers] recognized the importance of political and economic unity in Western Europe. It was accepted that in any negotiations that take place the essential interests of Commonwealth countries should be safeguarded and full account taken of the continuing importance of intra-Commonwealth trade.'[5] The commitment to 'safeguard the essential interests of the Commonwealth', a phrase

---

[3] This protocol provides that for certain listed countries the special treatment their goods enjoy in a member country will not be affected by the Treaty of Rome. Goods so imported are not, however, considered as being in 'free circulation' and therefore they do not receive the benefits of the tariff reductions on intra-Community trade if exported from one Community country to another.

[4] During his speech to the Council of Europe, cited above, Mr. Heath commented as follows on the Commonwealth meetings: 'We have recently taken advantage of the presence in London of the Commonwealth Finance Ministers to consider these problems with them. Because we ourselves have not yet made up our minds how to proceed, these talks were purely exploratory. . . . Some people seem to have been surprised that the other Commonwealth Ministers expressed so forcefully their preoccupations and their fears. We were not surprised: that was the object of the consultation. From these talks I have gained a very clear understanding of the difficulties and dangers which acceptance of the common tariff would be bound to have for the countries of the Commonwealth. And what is completely clear is that for us to sign the Treaty of Rome in its present form—and I underline these words—would be impossible. . . . I see no reason for thinking that the problem of the Commonwealth is insoluble.' Council of Europe, *Official Report of Debates*, p. 567.

[5] See *The Times*, 22 September 1960.

that was to recur time and again in later British statements, should
be noted, for it was very different in terms of the scope it left for
bargaining with the Six than were the earlier commitments to
maintain existing entry arrangements for food, drink, and tobacco.[6]

Having made a little progress with the Commonwealth in the
sense that some, at least, of the difficult questions were now being
officially raised, Mr. Heath turned to the Six and early in October
went to Paris for discussions with the Prime Minister, M. Debré,
and the Foreign Minister, M. Couve de Murville. The French
position had been the determining factor in the failure of the free
trade area negotiations and the French had been the strongest
opponents of the various forms of 'bridge-building' between the
Six and the Seven that were later discussed. Any re-examination
of British policy clearly had to take into account French views of
the British role in Europe. If the French Government was completely determined to keep the British off the Continent of Europe
and to keep to a minimum British influence in Europe, there was
little point in even contemplating the profound domestic upheaval (economic, political, and emotional) that a drastic reversal
of British policy and a decision to join the Six would entail. If,
on the other hand, the French were not irrevocably opposed to
some kind of compromise short of British membership in the
Community, the upheaval of a change in policy could also still
be avoided. But, if Gaullist policy, like 'European' policy, was
'join or stay out', then the fundamental problem would have to
be faced. Closely related to an assessment of French attitudes
was, of course, the assessment of how far French views would
prevail within the Six and, beyond that, how much support
they would find from the new United States Administration.

Mr. Heath's discussions in Paris were the first Anglo-French
talks at ministerial level since General de Gaulle's broadcast of
31 May and the French President's subsequent discussion with the
ministers of the Six about his plans for organizing Europe politically. The meetings were apparently cordial and produced no
fireworks. But neither did they yield any helpful suggestions for
ways round the British difficulties. It can be assumed that Mr.
Heath sought to convince his hosts that the British wanted a new
and close relationship with the Six but that the United Kingdom
had valid reasons for not being able simply to sign the Treaty of

[6] As indicated in Chapter IX, the 'food, drink, and tobacco' formulation was used
by Mr. Maudling in the July 1960 debate in the House of Commons.

Rome. It can also be assumed that Mr. Heath reiterated the British
view that any foreign policy and defence discussions among the
Six should be closely tied in to the WEU–NATO structure. It
seems probable that the main result of the discussions was to make
it clear that in the French view there were no half-way houses and
that full membership in the Common Market was a precondition of
participation in the political construction of the Six; and to put an
end to any hopes that General de Gaulle's opposition to the
'Europeans' might make an 'association' with the Common Market
easier. To some people there had seemed to be a contradiction in
de Gaulle's position. On the one hand, he was advocating a form
of European action, based on co-operation among states, that was
easier for the British to accept than was the 'supra-nationalism' of
the 'Europeans'. On the other hand, his conception of a European
confederation appeared to be confined to the Six and expressly to
exclude the United Kingdom. In General de Gaulle's mind there
was, presumably, no paradox: simply the conviction that it would
be more difficult for France to assume her rightful role as the
leading power on the Continent if the British were also part of the
construction. However, others in France, and perhaps also de
Gaulle himself, regarded a customs union as an essential element
even in a confederation; therefore, despite the fact that General de
Gaulle's plans for a confederation were rooted in respect for
national sovereignty, they saw no contradiction in requiring acceptance of the Common Market[7] as a condition of participation in
the political construction.

The position of the EFTA countries was another element in the
complicated equation that the British had set themselves to solve.
At the end of October (1960) the Ministerial Council of the EFTA
met in Berne. This was the second ministerial meeting since the
entry into force of the Stockholm Convention, and the first since
the first tariff cuts of 20 per cent. had been made on trade within
the group. There were two principal questions on the agenda: the

---

[7] For example, a leading article in *Le Monde* of 6 September 1960, after commenting on the apparent contradiction in the French position, pointed out
that the French Government could rest on an argument solid enough to resolve
the contradiction: 'An association, looking towards a confederation, has a
chance of success only if it is founded on a customs union, or better on an
economic community, as history has adequately demonstrated. So long as
the United Kingdom refuses the obligation such an undertaking implies, she
could not be admitted to a full part in any such confederal council.' (My
translation.)

possibility of a further cut in tariffs, ahead of the timetable laid down in the Convention, in order to keep pace with the accelerated timetable of the Six; and the consideration of relations with the Six. Austria, Norway, and Denmark were opposed to making another tariff cut so soon after the first, and the question of an acceleration was postponed for further consideration in the new year. Thus the principle of strict parallelism with the Six was abandoned.

On the second point, relations with the Six, the rest of the Seven, and the Swedes and Swiss in particular, appear to have been even more sceptical than were the British of the chances of any successful negotiations with the Six in the foreseeable future, and they were strongly in favour of building up the EFTA, by accelerating tariff cuts and in other ways. The British were in favour of accelerating the tariff-cutting within the EFTA to keep pace with the Six, but, although loyal to the EFTA, they did not have the same enthusiasm as, say, the Swiss for the EFTA as an end in itself. They would probably have put the priorities rather differently from the way they were put by the President of the Swiss Confederation, M. Max Petitpierre, in his opening address to the EFTA Council:

> We have to show that EFTA is an institution brought to life by a common will to make of it something alive and effective. We can no longer consider it essentially a means to enable our seven countries to embark on a negotiation with the European Economic Community. That objective remains valid. But it is necessary first of all for EFTA to be capable of attaining its own ends.[8]

However, although there were shades of difference, the general feeling appears to have been that the time was not ripe for a new negotiation with the Six. The rest of the Seven were content to let the British carry on exploratory talks with the Germans, but at this time they were neither sanguine nor fearful about the results.

In accordance with the agreement reached between Dr. Adenauer and Mr. Macmillan in August, technical discussions between British and German officials were held in Bonn early in November and, later in the month, in London. These talks were rather disappointing. In part this was because the British officials were bound by rather limited instructions: their task was, essentially, to explore the arrangements that might be made for Commonwealth imports if the United Kingdom were to join a customs

[8] Reprinted in the EFTA *Bulletin*, November 1960.

union with the Six. In part the talks were disappointing because the real question in the minds of the British was what the French attitude to various possible arrangements would be: German willingness to consider possibilities, such as tariff-free quotas and nil tariffs, although encouraging, was not enough, and there was little to suggest that the Germans had discussed with the French, in any very serious way, the kinds of arrangement being considered in the talks with the British. And there was a good deal to suggest that French reactions would be unsympathetic. In other contexts, the French were making it clear that they were unlikely to look with favour on any arrangements which substantially breached the common tariff. For example, in discussions within the Community on the association arrangement for Greece, the French were taking a tough line on the use of tariff quotas and it was generally assumed that this was, in part at least, to avoid setting any precedents that the British might exploit too liberally later on. Moreover, although the Germans might welcome the idea of reductions in the common external tariff, the more protectionist French were unlikely to do so. The postponement in 'acceleration' meant that the first step towards a common tariff had not yet been taken by the Six and the old fears that the British would use every possible device to turn the customs union into a free trade area (and that the Germans would be happy to see them do so) were also still very much alive in France, and in Community circles generally. Similarly, German willingness to consider special arrangements which would exclude agriculture from the Common Market was largely irrelevant, if not positively harmful to the British case, since the Germans were themselves opposed to many features of the common agricultural policy and could be counted on to welcome, rather than to resist, modifications in it. In contrast, the French regarded the commitment to a common agricultural policy as one of the most important aspects of the Treaty of Rome. Privileged access to the German market was, in the eyes of many Frenchmen, the logical and necessary counterpart of the opening of the French market to German industrial goods. Therefore, unless the Germans were prepared to talk seriously with the French, and to reflect French views in their explorations with the British, the Anglo-German talks were bound to be of limited usefulness.

There were a number of reasons why the Germans, although ready enough to talk with the British, were reluctant to carry matters to the point of pushing the French. There was still considerable tension and uncertainty between the two Governments, stemming from the Rambouillet discussions and from subsequent statements by General de Gaulle. The most disturbing aspect of the French position, in the eyes of the Germans, was General de Gaulle's attitude towards NATO and his insistence on the need for a French *force de frappe*. In his press conference of 5 September (1960), General de Gaulle had not only summarized his views on the further organization of the Six, but had spoken again of his views for reorganizing NATO, reverting to ideas he had put forward in a letter to President Eisenhower and Mr. Macmillan in September 1958 for extending the scope of NATO to cover other areas of the world but concentrating the power of decision in a three-power (American, British, and French) directorate. He had also indicated that, in his view, there was already too much integration in NATO and had stressed that the defence of a country must have 'a national character'. These views were anathema to Dr. Adenauer. During the autumn the French sought on several occasions to reassure the Germans that French policy was not based on a desire for any reduction in the American commitment to Europe, but simply on the prudent assumption that such a reduction might one day occur. Nevertheless, the German Government was uneasy lest the effect of French policy, whatever the intent behind it, would be a weakening of the United States' commitment. Moreover, Dr. Adenauer had always been conscious of the pressures within Germany for the re-establishment of Germany as an independent military power and he feared the effect in Germany of the French example.

These concerns were overriding, but connected with them was the Chancellor's conviction that the policy of European integration must be pursued and that there should be no weakening of the foundation that had been laid in the existing Communities, even though any new steps might have to be taken along the intergovernmental lines proposed by General de Gaulle. Accordingly, although during the summer Dr. Adenauer had seemed to be rather less solidly behind the Communities and the Brussels institutions than he had been formerly, the apparent weakening in his support was short-lived.[9]

---

[9] It should be noted that the German Embassy in London put out a statement after the Macmillan–Adenauer talks to counteract the impression that the German willingness to have bilateral talks reflected a down-grading in the position of the Communities. See also dispatch from Bonn in *The Times*, 6 October 1960, which read in part: 'The swing in official opinion away from the community's headquarters in Brussels has been arrested and there is a

And the fact that he was defending the Communities against French proposals which he felt would weaken them, inevitably made it more difficult for him, at the same time, to press the French to make concessions to the British, particularly concessions which many Frenchmen believed would undermine the Community. Thus, as had happened so many times during the long search for a settlement between the United Kingdom and the Six, internal arguments and differences of view among the Six had their inevitable repercussions on the problem of the British relationship. During the autumn of 1960 it became quite clear that the British problem and the question of the political construction of the Six were so closely interrelated that little progress could be made on either question until General de Gaulle and Dr. Adenauer could meet together to dispel the misunderstandings, and perhaps even mistrust, which had grown up between the two Heads of Government.

In October, in an attempt to improve relations, M. Debré and M. Couve de Murville visited Bonn, but these discussions appear to have resulted in little agreement.[10] The communiqué issued at the end of the talks contained the usual endorsements of closer European co-operation and of closer co-operation between Europe and North America but revealed little agreement on the way either was to be achieved. Dr. Adenauer was not yet ready to agree to General de Gaulle's detailed proposals for the construction of Europe, although he accepted the idea that heads of state (or government) should meet more often. After consulting the rest of the Six, it was accordingly agreed that a 'little Summit' of the Six should be held in Paris on 5 December and that Dr. Adenauer and General de Gaulle would meet with one another the day before to seek to resolve their own differences of view. There was a certain

tendency once again to support Professor Hallstein. Officials have given warning that this should not be interpreted as a new obstacle in the negotiations between west Germany and Britain. Their sincerity cannot be doubted, but the indications are that the initiative of Mr. Macmillan and Dr. Adenauer is likely to come to nothing because of French ambitions. . . . While Dr. Adenauer is anxious to find a solution for problems arising from the existence of two European trading groups, he is now being forced to fight a rearguard action.'

[10] General de Gaulle complicated the tasks of his emissaries by reiterating just at this time, in a series of talks in Savoy, the reasons why France needed an independent nuclear striking force. In the course of his talks he referred scornfully to those NATO countries that were not so equipped as 'integrated satellites'. See *The Times*, 11 October 1960.

amount of discussion among the Six about whether the British should be brought into these talks, and at one time there were press rumours that Mr. Macmillan might be invited to attend the Paris meetings. This never seemed very probable and the rumours ceased with the announcement that, at British invitation, Dr. Adenauer would visit London shortly after his talks in Paris. Unfortunately the hopes pinned on these December ministerial encounters were not realized, for early in December ill-health on the part of Dr. Adenauer led to the postponement of his visit to Paris, to the postponement of the 'little Summit', and to the postponement of his visit to London.

At the end of the year, however, numerous meetings in Paris offered an opportunity for exchanges of view at ministerial level: the signing of the OECD Convention and the inaugural meeting of the new organization took place on 14 December 1960, and beforehand the EEC Ministers held preparatory meetings among themselves. In addition the Ministerial Councils of the WEU and of the Council of Europe both met in Paris during December. It was rather unfortunate that Dr. Erhard (rather than Dr. Adenauer or his Foreign Minister, Herr von Brentano) was the German Minister who at this time described to the rest of the Six the nature of the discussions which had been taking place between the German and British experts. Given his own predilections,[11] it can be assumed that he not only emphasized the importance of a settlement with the Seven but also argued the feasibility of some form of modified customs union, presumably along the lines of the Mueller–Armack plan which was then receiving a certain amount of attention in Germany.[12]

The French had made it clear at various times, both in public and in private, that they were not disposed to negotiate in these terms and that they regarded a customs union with modifications as not significantly different from the free trade area proposal. It therefore seems probable that Dr. Erhard's presentation did little to counteract the prevailing French view that the British were still

[11] See Siegler, op. cit., p. 406.
[12] See *Financial Times*, 4 January 1961. According to this account the Mueller–Armack plan was a cross between a free trade area and a customs union. The Six and Seven would remain as separate organizations but would bring about a large measure of harmonization in their tariffs *vis-à-vis* third countries, and where this was achieved they would have free trade with one another. Special arrangements of various kinds, e.g., tariff-free quotas, nil duties, origin controls, were proposed to deal with Commonwealth imports. Agriculture was to be excluded from the arrangement.

searching for ways of obtaining the commercial advantages of the Common Market at minimum political cost. The French view under General de Gaulle, as before de Gaulle, was that the Common Market and the provisions of the Treaty of Rome represented a balanced collection of commitments, of advantages and disadvantages, an indivisible package which could only be accepted or rejected as a whole. Although the French did not entirely exclude some kind of European trading arrangement between the Community and the other European countries, they felt such an arrangement could not be contemplated until the customs union among the Six was much nearer completion. For the next few years at least, those European countries that were not prepared to accept the Treaty of Rome should, in the French view, abandon the search for a compromise and make use of the OECD for the discussion of particular trade difficulties and of the GATT for negotiations on a general lowering of tariff barriers.[13] As they frequently pointed out, examination by the Study Group set up by the Committee of Twenty-one had not revealed any great difficulties, and trade figures showed a steady expansion in trade between the Six and their European neighbours. This general approach to the question of relations between the Six and the Seven also prevailed at the headquarters of the Community in Brussels.

Although by the end of 1960 very little positive progress had been made towards an agreement with the Six, the discussions by the British and German experts and various exchanges at the diplomatic level had cleared away a certain amount of dead wood and had strengthened the views of those in the United Kingdom who believed that the choice before the United Kingdom was between joining the Community and being treated by the Community, for the foreseeable future at least, in the same way as any other friendly third country. In addition, a considerable evolution in thinking had taken place within the British Government during the latter part of 1960, and by the end of the year there was much wider recognition than there had been in the spring that the heart

[13] During the autumn of 1960 the GATT countries were negotiating under Article XXIV–6 of the General Agreement, that is, they were negotiating 'compensation' for the changes that the Six would have to make in 'bound' tariffs when they applied the common external tariff. The so-called 'Dillon round' of tariff negotiations, which it was hoped might result in a reduction of the order of 20 per cent. in the common external tariff was scheduled to begin early in 1961.

of the matter was political rather than economic. It was also coming to be much more widely appreciated that if a change in policy as profound as the willingness to join a customs union were to be made there would be clear advantages in going further and joining the Community and thus being in a position to influence decisions. This would have been true had the Six been talking of nothing more than a Common Market, but the fact that the Six were moving towards some kind of political construction underlined the advantages of being in a position to influence developments. Although the form the political construction would take was still very obscure, it was apparent that earlier British hopes that political discussions could be diverted into the WEU framework were not materializing and that membership in the European Economic Community would be the indispensable precondition of any real participation with the Six in the political field. Thus by the end of 1960, there seems to have been a considerable disenchantment in Government circles with the idea of a modified customs union, either as a link between the Six and the Seven or as a master arrangement in which the Six (but not the United Kingdom) would constitute the 'core' group.

At the risk of some over-simplification, it is reasonably accurate to characterize the years 1957 and 1958 as the years when the solution to the problem of the British relationship with the Six was sought on the basis of a free trade area; 1959 as the year of the construction of the EFTA and the period of the belief that the best hope of agreement lay in some kind of bridge arrangement between the two organizations; 1960 as the year in which 'bridge-building' tended to give way to concepts of modified customs unions, perhaps on the basis of an inner and an outer circle, with the British increasingly coming to feel that their place lay in the inner, 'core', group rather than in the peripheral group, and also as the year in which a few key people began to think in terms of joining the Community; 1961 as the year when the views of the British Government developed further and there was not simply a desire to be in the 'core' group but a willingness to accept the essential features of the Treaty of Rome; and, finally, 1962 as the year when the hard decisions implicit in joining the Community were faced by the Government and became the subject of intense national debate.

But this is anticipating. As the year 1961 opened two new factors were introduced into the European picture. In the first place, on

1 January, in accordance with the 'acceleration' decision agreed the previous May, the Six not only cut tariffs on trade among themselves by a further 10 per cent., thus bringing the total reduction to 40 per cent., but, and much more important, they took the first step in aligning their individual national tariffs with the agreed common external tariff and thus started the process of turning themselves into a customs union rather than a free trade area.

The other new factor was the inauguration of Mr. Kennedy as President of the United States. In the United Kingdom there was some hope that as a result of the change of administration the support for the Six, which during the Eisenhower–Dulles–Dillon period had sometimes seemed to the British to be rather emotional and short-sighted, would give way to a more 'balanced and objective' view of the European problem and to a greater willingness to recognize the political dangers that the British saw in a continuation of the division into the Six and the Seven. Those who harboured these hopes were undoubtedly encouraged by the signs of sympathy with the British case that had been apparent for some time in business and academic circles in the United States and, indeed, in some parts of the Administration. It was never realistic to hope that there would be any very great shift in the United States attitude, for the general policy of encouraging the unification of Europe on as deep and far-reaching a basis as possible had had strong bi-partisan support for many years. Moreover, although the Administration had changed, many of those most concerned with European policy were career men, or men like Mr. Dillon who continued to occupy positions of influence in the new Administration. Furthermore, the new Under Secretary of State for Economic Affairs (later to become Under Secretary) was Mr. George Ball, a close associate and intimate friend of M. Jean Monnet. Nevertheless, although presumably there was little expectation in Government circles that the United States would do an about face and come to favour the various kinds of 'bridges' that the previous Administration had opposed, a new Administration was bound to review policies and to re-examine priorities. It was obviously sensible for a British Government that was contemplating a radical change in its own policy to explore the ground in Washington before finally deciding on its own course of action.

Some months were to go by before Mr. Macmillan went to

Washington. Meanwhile, developments in Europe made it plainer with every week that passed that British hopes of negotiating a satisfactory arrangement (political and economic with the Six) depended on Britain's willingness to accept the main principles of the Treaty of Rome.

Early in February, the German Chancellor paid his delayed visit to Paris and the following day the 'little Summit' of the Six was held. During their discussions, General de Gaulle and Dr. Adenauer apparently reached a considerable measure of agreement on the next steps to be taken in the political field. General de Gaulle, for his part, reassured Dr. Adenauer on the two points that had earlier caused the Germans the most concern: the fear that the French were seeking to organize the Six in a way that would weaken the predominant role of NATO in defence matters and the fear that the French President was seeking to emasculate the European Communities. In return Dr. Adenauer appears to have indicated his readiness to abandon, for the time being at least, his earlier hope of giving a 'federal' character to the political construction, and to have agreed with General de Gaulle that there should be regular quarterly meetings of the Heads of Government and of the Foreign Ministers of the Six, these meetings to be prepared by a permanent secretariat composed of officials from the national governments.[14] The 'little Summit' meeting that followed (10 and 11 February) was less harmonious. Dr. Luns, the Dutch Foreign Minister, resented the French and German assumption that once the 'big two' had reached agreement, the rest of the Six would fall into line. Moreover, he felt that since the Six were not now talking of 'federal' or 'supra-national' action in the political field the British should be invited to participate in their discussions. The others, and in particular the French, were opposed to broadening the discussions to include the British. The Dutch, therefore, refused to agree to the modified French proposals (which the others as well as the Germans would probably have accepted) for regular meetings of the Heads of Government and of Foreign Ministers, prepared by a permanent secretariat. The results of a long and apparently acrimonious discussion were rather meagre. The communiqué issued at the end of the meeting was the first of a number of seemingly anodyne communiqués issued by the Six as their discussions on the political *relance* proceeded, communiqués which can be read intelligibly only if a gloss is provided for almost

[14] See *The Times*, 13 February 1961.

every word. Thus the key paragraph in the Paris communiqué read:

It was the purpose of the Conference to seek the methods by which closer political cooperation could be organised. In establishing links in other fields, the intention is to lay the foundation of a union which would develop progressively. It will be possible for this union, limited for the moment to the member states of the European Economic Community, to be extended later.

To the initiated this paragraph revealed a number of points. First, the other five had, for the time being at least, successfully resisted General de Gaulle's attempts to extend Six-country action to the defence field. Second, the political construction would not, initially, involve any 'supra-national' elements, but would respect national sovereignty and the right of veto ('political cooperation'). On the other hand, the fact that it was expressly stated that the union would 'develop progressively' indicated acceptance of the fact that it *might* (and in the minds of some of the drafters *must*) develop 'federally' at a later stage. Finally, the last sentence was an obvious attempt to find a compromise between the Dutch and the French on the question of British participation. But no amount of fine drafting could conceal the fact that the Six were very far from agreement on a number of crucial points and notably on whether or not any commitment to an eventual federal arrangement should be made. The most tangible result of the meeting was the decision to appoint a committee of representatives of the Six Governments (the Fouchet Committee) to try to formulate precise proposals for another meeting of the Heads of Governments to be held in Bonn on 19 May 1961.

The communiqué was at its most Delphic on the question of the British relationship with the Common Market:

The six governments are anxious to seek, in a spirit of goodwill and friendship, all agreements likely to maintain and develop trade with other European countries, and, in particular, with Great Britain, as well as with the other countries of the world. They will endeavour, in the same spirit, to find a solution to the problems arising from the existence of two economic groupings in Europe.[15]

This paragraph can probably best be translated by two words, 'no agreement'.

[15] The text of the communiqué is given in Roy Pryce, *The Political Future of the European Community* (London, 1962), p. 102.

The Dutch position at the Paris meeting—'no Europe à l'Anglaise sans les Anglais'—although, on the face of it, logical, was felt, and not only by the Gaullists but by many 'good Europeans' as well, to be unnecessarily obstructive, and there was some suspicion that the British had encouraged Dr. Luns to be stubborn and to keep the Six from taking any steps in the political field without British participation. It seems unlikely that the Dutch needed any prodding. However, the British were obviously becoming increasingly concerned at the political aspects of developments among the Six and, shortly after this meeting of the Six, Mr. Macmillan made it clear in the House of Commons that, if invited, he would be happy to take part in the political discussions among the Six.[16]

At the end of January, Mr. Macmillan visited General de Gaulle at Rambouillet and about a month later Dr. Adenauer visited Mr. Macmillan in London. Although very little was officially disclosed about either set of meetings it seems safe to conclude that these discussions confirmed a number of points; namely, that the French were opposed to plans like the Mueller-Armack scheme of a modified customs union for bringing the Six and Seven together, that General de Gaulle was unlikely to give serious consideration to any proposal short of a British request to join the Community, and that membership in the Common Market was now a precondition in Dr. Adenauer's mind, as well as in General de Gaulle's mind, for Britain's participating in the discussions on political union that the Six were having among themselves. In his talks with Mr. Macmillan, Dr. Adenauer was widely reported to have suggested that the WEU might form the political link between the Six and the United Kingdom. This was not a new idea but one the British had proposed to the Six in the autumn of 1959.[17] Discussions within the WEU had not developed in the way the British had hoped and this suggestion was not by this time regarded by the British as going nearly far enough.

A few days after the discussions with Dr. Adenauer, Mr. Heath made an important statement to the WEU Council in which he set out the British position on the political discussions. He divided the political question into several parts. So far as discussions arising from the business of the Communities were concerned, Mr. Heath recognized (as Mr. Selwyn Lloyd had done earlier) that

---

[16] *Hansard*, House of Commons, 16 February 1961, col. 1759. The *New York Times* of 17 February 1961 reported that the British had made their position plain to the Six before the 'little Summit' meeting.

[17] See Chapter VIII, p. 234.

these were the sole concern of the Six and that the United Kingdom could not expect to participate in them *'unless or until they had joined, or formed some association with, the communities'*. The qualification was significant, and he followed it up by pointing out that when an acceptable arrangement with the Communities was reached the United Kingdom would expect to participate fully in the institutions. He thus sought to put an end to thoughts thaᵢ certain groups among the Six were suspected of harbouring, that it might be desirable to include the British in an economic arrangement but to exclude them from the political construction.[18] Pending a settlement of the relationship between the United Kingdom and the Communities, the United Kingdom wanted to participate in any political discussions of 'broad European' and of 'world-wide' problems, and Mr. Heath indicated that here the WEU could be useful. He emphasized that 'the British government would not like to be excluded from European discussions of political questions in which they had a direct interest, such as East–West relations, the *political future of Europe*, questions of security and disarmament, relations with other continents, and so on'. He was obviously trying to drive home the point that it was not enough for the Six simply to inform the United Kingdom afterwards of the discussions which they had previously had on these matters among themselves, which was what the consultations in the WEU framework had amounted to all too frequently.[19]

In his long statement to the WEU Council, Mr. Heath also described the basis on which the British had been proceeding in their technical discussions with the Germans, with the Italians, and with the French.[20] (The opening round of talks with the French took place in London at the same time that Mr. Heath was speaking in Paris.) This was the first official confirmation of impressions that were then fairly widespread about the kind of concessions the British were ready to make. In the first place Mr. Heath confirmed that the United Kingdom was prepared to accept a common or harmonized external tariff and presumably—although on this

[18] Dr. Adenauer reverted to these ideas in the autumn of 1962.
[19] A summary of the statement made by Mr. Heath to the WEU Council on 27 February 1961 was released by the WEU headquarters in London following the meeting. The above quotations are from that release. (My italics.)
[20] The British had at one time hoped that the bilateral Anglo-German technical talks would become trilateral, Anglo-French–German, talks. The French turned down this idea but agreed to bilateral talks. Anglo-Italian bilateral talks were also held early in 1961. These were an outcome of Lord Home's visit to Rome in November 1960.

point he was not explicit—a common commercial policy in so far
as it flowed from this decision. But this commitment to a 'common
or harmonized' tariff was strictly limited and applied only to imports coming from countries other than the Commonwealth
countries and the EFTA countries. Thus, in the case of trade with
the Commonwealth countries, the United Kingdom was prepared
to take steps that would have eliminated the preference that
Commonwealth goods enjoyed in the British market, and to put
them on the same footing as goods coming from the Common
Market, but it was not yet prepared to establish a 'reverse preference' and to give the Common Market countries better treatment
than the Commonwealth. The second change in the United Kingdom position flowed from this first major change: British spokesmen were now authorized to indicate that they were ready to see
the Six and the Commonwealth countries concerned enter into
negotiations looking to the elimination of the preferences that
certain British goods enjoyed in other Commonwealth countries.[21]

The third change in the United Kingdom position was put
rather cryptically: Mr. Heath said that the British Government
also 'visualized special arrangements for tropical and agricultural
products', and he indicated they did so because 'they believed that
this was important not only for economic reasons but also to
prevent an extension of the division of Europe into Africa and
particularly into the newly emergent territories there'. At the end
of the year 1960 the Six were deep in consideration of the kind
of arrangements that should govern their relations with their
associated overseas territories when the five-year Convention
included in the Treaty of Rome came up for renewal in 1963. The
British hoped to work out arrangements with the Community to
reduce the discrimination against their own former colonies when
the Convention was renewed, whether or not progress could be
made on the broader problem of the United Kingdom's relationship with the Six. The United Kingdom had always been very
much alive to the problems these arrangements posed for their
own possessions and former possessions, particularly those in
Africa and the West Indies with economies similar to those of the
countries already associated with the Community.

[21] There were two ways in which the preference might be eliminated: either the
m.f.n. rate could be reduced to the British preference rate or the preference
rate could be raised to the m.f.n. rate. Extension of the preference rate to the
Six, which might well have seemed the most desirable solution to the Six,
would have been contrary to the 'no new preference rule' of the GATT.

Mr. Heath's bald statement that special arrangements were visualized for agricultural products went no further than the British had shown they were prepared to go during the EFTA negotiations. It seems probable, however, that the Government was ready to go beyond limited deals of that kind (and further than the proposals it put forward during the Maudling Committee negotiations), but that it was still hoping ways could be found to keep intact the entry arrangements for temperate-zone agricultural products from the Commonwealth. And it seems clear that the Government had, as yet, reached no decision on how far it was prepared to go in modifying domestic agricultural support arrangements.

In many ways the most revealing indication of the change that had taken place in the attitude of the British Government came when Mr. Heath was commenting on a proposal from the WEU Assembly that the United Kingdom should accede to the European Economic Community as a full member. The British Government, he said, did not wish to express a view on this resolution but they had an open mind and in this connexion the Government 'fully recognized that common institutions would be necessary to control a common or harmonized tariff' and they were 'not afraid of any such institutions'. Mr. Heath went out of his way to underline the point that far from wanting to steer clear of commitments with political overtones, 'no arrangements would be satisfactory to his Government which did not involve a political as well as an economic relationship with the Six'. And, as summarized above, later in his speech he outlined in some detail the British interest in the political discussions.

It seems clear that, by the time he came to make it, Mr. Heath's statement to the WEU Council was not a description of an approach in which the British Government still reposed much hope but rather a description of an approach which six months before they had thought might be fruitful but which had already been shown to be inadequate. Any lingering hopes that progress could be made in defining the kinds of arrangement the Six might be willing to accept in the absence of a prior political decision to accept the basic principles of the Treaty of Rome must, in any case, have been dashed by the French reactions during the first set of Anglo-French talks in London, at the WEU Council meeting, and, a few days later, at a meeting of the Consultative Assembly of the Council of Europe. In London, Paris, and Strasbourg the French made it plain that they felt it was premature to talk in any

detail about the special arrangements that might be made to meet
the Commonwealth and other problems until the United Kingdom
had reached its own decision. Although the French did not rule
out entirely some kind of association, the only kind they seemed
prepared to consider would have amounted to little more than an
agreement to make reciprocal tariff concessions in the GATT and
to exchange views on political questions in the WEU. Moreover,
it was abundantly clear that the French felt the new political construction should be limited to, and based on, membership in
the Common Market. Without mentioning the United Kingdom by name, M. Couve de Murville, the French Foreign
Minister, made it plain at Strasbourg that, in his view, the
right solution for the United Kingdom was to join the Economic
Community:

> Our partners in the Common Market and we ourselves have always
> said that the Common Market was, and always remained, open to any
> other European country which wished to join it. We persist in thinking
> that therein lies, for some at least, a valid possibility, and, doubtless,
> the only really satisfactory solution. We persist in hoping, furthermore,
> that certain refusals, although repeated, will not be maintained.[22]

The dilemma in which the British Government thus found
itself might easily have resulted in stalemate. Given the nature of
the problems that needed to be solved and the state of public
opinion, no British Government could at that time have taken an
unqualified decision to join the Community; on the other hand,
nothing short of a clear decision seemed likely to produce the
kind of discussion with the Six which would yield enough information on the arrangements that might be negotiable to make the
decision possible. The only way out of the dilemma was the way
eventually taken by Mr. Macmillan, that of a qualified acceptance
of the Treaty of Rome. This way out took great political courage
for, as discussed further below in Chapter XI, it had built into it
a number of difficulties which put the Government in a relatively
weak bargaining position vis-à-vis the Six and in a very vulnerable
domestic political position.

---

[22] Quotation taken from the press release issued by the French Embassy in
London giving the text of M. Couve de Murville's speech to the Consultative
Assembly on 2 March 1961. The British interpreted this statement to mean
not only that the French would oppose half-way measures but also that they
would respond favourably to a British application for membership. See Mr.
Heath's reference to this statement in Chapter XIV, p. 492.

During the spring of 1961 the feeling of suspense in London was almost tangible. Rumours of the imminence of a Cabinet decision abounded, and counting probable ministerial votes for and against joining was a common journalistic pastime. In addition to those who still doubted the wisdom of joining there were many who felt that the time was not ripe for beginning negotiations. There was great fear of another failure, and rightly so. Although the collapse of the free trade area negotiations had been a considerable shock to those most deeply involved in the negotiations, the failure had seemed to most people to be simply one unhappy episode in the search for the right relationship with the Six. It was still possible, and not too difficult, to try again. In contrast, a failure of a serious attempt to join the Community might mean that the United Kingdom had come to the end of a road that had been followed since the end of the war, albeit at times haltingly and without much conviction. And in the early months of 1961 there were very few encouraging omens. The French and the Commission (supported in varying degrees by the other member governments of the Community) had slammed every door that opened on a solution short of membership, but it was a very long leap from opposing solutions short of membership to wanting British participation enough to make concessions. Despite statements like those of M. Couve de Murville, it was difficult to believe that General de Gaulle's concept of an 'organized' Europe was one which embraced the United Kingdom. Moreover, in addition to the difficulties across the Channel, some of the EFTA countries were reluctant to contemplate bargaining separately with the Six. Ironically enough, although the desire to keep some of the other EFTA countries from making separate deals with the Six had been one of the main British motives for agreeing to the formation of the Seven, the advantage of sticking together and bargaining collectively was now an argument played back at the British when they suggested that more might be achieved by separate negotiations. In addition there was concern, verging on open opposition, from some parts of the Commonwealth. Finally, earlier attempts at 'bridge-building' had shown that the support, or opposition, of the United States might well be a crucial factor in the success or failure of a new negotiation. And the reactions of the United States had still to be tested.

In the winter of 1960-1, United States officials concerned with European questions tended to share the view that then prevailed in France and in Community circles in Brussels, namely that although the British were now obviously prepared to make various concessions which they had been unwilling to make during the free trade area negotiations, they were not yet seriously interested in becoming part of the main-stream of the movement for European integration and were not yet ready to accept the underlying concepts of the Treaty of Rome. At the end of March, however, the American Under Secretary of State for Economic Affairs (Mr. George Ball) visited London for a meeting of the Development Assistance Group (see Chapter VIII) and while in London he had discussions with Mr. Heath, Sir Frank Lee, and others, during which it became clear to him that the British were, in fact, thinking in new terms and had edged very close to a decision to apply for membership in the Communities.

Early in April, Mr. Macmillan went to Washington for talks with the new Administration. Although he had met the new President in January at Palm Beach in connexion with the Laos crisis, the April visit was the first opportunity for a general review of common problems, and Britain's relations with the Common Market was obviously one of the matters which Mr. Macmillan wanted to discuss. The available evidence suggests that Mr. Macmillan asked Mr. Kennedy a hypothetical question: 'What would be your reaction if we decided to join the EEC?' and that he was given an enthusiastic affirmative answer. There is no evidence to suggest that Mr. Macmillan was 'pushed' by Mr. Kennedy, as was alleged, and denied, at various times. But it is clear that Mr. Kennedy left no doubt in Mr. Macmillan's mind that a British decision to join the Six would be welcome and that Mr. Macmillan left Washington convinced that, far from straining Anglo-American relations, Britain's joining the Community might well lead to much closer and more far-reaching transatlantic links than the British could hope to achieve in other ways. The reflection that the shortest, and perhaps the only, way to a real Atlantic partnership lay through Britain's joining the Common Market seems to have been a very important—perhaps the controlling—element in Mr. Macmillan's own decision that the right course for the United Kingdom was to apply for membership.[23] Mr. Kennedy's warm

[23] See the speech that Mr. Macmillan made at the Massachusetts Institute of Technology on 7 April 1961 for an indication of the importance he attached to the need for a better organization of the free world and, in particular, for an 'imaginative partnership in the centre', that is, the Atlantic alliance, 'the core

response undoubtedly strengthened Mr. Macmillan's own conviction that joining was the right course of action and encouraged him to continue his efforts to bring the sceptics in the Cabinet to accept this view. Also, like the discussions with General de Gaulle and Dr. Adenauer earlier in the year, the discussions with the United States Administration underlined, once again, the fact that 'association' arrangements were not likely to be negotiable. It was clear that the United States was prepared to accept the additional commercial 'discrimination' against itself because of the political advantages it saw in British membership in the Community, but that it would be hostile to arrangements short of membership which, in its view, would simply increase 'discrimination' but would not, like full membership, add to the political stability of the Community or strengthen the 'Atlantic' orientation of the new power-complex the Six were clearly coming to be.

After Mr. Macmillan's visit to Washington there was pressure from Parliament and from the press for an early statement of the Government's position and there was some criticism of the Government for not being able to make up its mind. At the end of April, Mr. Maudling (then President of the Board of Trade) stated flatly in the House of Commons that the Cabinet had not yet reached a decision. However, there were increasing signs that the Cabinet was moving towards a decision, and on 17 May Mr. Heath, opening a debate in the House of Commons on foreign affairs, made the longest and most forthcoming statement that had yet been made on the Government's thinking about the European problem. Although he included 'a form of association with the Community' as one possible course of action, he spoke of it with little enthusiasm, and it was clear enough that the fourth possibility he listed—'that of full membership, provided that proper arrangements are made for Commonwealth trade and for our agricultural system ... and proper arrangements for our EFTA partners' —was the one that he found the most attractive and the one the Government were, in fact, most likely to adopt.[24] He made it clear that the Government were not going to be rushed into opening negotiations before they could see the main lines of a

of the free world'. It is also worth noting—in the light of later developments— that Mr. Macmillan pointed out that 'the health of our whole NATO alliance depends on finding a way of building a partnership in the nuclear as well as in the conventional field.' Official text released by Admiralty House.
[24] *Hansard*, House of Commons, 17 May 1961, col. 1398.

solution and were reasonably assured of success, and also that they had no intention of signing first and negotiating afterwards, as they were being urged to do by some of the most enthusiastic pro-'Europeans'.

Consultations with the Commonwealth

The uncertainties and doubts that existed within the Cabinet and the uncertainties and doubts felt by some of the other EFTA countries and by many of the Commonwealth countries inevitably nourished one another and, in these last days before the decision to negotiate was finally taken and announced, there was an un-fortunate, if understandable, temptation to promise too much to too many different interests. The promises made at this time added considerably to the difficulty of the negotiations. Moreover, they tended to perpetuate the confusion both at home and abroad about the Government's real objectives and to give substance to later charges of bad faith.

The Commonwealth aspects of the question overshadowed all others, politically, economically, emotionally. On one level the problem was whether, in fact, arrangements could be made so that the Commonwealth countries could be assured that the oppor-tunities for maintaining their existing level of exports, and for satisfying their reasonable hopes for expanding their exports, would not suffer as a consequence of Britain's joining the Common Market. But concern at a deeper and more fundamental level was also apparent during the spring of 1961, although it came much more to the fore in the autumn of 1962. This was the uncertainty whether the fabric of the Commonwealth was tough enough to stand the strain that would inevitably be placed upon it by the United Kingdom's entry into the European Community and by the drastic modification in the existing preferential trade arrange-ments that such a move would bring about, in the long run at any rate. The uncertainty about the relationship between the prefer-ential system and the cohesion of the Commonwealth had several parts. First, how important an ingredient in the cement that held the Commonwealth together were the trade arrangements? Second, was this importance based on real economic advantage or was it mainly psychological, that is, if other arrangements could be found to safeguard the trade, would there, or would there not, be a strain on the Commonwealth relationship? Third, were not Common-wealth economic relations changing in any case and would a United

Kingdom that stayed out of the Common Market, in fact, be able, or would it wish, to maintain the present trade arrangements for very much longer in any case? Finally, would some of the other Commonwealth countries want to maintain them for much longer, whatever Britain did? Reflections about the importance of the existing trading arrangements led on to further reflections about the importance of the Commonwealth. What were the essential characteristics of the Commonwealth that needed to be preserved? Understandably enough, no clear answer was found to this question, for the answer is not the same for all people. But this intangible, emotional aspect of the problem was, and continued to be, the most difficult aspect of the whole problem of the United Kingdom's relations with the Six. It could be demonstrated, and it was demonstrated time and again, that the Commonwealth was not an economic alternative to the Common Market; the countries of the Commonwealth had shown that they were not interested in forming a free trade area or a customs union with the United Kingdom. And it could be demonstrated that United Kingdom trade with the Commonwealth was declining while trade with the continent of Europe (despite the beginning of tariff 'discrimination' by the Six) was expanding. And it could be demonstrated that the preferential arrangements were constantly being eroded, and were being eroded not least by conscious policy decisions on the part of the Commonwealth countries themselves. And it could be demonstrated that, on certain and not too exaggeratedly optimistic assumptions, the Commonwealth countries might well gain more than they lost from the United Kingdom's joining the Community. Nevertheless, there was a nagging doubt and a strong undercurrent of feeling that, since the Commonwealth relationship was being changed, it was probably being changed for the worse.

If the Commonwealth countries had themselves taken the lead in urging Britain to join the Common Market, the Government's task would have been immeasurably easier, although even Commonwealth encouragement for such a move might not have been enough to persuade some of the most loyal Commonwealth partisans in the United Kingdom that it was really in the best interests of the Commonwealth for the United Kingdom to join the Six. But, for the most part, the Commonwealth countries did nothing to hide their concern. Early in March (1961), the Commonwealth Prime Ministers met in London. This meeting was almost entirely given

over to a discussion of the South African problem, that is, whether
once South Africa became a republic it would wish to remain in
the Commonwealth, and whether its continued membership would
be acceptable to the other members of the Commonwealth. The
discussions among the Prime Ministers, and the eventual decision
of the South African Prime Minister to withdraw the South
African application for continued membership, aroused many
misgivings and strong and conflicting emotions. The controversy
over South Africa underlined the fundamental lack of cohesion in
the Commonwealth and probably facilitated the decision to seek
to join the Common Market by making it easier for the British
Government to think in new terms about the whole basis of the
Commonwealth relationship. On the other hand, the controversy
seems to have increased the reluctance of some Prime Ministers—
and of Mr. Menzies, the Australian Prime Minister, in particular
—to see any further weakening of the ties between the United
Kingdom and the 'old dominions'.

As indicated above, the fact that the United Kingdom was
seriously considering a customs union with the Community and
might, in certain circumstances, even consider joining the Community, had been made clear to the Commonwealth Finance
Ministers in London in October 1960. It can be assumed that the
Commonwealth countries were kept informed of the technical
explorations which the British carried on during the winter and
spring of 1960–61, first with the Germans and then with the
Italians and the French. It must have been as clear to the
Commonwealth representatives as it was to any informed observer
that the Six were not prepared for any arrangement with the
United Kingdom which did not involve acceptance, in principle,
of the common external tariff, a common commercial policy, and a
common agricultural policy, and that any arrangements to safeguard Commonwealth interests would have to be taken within the
framework of these policies. In any case, at the end of May
Commonwealth economic experts met in London and, at this time,
United Kingdom officials reviewed with them, in some detail, the
kinds of arrangement they thought might be negotiable for the five
main categories of goods into which the problem of 'Commonwealth exports' had been divided: basic materials, temperate zone
foodstuffs, tropical products, manufactures from the developed
countries of the Commonwealth, and manufactures from the less-
developed parts of the Commonwealth. These discussions

strengthened the impression that the British Government was on the point of taking a decision in principle to join the Community, and there was pressure from some of the Commonwealth countries (Canada, in particular) and also in the House of Commons for high-level Commonwealth discussions, perhaps a Prime Ministers' conference, before any decision was taken. The Government was very cool to this idea but Commonwealth pressure for high-level consultations could not be ignored. Early in June, Mr. Macmillan, in reply to a series of questions in the House of Commons, indicated that, in his view, the interests of the Commonwealth countries differed so widely that separate consultations were more likely to be fruitful than was a full-dress Prime Ministers' conference, and soon thereafter it became known that a number of Cabinet Ministers were to make flying trips to the Commonwealth capitals for discussions on the Common Market.[25]

In addition to the point made by Mr. Macmillan, there was obviously no time to convene a Commonwealth Prime Ministers' meeting before a statement was made to the House of Commons, if a statement were to be made before the summer recess. And, for a number of reasons, if a decision to negotiate in terms of entry were to be taken it was desirable that it should be taken quickly so that negotiations could begin in earnest early in the autumn. In the first place, two of the Community's major policies and the two policies that had the most direct impact on the Commonwealth countries— the common agricultural policy and the arrangements to be made with the associated overseas countries and territories when the Convention came up for renewal in 1963—were then under discussion within the Community, and it was obviously desirable that if the British were to join the Community they should be in a position to take part in the formulation of policy on these key issues.[26] In the second place, tariffs within the Six were coming down even faster than the Treaty of Rome had specified, and the sooner the British joined the Community the lower the initial hurdle to be taken. At this time the Government had the following programme in mind: (1) a statement by the Prime Minister before

---

[25] *Hansard*, House of Commons, 1 June 1961, col. 415.

[26] In the event, the Six rushed through the decisions on the main provisions of the common agricultural policy so that they could negotiate collectively with the British from an agreed position on this crucial issue. See below, Chapter XI. The Six also pushed ahead with the renewal of the Convention on the overseas territories, although there was rather more informal consultation with the British on this question than there was on agriculture.

the House of Commons rose early in August indicating the Government's intention of opening negotiations with a view to joining the Community; (2) serious negotiations with the Six during the autumn and winter; (3) conclusion of negotiations in the spring of 1962; (4) ratification during the autumn of 1962; and (5) formal entry into the Community on 1 January 1963. Even if the negotiations had been successful this timetable would not have been met, but in the summer of 1961 it did not seem to be an unduly optimistic one. However, if the Prime Minister was to open the way to negotiations by a statement to the House before the summer recess, there was obviously no time for a full-dress Commonwealth meeting beforehand.

Mr. Diefenbaker, the Canadian Prime Minister, would clearly have preferred a Commonwealth Prime Ministers' meeting to the bilateral consultations suggested by Mr. Macmillan, and his views apparently found some support elsewhere in the Commonwealth.[27] For a time there was some confusion, for the British Government could not have ignored a clear demand for a Commonwealth conference. Presumably the British Government made it plain to the other Commonwealth Governments that Mr. Macmillan's statement to the House would not be a decision to enter the Common Market but simply a decision to negotiate to see whether the conditions required to meet the special problems of the United Kingdom, the Commonwealth, and the EFTA countries could be obtained. And it was no doubt pointed out that the Commonwealth countries would, in any case, have an opportunity for a collective discussion at the meeting of Commonwealth Finance Ministers already planned for September and that no real negotiations with the Six would have taken place before then.

In the end, the procedure of discussions with the emissaries from the British Cabinet was accepted, but Mr. Macmillan must have had a ticklish time getting his own way. Mr. Sandys, the Minister responsible for Commonwealth relations and one of the strongest 'Europeans' in the Cabinet, visited New Zealand, Australia, and Canada; Mr. Thorneycroft, then Minister of Aviation, and another of the known 'Europeans' in the Government (as President of the Board of Trade he had been one of the first to recognize the need to find some accommodation with the Six) visited India, Pakistan, Ceylon, and Malaya; and Mr. Hare, then Minister of Labour but

[27] See *Financial Times*, 12 June 1961, and also the report from Ottawa in *The Times* of 14 June 1961.

a former Minister of Agriculture and a 'dark horse' so far as his views on the Common Market were concerned, went to Sierra Leone, Ghana, Nigeria, and the Central African Federation. Lord Perth, Minister of State at the Foreign Office, went to the British West Indies and Mr. Heath to Cyprus.

These visits took place, for the most part, during the first fortnight in July. Beforehand, various statements emanating from the Commonwealth capitals indicated that the tasks of the emissaries would not be easy. A number of the Commonwealth countries clearly felt that, despite the repeated assurances that no decision had yet been taken, the British Cabinet had, in fact, already reached its decision and that the emissaries were being sent out to 'sell' to the Commonwealth the British case for joining the Common Market and not to have any real discussions of the advantages and disadvantages. This uneasiness and resentment was not the best atmosphere for the talks.

Very little, other than the formal communiqué issued at the end of each set of discussions, was officially revealed about the talks.[28] From the information available it seems probable that the British Ministers made it clear that, in their view, the long-term interest of the United Kingdom lay in joining the Common Market, provided, but only provided, suitable arrangements for the Commonwealth could be made; that they felt that they had come to the end of the line in exploratory discussions with the Six; and that the only way to discover whether or not adequate arrangements could, in fact, be made was by opening formal negotiations. It also seems probable that the British Ministers tried to get the Commonwealth countries to indicate, if only in a very general way, their approval for this course of action, since evidence of Commonwealth support would have been invaluable to the Prime Minister when he came to make his statement to the House of Commons.

Mr. Thorneycroft seems to have had a relatively easy passage. The Malayan Federation was reasonably optimistic that its two big export commodities—tin and rubber—would not suffer but might even expand as a result of the United Kingdom's joining the Common Market, since there was no Community tariff on either

---

[28] Mr. Gaitskell pressed the Prime Minister to issue a White Paper on the consultations, but the Prime Minister declined to do more than have the communiqués reproduced, saying that the talks were of a confidential character. The texts of the communiqués are in the White Paper, *Commonwealth Consultations on Britain's Relations with the European Economic Community*, Cmnd. 1449, H.M.S.O., July 1961.

item. In Pakistan he presumably found considerable understanding for the British position as well as some concern about the impact on Pakistan's exports of textiles and other manufactured and semi-manufactured goods. At the time when Mr. Thorneycroft was in Pakistan, President Ayub Khan was in London, and commented to the press: 'I think it would be a good thing if Britain joined the Common Market. . . . Although we, as members of the Common-wealth, enjoy certain privileges and we should like to see our interests safeguarded, we would not stand in the way of Britain's joining. We welcome any strength arising anywhere in the free world, and it would probably benefit us in the long run.'[29]

The Indians appear to have been less forthcoming than the Pakistanis. Like the Pakistanis they were worried lest British accesssion to the Community would mean that restrictions would be placed on their exports to the British market without any off-setting liberalization being made in the highly restrictive import régimes of some of the Six. In addition the Indians seem to have been concerned about the weakening in Commonwealth links which they felt would inevitably result from British membership in the Community. They also felt that, if some Commonwealth countries, such as the African countries, became associated with the Community, while others like India did not, undesirable divisions within the Commonwealth would be created.

Mr. Hare seems to have met with very little encouragement in Africa and the communiqués issued after most of his talks were ominously brief. The Ghanaian Government had long regarded the EEC with suspicion and the association of African countries with the Common Market as a thinly disguised form of neo-colonialism.[30] The Nigerians also viewed the association arrange-ments with misgivings although, unlike Ghana, Nigeria was not yet prepared to reject the possibility of an association.

The really difficult talks, however, were those undertaken by Mr. Sandys. This was inevitable, both because the emotional ties are strongest between the 'old' dominions and the United Kingdom and because the problems that Britain's joining the

[29] See *Financial Times,* 8 July 1961.
[30] According to the *Guardian* of 5 July 1961, President Nkrumah, in addressing the State Opening of the Ghanaian Parliament, said that he thought British membership in the Common Market would have a disruptive effect on the Commonwealth and that the EEC would 'perpetuate by economic means many artificial barriers which were imposed on Africa by European colonial powers'. He advocated an African Common Market.

Community posed for these countries were, in fact, very difficult ones to solve within the context of the Treaty of Rome and of the policies adopted by the Community. Press accounts of the talks and the communiqués themselves suggest that the talks were even more difficult than had been expected. On the eve of Mr. Sandys' arrival in Wellington, Mr. Holyoake, the Prime Minister, summed up the New Zealand position: 'We do not take a dog in the manger attitude. . . . We have, however, made the most detailed study and have so far been unable to discover an alternative that could compensate us for the loss of our existing contractual right of unrestricted and duty-free entry for our meat and dairy produce to the British market.'[31] The communiqué indicated clearly enough that Mr. Sandys had made little progress in trying to convince the New Zealanders that other ways of meeting their interests could be found and the relevant section of the communiqué closely paralleled Mr. Holyoake's statement: 'The New Zealand Ministers made it clear that they could not at present see any effective way of protecting New Zealand's vital interests other than by maintenance of unrestricted duty-free entry.' According to the communiqué, Mr. Sandys explained the difficulties of reconciling unrestricted duty-free entry into the United Kingdom with the concept of the Common Market and indicated that 'It might therefore be necessary in any negotiations to explore other methods of securing comparable outlets for New Zealand exports'. The use of the phrase 'comparable outlets' in the communiqué should be noted, for it was to figure prominently in the negotiations.[32] The communiqué then stated that: 'New Zealand Ministers said that while adhering to the views they had expressed they would be willing to examine any such alternative methods for protecting New Zealand interests which might emerge in the course of negotiations.'

The idea of an association between New Zealand and the Common Market may well have been one of the possibilities considered in Wellington, for Mr. Holyoake told the press that New Zealand was keeping a close watch on the negotiations for association with Greece, and indicated that, in certain circumstances, it might perhaps be a good thing if New Zealand could be associated in

[31] *Guardian*, 1 July 1961.
[32] It should also be noted that Mr. Sandys pointed out that even if Britain did not join the Common Market, New Zealand might well be faced with difficult problems in finding outlets for its 'increasing agricultural production' as there were limits to the British market. See communiqué reprinted in the White Paper.

some way.[33] The United Kingdom Government was not, however, thinking in these terms but rather of special free entry arrangements for key New Zealand products, such as dairy products and lamb.

From the United Kingdom's standpoint, the chief result of the discussions in Wellington was the acceptance by the New Zealanders of the British view that it would be fruitless to hold further exploratory talks with the Six and that the only way to find out whether acceptable conditions were obtainable was by opening formal negotiations. The New Zealanders, for their part, were given assurances of full consultation before and during the negotiations and of a thorough discussion of the results before a decision to join the Community was taken. Moreover, the communiqué specifically recorded that Britain would not feel able to join the European Economic Community unless special arrangements to protect the 'vital interests' of New Zealand were secured. Although the New Zealand Government stopped short of giving its approval to a British decision to open negotiations, the communiqué stated that 'in the light of these assurances they [the New Zealand Ministers] informed Mr. Sandys that they would understand it if, after considering the views of Commonwealth countries, the British Government should open negotiations with the European Economic Community'.

Mr. Sandys went from Wellington to Canberra, where he appears to have found great uneasiness and rather less willingness to look at the problem from the British point of view than he had in New Zealand. The Australian Government had wrung every ounce of meaning from the Wellington communiqué and had decided that the New Zealanders had gone too far in giving the United Kingdom a free hand in deciding what constituted adequate safeguards for the Commonwealth.[34] Moreover, the Australians had domestic political problems which made them loath to go even as far as the New Zealanders had gone in indicating 'understanding' of a British decision to open negotiations. Elections were in the offing and the Government was based on a coalition between the Conservatives and the Country Party (farmers). Mr. McEwen, the Deputy Prime Minister and Minister of Trade, was the leader of the Country Party and, therefore, particularly responsive to the

---

[33] See *Guardian*, 11 July 1961. M. Monnet was known to be thinking along similar lines at this time.

[34] See *Financial Times*, 8 July 1961, and *The Times*, 11 July 1961.

agricultural interests. Australian doubts were not, however, prompted solely by fears for their own trade. The Prime Minister, Mr. Menzies, was obviously sincerely troubled by the long-term political effects on the Commonwealth.

The communiqué took some ten hours to draft and satisfied no one. It did not give Mr. Sandys the encouragement he sought nor did it give the Australians any precise assurances. It followed the pattern of the Wellington communiqué in stating the views of both sides rather than agreed conclusions, and it is not difficult to read into it an even wider divergence of view about the basic questions than had existed in Wellington. Mr. Menzies could not swallow Mr. Sandys' argument that Britain's closer association with the Continent would be an added source of strength to the Commonwealth, and the communiqué formally recorded the Australian concern 'at the weakening effect they believed this development would have on the Commonwealth relationship'.[35] Mr. Sandys succeeded in extracting from the Australians the statement that 'As the whole question is of major importance for Britain and for decision by her, Australian Ministers did not feel entitled to object to the opening of negotiations by the British Government should it reach the conclusion that this was desirable.' However, the Australians saw to it that this statement was followed by another reading: 'but they made it clear that the absence of objection should in the circumstances not be interpreted as implying approval'—which left Mr. Sandys with very little. The statement in the Wellington communiqué that the United Kingdom would not feel able to join the EEC unless arrangements were secured to protect the vital interests of New Zealand was conspicuously lacking. The nearest counterpart was the assurance given by Mr. Sandys that the British Government 'fully shared its [the Australian Government's] concern to maintain the long-established flow of trade between their two countries. If negotiations took place, the intention would be to secure special arrangements to protect these important trading interests.' Although the New Zealanders had been ready to accept British assurances that they would be consulted throughout the negotiations and had not, apparently, pressed for direct participation, the Australians made it clear that they wanted to be directly represented at the negotiating table when arrangements affecting Australian trade were discussed. Since this was a matter

[35] It was reported in the press that the communiqué was drafted largely by Mr. Menzies.

for decision by the Six, as much as by the United Kingdom, Mr. Sandys could give no undertaking on this point. It should be noted that the Australians were invited to sit at the table at one stage during the negotiations, a right which the New Zealanders and Canadians did not claim, perhaps because they felt they would be in a stronger position to be critical of the arrangements agreed if they were not represented.

In a statement to the press after the discussions, Mr. Menzies elaborated on his concern at the long-term political implications for the Commonwealth:

> It is very difficult for me to believe that Britain, intimately involved in European politics for the first time, would remain so individual and detached as it is today. I am not saying that is good, bad, or indifferent —neither my colleagues nor I sit in judgment on that, but we record our view that the Commonwealth will not be quite the same. Mr. Sandys felt, no doubt with great conviction, that none of these things would affect Commonwealth relationships. Well, we think it will.[36]

After Canberra came Ottawa. For some time the Canadian Government had made no secret of its dislike of the idea that Britain might join the Six, and the British Government can have had little hope that Mr. Sandys would receive any encouragement in Ottawa. Unlike the situation with respect to New Zealand (and, to a less extent, Australia), there was little real uncertainty about the kind of arrangements that could be made for Canada's principal exports. Except for wheat (and here Canada was in a better position than Australia because Canadian hard wheat is not directly competitive with European wheat), Canadian exports stood to be affected mainly by the common external tariff of the Six rather than by the (as yet unsettled) common agricultural policy. Although there might be scope for negotiating tariff quotas, or nil duties, for some of Canada's important exports, such as aluminium and newsprint, it was abundantly clear that the Six would insist that, in principle, the common external tariff should be applied to British imports of Canadian manufactures and basic materials. There can thus have been very little to 'explore' with the Canadian Ministers except, perhaps, the timing and the technique of Commonwealth consultations.

Since taking office, Mr. Diefenbaker had tried in various ways to lessen Canadian economic dependence on the United States

[36] *The Times,* 13 July 1961.

and to re-direct some Canadian trade from the United States to the United Kingdom. He had resented the United Kingdom's counter of a free trade area to his earlier suggestion for a 'modest' redirection of trade, and he was now concerned lest the inevitable result of Britain's joining the Six would be to increase Canada's economic dependence on the United States. Moreover, as in the case of Australia, domestic political problems contributed to the tough line taken with Mr. Sandys. Elections were expected within the year and the position of the Conservative Government, which had never been very strong, seemed to be growing weaker. The economy was stagnant and the rate of unemployment very high. Anything that might contribute to Canada's own domestic economic difficulties was therefore more than usually unwelcome.

Although the main opposition party, the Liberal Party, and various business and banking groups in Canada were critical of the carping comments made by Mr. Fleming and by others in the Diefenbaker Government about the United Kingdom's movement towards Europe, their criticisms did little to soften the Canadian Government's strictures, although they doubtless somewhat blunted the impact on the British Government.[37] The fact that the Canadian Government was threatening to create new problems for British exporters by increasing tariffs on automobiles and by devaluing the Canadian dollar also tended to make some of the criticism less telling tha it might otherwise have been.

The Ottawa communiqué was very much shorter than the Wellington and Canberra communiqués and even blunter in tone. Moreover, the Canadian Government went even further than had the Australian Government in recording its disagreement with the British Government's assessment of the potential advantages and disadvantages of joining or staying out of the EEC. Although, like the other Commonwealth Governments, the Canadian Government formally recognized that the question of whether or not to negotiate was a matter for decision by the British Government, it also recorded in the communiqué 'the grave concern of the Canadian Government about the implications of possible negotiations between Britain and the European Economic

[37] Mr. Pearson, the leader of the Liberal Party, had apparently encouraged Mr. Macmillan to join the Common Market when the latter visited Ottawa in the spring. See *The Times*, 6 July 1961. Throughout the negotiations Mr. Pearson continued to criticize the negative attitude of the Diefenbaker Government.

Community, and about the political and economic effects which British membership in the European Economic Community would have on Canada and on the Commonwealth as a whole'.[38] There were no British commitments, except for further consultation, in the Ottawa communiqué, and even the customary statement that the British Government intended to safeguard the vital interests of the Commonwealth countries was missing.

Mr. Macmillan's desire to avoid a Commonwealth conference before making his statement to the House was understandable, but it is difficult to believe that the decision to send emissaries around the Commonwealth capitals before the Cabinet had taken its own decision was a wise one. The attitudes of the Commonwealth countries were well known in Whitehall, and these last-minute discussions simply invited the Commonwealth countries to add more requests for 'special arrangements' to the already almost un-negotiably high pile. Moreover, rather than reassuring the Conservative back-benchers who had been pressing for fuller Commonwealth consultations, the effect of the talks was probably to add to the ill-defined but very real political concern that the Commonwealth might be weakened if the United Kingdom were to join the Six.

There is nothing to suggest that any Commonwealth country put forward any alternative suggestions. The general impression created by the communiqués and by the press comment at the time was that the Commonwealth countries felt they had few obligations to, but strong claims on, the United Kingdom; in short, that the relationship was a rather one-sided one. It seems probable that by their hard bargaining and by a tendency to take a narrow national view of the questions at issue, the Australians and the Canadians tended to weaken rather than to strengthen their position with the British Government.[39] The New Zealanders, on the other hand, probably strengthened their position by showing a relatively greater understanding of the United Kingdom's position, even though their own situation was the most precarious of the three. However, although the views of the various Commonwealth countries can have done little to reassure those Cabinet Ministers who were already sceptical, they were not so negative as to make

[38] White Paper, p. 4.
[39] It should be noted, however, that Mr. Sandys was also criticized by Mr. Gaitskell and others for his tough handling of the Commonwealth countries, both at this time and, later, at the Commonwealth Prime Ministers' Conference in September 1962.

the Prime Minister abandon his own view that the right course was
to open negotiations.

Consultations with the EFTA countries

The process of discussion with the Commonwealth countries
that was carried on at various levels during 1960 and 1961 resulted in the gradual substitution of general formulae, such as
'safeguarding vital interests' and 'seeking to ensure "comparable"
outlets', for the earlier flat commitment to preserve existing entry
arrangements for food, drink, and tobacco. In contrast, the discussions with the EFTA countries in the spring and early summer
of 1961 resulted in a British commitment to the EFTA countries
that was much more precise than that contained in the Stockholm
Convention.

The EFTA Ministerial Council met in Geneva in February
1961. At this session, the Ministers were concerned with several
questions. The proposal for speeding up the tariff cuts in the
Free Trade Association, which had been discussed without agreement in the autumn of 1960, was considered again and it was
decided to bring forward to July (1961) the tariff cuts originally
scheduled for the end of the year. Thus the gap between the speeds
at which the Six were creating their customs union and the Seven
their free trade area was closed, although not for long, for the Six
'accelerated' again at the end of 1961. A second important question
discussed at the February meeting was the association of Finland.
It will be recalled that at their Lisbon meeting in May 1960 the
EFTA Council, under considerable pressure from the Swedish
delegation, had agreed, in principle, that Finland should become
associated with the EFTA. However, during the autumn of 1960,
as the form the association might take was examined in detail,
there was less and less enthusiasm on the part of some of the EFTA
countries, particularly the non-Scandinavian countries, for proceeding with the arrangement. It was clear that the Soviet Union
would only approve of Finnish association with the EFTA on
terms which would, in effect, give Russian goods rather better
access to the Finnish market than they were then receiving and it
was feared that the arrangements with the Russians might mean
that Finland would become a backdoor entrance to the EFTA for
Russian goods. Moreover, Switzerland and Austria—Austria in
particular—feared that if Finland were to make special arrangements with the Russians there would be Soviet pressure on them, as

neutral countries, to make similar arrangements. There was also some feeling on the part of the United Kingdom, although rather less than one might suppose, that an arrangement between the EFTA and Finland would complicate the problem of finding the right relationship between the Six and the Seven. These aspects of the question were examined by officials and the EFTA secretariat during the autumn and winter. At the February meeting the Ministers agreed that enough ways had been found to guard against the most serious difficulties so that the negotiations with Finland could be concluded.[40]

Mr. Heath then reported to the EFTA Council on the progress made in the technical talks with the Germans and Italians, and the general question of relations with the Six was discussed. At this time the EFTA countries were of several minds about the problems of relations with the Six. At one extreme the Austrians and the Danes were pressing hard for a resumption of efforts at 'bridge-building' between the EFTA (as a group) and the EEC. At the other extreme, the Swedes and the Swiss wanted to leave it to the Six to come up with some new proposals and to concentrate, for the time being, on the building up of the EFTA. They were not optimistic about the prospects for 'bridge-building' and they were sceptical of the usefulness of the exploratory talks the British had been holding. The kind of eventual arrangement that the EFTA countries generally still felt to be not only the most probable but also the most desirable was an agreement between the EFTA, as a group, and the EEC, as a group. Although, as discussed above, doubts were growing within the British Government about the feasibility (and desirability) of this kind of 'bridge-building', it is worth noting that at the press conference at the end of the February Council meeting, Mr. Maudling, then President of the Board of Trade, said in reply to a question 'There were differences of approach in the way the Six and the Seven respectively looked at integration. One should think of the two groups concluding an agreement rather than merging.'[41] Although

---

[40] The agreement on association with Finland was signed at Helsinki on 27 March 1961.

[41] See EFTA *Bulletin*, March 1961, p. 9. The editorial at the beginning of that *Bulletin* is also worth reading because it makes it abundantly clear that the author (presumably the Secretary-General) felt the kind of arrangements evolved in the EFTA would be the prototype for future arrangements between the Community and other European countries, including the United Kingdom. 'The relations between all the other countries of Europe outside the Six,

this may well have been Mr. Maudling's view, it is unlikely that the Prime Minister and others in the 'European' Group within the Cabinet would, at this time, have put it as their preferred arrangement.

During the spring, as signs of a change in the British attitude multiplied and as it became clear that the Government was seriously considering membership in the Community, the other EFTA countries, understandably enough, became increasingly uneasy. There was no particular secrecy about the kind of arrangements the British felt should be made for the other EFTA countries if the United Kingdom eventually decided to join the Six. It was assumed that Denmark and probably Norway would also seek to join the Community, that an arrangement similar to the one under discussion between the Six and Greece might be made between the enlarged Community and Portugal, and that some kind of non-political customs union, or, more probably, a free trade area with a largely harmonized tariff, could be arranged between the enlarged Community and the three neutrals.[42] This kind of arrangement would have been acceptable enough to the Danes, who throughout the spring made no secret of the fact that they desperately wanted the United Kingdom to apply to join the Community and that they would, themselves, immediately follow suit. Some of the other EFTA countries and, in particular, the neutrals, were much more dubious, both about the desirability and about the negotiability of arrangements of this kind. They found the earlier EFTA plan of an agreement between the EFTA as a group and the EEC as a group much more attractive since it would yield the economic advantages of a large common market while enabling them to work within the loose institutional framework of the EFTA which was congenial to them. This solution also raised no problems of conflict with their neutrality. Moreover, it was as clear to the neutrals as it was to the British that a country associated with the Community on any basis to which the Six were apt to agree, although it might have the illusion of freedom of action, would, in

---

and between those other countries and the European Economic Community itself must be different from those between the Members of that Community. Indeed, if they were not, the creation of an all-European market might weaken the coherence and integrity of the Community.' (*Bulletin*, p. 3.)

[42] The second approach outlined in my pamphlet *Four Approaches to the European Problem* (O.P. 12) (Political and Economic Planning, March 1961) was very similar to the kind of scheme that was being fairly openly discussed in Whitehall at this time.

fact, find that it had either to follow the Community line in setting its own tariffs and in formulating its own commercial policy, or it would lose the benefits of free trade with the Community. Although there was considerable agreement with the British diagnosis that the only kind of approach to the Six that stood a chance of being negotiable at that time was the one the British were now considering, the Swiss, and others, were very doubtful whether a negotiation—in any terms—would suceed. And a number of countries felt that it would be better to hold off opening negotiations for a year or two in the hope that the arrangement preferred by many EFTA countries would, then, prove to be negotiable.

During the spring of 1961 high officials of the EFTA countries held a number of meetings at which tactics and objectives *vis-à-vis* the Six were exhaustively discussed. The British must have found themselves in a rather awkward position in these discussions, for some of the arguments that had led them to think in terms of joining the Community, rather than seeking an association with it, were the very reasons why the neutrals found an association arrangement for themselves less attractive than an arrangement between the EFTA and the EEC. At this time there was little concern about the willingness of the Six to agree to association arrangements. Later, as it became apparent that certain groups within the Six and also the United States were decidedly cool to an association between the neutrals and the Community, the anxieties of the neutrals became much more acute.

The EFTA convention, unlike the Treaty of Rome, contains a one-year abrogation clause and, from time to time during the spring, there were rumours that the United Kingdom might make a separate deal with the Six and then simply pull out of EFTA. British ministers and officials repeatedly made it clear that they had no such intention, but there was considerable uneasiness in some of the EFTA countries which continued until the Ministerial Council of the EFTA met in London from 27 to 29 June 1961. The June meeting was an important one. The British, in effect, sought the approval of their EFTA partners for their decision to open negotiations with the Community. As in the case of their discussions with the Commonwealth countries, the British were careful to avoid putting the EFTA countries in a position of having to agree to or to veto a British decision. However, the British Government was under a very strong moral obligation to consult the other EFTA countries before it reached its own decision and then to act in a way which was consistent with the agreed objective of the EFTA, that is, the achievement of a single European market. Apparently most, although not all, of the other EFTA Ministers had by this time come to feel that a British decision to open negotiations was right, both tactically and substantively; those who still had doubts either about the timing or about the action itself were not prepared to press their doubts to the point of seeking to dissuade the United Kingdom from opening negotiations. However, a number of the EFTA countries had considerable fear that they might find themselves left in the lurch, not as a result of a deliberate decision by the United Kingdom but rather as a result of an inevitable British preoccupation, once negotiations had begun, with finding solutions to their own domestic problems and to those of the Commonwealth countries. Various procedural questions were thoroughly discussed, such as the timing and method to be followed in applying for membership or association, the arrangements that the EFTA countries would make to co-ordinate their action among themselves during the negotiations, and whether negotiations should be carried on jointly or separately. Those countries that were still sceptical about the outcome of the negotiations wanted reassurance that there would be no running-down of the EFTA during the negotiations. Most important of all, the British were pressed to make it clear that there would be no abandonment of the EFTA until satisfactory arrangements for all the member countries had been worked out. The precise wording of the key paragraphs in the communiqué, which became known as the 'London Agreement', are worth quoting in full, for the shades of meaning attached to these commitments later assumed considerable importance:

Ministers considered whether their common objective—a single European market embracing all the Members of EFTA—could be achieved by way of negotiation for membership of, or association with the European Economic Community. They concluded that it was premature to judge whether this was possible or was likely to be successful; they decided to re-examine the question at their next meeting.

Ministers agreed that if such a course should then appear possible, the Members of EFTA should coordinate their actions and remain united throughout the negotiations. Ministers resolved that the European Free Trade Association, the obligations created by the Convention between the Members, and the momentum towards integration within the Association, would be maintained at least until satisfactory arrangements have been worked out in negotiations to meet the various legitimate interests of all Members of EFTA, and thus enable them all to participate from the same date in an integrated European market. They agreed that a partial solution which created new economic division within Western Europe could not in any circumstances be regarded as satisfactory.[43]

These undertakings, not surprisingly, reassured the other EFTA countries that their own bargaining power would not be compromised by Britain's decision to negotiate with the Six and that the added strength each had hoped to achieve by forming EFTA was not being jettisoned by one partner. A few voices (but surprisingly few) were raised in the United Kingdom to question the wisdom of having gone quite so far, and in quite so much detail, in strengthening the commitment to the EFTA. No one in the United Kingdom questioned the fact that the British Government had a strong moral obligation, given the history of the EFTA, to do whatever lay within its power to see that the other EFTA countries succeeded in their own negotiations, but the London Agreement went very near to stating that the United Kingdom would not join the Six unless and until the Six agreed on a single market of the Thirteen.

The wording in the first paragraph quoted above reflected the fact that the decision of the British Cabinet could not be finally taken until after the 'emissaries' had made their rounds of the Commonwealth countries and the results of their discussions had been considered by the Cabinet. However, little remained for the next EFTA meeting—which was held in Geneva at the end of July—but to hear from Mr. Heath the terms in which the Prime Minister would make his statement in the House of Commons and to agree on the statement that was issued by the EFTA Ministerial Council immediately the announcement had been made.[44]

The decision to open negotiations

Mr. Macmillan's announcement of the Government's decision to open negotiations with the Six Governments was finally made

---

[43] EFTA, *Bulletin*, July 1961, p. 8.
[44] The July declaration of the EFTA countries reaffirmed the London Agreement and stated that 'All Member States of EFTA declare their intention to examine, with the European Economic Community, the ways and means by which all Members of EFTA could take part together in a single market embracing some 300 million people.' See EFTA, *Bulletin*, August–September 1961, p. 7.

to the House of Commons on Monday 31 July and, later in the week, long debates on the decision were held in the House of Commons and in the House of Lords. Mr. Macmillan's announcement was fairly brief and, considering the historic importance of the occasion, it was delivered in a surprisingly uninspired way. This seems to have been a product of fatigue rather than of lack of conviction; nevertheless it detracted somewhat from the occasion. The main exposition of the Government's case and a considerably more enthusiastic presentation was given by Mr. Macmillan in opening the main debate in the House of Commons two days later. Several points made by the Prime Minister in his first brief statement on 31 July should be noted. First, Mr. Macmillan made it clear that he looked upon the problem of relations between the United Kingdom and the EEC and the closely-related question of the effect a closer relationship with the Community might have on relations with the Commonwealth in essentially political terms:

... In this modern world the tendency towards larger groups of nations acting together in the common interest leads to greater unity and thus adds to our strength in the struggle for freedom. I believe that it is both our duty and our interest to contribute towards that strength by securing the closest possible unity within Europe. At the same time, if a closer relationship between the United Kingdom and the countries of the European Economic Community were to disrupt the long-standing and historic ties between the United Kingdom and the other nations of the Commonwealth the loss would be greater than the gain.[45]

Second, he clearly rejected the idea which had been current in some quarters, and was at times urged on the British from influential sources in the Six, that the United Kingdom should, in effect, join the Community and then, from inside, settle the problems arising from its commitments to the EFTA, to the Commonwealth, and to British agriculture. Third, he made it clear that the exploratory talks that had been going on had carried the matter as far as they could and that no clear picture of the conditions on which the United Kingdom could join would emerge unless a formal application for membership under Article 237 of the Treaty of Rome were made. He emphasized that, although he was now asking the House to approve the decision to open negotiations, the decision to join or not to join would not be made until after the negotiations had been concluded: 'No agreement will be entered

[45] *Hansard*, House of Commons, 31 July 1961, cols. 928–31.

into until it has been approved by the House after full consultation with other Commonwealth countries by whatever procedure
they may generally agree.' Although Mr. Gaitskell deferred most
of his main points until the full-dress debate later in the week, he
pressed the Prime Minister to give the Commonwealth as firm a
commitment as the London Agreement appeared to give the EFTA
countries, a point he pursued further during the debate. On both
occasions, Government spokesmen, although ready to state that
they would not join the Six unless satisfactory arrangements for
the Commonwealth had been made, were careful to keep in their
own hands the final judgement as to what was satisfactory and not
to give the Commonwealth countries a veto over the British decision.[46] In reply to a question from Mr. Turton, Mr. Macmillan
also made it quite clear why the Government had chosen to apply
under Article 237 (membership) rather than Article 238 (association): 'If we were to apply to be an associate member under Article
238 we should have all the same economic difficulties for the Commonwealth—not one single one of them would be made easier—
and we would have no influence in Europe.' In reply to other
questions, Mr. Macmillan expressed himself as 'hopeful' but not
'confident' of a favourable outcome of the negotiations but sure in
his own mind that it was now better to bring matters to a head
and to open negotiations than to postpone negotiations until the
omens, and in particular the attitude of the French Government,
were more clearly propitious.[47]

In opening the full-dress debate in the House of Commons on
2 August, Mr. Macmillan reiterated that 'the moment of decision'
had not yet come and repeated his promise that the results of the
negotiation would be brought back for the House to judge.[48]

---

[46] Mr. Maudling, in winding up the first day's debate, made and repeated the
following statement on the commitments to EFTA and the Commonwealth,
a statement which had clearly been drafted with some care: 'We have given
the same undertaking to our Commonwealth partners and to the other EFTA
countries, namely, that we will not join the Community unless special
arrangements have been worked out in negotiations to protect their essential
interests.' *Hansard*, House of Commons, 2 August 1961, cols. 1601 and 1602.
Mr. Maudling also made it clear that the situation of the EFTA countries was
rather different from that of the Commonwealth countries inasmuch as the
other EFTA countries would themselves be negotiating with the Six.

[47] *Hansard*, House of Commons, 31 July 1961, cols. 928–42.

[48] The Government's motion read as follows: 'That this House supports the
decision of Her Majesty's Government to make formal application under
Article 237 of the Treaty of Rome in order to initiate negotiations to see if
satisfactory arrangements can be made to meet the special interests of the

Nevertheless, despite the general recognition and acceptance of this formal position, the debate was a critical one, for everyone realized that once the Government's motion had been approved it would be extremely difficult for the House to oppose entry unless the arrangements negotiated were clearly unsatisfactory.

In his opening speech Mr. Macmillan made it clear again that the dominant considerations in his mind were political ones: that the United Kingdom would be affected by whatever happened on the Continent, that there was no security in isolation, and that it was better to 'play our role to the full and use the influence we have for the free development of the life and thought of Europe'; and that 'our right place is in the vanguard of the movement towards the greater unity of the free world, and that we can lead better from within than outside'.[49] He admitted that it would be dangerous for the United Kingdom to join in a 'little Europe' movement looking inwards on itself—'certainly, this island could never join an association which believed in such medieval dreams' —but he felt that the leading men and the Governments on the Continent did not have such a narrow view and that, in any case, it was the duty of the United Kingdom to add its weight to the majority of Europeans who 'see the true prospective [*sic*] of events'. When he turned to review the three big familiar problems —the Commonwealth, EFTA, and British agriculture—he added nothing new to what had previously been said on the EFTA but revealed a little more about Government thinking about the Commonwealth and the problem of domestic agriculture. On the first, Mr. Macmillan made it clear that the Ottawa agreements had been responsive to the different needs of a different age. Although he reiterated the Government's intention to try to meet the special interests of the Commonwealth, it was plain that he did not feel under any obligation to seek to preserve the Ottawa system as such. Similarly, when he turned to British agriculture, the Prime Minister was unequivocal in stating that the objective

---

United Kingdom, of the Commonwealth and of the European Free Trade Association; and further accepts the undertaking of Her Majesty's Government that no agreement affecting these special interests or involving British sovereignty will be entered into until it has been approved by this House after full consultation with other Commonwealth countries, by whatever procedure they may generally agree.' *Hansard*, House of Commons, 2 August 1961, col. 1480.

[49] *Hansard*, House of Commons, 2 August 1961. The Prime Minister's opening speech is in cols. 1480–94.

was a 'prosperous, stable and efficient agricultural industry, organised to provide a good life for those who live and work in the countryside', but he indicated that the 'method' for achieving this end might well have to be changed, and changed whether or not the United Kingdom joined the Gommon Market.

Mr. Macmillan's comments on the problem of sovereignty and on the related question of political unity in Europe should also be noted. He made it clear that the amount of sovereignty which would be delegated by accepting the Treaty of Rome did not seem to him to be very great. He recognized that there were forces in Europe working towards a federalist system, 'a sort of United States' of Europe, and he did not hide the fact that he felt they were on the wrong track. On the contrary, he went out of his way to agree with General de Gaulle that the only practical concept, and 'one with which we could associate willingly and wholeheartedly', would be a 'confederation, a commonwealth if hon. Members would like to call it that—what I think General de Gaulle has called *Europe des patries*—which would retain the great traditions and the pride of individual nations while working together in clearly defined spheres for their common interest'.

Mr. Gaitskell, the leader of the Labour Party, opened for the Opposition and moved an amendment to the Government's motion, but in doing so made it clear that even if the amendment were defeated the Labour Party would not oppose the substantive part of the Government's motion, that is, the decision to open negotiations to see what, in fact, the terms of accession might be.[50] Although, as leader of the Opposition, Mr. Gaitskell inevitably found it necessary to criticize the Government's handling of past negotiations with the European countries and to point out that it would have been very much easier to negotiate entry if the attempt had been made earlier, the Labour Party was in no position to

---

[50] The Opposition's amendment read as follows: 'To strike everything after House and substitute "notes the decision of Her Majesty's Government to make formal application under Article 237 of the Treaty of Rome in order to initiate negotiations to see if satisfactory arrangements can be made to meet the special interests of the United Kingdom, of the Commonwealth and of the European Free Trade Association; regrets that Her Majesty's Government will be conducting these negotiations from a position of grave weakness; and declares that Great Britain should enter the European Economic Community only if this House gives its approval and if the conditions negotiated are generally acceptable to a Commonwealth Prime Ministers' Conference and accord with our obligations and pledges to other members of the European Free Trade Association.' *Hansard*, House of Commons, 2 August 1961, col. 1494.

make much of either of these points, since it had agreed, broadly, with the kinds of arrangement the Government had previously sought to negotiate, and had, as a party, shown even less enthusiasm than had the Conservative Party for joining the Six. Very few major differences were detectable between Mr. Gaitskell and Mr. Macmillan. Mr. Gaitskell was more emphatic than the Prime Minister that 'there is no question whatever of Britain entering into a federal Europe now. British opinion simply is not ripe for this, and in any event it is surely completely incompatible with all the pledges and promises which have been made about the Commonwealth. I am not saying that we have to commit ourselves for all time, for twenty, fifty or a hundred years hence.' And, unlike the Prime Minister, he went out of his way to comment that he thought if the Assembly of the European Community were to be directly elected (as had already been proposed by the European Parliamentary Assembly and advocated by many 'Europeans'), this would be a very long step towards a federal Europe. He also made clear his own dislike for the independent character of the European Commission, a point to which he was to return in the future. He was apparently not opposed, in principle, to qualified majority voting, although he thought the allocation of votes was clearly a point of great importance. Like Mr. Macmillan, he tended to feel that the British farmer had little to fear. And, as he had done earlier in the week, he pressed Mr. Macmillan to give a more precise commitment to the Commonwealth, something more akin to the pledge given to the EFTA countries, with which he expressed his full agreement. Mr. Gaitskell conceded that the Government should not give a 'right of absolute veto on any [sic] detail to any member of the Commonwealth' but felt that—as proposed in the Labour amendment—a commitment should be made that the conditions of entry should be 'generally acceptable' to a conference of Commonwealth Prime Ministers.

The debate was too long (thirteen hours) to be summarized in detail here but a few generalizations can be made and a few specific points should be noted. Sir Derek Walker-Smith undoubtedly made the most eloquent and the most elegant speech against the Government's decision. As a former Conservative minister and the leading Conservative back-bencher opposing entry, he was probably the critic that the Government feared the most. Essentially his case was that one should not blink at the long-term implications of what the Six were doing and that what was right for the Six was not necessarily right for the United Kingdom: 'The Six share their constitutional outlook and practices with each other, but not with us. Their evolution has been continental and collective. Ours has been insular and imperial. Therefore, for them political union would be a reunion and a rediscovery, while for us it would be a departure and a divergence.' With considerable effect Sir Derek Walker-Smith warned the Government against a 'sophisti-cated exercise in seeking to ease us into political union in the wake of economic union' and made the very real point that if the Government were not prepared to go the full way with the Six, whatever that might be, and had at some stage to say that they would have to withdraw, 'the last state of our relations with Europe would be worse than the first'. Like other speakers in the debate who were critical of the Government's decision, he was better at pointing out the difficulties than in suggesting alternative courses of action. Like a number of others, he hoped that an association arrangement under Article 238 might yet be possible and, like others, although with more circumspection and clearly with more awareness of the difficulties, he urged a closer economic and poli-tical association with the Commonwealth.

As Mr. Macmillan had done earlier, Mr. Heath in the course of the debate made it clear enough that the Government had con-sidered but had ruled out an association under Article 238 on two grounds: first, it raised suspicions in the Six that the United Kingdom wanted to get the advantages of the Common Market without undertaking the obligations of the other members of the Community and was, in consequence, unlikely to be negotiable; and second, that since the Six would insist that any association arrangement with the United Kingdom would have to take the form of a customs union, the United Kingdom would be in a better position as a member than as an associate.[51]

Mr. Heath also tried to deal with the concern expressed by Sir Derek Walker-Smith and many others about the implications for British sovereignty. He divided the question into three parts: the effect of accepting the actual provisions of the Treaty of Rome;

[51] 'As it would be a Customs union, there would be a common tariff. But as an associate member, we should not have representation in the organs which decided that common tariff. Therefore, we should be giving up our sovereignty for a common tariff but we should not have a say in how it was fixed. To that extent, our position *vis-à-vis* sovereignty would be worse than if we were a member fixing these things and had our full share as to how they were ar-ranged.' *Hansard*, House of Commons, 3 August 1961, col. 1684.

the effect of participating in the political consultations already occurring among the Six; and the position with respect to the discussions then occurring within the Six looking towards further action in the political field.[52] The first he characterized as a pooling, rather than a sacrifice, of sovereignty for a specific purpose and argued that it was no different in kind from the pooling of sovereignty already occurring in numerous other contexts, in the NATO, the GATT, the ILO;[53] on the second, he pointed out that this was occurring on a purely 'consultational' level. On the third point he relied on the fact that in the Treaty of Rome 'there is no commitment either explicit or implicit leading to any particular form of constitutional development above the Rome Treaty itself', and on the fact that any new commitment to a particular form of unity would have to be agreed unanimously.

The debate was well attended and, in the main, on a very high level. Although the formal question before the House was whether or not negotiations should be opened to see whether joining was feasible, almost every speaker rightly addressed himself to the substantive question of whether joining was the right course of action and, if so, the conditions that should be obtained. The Commonwealth aspect of the question, both economic and political, loomed the largest, with the implications for sovereignty coming a close second, and the implications for British farmers coming a very poor third. There was general recognition that for the most part British farmers were as efficient as, or more efficient than, continental farmers, that continental farmers were more important numerically (and therefore more powerful politically) than British farmers and could be counted on to press for the protection of agricultural interests, and that existing British agricultural support schemes were almost sure to be changed in the

---

[52] Various speakers in the debate referred to the Bonn communiqué which had been issued by the Heads of State or Government of the EEC countries on 18 July 1961. In this communiqué the Six stated that they had decided 'To give shape to the will for political union already implicit in the Treaties establishing the European Communities, and for this purpose to organise their cooperation, to provide for its development and to secure for it the regularity which will progressively create the conditions for a common policy and will ultimately make it possible to embody in institutions the work undertaken'. The Six also asked the Fouchet Committee, which had been discussing this problem, to submit proposals to 'enable a statutory character to be given to the union of their peoples'. The full text of the communiqué is in Appendix B, p. 523.

[53] But compare Lord Home, below, pp. 365–6.

relatively near future whether or not Britain joined the Common Market.

The sovereignty issue has been commented on above but it should be noted that many speakers from both sides of the House, and many who favoured joining as well as those who opposed joining, went out of their way to oppose a federal form of unity in Europe and to endorse, instead, the general approach of General de Gaulle. A Liberal speaker, Mr. Holt, was the sole advocate of 'federalism', although Mr. Heath was noticeably silent on the subject. The strange alliance between the extreme right of the Conservative Party and the extreme left of the Labour Party, both of which strongly opposed the Government's decision, was commented on by many speakers.[54] But although the two extremes found a measure of common ground in advocating the strengthening of Commonwealth ties as an alternative to joining the Common Market, neither extreme produced any very good idea of how this was to be done. This was not surprising for, as more than one advocate of joining the Six pointed out, the alternative of a Commonwealth free trade area or customs union was an illusion, since the Commonwealth countries themselves were not interested in any such arrangement. Moreover, it was noticeable that 'the Commonwealth' which the Conservative back-benchers were interested in strengthening was the 'old, white' Commonwealth, while the left wing of the Labour Party was far more concerned to maintain and strengthen British influence with the 'new, black' Commonwealth.

Although the opposition on the Conservative back-benches was less widespread, and less uncompromising, than had been feared and the Government's motion was carried easily, the debate produced relatively few strong 'pro-European' speeches.[55] In general the prevailing feeling seemed to be that joining the Common Market was probably right in view of the lack of other good alternatives and that the Government having missed the bus before

[54] As noted above, in Chapter III, a similar alliance in the French Assembly had opposed the Treaty of Rome.
[55] Among the most 'European' were those of Mr. Roy Jenkins (Labour), Mr. Peter Smithers (Conservative), Mr. Pannell (Labour). Mr. Heath's speech was notable for its full understanding of and considerable sympathy with the 'European' standpoint; Mr. Maudling's for his inability to hide his own personal preference for other kinds of arrangement. It is worth noting that Mr. Jenkins resigned from the Front Bench of the Labour Party to have greater freedom to speak on European questions and that Mr. Smithers was made a junior minister in the Foreign Office in 1962.

had better not do so a second time. Moreover, although many Members undoubtedly privately agreed with Michael Foot that 'the real decision as to whether this country is to go into the Common Market will be made tonight',[56] the House was determined to keep the position as open as possible and to preserve for itself every right to judge, on their merits and without any previous implicit approval, whatever arrangements emerged from the negotiations.

One of the best speeches made on the subject was given not in the House of Commons but in the House of Lords, by Lord Chandos (Oliver Lyttelton). He went out of his way to brush aside the reassuring statements that had been made by Government spokesmen and by other advocates of joining the Common Market and painted as stark a picture as he could, not only of the short-run economic difficulties that joining the Common Market might entail but also of the far-reaching inroads on sovereignty that he thought might result in the long run. Nevertheless, having done his best to counteract the 'tranquillizers' which, in his view, Lord Gladwyn and others had been administering, he concluded:

... in my belief, the Common Market will either disintegrate, or it will lead to wide, though I hope not total, political integration. I find it difficult to imagine what Europe and the world will look like when this has been achieved. We may be taking a step here of far greater importance in the national life than any single measure of which I can readily think, even the repeal of the Corn Laws. Perhaps men of my age will console themselves by saying: 'We shall not live through some of the changes which await us; while there's death, there's hope.' Agonising reappraisals, my Lords, are going to be as common as popcorn, but I remain convinced that, whatever the agony, they must be faced, and that in the issue we shall be stronger, richer and happier by joining the Common Market.[57]

The Foreign Secretary, Lord Home, although not quite as outspoken as Lord Chandos, was very forthright in his approach to the sovereignty question:

We should not make sovereignty into a shibboleth. It is harmful to surrender it if the results damage the nation, but it is not harmful if, on balance, the results are beneficial to it. ... Let me admit at once that the Treaty of Rome would involve considerable derogation of sovereignty. Let me say also that the field in which there could be

[56] *Hansard*, House of Commons, 3 August 1961, col. 1751.
[57] *Hansard*, House of Lords, 3 August 1961, cols. 253–4.

surrender of sovereignty is clearly defined and restricted to economic matters. . . . I think I must say to Lord Strang that he is right in saying that, within this restricted field, derogations of sovereignty will be different in kind from any contract into which we have entered before. It is well that people should realise that, although I cannot forecast whether these derogations would be substantial or whether in any particular case the derogation of sovereignty would act against us or for us.[58]

In general the speakers in the House of Lords were more concerned with the long-term implications of joining the Common Market than with the conditions of membership and, perhaps for that reason, the essential arguments for joining came out rather more clearly than they did in the House of Commons debate. In particular both the negative point, that if the United Kingdom were to stand aside it would inevitably lose power relative to the Six, and the positive point, that by joining the Six the way would be opened to a genuine Atlantic partnership based on a relationship of approximately equal power between the United States and Europe, were effectively made by Lord Home and by a number of other speakers. The Lord Chancellor (Lord Kilmuir), in concluding the debate, was particularly forthright:

At a time when the Soviet Union would dearly like to foment divisions in the Western Alliance I believe that the Bonn declaration is a source of great comfort and strength to the free nations. The unity of the EEC Powers in the political as well as the economic sphere is a vital element in the Atlantic Alliance. If we and some of our EFTA partners can extend the area of that unity without weakening its cohesion or diluting it in any way, then we shall be making a major contribution to the strength of NATO and to the partnership between Western Europe and North America. This is the guarantee of our liberties. It is, my Lords, also the hope of the world.[59]

[58] *Hansard*, House of Lords, 2 August 1961, cols. 119–20.
[59] Ibid., 3 August 1961, col. 306.

XI

THE FIRST STAGE OF
THE NEGOTIATIONS ON BRITISH
ACCESSION

(September 1961–August 1962)

The opening moves

It is hard to imagine a more difficult negotiating situation than the one that confronted the British Government in the autumn of 1961. Numerous and often conflicting interests had to be satisfied and the Government had to negotiate simultaneously on many fronts—with the Commonwealth countries, with the EFTA, and at times with the United States and other third countries, as well as with the Six. It had to try to reassure both those in the United Kingdom and the Commonwealth who felt that the Government was going too far and too fast and those in the United Kingdom and the Six who felt that it was being a too reluctant suitor. It had to convince the Six that the British were no longer seeking a special position which would enable them to be in Europe for some purposes and out of Europe for other purposes, and to make it plain that the United Kingdom was now ready to become a full partner in the search for European unity; and it had at the same time to reassure the Commonwealth countries that it had no intention of sacrificing them in order to join the Six, and to re-assure the EFTA countries that it remained loyal to the London Agreement. Moreover, as well as negotiating on several fronts it had to negotiate against the background of uncertain domestic support and at a time when opinion within the Government itself, as well as within the country at large, was still evolving. Mr. Heath was not only negotiating with an institution (the European Community) that was itself constantly developing—a kind of moving belt, as he once described it to the House of Commons—but he

was standing on a moving staircase while doing so. As indicated in
the previous chapters, Mr. Macmillan, a few other ministers, and a
few top civil servants had been a year or so ahead of the Government as a whole in coming to the conclusion that it might be in
the British interest to join the Community. When the negotiations
began, the Government was well ahead of the country, and it was
in the very difficult position of having to act on the assumption
that by the time it had completed its negotiations public opinion
would have developed to the point where the country would be
prepared to accept the kind of arrangements that were apt to be
negotiable. It must have been quite plain to Mr. Macmillan, Mr.
Heath, and others that the kind of agreement that would be
negotiable, even on reasonably optimistic terms, would not, in the
summer of 1961, have seemed good enough to the House of
Commons. The Government, and the Prime Minister in particular,
took an enormous, but necessary, gamble on the development of
British opinion.

In this complicated situation it is understandable that Government spokesmen emphasized different things to different people,
but the resulting ambiguities in the Government's position made
a difficult negotiation even more difficult. Some of the ambiguities
were probably unavoidable, others could have been avoided by
plain speaking which, even though politically difficult, might well
have been politically wise. One ambiguity arose from the fact that
for domestic political reasons and for the sake of harmonious
relations with the Commonwealth (these were, of course, two sides
of the same coin) Government spokesmen felt they had to say
repeatedly that there was no question of a choice between Europe
and the Commonwealth. These statements fed doubts on the
Continent about British intentions, for the Continentals felt that it
was precisely that choice that the United Kingdom must make.
For many years, in explaining why the United Kingdom could not
join the Common Market and why the free trade area was the only
arrangement they could contemplate, Government spokesmen had
repeatedly said that joining the Common Market would mean
'choosing' Europe in preference to the Commonwealth and that,
although they hoped this choice would never arise, if it did they
would always and unhesitatingly choose the Commonwealth.
Once the decision to negotiate with the Six had been taken, the
formula changed. Now British ministers said, and said repeatedly,
that there was no question of a 'choice', because joining Europe

was in no way incompatible with membership of the Commonwealth; on the contrary, they said, a strong Commonwealth had an interest in a strong Europe and vice versa, and the United Kingdom's joining Europe would strengthen both groups. This may be true, but it is only true if a rather special meaning is given to the phrase 'strengthening the Commonwealth'. Prosperity in Europe and a faster rate of growth in the United Kingdom would benefit the Commonwealth countries but 'the Commonwealth' was bound to be a different and more diffuse 'institution' as a result of Britain's joining the Six.

A somewhat similar difficulty arose with respect to the other EFTA countries. Here, as in the case of the Commonwealth countries, there were not only very real negotiating problems but psychological and emotional problems as well. The way particular points about the EFTA arrangement were presented to the Six jarred on the ears of the other EFTA countries, and perhaps even more harshly the other way round. The Six regarded the British decision to negotiate as evidence that they (the Six) had been right and that the free trade area was an inadequate concept. They did not see the British decision as opening the way to a single European market embracing both the Six and the Seven, but as an essentially political decision on the part of the British. The Seven, on the other hand, had had to be persuaded that the result of the British decision would be progress towards the objective that the EFTA had set out to achieve, that is, the creation of a single European market. Again, as in the case of the Commonwealth, the conflicting positions could just be reconciled, but many statements about the EFTA, as well as about the Commonwealth, were not formulated with enough precision. Moreover, in both cases, the reconciliation of conflicting viewpoints could only be achieved at such a sophisticated level that it was difficult to avoid being either disingenuous or misleading.

Another ambiguity arose over the question of the 'terms'. Mr. Macmillan was obviously sincere when he told the House of Commons in July 1961 that no final decision would be taken until after the terms were known, for there were still unresolved differences of view within the Cabinet about the kind of arrangements that would be acceptable and the agreement to open negotiations could only be reached by reserving the final judgement until later. Nevertheless it was clear enough that once embarked on negotiations it would be extremely difficult for the Government to admit defeat and to withdraw. Moreover it was also true that, irrespective of the 'terms', a fundamental choice had to be made between two ways of working out the future of the country: the Government and people had to decide whether they *wanted* to become part of the new complex that was developing on the Continent, with the prospects that held of economic strength and political power, but at the price of some loss of freedom of action and some changes in political and economic relationships, or whether they preferred to stand aside, seeking to maintain existing relationships and freedom of action, but almost inevitably seeing their economic and political power decline relative to that of the Six. It would be politically easier to join the Six if the terms of accession were good and, given the commitments the Government had made and the strong emotional pull of the Commonwealth, it might become politically impossible to join the Community if the terms were very poor. Thus, given the state of British public opinion, the 'terms' were, in fact, considerably more important than many 'Europeans' recognized. Nevertheless the 'Europeans' were right: regardless of the terms, there was still a prior choice that had to be made, intellectually and emotionally. And the fact that the answer to this prior question seemed to be in doubt—not, as was commonly said, particularly by the Opposition, because the Government had no alternative—was probably the major weakness in the Government's negotiating position.

It was clear that Mr. Macmillan, and the ministers and officials most directly concerned with the decision to open negotiations, had made a choice and were prepared to accept the implications of their choice, but the Prime Minister clearly did not feel sure enough of support from his own party, or from the country at large, to make the full implications of joining the Community plain until the autumn of 1962. Had the Government felt sure enough of support to take a more positive approach from the start, the advantages gained for Mr. Heath in Brussels might have been considerable, for it would then have been much more difficult for the French to have exploited—as they did with great effectiveness— the doubts that still existed in the minds of the Six about the depth of the new British commitment to Europe. Moreover British public opinion, although divided, was not for the most part deeply 'committed' one way or the other, and a stronger lead from the Government—particularly if the issue had throughout been treated as a non-partisan question—might well have produced a much more understanding public response than the Government feared.[1]

In addition to the difficulties arising from having to negotiate on many fronts and at a time when, for the most part, public opinion lagged behind the Government, there was the additional problem that British membership of the Communities was unlikely to be welcome to the French Government. Somewhat to their own surprise the French had emerged as the strong power within the Community. Owing to the skill of the French negotiators the Treaty of Rome had been nicely tailored to French specifications, for the French had exploited to the full the advantages of negotiating from weakness, an art the British seem not to have mastered. Moreover, the fact that the French negotiators had had a coherent concept of the new pattern of relationships they were seeking to establish meant that the structure of the Community, even where it was not deliberately shaped to meet French needs, reflected French ideas and methods. British accession would inevitably have affected the balance of the treaty and would have meant some dilution of French influence in the Community. These considerations would have affected the position of any French Government. But the fact that during the period of the negotiations General de Gaulle was the Government of France added a new, incalculable difficulty. On the one hand, he had made it plain that he had little use for 'supra-nationalism' and the 'Community method' of the 'Europeans' and, therefore, fears that British accession might slow down the move towards unity on the Community pattern—a consideration which would have counted with some French Governments—were not apt to weigh with the Fifth Republic. On the other hand, as General de Gaulle had made unmistakably clear in his memoirs, the mainspring of his whole life has been the determination to secure a position for France that would be consistent with its past tradition of greatness. And, as he had also made clear, for him that meant that France must be the dominant power in Western Europe.[2] France, particularly if General de Gaulle could consolidate the French position as the

---

[1] The Government was in part deterred from giving a strong lead to public opinion by the fear that any show of enthusiasm for joining the Community would simply cause the Six to harden the terms. Informed people among the Six have always disputed this view.

[2] Charles de Gaulle, *War Memoirs* (3 vols., Eng. trans., Weidenfeld and Nicolson). See, in particular, the opening paragraphs of Volume I, *The Call to Honour*, and the first pages of Chapter 5 of Volume III, *Salvation*.

political leader of the Six, would clearly be in a relatively stronger position if the United Kingdom were not a part of the European construction. The British therefore knew from the start that they could expect little help from the French Government. They were prepared for hard bargaining and perhaps some deliberate obstruction but, like M. Monnet, M. Spaak, and others in the Six who were encouraging them to join, they did not anticipate a unilateral French veto.

In the circumstances, it would have been hard to settle easy problems, but many of the problems that had to be solved were complicated and difficult. Moreover, some of the problems and, more important, the reasons for each other's attitudes were not fully understood by either side before the negotiations began, and this led, at times, to the taking of premature positions which were then difficult to abandon gracefully. For example, there was widespread misunderstanding among the Six about the nature and extent of the Commonwealth arrangements: 'free entry' and preference' were not infrequently confused, and there was little real understanding of the depth of feeling the Commonwealth connexion aroused in the United Kingdom. The Six seemed largely unaware of the fact that—for domestic political reasons—the British Government could not simply assert but had to demonstrate to their own people that certain kinds of arrangement for the Commonwealth were not negotiable. For their part, the British did not fully appreciate how difficult it was, simply procedurally, for the Six to be flexible, or the primacy the Six gave to finding and holding a common front, even when this meant a more negative attitude than the majority favoured. Rather strangely, in view of all that had gone before, the British also seem to have expected that the negotiations would take the form of seven governments trying to work out solutions in concert (much as the Six had done in drafting the Treaty of Rome), rather than that of one government negotiating with the Six as a group. Moreover, when they took the decision to open negotiations, the British had also assumed that there would be a readiness on the part of the Six to interpret, and to stretch, the Treaty of Rome, and to rewrite, if not the treaty itself, at least some of the regulations implementing the treaty. They had also assumed that they would participate with the Six in the drafting of the crucially important Community regulations on agriculture. And they had assumed that the Six would be far less concerned with the details of the transitional arrangements than proved to be the case. This difference of view between the United Kingdom and the Six about the purposes of the transition period and the way it should be used was at the root of some of the most difficult aspects of the negotiations. When they began negotiating the British assumed that once they had unequivocally accepted a common external tariff, a common commercial policy, a common agricultural policy, and the other important principles of the Treaty of Rome, the Six would be tolerant of the arrangements made during the transition period provided that at the end of it the British were in the same position as other member countries. The Six, however, soon made it clear that they regarded the transition period not as a period of grace, during which the British would have considerable latitude to make their own adjustments in their own way, but, very literally, as a period of transition during which all aspects of the eventual system should be progressively brought into force.

However, although the British Government may have begun the negotiations under certain illusions about the kinds of arrangement that could be negotiated, they knew the negotiations would be long and difficult. And, for the most part, they seem to have drawn the right conclusions from the tactical and presentational mistakes that they had made during the free trade area negotiations. The accession negotiations were given an overriding priority; they were not done with the left hand while thinking about something else. Other actions and policies were usually considered from the standpoint of the side effects they might have on the negotiations, although, in December 1962, there appears to have been a critical failure on Mr. Macmillan's part to appreciate the effect the agreement made at Nassau with President Kennedy might have on General de Gaulle's attitude towards the Brussels negotiations. In their approach to the accession negotiations the British also showed far more sensitivity to the 'European' viewpoint and far more appreciation of the weakness in their own bargaining position than they had shown in the free trade area negotiations. This time there were no White Papers outlining the terms in advance of negotiations. There was little frittering away of bargaining power on unimportant procedural arrangements and, in the opening stages at least, no pressures, no deadlines, and no warnings about the consequences of failure, although these signs of a fear of failure began to appear towards the end of the negotiation. Above all there was an attempt, and a reasonably successful attempt, to talk the same language as the 'Europeans'.[3]

Great care was taken to see that the right ministers were in the right positions in London. As indicated in the last chapter, in the summer of 1960 the Prime Minister had reshuffled his Cabinet and, as a result, a 'European', Mr. Sandys, was at the crucially important Commonwealth Relations Office and another, Mr. Soames, at the almost equally important Ministry of Agriculture. Mr. Thorneycroft had been brought back into the Government as Minister for Aviation in the summer of 1960, and, in the summer of 1961, he was moved to the much more important post of Minister of Defence and brought into the Cabinet. Lord Amory (Derick Heathcoat Amory) was named British High Commissioner in Canada, an appointment which seems to have been not un-related to the negotiations. One of the most astute of Mr. Mac-millan's moves was his decision to put Mr. Butler in charge of the ministerial committee that was back-stopping negotiations. Mr. Butler was known to be, at best, lukewarm about the decision to seek to join the Community; as the minister responsible for co-or-dinating Cabinet views on the negotiations his unquestioned talents would be engaged in trying to make the negotiations succeed rather than used in casting doubt from the sidelines. Finally, the decision to entrust the actual negotiations to Mr. Heath, who had done so much of the exploratory discussions with the Six, was one which was never regretted. The negotiating team was also carefully chosen, not only for its ability and technical competence, but for other qualities as well, such as experience in negotiating with the key country, France, knowledge of French and German, known sympathies with the 'Europeans', and past familiarity with problems of European unity and with the people who had been dealing with them.[4] And, in London, Sir Frank Lee continued to

---

[3] During the free trade area negotiations Mr. Maudling had caused a good deal of ill-will among the 'Europeans' by ignoring Prof. Hallstein and the rest of the Commission. Mr. Heath's relations with the Commission were very cordial. The Commission played a much more important role in the accession negotia-tions than it had in the free trade area negotiations.

[4] Sir Pierson Dixon, the British Ambassador in Paris, was made head of the delegation at official level; Sir Eric Roll, trilingual, a close friend of M. Marjolin, and a member of the British delegation to the OEEC in its happiest days, was the deputy head. Sir Roderick Barclay, who had conducted the pre-liminary bilateral discussions with the Germans, French, and Italians, was the Foreign Office representative on the delegation. The Commonwealth

serve as the linch-pin of the whole negotiating structure until his retirement from the Civil Service in the autumn of 1962.

During the summer of 1961 British officials were busy working out the details of the arrangements they would seek to negotiate. These proposals were further refined (and, rather ill-advisedly, toughened up) after discussions with the Commonwealth economic experts in London early in the autumn. Before these detailed discussions with the Commonwealth experts took place, the annual Commonwealth Finance Ministers' meeting (i.e. the usual meeting before the Bank and Fund meetings) had been held at Accra in Ghana. Rather to the surprise of the British, the Canadian Minister of Finance, Mr. Fleming, took the occasion to be outspokenly critical of the British decision to open negotiations.[5] Although this led to a certain amount of unexpected discussion of the Common Market question—and a good deal of acrimony—at Accra, the detailed work in preparation for the negotiation was done, more quietly, with the experts who met in London shortly thereafter.

During the two months between Mr. Macmillan's announcement and Mr. Heath's first meeting with the Six, there was also much discussion among the Six and, informally, between the Six and the United Kingdom, about how the negotiations should be carried on. For a time the possibility was discussed of putting a key figure in charge of the negotiations in a role similar to that played by M. Spaak during the drafting of the Rome Treaty. M. Spaak was known to be ready to take on the task, but the French were strongly opposed to his doing so, for a number of reasons, mostly, perhaps, because they knew M. Spaak would be eager to bring the negotiations to a successful conclusion and might push for more concessions than they, at least, would feel it desirable to make.

Relations Office representative was Sir Henry Lintott, who was also a close friend and former colleague of M. Marjolin, having been Deputy Secretary-General of OEEC while M. Marjolin was Secretary-General. The fifth knight, Sir William Gorell Barnes of the Colonial Office, was fluent in French and 'European' in his sympathies and had worked with M. Monnet during the war. The Board of Trade representative—Herbert Andrew—should also be mentioned, for his fair-minded toughness earned him much affectionate respect in the Commission.

[5] The opposition shown at Accra, particularly by the Canadians, was felt by the British to be unreasonable and, for a period, British–Canadian relations on the Common Market question were rather strained. Mr. Heath's visit to Ottawa in January 1962, as well as Lord Amory's activities in Canada, seem to have contributed to an improved relationship during the early months of 1962.

There was also considerable argument about the role of the Commission. The Treaty of Rome (Article 237) was clear that a European state wishing to become a member of the Community addressed its application to the Council and that the Council, after obtaining the opinion of the Commission, decided unanimously on the application. It was also clear that the conditions of admission and the adjustments to the treaty necessitated by the addition of a new member should be the 'subject of an agreement between the Member States and the applicant State'. But the treaty was silent about how the actual negotiations were to be carried on. Probably none of the Six would have been willing to entrust the task to the Commission, but none of the rest were prepared to go as far as the French, who at one time argued that members of the Commission should not even be present in the room during the negotiations. In the end it was agreed that the negotiations should be carried on by ministers of the Six Governments, acting as representatives of their Governments and not as the Council of Ministers of the Community, and that the Commission would be present as observers and could be called upon for technical work. In the event, the Commission, which enjoyed the confidence of the delegations and had better resources than the Governments to do much of the technical work, played a major part in the negotiations—in both the actual negotiations with the British and, more particularly, in the frequently even more difficult prior negotiations among the Six. Rather ironically, the French profited the most from not having had their way, for the Commission representatives were powerful supporters of the French in urging the rest of the Six to reject British proposals which, if adopted, might have stretched the Treaty of Rome or strained the cohesion of the Community. There was also disagreement about the site of the negotiations. The French wanted to meet in Paris rather than Brussels, partly because they always prefer Paris, partly, no doubt, because it was consistent with General de Gaulle's view that governments were what mattered and that the institutions of the Community should be cut down to size.

Throughout all these procedural arguments the British conducted themselves with exemplary patience and goodwill and, generally, were ready to accept any arrangements the Six could agree upon among themselves. The only point at which the British rightly drew the line was when the French suggested that, as a first move, the British Government should submit a detailed statement of the arrangements they would have to have; on the basis of this statement, the Six would then decide whether or not to open negotiations. Such a procedure would have put the British in an impossible negotiating position and the suggestion was withdrawn. Eventually, on 26 September, the Council of Ministers formally accepted the British request for negotiations and proposed that the United Kingdom make an introductory statement at a ministerial conference to be held in Paris on 10 October.[6]

Mr. Heath's statement on 10 October 1961 was designed for 'European' ears in contrast to Mr. Macmillan's statement in the House of Commons, which had been addressed primarily (although not exclusively) to his domestic audience. Mr. Heath's statement was a very long one and very skilfully drawn.[7] In it he managed, with remarkable success, to sound convinced of the need for European unity, of the wisdom of the course the Six were pursuing, and of the advantages that would accrue both to them and to the United Kingdom if Britain were to join the Community, yet, at the same time, he gave nothing away that had not already been implicitly given away by the British application or by Mr. Macmillan in his statement to the House of Commons. The Lord Privy Seal skated with great confidence on very thin ice and somehow made sense out of the doubtful proposition that it was possible to have a real negotiation on a matter of such far-reaching importance and yet formally still to be sufficiently uncommitted so that either side could withdraw if it became clear that mutually satisfactory arrangements could not be made. Somehow he managed to make it seem plausible to say, on the one hand, that the British had already made a major decision of principle but, on the other, that the decision must be conditional on the outcome of the negotiations.

Almost every word in Mr. Heath's statement was important and it should be read in its entirety. In the first part, he set the tone of the British approach; in the second, he outlined the scope of the negotiations. He made it unmistakably clear that the British approach to the Six was not a tactical gambit, or a half-hearted

---

[6] Before this, the Council of Ministers had formally requested an opinion from the Commission; the Commission had replied that it could not give its view until it knew what the conditions of membership would be, i.e., until the negotiations had been concluded.

[7] Mr. Heath's speech was issued as a White Paper, *The United Kingdom and the European Economic Community* (Cmnd. 1565, H.M.S.O., November 1961).

move, but was born of the conviction that 'our destiny is intimately linked with yours':

> The British Government and the British people have been through a searching debate during the last few years on the subject of their relations with Europe. The result of the debate has been our present application. It was a decision arrived at, not on any narrow or short-term grounds, but as a result of a thorough assessment over a considerable period of the needs of our own country, of Europe and of the Free World as a whole. We recognise it as a great decision, a turning point in our history, and we take it in all seriousness. In saying that we wish to join the E.E.C., we mean that we desire to become full, wholehearted and active members of the European Community in its widest sense and to go forward with you in the building of a new Europe.[8]

Although in the first part of his speech Mr. Heath was clearly seeking to dispel doubt and to underline that the British Government had taken a far-reaching decision, he nevertheless made it clear that an important element in that decision had been their conviction that they could join the Community without damaging the 'essential interests' of the Commonwealth countries: 'Some people in the United Kingdom have been inclined to wonder whether membership of the Community could in fact be reconciled with membership of the Commonwealth. The task of reconciliation is complex, but we are confident that solutions can be found to Commonwealth problems fully compatible with the substance and the spirit of the Treaty of Rome.'[9] Thus, although in this first atmosphere-creating section of the speech nothing was said about conditions, or about circumstances in which the British might not feel able to join, it was nevertheless made quite clear that the United Kingdom was operating on the assumption that the Six shared the British view that the Commonwealth made an essential contribution to the strength and stability of the world and that adequate solutions for the problems of the Commonwealth countries could be found.

When he turned to the specific points on which there would have to be negotiations, Mr. Heath first made it clear that the British Government accepted, without qualification, the objectives laid down in Articles 2 and 3 of the Treaty of Rome, including the elimination of internal tariffs, the adoption of a common customs tariff and a common commercial policy, and the adoption of a common agricultural policy, and that the British Government was

---

[8] White Paper, para. 3.   [9] Ibid., para. 7.

ready to accept and to play a full part in the institutions of the Community. He indicated that the British Government thought no formal amendments to the text of the treaty would be necessary, simply certain adaptations consequent on the admission of a new member.[10]

Before the negotiations opened there had been considerable fear in Community circles that the British application would slow down the pace of European unification. This was both a generalized worry based on the feeling that the British were not yet really 'European-minded' and would be a brake on the further evolution of the Community and on the move towards unity in the political field, and a more specific fear that progress in implementing the Treaty of Rome would be held up until after the lengthy negotiations with the British had been completed, and perhaps even beyond that, during a transition period while the British were adjusting themselves to the Community. Mr. Heath sought to reassure the Six on both counts: he went out of his way to endorse the Bonn declaration of the Six and to stress the British desire to 'contribute to the unifying process of this great European Community'.[11] He also referred to the willingness of the British to cut their own tariffs immediately on joining the Community, by whatever amount the Six had already achieved, and to accept the structure of the common external tariff.[12]

Mr. Heath then turned to the three major problems: Commonwealth trade, British agriculture, and the EFTA arrangements. He prefaced his specific comments on these three problems with the general assurance that the United Kingdom was not seeking a privileged position—a charge that had been made repeatedly and

[10] For a time there had been some confusion arising from the fact that the unofficial English version of the treaty had translated the French word 'adaptations' as 'amendments'. Mr. Heath was, *inter alia*, making it plain that he recognized that 'adaptations' was a more accurate English equivalent.

[11] See White Paper, para. 22. Here again the wording in the statement is very dexterous, displaying a full awareness of the differences of view and of the nuances that particular words had acquired within the Six. For a discussion of the Bonn declaration see Chapter XII.

[12] Under the rules of the GATT, other GATT countries could have argued that British accession to the Community required a re-negotiation of the common external tariff if the common tariff was more restrictive than the previous separate tariffs of the United Kingdom and the Six. To meet this point without the time-consuming task of re-negotiation, the United Kingdom indicated that it accepted the 20 per cent. reduction in the common external tariff that the Six had in any case proposed as part of the acceleration decision. See Chapter VIII.

with some justice during the free trade area negotiations—and that the British Government fully recognized that the solutions to these problems must be compatible with, and not disruptive of, the Common Market. That said, he turned to the biggest problem— Commonwealth trade. Throughout his speech, although he made very clear the points to which the British Government attached particular importance, he was very careful not to reveal what constituted the irreducible hard core of the British request. It was made plain that there was a reserve price, but not what it was. This was partly elementary prudence at the start of a very tough negotiation, but it was partly because the separate points requiring negotiation were very closely interrelated. What might be acceptable on one point depended on what was negotiable on other points: for example, a good arrangement for Australian wheat would make a relatively poor arrangement for Australian canned fruit easier to accept, and vice versa. Mr. Heath said very flatly: 'I am sure that you will understand that Britain could not join the E.E.C. under conditions in which this trade connection [between the Commonwealth and Britain] was cut with grave loss and even ruin for some of the Commonwealth countries.'[13] From the rest of his remarks it was clear that his approach was not simply—as this statement might suggest—to provide for the minimum essential needs of the Commonwealth, but, rather, to find a system under which the Commonwealth would not suffer as a result of the change in British policy.

In introducing his specific comments on the arrangements that might be made for the Commonwealth, Mr. Heath drew attention to the fact that when the Treaty of Rome was negotiated the Six had dealt with problems arising from the special arrangements that France, and others, then had with overseas countries and territories 'without damage to the interests of the countries concerned, and in some cases with considerable advantage to them'. He also made the point 'that in no case was a tariff imposed on trade where one had not been in force before the Treaty was signed'.[14] Some countries, such as Morocco and Tunisia, were, under the terms of a special protocol, allowed to maintain, unimpaired by the treaty, their right of access to the French market, others were associated with the Community and thus gained a preferential position for their exports in the Common Market as a whole. Mr. Heath's reference to the Morocco Protocol was a perfectly fair

[13] White Paper, para. 29.   [14] Ibid., para. 30.

point to make, but it was not one which the Six wanted to hear made. When speculating about the kinds of arrangement that might be made for the Commonwealth, Community representatives always steered clear of the Morocco Protocol, for it created a precedent which, if extended to the Commonwealth *en masse*, would have meant a major breach in the common external tariff and in the common agricultural policy. The possibility of associating new countries with the Community was also one that the Six treated with circumspection and at no time was there any indication that the Community would contemplate associating the developed countries of the Commonwealth.[15] The British were well aware that the Six would not contemplate using either the Morocco Protocol or 'association' as a complete solution, and Mr. Heath wisely admitted as much.

All expositions and examinations of the Commonwealth problem soon break down into a discussion of several quite different problems. Sometimes the problem is divided up by country, or by groups of countries, sometimes by commodity categories. Mr. Heath—doubtless for tactical reasons—began rather more broadly than usual by commenting first on the needs of the large group of less-developed Commonwealth countries and of the territories (for the most part underdeveloped) that were not yet independent. For these countries and for the dependencies the British responsibility was clearest, the need for special arrangements was apt to be felt by the Community to be the most persuasive, and the analogy with the existing overseas associates the closest.[16] Although Mr. Heath expressed some doubt as to whether all the countries in these categories would, in fact, want to apply for association, he suggested that they all ought to be given an opportunity to enter into association with the Community on the same terms that would be available, in the future, to the present associates. The list was a massive one, and apart from the fact that some of the countries on it, such as India and Ghana, had already made it quite clear that association was not the answer to their problems, the British knew that the Six would be unlikely to offer association to the whole list. It was clear from the informal talks

[15] New Zealand was always regarded as being a special case and from time to time 'association' was clearly thought of as a possible solution, although it was never actually put forward by Britain, by New Zealand, or by the Six.

[16] The Community has from the start been concerned about its 'image' in the underdeveloped countries and has been sensitive to criticism that the Community is a 'rich man's club'.

that had been held earlier in the year between British and French officials that one test for association would certainly be the fact that a country was underdeveloped, but it was not yet clear what other tests the Six would apply. Therefore, it seemed to the British to be sensible to list all conceivable candidates. This proved to be a rather dubious tactic, for it gave rise to complaints within the Community that the British approach was 'unrealistic'. However, the British were sufficiently 'realistic' to comment as well on the arrangements that might be made, short of association, even for countries on this list, as well as for the more developed members of the Commonwealth. Accordingly, at this point in his speech, and after another admiring glance at the Morocco Protocol, Mr. Heath broke the problem down into the conventional commodity classification: tropical products, materials, manufactures from the developed Commonwealth countries, the so-called 'low cost manufactures' from the less-developed, mostly Asian, Commonwealth countries, and temperate zone foodstuffs.

The British were reasonably hopeful that association would be offered to the Commonwealth countries in Africa and to the British West Indies. But they knew that Ghana would almost certainly reject it and that the Six would be very unlikely to offer it to the Asians. Mr. Heath therefore suggested two alternatives to association for producers of tropical products: first, where the country concerned needed protection, as well as equality of treatment, he proposed that the country should be given the right of free entry into the United Kingdom market (but not into the markets of the Six) and that the common external tariff should be re-negotiated so that it would give protection both to the Commonwealth country concerned and to the countries associated with the Community; in other cases, he suggested that the common tariff should be lowered or perhaps eliminated altogether. Under the second heading, he mentioned tea from India and Ceylon and cocoa from Ghana as cases in point.

Most raw materials already enter the Community duty-free and exports of tin and rubber would obviously not be disadvantaged by Britain's joining the Six and might even benefit if economic expansion in the United Kingdom were accelerated. Australian wool was another commodity which would probably gain rather than lose markets if Britain joined the Community. But, as Mr. Heath pointed out, there was a handful of raw materials on which the common external tariff was substantial and the Commonwealth producers of these commodities stood to lose if no provision were made, since they would not only lose their preference in the British market (in those cases where they had a preference) but would be confronted by a 'reverse preference', that is, by a tariff against themselves which conferred a substantial benefit on their competitors within the Six. Accordingly, Mr. Heath indicated that the British would seek a zero tariff for five important raw materials —aluminium, woodpulp, newsprint, lead, and zinc—as well as for some less important commodities.

When he turned to the problem of manufactures, Mr. Heath discussed, first, the problem that would face the developed countries of the Commonwealth—Australia, Canada, and New Zealand—if their industries which had been developed on the basis of free, or preferential, entry to the British market were now not only to lose these advantages but to be confronted with 'reverse preferences'. However, he recognized that 'the indefinite and un-limited continuation of free entry might not be acceptable', and he indicated a willingness to negotiate on this question. Again, it would doubtless have helped him with the Six had he bowed to the inevitable rather more vigorously. The problem of low-cost manu-factures from the less-developed countries of the Commonwealth he put in a separate category. As Mr. Heath pointed out, no problems would arise if the Asian Commonwealth countries and Hong Kong were to become associated under Part Four of the treaty, but except, perhaps, for the Colony of Hong Kong, he clearly had no real hope that this would be possible. Although Mr. Heath suggested no specific alternatives, he did draw attention to 'the increasing international recognition that developed countries have a duty to facilitate international trade in this field as much as they can', and added: 'You will probably agree that it would not be in the general interest that the United Kingdom should erect fresh barriers to cut back such trade.' The common external tariff on most textiles (the principal item in question) was high (and imports into some countries of the Six were also drastically restricted by quotas), while the United Kingdom had a nil tariff and a liberal import régime for most textiles imported from the Common-wealth countries. Mr. Heath's statement, therefore, implied a number of possible solutions: Morocco Protocol, tariff quotas, reduction of the common external tariff; but he was not explicit.

Finally, Mr. Heath turned to the problem of temperate-zone foodstuffs. 'Australia, New Zealand, and Canada, in particular, have vital interests in this field for which special arrangements must be made.' He gave figures illustrating the extreme dependence of New Zealand on the British market for mutton, lamb, butter, and cheese, and stated quite flatly that 'If in the future New Zealand cannot, by one means or another, be assured of comparable outlets for them, her whole economy will be shattered.' Although New Zealand was the extreme case he pointed out that other Commonwealth commodity problems 'are the same in kind if not in degree'. In a key paragraph, Mr. Heath enunciated the doctrine of 'comparable outlets', which was to prove to be highly contentious: 'I therefore hope that we can reach agreement in principle that full regard should be paid to the interests of the Commonwealth producers concerned, and that they should be given in the future the opportunity of outlets for their produce comparable to those they now enjoy.'[17] It should be noted that he spoke in terms not of a guaranteed market but of 'comparable opportunities', but just what was meant by 'comparable' was not spelled out. Mr. Heath then made it very clear that since the 'precise form of the special arrangements needed to protect vital interests of Commonwealth countries' would depend on the common agricultural policy, the British wanted to work jointly with the Six 'in examining these problems and their relation to the common agricultural policy'.[18] Among the special arrangements that might be considered he mentioned, once again, a Morocco-type protocol, and also duty-free, levy-free, or preferential quotas, market-sharing agreements, and long-term contracts. He did not, at this time, indicate any specific solutions, but expressed his confidence that it should be possible to find agreements on detailed arrangements 'if you are prepared to accept the basic principle of comparable outlets'. As discussed further below, the Six, for a number of reasons, unanimously refused to accept this concept.

This presentation of the problems British membership posed for the Commonwealth countries and of the kinds of solution that the British had in mind took up a large part of Mr. Heath's speech. British agriculture and the EFTA, although important, clearly seemed to him to be easier to deal with. In discussing agriculture, Mr. Heath made it clear at the outset that the British Government 'fully accept that the Common Market must extend to agriculture and trade in agricultural products'. He then outlined the British system of agricultural support and emphasized the advantages it

---

[17] White Paper. para. 45.   [18] Ibid., para. 46.

held, for both the farmer and the consumer. He indicated that the British were nevertheless ready to 'move towards' the very different continental method of support. However, it was clear that he assumed the British would, in fact, be able to have a hand in shaping the common agricultural policy, the details of which were still under discussion within the Community, and that, as a result, the common agricultural policy might well have some of the characteristics of the British system: 'I am sure that the pooling of ideas and experience will have fruitful results; indeed, some features of our arrangements may prove attractive to you. Our object will be to consider with you how the essential interests of our farmers can be effectively safeguarded within the framework of the Treaty of Rome and in consonance with the objectives of the common agricultural policy.'[19] On this point, too, British hopes were to be disappointed, for the Six, under pressure from the French, pushed ahead with the formulation of detailed agricultural regulations and only began discussions with the British after they had reached agreement among themselves. In his comments on agriculture Mr. Heath also laid great stress on the need for making adjustments gradually and he made the point that 'the conditions under which our agriculture is brought within the common policy should not be more onerous than those which were open to you when the Treaty of Rome entered into force. On this basis the transitional arrangements for the United Kingdom could, where necessary, continue for a period of between 12 and 15 years from when we join.'[20] On this point, also, Mr. Heath was to meet strong opposition from the Six.

When he turned to the question of the EFTA countries, Mr. Heath pointed out that the United Kingdom had always deplored the division of Europe into two economic groups and that it now hoped that the division would be brought to an end through some countries joining the Community and others becoming associated with it. He pointed out that the EFTA countries had agreed to maintain the EFTA until, in the words of the London communiqué, 'satisfactory arrangements have been worked out . . . to meet the various legitimate interests of all members of E.F.T.A., and thus enable them all to participate from the same date in an integrated European market'. He then recapitulated—but slightly reinterpreted—this commitment: 'Her Majesty's Government earnestly trust that, when the other E.F.T.A. countries have

[19] White Paper, para. 53.   [20] Ibid., para. 54.

explained where they stand, it will be possible to agree on ways and means of meeting their legitimate interests. I am sure you will appreciate that, given our obligations to our E.F.T.A. partners, we should not ourselves be able to join the Community until this has been done.'[21] There is a strong suggestion in the formulation in the London Agreement that a situation in which all EFTA members 'participate from the same date in an integrated European market' is synonymous with 'legitimate interests', and the omission of this phrase from Mr. Heath's second formulation was probably significant, although he made it clear that he hoped that a single market would be the result. By this time there had been enough signs of the difficulties that lay ahead for the neutrals, so that the British, although still loyal to their EFTA partners, presumably hoped that some of the EFTA countries might in the end decide that their 'legitimate interests' had been satisfied by something less than a situation in which all participated from the same date in an integrated market.

Mr. Heath had copies of his speech available for the delegates, not simply in English but also in French, German, Dutch, and Italian, an indication of the new attention being given to 'European' details. A fairly full summary of Mr. Heath's speech was released to the press and given to the Commonwealth and other diplomatic missions. The reason given for releasing a summary rather than the full text was to avoid setting a precedent for other conference documents. Presumably the British also felt that the speech, having been written primarily for 'European' consumption, might give rise to awkward questions and possibly to misunderstandings. Inevitably, however, the speech leaked and for a time there was a rather pointless controversy, stirred up by the Canadians, over the decision to keep the full text secret. Eventually the full text was 'found' and published by Reuters and, following its appearance in the press, it was issued as a White Paper. The reaction to the full text was, in the main, one of surprise that it had not been published at the time it was given, for it was generally conceded to have been a masterly exposition of the British case.[22]

Within the Six there was great satisfaction with the positive tone

---

[21] White Paper, para. 59.

[22] See for example the *Times* leader, 28 November 1961. On the other hand, Richard Crossman (an opponent of joining the Common Market) reacted predictably, saying that it had obviously been kept secret to conceal from the British public the extent to which the Government had sold out to the 'Europeans'. See *Guardian*, 1 December 1961.

of the British statement but, as was to be anticipated, every word and phrase was subjected to the most minute analysis. It was clear enough that the British were now prepared to negotiate in terms of joining the Common Market, but it was also true that their opening statement could be read to mean that they were going to seek such sweeping exceptions for the Commonwealth that their acceptance, in principle, of the common external tariff and the common agricultural policy would mean very little in practice. It could also, and more charitably, be read to mean that they were prepared to go very far in accepting the system of the Six. It was read by different people in both these ways. But, although a few hardened cynics considered that it was little more than a bid for the free trade area all over again, the prevailing view was that the speech reflected a real change in policy and that it was an extremely skilful, and encouraging, opening to what would doubtless be a long and difficult negotiation.

The substance of Mr. Heath's speech was not discussed at the October meeting and the next ministerial meeting did not take place until a month later (8 and 9 November). By this time it was clear that the negotiation would not really get under way until early in 1962, for the Six were not prepared to discuss any aspect of the negotiation which was affected by the common agricultural policy until they had reached fairly detailed agreements among themselves on the main features of the agricultural policy. The Six took this position for two main reasons. In the first place, the French, with considerable support from the Dutch, had made it clear that they would not agree to the passage to the second stage of the transition period on 1 January 1962 unless substantial agreement had been reached on the details of the agricultural policy. The Treaty of Rome provided that before passing to the second stage the Council must find unanimously that the objectives laid down for fulfilment during the first stage had been achieved. Failing unanimous agreement, the first stage would have been automatically extended for another year. Although the Treaty of Rome was somewhat imprecise about the timetable for the common agricultural policy, it was clear enough that the French could find an adequate basis for a veto if no substantial progress were made on agriculture before the end of the year. The Commission had made proposals to the Council as long ago as June 1960; there had been several discussions on them by the Council; and they had been debated by the Assembly. But the Germans had been reluctant to begin any serious discussions until after their elections in the autumn of 1961. Once the German elections were over, the settlement of the details of the common agricultural policy clearly had first claim on the time of the Council of Ministers of the Six, for the passage to the second stage of the transition period had acquired great symbolic importance, and failure to begin the second stage in January 1962 would have been regarded as a tremendous setback. The second reason for giving priority to settling the common agricultural policy was to enable the Six to negotiate with the British collectively and with a single voice: both the problem of the arrangements to govern the import of temperate zone agricultural products from the Commonwealth and the question of the adjustments to be made in British agriculture depended directly on the common agricultural policy. Moreover, in addition to the general desire of the Six to be able to act together, the French were anxious to have certain aspects of the proposed policy accepted by the others and by the Germans, in particular, before the British joined the Community. With some reason, they felt that if decisions on the agricultural policy became mixed up with the accession negotiations, or were left for decision after British accession, the Germans and the British—the two big importing countries—would join forces and block the adoption of the kind of agricultural policy for which the French were pressing.

The Six were also not yet ready for serious discussion on the possibility of associating certain Commonwealth countries with the Community. The special convention on the arrangements governing the association of the former French, Belgian, and Dutch colonies was due to expire at the end of 1962 and the Six were in the process of discussing the terms of a new convention with their associates. They were understandably reluctant to begin negotiations on the extension of association arrangements to additional countries until they had decided on the shape of the new convention: partly, again, because of the overriding priority they gave to speaking with one voice in the negotiations with the British, and partly because the prospect of new associates complicated the negotiations with the existing associates.[23]

---

[23] The coolness of the existing associates towards new associates arose partly from their reluctance to see more claimants on the Development Fund—even though there would also be an important new contributor to the Fund—and, probably more important, from the fact that the value of the preferences the

As indicated above, the British had hoped that the policies on agriculture and on association would be worked out in conjunction with them, and in a way that would make participation in the Community easier to reconcile with their commitments to the Commonwealth and to British farmers. Useful exchanges of views took place informally between the British and the Six about the new convention on association, but British attempts to influence the shape of future agricultural policies had little, if any, effect. Moreover, although the British had, apparently, been given assurances that the Community's agricultural regulations could be modified later to take account of the new situation created by British entry, the Six (and, in particular, the French and the Commission) became strongly opposed to the reopening of any of the principal points once agreement among the Six had been achieved.

At the ministerial meeting early in November, Mr. Heath and the Six agreed that experts should begin work on the problems raised by the British acceptance of the common external tariff, and, at a second ministerial meeting held later in the month, Mr. Heath tabled a list of twenty-seven items (including the 'big five', aluminium, woodpulp, newsprint, lead, and zinc), on which the British requested that the common external tariff be reduced to zero. The third ministerial meeting was held on 8 December. Between the ministerial meetings the deputies and committees of experts met frequently and a mass of detailed information was compiled. Progress was made in separating the Commonwealth problem into its component parts, that is, the problems posed by the common external tariff, by the adoption of the common agricultural policy, and by the Community's association arrangements. The mere classification of problems in this way underlined what had been clear enough from the start: that is, that 'association' was, in practice, a sensible arrangement only for dependent territories and for those Commonwealth countries that, in terms of production patterns and stage of development, were directly comparable with countries already associated with the Community, in short the Commonwealth countries in Africa, the British West Indies, and a few scattered dependencies.

By the end of the year 1961, although it was clear enough that

---

existing associates enjoyed in the Community market would be greatly diminished if they had to compete on equal terms with the frequently more efficient producers in 'British Africa'.

certain arrangements would not be negotiable, no real negotiations had yet taken place and no positions had been abandoned by either side. Both sides were still testing the water and neither wanted to be the first to offer compromises. The Six felt, not unreasonably, that it was up to the British—as the applicant for admission—to put forward specific proposals. Moreover, it was easier (although still difficult) for the Six to respond with a common voice to proposals made by the British than it was for the Six to reach agreement among themselves on compromises to put forward. But the British had problems of their own in putting forward compromises, for it was obviously easier for them to persuade a Commonwealth country that an offer made by the Six would have to be accepted than it was to convince a Commonwealth country that the British should themselves suggest any arrangement that fell short of the Commonwealth country's own maximum demands. In addition to these difficulties, the fact that all aspects of negotiation were closely interrelated meant that it was difficult to begin the process of compromise on a piecemeal basis. The British Government knew well enough that it stood no chance of satisfying every Commonwealth country on every count, and that the best it could hope for was a total package that would look reasonable to the Commonwealth and to the House of Commons. Therefore until the Six were prepared to begin discussing the key questions, and, in particular, those affecting imports of temperate-zone agricultural commodities, it was difficult for any real negotiations to begin. Accordingly, during December and January the important negotiations were those among the Six on the common agricultural policy, rather than the preliminary exchanges between the United Kingdom and the Six.

Discussions among the Six on agriculture

On 18 December, the Council of Ministers of the Six met to discuss various questions related to the decision on the passage to the second stage of the transition period. The Germans and the Dutch had made the Council's approval of the cartel regulations a condition of their agreement; the French and the Dutch had made settlement of the common agricultural policy a condition of their agreement; and the French had also pointed out that equal pay for men and women (which was supposed to have been achieved during the first stage) was not yet the practice in some countries of the Six. By 24 December, when the Council of Ministers adjourned for Christmas, the only remaining objection to passing to the second stage came from the French, who insisted that further details of the agricultural policy had first to be agreed. On 29 December, the Council of Ministers reconvened to make a desperate last-minute attempt to reach agreement before the year ended. On 31 December, they decided to 'stop the clock' and to reconvene again on 4 January. From then until 14 January the ministers sat in almost continuous session. Finally after twenty-three days of discussions, many late-night sessions, and one all-night session, the Council reached agreement and the way was clear to the second stage. The formal decision to pass to the second stage was taken and made retroactive to 1 January 1962.

Herr Lahr, the Under-Secretary of State in the German Ministry of Foreign Affairs, described the agricultural agreements reached at this time as 'a new Treaty of Rome' and Dr. Adenauer called the settlement 'one of the most important happenings of European history of the last few hundred years'.[24] Both statements were exaggerations, but they illustrate the high sense of achievement the Six felt at the time, and with reason, for agreement on common policies for agriculture had heretofore always eluded governments. The Green Pool had been stillborn and the Benelux Economic Union, even today, largely excludes agriculture. Agreement among the Six was only reached because their ability to overcome the agricultural hurdle came to be regarded as the acid test of their willingness to make the Community succeed. Fortunately the negotiations covered a wide enough range of issues, so that it was possible for each country to gain on some points while yielding on others, although the French undoubtedly gained the most and yielded the least. Nevertheless, in the last resort each of the Six countries gave the common interest priority over purely national interests. Moreover, although concern for the French farmer undoubtedly ranked considerably higher in M. Pisani's scheme of things than did the consolidation of the Community, the result of French stubbornness and of their insistence on reaching detailed agreements before moving to the second stage was the taking of a long step forward towards full economic union. The agricultural regulations that were adopted can be criticized on a number of counts,[25] and the wisdom of determining policy in this field before

[24] See *The Times*, 18 January 1962.
[25] Principally on the grounds that they showed a strong bias towards autarchy and appeared to be administratively cumbersome.

knowing whether or not the British were to become members of the Community is open to question, since the addition of the United Kingdom would have altered profoundly the demand–supply situation for a number of the most important products. Nevertheless, the difficulties of the negotiation and the persistence with which the Six worked their way to final agreement further consolidated the Six and provided them not only with a set of specific regulations but with a body of doctrine on agricultural questions without which they would have had the greatest difficulty in maintaining any kind of common front in their negotiations with the British. The agreements reached also reinforced two essential characteristics of the Community, characteristics which the Six fought hard to preserve throughout the negotiations with the British: first, the fact that all members of the Community are to be treated equally and farmers of one nationality cannot, therefore, have better guarantees than farmers of another nationality; and second, the fact that members of the Community are to be treated differently from—and better than—outsiders, that is, the principle of Community preference.

The agreements reached in January followed, in the main, the proposals that had been made by the Commission, and the similarity between the final agreement and the Commission's proposals is an impressive example of the extent to which the Commission's power to propose has enabled it to play an important and, at times determining, role in the decision-making process. The regulations agreed in January are too lengthy and complicated to be summarized in detail here, but a few key points should be noted, for they set the limits to what was possible in the British negotiation.[26]

A system of variable import levies was adopted for grain, pigmeat, eggs, and poultry. This levy system takes the place of all existing forms of protection. During the transition period, levies are to be applied to trade within the market as well as to trade with third countries, but a fixed sum (*montant forfaitaire*) is to be deducted from the levies on intra-Community trade in order to give a preference to Community suppliers. The intra-Community levies will progressively diminish, and will disappear entirely by the end of the transition period. The amount of the

---

[26] A summary of the 14 January decisions was put out by the Commission in a brochure, *A Farm Policy for Europe* (January 1962). The detailed regulations can be found in the *Journal Officiel des Communautés Européens*, 20 April 1962.

levy is to be calculated in different ways for different commodities. For grains, target prices will be set, first nationally, and later on a Community basis. Producers will be guaranteed approximately these prices, since the Community will intervene in the market when prices fall by more than a certain specified percentage below the target prices and the levies at the Community's frontier will bring the price of imports up to the internal price. For pig-meat, eggs, and poultry there will be no target and intervention prices and therefore no 'guaranteed prices'. However, there will be what are called 'sluicegate' prices; in effect these are minimum prices, and imports can only be made at this price or above. The levy, in the case of these three products, is a fixed amount and is to be made up partly of a fixed amount to compensate for differences in the cost of feeding stuffs, and partly of a fixed amount corresponding to a protective duty. For pig-meat, but not for eggs or poultry, there will be an intra-Community 'sluicegate' price during the transition period. Prices throughout the Community for pig-meat, eggs, and poultry will eventually be similar as a result of the working of normal market forces and the absence of any protection within the Community.

In the case of grains, although the target prices will, in the first instance, be set by national authorities, national prices will be progressively 'approximated', and eventually there will be 'Community' target prices. Clearly the key decision will be the decision on the price level that the Community will maintain internally. If it is high, the levy system will be very protective and will stimulate production within the Community. If it is low, the system will be liberal and will discourage additional domestic production. Although the principle of 'approximation' (i.e. the bringing into line of national prices) was accepted in January 1962, a decision on the first approximation was put off until the spring of 1963.[27]

It was also agreed, in principle, that the levy system should be applied to dairy products. However, although the Council was supposed to have taken a decision by the end of July 1962 on the detailed arrangements to give effect to this decision, no agreement had been reached by the summer of 1963. The arrangements to

---

[27] After the breakdown in the negotiations with the British, the rest of the Six deliberately tied decisions on the outstanding agricultural questions which were of particular interest to France to French concessions in the 'Kennedy round' of tariff negotiations in the GATT and to the establishment of relations between the Six and the United Kingdom. The result was a stalemate which had not been broken when this book went to press in August 1963.

govern trade in rice and sugar were also to have been decided
during 1962 but, again, no decisions had been taken by the time
this book went to press.

It was also agreed that intra-Community trade in fruit and
vegetables will be free from restriction, except for the restrictions
implicit in rather elaborate quality controls, and a timetable was
laid down for the removal of existing restrictions such as tariffs,
quotas, and minimum prices. Imports of fruit and vegetables from
third countries will, however, be subject to the common external
tariff and, in exceptional circumstances, minimum prices and
compensating levies may be used to protect the market.

In addition to these regulations and declarations of principle,
the Council of Ministers also agreed that a 'European Agricultural
Guidance and Guarantee Fund' should be established to be used
for three purposes: to subsidize agricultural exports, to support
prices by interventions on the internal market, and to promote
structural change in agriculture within the Community. However,
both the way the Fund was to be used and the way it was to be
fed gave rise to heated and prolonged controversy. The importing
countries, Germany and the Netherlands in particular, obviously
wanted the Fund to be fed by budgetary contributions as well as
by levies on imports, and wanted the Fund to be available for
promoting structural reform as well as for subsidizing exports.
France, in contrast, had an interest in all the levies going to the
Fund and in having the Fund available as necessary to subsidize
exports. A compromise was eventually reached on the proportions
to be contributed and to be spent for various purposes for the
period until 1965. The Council was to reach another decision on
the scale for contributions and expenditures for the period from
1965 until the end of the transition period. It was understood that
the proceeds of the levies would go to the Community for Community expenditure in the Common Market period, that is, at the
end of the transition period. However, it was not altogether clear
what aspects of the post-1970 arrangement required further consideration by the Council, and differences of view on this point later
gave rise to difficulties in the negotiations with the British.

Negotiations during the spring and summer, 1962

When Mr. Heath met again with the Ministers of the Six on
18 January 1962, Mr. Mansholt (the member of the Commission
responsible for agriculture) described the agricultural decisions

which the Six had taken, but the texts were not yet available and
there was little detailed discussion of the proposed arrangements.
Each side was still waiting for the other to make the first move
towards real negotiation and the meeting was a short and unproductive one. Public interest inevitably centred on the meetings
between Mr. Heath and the Ministers of the Six, and it was after
the ministerial conferences that Mr. Heath normally made reports
on progress to the House of Commons. However, although it is
convenient to describe progress in relation to the decisions reached
at the ministerial meetings, this inevitably gives a rather false
impression of the way the negotiations proceeded, for the United
Kingdom and the Six were meeting together at deputy and high
official level almost continuously throughout the period of the
negotiations.

Early in the new year (1962) there were signs that the British
hoped to speed up the negotiations, and it was assumed by the
press, probably rightly, that this was one of the topics discussed
by Mr. Macmillan with Dr. Adenauer during their meeting in
Bonn early in January, and again with Dr. Erhard during his visit
to London towards the end of January. Dr. Erhard was very
anxious to see the negotiations concluded as soon as possible, but
there is little to suggest that his views in this matter carried any
more weight with the Chancellor, or with the French, than had his
earlier advocacy of the free trade area. On the contrary, like his
earlier enthusiasm for the free trade area, his enthusiasm for
British membership may well have been counter-productive. At
the end of his visit to London he prophesied, with some confidence,
that an agreement would be reached in the summer and that the
United Kingdom would be a member of the Community by
January 1963. The British were themselves still hoping that
roughly this schedule could be met, although they were less
sanguine than Dr. Erhard and much more cautious about setting
dates. Although the British were seeking ways to speed the
negotiations they were anxious to avoid giving any impression of
over-eagerness or of being bound by a particular timetable, or
deadline, for they felt that signs of either might weaken their
already far from strong bargaining position with the Six. From the
start of the negotiations the British had felt handicapped by the
fact that the French, in particular, but others within the Six as
well, seemed convinced that the British Government was prepared
to pay almost any price to join the Community. And the British

Government's feeling that it was desirable to try to counteract this impression of inevitability and better to appear to be not too eager made them reluctant to be the ones to begin the process of making compromises. The Government was caught in a difficult public relations situation and almost anything it did seemed likely to boomerang. If it showed enthusiasm for joining the Six, there was the danger that the Six would simply harden the terms; but if it appeared to lack enthusiasm, the Six were quick to suspect that the British were not sincere. Similarly there were difficulties at home whichever course was pursued. Enthusiasm and a sense of urgency led to charges that the Government was determined to join at any price and that it was not being honest when it said the terms had to be right. But silence led to the criticism that the Government was not educating the country to the implications of joining 'Europe' and that it was letting the anti-Common Market propagandists make the running.

Nevertheless, despite the risks involved, during the spring of 1962 the British took the lead in pressing for the delegation of more work to the deputies and for more frequent ministerial meetings, and eventually—although rather late in the day—Mr. Heath began the process of making concessions. Ministerial meetings were held on 22 February and 22 March. During these meetings the full range of problems was reviewed and, as had been anticipated, the two points that emerged as the ones which would prove to be the most difficult were, first, the problem of imports of temperate-zone foodstuffs from the Commonwealth, and, second, the timing and procedure of the changeover from the British system of deficiency payments to the Community support system. The main argument over British agriculture did not really come until the autumn, but the battle on the import régime for temperate-zone foodstuffs was joined in the spring and had largely been settled by the time the negotiations were adjourned early in August.

At their meeting on 22 March, the Ministers had asked the deputies to prepare a detailed progress report which could be circulated to the seven negotiating governments before Easter. This report was in no sense an 'outline' agreement: where positions differed the two points of view were given and no attempt was made to suggest compromises. Nevertheless, over quite a wide range of matters positions were close enough together so that the nature of the final arrangement was reasonably apparent. And when the Ministers met again, on 8 May, a period of real negotiation finally began which continued until the summer adjournment early in August.

The first specific agreement to be reached was on the timetable for the application of the common external tariff to the import of industrial goods from the developed countries of the Commonwealth. Although it had been clear from the moment of Mr. Macmillan's statement in the House of Commons that if the British entry into the Common Market meant anything it meant the application of the common external tariff to this group of products, the British, under pressure from the Commonwealth, had earlier put forward the case for continued free entry. It was clear to everyone, however, that this stood no chance of being negotiable and that the most the British Government could achieve for these Commonwealth products was some phasing of the application of the common external tariff.[28] Accordingly the British did not press the case for free entry but sought instead freedom to apply the common external tariff gradually and an undertaking that the development of trade would be kept under review and the schedule modified if hardship resulted. Although the Six proposed a slightly different rate of application and a slightly different review formula, this problem was settled with no very great difficulty. Rather surprisingly, in view of the fact that they could have been under no illusion about the eventual application of the common tariff to these goods, Mr. Menzies and Mr. Marshall (the Deputy-Prime Minister of New Zealand), who were then in London, issued a statement when news of the agreement was published, criticizing the arrangement as a 'disturbing development' and emphasizing that it should not be a precedent for other, more important, products.[29]

Later in May the British also made proposals on the arrangements that should govern trade with the Asian countries—India,

---

[28] Mr. Gaitskell, in his statement in the House of Commons in June, acknowledged that the application of the common external tariff to these products was unavoidable and obvious from the very beginning. See *Hansard*, House of Commons, 6 June 1962, cols. 509–10.

[29] It was agreed that the British preference rates would be brought into line with the common external tariff on the following schedule: 30 per cent. on accession, 30 per cent. on 1 January 1967, final alignment on 1 January 1970. Many more Canadian exports were affected by the application of the external tariff than Australian and New Zealand exports. Mr. Heath had visited Ottawa at the end of March 1962, when, presumably, he had convinced the Canadians of the need for the British to put forward proposals in order to get the negotiations off dead-centre.

Pakistan, and Ceylon—and again the Six responded with counter-proposals which were close enough to offer room for a reasonable compromise, although, again, the Commonwealth countries concerned (in this case India, in particular) were quick to make it plain that the arrangement agreed was not wholly satisfactory. During this period, May and early June, negotiations finally seemed to be under way, and there was considerable optimism in London that it should be possible to have a fairly complete outline agreement by the end of the summer in time for the Commonwealth Prime Ministers' meeting which had been set for 10 September. It was hoped that the negotiations could then be finished by the end of the year, ratification completed during the spring, and British entry into the Community take place on 1 July 1963, only six months later than the date in the first tentative timetable.

The feeling that the negotiations were, at last, beginning to gain momentum was given a fillip by the Prime Minister's talks with General de Gaulle at the Chateau de Champs on 1 and 2 June. During these discussions, Mr. Macmillan seemed to have persuaded General de Gaulle that the British shift in policy was a real one and, at the time, the meeting was regarded—on both sides of the Channel—as having been a considerable success.[30] However, British hopes that the meeting might lead to some softening of the French position in Brussels were disappointed. The French position still appeared to be what it had been from the start, namely that if the British were ready fully to join the Community they must be accepted, but that there was no reason to make the task of entry easy for them and every reason to insist that the British should take steps on entry which would constitute hard evidence of the sincerity of their intentions.

As noted earlier, French domestic interests could frequently be served by insisting on acceptance of the letter of the treaty and as the negotiations proceeded, the British tended to feel that the French defence of the treaty and particularly of the regulations already adopted by the Community was a completely cynical one. However, although self-interest doubtless contributed to the zeal with which the French defended the treaty, they could not have held the Six together—which they did with conspicuous success until the crisis in January 1963—if their arguments had rested

[30] This meeting between Mr. Macmillan and General de Gaulle is commented on in more detail on pp. 428–9.

simply on the need to secure advantages for France. Moreover, within the Six there was considerable agreement with the French argument that unless the British were obliged, on entry, to make changes in their relations with the Commonwealth countries and in their domestic agricultural support schemes so that there could be no going back, they would use the transition period not to adapt their methods to Community methods but to reshape the Community to satisfy their own requirements.[31]

Although at the start of the negotiations the British Government had been determined to avoid deadlines, once they had set the date for the Commonwealth Prime Ministers' meeting, they had, in fact, imposed a kind of deadline. The British were ready to sit well into August if that proved to be necessary to achieve an outline agreement, but it was clear that they could not hope to persuade the Six to remain in session much after the first of August, for little work is ever done in August, the traditional vacation month. In addition the French felt no particular urgency about completing the negotiations and suspected that their partners would be too prone to compromise if the importance of an agreement before the adjournment were dramatized or made to appear decisive. Nevertheless, most of the delegates clearly hoped that a fairly complete outline of the final agreement could be achieved before adjourning, and during June and July the Ministers held a number of long sessions. When the conference was adjourned early in the morning of 5 August, after an all-night sitting, the hoped-for 'outline' agreement had not been achieved, but enough agreement had been reached on the points that affected the Commonwealth so that the Prime Ministers' Conference could be held as planned. The lion's share of the time at the July and August meetings was spent on the arrangements to govern the import of temperate-zone foodstuffs. The main points at issue between the Six and the United Kingdom and the agreements reached on this problem are worth describing in some detail; this was probably the most difficult problem in the negotiation, the amount of trade likely to be affected was substantial, and the issues involved posed more clearly and more inescapably than did most of the others a 'choice' between Europe and the Commonwealth.

As indicated above, page 384, Mr. Heath had said in his opening

---

[31] The British had not helped their own case by privately predicting that the Community would, in fact, be a 'different animal' once they were inside and that the agricultural policy would almost inevitably break down.

statement that 'if you [the Six] are prepared to accept the basic principle of comparable outlets which I have put forward, then agreement on the detailed arrangements required should be possible'. Mr. Heath was doubtless right in his conclusion that had the Six been prepared to accept the principle of ensuring comparable outlets to Commonwealth suppliers it would have been relatively easy to have found ways of doing so. But the Six were not prepared to accept the principle. They thought that for some important products (cereals and dairy products) it was inevitable (and desirable) that, over time, the quantities of Commonwealth goods sold in Europe should decline relatively, and perhaps absolutely, and that Australia and New Zealand should increasingly develop new markets in the Far East. For reasons of principle, as well as of self-interest, they opposed all proposals which might 'freeze' world trade patterns or nullify the advantages for domestic producers that were inherent in the common agricultural policy, which, as it had been elaborated at the turn of the year, was expressly designed to give a substantial 'Community preference' to Community producers. Throughout the negotiations the Six were steadfast in their refusal to contemplate arrangements which guaranteed any specific level of imports, which put the Commonwealth countries in as good a position as the other members of the Six—even during the transition period—, or which gave the Commonwealth countries better treatment than other third countries after the end of the transition period. Many of the British proposals would have created one or more of these situations, for it was impossible to give any substance to the concept of 'comparable outlets' without doing so. The British eventually shifted their position and, in effect, sought to ensure that Commonwealth suppliers would have 'reasonable access' to the expanded Community. Although there was room for much argument about what constituted 'reasonable access', it was a concept that was clearly consistent with the common agricultural policy, and the British, once they had shifted position, were on much stronger ground.

There was considerable agreement between the British and the Six about the nature of the agricultural problem, and it was quickly agreed that the biggest problems arose in connexion with cereals (wheat and coarse grains), with dairy products coming a close second. It was generally accepted that in those products, at least, there were trade problems that would require international action, irrespective of British accession to the Community, but that

British accession would measurably accentuate the problems.[32] It was recognized that the basic difficulties arose from the fact that in terms of effective demand there was already over-production of cereals and soon would be of dairy products. For social reasons, most producing countries subsidized their farmers, in one form or another, and world cereal prices therefore bore little relation either to the real costs of production or to the market situation. Moreover, although the non-Communist world's major producers were burdened with surpluses, half the world's population was undernourished. Accession of the United Kingdom to the Community and the acceptance by the United Kingdom of the levy system would give Common Market producers a market in the United Kingdom at the expense of Commonwealth, and other third country, producers, and would stimulate production in the United Kingdom, thus intensifying the existing anomaly of too much food in one half of the world and too little in the other.

So far there was general agreement. There was also agreement that it would be desirable to bring about a more rational pattern of production and trade in agricultural commodities by means of world-wide agreements between the major suppliers and the major producers, covering not only trade but also price, subsidy, and production policies—although the British were considerably more sceptical than the Six about the feasibility of negotiating world agreements. However, views differed sharply about the extent to which Commonwealth producers were entitled to, or needed, special safeguards for their trade with the expanded Community—especially if the world agreements did not materialize—, about the kinds of safeguards considered to be suitable, and about the phasing out of the Commonwealth preferences and the phasing in of the Community system.

At first, and in accordance with Mr. Heath's statement that they would seek 'comparable outlets' for the Commonwealth, the British proposed that the enlarged Community give the Commonwealth suppliers a right of access 'on level terms' with Community suppliers up to a specified amount, the amount to be roughly that currently imported by the United Kingdom, or by the enlarged Community.[33] In making their proposals the British assumed that

[32] The Contracting Parties of the GATT had already recognized the existence of a problem and had set up a special agricultural committee.

[33] The British were intentionally vague on this point since they did not know which formulation the Community would prefer. Access to the United

'world-wide' agreements, when concluded, would supersede these 'access' guarantees. However, to protect the Commonwealth's bargaining position in the negotiation of world-wide agreements and to safeguard Commonwealth trade if no world-wide agreements had been concluded by the end of the transition period, the United Kingdom proposed that these special 'access' arrangements should not be limited to the transition period but should continue until they were superseded—by mutual agreement— by other arrangements. The British suggested that before the end of the transition period the working of the special 'access' arrangements should be reviewed to see whether they should be continued in their original form, or modified in the light of other developments. The British also proposed that this review should be carried on in consultation with the Commonwealth countries concerned, and that the objective of ensuring 'comparable outlets' should be accepted as of continuing validity. Thus, under the British proposal, the negotiation of world agreements could take place at any time without prejudicing the Commonwealth's bargaining position, since special arrangements, of some sort, would continue until superseded by other arrangements. It should be noted that what the British were requesting was an 'access' guarantee, not that the Community should give the Commonwealth countries a firm commitment that they would purchase any given amount.

The Six were unanimous in feeling that this British proposal was completely unacceptable. They had a number of reasons for their view. In the first place they felt that the British were asking the Community to give the Commonwealth countries a firmer and longer-term commitment than any the British had themselves been willing to give. In the second place, access on 'level terms' would have been inconsistent with the principle of Community preference. In the third place, the Six felt that the open-ended commitment to give special treatment to the Commonwealth countries until those countries were satisfied that their needs had been met through world-wide agreements would tend to freeze the pattern of world trade and to inhibit the Commonwealth countries from seeking new outlets, particularly in Asia, as energetically as they

---

Kingdom only would have been quantitatively a somewhat smaller commitment, but a 'Community' commitment would have been more compatible with the spirit of the Treaty of Rome.

might otherwise do. Moreover, a commitment extending beyond the end of the transition period ran counter to the principle that, at the end of the transition period, Commonwealth countries should be treated in the same way as other third countries. Finally, of course, any such commitment would have put the Commonwealth countries in a very strong position at the conference negotiating world agreements.

In addition to these specific reasons for opposing the British opening request for 'comparable outlets', some of the Six, and particularly the French and the Commission, suspected that the British hoped to avoid having to adopt the levy system and that they were therefore seeking to negotiate arrangements which would enable them to avoid having to do so for several years; that once inside the Community they would seek to modify the system; and that they would doubtless obtain help in doing so from the Germans. This suspicion was not unreasonable for there was much British criticism of the levy system, which many people felt was not only unsuitable but probably unworkable in the expanded Community.[34] The French and the Commission in particular, but with the support of the rest of the Six, were therefore loath to agree to any proposals that relieved the United Kingdom of the obligation to take, on entry, the first steps in applying the agricultural policy, and, in particular, the levy system. (The same suspicions of British intentions were also conspicuous during the negotiations on the arrangements to be made for British agriculture. See Chapter XIV.)

There were two elements in the British concept of 'comparable outlets' which tended to be confused in much of the comment on the negotiations, but which, although they were closely related, should be distinguished in so far as possible. The first was the 'preference' aspect; the second the 'access' aspect. In their opening bid, the British contributed to the confusion because they did not themselves draw a distinction between commodities enjoying preference and other commodities. For all the major temperate-zone agricultural commodities they were, in effect, asking for the 'Community preference' until the Commonwealth countries were themselves prepared to give it up. The Six were ready to recognize that in so far as certain Commonwealth trade enjoyed a preference

---

[34] See, for example, the discussion of the levy system in Political and Economic Planning, Occasional Paper No. 14, *Agriculture, the Commonwealth and EEC*, pp. 52–53.

in the British market, there was a case for treating that trade somewhat more favourably than other third country trade during the transition period. But the Six were clear, from the first, that any special advantages given the Commonwealth should be degressive and should have tapered off entirely by the end of the transition period. For a long time the British held out against the principle of degression, not because they were against the general principle of phasing out Commonwealth preferences—a principle which in other contexts they had already accepted—but because, where the Community could expand production, the only way to give the Commonwealth countries any real assurance that they could maintain their existing markets was by giving them access to the United Kingdom market (or the Community market) on the same basis as the Community suppliers, that is, with the same degree of 'preference'. It was only after the British had finally abandoned their request for levy-free arrangements to guarantee access that they were willing to disentangle the two aspects of the question and to agree, in principle, to the degressivity of the preference element.

The heart of the negotiations on temperate-zone foodstuffs was not, however, the extent to which the Commonwealth countries should receive better treatment than other third countries but the 'access' question. This was not a question that could logically be limited to the transition period, nor was it a question that could be regarded as simply of interest to the Commonwealth countries. The crucial question was the extent to which the policies of the enlarged Community would stimulate Community production at the expense of more efficient production in the Commonwealth and other third countries, e.g. the United States and the Argentine. From the start of the discussions on temperate-zone agriculture the Six had argued that the levy system was not inherently restrictive: whether or not it proved to be restrictive would depend on the price levels adopted by the Community. They also argued that by substituting a single device—the levy—for the multiplicity of devices formerly used to protect agriculture, the Six countries were making it easier for third countries to negotiate for a liberal agricultural support system, since all their energies could be focused on the key question—the size of the levy, or, more accurately, the Community's target price. The Six felt that the result of the target price–import levy system would probably be to increase world prices somewhat and there was considerable feeling in Community circles that some rise in world prices was, in fact, desirable, since this would make it easier for other producing countries, like the United States, to abolish, or to reduce, producer subsidies.[35] Moreover, the Six felt that the Australians, Canadians, and New Zealanders might in this way derive approximately the same level of revenue from their exports to the Community even though the quantities exported declined. Although the Commonwealth countries were not unhappy at the prospect of an increase in the price of cereals and dairy products, they were decidedly cool to suggestions that there would be no 'Commonwealth problem' if prices rose enough to give them the same revenue for a smaller volume of exports. Moreover, the Australians, at least, did not share the assumption that world prices would tend to rise. On the contrary, they feared that the levy system would have what they called a 'ratchet' effect—screwing down world prices rather than pushing them up.

The Six were, of course, right in arguing that price was the key to the access question. But it was difficult for the British to accept this argument because it seemed highly unlikely that any price which it was politically feasible for the Community to adopt would be low enough to maintain imports at current levels, let alone to allow for any increase. The only way really to ensure that Commonwealth trade was maintained at current levels was, as the British had proposed, by giving the Commonwealth producers access on the same terms as Community producers, wherever they were directly competitive. Nevertheless, once it was completely clear that the British stood no chance of getting the kind of access guarantee they wanted, they switched ground. They accepted the main argument of the Six but tried to achieve their objective of ensuring that Commonwealth trade would not be adversely affected by obtaining explicit commitments on two counts: first, a commitment that the price policy of the Community would take account of the interests of 'traditional' suppliers and be designed

[35] In the background of the negotiations was the plan that the French had outlined during the GATT discussions in the autumn of 1961. This plan, the 'Baumgartner plan', in essence envisaged an increase in world prices to an 'economic' price (probably the French price) and the abolition of national subsidy arrangements. The export of surpluses produced at this price by France, the U.S., and others would be internationally subsidized to those countries that were unable to pay the market price. This scheme found considerable support in Commission circles and was well received by the Australians. The British were very cool to it for the obvious reason that they saw themselves becoming the principal financiers of the plan.

to ensure access; and second, that if there were an important decrease in imports from the Commonwealth countries, the Community would agree not only to consult with the countries affected but to take appropriate remedial action. However, again, they asked for more than the Six thought was reasonable. The Six felt that such a firm commitment to third countries would weaken the Community's future bargaining position. They also felt that, like a 'quantity' guarantee, a commitment to take corrective action if trade deteriorated would tend to freeze patterns of trade and to undermine the Community preference. Nevertheless, once the British began arguing on the ground chosen by the Six it became much more difficult for the Six to stick together, and there was considerable restlessness among the Six at the obduracy of the French, who, for reasons of both principle and domestic self-interest, were throughout the least inclined to compromise.[36] Eventually a formula on price policy was found which, although it did little more than recite two articles (39 and 110) of the Treaty of Rome, went some way to meet the British by stating that the Community intended to pursue a 'reasonable price policy' and by putting the development of world trade on an equal footing with the protection of domestic agriculture.[37] Moreover, although the Six were not prepared to accept as far-reaching a commitment to take remedial action if trade deteriorated as the British would have liked, they did agree to a limited commitment for the transition period. Thus they stated that it was their intention 'to ensure that

[36] Throughout the period of the negotiations there was much discontent among French farmers—which at times reached the point of open rioting—and this difficult domestic situation presumably contributed to the toughness of the position taken by the French Government in the Brussels negotiations.
[37] See paras. 16, 17, and 18 of *The United Kingdom and the European Economic Community*, Cmnd. 1805, H.M.S.O., August 1962. Article 39 (1) of the Treaty states the general objectives of the common agricultural policy, namely: '(a) to increase agricultural productivity by developing technical progress and by ensuring the rational development of agricultural production and the optimum utilisation of the factors of production, in particular labour; (b) to ensure thereby a fair standard of living for the agricultural population, particularly by the increasing of the individual earnings of persons engaged in agriculture; (c) to stabilise markets; (d) to guarantee regular supplies; (e) to ensure reasonable prices in supplies to consumers'. The relevant section of article 110 of the Treaty states the Community's intention of contributing to the general expansion of world trade: 'By establishing a customs union between themselves the Member States intend to contribute, in conformity with the common interest, to the harmonious development of world trade, the progressive abolition of restrictions on international exchanges and the lowering of customs barriers.'

the operation of the intra-Community preference would not lead to sudden and considerable alteration in trade patterns', and that if this were to occur 'the Community would review the operation of the intra-Community preference in consultation with Commonwealth countries'.[38]

The Six resisted British suggestions that the Community should undertake to discuss its price policy with the Commonwealth countries (or traditional suppliers[39]), which they felt was something no large producing country had ever agreed to do, but they agreed that, if other major producing countries were ready to do the same, a 'confrontation' of price policies should take place within the framework of the proposed world-wide agreements.

One of the main arguments that the Six had used to rebuff the original British proposal for an 'access guarantee' in quantitative terms was that they were opposed to any use of quantitative controls, either to ensure access or to limit access, and they pointed out that they did not propose to use them within the Community. Therefore, in addition to the assurances that the price policy of the Community would have regard for third country suppliers, the Six, as a part of the agreed paper on temperate-zone agriculture, confirmed that their agricultural regulations required the abolition of quantitative restrictions on imports from third countries as well as on internal trade 'subject to exceptional provision in the event of grave disturbance'.[40]

From the start of the negotiations the Commonwealth countries had recognized that it would be considerably easier for the British to negotiate special safeguards for Commonwealth trade during the transition period than for the definitive common market period. During the spring and early summer much was heard, particularly from the Australians, about the 'precipice' which would exist at the end of the transition period if the special arrangements negotiated for that period ended abruptly. To meet this point the British, as noted above, had originally suggested that some special arrangements should continue until superseded by world agreements, although they recognized that any special arrangements extending beyond the transition period might be different from

[38] See White Paper (Cmnd. 1805), para. 20
[39] Although obviously bargaining for the Commonwealth the British were usually prepared to see the same arrangements given to other 'traditional' suppliers.
[40] See White Paper, para. 18.

those agreed for the transition period.[41] The Six had rejected any open-ended guarantee or special arrangements extending beyond the transition period but to meet the 'precipice' argument they had proposed that the negotiation on world-wide agreements begin as soon as possible, perhaps as early as 1963. The problem then became not one of the régime to be followed if there were a gap between the end of the transition period and the conclusion of world agreements, but, rather, the régime to be followed if it did not prove possible to negotiate world-wide agreements. This problem, the so-called question of the 'hinge', was for a time a major issue. In the end the Six stated that they would be ready to conclude agreements 'for the same purpose' (as the world-wide agreements) with 'those countries that wished to do so and, in particular, the Commonwealth countries'. This, of course, gave little real guarantee to the Commonwealth, for obviously they and the Six might not be able to agree on the provisions of agreements to take the place of 'world-wide' agreements.

During the discussions on the arrangements to be made for imports of temperate-zone foodstuffs, there was general recognition of the fact that New Zealand's dependence on the United Kingdom market was of a different order of magnitude from that of Canada or Australia and that a sharp decline in its trade with the United Kingdom would have serious repercussions on the New Zealand economy. However, until the very end of this phase of the negotiations, the British were unwilling to have New Zealand's case considered separately, partly because they hoped to get better arrangements for the whole group of Commonwealth countries by treating them together; partly because it was politically difficult for Australia, for example, to be given demonstrably worse treatment than New Zealand. When it became apparent that the British could not obtain quantitative access guarantees, but simply a commitment that the Six intended to give third countries reasonable access to Community markets, it was clear that something firmer would have to be obtained for New Zealand. Just how much underpinning would be required could not be determined until the Community's regulations on dairy products, lamb, and mutton had been decided. However, before the

---

[41] The British knew the Six were very unlikely to agree to any special arrangements extending beyond the transition period and apparently put the suggestion forward—against their own better judgement—in response to Commonwealth pressure.

summer recess, the Six expressed their readiness to consider special arrangements for New Zealand, although the need to recognize New Zealand's special difficulties appears to have been the subject of an internal dispute between the French and the rest of the Six and was, later, called in question by the French.

Considerable tension (both between the United Kingdom and the Six and among the Six) built up during the discussion of the temperate-zone foodstuffs problem. Two episodes are perhaps worth noting. At the end of July, after they had abandoned their opening position on 'comparable outlets' and had agreed to take the paper put forward by the Six as the basis for discussion, the British proposed a large number of amendments to the paper. Some of these amendments were trivial, but many of them were substantial. The Six apparently had considerable trouble in reaching agreement among themselves on the response to make to these suggestions and for a time it looked as though there would be a crack in the united front which until then they had maintained without much difficulty. The other five were disposed to compromise on points the French felt to be fundamental, and the French were apparently reluctant to give way even on points which they knew to be simply presentational. At one stage M. Spaak threatened to break the united front unless the French showed some disposition to compromise. After this explosion the Six reached agreement and some progress was made with the British. But at about midnight on 4 August another episode heightened the tension and caused a certain amount of bad blood. As indicated above, an ambiguity existed in the interpretation of the financial regulation which the Six had agreed among themselves in January 1962. The British, in commenting on the regulation earlier in the negotiations, had apparently raised doubts in the minds of some of the Six—the French in particular—about whether or not they (the British) accepted the principle that the levies would become the property of the Community at the end of the transition period. With a view to killing two birds with one stone and both clearing up the ambiguity among the Six and committing the British to the 'correct' interpretation, a detailed paper on the financial regulation which had been drawn up by Sr. Colombo and M. Marjolin was unexpectedly circulated for approval. The British refused to discuss the paper on the grounds that it had been sprung on them and that they needed time to study it. They then further annoyed the French and the Commission (both of whom wanted the paper adopted) by pointing out certain implications in the document to the Germans and the Dutch, who then withdrew the approval they had previously given to the paper.

The conference adjourned for the summer holidays a few hours after this incident. M. Couve de Murville, the French Foreign Secretary, formally reserved the French position on the agreements that had been reached on the import arrangements for temperate-zone agricultural products pending a satisfactory settlement of the controversy over the financial regulation. Mr. Heath, for his part, 'noted' the formula agreed on the price policy of the Community pending further Cabinet consultations.

It is more difficult to make an impartial judgement on the settlement reached on the import of temperate-zone agricultural products than it is on the other agreements reached in the course of the negotiations, for the judgement depends on the premises one adopts. Most of the arrangements put forward by the British during the discussions on temperate-zone imports would have made the Community more liberal, and would have gone considerably further to ensure that the Commonwealth countries and other traditional exporters maintained their position in the markets of the enlarged Community, than would the commitments to adopt reasonable price policies, to negotiate world agreements, and to renounce the use of quotas, which were proposed by the Six, and, in a somewhat improved form, ultimately accepted by the British. However, if one accepts the dominant view of the Six (the view that was held most strongly by the French, the Italians, and the Commission but which was not openly challenged by the others) that the problem was to find a way of adapting the existing arrangements with the Commonwealth to conform with the principles of the common agricultural policy agreed among the Six in January 1962, the kind of commitments and understandings the Six were prepared to subscribe to went about as far as could be expected. The Six, however, could have been more generous in matters of detail and presentation. For example, they could have been more forthcoming in offering to consult others, and readier to *consider*, if not to commit themselves to *take*, corrective measures if the trade of 'traditional' exporters was badly hit by the operation of the levy system. The unwillingness, or inability, of the Six to act generously was the result partly of the fact that they had first to agree among themselves and therefore one objection was enough to kill a generous impulse, and partly of the fear that the British if given an inch would take a mile. In addition, in a situation in which the Six were still formulating and developing their own doctrines—and particularly on a question like agriculture, where they had strong conflicting views among themselves and governments were subject to strong domestic political pressures—it was perhaps not surprising that the Six, as a group, did not take as relaxed a view of minor exceptions, or of stretched interpretations, as a more mature and self-confident Community might have done.

The British, for their part, tried for too much initially and then held on for too long to positions which they knew they would ultimately have to abandon. It was a mistake for them to have yielded to Commonwealth pressure and, against their own better judgement, to have tried for open-ended commitments rather than differentiating sharply between the transition period and the 'common market' period. More fundamentally, the concept of 'comparable outlets' was in contradiction to the underlying philosophy of the particular kind of common agricultural policy adopted by the Six. When the formula was used in Mr. Heath's opening speech this conflict had not become clear, but it was clear by the time the British put forward specific proposals in the late spring of 1962. It would have been better to have recognized the basic conflict and to have accepted the fact that on this point a major concession would have to be made if the negotiations were to succeed, and, above all, to have made it earlier. Six weeks saved in the summer of 1962 might have made the difference between failure and success.

By the time the conference adjourned on 5 August, all the points affecting the Commonwealth had been discussed in enough detail so that the British had a clear idea of the arrangements they would be able to negotiate. And many pieces of the jigsaw were already in place, or almost in place. The principles that would be applied to temperate-zone agricultural imports were settled, although many loose ends, and some very important loose ends, remained to be tied up. The arrangements for manufactures from the developed countries of the Commonwealth had been agreed. The arrangements to be made for imports from India, Pakistan, and Ceylon were largely agreed.[42] With a few exceptions, it was

---

[42] The arrangements that had been agreed upon during the ministerial meeting from 1–5 August 1962 were reported to Parliament by the Lord Privy Seal in a White Paper, *The United Kingdom and the European Economic Community* (Cmnd. 1805, August 1962). The main points in the arrangements agreed for imports from India, Pakistan, and Ceylon are worth summarizing for they were

clear which Commonwealth countries would be offered association, and the Six were far enough along with their own associates in agreeing on the terms of the new association convention, so that it was reasonably clear what, in fact, 'association' meant.[43] Apart from the important nil duty requests, on which little progress had been made, and the treatment to be given to certain processed foodstuffs, in particular canned and dried fruit and canned salmon, those aspects of the negotiation that particularly affected the Commonwealth countries had been largely settled. Thus, although Mr. Heath's objective of an 'outline' agreement had not been reached, there was plenty for the Commonwealth Prime Ministers to discuss.

---

subject to considerable criticism both from the Commonwealth countries affected and from the Labour Party. This was rather surprising as the agreement was a reasonably generous one. The ministers of the United Kingdom and the Six recognized that in defining the future commercial policy of the enlarged Community account should be taken of the necessity for India, Pakistan, and Ceylon to increase and diversify their production. With this in mind, it was agreed that the enlarged Community would seek to negotiate comprehensive trade agreements with the three countries by the end of 1966, at the latest. The objective of these agreements would be 'to develop trade and so to maintain and increase the foreign currency earnings of these countries and in general to facilitate the implementation of their development plans'. A specific agreement was reached to abolish the existing common external tariff of 18 per cent. on tea and a few other less important tariffs were to be abolished or suspended. Special arrangements were to be made for imports of cotton textiles from these countries: although the common external tariff would be progressively applied, it would be applied according to a special rate—20 per cent. on British accession, 20 per cent. more eighteen months later, 30 per cent. more a year thereafter, and the final 30 per cent. whenever the common external tariff was fully applied by the Community. Moreover, it was agreed that until the end of 1966 (or the conclusion of the comprehensive trade agreement) the enlarged Community would take steps to restore the situation if, as a result of the progressive application of the common external tariff by the United Kingdom, exports from these Asian countries to the enlarged Community were to decline. For imports of other manufactured goods from these three countries the so-called 'soft décalage' would be applied, that is, the British would progressively apply the common external tariff at the following rate: 15 per cent. on accession, 15 per cent. more on 1 July 1965, 20 per cent. more on 1 January 1967, 20 per cent. more on 1 July 1968, and the full rate on 1 January 1970. This was in contrast with the faster rate of application of the common tariff which had earlier been agreed for imports of manufactured goods from Canada, Australia, and New Zealand. (See footnote, p. 397, above.)

[43] Generally speaking, association was agreed to be a suitable arrangement for Commonwealth countries in Africa and the Caribbean and for most of the British dependencies. Hong Kong presented special problems which were discussed further during the autumn. The arrangement to be made for the Federation of Rhodesia and Nyasaland was deliberately left aside for later consideration since the break-up of the Federation appeared to be imminent.

The initial disappointment in the British Government at having had to adjourn for the summer holiday without the 'outline' agreement soon gave way to the more cheerful reflection that it might well be psychologically better to have the discussions with the Commonwealth Prime Ministers on the basis of an unfinished interim report. Conservative back-benchers, as well as the Opposition, had cautioned the Government against confronting the Commonwealth with a cut-and-dried, take-it-or-leave-it proposition and in this situation the interim character of the August White Paper was seen to have certain advantages. However, although the failure to reach agreement may have reassured those who feared that the Government was going too fast, and thus have had certain short-term political advantages, the dangers in the slowing down in the timetable which resulted from the failure to reach an outline agreement by August became apparent when the negotiations resumed in October.

XII

DISCUSSIONS ON POLITICAL UNION

Stalemate among the Six

Although the negotiations among the Six about political union were kept separate from the negotiations on British accession to the Community, the two sets of discussions interacted in a number of ways. As indicated in Chapters IX and X, the fact that the Six were discussing moves in the political field was an important factor in the British Government's decision to apply for membership and was a reason for its deciding to open negotiations in August 1961, rather than waiting for a more propitious climate on the Continent, particularly in France.[1] In turn, the British Government's desire to participate in the political discussions among the Six once the United Kingdom had become a member of the EEC— and to be kept fully informed of developments prior to that time— affected the discussions among the Six on political union. The obvious unreadiness of most of the British public for anything approaching political federation with the Continent, and the criticisms by the Labour Party of even the cautious endorsements given by the Government to the goal of political union, undoubtedly made Mr. Heath's task more difficult by casting doubt on Britain's long-term intentions and on the sincerity and the durability of the British Government's professed desire to become a full and active member of the European Community. Finally, the differences of view on political union—between 'Gaullists' and 'Europeans' and between each of them and the British—helped to create the political climate in which the breakdown of the negotiations occurred in January 1963.

As described in Chapter X, in the spring of 1961 a committee of government representatives (called first the Fouchet Committee

---

[1] This point was made by Mr. Heath in the debate in the House of Commons on 3 August 1961.

and later the Cattani Committee, after successive chairmen) had
been appointed by a 'Summit' meeting of the Six to formulate proposals for organizing co-operation in the political field. This was
not easy, for the Six disagreed on a number of fundamental points
and, in July (1961), a second 'Summit' meeting was held to try to
resolve these differences. The Bonn Declaration[2] issued at the
end of this meeting was ambiguous on a number of points, but it
represented an advance towards a common position. In particular,
the French had apparently gone some way to allay the fears of the
other Five that the kind of action wanted by General de Gaulle
would weaken the Atlantic Alliance and would undermine the
European Communities. Thus, the Bonn Declaration contained
affirmations, albeit in rather parenthetical terms, that a united
Europe would remain allied with the United States and would
serve to strengthen the Atlantic Alliance, and that by 'organising
their co-operation', the Six Governments would 'further the
application of the Rome and Paris Treaties'. Although there was no
specific commitment to move to a more 'federal' system at a later
date, such a move was not foreclosed by the Declaration and
could, at a pinch, be read into the first operative paragraph, which
said that the Heads of State, or Government, had decided 'to give
shape to the will for political union already implicit in the Treaties
establishing the European Communities, and for this purpose to
organise their co-operation, to provide for its development and to
secure for it the regularity which will progressively create the
conditions for a common policy and will ultimately make it
possible to embody in institutions the work undertaken'. However, it was clear from the second operative paragraph that, for
the present, the most that the French would contemplate was
'organised co-operation' through regular meetings of the Heads of
State, or Government. 'Necessary practical measures' would be
taken to prepare these meetings and the practice of holding periodic
meetings of Foreign Ministers (begun in 1960) would be continued.
It was also envisaged that other ministers would meet from time to
time, thus extending co-operation to the spheres of education,
culture, and research. The Fouchet Committee was instructed to
submit proposals to the Heads of State, or Government 'on the
means which will as soon as possible enable a statutory character
to be given to the union of their peoples'.

As already noted, Mr. Macmillan had commented approvingly

[2] The text of the Bonn Declaration is reproduced in Appendix B, p. 523.

on the Bonn Declaration during the debate in the House of
Commons on the British decision to apply to join the Community,
as had Mr. Heath in the statement he made to the Six on 10 October 1961. Both were careful to avoid giving offence to any in the
Six by attempting to construe the Declaration, but both made it
clear that they were following the political discussions closely and
that the British intended to play an active part in the political
construction once they had joined the Community.

The amount of real agreement represented by the Declaration
was rather less substantial than it seemed to be at the time of the
Bonn meeting and the Fouchet Committee made little progress.
In November 1961 the French submitted to the other members of
the Committee a draft treaty establishing a Union of States. The
Five felt this draft represented some back-sliding from the Bonn
Declaration and they proposed numerous modifications during
the Committee's discussions that autumn and winter.[3] The main
points at issue among the Six were variants of those that had been
at issue from the time General de Gaulle made his first proposals
for political co-operation in the summer of 1960: the institutional
arrangements, the relationship between any new institutions and
the existing Communities, the provisions for the accession of new
members and, in particular, of the United Kingdom, and the
connexion between any action on defence questions and the work
of the NATO. The French draft treaty seemed to the other Five to
be unsatisfactory on all these counts. Even the title proposed by the
French—'Union of States'—was unsatisfactory, for it reflected the
Gaullist concept that the important unit was the nation state, and
seemed to the others to represent a retreat from the phrase 'union
of their peoples' which had been used in the Bonn Declaration.

The institutional arrangements proposed by the French were
very much in line with the earlier proposals made by General de
Gaulle: a Council which would meet every four months at the
level of Heads of State, or of Government, and during the intervening period at least once at the level of Foreign Ministers, and
which would consider any matter proposed by a member state and
would take its decisions unanimously; a European Political
Commission, composed of high officials from the Ministries of
Foreign Affairs, which would sit in Paris and would prepare and

---

[3] The text of the French draft treaty and accounts of the objections raised by the
Five to this draft are contained in P.E.P., *The Negotiations on Political Union*,
Planning, Vol. XXVIII, No. 465, 1 October 1962, and in Pryce, op. cit.

carry out the Council's decisions; a European Parliament (the existing European Parliament), which would discuss matters concerning the aims of the Union. The Parliament could address oral or written questions to the Council and make recommendations to it. The Council would be required to let the Parliament know, within six months, what action it intended to take on these recommendations and to make an annual report to the Parliament, but it was clear enough that—in the French conception—the Parliament would be a purely advisory body with no real powers. Although there was a revision clause in the draft treaty which could be read as holding open the possibility of a later evolution towards a form of action comparable to that of the existing Communities, it could also be read, and read rather more easily, as indicating an intention to absorb the existing Communities into the institutional framework proposed for the political union.[4] In any case revisions could only be made by unanimity, so that so long as the Gaullist view prevailed in France there was no promise of an evolution towards the Community concept to which the rest of the Six attached importance. The Union was to be open to members of the Council of Europe provided they had previously become members of the European Communities; admission was not automatic, however, for the Council had to approve new members unanimously. Thus although participation in the European Communities was clearly a prior condition for membership in the political union, it would not ensure membership. There was no reference to the NATO or to the Atlantic Alliance in the French draft, although it could, with some difficulty, be read into the statement of one of the aims of the Union: 'To reinforce, in co-operation with the other free nations, the security of member states against any aggression by means of a common defence policy.'

During the discussions in the Fouchet Committee, the rest of the Six put forward various proposals designed to give the political union some of the characteristics of the existing Communities; to

---

[4] Article XVI of the draft treaty read as follows: 'Three years after the entry into force of the present treaty it will be submitted to a general revision which will have for its aim the examination of methods suitable to reinforce the Union, account having been taken of the progress already accomplished.

'This revision should have for its principal aims the achievement of a unified foreign policy and the progressive establishment of an organisation centralising, in the framework of the Union, the European Communities mentioned in the preamble to the present treaty. Amendments will be adopted by the procedure laid down in Article XV.' P.E.P., op. cit., p. 324.

emphasize the primary role of the NATO in the defence field; and to hold the door open to the British. Thus they suggested that there be an independent secretary-general with powers of initiative, assisted by an independent secretariat. This was not a 'Commission', but it was a step away from the French concept of a committee of national officials. They also suggested that when the treaty was revised after three years, majority voting for certain decisions should be introduced and the powers of the Parliament increased. Some of the Five also wanted to provide for direct elections to the Parliament at that time. It was also suggested that, even before the formal revision of the treaty, the Council could, by unanimity, agree to take certain kinds of decision by qualified majority voting. The Five also attached importance to making it clear that when the existing Communities were merged with the Union there should be no restrictions on the powers of the existing Communities. And the Five also made various proposals to ensure that the common defence policy would be carried out within the framework of the NATO. Finally, they sought to make membership of the political union automatic for members of the existing Communities.

There was little common ground between the French and the rest, and the tensions between them were exacerbated early in the new year (1962) when the French put forward a revised draft treaty which, far from taking account of the objections of the others, seemed to the Five to be even worse in many respects than the first draft.[5] There was still no mention of the NATO, and there was a suggestion that economic questions should come within the scope of the political union. This was interpreted—probably rightly—by the Five as a move against the powers of the existing Communities. In February 1962, General de Gaulle and Dr. Adenauer met in Baden-Baden in an attempt to try to find a way out of the stalemate that had been reached in the Fouchet Committee. This meeting was followed by another meeting of the Foreign Ministers of the Six in Luxembourg in March, and, in April, by the visit of General de Gaulle to Rome, and by talks between President Fanfani and Chancellor Adenauer. During this period there were frequent bilateral discussions within the Six, at various levels, as well as further attempts by the Fouchet (now Cattani) Committee to reach agreement on a draft statute. Finally, on 17 April 1962, the Foreign Ministers of the Six held an

[5] General de Gaulle was assumed to have been responsible for the revised draft.

important meeting in Paris. Some progress was made on the defence question and also on the need to respect the integrity of the existing Communities. It was agreed that the following specific reference to the Atlantic alliance should be inserted in the preamble: 'Holding that security should be maintained by common action in the field of defence which would contribute to the strengthening of the Atlantic alliance.' And a formula was found which met the French point that the Union—composed as it was of Heads of State—must be able to discuss economic questions, but reassured the rest that this would not be at the expense of the Communities by stating explicitly that the provisions of the new treaty should not affect the commitments in the Treaties of Paris and Rome and, in particular, 'the powers of the institutions and the working rules of the Communities'.[6] However, no agreement could be found on the revision clause. Moreover the Belgians and the Dutch were becoming worried lest the French Government, perhaps assisted by Dr. Adenauer, might try to keep the United Kingdom out of a future political union either by making it impossible for the British to join the Common Market or by subsequently refusing to agree to British participation in the political union. Accordingly they refused to sign any treaty until the British had joined the European Economic Community and could take part in the political discussions.

A French suggestion that the treaty be shown to the British and only signed by the Six if the United Kingdom indicated that the terms were acceptable was not felt by the Benelux ministers to be a guarantee against a later French or German 'blackball'. Moreover there was some suspicion that the French, aware of the British Government's domestic problems, were simply trying to make the British accession to the European Community more difficult by forcing the question of political union while the British negotiations on the Treaty of Rome were still in progress.

The kind of treaty the French wanted, and which the Germans, and probably the Italians, were now ready to accept, contained none of the 'supra-national' characteristics which had formerly been the essence of the difference in approach to European unity between the Six and the United Kingdom. But the Belgians and the Dutch, although they might well have gone ahead without the British with the signing of a political treaty founded on the 'Community' pattern, were only prepared to accept the kind of

[6] See P.E.P., op. cit., pp. 310–11.

treaty now under consideration if it was clear that the British
would become members. The Foreign Ministers adjourned, in
disagreement. No instructions for further work were given to the
Cattani Committee and no date was fixed for further ministerial
discussions of a draft treaty.

British views on political union

The British had been kept informed of the discussions in the
Fouchet Committee and just a week before the 17 April meeting
of the Six Foreign Ministers, Mr. Heath made a second long statement to the WEU Council on the British views about political
union, in the course of which he made it very plain that the United
Kingdom would like to be asked to take part in the discussions.
Like his earlier statement to the WEU Council in February 1961,
this statement was apparently resented by the French, who saw in
it an attempt to strengthen the Belgian and the Dutch resistance to
reaching an agreement without the British. At the time the WEU
meeting was arranged, it had been anticipated that the Six would
have reached agreement among themselves on the draft treaty
before the WEU meeting, and that the British would be giving
their views on an agreed draft. In the light of the continuing disagreement among the Six, it was, perhaps, not a very auspicious
time for a British statement. However, Mr. Heath displayed his
customary tact, and it is difficult to believe that the British statement
had as much to do with the stiff position taken by M. Spaak and
Mr. Luns as did their own suspicions about French motives and
their resentment at the Franco-German assumption that prior
agreements reached by the two big countries (and sometimes with
Italy) would, in the end, be accepted by the Benelux countries.[7]
    Although Mr. Heath, in his statement to the WEU Council on
10 April,[8] said that he was taking care not to comment on the texts
under discussion by the Six, he nevertheless made the British
position clear on a number of points known to be in dispute among

[7] The French Government was at this time refusing to consider various proposals for a NATO nuclear deterrent, and renewed uncertainty about the
French commitment to NATO added to the reluctance of the Benelux countries to commit themselves to a union without the United Kingdom. See
Financial Times, 18 April 1962.
[8] Mr. Heath's statement to the WEU Council, which was published as a White
Paper, *European Political Union* (Cmnd. 1720, H.M.S.O., 10 April 1962), is
reproduced in Appendix C, p. 525.

the Six as well as on one or two other points on which the British view was somewhat different from that of the Six as a group. In the first place he made it plain that the British assumed that the existing Communities would be the foundation on which 'Europe would be built'. 'We see the existing Communities continuing and expanding their work but knit together with the new political structure in a coherent and effective whole.' Although he was deliberately obscure about how the two would be knit together, he was clearly assuming that the powers of the existing Communities would not be diminished. In the second place he made it plain that the kind of Europe the British envisaged would stand 'shoulder to shoulder with the United States'. He indicated that the British felt that the European political union would inevitably be concerned with defence matters and that a European point of view on defence would emerge. However, although he agreed with the French that defence must, inescapably, be the concern of a political union, he came down very hard on the side of those who had been arguing that European defence arrangements must take place within an 'Atlantic' context: 'We must make it clear beyond all doubt that the object of our common policy is to defend and strengthen the liberties for which the Atlantic Alliance is the indispensable shield.'

Later in his speech Mr. Heath touched on the contentious issue of the revision clause. Here, the British unwillingness to commit themselves to a particular form of future development for the political union was closer to the French position than to that of the Five. However, he sought to reassure the Five by making it plain that he expected British views would evolve quite quickly: 'We do not think that at this stage it is wise to try to lay down the exact rhythm of future political developments. We are all politicians and we have to take account of present limitations as well as of future possibilities. . . . The element of caution in our present outlook might impose on us an attitude of reserve if we were asked to commit ourselves now to specific forms of political machinery, or to particular courses of action at a fixed moment in the future—whereas when we reach that moment we may well find that the course of action seems quite natural and perfectly obvious.' And he gave point to his assumption that British opinion would develop rapidly: 'As members of the Community we will, I am sure, want to see the European Parliament playing an important part. But it is not easy for us to commit ourselves, at this stage and before we have participated in the work of the Assembly, as to what that part should be or as to how it should be accomplished.' Mr. Heath made it abundantly clear that the British wanted to join the political union at the same time as they joined the European Economic Community and that (in accordance with assurances they had already been given) they expected to be consulted before the treaty was finally agreed. He then went on to suggest that the British, 'as impending members of the European Economic Community', be asked to join the Six in their discussions 'about the future political framework of Europe'.

In addition to these comments which were directly related to points then under discussion among the Six, Mr. Heath also put on record the British position on two other points. In the first place he indicated that the 'European' neutrals had a part to play in the 'new Europe'. He assumed they would not be part of the 'central core', but he felt they should be associated with the Community and that this could be done in such a way 'as not to weaken the political and economic cohesion of the central nucleus of full members'. At this time there was considerable discussion among the Six on the arrangements to be made for the neutrals in the context of the Brussels negotiations, and M. Spaak, in particular, had recently indicated fairly strong opposition to any form of association.[9] Mr. Heath also went out of his way to make it clear that he saw no conflict between British membership in a political union and the Commonwealth connexion: 'We shall, of course, retain our constitutional ties and the arrangements for consultation with the Commonwealth, which we have worked out. In my judgement these will be a source of strength to Europe. They will in no way prevent us from participating fully in the growth of a new Europe, and this in its turn will give fresh vitality to our Commonwealth connexions.'

Mr. Heath's statement to the WEU Council was the most complete statement of the British Government's views about the political development of the Community that was made during the negotiations. Although he did not formally commit the

---

[9] M. Spaak expressed doubts about the desirability of having the neutrals associated with the Community on a number of occasions: in a speech to a meeting in Brussels of trade union representatives from the Six on 10 January 1962 (see *Le Soir*, 16 January 1962); in a speech to the Belgian Chamber of Commerce in New York on 25 January 1962 (see *New York Times*, 26 January 1962); and, later, in May 1962, to the Assembly of the Council of Europe.

Government to anything, his clear recognition of the political aspirations of the founders of the Community, his acceptance of the logic of the extension of the Community to the fields of foreign policy and defence, and his open-mindedness about future institutional development contrasted sharply with the excessive caution previously shown by all British Governments to European plans for political union. Moreover, although Mr. Heath's statement to the WEU Council corresponded fairly closely to the views of what might be called the 'European élite' in the United Kingdom, it was substantially in advance of public opinion generally.

In particular, Mr. Gaitskell and other Labour Party leaders were not only outspokenly opposed to participation in a 'federal Europe' but were even critical of the very mild dose of 'supranationalism' in the existing Communities, an attitude the Socialists on the Continent, who were for the most part strong 'Europeans', found hard to understand. At various times Mr. Gaitskell advocated greater control by the Council of Ministers over the Commission and a weakening in the two-thirds majority rule, two moves which ran directly counter to steps M. Spaak and other European Socialists were advocating in order to strengthen the Communities. It was clear that the kind of Europe of which Mr. Gaitskell approved was very different from the Europe of the 'Europeans'. Mr. Gaitskell's Europe, as it emerged from his various speeches during the summer and autumn of 1962, was a Europe based essentially on co-operation among states, a Europe whose outer edges were fuzzy and intentionally not very clearly drawn (inclusiveness was prized above cohesiveness), a Europe whose members were loosely joined together in a customs union but maintained economic links with other countries as well, a Europe which was low-tariff and liberal in its external policies, a Europe that made no attempt to plan or to use its resources as common resources, and a Europe which—although the members' policies might be loosely co-ordinated—did not seek to act as a unit in its relations with third countries and was not interested in becoming a political or military bloc.[10]

To many of the Continentals, both 'Europeans' and Gaullists, the Gaitskell concept was little more than the 'Europe of the OEEC' which both these groups, although for different reasons,

---

[10] See particularly Mr. Gaitskell's speech at Brighton, his speech in the debate in the House of Commons on 7 November 1962, and his speech to the Anglo-American Press Association in Paris on 3 December 1962.

considered inadequate, irrelevant, and not what the negotiations in Brussels were about.[11] Although Mr. Heath's speech to the WEU Council was clearly a considered statement of policy by the British Government, Mr. Gaitskell's Europe was fairly close to the Europe favoured by much of the Conservative Party as well as by most of the Labour Party. In consequence, when speaking to British audiences Government spokesmen tended to be more cautious and circumspect than Mr. Heath had been and to emphasize the limited nature of the commitments being undertaken in the Treaty of Rome and the need for unanimity before any extension of the Community's activities into the political realm could take place.[12] Similarly, when discussing the contentious issue of 'sovereignty', Government spokesmen normally played safe and emphasized the strictly limited infringement of sovereignty represented by the Treaty of Rome. There was little inclination to paint the positive advantages of transcending sovereignty by moving to a new kind of relationship among states.[13]

[11] Sharp differences of view about Europe between the leaders of the British Labour Party and the European Socialists were aired in July 1962 during a meeting in Brussels at which Mr. Gaitskell and M. Spaak found themselves in fairly complete disagreement. The difference of view between the European Socialists and the British Socialists also seems to have been the reason that M. Mollet suggested to Mr. Gaitskell during their discussions in Paris in December 1962 that 'association' might be a better arrangement than membership for the United Kingdom. The Labour Party's views on Europe are discussed further in Chapter XIII.

[12] See for example Mr. Macmillan's statements on 17 July 1962 in the House of Commons, *Hansard*, cols. 226–9. In his principal speech at the Conservative Party Conference at Llandudno Mr. Macmillan said: 'It is true that the governments of the Six are anxious to move forward from an economic to some form of political union and we want to play our part in devising these new arrangements. But so far there is no agreement as to the form they should take. Mr. Gaitskell now prattles about our being reduced to the status of Texas or California. What nonsense! . . . Certainly if I believed that I would not touch it on any terms. The approach of the six existing members of the Community is gradual and pragmatic—as our own has been on constitutional development. In any case, any agreement reached in this field must be by unanimous consent. There can be no question, therefore, of Britain being outvoted into some arrangement which we found incompatible with our needs and responsibilities and traditions.' *The Times*, 15 October 1962.

[13] It is worth noting here that on 2 August 1962 the Lord Chancellor (Lord Dilhorne) made a statement in the House of Lords describing in detail the implications of the Treaty of Rome for the Crown, Parliament, the Executive, and the Courts. In the course of his long, precise, legal exposition he made the point that an Act of Parliament would be required to apply the treaty and that like any other Act of Parliament that Act could be repealed by a subsequent Act. He went out of his way to make it clear that although 'Parliament's power to repeal the Act applying the treaty remains, and cannot be

General de Gaulle's views

The Continentals, as well as the British, were uncertain and divided in their views on political union, but on the Continent the divisions were, as outlined above, about the form a European political union should take and about the political orientation of such a union rather than, as so often in the United Kingdom, about whether any kind of political union was desirable. However, by the spring of 1962, the Benelux countries had decided that, despite the all too apparent differences of view in the United Kingdom, the kind of evolutionary pragmatism advocated by the British Government offered some prospect for development in the political field and that it was, at least, less of a threat to the integrity of the Community, on the one hand, and the NATO alliance, on the other, than was the kind of political construction advocated by General de Gaulle. The Benelux Governments were confirmed in their view that the 'Europe' of General de Gaulle was in direct conflict with their own 'Europe' by the long statement on the subject which General de Gaulle made at his press conference on 15 May 1962. At this press conference, General de Gaulle gave the first instalment of his views on Europe. At his press conference of 14 January 1963, when he dealt with the subject of British membership, he gave the second instalment: this followed logically from the first and his two long statements should be read together (see below, Chapter XIV).

In his press conference on 15 May, General de Gaulle first described the proposals that the French had made to the Fouchet Committee and then, in response to a question about the objections that had been raised to the French plan, 'notably by M. Paul-Henri Spaak' and also during the recent debate in the French National Assembly, he made the following points. First he said he had never used the term *l'Europe des patries* which was frequently attributed to him but that he nevertheless agreed that at the present time there could be no other Europe than the 'Europe

---

fettered', such a step would only be justified in exceptional circumstances and that 'if it were taken without justification and without the approval of other member countries, it would be a breach of the international obligation assumed on entry into the Common Market'. (See *Hansard*, House of Lords, 2 August 1962, cols. 416–26.) Nevertheless this section of his statement caused considerable consternation in some circles on the Continent and apparently contributed to Dr. Adenauer's growing coolness towards British membership.

of the states', apart, of course, from the 'myths, stories and parades', by which he meant the conception of the 'Europeans'. He then rubbed salt into the wounds by a brutal description of the degree to which the European Community was still dependent on political decisions of governments, which, although technically accurate, discounted to a rather unfair extent the role of the Commission. He then ridiculed the ideas which M. Spaak held and which the Five generally had been advocating in the Fouchet Committee.

There were those who said 'Let us merge the six states into a supra-national entity; this way, things will be quite simple and practical.' But such an entity cannot be found without there being in Europe today a federator with sufficient power, authority and skill. That is why one falls back on a type of hybrid, in which the six states would undertake to comply with what will be decided upon by a certain majority. . . . These are ideas that may, perhaps, beguile certain minds, but I certainly do not see how they could be carried out in practice, even if there were six signatures on the dotted line. . . . It is true that in this 'integrated' Europe, as they say, there would perhaps be no policy at all. This would simplify things a great deal. Indeed, once there would be no France and no Europe, once there would be no policy—since no one policy could be imposed on each of the six states—one would refrain from making any policies at all. But then, perhaps, this world would follow the lead of some outsider who did have a policy. There would perhaps be a federator, but the federator would not be European. And it would not be an integrated Europe, it would be something quite different, much broader and much more extensive with, I repeat, a federator. Perhaps it is this which, sometimes and to a certain degree, is at the basis of some remarks of such or such an advocate of European integration. In that case, it would be best to say so.[14]

This was a double-barrelled attack on the 'Europeans'. First, it accused them of unreality; secondly, of being dupes of the United States (the federator), a foreshadowing of the Trojan Horse theme that was to become a prominent feature of the Gaullist line later in the year (see Chapter XIV). This speech produced strong reactions on the part of the 'Europeans'. In France, M. Pflimlin and the other four MRP ministers in M. Pompidou's Government resigned in protest.[15] Early in June, 293 deputies signed a manifesto setting forth their views on European union, which were clearly opposed

[14] The quotations are from the English text supplied by the French Embassy, London, and the French Information Service, New York, Speeches and Press Conferences, No. 175, 15 May 1962.
[15] See The Times, 17 May 1962.

to the de Gaulle view, for they favoured a 'democratic community of peoples' rather than a series of conferences between governments 'in the diplomatic style of yesterday'.[16] At the end of the month, M. Monnet's Action Committee for the United States of Europe also took issue with the conception of General de Gaulle, pointing out that the true 'federator' was not some outside power, as General de Gaulle had implied, but the 'new method of collective action' which operated within the European Community. In their declaration the Committee also, in effect, endorsed the kind of political Community that the Five had pressed for during the Fouchet Committee discussions and called for the rapid conclusion of a treaty initiating a political union and also of the negotiations on British entry into the European Community.[17]

There was at this time considerable feeling both in Westminster and in Whitehall that British views on political union were closer to those of General de Gaulle than they were to those of the 'Europeans' and that this similarity in view should make British membership in the Common Market more welcome to General de Gaulle. As was to become plain later, this was an illusion, for although General de Gaulle and the British agreed that co-operation among states must be the basis on which political union should be built, they disagreed much more profoundly than did the British and the 'Europeans' about the orientation of an eventual political union. Moreover the apparently similar dislike of

[16] See *The Times*, 14 June 1962.
[17] Action Committee for the United States of Europe, *Joint Declaration* of 26 June 1962. The section on political union read as follows: 'Just as we have had to change outmoded forms of national economic relations in order to arrive at a European Common Market, so the forms of national political relations will have to be gradually changed before a unified political outlook is achieved.

'At present, it is still not possible to apply to foreign policy rules and institutions such as are suitable for dealing with the material problems of the economy.

'Any agreement organising the system of cooperation that will be necessary at the outset must clearly guarantee the continuity and future of economic integration, which is the basis of political union. This economic integration cannot be called in question, either now or in the future.

'Thus, when Heads of State and Government confer together about questions which are matters for the Communities they must necessarily be bound by the rules and procedures adopted under these treaties drawn up by the member States.

'It should now be made clear that after the initial period of cooperation the revision of the commitments entered into by the States should provide for the gradual adaptation to the political sphere of the method which has already made it possible to achieve the economic integration of Europe.'

'supra-national institutions' was rather different in motivation: the British were worried about the spectre of government by bureaucracy without parliamentary control, as well as about the loss of their own freedom of action; the Gaullists were concerned by the threat that supra-nationalism posed to their own power to fashion Europe to their own design—the same concern that was the root of their opposition to British membership in the Community. The British tendency to over-simplify the similarities between their own views and those of General de Gaulle caused some needless concern to their 'European' friends, but cut little ice with General de Gaulle.[18]

Shortly after General de Gaulle's press conference of 15 May, Mr. Macmillan visited him at the Château de Champs. Despite the clear differences between General de Gaulle and the Five about the kind of Europe they wanted, both 'Europeans' and Gaullists shared doubts about whether the British were really prepared to become European, in either the 'European' or the Gaullist sense, and these doubts were hampering the negotiations in Brussels as well as blocking British participation in the negotiations on political union. At the Champs meeting on 1 and 2 June, Mr. Macmillan sought to convince General de Gaulle of the depth of the British decision to join the Community and tried to make it clear that the British Government was prepared to follow the policy of unity with Europe to its logical conclusions. Although the more extravagant statements that appeared in the French press were rather wide of the mark, General de Gaulle was apparently genuinely surprised to find how far Mr. Macmillan was prepared to go to give priority to Britain's European role and to accept the consequential changes in British relations with the Commonwealth and the United States.[19] From the information available it seems clear that, looking ahead, Mr. Macmillan indicated that he saw much the same kind of development in Europe as General de Gaulle was known to want: a confederal Europe possessing the means of its own defence and capable of dealing on equal terms with the United States. As he later made plain, General de Gaulle did not share Mr. Macmillan's conviction that a stronger and more unified Europe must necessarily work in close partnership with

[18] Some of the oversimplification arose from the fact that the British Government found it convenient to reassure those in the United Kingdom who were opposed to any form of political federation by pointing to General de Gaulle's opposition as sufficient guarantee against any such development.

[19] See *Financial Times*, 10 June 1962.

the United States but—at this meeting—this difference seems not to have been pursued, for within the limits of the matters discussed there appears to have been no great divergence of view about the kind of development that was desirable and might reasonably be expected to occur in Europe. And, contrary to expectations, a short communiqué was issued after the meeting indicating that the two Heads of Government had agreed on 'the community of interests' between Britain and France.

Before the Champs meeting there had been much speculation in the British press that General de Gaulle would exact some promise on the sharing of nuclear secrets as the price of British participation in the Community, and this appears to have been a possibility that worried the British Government. There was very little that the British could have given to the French without American agreement and it was unlikely that the United States would have looked with favour on the British giving to the French information which they themselves had recently once again decided not to give, despite strong pressure from the French and some pressure from within the United States Administration. In the event General de Gaulle did not raise the question, as might have been foreseen, for he is not one to put himself in the position of suppliant. However, the British relief that the nuclear question did not figure prominently in the discussions was, perhaps, shortsighted. Although it was a crude oversimplification to argue, as some commentators did, that the British could and should buy their way into Europe with their nuclear weapons, it was clear that General de Gaulle's interest in an organized Europe was a military-political interest and that in his mind the acid test of whether or not the British were European would be the way they looked at the problem of defence. But at Champs in June 1962, and again at Rambouillet in December 1962, the known areas of disagreement in the defence field seem to have been skirted rather than probed. Perhaps Mr. Macmillan's principal achievement at Champs was to make General de Gaulle realize that the British Government was prepared to go very far indeed to meet the conditions on which the Six were insisting. However, since the result seems to have been to start the General thinking more deeply than before about the implications for France of an expansion of the Community, Champs, in retrospect, was perhaps not the success it seemed to be at the time.[20]

[20] See *Financial Times*, 10 June 1962, and also *The Times*, 14 June 1962.

Shortly after the Champs meeting, M. Couve de Murville made a long statement to the National Assembly covering both the question of British membership in the Community and French ideas on political union. His statement seemed to reflect a new French feeling that the Brussels negotiations might, in fact, succeed, although he continued to emphasize the difficulty of the choice facing the British and made it clear that, in the view of France and her partners in the Community, Britain must truly enter the Common Market as an integral member and not just be 'juxtaposed to it'. However, although he felt the initial positions of the British and of the Six had been far apart, he felt that they were 'perhaps not irreconcilable, if we asked only the normal and if the British intended sincerely to become Europeans'. Moreover, he added: 'We French can only welcome her with friendship if she chooses the path—for Britain, difficult and courageous—that leads to Europe.' He pointed out that: 'This united Europe will certainly be more modest, but also more cohesive, if it remains limited to the Six; it will be looser, but perhaps more impressive, if Britain and the other nations find their places.' M. Couve de Murville made it clear that France intended to pursue the task of European construction whether or not the Community was extended, and he made it clear enough that the Gaullist Europe was to be a new power group which would have to define and practise a common foreign policy, and must have a defence policy. Little by little Europe would become, within the Atlantic Alliance, an equal partner of the United States. And finally the creation of Europe would lead to *règlement pacifique* from 'the Atlantic to the Urals'. Because of the fact that the Europe expanded to include the United Kingdom and perhaps others (he mentioned Denmark and Norway) would be a different, less cohesive Europe from that which had originally been conceived, M. Couve de Murville also made it clear that the French saw little point in trying to push ahead with the discussions about political union until it was known whether or not Britain was to join the Community, a question which he then thought would be answered one way or the other by the autumn.[21]

In his press conference on 15 May 1962 General de Gaulle, as well as outlining his ideas for the political construction of Europe, had also commented at some length on the NATO. As he had

[21] See *The Times*, 14 June 1962, and Assemblée Nationale, *Journal Officiel*, 13 June 1962, pp. 1664–6.

done on numerous occasions he reaffirmed that the Atlantic Alliance must be maintained for as long as Soviet power threatened the world and made it clear that if the free world were attacked France would take part in the common defence with all the means at her disposal. Nevertheless he also made it clear that an 'integrated' NATO force was in his eyes simply a polite way of describing American domination and that it was 'both morally and politically indispensable' for the defence of France 'to become once again a national defence'. Although, as noted above, M. Couve de Murville had used the language of the 'Europeans' and had talked about a 'Europe' that would become an 'equal partner' with the United States within the Alliance, it was clear enough already—and became clearer as the year wore on—that General de Gaulle's over-riding concern was not with the formation of a partnership but with the achievement of equality. It was also plain that for General de Gaulle 'independence' and 'nationalism' had reality, whereas 'interdependence' and 'integration' were woolly abstractions cloaking continued dependence on the United States. For this reason President Kennedy's speech on 4 July 1962, in which he stressed the need for 'interdependence' and spoke more forcefully and authoritatively than had yet been done of the prospect of an 'equal partnership' between the United States and 'a strong and united Europe', may well have had a different effect from that intended. It seems probable that rather than being a stimulus to the rapid consolidation of Europe the speech contributed to the General's conviction that British membership in the European Community would prejudice his own design for Europe.

Partly, at least, because of the prevailing feeling that it would be clear by the autumn whether or not the United Kingdom was to become the seventh member of the EEC, the Six abandoned their own efforts to try to come to some agreement on political union during the summer. But by the autumn the question of British membership was still unsettled, and both General de Gaulle and Dr. Adenauer had become less interested in pursuing the question on a Six-country basis than they were in pushing ahead bilaterally.[22]

[22] Apparently the idea of a Franco-German treaty was suggested by General de Gaulle very soon after the stalemate of 17 April 1962 in the discussions among the Six on the Fouchet plan. In the light of later events, it seems possible that General de Gaulle lost interest in pushing ahead with the Fouchet plan less because of the Belgian and Dutch opposition than because it was plain from Mr. Heath's statement to the WEU Council on 10 April 1962 that the British Government would, in fact, have been ready to accept the Fouchet plan.

Early in July, Dr. Adenauer paid a highly successful state visit to France which culminated dramatically in a High Mass in Rheims Cathedral. In September, General de Gaulle paid a triumphal return visit to Germany, during which it became clear that the relationship between the two countries was entering a new stage. The 'Great Reconciliation' had been achieved: the two Heads of Government had a new objective, that of a political union between their two countries as the basis of a European union.

Despite his long attachment to the concepts of the 'Europeans' and his earlier suspicions of General de Gaulle, Dr. Adenauer had become increasingly impatient with the rest of the Six and by mid-1962 he attached more importance to making progress on some form of political union before his retirement than he did to the preservation of the 'Community' method. He had also become increasingly cool to the expansion of the Community to include the British, and he was annoyed with the Benelux countries for holding up the political discussions until the question of British membership was clearer.[23] At a state banquet at Bruhl, near Bonn, on 4 September General de Gaulle made it clear that in his view France and Germany should not wait for the rest of the Six but should proceed with a union between themselves on the basis of the plan proposed by the French in the Fouchet Committee. A few days later, Dr. Adenauer referred to these remarks of General de Gaulle, and indicated that he, too, felt the two countries should go ahead together, although he was apparently convinced that others would soon join.[24] Other German and French ministers were more sensitive than were the two leaders to the objections of the rest of the Six to the formation of a Bonn–Paris axis, and they sought to play down the significance of these statements and to deny that institutional arrangements between the two countries were under consideration. The final communiqué simply referred to the desire of the two statesmen 'to continue and accelerate an evolution which meets not only the interests of the two countries, but also those of all peace-loving peoples', and indicated that 'practical steps will be taken by the two Governments to strengthen effectively the bonds which already exist in a great number of spheres'.[25]

[23] Dr. Adenauer apparently felt that although British membership in the Economic Community might be inevitable, membership in a political community or union need not follow automatically. See the account of his television interview in *The Times*, 30 August 1962.

[24] See *The Times*, 6 and 7 September 1962.

[25] For the text of the communiqué see *The Times*, 8 September 1962.

However, during the autumn French and German officials drafted an agreement on political co-operation which, at the initiative of the German Government, was given the form of a treaty. The treaty was signed during Dr. Adenauer's visit to Paris in January 1963. By that time, General de Gaulle had made clear his decision to exclude the British from the European Community and the strength of the new bond between Dr. Adenauer and General de Gaulle had taken on a new significance.

XIII

THE COMMONWEALTH PRIME MINISTERS' MEETING AND THE PARTY CONFERENCES

THE conference of Commonwealth Prime Ministers was held in September (1962) while the Brussels negotiations were adjourned for the summer vacation. The annual conferences of the three political parties followed in quick succession. The Commonwealth conference and the Conservative Party conference had come to be regarded as key tests of the British Government's decision to seek to join the Community. If these meetings passed off uneventfully, it was assumed that the Macmillan Government would have little difficulty in obtaining support for any agreement it felt able to sign. It was less clear what would happen if strong opposition developed at either conference, a possibility no minister liked to contemplate. The first hurdle, the Commonwealth meeting, was taken with determination but not without difficulty; the second hurdle, the Conservative Party conference, was taken with surprising ease, thanks, in part, to the strictures of Mr. Gaitskell and the hardening of the Labour Party's position against entry, which inevitably tended to mute Conservative criticisms.

The Commonwealth Prime Ministers' meeting

The Prime Ministers of the Commonwealth countries traditionally meet together from time to time, not on an annual basis (as it has become customary for the Finance Ministers to do) but when there is a general feeling that it would be useful to do so, and usually at the initiative of the United Kingdom Government. During the spring of 1961 there was some pressure from the Commonwealth and some domestic political pressure in the United Kingdom for the convening of a Prime Ministers' meeting before any decision was taken to open negotiations with the Six. Although that proposal was successfully headed off by Mr. Macmillan it was clear that a full-dress conference would generally be felt to be desirable before any final decision was taken to join the Community. And when he announced the Government's decision to open negotiations Mr. Macmillan indicated that he thought the Commonwealth Prime Ministers would wish to meet 'when the negotiations had reached a certain stage before any final decisions were put before Parliament and this country'.[1]

Fairly early in 1962, Opposition spokesmen in the House of Commons began pressing the Government to set a firm date, and on 19 April, Mr. Macmillan announced in the House of Commons that the Prime Ministers would meet on 10 September 1962. He was taking a considerable risk in setting a date, for at this time no agreements had been reached in the negotiations in Brussels on any of the questions affecting the Commonwealth. The kind of compromise that would be found for some questions was reasonably clear, but it was not at all clear what arrangements would be found for the single most difficult problem, temperate-zone agriculture. Nevertheless it was a risk that had to be taken, for it is difficult to call Prime Ministers together at short notice and the timetable on which the British Government was operating was a tight one. Moreover, despite the British reluctance to set deadlines at the start of the negotiations, there was considerable feeling during the spring of 1962 that unless some objective, such as the achievement of 'outline' agreement before September, were adopted, the negotiations might never come into focus, but drag on interminably, with more studies being called for whenever difficulties were encountered. The objective of an 'outline' agreement was not attained, but the general nature of the arrangements that could be made for the Commonwealth countries was clear enough by the time the negotiating conference was adjourned in August, although some things which the British had hoped to negotiate to make the package sweeter, such as nil or reduced tariffs, were still undecided.

Normally the greatest discretion surrounds the Commonwealth Prime Ministers' meetings, the communiqués are short and perfunctory, and great care is taken to preserve an atmosphere of frank, friendly, and confidential discussion. The Prime Ministers' meeting that began on 10 September 1962 broke sharply with this tradition. Long summaries, or full texts, of most of the opening and closing speeches by the assembled Prime Ministers were

[1] *Hansard*, House of Commons, 31 July 1961, cols. 932–3.

released to the press and no attempt was made to disguise the fact that, at times, the atmosphere was highly charged. It is arguable that it would have been better if the press had been allowed in the conference chamber, at least for the opening and closing discussions, since the drama seems to have been heightened in the retelling. Mr. Macmillan opened the conference with a long statement on the reasons for joining the Community. This was the most forthright and strongest statement of the Government's political and economic reasons for applying for membership that had yet been presented to any group. It was the hope of the British Government that, by opening the conference in these terms, it could lift the discussion above the details of the negotiation and persuade the other Commonwealth Prime Ministers to look at the crucial problem of Britain's future role in the world in a broad and understanding way, and that the other Prime Ministers would be ready to discuss the terms of entry not as a static calculation of gains and losses but as part of a dynamic process. The case that the Prime Minister put to the conference in his opening statement was essentially the same as the one he put forward in the pamphlet he wrote shortly afterwards for circulation by the Conservative Central Office.[2] It was also substantially the same as the case he made in his broadcast to the country after the Prime Ministers' meeting and that he later made to the Conservative Party conference at Llandudno.

Mr. Macmillan's statement to the Commonwealth conference, which he subsequently made to the country, was a much more outspoken and 'committed' statement than the one he had made in the House of Commons in the summer of 1961, but, in essence, it was a further development of views that were generally known to have been at the root of his decision. It was above all a political case and one that was based not on a static view of the world but on a long-term evolutionary view, taking full account of trends within

[2] Harold Macmillan, *Britain, the Commonwealth and Europe*, published by the Conservative Central Office, undated (September 1962). In the introduction Mr. Macmillan stated that at the Commonwealth conference British ministers were able to explain in detail to the Commonwealth leaders 'the reasons why, in our view, British membership of the European Community would be a source of new strength, not only to this country, but to the Commonwealth as a whole; and conversely, why a Britain detached from Europe would mean inflicting permanent injury on our common cause. Now that the Conference is over I would like to put the same arguments before the British public, for I believe that they can help to remove many of the misunderstandings which have arisen over this great issue' (p. 3).

the Commonwealth, within Europe, and in the rest of the world. Inevitably, perhaps, Mr. Macmillan once again denied that Britain was faced with a 'choice' between the Commonwealth and Europe, but for the first time he made it plain that the reason there was no choice was because the Commonwealth and the European Community were two 'entirely different types of organization', and he stressed in a way that had not been done before that the Commonwealth was not a single economic unity and that there was no 'practical possibility of making it one'.[3] He pointed out the changes that had taken place since the Ottawa Agreements had been signed some thirty years earlier and made it plain that, although British entry into the Common Market would mean the end of the present system of free entry and preferential treatment for Commonwealth goods, the British market was not big enough to 'absorb the growing production of the Commonwealth countries'. What the Commonwealth needed was more capital and larger markets, and the United Kingdom could be more influential acting as a member of the Community than it could be acting alone in securing a 'fundamental reshaping of the present framework of world trade'. To those who feared that the Commonwealth would never be the same again if Britain joined the Community, he pointed out that the Commonwealth was not the same today as it had been 'ten or even five years ago'.

In reviewing the reasons for joining, Mr. Macmillan made it clear that, in his view, this was the way not only for the United Kingdom to 'gain a new stature in Europe, but also increase its standing and influence in the councils of the world'. A united Europe would be able 'to stand on an equal footing with the great power groupings of the world'. If the United Kingdom held aloof it seemed to him inevitable that the United States would increasingly concert its policies with the Community and pay much less attention to British views. 'To lose influence both in Europe and Washington . . . would seriously undermine our international position and hence, one must add, our usefulness to the Commonwealth.' Although Mr. Macmillan acknowledged that political unity was the central aim of the European countries and that 'we would naturally accept that ultimate goal', he rather played down the implications of political unity and again made it clear that, as a member, the United Kingdom would be in a position to influence developments, whereas by remaining outside 'we could be faced

[3] Macmillan, op. cit., p. 4.

with a political solution in Europe which ran counter to our views and interests but which we could do nothing to influence'.

Mr. Macmillan's speech to the Commonwealth Prime Ministers was made against the background of considerable debunking of the economic advantages of joining the Common Market. At the start of the debate in the United Kingdom those who advocated British membership had undoubtedly overplayed the economic advantages of joining and had over-dramatized the economic consequences of staying out. Professional economists were rather slow to make predictions one way or the other, but when they began they tended to take issue with the earlier exaggerated statements. No forecasting was worth very much since to a large extent the economic calculation was based on subjective judgements about how British industry would respond to the new situation and equally hazardous guesses about the alternative actions that might be taken if the United Kingdom did not join. However, once the pendulum began to swing, the tendency was not simply to correct but to overcorrect the earlier optimistic forecasts. Mr. Macmillan sought to reinstate the economic argument by making it clear that the Government did not take the cautious, and at that time fashionable, view that the economic advantages and disadvantages were evenly balanced, but believed that the 'economic opportunities which the Common Market offers to Britain greatly outweigh the risks involved'.[4]

Mr. Macmillan was followed by Mr. Heath, who gave a detailed account of the state of the negotiations in Brussels. Unfortunately for the British, Mr. Diefenbaker (Canada) was the first of the visiting Prime Ministers to comment. As he had done on Mr. Sandys' visit to Canada before the British opened negotiations, he challenged Mr. Macmillan's basic assumption that the right role for the United Kingdom—and the one which would enable the British to play the most constructive role in the world—was as a member of the European Community. He felt that Commonwealth links would inevitably be weakened and that the consequence for Canada, at least, might well be that she would be drawn increasingly into the orbit of the United States. Mr. Diefenbaker, like most of the Prime Ministers who followed him, felt the terms of entry were too imprecise for any final judgement, but that in so far as they were now known they were inadequate. To the considerable annoyance of the British Ministers, he pointedly quoted a number of their earlier flat assertions that no British Government

4 Macmillan, op. cit., p. 7.

could contemplate joining the European Common Market because of the inevitable damage to the Commonwealth.

Although Mr. Diefenbaker was the most critical, the only Ministers who seemed content with the course of the negotiations were Tun Abdul Razak of Malaya and Dr. Williams of Trinidad and Tobago. Mr. Holyoake, the New Zealand Prime Minister, impressed British Ministers, as he had throughout the formal and informal consultations with the Commonwealth countries, by his reasonableness and by his willingness to accept the British case for entry, although he, too, made it clear enough that the terms thus far agreed were too vague to give New Zealand the assurances needed to save her from 'economic disaster', a term that he said he was using modestly. He indicated that if at the end of the negotiations New Zealand's vital interests had been assured, he would support British entry, although, like others, he expressed doubts about the effect on the Commonwealth if the United Kingdom were increasingly to become sucked into a united Europe. Mr. Menzies (Australia) had much more pronounced doubts on this score; speaking as a representative of a federal state he felt it was an illusion to suppose that once the process of integration with Europe had begun the United Kingdom would be able to play for long a leading role in the Commonwealth. On his return to Australia, Mr. Menzies commented on the paragraph in the Commonwealth Prime Ministers' communiqué which stated: 'They trusted that should there be closer association between Britain and Europe it would not be allowed, as it developed, to weaken the cohesion of the Commonwealth.' 'Now that', he said, 'is putting in the language of diplomacy the view that federation, as we understand the term, is not to be desired.' According to the account in The Times, he said he had given a warning in London that history showed that when nations became associated in some form of political confederation, the confederation either developed into a federation or broke up.[5] Mr. Menzies was also highly critical of the terms thus far agreed, criticizing them both for their vagueness and because too much of the final price seemed to be payable by the Commonwealth.[6]

After the three old Dominions—Canada, Australia, New Zealand—the Commonwealth countries that carry the most weight in the House of Commons, and in the United Kingdom generally,

[5] See The Times, 1 October 1962.
[6] Ibid., 12 September 1962.

are India and Pakistan. Before the conference opened, Mr. Gaitskell had met with the leaders of the Labour Parties from a number of the Commonwealth countries, and following these discussions a communiqué had been issued which was highly critical of the agreements set out in the August White Paper. The Government's task was undoubtedly complicated by this semi-official ventilation of Commonwealth attitudes on the eve of the formal conference, for the Prime Ministers had, inevitably, to be as forthright in the defence of their own national interests as the leaders of their opposition parties. Perhaps the person who made the biggest impact in these preliminary discussions (particularly on Mr. Gaitskell) was Mr. Lall (the Indian Ambassador in Brussels), who had been sharply critical of the fact that Mr. Heath had provisionally agreed to start applying the common external tariff to Asian manufactures before the promised negotiations on trade agreements with the Asian countries were undertaken by the enlarged Community.

During the Prime Ministers' conference, both the Pakistan Prime Minister and Mr. Nehru attacked this same point. Mr. Ayub Khan apparently made the more forceful speech, placing great emphasis on the need for a radical reshaping of world trade patterns, so that the developing countries could find markets for their relatively simple, labour-intensive manufactures, while the developed countries concentrated increasingly on more advanced types of manufacture. Mr. Ayub Khan was also the most critical of any of the Prime Ministers of the protectionist tendencies of the Six. Mr. Nehru, although sharing Mr. Ayub Khan's view that the proposed trading arrangements were not good enough, was apparently more concerned about broad political questions than about the commercial implications: he felt that Britain's joining the Community might add to the tensions between East and West.

Of the three main groups at the conference—the old Dominions, the Asians, and the Africans—the African group was the one the British Government thought had least cause for being critical of Mr. Heath's achievements since they were to be offered association with the enlarged Community on the same basis as the existing associates. Nevertheless even the African Prime Ministers were for the most part dissatisfied. The Ghanaians had always made it plain that they were opposed to becoming associated with the Community and Mr. Nkrumah had constantly denounced 'association' as a pernicious form of neo-colonialism, but the British had hoped that 'association' would be attractive to the other countries in Africa and to the British West Indies. However, the Nigerian Prime Minister, Sir Abubakar Tafawa Balewa, flatly rejected it on political grounds, as did the Tanganyikan Prime Minister, Mr. Kawawa, who indicated that he was speaking for Uganda and Kenya as well.[7] Sir Milton Margai from Sierra Leone was non-committal at the time, although Sierra Leone eventually decided to accept association. Only Sir Roy Welensky (Federation of Rhodesia and Nyasaland) from the African countries was prepared to welcome association as a desirable arrangement and his position can hardly have improved matters with the rest of the Africans.[8]

There seem to have been a number of reasons why the African response was so cool. In the first place there were misunderstandings about the nature of the 'association' arrangements, and concern lest 'association' with the Community would prevent, or impede, the formation of an African Common Market. To some extent, the British may have been to blame for not having made the implications of association clear to the Africans rather earlier than they did, but they were somewhat hampered by the fact that the terms of association were under negotiation between the Community and its own associates. Perhaps of more importance was the fact that, until they had decided to join the Community and to seek association for certain members of the Commonwealth, the British had been strong critics of the association arrangements, particularly in the GATT discussions, and the Africans smelt something fishy in such an abrupt reversal of position. Finally, of course, although it was true that the trade and aid arrangements proposed for the associates were advantageous, it could not really be denied that association had some political overtones, both in terms of the East–West struggle and in terms of perpetuating a special relationship with former colonial powers.

Before the conference convened it seemed unlikely that the Prime Ministers would say anything that would be positively helpful to the British Government. The hope was that the conference would be uneventful and do nothing to inflame the anti-Common Market men on the back benches of the Conservative Party or to provide the Labour Party with new sticks with which

[7] There was some confusion on this point at the time, but the opposition of all three countries to 'association' was later confirmed.
[8] Moreover, it was far from clear that the Six would agree to the association of Rhodesia. As noted above (p. 412), the question of Rhodesia had not been settled before the adjournment in August.

to beat the Government. The tradition of past Commonwealth meetings, the restraining influence of meeting in London, and Mr. Macmillan's own efforts were counted on to keep the temperature low. But the combined effects of Mr. Gaitskell's curtain-raiser with the leaders of the opposition in a number of important Commonwealth countries, of the fact that two of the key Prime Ministers—Mr. Diefenbaker and Mr. Menzies—were politically vulnerable at home, and of the fact that the press—the pro-Common Market papers as well as the anti-Common Market papers—were out for every scrap of news they could get, meant that these hopes were soon exploded. Moreover, most of the Commonwealth Prime Ministers had arrived convinced that the British Government was determined to join the Community, an impression that was confirmed by Mr. Macmillan's opening speech. The conviction that what they said would not materially affect the outcome reduced any feeling of responsibility and increased the temptation to speak primarily for home consumption. There was, however, no conniving with the anti-Common Market groups in the United Kingdom. On the contrary, Mr. Menzies and Mr. Diefenbaker were at pains to avoid being linked in any way with these groups. None of the Commonwealth Prime Ministers were seeking to embarrass the British Government; they were simply putting their own domestic interests first. In addition, particularly to the representatives of the old Dominions, the British wish to join Europe seemed to mark the end of an old relationship. Although it was clear that the Commonwealth was changing in any case, the very fact that it was doing so and that it was changing in ways that were not altogether pleasing to Mr. Menzies and Mr. Diefenbaker made it even harder for them to accept the British action. And the feeling that this was the end of a chapter presumably made it seem less important to try to preserve the conventions normally observed at Commonwealth meetings.

After the opening speeches the conference met in committees for detailed examination of the main Commonwealth problems: temperate-zone foodstuffs, 'association', Asian exports, and a few special items, such as sugar. Although before the conference began there had been considerable doubt in British minds about the need, or usefulness, of a communiqué, the unfavourable tone of much of the press comment and the inflammatory nature of some of it apparently convinced Government leaders that it would be desirable for the conference to put out an agreed statement that was moderate enough in tone to counteract some of the wilder rumours about Commonwealth attitudes. A first draft prepared by the United Kingdom was felt by some of the delegations, and by the Canadians in particular, to go too far in implying approval of the British decision to apply for entry. The final draft gave no encouragement to the British but neither did it tie Mr. Heath's hands in the subsequent negotiations in Brussels by enumerating all the ways in which the Commonwealth countries felt the terms should be improved. In his summing-up speech, Mr. Macmillan noted that the conference was in agreement on four main themes: the need to work for an expansion in world trade; the need to improve the organization of the world market in primary foodstuffs, and in this connexion to make a fresh approach to international commodity agreements; the need for recognition by the developed countries that increased chances for trade were no less important than financial help for the developing nations; and the need to regulate the disposal of any agricultural surplus to meet the needs of those people of the world who were in want.[9] These principles, formulated with rather more precision and with somewhat more emphasis on the needs of the developing countries, found their place in the communiqué. In it the other Commonwealth countries 'freely acknowledged' that the British Government had made strenuous efforts to ensure that the Six understood the safeguards needed if British entry into the Community was not to impair the vital interests of the Commonwealth. But they said nothing which could be read as implying that this had been achieved. On the contrary, the communiqué recorded that the Commonwealth Prime Ministers had 'explained the economic points of special concern to their respective countries and the extent to which their interests had not so far been met in the Brussels negotiations'.[10] According to a statement made to the press by Mr. Diefenbaker, the most important paragraph in the whole communiqué was that which recorded that: 'The Prime Ministers took note that the negotiations in Brussels were incomplete and that a number of important questions had still to be negotiated. Only when the full terms were known would it be possible to form a final judgement.'[11]

Although the communiqué was cold comfort for the British

[9] See *The Times*, 18 September 1962.
[10] For the text of the communiqué see *The Times*, 20 September 1962.
[11] See *Guardian*, 20 September 1962.

Government, the Commonwealth Prime Ministers had recorded, once again, that the decision was one for the British Government alone to make and the three things that had worried the British most had been avoided; that is, an outright rejection of the terms thus far negotiated, a communiqué which would have required Mr. Heath to re-open points of principle already settled in Brussels, and a call for a further Commonwealth Prime Ministers' meeting.

A bad communiqué would have been very damaging to the British Government but the non-controversial one that was finally agreed seems to have made little impact, for it was too late to dispel the impressions of the conference that had been created. The impressions that stuck in the public mind were: first, that the Commonwealth countries were dissatisfied but that the British Government was determined to go ahead despite the strongly expressed reservations from the Commonwealth; second, that the Commonwealth countries, although critical of the British move, had offered no alternative; and third, that the conference had marked a turning-point in Commonwealth affairs and that, even if the negotiations in Brussels failed, a phase in Commonwealth relationships was over and a new and uncharted relationship was beginning.

The Liberal Party conference

The first of the three annual party conferences, that of the Liberal Party, opened late in September just as the Commonwealth conference was finishing. The Liberals had advocated joining the Common Market for many years, and, although they frequently denied that they were in favour of joining regardless of the terms, their advocacy was uninhibited in contrast to the caution that customarily prevailed in the two major parties. As Mr. Grimond, the leader of the party, had pointed out, one did not start haggling over the price of a house unless one liked it and wanted to buy it. The Liberals liked the house enormously, and the party conference once again strongly supported entry into the Economic Community and also showed considerable spontaneous enthusiasm for British participation in a fully-fledged federal Europe.[12] Both the Conservative and the Labour Party leaders

[12] The motion put forward by the executive of the Liberal Party, and Mr. Mark Bonham Carter's speech in support of it, were much more cautious than was the spontaneous and somewhat emotional endorsement of 'federalism' given

derided the enthusiasm of the Liberals, for it embarrassed both major parties in different ways. It was awkward for the Conservative Government to have the strongest support for its policies coming from an opposition party and for this support to be, at times, faintly fanatical, and it was awkward for Mr. Gaitskell to have so obvious an alternative ready to receive any members of his own party who could not be held to the Labour Party line.

Labour Party views and the party conference

The British Government's decision to open negotiations with the European Economic Community had placed strains on the cohesion of the Conservative Party, but it had placed far greater strains on the Labour Party. Opinions within the Labour Party ranged from strong support to bitter opposition, and the differences of view grew sharper as the negotiations proceeded and as the implications of joining became more widely understood. Mr. Roy Jenkins and a group of about thirty Labour Members felt the Government's decision had been correct, if belated, and they made no secret of their warm support. Mr. Michael Foot and a few others on the extreme left wing of the Labour Party were adamantly opposed to joining on any terms. A much more important group, which included Mr. Douglas Jay from the front bench of the Labour Party and was of roughly the same size as Mr. Jenkins' group, was clearly opposed to joining on any terms that could conceivably be negotiated. Both this 'moderate' anti-Common Market group and Mr. Jenkins' pro-Common Market group were more or less formally committed to sitting on the fence until the final terms of entry were known, but they expressed their views freely, and it was clear that Mr. Jenkins and some of the other strong supporters of entry would have difficulty remaining in the party if that meant voting against entry into the Common Market.

Apart from Mr. Jenkins and his friends (whose position was very close to that of the Liberals), there was very little enthusiasm in the Labour Party for the Community as a political and economic experiment and still less for Britain's taking part in the experiment. There was fairly widespread acceptance of the fact that some way

---

by the conference. Mr. Mark Bonham Carter's views were probably not very different from those held privately, at least, by the Prime Minister, although it was obviously considerably easier for Mr. Bonham Carter to be candid. See the account in *The Times*, 21 September 1962.

must be found to live amicably with the Six but there was considerable rather unreal nostalgia for some kind of loose economic association with the Community. There was a strong feeling that the Community was too much a part of the cold war, a feeling which was nourished by the hard line taken by the Community on the application of the neutrals for association and, to some extent, by the obvious American enthusiasm for British membership. This was, of course, particularly apparent in the left wing of the party where neutralism and anti-Americanism were prevalent, but even in the centre or on the right of the party many people, like Denis Healey, who were strong supporters of the NATO and of the American connexion, felt that the United Kingdom as a member of the Community would have to adopt a more intransigent line on many questions than was wise. There was some feeling that the rot had already set in and that Mr. Macmillan had modified his own position on Berlin to please Dr. Adenauer and General de Gaulle and thus to ease Mr. Heath's task in Brussels. The argument that Britain could best retain its position of influence in the world by becoming a part of a European power complex was one that left most of the Labour Party unmoved. And, as has already been noted in Chapter XII, the Labour Party was deeply suspicious of any discussion with the Continent about 'political union'.

There were also widespread reservations in the Labour Party about the economic implications of joining the Common Market. The most pervasive reservation was, at bottom, a reluctance to see any weakening of the powers which a future Labour Government might wish to use to control or direct the economy. Combined with a natural 'socialist' reluctance to see the scope for direct controls reduced, there was a 'nationalist' reluctance to see controls removed from British hands. Thus, Labour spokesmen seldom addressed themselves to the question of whether the Community institutions would be able to stimulate appropriate policies for full employment, area development, etc., but concentrated, instead, on the risks of a British Government having less power to do so on a national basis.[13] This, like many of the Labour Party's reservations about Europe, was more understandable in the early days when the 'Europeans' on the Continent drew their

[13] Mr. Gaitskell in his speech to the Labour Party conference admitted that some Labour spokesmen had made unsound arguments on this point. See p. 14 of the pamphlet containing the text of his speech, *Britain and the Common Market*, published by the Labour Party.

support from the conservative Christian Democrats than it was after the Treaties of Rome had been ratified with strong support from the Socialists.

'Liberals' in the Labour Party, like 'liberals' in the Conservative Party, were concerned at the signs of restrictionism among the Six and these criticisms became sharper as the details of the agricultural policy of the Six became known.[14] The Common Market was frequently criticized for being a 'rich man's club', for having the wrong priorities, and for improving trading conditions among the member countries at the expense of the underdeveloped countries. There were good grounds for criticizing some of the policies of the Community, but much of the criticism of the economic 'liberals' would have been more effective—and would have been more sympathetically received on the other side of the Channel—if it had been directed to the problem of how to achieve *common* policies that were 'liberal' in their impact on third countries, rather than being entangled, as was often the case, with criticisms that stemmed essentially from the fact that the Six were giving a higher priority to the achievement of economic unity than to steps which would promote better trading conditions on a world-wide basis. The latter criticism seemed to the Six to reflect an unwillingness to accept the fundamental purpose of the Treaty of Rome, and a nostalgia for a free trade area. This strand in Mr. Gaitskell's own position detracted from the force of many of the criticisms he made about the restrictionist policies of the Six.

Some of the Labour Party criticism, particularly criticism of the terms of entry, was undoubtedly prompted by a desire to strengthen the Government's bargaining position. Many of those who were not opposed to joining or were even mildly in favour of joining felt that the Government was being pushed by the Six to make unreasonable concessions and that it would be helped by some show of strong political opposition. This was a miscalculation of how the Six were apt to react and tended to be counter-productive. The Labour Party's growing opposition produced misgivings among some of Britain's best friends on the Continent and made them more willing than they might otherwise have been to agree with the French that the British must show their good faith by making changes in policy on the day of entry, rather than being

[14] For an exposition of the reservations felt by many 'liberals' in all parties, see James E. Meade, *United Kingdom, Commonwealth and Common Market* (Hobart Paper No. 17, London, April 1962).

given leeway to make more gradual adjustments. However, although tactics played some part in the Labour opposition, there is no blinking the fact that the dominant Labour view was one of suspicion and instinctive dislike of the Common Market. The Labour Party, for the most part, saw the dangers in the Community—some of which were real enough—but not the promises which were also there. Although there is a strong streak of idealism in the Labour Party, it did not respond to the strong streak of idealism which is also characteristic of the 'Europeans'. And too much of the Labour Party criticism was not based on a reasoned appraisal of the economic and political consequences of joining the Common Market but was parochial in tone and revealed an innate distrust of foreigners.[15] Although there were refreshing exceptions, Labour Party spokesmen as a rule preferred the United Nations to the Community and World Government to the institutions of the Six and did so in terms which made it difficult to avoid the conclusion that their preferences owed something to the fact that the United Nations was weak and World Government comfortably far away.

By its insistence that it was not negotiating to join the Six but to see whether or not terms could be obtained that would make joining possible, the Government had made it easy for the Labour Party to sit on the fence. However, by the spring of 1962 it was clear that whatever the formal position might be, the country was in the throes of debating the fundamental question whether or not it wanted to become a part of the European Community, and the leadership of the Labour Party was subjected to growing criticism for not taking a clear position. Early in May, Mr. Gaitskell, in a political broadcast, defended the Labour Party's position and summed up his own view in the following words: 'To go in on good terms would, I believe, be the best solution to this difficult problem. And let's hope we can get them. Not to go in would be a pity, but it would not be a catastrophe. To go in on bad terms which really meant the end of the Commonwealth would be a step which I think we would regret all our lives, and for which history would not forgive us.'[16]

The Labour Party's first three conditions were broadly the same

[15] Mr. Dingle Foot (Labour) commented on this undercurrent of simple dislike of foreigners in much of the Labour opposition in an excellent speech in the debate in the House of Commons on 7 November 1962. *Hansard*, House of Commons, 7 November 1962, col. 1066.
[16] See *Guardian*, 9 May 1962.

as the Government's conditions: safeguards for the Commonwealth, adequate arrangements for the other EFTA countries, and suitable arrangements for British agriculture. To these three, the Labour Party added two more: freedom to pursue an independent foreign policy and freedom to formulate and carry out national economic planning. In his May broadcast, Mr. Gaitskell indicated that he thought the economic arguments for and against entry were fairly evenly balanced, although he was, at that time, prepared to be more optimistic than some of his advisers and to feel that in the long run and on the right conditions the economic case for entry was the stronger. Although he dismissed as 'rubbish' the fear that the United Kingdom would be finished as an independent power as a result of accession to the Treaty of Rome, he did not hide his total opposition to participation in a 'federal' European state or the fact that a strong reason for this opposition was that this would mean the end of the Commonwealth.

This speech was generally taken as evidence that Mr. Gaitskell was, himself, a 'pro-European' although a rather mild one, and this impression seemed to be confirmed by his remarks in the House of Commons early in June, in which he spelled out, in rather more detail, what he meant by fulfilling the obligations to the Commonwealth countries and to the EFTA. In the June debate his comments on the specific arrangements he hoped the Lord Privy Seal would make were not very different from the arrangements Mr. Heath was then seeking to negotiate. Mr. Gaitskell was (as was the Government) highly critical of the Community's variable levy system on agricultural imports and quite dogmatic in his view that the Government should not in any circumstances agree to adopt it. Mr. Gaitskell was also very outspoken on the inadequacy of purely temporary safeguard arrangements for the Commonwealth. He felt, too, that international commodity agreements, although desirable, might prove to be impossible to negotiate: 'I hope we shall not be fobbed off with a meaningless phrase which is meant to disguise the fact—and let us not beat about the bush—that we are selling the Commonwealth down the river on this issue.'[17]

During the summer both Mr. Gaitskell's view and the attitude of the large undecided group in the Labour Party showed signs of hardening against joining the Community. This seems to have

[17] *Hansard*, House of Commons, 6 November 1962, col. 523.

been the product of a number of factors. In the first place, it was becoming clear that the conditions on which the precarious Labour Party agreement to support entry rested were not likely to be attained, and the Labour Party would have had small chance of avoiding another damaging division had the leadership sought to carry the party with it in advocating membership on terms which clearly fell short of their conditions. In the second place, the Conservatives had swung into a clearer position of support for joining and were showing an increasing tendency to turn the question into a party issue.[18] There was no place for the Labour Party to go except into opposition, since Mr. Grimond had already pre-empted the role of chiding Mr. Macmillan for being insufficiently 'European'. In the third place, the talks that Mr. Gaitskell had had in Brussels in July with M. Spaak and other continental Socialist leaders had gone very badly and had revealed fundamental disagreements between the British and the continental Socialists about the nature of the European experiment. Finally, the discussions with the Labour Party leaders from the Commonwealth and the meeting of the Commonwealth Prime Ministers had revealed strong dissatisfaction in the Commonwealth with the terms emerging from Brussels; this appears to have made a deep impression on Mr. Gaitskell personally.

At the conclusion of the talks between Mr. Gaitskell and the Labour leaders from other Commonwealth countries not only was a joint statement issued which was highly critical of the terms thus far obtained, but Mr. Gaitskell, speaking for the British Labour Party, indicated that he would press for a General Election if the Government sought to join the Common Market on terms that the Labour Party regarded as wholly unacceptable. And, following the Commonwealth Prime Ministers' meeting, Mr. Gaitskell (as well as Mr. Macmillan[19]) appeared on television. Mr. Gaitskell again attacked the terms, as then known, for being too vague and

[18] Some time during the summer of 1962, Mr. Macleod, the chairman of the Conservative Party organization, apparently decided that the Common Market was a potential election winner. Although there is no evidence to suggest that Mr. Macmillan tried to make the issue a 'bipartisan' one, it was not until the summer of 1962 that it began to turn into a party question. During the spring of 1962, Mr. Heath had apparently offered to give Mr. Gaitskell full information on the negotiations as they proceeded, but Mr. Gaitskell declined the offer, since he wanted to retain full freedom to criticize the Government's handling of the negotiations.

[19] Mr. Macmillan's statement was similar to that in his pamphlet cited above, p. 436.

outlined ways in which they could be made specific enough to meet Labour's main conditions.[20] He also attacked even more vigorously than he had done previously the idea of a European federation and, to the consternation of many Socialists on the Continent, he made the point that a strong reason for joining the Community would be to see that 'a loose association' took the place of a political federation. Both the tone and the content of Mr. Gaitskell's comments on the Community were too unsympathetic to suit the pro-Common Market element in the Labour Party and on the eve of the Labour Party conference there was much press speculation about whether the deep differences of view within the party would be reconciled and an open division avoided. After many hours of work, a long statement on the Common Market was agreed on by the National Executive of the Labour Party. The pro-Common Market group had succeeded in giving the document a much more positive tone than that which had marked Mr. Gaitskell's most recent statements but there was no easing of Labour's five conditions and the document was carefully balanced between the pros and the cons, with the opposing views set out antiphonally. The statement reiterated Mr. Gaitskell's proposal that negotiations on world commodity arrangements, on special arrangements for New Zealand, on trade agreements with India, Pakistan, and Ceylon, and on arrangements to safeguard the trade of African and Caribbean Commonwealth countries should be begun immediately, and stated flatly that until these negotiations resulted in satisfactory arrangements the present system of Commonwealth preference should remain unimpaired. The statement also reiterated Labour's other conditions: 'At the same time the Government must show . . . that it has no intention of deserting its partners in EFTA; that it will really insist on firm guarantees for British agriculture; that it will retain the right to pursue an independent British foreign policy; and that it means to retain for the British Government effective powers for safeguarding full employment and the balance of payments.' The statement then said, very flatly, that if these demands were met 'as we still hope', Britain should join the Common Market, but 'should they be

[20] The principal suggestion made by Mr. Gaitskell was that the various arrangements that the Six and the United Kingdom had agreed to negotiate after British accession—trade agreements with India and Pakistan, world cereals agreements—should be negotiated *before* British accession. This proposal, as Mr. Gaitskell was well aware, would have upset the Government's plan for concluding the negotiations before the General Election.

rejected, then Britain should not enter and the present negotiations should be brought to a halt.'[21]

The pro-Common Market group in the Labour Party was not very pleased with the statement but felt that they could just accept it. However, Mr. Gaitskell in his main speech to the conference seemed to depart from the spirit if not the words of the text and to reveal not simply profound doubts but a basically hostile attitude to the Six and to participation in the Common Market.[22] Mr. Brown, the Labour Party spokesman on foreign policy and a 'European', tried to counteract the impression left by Mr. Gaitskell, but the judgement of all political commentators was that the anti-Common Market group in the Labour Party had won the day, that the Labour Party had come off the fence and was now opposed to membership, and that unless their terms were met, the Labour Party would press for a general election on the Common Market issue.[23] Although Mr. Crossman and others on the left wing of the Labour Party were pushing Mr. Gaitskell to go even further and to indicate that he would repudiate a treaty of accession if the Government forced one through prior to an election and in the face of Labour opposition, Mr. Gaitskell never made this threat. To the end he continued to maintain his view that although the terms thus far negotiated were inadequate, no final judgement could be made until the final conditions were known, that, contrary to the general view, acceptable conditions might still be negotiable, but that if the Government sought to enter on conditions that the Labour Party considered inadequate, the 'only right and proper and democratic thing is to let the people decide the issue'.[24]

The Conservative Party conference

The Conservative Party conference at Llandudno came a few days after the Labour Party conference had closed. Before it

[21] The policy statement and the speeches made on the policy statement by Mr. Gaitskell and by Mr. George Brown are set out in a brochure, *Britain and the Common Market*, available from the Labour Party Headquarters.

[22] For an account of the emotions aroused by Mr. Gaitskell's handling of the Common Market issue at the Brighton Conference and the sense of 'betrayal' felt by the pro-Common Market group, see the *New Statesman*, 5 October 1962.

[23] It should be noted that many of the trade unions were in favour of joining the Common Market and that the statement of policy adopted by the T.U.C. at its annual conference, although it formally reserved judgement, was slightly warmer in tone than that of the Labour Party statement adopted at Brighton.

[24] The quotation is from the text of Mr. Gaitskell's major speech to the Labour Party conference.

opened the Conservatives had fired two big shots in active support
of the decision to join the Community—Mr. Macmillan's television broadcast and his pamphlet—and it was clear that the
much-heralded and long-awaited Conservative campaign to gain
public support for joining the Community had opened at last. The
party conference, which had been regarded by the Government as
its second big hurdle (the first being the Commonwealth Prime
Ministers' meeting), was taken with ease and for a time the
Government felt, wrongly, that its troubles, if not completely over,
were far less formidable than it had feared. Mr. Macmillan was, of
course, greatly helped at Llandudno by Mr. Gaitskell's flat statement that the terms thus far negotiated did not meet the Government's pledges to the Commonwealth, for most of those Conservatives—and they were probably more than they appeared to
be at Llandudno—who shared Mr. Gaitskell's view were forced
into silence by the position taken by the Labour Party. In the
Conservative Party the strongest Commonwealth men and the
strongest anti-Common Market men (the two groups were
practically coterminous) were well to the right, and much as they
might dislike Mr. Macmillan's policy they were not prepared to go
very far in making common cause with Mr. Gaitskell. Moreover,
Conservative Party conferences are traditionally very different
affairs from Labour Party conferences, and the policies of the
leadership are normally endorsed rather than modified in the
conference hall.[25] Nevertheless the enthusiasm of the conference
for the Government's European policy came as a welcome surprise. The anti-Common Market group led by two former ministers—Sir Derek Walker-Smith and Mr. Turton—commanded
little support. A motion welcoming the progress being made in
Brussels, expressing confidence in the Government's determination
to find adequate safeguards for British, Commonwealth, and
EFTA interests, and stressing the 'importance of a successful
outcome to the negotiations for the strength and unity of the free
world and the future prosperity of the United Kingdom, the
Commonwealth and Western Europe', was endorsed overwhelmingly by a show of hands. Somewhat surprisingly, Mr. Butler,

[25] A special article in the *Sunday Times* of 14 October 1962 described the difference between the two party conferences in the following terms: 'Whereas the
Labour Party Conference is a gathering of rival armies arranging the terms
of their alliance for the coming year, the Conservatives settle these troubles
elsewhere, and at their conference get down to four days of supercharged
togetherness.'

who had been one of the leading sceptics, perhaps best epitomized the exhilarated mood of the conference when in his opening speech on the Common Market he commented that: 'The Socialists have decided to look backward and to leave the future to us. For them a thousand years of history books. For us the future.'[26]

The state of euphoria in which the Conservatives left Llandudno was very short-lived. The public opinion polls soon began to show a sharp swing away from the Conservatives and a hardening of British opinion against entry into the Common Market. The Conservative candidates did very badly in a series of five by-elections in November. The negotiations in Brussels lost momentum and entered into a particularly difficult patch during which each side felt the other was stalling and adopting unrealistic bargaining positions. And the Cuban crisis added a new element to the negotiations which it is hard to assess but which was clearly important. In the United Kingdom it helped to create the uncertain and somewhat xenophobic mood that prevailed during the late autumn. In this atmosphere opponents of the Common Market found it easy to twist any British concession made in Brussels into a humiliating defeat, thus greatly handicapping Mr. Heath's attempts to conduct a sensible negotiation. More fundamentally, the Cuban crisis dramatized the inequality and the lack of balance in the Alliance and precipitated the whole question of Europe's role in determining the policies of the Alliance, thus helping to set the stage for the final breakdown.

[26] For the text of the motion and excerpts from the main speeches see *The Times*, 12 October 1962.

XIV

THE LAST PHASE OF THE ACCESSION NEGOTIATIONS

(October 1962–January 1963)

The negotiations in Brussels: October–December 1962

Negotiations at the official level between the United Kingdom and the Six were resumed late in September 1962. Before the first ministerial conference—on 8 October—Mr. Heath had made the round of the capitals of the Six to make it clear that the British were not intending to reopen any major points of principle as a result of the views expressed at the Commonwealth conference and to do what he could to see that the momentum the negotiations had finally acquired before the summer recess would be maintained, so that an agreement could be reached before Christmas or shortly thereafter. At the first, rather brief, ministerial meeting early in October, Mr. Heath gave an account of the Commonwealth conference and indicated ways in which some of the fears expressed by the Commonwealth countries could be dispelled. In this connexion, he pointed to the importance of a liberal response to the British requests for nil tariffs on lead, zinc, newsprint, and aluminium, and on a group of items of particular interest to the Asian countries—heavy jute goods, hand-knotted carpets, coir mats and matting, and East Indian kips. He also stressed the importance of a substantial reduction in the tariffs on processed foodstuffs, for canned and dried fruit were of great interest to Australia, and canned salmon of importance to Canada. He came closest to reopening a decision reached before the August recess when he commented on the reactions of the Indians and the Pakistanis to the arrangements that had been provisionally agreed for them. He suggested that the Community agree to begin negotiations on the trade agreements that were to be concluded with these countries as soon as possible after the British joined the Community and that the progressive application of the common external tariff—to which he had provisionally agreed—should be suspended until after the negotiations had been concluded. Mr. Heath also pointed out that since most of the African countries had, mistakenly in his view, rejected association, it would be necessary to look at other arrangements for these countries.

During the autumn some progress was made on all these points. A satisfactory understanding was reached on the arrangements to be made for those countries who were eligible fo association but as yet unwilling to accept it.[1] The Six agreed to open negotiations with the Indians and Pakistanis as soon as possible after the British became members of the Community, but they turned down the request for a suspension of the common external tariff, which they felt involved a point of principle. Some minor tariff items were settled, although little progress had been made on most of the important requests for nil or reduced tariffs by the time the negotiations were broken off. However, this was not, for the most part, because there were important points of principle at stake but because the concessions on tariffs were looked at—by both sides—as concessions which would be made as part of a final package settlement.[2] Although these and various other points affecting the Commonwealth (e.g. Hong Kong) were pursued at official and ministerial level during the autumn, the major issue under discussion from October until the breakdown in January was the method and rate by which British agricultural policies would be conformed to those of the Six.

Before the August adjournment there had been some pre-

---

[1] Briefly, the agreement was that the possibility of association would remain open to these countries, that trade agreements would be negotiated with them, and that the United Kingdom in applying the common external tariff to the trade of these countries would do so at the same rate as had been agreed for manufactured goods from India and Pakistan, that is, according to the so-called 'soft décalage', a slower rate than that applied to Canada, Australia, and New Zealand. See European Economic Community, Commission, *Report to the European Parliament on the State of the Negotiations with the United Kingdom* (Brussels, 26 February 1963), pp. 47–48.

[2] It is worth noting that on some of the important tariff items negotiations were held up because of disagreements within the Six and that the objections to reductions came not simply from the French but also from others in the Six who were interested in protecting their own industries. See Commission, *Report*, pp. 15–21. It is also worth noting that a complicating factor in the discussion on tariff reductions was the imminence of the 'Kennedy round'. Although behind the scenes the United States was in certain cases offering to 'take account' of tariff reductions made in the accession negotiations, there was an understandable reluctance to give up bargaining power in advance of a new GATT tariff negotiation without a more specific *quid pro quo*.

liminary discussion of the arrangements to be made for British agriculture and the Six had made it clear that they would oppose the British request for a twelve-year transition period, from the date of British entry into the Community, for the adjustment of their agriculture. The Six were united in their view that all special arrangements must end by 1970, at the latest. They countered the argument that since the Six had had twelve years for adjustments the British should have the same by pointing out that there had been no common agricultural policy during the first four years, so that the actual time for adjustment available to the British was substantially the same as that available to the Six themselves. Moreover, British agriculture was, they felt, at least as efficient as agriculture within the Six and in some respects more efficient. The British reply to these arguments was that although their agriculture might well be just as efficient, its cost structure was very different from that on the Continent; that the common agricultural policy bore a close resemblance to existing arrangements on the Continent but was totally different from the British system; and that for these reasons the order of magnitude of the change involved for the British was not comparable with that for the Six. These opposing views about the length of the transition period were well known, and unresolved, when the negotiations on British agriculture began in earnest in the autumn.[3] However, other even more fundamental differences of view quickly became apparent.

At the first ministerial discussions on agriculture late in October, the Six put forward counter-proposals to a British paper which

---

[3] Before the summer holiday the British and the Six had agreed on only one aspect of the British proposals on agriculture; that was the 'annual review'. The British had proposed that there should be national annual reviews similar to those carried on in the United Kingdom to determine, among other things, whether farm incomes bore a 'fair' relationship to total national income. The results of these national reviews would be sent to the Commission which would then draw up an annual Community review. If the review showed that the agricultural population of a member country was not assured a 'fair' standard in any member country, that country could ask the Commission to submit proposals to the Council to remedy the situation. The Six accepted the idea of an annual review but felt the survey of farm incomes should be made at a Community, rather than a national level, that the Commission should decide whether action was called for, and that any measures taken should be Community measures rather than national measures. The British agreed to the Community proposals, modified to make clear their own right to carry out a national review—in addition to the Commission's review—and tightened up to give a greater guarantee to farmers that action would, in fact, be taken if incomes became out of line. See Commission, *Report*, pp. 170–1.

had been circulated earlier and which had been discussed, inconclusively, at official level. Mr. Heath reacted strongly, and adversely, to the proposals put forward by the Six, which he considered to be totally unacceptable. The discussion among the ministers achieved nothing and the negotiations, far from resuming where they had left off in the summer, seemed to be in danger of slipping into immobility, with both sides imprisoned in rigid positions.

Apart from their request for a longer transition period, the main points in the British paper—to which the Six were reacting at this October session—were as follows. The British proposed to maintain their system of guaranteed prices and deficiency payments during the transition period but to bring the operation of the system progressively into line with the system of the Six and to make a complete change-over to the system of the Six at the end of a transition period. To this end, the British proposed that levies on imports should be progressively imposed and British market prices should be progressively brought to the level of Community prices. Although the British guaranteed prices would remain, in principle, until the end of the transition period, the *differences* between the guaranteed price and the market price would decrease and would probably disappear well before the end of the transition period. The burden of supporting the farmer would thus be shifted progressively from the Treasury to the consumer, through the price mechanism. In addition to this general plan for progressively adapting their system to that of the Six, the British made a few important proposals for specific commodities. They felt that the pig market and probably the egg market would be over-supplied once the United Kingdom, Denmark, and probably Ireland joined the Community and that if the farmers' incomes were to be maintained at current levels it would be necessary for the Community to institute intervention prices for these products as they had done for wheat. They also proposed that the British target price for wheat should be set initially at £25 a ton (as compared with an existing British market price of about £20 and a French price of about £34). British wheat prices would be raised, by stages, and, like the wheat price in other Community countries, would be aligned on an agreed 'Community' price at the end of an agreed transition period. The British also proposed certain special arrangements for horticulture.[4] Dis-

---

[4] The British proposals on horticulture and the reactions of the Six are summarized in the Commission's *Report*, pp. 85–86.

cussion of the arrangements for horticulture had not progressed
very far by the time the negotiations broke down; the main arguments during the autumn and winter centred on the arrangements
to be made for wheat and coarse grains, and for pigs, eggs, and
poultry.[5]

When the Six put forward their counter-proposals to these
British proposals, they reiterated, as had been anticipated, the
sanctity of 1 January 1970 as the terminal date for all transitional
arrangements. But to the consternation of the British, they insisted
that the British should make the change-over from their system of
guaranteed prices and deficiency payments to the system of the
common agricultural policy on the day of entry into the Common
Market. They also insisted that, on entry, the British target price
for wheat should be set at the lowest price prevailing within the
Community, i.e. at the French price, rather than, as the British
had proposed, at a price substantially below the lowest Community price. The Six recognized that such an abrupt increase in
the wheat price might be politically impossible for any government
to accept and they therefore suggested that difficulties arising from
the sharp price increase might be alleviated by consumer subsidies
(presumably subsidies to the millers) which would be progressively
reduced during the transition period. Although the French, in
particular, were reluctant to do so, the Six also indicated that in
certain exceptional cases they might agree to the use of producer
subsidies, apparently mainly to help pig producers caught by the
rising cost of feeding stuffs,[6] on the one hand, and greater dependence on the market, on the other. Finally the Six indicated that
they felt there was no need to provide for intervention in the pig
and egg markets as the British had proposed. On this issue the
usual roles were curiously reversed: the Six argued the advantages
of a free market and warned of the dangers of stimulating

[5] The Six had not yet agreed among themselves on the details of their policies
for beef, veal, dairy products, mutton, lamb, rice, and sugar. Although the
British put forward some views on the arrangements to be made for these
products, real negotiations between the Six and the United Kingdom were
held up until the Six could reach agreement among themselves. The policy to
be adopted for dairy products was the subject of much internal argument
among the Six during the autumn and had not been settled when the negotiations broke down. On some of these products there were no important
problems, but arrangements for dairy products would, almost certainly, have
proved to be a controversial issue between the United Kingdom and the Six,
since the British desire to safeguard New Zealand's butter exports would have
come into direct conflict with the principle of community preference.

[6] Coarse grain prices are linked to wheat prices.

uneconomic production; the British stressed the dangers of excessive competition.

It is hardly surprising that the British reacted strongly to the counter-proposals of the Six and particularly to the demand for the immediate abolition of the deficiency payments system and for an immediate sharp increase in the wheat price. Their indignation, although understandable, was, however, much too indiscriminate. On some points, and particularly on questions of timing, the Six were gratuitously tough, but some of their objections to the British proposals were more reasonable than they were made to appear in most British accounts of the controversy. As in the earlier argument over Commonwealth imports of temperate-zone products, part of the difficulty arose because both sides opened with positions that were too extreme and then each side over-reacted against the exaggerations in the other side's position. There were, essentially, two main points at issue—the continuation of guaranteed prices, and the price to be adopted as the target price for wheat. The Six felt that the way the British proposed to phase out their deficiency payments systems would put British farmers in a better position than other Community farmers, since British farmers could count on a *guaranteed* price, independent of the market price, until the end of the transition period. This was true, for although under the British proposal market prices would be allowed to rise and deficiency payments would disappear when market prices reached the guaranteed price, the *guarantee* to the farmers of a particular price would remain intact until the end of the transition period. Thus, for commodities except those, like wheat, for which the Community had intervention prices, British farmers would be effectively protected against a collapse of the market in a way continental farmers would not.

On the second main point at issue, the question of the wheat price, the British were on much stronger ground than they were in the argument over the retention of the deficiency payments – guaranteed price system, since there was no principle that the Six could invoke to back up their insistence that the British should fix their initial target price within the *fourchette*.[7] On the contrary, under the agreements on the common agricultural policy reached in January 1962, the Six had all, initially, set their target prices at their own domestic price, and it was difficult to argue that the

---

[7] The *fourchette*, or fork, was the spread between the lowest Community price (the French price) and the highest Community price (the German price).

British must immediately set their target price at a price within the *fourchette*.[8] One reason for the position of the Six was that any widening of the *fourchette* would have increased the difficulty of ultimately agreeing on a Community price. The Germans were strongly opposed to having the lower limit reduced. The French, who might have been expected to welcome this support for an eventual agreement on a Community price nearer the French price than the German price, were opposed to anything that might make the agreement on a unified wheat price more difficult. Moreover, the sooner the British price was raised to the French price the sooner the French could expect to export wheat to the British market without a subsidy. The British, as well as having precedent on their side, had a number of very good reasons for opposing too sudden and too steep an increase in the wheat price. In the first place, a rapid rise in wheat prices would have affected the cost of living, wages, and hence industrial costs, just at a time when the British were hoping to hold costs steady in order to reap the rewards (and to withstand the jolt) of joining the Common Market. In the second place, coarse grain prices are linked to wheat prices and a rapid increase in the price of wheat would have raised the prices of the feeding-stuffs used by the pig and poultry producers, thus increasing their costs just at the time when they were to become more dependent on the market for their income. Finally, of course, a higher price for wheat would have been bad for the Commonwealth, and third countries generally, since it would not only have made it easier for unsubsidized French wheat to find a market in the United Kingdom but would have been likely to stimulate additional production of British wheat.

The negotiation on British agriculture was bound to be difficult because of the wide differences between British and continental methods of supporting the farmers. But the fact that domestic politics and national self-interest were involved on every side made this phase of the negotiations doubly difficult. In France, the discontent of the farmers was the single most serious internal domestic problem then facing the de Gaulle Government. In Germany, Dr. Adenauer's party, the CDU, depended heavily on the farm vote and the farmers had recently been openly rioting over reports from Brussels that the common agricultural policy

[8] The question was complicated by the fact that there was no 'British' price in the sense that the Six had prices, since neither the market price in the United Kingdom, which was the world price, nor the British guaranteed price was the equivalent of a market price on the Continent.

462   ACCESSION NEGOTIATIONS: LAST PHASE

meant lower farm prices.[9] In the United Kingdom the powerful National Farmers' Union had become increasingly critical of entry into the Common Market, although many large farmers, particularly, of course, the wheat and barley growers, were in favour of joining the Community. The importance to the Conservative Party of the agricultural vote in anything up to a hundred constituencies is part of the folklore of British politics and it is hard to separate fact from superstition. Nevertheless the poor showing of the Conservative Party candidates in agricultural constituencies in the November by-elections was a portent. Another, more ominous, sign was the strong opposition of Sir Anthony Hurd, the Chairman of the Conservative Party's Agricultural Committee, to the proposals put forward by the Six.[10] Moreover, apart from strong domestic political pressures on all sides, the negotiation on agriculture was considerably complicated by the growing criticism of the Macmillan Government and the feeling in the United Kingdom that the Six, under pressure from the French, were exploiting the support given to the Government's European policy by the Conservative Party conference and were responding to the Government's decision not to be deterred by criticisms made at the Commonwealth Prime Ministers' conference by hardening the terms of entry.

During the autumn, as the domestic problems facing the British Government multiplied, the Six were far less understanding of Mr. Macmillan's political problems than they had been of each others' difficulties during the Treaty of Rome negotiations. In the light of later events, it seems probable that the French were at this time deliberately seeking to harden the terms to the point where they would be rejected. But insensitivity to British difficulties

[9] See *Financial Times*, 12 October 1962, and *Guardian*, 18 October 1962.

[10] On 23 November 1962, Sir Anthony Hurd, speaking in Berkshire, said in part: 'The Council of Ministers will also have to heed the facts of life in British politics. The results of this week's by-elections show no joy in the reports from Brussels, and anyway Europe's ambassadors here can surely discern what Mr. Heath must have told the Six in Brussels—that the British electorate just would not take sharply increased food prices on our entry into the Common Market. Nor will the Conservative Party put back a network of food subsidies as a palliative for high consumer prices. It is well to say this bluntly.' *The Times*, 24 November 1962. Later, on 13 December 1962, Sir Anthony Hurd was among a group of forty-seven Conservative M.P.s who tabled a motion congratulating Mr. Heath on his firmness in dealing with the Common Market's agricultural proposals, and urging equal firmness on other matters, even though firmness might mean a breakdown. See *The Times*, 24 November and 14 December 1962.

was not confined to the French, and the rest of the Six and the Commission, although they made some efforts to keep the French from pushing the price too high, tended to underrate the very real difficulties confronting the Macmillan Government. There was a lack of generosity and of largeness of spirit on the part of the Six which seemed out of place in the final stages of a negotiation of such vast importance and one in which, on most issues, the British had already shown themselves willing to meet the terms of the Six.

However, the faults were not all on one side; the British were dotting 'i's and crossing 't's as well. Moreover, during the autumn of 1962 the British were in a mood to be touchy and to see slights and humiliations where none were intended.[11] The Cuban crisis had brought home to the British in a new and profoundly unpleasant way the extent to which their status in the world had changed since the end of the war. It had been far easier for the continental Europeans to recognize, to accept, and to draw conclusions from their decline in power, for the change and the adjustment had been a part of the massive upheaval of the war and its aftermath. The war had been different for the British and it left them not with a sense of failure and a feeling of inadequacy, but with a sense of achievement and the illusion of power. The 'Europeans' on the Continent tended to be rather contemptuous of the debate the British were carrying on with themselves about the implication of their changed circumstances, and they pointed out that no such pining after the past accompanied their own clear-eyed decisions on the Common Market. These complacent assertions ignored the fact that the crisis in France on whether or not to pursue a 'European' course came over the EDC; the Common Market slid home without attracting much attention in large measure because the emotional tensions had been pushed to explosion-point earlier. Nevertheless, although the somewhat xenophobic mood that was apparent in the United Kingdom during November and December can be explained by the fact that both Cuba and the Common Market negotiations were underlining, in different ways, a changed situation which had been accepted intellectually, but not yet emotionally, the mood of the country undoubtedly made it difficult for the British Government to make concessions in the negotiations. And this difficulty was

[11] The British reaction to Mr. Acheson's speech at West Point on 5 December 1962 was a particularly striking case in point. See comment in *The Times*, and other papers.

sensibly increased by the fact that both the Labour Party and, on the other flank, the Beaverbrook press were assiduously portraying the negotiations as a long series of humiliating surrenders. Unfortunately there was an undercurrent of feeling, on the part of at least some of the Six, that it was not inappropriate for the United Kingdom as a late-comer to grovel a little before entry, and this gave colour to these assertions, but the picture of the negotiations as simply a succession of surrenders was largely an optical illusion. As indicated above, on a number of key questions the British had opened with a position which they knew they could not sustain but which they felt they had to demonstrate to the Commonwealth countries or to their own farmers was non-negotiable before they could move to a more realistic position. Moreover, as the spokesmen for the Six never tired of pointing out, this was not a negotiation where the right answer could be presumed to lie half-way between two opposing views, since the problem was not to create a new system having some of the characteristics of the British system and some of the characteristics of the Community system but to agree on ways to fit the United Kingdom into the Community system.

By late November 1962 it was clear that the atmosphere in Brussels, as well as in London, had deteriorated dangerously and that the negotiations might run into the sand. The Six were making slow progress in agreeing among themselves on the crucial question of the financial regulation, on the details of the common policy for dairy products, and on various other matters, such as the levels of particular tariffs, on which prior agreement within the Six was necessary before discussions with the United Kingdom could be undertaken. The French were now being suspected—by their partners as well as by the British—of deliberately trying to drag out the negotiations in the hope that the British would have to break them off because of the imminence of their elections. This was a suspicion, not a fact that could be documented, for the French were being careful to abide by the rules and to justify their positions with arguments solidly rooted in Community 'doctrine'. However, it was apparent to everyone that time was running out and that the British Government would soon have either to show that success was imminent or to withdraw its application.[12]

[12] On 12 December 1962 the *Daily Telegraph* gave the results of a Gallup poll showing that since October 1962 the percentage of those in favour of joining 'on the facts as you know them at present' had declined from 41 to 29 and the percentage against joining had risen from 28 to 37. The poll also showed that

Early in December, the Belgians proposed to their partners in the Community that two long ministerial sessions should be held early in the new year. Under the system of rotation agreed upon at the start of the negotiations, the Belgian Foreign Minister would then be in the chair, and M. Spaak hoped to be able to give the negotiations the impetus needed to break the back of the remaining problems.[13] It is worth noting that although the French agreed to the 'marathon meetings', they made it plain that some of the remaining problems would take more time to settle than the Belgians implied, and M. Couve de Murville apparently pointed out that the Seven (i.e. the United Kingdom and the Six) could not really consider the New Zealand question until after the Six had reached agreement among themselves on a dairy products policy.[14]

Mr. Heath met with the ministers of the Six for a three-day session in mid-November and for two shorter sessions in December. At the November meeting agriculture was not discussed, but some progress was made on other, less controversial, aspects of the negotiations.[15] By the time the December meetings were held the possibility of progress before the marathon meetings scheduled for January had been largely discounted. The prevailing feeling in the United Kingdom was that neither side would make any real concession on the important unresolved points until a decisive final encounter, but that in January or February there would be a non-stop session, such as the Six themselves had had on agriculture the previous year, and at dawn in a smoke-filled room the final deals would be done, or the negotiations would break down. Just before the ministerial meeting of 10–11 December both Mr. Maudling (the Chancellor of the Exchequer) and Mr. Erroll (the President of the Board of Trade) had made statements to the effect that although the British Government still hoped it would be

---

42 per cent. as against 37 per cent. in October expected the Labour Party to win the next election. And, more disturbing still for the Government, the percentage expecting the Conservatives to win had fallen from 37 to 29.

[13] Although M. Spaak originally intended to take the chair himself, it was later decided that it would be more prudent for M. Fayat, the Deputy-Foreign Minister, to do so. M. Spaak was too zealous an advocate of British membership to suit the French, as well as being openly opposed to General de Gaulle's ideas about political union.

[14] See *Guardian*, 5 December 1962.

[15] A statement on the main agreements reached at this meeting is contained in Mr. Heath's report to Parliament, published as a White Paper, *The United Kingdom and the European Communities* (Cmnd. 1882, November 1962).

possible to join the Common Market it would not be a disaster if the negotiations failed. Presumably the intention behind these remarks was partly to strengthen Mr. Heath's position in Brussels (although it seems unlikely that the statements had this effect), and partly to begin the process of preparing British public opinion for a possible failure.

At the 10–11 December meeting, agriculture was discussed at ministerial level for the first time since the completely unproductive session at the end of October. Before the December meeting the Foreign Ministers and the Agricultural Ministers of the Six held several long sessions to try to agree on a common position. During these discussions the French took a very hard line against making any concessions to the British, and they apparently had considerable difficulty in holding the other Five to the position put forward in October.[16] The French finally agreed with the others that the British Government had to be given enough leeway to enable it to live up to the specific commitment it had made that support prices would only be changed within narrow limits during the lifetime of the present Parliament, but in other respects the French views—supported by the Commission—prevailed. Accordingly, at the 10–11 December meeting, the Six insisted again that the British accept the principle of an immediate change-over to the Community agricultural support system, although they confirmed their willingness to allow the British to defer the taking of steps that conflicted with the commitment made on support prices until a new Parliament had been elected.[17] Assuming that British entry into the Community took place on 1 January 1964 (the date that then seemed most probable), this would have given the British, at most, only one year of grace, since the elections had to be held by the autumn of 1964, at the latest. Thus the concession, although important politically to the British, was not one that it cost the Six very much to make. A more significant development was the decision to form a ministerial committee, under the chairmanship of Mr. Mansholt (the member of the Commission who was responsible for agriculture), to examine the economic effects of the agricultural proposals made by the British and of the

---

[16] See *Le Monde*, 5 and 6 December 1962.

[17] The Government had promised that during the lifetime of the present Parliament it would not change the commitment contained in the Agriculture Act of 1957 to maintain the total value of the guaranteed prices at not less than 97½ per cent. of their value in the preceding year, the guaranteed price for each commodity to be not less than 96 per cent. of the previous year's price.

counter-proposals made by the Six. There was some argument about whether the Mansholt Committee should examine the economic effects of both sets of proposals, or of only the proposals put forward by the Six, the French maintaining that only the latter were under consideration. In practice, the Mansholt Committee produced material responsive to questions arising from both sets of proposals.

The appointment of the Mansholt Committee gave rise to a wave of optimism, the first since the resumption of negotiations in October. Many people had felt that, given the difficulty both sides faced in putting forward compromises, progress would have been easier and more rapid if, throughout the negotiations, the Commission had been given more power to propose solutions.[18] Although the mandate to the Mansholt Committee stopped short of empowering the committee to propose solutions to the points at issue, it was generally assumed that the outline of a settlement on agriculture would emerge from the committee's work. And the fact that the British and the French had agreed to the setting-up of the Mansholt Committee reassured both those who had become sceptical of French intentions and those who had become doubtful whether the British were yet ready to make the concessions that were clearly necessary for a settlement. The Mansholt Committee began work a day or two later but agriculture was not discussed again by the ministers until January.

The ministerial meeting on 19 and 20 December 1962 settled a few outstanding questions relating to Malta, Cyprus, and the African protectorates. In addition, Mr. Heath gave the British view on a number of institutional questions. In particular he made it clear that the United Kingdom, while expecting the same voting rights as the three big countries, France, Germany, and Italy, accepted that a qualified majority was, in principle, a two-thirds majority. This was in accord with the situation then prevailing in the Community but it was different from Mr. Gaitskell's position that one large and one small country should be enough to block action. In the Community of the Six a

[18] This was a point that had been made very frequently by M. Monnet. His Action Committee for a United States of Europe was at this time about to recommend a change in the negotiating method to give a greater role to the Commission. However, in view of the decision to appoint the Mansholt Committee, the Action Committee simply welcomed this development and recommended it as a procedure to be followed in settling other problems. See Action Committee for the United States of Europe, *Joint Declaration* (Paris, 17 and 18 December 1962).

'qualified majority' is a two-thirds vote but, at the same time, one large and one small country acting together are enough to make a two-thirds majority unattainable. This would not have been the case in the enlarged community, however, and Mr. Heath's acceptance of the two-thirds majority principle was therefore very well received by the 'Europeans'.[19]

The ministerial conference of the Seven did not meet again until 14 January 1963, the day that General de Gaulle announced at his press conference that in his opinion the British were not yet ready to become European. It had become apparent during the Christmas interval that the negotiations were building up to a climax. But it was far from clear whether the January meetings would see the negotiations finally into their last lap, or, as proved to be the case, in collapse. There were indicators pointing in both directions, although early in January the danger signals were more prominent than the encouraging signs. On the positive side there was the appointment of the Mansholt Committee. In addition, it had become apparent from a series of discussions that Mr. Heath held just after Christmas with the ministers from the Six that the British Government was now ready to begin the process of final bargaining. And the prevailing view appeared to be that the British would make enough concessions on the points in dispute on agriculture so that there was a reasonable prospect that the deadlock on agriculture could be broken as part of a final 'package' deal. However, by the end of the year disturbing signs that General de Gaulle would not welcome a successful outcome overshadowed these indications that success might be near.

Opposition from General de Gaulle

On 15 December, Mr. Macmillan visited General de Gaulle at Rambouillet. This meeting seems to have been very different in atmosphere from that at the Château de Champs in June. Once again, as he had done on numerous previous occasions, and as he was to do in his press conference on 14 January, General de Gaulle expressed his doubts about whether the British could actually make the adjustments in policy and attitude that joining the European Community implied. Mr. Macmillan sought to dispel, and to correct, these misconceptions but he apparently made less impression upon the French President than he had at their June

[19] See White Paper, *The United Kingdom and the European Communities* (Cmnd. 1910, December 1962).

meeting. Although there had been press speculation before the meeting that General de Gaulle might suggest to Mr. Macmillan that 'association' with the Common Market might be a better solution than membership, this possibility was apparently not put forward.[20] The Rambouillet meeting took place after it had become known that the United States would probably soon discontinue its support for the Skybolt missile, and after it had become clear that the problems this posed for the British would be discussed between Mr. Macmillan and Mr. Kennedy at Nassau a few days after the Rambouillet meeting. The available evidence indicates that Mr. Macmillan told General de Gaulle that he expected to discuss this matter with President Kennedy and that he would probably accept Polaris missiles in substitution for Skybolt missiles, and, further, that he would assume that these would normally operate within the NATO framework, although the British would want to have the right of unilateral control over them in time of crisis.[21] However, European defence arrangements do not appear to have figured prominently in the Rambouillet discussions, and there were apparently no suggestions made, from either side, for merging the British and French nuclear efforts.[22] The fact that General de Gaulle did not himself propose a nuclear deal and apparently made no comments on Mr. Macmillan's remarks on his own plans about a successor to Skybolt is not, of course, evidence that he might not have changed his views about the British acceptability as a member of the Community had the suggestion come from the British side.

[20] Mr. Gaitskell visited Paris early in December 1962 and in a speech to the Anglo-American Press Association was not only very critical of the concessions made by the British Government during the negotiations but very outspoken about the dangers he saw in a European federation. He also had talks with M. Mollet, M. Pompidou, and M. Couve de Murville. After these talks, suggestions began to appear (emanating apparently from both M. Mollet and French Government sources) that it might be better for the British to be associated in some way with the Common Market rather than to become members. Some people have felt that Mr. Gaitskell's talks in Paris at this time contributed significantly to General de Gaulle's decision to veto British membership in the EEC. This seems improbable. On the other hand, Mr. Gaitskell's views lent useful verisimilitude to General de Gaulle's case against the British and may well have made him feel that there would be less criticism—from Socialists in France and elsewhere in the Six—of his decision to exclude the British than in fact materialized.
[21] See Mr. Macmillan's statement in the House of Commons debate on defence on 31 January 1963. *Hansard*, House of Commons, col. 1255. See also his Liverpool speech discussed below, p. 487.
[22] See *The Times*, 17 December 1962.

Although little that General de Gaulle said at Rambouillet was new, the fact that far from modifying his earlier views he now apparently held them even more strongly, despite the considerable progress that had been made during the negotiations in July and August, must have raised grave doubts in Mr. Macmillan's mind about the probability of the negotiations in fact succeeding. And additional signs of trouble soon began to appear. In his New Year's Eve address to the French people, General de Gaulle in a few compressed sentences foreshadowed the views he later expressed in far greater detail at his press conference.[23]

Moreover, although the first French reactions to the Nassau conference and to Mr. Kennedy's offer of Polaris missiles to the French on the same basis on which they had been offered to the United Kingdom had been circumspect, the tone of French press and official comment soon changed.[24] By the beginning of the year, the Nassau agreement was being interpreted as a complete capitulation by the British to the United States, and the possibility of the British, in fact, being able to use Polaris for their own purposes was being dismissed as 'purely theoretical'. Far from having terminated their supposed special relationship, the British were felt to have tied themselves more securely than ever to the United States. The parallel offer to France was dismissed as irrelevant, since the French were in no position to supply either launchers or war-heads.[25] In its issue of 10 January 1963, *Le*

[23] In his broadcast on 31 December 1962, General de Gaulle referred to various fields in which he looked for progress. The paragraph on international action read as follows: 'International progress, especially in the two directions where our main effort is exerted abroad. In the first place, the union of Western Europe with respect to its economy, its policies, its defence, its culture, thus establishing a balance with the United States, reinforcing thereby the alliance of the free world, ready to receive in the future a Britain which could and would join it without reservation and definitively, aiming at organizing with the countries of the East—should they one day come to a complete easing of the tension—the peace and the life of our whole continent.' (Press Release by the French Embassy, London.)

[24] Nora Beloff in the *Observer*, 30 December 1962, reported that: 'Gaullist circles who would not venture too far from the General's known beliefs are castigating the Polaris offer as, among other things, a trap, a nonsense, an insult, and a joke.'

[25] On 3 January 1963 the Polaris offer was discussed at a meeting of the French Council of Ministers presided over by General de Gaulle, after which the Minister of Information, M. Peyrefitte, reported to the press that no immediate decision on the question had seemed necessary since France had no launchers or war-heads and therefore the offer was not 'actual'. He added that France was engaged on her own nuclear programme and remained attached to the principle of independence for its own defence. See *Le Monde*, 4 January 1963.

Monde carried two articles which gave warning that British entry into the Common Market was being looked upon as a means of increasing American control over Europe in both defence and economic matters. The first, by M. André Fontaine, indicated that the tightening of the 'special links' between London and Washington which the Nassau agreements were felt to have brought about had led to the conclusion 'in high places' that the entry of the United Kingdom into the Common Market would carry a great risk of opening the doors to an American 'Trojan horse'. The same article also pointed out that in Paris the familiar fear was still alive that—under the influence of Britain and of 'the caravan' that she would bring with her—the Community would degenerate into a vast free trade area. The second article, by M. Duverger, was primarily concerned with the 'Grand Design' of the Kennedy Administration, which he saw as a plan to absorb the European Community in an Atlantic Community run by the United States. This concept was very different from the concept which, he felt, was fundamental to the Treaty of Rome (and to the other efforts of the Six), which was to create a European 'super-power' *vis-à-vis* the American 'superpower'. He said that 'some people' feared that the entry of the United Kingdom into the Common Market would lead to the progressive modification of the system in the direction wanted by the United States and that these people were 'not far from seeing in England the Trojan horse of the United States'. He himself thought American invest-ment in Europe and the policy of post-Adenauer Germany might be even more powerful Trojan horses. However, he emphasized that Europe now faced a choice between a capitalist, free trade economy dominated by the United States and an organized, planned, autonomous common market, and that British entry must be considered in the light of this choice.[26]

Before the resumption of negotiations in Brussels on 14 January 1963, Mr. Heath again held a round of bilateral discussions with the ministers of the Six and, on 11 January, he visited Paris for discussions with M. Couve de Murville. Against the background of press comment and rumours that a French veto might be in the offing, Mr. Heath is reported to have asked the French Foreign Minister, point blank, whether if the technical problems could be solved the French Government would veto British member-ship, and to have received the unequivocal answer, 'Certainly

[26] See *Le Monde*, 10 January 1963.

not'.[27] At about the same time, the French Prime Minister, M. Pompidou, also denied that there were any political objections to British entry, although his comments were in other respects a little ambiguous.[28]

On the eve of the resumption of the negotiations, the prevailing view was that the French would make no concessions on agriculture, that they would seek to exploit any opportunity to get Britain to break off the negotiations, and that they would probably try to drag out the negotiations to the point where the British had to abandon them for domestic political reasons, but that they would not openly block British membership or put themselves in the position of being clearly responsible for a breakdown.[29]

The meeting between Mr. Heath and the Six on 14 January was a very brief one because the key question—agriculture—had been held over until the following day to enable the Mansholt Committee to complete its report. When the conference resumed on 15 January it was against the background of General de Gaulle's press conference and in the full knowledge that the French President was opposed to British membership in the Community.

General de Gaulle has customarily used his infrequent press conferences to make major statements of foreign policy. At his last previous press conference, on 15 May 1962, he had elaborated his views on European political integration, on the German problem, on NATO, on the Geneva disarmament conference, and on French–African relations, but he had not dealt with the Brussels negotiations, or with Britain's role in Europe, although this omission was, in itself, of some significance.[30] The British question, further reflections on NATO, his reactions to the Nassau con-

[27] See Nora Beloff in the *Observer*, 20 January 1963. Also see *Le Monde*, 13–14 January 1963.

[28] In *Le Monde* of 13–14 January 1963, M. Pompidou was quoted as follows: 'Les thèses britanniques restent catégoriques. Nous n'arrivons pas à établir de rapprochement entre les Britanniques et nous, c'est-à-dire la France et ses partenaires européens. On ne peut pas dire pour l'instant que les points de vue se soient rapprochés. La France n'a aucune objection politique à l'entrée de la Grande Bretagne dans le Marché Commun. Cependant les difficultés actuelles relèvent non pas d'un problème technique, mais d'un problème de conception même du Marché Commun et de son avenir.'

[29] See *Observer*, 13 January 1963. See also the article by the Foreign Editor, *Financial Times*, 14 January 1963: 'One point only seems to be clear at this stage. Whether the French intention is to screw up the entrance fee, or whether General de Gaulle is determined to block British entry, the chances are that the French team here will continue to play for time.'

[30] See Chapter XII.

ference between Mr. Macmillan and Mr. Kennedy and to Mr. Kennedy's subsequent proposals to France, and Franco-German co-operation, provided the main themes for his 14 January press conference.[31] The grouping together of these subjects was not accidental, for it was clear that in the General's mind they were all interrelated. He commented first, and at length, on the negotiations with the British. His remarks must be read with the point the negotiations had reached in mind, for, coming on the eve of what was generally assumed to be the final stage of the negotiations, his comments amounted to a unilateral and arrogant pre-judgement of the outcome which deeply disturbed even those in France, and elsewhere in the Six, who might have accepted the failure of the negotiations with equanimity. As *Le Monde* pointed out, his pronouncement came either too late or too soon. If General de Gaulle was opposed, in principle, to British membership, he should have said so at the start. But if his real objection was that the British had failed to meet the conditions of the Six, he should have waited until after Mr. Heath had played his last cards.[32]

The technique used at General de Gaulle's press conferences is either for questions to be planted or for General de Gaulle to take a group of questions and to reformulate them so that they put to him the points on which he wants to make a statement of policy. The question he was answering on 14 January was: 'Can you explicitly define France's position concerning the entry of Britain into the Common Market and the political evolution of Europe?', and it can safely be assumed that he wanted the question formulated in this way in order to put the question of British entry into the Common Market into a political framework. General de Gaulle's reply was a long one and well worth reading in full. He began by recalling that the Treaty of Rome was concluded by six adjacent continental states which had similar economic structures and similar commercial traditions, and which were developing economically and socially at roughly the same rate. 'The very fact of grouping them and linking them together in such a way that what they produce, buy, sell, and consume, they produce, buy, sell, and consume by preference within their own grouping thus conforms to reality.' 'Furthermore,' he continued, 'it happens that there exists between them no kind of political grievance, no border

[31] The press conference began with a question about the French economy, but the rest of it was devoted to foreign policy questions.
[32] See leading article 'Trop Tôt ou Trop Tard', *Le Monde*, 20–21 January 1963.

disputes, no rivalry for domination or power', and 'they have a feeling of solidarity because not one of them is linked on the outside by any special political or military agreement'.

After noting that even with these similarities the formation of an economic Community among the Six had not been without difficulty, he emphasized that the Treaty of Rome had not been 'complete' until the agricultural regulations had been worked out, and, in this connexion, he emphasized that 'We cannot conceive of a Common Market in which French agriculture would not find outlets commensurate with its production.' After commenting, in passing, that the United Kingdom had refused to participate in the formation of the Community and had then 'put some pressure on the Six in order to prevent the application of the Common Market from really getting started', he turned specifically to the problems 'of a very great dimension' raised by British membership. 'England is, in effect, insular, maritime, linked through its trade, markets, and food supply to very diverse and often very distant countries. Its activities are essentially industrial and commercial, and only slightly agricultural. It has, throughout its work, very marked and original customs and traditions. In short, the nature, structure, and economic context of England differ profoundly from those of the other States of the Continent.' General de Gaulle then referred particularly to the fact that the British imported food at low prices and granted large subsidies to British farmers, which was 'obviously incompatible with the system the Six have quite naturally set up for themselves', a system which he then briefly characterized in the following way: 'The system of the Six consists of making a pool of the agricultural products of the entire Community, of strictly determining their prices, of forbidding subsidizing, of organizing their consumption between all the members and of making it obligatory for each of these members to pay to the Community any savings they might make by having foodstuffs brought in from outside instead of consuming those offered by the Common Market.' This was an accurate and unvarnished description of the agricultural policy as the French intended to make it work, although Mr. Mansholt might have described it somewhat differently. After referring to the fact that 'One was sometimes led to believe that our British friends, in applying for membership in the Common Market, agreed to change their own ways even to the point of applying all the conditions accepted and practised by the Six', presumably a reference to the attempts Mr. Macmillan had made at Champs and at Rambouillet to convince him of British willingness to accept fully the implications of membership, General de Gaulle made it clear that in his own view the British were not ready to accept the conditions of membership as he understood them. The question is whether 'Great Britain can at present place itself, with the Continent and like it, within a tariff that is truly common, give up all preference with regard to the Commonwealth, cease to claim that its agriculture be privileged and, even more, consider as null and void the commitments it has made with the countries that are part of its free trade area. That question is the one at issue. One cannot say that it has now been resolved. Will it be so one day? Obviously Britain alone can answer that.'

General de Gaulle then clearly revealed that he was not concerned simply at the prospect of British entry and the changes that this would inevitably bring in its train, but at the prospect of a further expansion of the Common Market to eleven, thirteen, or perhaps eighteen members, and at the orientation of an enlarged Community. He foresaw that in such a Community 'the cohesion of all its members, who would be very numerous and very diverse, would not hold for long and that in the end there would appear a colossal Atlantic Community, under American leadership and dependent on the United States, which would soon completely 'swallow up the European Community'. 'This', he said, 'is an assumption that can be perfectly justified in the eyes of some, but it is not at all what France wanted to do and what France is doing, which is a strictly European construction.' General de Gaulle then referred once again to the possibility that Britain might 'one day come round to transforming itself enough to belong to the European Community without restriction and without reservation, and placing it ahead of anything else', and he emphasized that then 'France would place no obstacle in its path'. But, once again, he gave his view that a British decision to join without reservation was some distance in the future: 'It is also possible that England is not yet prepared to do this, and that indeed appears to be the outcome of the long, long Brussels talks.'

Having thus given his judgement on the outcome of the Brussels negotiations, General de Gaulle indicated that, in his view, a failure of the negotiations need not disturb relations between France and the United Kingdom. Although presumably well-intentioned, the tributes he then paid to 'the resolution, the solidity, and the courage of the British people' during the war struck a rather sour note. General de Gaulle indicated that 'if the Brussels negotiations were not to succeed at this time, nothing would prevent the conclusion of an agreement of association between the Common Market and Great Britain in such a way as to safeguard trade'. Finally, he once again referred to the probability of eventual membership at some unspecified but distant date, and again he sounded a discordant note by congratulating Mr. Macmillan on having shown political wisdom and courage. 'Lastly, it is highly possible that Great Britain's own evolution and the evolution of the world would lead the British to the Continent, whatever may be the delays before complete realization. For my part, this is what I am inclined to believe, and that is why, in my opinion, it will be in any case a great honour for the British Prime Minister, for my friend Harold Macmillan, and for his Government, to have perceived this so early, to have had enough political courage to proclaim it and to have had their country take the first steps along the path that, one day perhaps, will bring it to make fast to the Continent.'[33]

A number of things emerged clearly from General de Gaulle's comments in addition to the central fact that so far as he was concerned British membership in the Community was premature and the negotiations in Brussels over. In the first place it was clear that he regarded the United Kingdom as a potential rival to France on the Continent. Throughout the whole period reviewed in this book, the negotiations on European economic arrangements have been complicated by the existence of an unacknowledged power struggle between the British and the French. In all the negotiations in which the two countries were involved the French and the British have been the protagonists. However, leaders on both sides, if asked, would have denied that a wish to be the dominant power in Europe was behind the positions they took in the negotiations, and, to a large extent, they would have been honest in their denials, for the negotiations have explicitly taken place on the economic and technical plane and there have been genuine economic and technical differences. But the implications in terms of political

[33] All quotations have been taken from the English translation of General de Gaulle's press conference issued by the French Embassy, London, and by the French Press and Information Service, New York, *Seventh Major News Conference held by General de Gaulle as President of the French Republic on January 14, 1963* (Speeches and Press Conferences, No. 185).

power have been there as well. The power implications have probably always been more obvious to the French than to the British, not because the French are more cunning but because they tend to think in a longer time-period and to work to a plan rather than by responding to circumstances and relying on improvisation as the British do.

In the second place, it was clear from General de Gaulle's comments that if he had his way the European Community would become not only an economic unit but a fairly protectionist economic unit, putting its own interests at all times ahead of the interests of others. As has been pointed out above, throughout the negotiations between Britain and the Six (on the free trade area, on 'bridge-building', on accession) the phrases 'inward-looking' and 'outward-looking' have been used and misused until they have lost much of their meaning and acquired pejorative overtones. The British have not infrequently condemned, as 'inward-looking', policies of the Six which, although they were less favourable to third countries than the policies the British were advocating, were nevertheless policies that the Six had to adopt if six economies were really to be merged into a single economy. Thus a common external tariff and a common agricultural policy are indisputable ingredients of the Community concept of the Six. So, too, is the concept of 'Community preference'. None of these things can, in and of itself, fairly be characterized as 'inward-looking', despite the fact that the adoption of a common policy may lead to a re-channelling of trade to the advantage of the members and to the disadvantage of third countries. Whether the Community is 'inward-looking' or 'outward-looking' depends not on the existence of a common external tariff and a common agricultural policy embodying the principle of 'Community preference', but on the height of the tariff and other barriers (e.g. levies) that surround the Community, that is, on the *degree* of Community preference that is sought. The conclusion to be drawn from General de Gaulle's remarks, particularly his remark about agriculture, was that he would put the *complete* satisfaction of the market needs of Community producers before *any* satisfaction of the needs of third countries; this can fairly be called a protectionist or 'inward-looking' goal.

In the third place, although ostensibly defending the Community, General de Gaulle gave fresh evidence of his basic contempt for the 'Community concepts' that were dear to the hearts of the 'Europeans' in France and elsewhere in the Six. He made an unnecessary gibe (dressed up as a compliment)[34] at the Commission but, of more importance, he offended against the basic concept of the Community by prejudging an issue that was before the Community as a whole and by stating his own views without prior consultation or notification to his partners and without any suggestion that this was a question which was not simply one for France alone to decide irrespective of the views of its partners.

Finally, he made it clear beyond any doubt that his most fundamental objection to the admission of the United Kingdom arose from his conviction that the British were too closely tied to the United States and that, as members of the Community, they would see that the Community developed in ways that were consonant with American interests and purposes. This was not the way in which he wanted to see the Community develop. In his press conference on 15 May, General de Gaulle, when contrasting his ideas of a political union of European states with the 'myths, stories, and parades' of those who advocated a 'supra-national Europe', had said that an integrated Europe on supra-national lines would, in effect, have no policies except perhaps that of an outsider: 'There would perhaps be a federator, but the federator would not be European. And it would not be an integrated Europe, it would be something quite different, much broader and much more extensive with, I repeat, a federator.'[35] In his 14 January press conference, the danger of the European Community being swallowed up and losing its identity in a 'colossal Atlantic Community' under United States leadership was again stressed but now not as the result of the pursuit of the 'myth' of 'supra-nationalism' but as the consequence of the accession of the British, and others in their train.

When General de Gaulle answered the next question: 'What is France's position concerning the Kennedy multilateral formula, that is to say, concerning the Nassau agreements?', he again made it plain that his essential objection to British membership was his conviction that the British were too closely tied to the United

---

[34] 'I will note in passing that, in this vast undertaking [the elaboration of the agricultural regulations], all the decisions taken were taken by the Governments, for nowhere else is there any authority or responsibility. But I should say that, in order to prepare and clarify matters, the Brussels Commission worked in a highly objective and pertinent fashion.'

[35] *Text of President de Gaulle's Sixth Press Conference, May 15, 1962*, issued by the French Embassy's Press and Information Service in New York, No. 175. See Chapter XII.

States and too ready to remain dependent on the United States. General de Gaulle began by restating the reasons why France needed a 'nuclear arsenal' of its own, and it is clear that his convictions had been greatly strengthened by the Cuban crisis (to which he refers four times): 'The Americans, finding themselves exposed to a direct atomic attack from the Caribbean, acted in such a way as to rid themselves of that menace and, if it had been necessary, to crush it without its having occurred either to them or to anyone else that the game would necessarily be played in Europe and without recourse to the direct assistance of the Europeans.' In addition, the fact that the Russians now had a 'nuclear arsenal powerful enough to endanger the very life of America' meant, he said, that 'no one in the world—particularly no one in America—can say if, where, when, how and to what extent the American nuclear weapons would be employed to defend Europe'. And, he continued: 'Thus principles and realities combine to lead France to equip itself with an atomic force of its own. This does not at all exclude, of course, the combination of the action of this force with the action of the similar forces of its allies. But, for us, in this specific case, integration is something that is unimaginable.'

General de Gaulle then described the Nassau agreement, pointing out that the bulk of American nuclear weapons would remain outside the multilateral force and under the direct orders of the President. He also referred to the special arrangements for sharing knowledge in the atomic energy field, in a way that made it clear enough that this was still a thorn in his flesh: 'To build these submarines and warheads, the British receive privileged assistance from the Americans. You know—I say this in passing—that this assistance was never offered to us and you should know, despite what some report, that we have never asked for it.' General de Gaulle then pointed out that France could not subscribe to the Nassau agreement. In terms of technology it would not be useful to buy Polaris missiles, since France had neither the submarines to launch them nor the thermonuclear warheads to arm them, and by the time France did produce these, it would probably have missiles of its own. However, it was clearly of greater importance to General de Gaulle that the Nassau proposals did not meet his 'principle' that France must be able to dispose 'in our own right of our deterrent force'. Although, like the British, the French would have had the formal right to withdraw their force in time of

supreme crisis, General de Gaulle made it plain that he thought
this right would in practice prove to be illusory. General de Gaulle
thus made it clear enough that, although Mr. Macmillan might see
the Nassau agreement as a step towards 'inter-dependence', he
saw it as a step towards greater British dependence on the United
States. It was the kind of relationship which—for France—he
would reject.

General de Gaulle then turned to the question of French–
German relations. Although he sought to dispel the suspicions of
an exclusive Franco-German relationship, suspicions that the
Benelux countries had had for a long time and which the Italians
had come to share, the warmth of his remarks and the enthusiasm
he showed for going ahead with organized bilateral co-operation
with the Germans overshadowed his reassurances that Franco-
German *rapprochement* need not affect relations with the rest of
the Six.

After this cannonade from General de Gaulle, there were three
courses of action open to the British Government. They could
have withdrawn their application to join the Community on the
ground that they had been negotiating on the assumption that all
the negotiating countries wanted the negotiations to succeed and
that this assumption had now been shown to be invalid. They
could have continued to negotiate, thus forcing the French to
bring the negotiations to an end. This was the course chosen. Or
they could have called for a 'Summit' meeting, either of the Six
and themselves or of the NATO countries, on the ground that
General de Gaulle had called into question the basic assumption
that a strong European Community would act in partnership with
the United States. The British were clearly right to reject the first
course of action, but it is arguable that the third course might have
been better than the second, since it would have met General de
Gaulle on his chosen ground—the political–military plane—and
would have forced a confrontation on the fundamental issues.
However, the third course contained the risk that it might simply
have hardened differences. It also held less hope of achieving
the immediate objective of British membership in the Community
than the second course appeared to do. Moreover the second
course of action was the one strongly preferred by the rest of the
Six.

For a short time there was some hope that General de Gaulle
might simply be bargaining and that his objective might not be

the exclusion of the British but British entry on French terms. M. Couve de Murville soon made it plain that General de Gaulle was not bargaining. But, even so, there was for a time a kind of stunned inability to believe that the French would be prepared to force a breakdown against the clear opposition of the rest of the Six and the Commission, and in the face of hard evidence that the British had in fact already accepted arrangements which General de Gaulle had said they were not yet ready to accept.

The British Government made no formal comment on the press conference during the next few days, although Mr. Heath, in response to a press question, made it clear that the British were negotiating for full membership in the Community and that an association, as suggested by General de Gaulle, would be an inadequate arrangement.[36] The Five, however, all made statements to the press contradicting General de Gaulle's assertion that the negotiations had yielded little progress, confirming their own desire for the British to join the Community, and expressing their confidence that acceptable solutions could be found to the remaining problems. M. Monnet also took issue with General de Gaulle.[37]

The day after the press conference, 15 January, Mr. Heath met with the Ministers of the Six as planned. After Mr. Mansholt had presented the report of his committee, Mr. Heath—in response to a direct, and prearranged, question from M. Spaak—made it plain that, provided agreement could be reached on the substantive aspects of the transitional arrangements for agriculture, he would accept 31 December 1969 as the terminal date for any special arrangements.[38] This was an important step forward, although it was one that many people felt the British would have done well to have taken earlier. This cool, apparently nerveless, continuation of the business in hand was, presumably, not the reaction that General de Gaulle had anticipated. The next day, 16 January, the conference of the Seven again met as planned and again Mr. Heath continued as though nothing untoward had happened and put forward a 'package' proposal covering most of the unresolved tariff questions. The Six met among themselves later in the day to continue their discussions on the financial regulation and on other questions preparatory to further meetings with the British the

[36] See *The Times*, 15 January 1963.
[37] Ibid., 16 January 1963, and *Financial Times*, 16 January 1963, and, for M. Monnet's statement, *The Times*, 17 January 1963.
[38] Horticulture was not under discussion at this meeting and was not covered by Mr. Heath's statement.

following day. But there were no meetings with the British on 17 January, for M. Couve de Murville asked that the Six meet alone to consider the future programme of work and it soon became clear that by this he meant the termination of the negotiations.

The Ministers of the Six held long discussions in private on 17 and 18 January. From the obviously well-informed accounts appearing in the continental and British press, it seems clear that M. Couve de Murville had instructions to bring the negotiations to an end but that he hoped to do so in a way that would not leave France isolated. When the discussion turned to the French assertion that the negotiations were simply going round in circles, the President of the Commission, Dr. Hallstein, was asked to join the Ministers. Throughout the negotiations the French and the Commission had usually held positions that were fairly close together, but Dr. Hallstein now sided with the Five, and was not prepared to underwrite the French estimate of the progress made or to subscribe to French assertions that there was little prospect of solving the remaining questions. There was also no support from the Five, or from the Commission, for pursuing General de Gaulle's suggestion of an association between the Six and the United Kingdom.[39] The Five tried, without success, to get M. Couve de Murville to agree to various proposals designed to demonstrate to General de Gaulle that his assumptions about the negotiations were wrong, in the rather forlorn hope that, provided the probability of real progress in the near future could be amply demonstrated, he would not block British entry. To this end the Five proposed that a working group drawn from the Commission and the seven delegations (the United Kingdom plus the Six), meeting under the chairmanship of Sr. Colombo (the Minister most likely to be acceptable to the French), should be asked to produce a report for the ministerial meeting of the negotiating conference which had been scheduled for 28 January. The Five proposed that this report should show what had already been agreed, and suggest solutions for the outstanding problems. This proposal clearly went too far for M. Couve de Murville, who was ready to have a committee perform a post mortem on the negotiations but not to have it suggest ways around the remaining difficulties. In an attempt at compromise, the Germans proposed that Sr.

---

[39] The Commission, as well as the French, had been among the severest critics of the concept of 'association' two years earlier.

Colombo should prepare the report by himself, but this, also, was too positive for M. Couve de Murville, who wanted the negotiations suspended, not given a new lease of life, however tenuous. By Friday, 18 January, the Five, in their efforts to find some way to persuade the French to continue with the negotiations, had resorted to threats of counter-measures—despite the strong Community tradition against this kind of bargaining. Thus, unless the French agreed to continue the negotiations with the British, the Five threatened to block action within the Community on those questions in which the French were particularly interested: the financial regulation on agriculture, the common policy for dairy products, the renewal of the Convention for the Association of the Overseas Territories, and the arrangements needed to carry out French commitments to Algeria. After seeking further instructions from Paris, the most that M. Couve de Murville would concede was that the conference should meet again, as had earlier been agreed, on 28 January, but he insisted that the French proposal for a suspension of negotiations should be considered again at that time.

Throughout these discussions among the Six, Mr. Heath re-mained in the background, although he was kept fully informed by the Five. He joined the Six briefly at the conclusion of their discussions and M. Fayat (the Belgian deputy Foreign Minister and chairman of the conference) made the following formal state-ment, which, being acceptable to the conference as a whole, was subsequently released to the press: 'At the Sixteenth Session of the Conference the French delegation asked for the negotiations with the United Kingdom to be suspended. The five other delegations of the European Economic Community and the British delega-tion opposed this suggestion. Discussion of this matter will be continued at the next meeting of the Conference on January 28th.'[40] M. Fayat added that the Working Party on Hong Kong and the discussion in Luxembourg on problems connected with British entry into the ECSC would take place later that week, as scheduled, and the French Government would decide whether or not French experts would attend.[41] The negotiations had been granted a stay

---

[40] See *The Times*, *Financial Times*, *Guardian*, *Le Monde*, 18 and 19 January, and *Sunday Times*, 20 January 1963. The *Observer*, 20 January 1963, has an interesting chronological account of the developments from 11–19 January by Nora Beloff. The quotation is from Agence Internationale d'Information pour la Presse, Luxembourg, *EUROPE, Documents*, No. 186/187, 5 February 1963.

[41] French experts did not attend.

of execution. But it was clear that unless Dr. Adenauer were prepared to put real pressure on General de Gaulle the conference would meet again only to break down.

Dr. Adenauer's visit to Paris from 20 to 23 January had been arranged for some time and its coincidence with the crisis in the Brussels negotiations was accidental in so far as the Germans were concerned. General de Gaulle must have had Dr. Adenauer's visit in mind when he set the date for his press conference but he presumably thought that by the time the Chancellor arrived the negotiations would be over rather than in a state of suspended animation. In the event, the visit acquired an unexpected importance, and great pressure was brought on Dr. Adenauer to use his influence to bring about a change in General de Gaulle's position. The Social Democrats wanted him to postpone his visit to Paris as an indication of his disapproval and in the hope that this would induce General de Gaulle to change his mind. The other German political parties (the CDU and the FDP) wanted him to go to Paris as planned, but like the Social Democrats they urged him to use his influence with General de Gaulle to keep the negotiations going. M. Monnet (who at one time had had considerable influence with the Chancellor) also urged Dr. Adenauer to work for a resumption of negotiations. Mr. Kennedy sent a personal message to Dr. Adenauer. But Dr. Adenauer was himself doubtful about the need for British membership and it is not clear how much of an effort he made to change General de Gaulle's mind.

At the time of the visit there was considerable feeling—outside Germany—that Dr. Adenauer should bring pressure on General de Gaulle by refusing to sign the Franco-German treaty unless the French would agree to a continuation of the negotiations. This was too much to expect of the Germans, and particularly of Dr. Adenauer, and it is worth noting that in Germany itself the prevailing view, even among those who were strongly in favour of British membership, was that the signature of the treaty should take place as planned, although there was some suggestion that the need for ratification by the Bundestag might later be a means of bringing useful pressure on the French.[42] Reconciliation with France was the single achievement of which Dr. Adenauer was most proud. His highly successful visit to France in July, and General de Gaulle's even more triumphant return visit in September had demonstrated that there was strong popular support

[42] See *The Times* and *Financial Times*, 21 January 1963.

for the policy even in the border areas where memories of two wars might have been expected to be longest. Although cynics might say that the Franco-German Treaty was the product of a failure by the Six to launch a more ambitious scheme, it seems probable that the Chancellor had largely forgotten the antecedents of the treaty and that by the time he went to Paris it had become, for him at least, the documentary proof of his greatest success.

However, although the German Government was not prepared to use the treaty as a bargaining counter, efforts were made by Dr. Schroeder (the Foreign Secretary), who accompanied Dr. Adenauer, to get the French to accept some kind of formula which would allow the negotiations to proceed. Prof. Hallstein had been among those who had talked with Dr. Adenauer before his visit to Paris and he, M. Monnet, and others were at this time urging that the Commission be given a mandate to summarize the progress already made in the negotiations and to make recommendations on the settlement of the outstanding points. Since the Commission and the French had had similar views on most issues during the negotiations, this proposal might have appealed to the French had their real concern been with the terms of entry rather than with the principle of entry. The Germans apparently left Paris with the impression that some agreement on a mandate to the Commission had been reached, although press reports suggested that the French had a very different kind of mandate in mind from that advocated by Prof. Hallstein and others, reports that soon proved to be accurate.

Before the Ministers of the Six met again in Brussels on 28 January there was much discussion among the Five and between the Five and the United Kingdom about how best to proceed if the French continued to oppose the continuation of the negotiations. For a time the Benelux countries advocated proceeding on an 'empty chair' basis, that is, for continuing the negotiations between the Five and the British, without the French. Rather surprisingly, both M. Spaak and M. Monnet for a time supported this approach, although, in other contexts, both of them had formerly been strongly opposed to tactical moves which isolated the French. However, the 'empty chair' approach found little favour with the Germans, the Italians, or the Commission. The British were also reluctant to proceed on this basis for they wanted to avoid any charges of seeking to break up the Six. Moreover, there were difficulties from their own standpoint, for although they were prepared to make some further concessions to join the Community, they did not want to make 'final' concessions in negotiations with the Five, only to be pressed for still more 'final' concessions in any subsequent bargaining with the French. In the highly emotional atmosphere that existed during the last days of the negotiations some delegates from the Five were ready to contemplate breaking the Community and forming a Common Market with the United Kingdom instead of with the French, but this was never the official position of any of the Five Governments. Although there was little real hope that the French would agree to any report by the Commission that was designed to advance negotiations, hopes were pinned on this proposal for lack of any better plan. Just before the Six resumed their formal discussions on 28 January the British made it clear that they would accept such a proposal provided the time allowed for the report was relatively brief (they did not want the proposal for a report to be simply a stalling device), provided the Commission took its instructions from the Seven (i.e. the United Kingdom and the Six) and that the report was presented to the Seven, not the Six, and provided it was clear that the negotiations would be continued on completion of the report. The British also felt that pending the completion of the report, the negotiations at the official level on various non-controversial questions should be continued.[43]

As noted above, the British Government did not comment immediately on General de Gaulle's press conference. However, on 21 January, in the course of a speech at Liverpool, Mr. Macmillan sought to make plain the nature of the difference between himself and General de Gaulle and to set the record straight. Although M. Couve de Murville, in the discussions in Brussels, had formally based the French case for a suspension of negotiations on the fact that the negotiations were going round in circles, owing to British unwillingness to accept the Treaty of Rome and agreed Community policies, General de Gaulle had made it clear that a large part of his objection to British membership was unrelated to the course of the negotiations. Various rumours were circulating about what had transpired at Rambouillet and Nassau and there were allegations in the continental press, which apparently emanated from sources in the French Government, that Mr. Kennedy and Mr. Macmillan had reached secret agreements affecting the future of Europe. In his speech at Liverpool, Mr.

[43] See *Observer*, 27 January 1963.

Macmillan dealt first with the formal argument and reiterated that the British Government accepted the Treaty of Rome and 'aligned' itself with the political implications as well as the economic content of the treaty. He made it clear that a large measure of agreement had already been reached and that 'when after long months of negotiation this last round started a week ago it was recognised on all sides that the few outstanding problems were capable of solution'. He pointed out that everyone knew that the negotiations would be long and complicated and that had there been 'an objection in principle' he should have been told so at the beginning. He then turned to various statements that had been made about the Rambouillet and Nassau meetings

. . . it has been suggested that by making the Polaris arrangement with President Kennedy a few days after I had seen General de Gaulle himself at Rambouillet I did not treat him with absolute sincerity. On the contrary we discussed this question and I explained that if the Americans decided to abandon Skybolt as unlikely to prove satisfactory I would do my utmost at Nassau to obtain an effective alternative. I explained to him in some detail my view of the relations between interdependence and independence, and said that we must have a British deterrent available for independent use if need be. I am sure he fully understood our position. This impression was confirmed through diplomatic contacts after the Nassau agreement had been announced. I do not feel called upon to deal with some of the other rumours which I have seen quoted, rumours about new secret undertakings given by me at Nassau and so forth. All these are false.

The main interest of Mr. Macmillan's speech lay in the emphasis he put on 'interdependence', on 'alliance', and on 'partnership', in contrast to the emphasis put by General de Gaulle on national power and independence:

I do not believe that in the second half of this century there can be or ought to be domination or the pursuit of the concepts of hegemony by any one free state over other equally free states. Nor can any country in these days stand entirely on its own. Alliances are essential to security. We must have interdependence to meet the needs of modern defence. We must have it too in the field of economic and monetary development but each nation must also preserve that independence, without which it cannot be worthy of itself or make a full contribution to the alliance. . . . It is because our people have felt something new was wanted, something more generous, more noble and more up-to-date, more in tune with the aspirations of youth as well as more long-sighted, that we have been able to get a general acceptance, first for the NATO policies, then for the policies of European unity generally, and now for our application to join the Economic Community. In other words, our aim is to make a true European unity. Then and only then will Europe be great and strong enough to build a more equal and worthy partnership with North America. The right relationship between friends and allies is the relationship of equal balance and co-operation in which no partner seeks to dominate the others or dictate to the others.[44]

On 28 January the Foreign Ministers of the Six met together again in Brussels to try to agree to a proposal which they could put to the British. The Five were agreed that the Commission should be asked to make a report to the seven negotiating governments indicating the agreements already reached and proposing solutions for the remaining problems. They were also agreed that the Commission should be given three weeks to draw up the report and that the negotiations with the British should be resumed not later than ten days after the report had been submitted. However, although the French had agreed with the Germans to give the Commission a mandate, M. Couve de Murville made clear that the kind of mandate they had in mind was very different from the one favoured by the rest of the Six and the Commission. He proposed that the Commission should be asked to report on the consequences of enlarging the Community and that, in doing so, the Commission might well consider the advantages of completing certain parts of the Community's policy before including new members. In addition, the French Foreign Minister made it clear that although he was ready for the Commission to list the points agreed and the points still outstanding in the negotiations, he was not prepared to allow the Commission to suggest answers to the remaining questions. M. Couve de Murville further maintained that any Commission report must be a report to the Six, not to the seven negotiating governments. Finally, he was not prepared to accept an advance commitment to resume negotiations, maintaining that the Six should 'reflect' on the wisdom of continuing the negotiations in the light of the Commission's report. A report along the lines proposed by the French was clearly intended to gain recruits from the Commission and from the Five for the French position and to obscure the reasons for the eventual breakdown, not to offer any hope of bringing the negotiations to a successful conclusion.

[44] The quotations are taken from the text contained in *EUROPE, Documents*, loc. cit.

After two days of fruitless and sometimes acrimonious discussion the ministers of the Six accepted the fact that they could not reach agreement and, in the late afternoon of 29 January, Mr. Heath was asked to join the Six for the last time. M. Fayat, the chairman, formally told him of the proposal agreed by the Five and rejected by the French.[45] After his short factual statement the ministers of each of the Seven countries, and Prof. Hallstein for the Commission, spoke briefly in an atmosphere that was highly charged with emotion. M. Spaak spoke first. He was in a unique position as the 'father of the Treaty of Rome' and the man who had presided over the meeting in November 1955 when the British and the Six chose divergent paths. He of all the ministers present had the most impressive record of achievement in the cause of European unity and could not be accused (as some accused Mr. Luns, the Dutch Foreign Minister) of putting a higher priority on British membership than on European unity. His obvious regret at the exclusion of the British and his deep anger at the way it had been done were not superficial or momentary reactions. However, although he was obviously sincere in his desire for British membership it was clear that what troubled him most deeply was the fact that one of the Community countries was forcing its will on the others:

... Great Britain has been excluded, without valid reason in the opinion of five of the delegations of the Common Market, from the negotiations over its entry. ... When we made the Rome Treaty we proclaimed without cease that the Community we were forming was an open Community. This is written into the text of the Treaty. Today, without being able to explain our attitude to Great Britain we are forced, some of us against our wishes, against our will, against our hopes, not to respect the policy we laid down. ... what is happening today is unfortunately much bigger and more important than the question of the negotiations between the Community and Great Britain. It is the foreign policy of the Community countries which has suddenly been altered. It should be remembered that for over a year each of us, including the French delegation, has ceaselessly maintained that our

[45] The text of the mandate agreed by the Five was as follows: 'The EEC Commission is asked to draw up a report during the next three weeks on the present state of the negotiations between Great Britain and the six States of the European Economic Community, concerning accession; in this report it should outline the results already obtained, the questions still pending, and it should give its opinion on the latter. This report will be submitted to each of the seven delegations making up the Conference. The work of the conference will be resumed not later than ten days after this report has been submitted.' *EUROPE, Documents*, loc. cit.

aim was to receive Great Britain into the Community, and that in order to succeed we would conduct the negotiations loyally. On 14th January, we were faced with a spectacular reversal of French policy demanding a spectacular reversal of our own policy, without being forewarned by any of the diplomatic means at the disposal of our countries, and without even being permitted to discuss the reasons leading up to this event. . . . As soon as one member of a Community wishes to compel all the others to take decisions which are of capital importance for its life, the Community spirit ceases to exist. It will be extremely difficult, I am convinced, to continue to develop the economic Europe. As for the political Europe about which we had dreamed as a necessary consequence of economic organisation, I do not know when it will be possible to speak of this again, since there is incontestably no more confidence. . . . In closing I wish to express my deep regret at what happened and my solemn protest against the way in which this decision has been imposed upon us.[46]

Mr. Schaus for Luxembourg, Sr. Colombo for Italy, and Mr. Luns for the Netherlands followed with short but outspoken statements emphasizing their disagreement with the substance of the French position and with the means employed to bring the negotiations to an end, and, like M. Spaak, expressing their concern for the future of the Community itself. Herr Schroeder then spoke for Germany. He, like the rest of the Five, recorded his view that solutions could have been found to the outstanding problems and expressed his disappointment at the outcome. But he was rather less critical of the French and less gloomy about the future of the Community than the others had been. He emphasized that at the time the Treaty of Rome was ratified, the German Government had promised the Bundestag that it would try to widen the membership and that this policy remained unchanged. He expressed regret that the proposal for a Commission report ('which could have done no harm') had not been acceptable. He promised that the German Government would not give up the idea of British entry but admitted that for the time being he did not see what there was to be done. And, he concluded, 'The only hope I can express is that the movement towards us which has started in Great Britain will not die suddenly as a result of this event, and that, despite today's setback, the movement may stay alive. If so I—and I say this on behalf of my government—am convinced that the day will come when we will be able to settle this problem.'[47]

Prof. Hallstein, the President of the Commission, was even more

[46] EUROPE, Documents, loc. cit.   [47] Ibid.

circumspect in his remarks and apparently principally concerned to safeguard the position of the Commission. He expressed the Commission's regret 'at the way in which the conference has moved, so that we are no longer able to continue negotiating as we have done up till now' and he noted that the Commission was 'aware that the Community is not a concern to serve the egoistical interests of its members, but that it has a responsibility towards the other whose fate is affected by its actions and its failure to act'.[48] These were rather timid and tortuous comments, given the fact that, as M. Spaak had pointed out so clearly, the fundamental concept of the Community had been directly challenged by one of the members.[49]

M. Couve de Murville, who was the last of the Six to speak, stuck to General de Gaulle's contention that the French were simply looking facts in the face: the negotiations have been going around in circles since October and Great Britain was not yet ready to accept the disciplines of the treaty, notably those of the agricultural policy. He then spoke briefly about the kind of Commission report the French had advocated and commented scornfully on the suggestion of the Five that the Commission, an organ of the Six, should be asked to make a report for the Seven: 'I still fail to understand how such a suggestion could ever have been made.' This was, perhaps, a useful debating point but no more. He concluded by reaffirming the French official position that the burden of proof lay on the United Kingdom, not on France. 'We are not saying "England must not join the Common Market". We are saying "are the conditions fulfilled?" '[50] But he convinced none of his hearers.

Mr. Heath concluded the round of ministerial comments with a long, forthright, and moving statement, which put the blame for the breakdown squarely on the French, but did so without vindictiveness. Mr. Heath began by confirming what was already well known, that is, that had the Six accepted the proposal for a Commission report in the terms described by M. Fayat, the British would have done so as well. Then, after briefly recalling the assumptions and the hopes on which the negotiations had opened, he turned to the allegations General de Gaulle had made about the

[48] *EUROPE, Documents,* loc. cit.
[49] Of the members of the Commission, Dr. Mansholt publicly took the strongest line against the French position. He was also the first to speak out publicly. See his speech in Louvain on 22 January 1963 (EEC Press Release).
[50] *EUROPE, Documents,* loc. cit.

lack of progress in the negotiations and about Britain's unwillingness to accept the full implications of the Treaty of Rome, and refuted them one by one. He then said:

The plain fact is that the time had come when the negotiations were, for some, too near to success. It is clear to the world that they have been halted, not for any technical or economic reasons, but on purely political grounds and on the insistence of a single Government. I find the attitude of that Government irreconcilable both with the terms of the Treaty of Rome, which in its preamble and in Article 237 extends an open invitation to other European States to join the Community, and with what that Government has itself said in the past. I should like to remind the Leader of the French Delegation of the speech he made in the Consultative Assembly of the Council of Europe on 2 March 1961, a speech which was read at the time with the deepest interest throughout Europe and especially in my own country. . . .[51] There was, of course, a response to that speech. It was because, as M. Couve [sic] had said, full membership of the Community was the only satisfactory solution, and because as we have always made plain, our purposes were political as well as economic, that I spoke as I did on 10 October 1961.

Mr. Heath then thanked the chairman, the other delegations, the Commission and the Secretariat, and, not least, the Governments of the Commonwealth countries, for the care and effort they had all put into the negotiations. In conclusion he expressed what were very clearly his own deeply-felt convictions as well as the policy of the British Government:

Mr. Chairman, as my colleagues have said this afternoon, the events of the last few weeks have placed in jeopardy progress towards that true European unity which, I believe, many millions of people desire. But although, as has just been said, this is a sad moment for European unity, I should like straight away to say one thing. We told you, at the very beginning of these negotiations, that we wanted to go forward with you in the building of a new Europe. Our words were very carefully weighed. They remain true today. We have been encouraged by the upsurge of support for the fullest British participation in a united Europe which has been demonstrated in so many quarters in these recent weeks. And so I would say to my colleagues: they should have no fear. We in Britain are not going to turn our backs on the mainland of Europe or on the countries of the Community. We are a part of Europe: by geography, tradition, history, culture and civilisation. We shall continue to work with all our friends in Europe for the true unity and strength of this continent.[52]

[51] See above, p. 334.   [52] *EUROPE, Documents,* loc. cit.

The seventeenth ministerial session was formally closed by M. Fayat, who went out of his way in doing so to pay a special tribute to Mr. Heath and the British delegation. The negotiations had ended in failure, but they had gone far to wipe out the feeling that had persisted since 1955 that the British were at worst hostile and, at best, unsympathetic to the unity of Europe. And Mr. Heath had earned more genuine respect and affection from his European colleagues than had any British minister concerned with European questions since the end of the war.

The state of the negotiations at the time of the breakdown

Although the conference had been unable to reach agreement on a mandate to the Commission, less than a month after the negotiations ended the Commission in fact produced a report in response to a request from the European Parliament.[53] In accordance with the terms of the Parliament's resolution, the report set out 'both the results already obtained and the problems still outstanding' and gave the Commission's 'opinion on the latter'. The report amply refuted the French assertion that the British Government had been unwilling to accept the disciplines of the treaty and supported the contention of the Five, the British, and the Commission, that substantial progress had been made and that the remaining problems were capable of solution. The problems outstanding were, however, potentially rather more troublesome than some of the statements made by Mr. Macmillan and Mr. Heath seemed to suggest.

The principal agreements reached in the negotiations have been commented on above. The problems remaining to be solved fell into several categories. There were the 'nil' and reduced tariff requests. These were clearly on their way to a settlement when the negotiations broke down, and the reasons for delay were as much the result of disagreement among the Six as between the Six and the United Kingdom. There were certain details about the phasing out of Commonwealth preferences and the phasing in of Community preferences that still had to be agreed, but no important principles were involved and this could have been settled without difficulty. The arrangement for Hong Kong had still to be settled. At the time of the breakdown the British had put forward a

[53] European Economic Community, Commission, *Report to the European Parliament on the State of the Negotiations with the United Kingdom* (Brussels, 26 February 1963).

proposal to which the Six had not formally responded, but the Commission's report suggested the line they would presumably have taken. From this it seems probable that a compromise would have been found which would have given Hong Kong treatment similar to that agreed for India and Pakistan, with certain additional understandings linking gradual liberalization of trade between the expanded Community and Hong Kong with commitments on origin controls in Hong Kong.[54] The arrangements to be applied to the Federation of Rhodesia and Nyasaland had not been discussed in any detail because of the uncertainty over the future of the Federation. The Commission in its report simply recorded this fact without making any forecast of the outcome but it seems safe to assume that, after the break-up of the Federation, Nyasaland would have been offered association, but that difficulties would have arisen had Rhodesia pressed a claim for association. Conceivably some arrangement might have been made for tobacco but even this would have been difficult because of the conflicting interests of Greece (already associated with the Community) and pressure from the United States for non-discriminatory treatment.

The position reached in the discussion on British agriculture has already been described. As a result of the work of the Mansholt Committee it seems probable that compromises were in sight on the products under review. The Commission's report was not very explicit, but it seemed to suggest that the British would have accepted the 'principles' put forward by the Six, that the Six would have made some concession on the timing of the alignment of cereal prices, and that the Six would have agreed to review the desirability of intervention on the pig and egg markets after the British, and others, had become members of the Common Market. Various agricultural problems affecting both Commonwealth trade and the adjustments to be made in British agriculture had not been discussed, since the Six had not yet agreed on their own common policy. The British and the Six had discussed in a preliminary way an 'interim procedure' that might have been adopted to deal with these and the other outstanding questions during the interval between the initialling of an agreement and Britain's actual joining of the Community, a period which might well have covered almost a year. If a suitable interim procedure could have been agreed, it would have been possible to leave many of the details (as well as various questions that were not yet ripe for discussion) to have

[54] See Commission, *Report*, pp. 44-45.

been settled during this period. Presumably Mr. Heath and Mr. Macmillan assumed that some such arrangement would be made when they spoke of the possibility of a quick agreement.

There were, however, two big unsettled problems, in addition to British agriculture, on which something would have had to have been agreed before any British Government could have put an agreement to the House of Commons. The first was the arrangements to be made for New Zealand and the second was the arrangement to be made for the other EFTA countries. The problem of New Zealand was, of course, directly tied to the common policy to be adopted for dairy products and for lamb, neither of which had been settled by the Six themselves. Moreover within the Six there were differences of view about the need for special arrangements for New Zealand. The Commission, in its report, in effect accepted the fact that for butter, but only for butter, New Zealand had a special problem that must be recognized, but its comment on a solution was so cautious as to be almost meaningless: 'In this connection the Commission considers that the Conference should have sought the best practical means by which New Zealand could gradually adjust itself to the new situation that would have been created by United Kingdom membership in the Common Market.' The report then referred rather cryptically to the fact that an 'appraisal of any solution consonant with such an objective' depended not only on the common policy for dairy products but also on the financial regulation. From this and comments made earlier, it seems probable that the Six were thinking in terms of some kind of an 'income guarantee' for New Zealand exports of butter, presumably for a limited period. Whether this would have been considered adequate by the New Zealand Government, and hence by the House of Commons, remains a question for speculation.

The arrangements to be made for the other EFTA countries was potentially an even more troublesome problem. Denmark and Norway had opened negotiations with the Community looking towards full membership. So, too, had Ireland, which although not a member of EFTA was closely tied to the United Kingdom economically. Only the negotiations with the Danes had proceeded very far by the time the negotiations with the United Kingdom broke down, but it seems unlikely that, had Britain's negotiation been successful, insuperable difficulties would have arisen with respect to any of these three countries.[55] The problems raised by

[55] See Commission, *Report*, pp. 94 ff.

the applications of the three neutrals (Austria, Sweden, Switzer-land) were potentially much more difficult because of the doctrine the Six had evolved on 'association'—the arrangement for which these countries had applied—and also because of the Community's related views about neutrality. The Portuguese application also posed problems. Although there is nothing in Article 238 to limit association to countries like Greece that are in the process of development and are unable for that reason (but for that reason only) to undertake the full commitments of the Treaty of Rome, there has been a disposition in Community circles to interpret the article in that way. Portugal, by analogy with Greece, and being both a NATO member and an underdeveloped country, was in some respects the strongest candidate for association. But an association arrangement with Portugal raised two issues which the Community wanted to avoid: first, the problem of the Portuguese territories in Africa—Mozambique and Angola—and second, the precedent that would be created for an association arrangement with Spain.[56]

An association with the neutrals raised problems of a different order. As the Commission pointed out in its report: 'From the Community point of view, it has always been maintained that the customs union was not to be thought of as an arrangement in isolation; it only made sense and had practical prospects of success if it were embedded in an economic union.' This concept clearly raised problems both for the neutrals and for the Community. The question for the neutrals was essentially how far they could go in accepting common policies with the Six and, in particular, a common commercial policy including a common tariff. The questions for the Six were partly institutional and partly the familiar ones of how to maintain the identity, forward drive, and cohesion of the Community if certain countries had all the econo-mic benefits of membership without all the obligations of mem-bership. In addition, if an association agreement were made with the three neutrals, the problem of controlling the precedent would arise, for Article 238 (unlike Article 237—membership) is not limited to European countries. Beyond these very real problems there was also an emotional reluctance to accom-modate the Swedes and Swiss, based on the feeling that these

[56] On 9 February 1962 Spain had applied for association with the Community, with a view to complete integration at a later date. The Community had taken no action on the Spanish application by the time the negotiations with the British broke down.

countries had profited from their neutrality in the last war and now wanted to enjoy the advantages of NATO protection without assuming any of the obligations.[57] The Six were more tolerant of the Austrian position since, although her neutrality was formally a matter of choice, it was recognized that Austria, unlike Sweden and Switzerland, had no effective option save neutrality. Moreover, Austria was much more dependent economically on the Community than were the other two neutrals.

During the eighteen months that the British were negotiating, the three neutrals had given much thought to the problem of association and had defined with some precision the points of conflict between accepting the Treaty of Rome and maintaining a policy of neutrality. They had also examined ways of meeting the legitimate insistence of the Six that any arrangement must be a balanced one, giving equal rights and obligations to both sides, and that·the institutional arrangements should not prejudice the development of the Community. In essence the neutrals wanted an arrangement between themselves and the Community under which they would accept the same economic commitments as members and enjoy the same economic advantages as members but which would permit them to arrive at these results in their own way. To be consistent with their policy of neutrality the neutrals felt that they could not sign a permanent treaty but had to be free to withdraw from their association with the Community at any time. Moreover they had to retain the right to determine their policies unilaterally and independently. Thus, although the neutrals were prepared to go very far in adopting a tariff identical with the common tariff, and policies identical with those pursued by the Community, both internally and with respect to third countries,[58] the adoption of these policies had to be by their own decision and could not result automatically from a

[57] Although there was some basis for this view, it ignored the very large percentage of their gross national product that Sweden and Switzerland contribute to defence.

[58] Although over a wide range of questions the neutrals would have had little difficulty in aligning their tariffs and commercial policies with those of the Community, there were a few potentially very difficult problems. For example, Sweden was unlikely to agree to limit its imports of Soviet oil as severely as the Community countries would probably have decided to limit their own imports (this question was then under discussion in the Community). Where their tariffs or policies differed from those of the Community, the neutrals were ready to agree to take measures to prevent trade diversion, but this might not have seemed adequate to the Six.

Community decision or be the product of a majority decision. In addition to these two major points of principle, each of the neutral countries also had particular points on which, for reasons unconnected with its neutrality, it wanted to negotiate special arrangements. Of these the most difficult was the Swiss desire to maintain its highly subsidized system of farming.

Within the Six, opinion was divided on what, if anything, should be done about the neutrals. As indicated above, some arrangement could doubtless have been agreed upon for Austria.[59] In Germany, the industrialists were actively pressing for an arrangement, particularly with Sweden. The French Government had recently had reason to be grateful for the neutrality of Switzerland in connexion with the Algerian settlement, but French industry was opposed to free trade with the neutrals, perhaps particularly with Sweden because the paper industry feared Swedish competition. The Benelux and Italian industrialists were generally in favour of some kind of arrangement with all three countries. However, the positions of the Governments had not yet been made clear and in all the Six countries the strongest 'Europeans', like M. Spaak and M. Monnet, tended to take a hard line against any formal association with the neutrals, largely on the grounds that special arrangements of this kind would weaken the cohesion of the Community and impede its evolution into a politically effective unit. This position was strongly held by influential people in the Commission and also attracted support from the United States Administration. Because of these differences of view it is clear that no quick solution to the problem of the neutrals was in sight. Probably the most that the Six would have agreed to was a tariff 'standstill' until after the forthcoming 'Kennedy round' of GATT tariff negotiations and an undertaking to re-examine the question at some later date in the light of the results of the 'Kennedy round' and other developments. Under such an arrangement, the United Kingdom could not have made any further cuts in its tariffs on EFTA trade, but it could have postponed raising its tariffs against the neutrals (and presumably any other EFTA country for which no other arrangement had been agreed) at least until after the GATT tariff negotiations had been concluded.[60] Although agreement on a 'standstill' would

---

[59] During the spring of 1963—after the breakdown—the Six indicated their willingness to discuss an arrangement with Austria.

[60] There was some hope that the 'Kennedy round' would result in a substantial enough reduction in the common external tariff so that it would not have been

not have met the terms of the London Agreement, it seems probable that the neutrals would themselves have decided that it was in their own interest for the British to join the Community, partly because there would then be a powerful advocate for their 'association' within the Community, partly because the British could have exerted pressure for liberal commercial policies from within the Community. Had the neutrals themselves formally released the British Government from the terms of the London Agreement it would have been difficult for critics in the House of Commons to accuse the Government of 'betraying EFTA', although, as in the case of the Commonwealth, many of the domestic critics of the Government's actions tended to be more zealous than the countries they were defending. All this is speculation. The EFTA question was one on which it might well have been possible for the French Government to have broken the negotiations in a way that would have left the record muddy and opinion divided on where the fault for failure lay. But such a course, although, perhaps, it might have been more welcome to many Frenchmen, was less consistent with the nature of General de Gaulle than the more brutal but less uncertain way he chose to end the negotiations.

The reasons for the breakdown

General de Gaulle has never concealed the fact that he thinks of Europe in continental or, rather, in Carolingian terms, and that he regards the United Kingdom not as a natural part of Europe but as a part of a rival Anglo-Saxon power group. The British Government knew from the start of the negotiations that at some point they might face a French political veto. However, the French Government, like the Governments of the other members of the Community, had repeatedly emphasized that the EEC was an 'open' Community and had said that they would welcome a British decision to join the Community. And the French Government, as Mr. Heath and the Five pointed out, had joined with the other Governments of the Community in accepting the British application and in agreeing to the opening of formal negotiations.[61] On

---

appreciably different from the reduced tariff applied by the United Kingdom to imports from the EFTA countries, thus eliminating the need to raise these rates.

[61] Both the British and the French Governments were guilty of equivocation on the point of whether the negotiations were negotiations to join, or simply negotiations to see whether it was feasible to take the decision to join. Both Governments described the negotiations in different ways at different times.

the evidence now available, it is difficult to avoid the conclusion that the Government of General de Gaulle advocated membership for the United Kingdom when they were confident that there was no chance that the British Government would apply to join, and that they subsequently acted on the assumption that the British Government would not, in fact, be willing, or politically strong enough, to accept the terms which a strict reading of the Treaty of Rome and of the subsequent decisions of the Community implied. It is not clear whether the French tactic of insisting on the need for strict conformity with the Treaty (and full acceptance of the policies subsequently elaborated by the Community) was adopted for the express purpose of keeping the British out of the Community, or was simply a means of ensuring that if—contrary to expectations—the British did join, they would do so on terms that would be as advantageous as possible for France.[62] In either case it seems clear enough that the French Government assumed, until fairly late in the day, that there was little chance of the British being able to swallow the kind of terms that not only they, but the Commission, and the rest of the Six, with varying degrees of enthusiasm, would agree to be necessary. The fact that the promotion of French self-interest coincided to such a large extent with the defence of Community principles meant that the French motives were never clear either to their partners in the Six or to the United Kingdom. It seems probable that there was also confusion among the French themselves, for many, if not all, of the French officials most directly concerned appear to have been negotiating in good faith.

[62] In June 1962 the Agence Internationale d'Information pour la Presse in Luxembourg reproduced a memorandum on how to sell the Gaullist conception of a European confederation which, it said, had been written in the summer of 1960 by M. Alain Peyrefitte, who was at that time a Gaullist Deputy but later became the French Minister of Information. In this memorandum ways of exploiting the hopes and making use of the forms and language of the 'Europeans' to attain Gaullist ends were very cynically outlined. A strategy with respect to the United Kingdom which corresponded fairly closely with that in fact followed by the French Government was also suggested. In particular, the author argued the advantages of pushing the United Kingdom into a position of either having to join the Six without reservations or of having to remain on the outside, but without being in a position to complain of being left out. He felt that confronted with this choice the United Kingdom would remain outside. He made it clear that the British were not wanted 'during the first stage' of the development of the Gaullist plan for Europe although, like General de Gaulle, he seemed to suggest that at some much later date they might become a member of a European confederation. See *EUROPE, Documents*, No. 142, 6 June 1962.

The controlling factor in French policy was not, however, what particular French ministers or civil servants thought but what General de Gaulle thought. During his talks with Mr. Macmillan at the Château de Champs in June 1962, General de Gaulle was apparently genuinely surprised by Mr. Macmillan's view that, in the future, Britain's role should be a primarily European one, and he seems, for the first time, to have realized that the British application to join the Community represented a fundamental change in British policy and a willingness to see the United Kingdom's economic ties with the Commonwealth countries altered profoundly. It seems probable that this conversation, and perhaps reports from his ministers about the extent of the concessions the British were making during the first week of August, led him to feel that, contrary to his original expectation, the British might really be in the process of reorienting their policies. It seems probable that General de Gaulle had evolved his own policy for Europe on the assumption that this process of readaptation in British thought and policy would take some time, and it seems not improbable that his various remarks about the relatively distant date at which Britain might become a part of Europe were a reasonably accurate reflection of his own assumptions about the speed with which the British were going to change.[63] When these assumptions were on the point of being proved to be false, General de Gaulle had two choices: to change his own policy to take account of British membership, or to take action to give his assumptions continuing validity. It is in character that he chose the latter. If, as seems probable, General de Gaulle did not consider British membership to be 'real', until the summer of 1962, it seems reasonable to conclude that there was no long-standing French 'plot' to impose a political veto if all else failed, and that General de Gaulle's decision to bring the negotiations to an end came as a genuine surprise, although perhaps not a particularly unpleasant one, to his principal

[63] In June 1962, Lord Avon (formerly Sir Anthony Eden) paid a personal visit to General de Gaulle and apparently his talks with the French President contributed to General de Gaulle's feeling that even though Mr. Macmillan might be sincere in his wish to take the United Kingdom into the Community, he would not be able to carry the country. Lord Avon has never changed the views he expressed in a speech at Columbia University in January 1952, when explaining why the British would not participate in the EDC: 'You will realize that I am speaking of the frequent suggestions that the United Kingdom should join a federation on the continent of Europe. This is something which we know, in our bones, we cannot do.' *Memoirs*, Vol. III, *Full Circle* (London, 1960), p. 36.

ministers, including M. Couve de Murville, the Foreign Minister, and to the French negotiators at the official level. It seems probable that under another leader the French would have pressed for as stiff terms as did M. Couve de Murville and M. Olivier Wormser —and that they would have been relatively untroubled by the thought that these terms might result in the failure of the negotiations—but it also seems probable that no other French leader would have been willing to break the negotiations in the face of solid opposition from the other five members of the Community and from the Commission. It also seems probable that, although General de Gaulle was willing to take responsibility for the breakdown at the beginning of 1963, even he would not have felt strong enough to do so earlier in the year before the elections in France had effectively eliminated potential opposition in France and before he had assured himself that Dr. Adenauer would offer little real resistance.

At his press conference General de Gaulle was wrong in much of what he said about the state of the negotiations, but the main point he was making was true. This was, quite simply, that the British had one concept of Europe and he had another, and that although the British might one day be prepared to look at the political, military, and economic problems of Europe as he did, they were not yet ready to do so. Many people in all the Six countries shared General de Gaulle's scepticism about the readiness of the British fully to accept a 'European' point of view and agreed with him that the British had given fresh evidence at Nassau that they thought first of their Atlantic links and second of their European links. Many people on the Continent also shared General de Gaulle's desire for a Europe that would be a power group that could deal as an equal with the United States, and many agreed with him that the Nassau agreement did not respond to the need for a more effective European voice in decisions affecting the very existence of the peoples of Europe. On the surface General de Gaulle was, as he himself said, only drawing attention to the obvious. But there were serious flaws in General de Gaulle's position which made his case against the British ring false. The question at issue in the Brussels negotiations was not whether or not the British would accept General de Gaulle's vision of Europe but whether or not they could accept the Treaty of Rome and its implications. There were strong doubts in all of the Six Governments about the depth of the new British commitment to Europe, but there were also very strong reservations in the other five Community countries (and in France outside Gaullist circles) about the kind of Europe that General de Gaulle wanted. He had made it plain enough that in his Europe the dialogue between the Commission and the Council of Ministers—which seemed to the 'Europeans' to be the essence of the Community method—would be replaced by a return to intergovernmental action. The Europe he sought would either be dominated by a strong autocratic France, or it would be impotent. Many of the leading 'Europeans' had concluded that the British, despite their hesitations and lack of enthusiasm for 'supra-nationalism', would want the Community (once they had become members) to function effectively and democratically, and that the pursuit of these objectives would lead to less undermining of the Community method than would the undemocratic nationalism of the Gaullists.

The other five governments also had strong reservations about the role General de Gaulle saw for France and for Europe in the field of defence. They disliked his determination to persevere with the French *force de frappe* and they felt that the realities of power made the Atlantic Alliance indispensable, not just for the present—as General de Gaulle was prepared to concede—but for the foreseeable future. They were critical of the structure of the NATO, and of the imbalance within the alliance, but they were not prepared to follow the Gaullist line of refusing to co-operate with an imperfect structure. Like General de Gaulle, they wanted a strong Europe but, like the British, the other five governments all accepted the overriding need for maintaining and strengthening links with the United States at the same time that greater strength was being built in Europe. General de Gaulle, in vetoing British membership on the grounds that the United Kingdom was not yet ready to become 'European', was not only offending against the essence of the Community method by imposing a decision unilaterally and in the face of concerted opposition, but he was falsely equating his own concept of what 'being European' meant with that of the rest of the Six.

As he had made abundantly clear in his press conferences on 15 May 1962 and 14 January 1963, concepts like 'interdependence' and 'integration', whether on a European or on an Atlantic scale, have no reality for General de Gaulle. For him they are not desirable goals which, although difficult to attain, are nevertheless worth pursuing, but myths or stratagems to be ridiculed and exposed. British membership in the Community was thus a double threat to French power as conceived by General de Gaulle. It was an immediate threat to French dominance on the Continent. And it was a continuing threat to the emergence of a Gaullist 'third force' Europe, for it was clear that a compelling reason for the British decision to join the Community had been the conviction that the shortest route to a genuine Atlantic partnership led through British membership in the European Community. Nassau had underlined the fact that this further goal was never far from British thoughts. Had General de Gaulle shared the goal of the 'Europeans' and wanted to create a truly integrated Europe, the prospect of British 'rivalry' in the Community would have been irrelevant. Had he shared the aspirations of those who wanted to construct a more durable and more intimate partnership with the United States, British membership would have been accepted as a welcome step in that direction. Since he accepted neither goal, British membership could only mean a diminution in the role of France and a threat to Gaullist plans. The simple, if crude, arithmetic of power politics is explanation enough for his decision to keep Britain out.[64]

In deciding that the British were not 'ready' to become members of the European Community, General de Gaulle was not only substituting his judgement for the collective judgement of the Six; he was also substituting his judgement about the state of British public opinion for the judgement of the British Government. Had the rest of the Six accepted General de Gaulle's views about Europe and the Atlantic Alliance, this aspect of his action might not have troubled them, for others on the Continent who had reservations about the degree to which the British were prepared to become European were also basing themselves—for the

[64] At various times during the negotiations (and after their collapse) there was criticism of the British Government—from those on the Continent and in the United Kingdom who hoped for the success of the negotiations—for not having done a 'nuclear deal' with General de Gaulle. Apart from the impossibility of doing a deal without American consent (which would probably not have been forthcoming) or without violating agreements with the United States, those who argued this way appeared to ignore the fact that everything that General de Gaulle has said suggests that the only kinds of deal which he would have found attractive would have forced into the open all the latent differences of view about 'Europe' and about European relations with the United States which he precipitated by his statements of 14 January. Perhaps it was an illusion to think that these issues could be finessed, but it is difficult to see how bringing them to the surface earlier would have led to a successful outcome to the negotiations.

most part—not on what Government spokesmen said but on what various public figures such as Lord Avon, General Montgomery, and Lord Attlee said, on the antipathy to the whole idea of participating in a new power group which had been shown by Mr. Gaitskell and other prominent Labour leaders, and, more generally, on the doubts that the British were showing in the great debate they were carrying on with themselves about the question of joining the Community. There are several difficulties with this way of conducting international negotiations, the principal one being that the judge of the readiness of a country for any particular course of action can only be its own government, for it is only against its own government that the people have recourse if the judgement is wrong. Another objection to the tendency of most of the Continentals, not simply General de Gaulle, to be their own judge of what the British were or were not ready to do was the fact that they were applying tests to the British that they never applied to themselves. In none of the Six countries had the Schuman Plan, the EDC, Euratom or the Common Market been a matter for public referendum. The EDC, which was the only one of the plans to be the subject of prolonged and intensive public discussion, was rejected by the French. The other plans were negotiated for the most part secretly and with none of the glare of publicity that attended the British negotiations with the Six. In France, the Schuman Plan had been deliberately rushed through before its full import was generally understood. Moreover, as the Six themselves have amply demonstrated, loyalty to the Community comes, in large measure, from the experience of working closely together. The appetite grows with eating. The 'Europeans' among the Six might well have tempered their criticisms of the Labour Party by reflecting on the SPD's strong opposition to the Schuman Plan. General de Gaulle's own strictures must be viewed against his own opposition to all the plans of the Six which he was now defending against the 'unready' British.

Strictly speaking, so far as the negotiations in Brussels were concerned, what counted—or should have counted—was not what the British people thought and felt but what the British Government was prepared to accept. Mr. Macmillan's judgement about the British people might have been proved wrong, but it had not been proved wrong when the negotiations were brought to an end. The British people clearly had their doubts about 'joining Europe', and one of the dominant reactions to the failure of the negotiations

was relief at not having to get mixed up in 'all that'. But the great
bulk of British opinion was not committed one way or the other.
It was for this reason that the terms of entry were, in fact, more
important than seemed sensible to continental logicians. And it
was for this reason too that mood counted for so much; thus in
the uncertainty and malaise that prevailed in the United Kingdom
during the autumn, after the Cuban crisis, opinion was shifting
against the Common Market. The enthusiastic supporters of joining the Community were better organized and more influential
than were the strong advocates of staying out, who came from
groups on the extreme right and extreme left and were too dis-
parate in all other respects to be effective. But neither group of
enthusiasts was very large. The influential press was for joining
and so was the industrial élite, and both were important. But the
real strength of the Government's position lay in the fact that
although there was little real enthusiasm, there was widespread
acceptance of the inevitability of 'becoming European'. This was
particularly true among intellectuals and in the generation just
coming to power in industry and government. In this situation a
strong lead by the Government might well have called forth a
stronger response than the surface argument suggested.

Looking to the future, the most significant point about the
British debate was that the division by age was clear: a primarily
European role for the United Kingdom was accepted by the post-
war generation in a way their elders still found difficult. Any judgement on what might have been is hazardous. But it seems probable
that, save for the intervention of General de Gaulle, the negotiations would have resulted in an agreement, that the agreement
would have been ratified, and that—regardless of which political
party was then in power—the United Kingdom would have become
the seventh member of the European Community.

XV

A FEW CONCLUSIONS

DURING the first few years after the war, the British Government, had it taken the lead and tried to create a strong, unified Europe, could have played the determining role in shaping the new Europe —in defining its scope, in setting its institutional pattern, and in establishing its ethos. But, partly because they underestimated the revival power of continental Europe and misjudged the strength of the post-war drive towards unity, partly because they were pre-occupied with other, apparently more urgent, problems, and partly because they were slow to recognize—and to absorb emotionally— the implications of the shift in world power and of their own rela-tive weakness, the British missed the opportunity to create the kind of Europe they later wanted. An analysis of the missed opportuni-ties of the first post-war decade is outside the scope of this book, but it is clear from the record of the negotiations between the United Kingdom and the Six since Messina that all British Governments (Labour and Conservative) should have given a far higher priority to European relationships during the earlier period when the leadership of the Continent was theirs for the asking.

Throughout most of the period that has been reviewed here, the British Government had lost the initiative and was reacting to European situations created by others; it was not itself setting the pace. During this time the French were—for the most part —both the innovators and the pace-setters. The French Govern-ment has alternated between being the leader and the laggard of the European movement, but the concepts of the Treaty of Paris and of the two Treaties of Rome, the structure of the Community, and the elaboration of Community doctrine have been, preponderantly, the work of Frenchmen such as M. Monnet M. Marjolin, M. Uri, M. Maurice Faure, M. Hirsch, M. Gaudet' to name only a handful of the more conspicuous architects. Others' like M. Spaak (Belgium), Prof. Hallstein (Germany) and Dr. Mansholt (the Netherlands), have also played important roles but, for the most part, it has been Frenchmen who have been the innovators and the ones who have given a formal, logical content to the construction.

There were times during the period covered by this book when the British might have regained the initiative by adopting a few years earlier a position they were later to accept. And an earlier decision to 'join Europe' would have been a much easier step to take because 'Europe' was until recently largely unformed and very malleable. At the time of the Spaak Committee negotiations and again during the free trade area negotiations, had the British Government been ready to negotiate in terms of a customs union, it would presumably have had little trouble in obtaining sweeping exceptions for Commonwealth trade and for British agriculture. By the time of the accession negotiations, the bones had begun to set. And, rather ironically, the single factor that has probably contributed the most to the forming and hardening of the system of the Six has been the long series of negotiations with the British—first the free trade area negotiations, then the sparring over 'bridge-building' and the soundings on 'close association', and, finally, the abortive negotiations for accession.

Throughout the period covered by this book two processes have been at work which have interacted on one another: the British have been groping for the right relationship between themselves and the Six; the Six have been seeking to define and to establish the identity of the European Community. Neither process is yet complete. The successive negotiations with the British, although they not infrequently created dissensions among the Six, also had a catalytic effect on the development of the Community, since they caused the Six to develop the Community's external policies— and its internal policies where, as in agriculture, they intimately affected external policy—much more rapidly than would otherwise have been probable. In certain instances—again agriculture is a case in point—this forced growth led to the taking of decisions which not only accentuated the problems of Britain's coming to terms with the Six but created difficulties and tensions within the Community. But, for the most part, the long dialogue with the British has played an important role in consolidating the Community, in giving the Six the incentive to fill in the outline drawn in the Treaty of Rome, and in giving the Six a sense of cohesion. And, conversely, the rapid development of the Community and the sharpening of its edges have given urgency to the evolution of a new British policy towards Europe.

Although the free trade area negotiations generated considerable ill will and acrimony and ended in failure, they made an important contribution to both these developments: the forming of the Community and the evolution of a new British policy towards Europe. The proposal for a European free trade area was neither as well conceived as it seemed to be at the time to the British Government nor as blind and misguided a proposal as its critics—and not least its British critics—have made it appear to be in retrospect. It was true enough, as the 'Europeans' complained, that the free trade area involved no 'choice' for the British Government and people. Nevertheless it represented a real and substantial shift in the British Government's attitude towards Europe and the beginning of a questioning of the priorities that had hitherto conditioned all official, and most unofficial, thinking about the United Kingdom's external relations: Europe began to move up the scale, the Commonwealth to move down, and the nature of the British relationship with the United States began to come into better perspective. It was also true, as 'European' critics pointed out, that the free trade area proposal was primarily a plan for exchanging commercial advantages. But, as the Six were themselves discovering, commercial advantage was cementing the foundation of the Common Market and without the strong British industrial interest in Europe which the free trade area negotiations awakened, the later decision to seek to join the Community could not have become practical politics. Although the essentially commercial character of the plan limited its appeal to the 'Europeans' and contributed to the failure of the negotiations, this awakening of British industrial interest in Europe was a necessary preliminary to a new policy. And, on the Continent, the continued emphasis during almost two years of negotiation on those aspects of their own plan that went beyond the free trade area proposal inevitably created within the Six a much clearer commitment to the goal of economic union, not simply that of a customs union, than had existed when the negotiations began.

By the end of the negotiations on the free trade area it was apparent that there was a conflict between two concepts of Europe and that the 'completing' of the Common Market of the Six with a free trade area of the Seventeen was almost bound to result in either the system of the Six or the system of the Seventeen becoming the dominant one. The 'Europeans', in particular, became convinced, probably rightly so, that at least in the formative period of the Common Market two European circles—an inner hub and an outer wheel—could not coexist and that the pull would be towards the outer, looser arrangement. But this was not clear either to the British or to the 'Europeans' at the start of the negotiations, and the desire to 'undermine' or to 'dissolve' the Common Market was not—as so many on the Continent continue to believe —the motive that prompted the British Government to put forward the proposal. The free trade area proposal was ineptly presented and badly negotiated but it was not maliciously conceived.

Throughout the period covered by this book the negotiations between the United Kingdom and the Six have been explicitly about tariffs, quotas, and other aspects of commercial and economic policy. These problems have been real, and conflicting domestic interests have made them difficult to solve. But implicitly the negotiations have also been about the future shape of Europe. And on this level the argument has been complicated by the long, sometimes submerged, but sometimes all too apparent rivalry between France and Britain. It is not much of an oversimplification to say that during the first decade after the war the difference of view between Britain and the countries that formed the European Communities was over whether or not there should be some form of European unity and that during the second decade it has been over the kind of European unity that should be sought. In the course of this long debate, views have been constantly shifting and evolving and no group of countries nor any single country has been as monolithic in its attitude as any summary of the main differences between the British and the Six suggests. Nevertheless, beneath most of the technical arguments over quotas, tariffs, commercial policy, and agricultural policy there have been broad differences of outlook about the organization of Europe which have conditioned the positions taken on the detailed points at issue by the British on the one hand and by the Six, more or less collectively, on the other.

During the free trade area negotiations, and rather more clearly during the exploratory talks that were carried on after the breakdown in the free trade area negotiations and before the British Government took the decision to seek to join the Community, the central difference between the British and the Six underlying most of the technical arguments was whether or not the 'European unity' that they all said they wanted should act as a single entity in its external commercial and economic relations. At the start of the period covered by this book the British, when they professed their attachment to 'European unity', meant very little more than the maintenance of close and friendly relations and *ad hoc* co-operation on questions, primarily economic questions, of mutual interest. They clearly did not mean that they were ready to establish a relationship with other European countries that by its nature would inevitably restrict their freedom to maintain their own policies and their own relations with third countries.

By the time the free trade area negotiations collapsed, the British Government, although not yet prepared to accept the compulsion of a common commercial policy and a common tariff, was ready to risk the 'sucking' process which the combined pressures of free trade with other European countries, wide-ranging commitments to prior consultation, and substantial tariff harmonization would have set in motion. After the collapse of the free trade area negotiations the formation of the EFTA was a holding action, a step sideways which represented neither progress nor retrogression in the development of British policy towards Europe, although it was interpreted in both ways by different people. It served to maintain British interest in an arrangement with the Six, but it involved no new move towards Europe nor any significant new policy decision.

However, during the two and a half years between the breakdown in the free trade area negotiations and the decision to seek to join the Community, the views of the British about the kind of Western European system they favoured evolved considerably. The British concept of European unity was still fuzzy and ill-defined but it was no longer devoid of meaning and it accepted the fact, or, rather, rested on the assertion that the European countries should have a relationship with one another that was closer and different in kind from the relationship they maintained with other countries. In economic terms the British 'Europe' came to look more and more like a customs union, with some exceptional arrangements, rather than like a free trade area. The 'larger Europe' advocated by the British was inclusive rather than exclusive, its ultimate shape was vague, participation involved no immediate drastic 'choices', but no eventual developments—economic or political—were ruled out. The approach was a pragmatic, evolutionary one which reflected not only British uncertainties about how far into Europe it was wise to go but also the conviction that it was wise to go a good deal further than had ever before been contemplated. In the British view, there were a number of possible forms for this 'larger Europe'—it might be a system in which the Six would fit as a unit, or an arrangement between the Six as a group and the Seven as a group, or a 'close association' between the United Kingdom and the Six with a looser association between this inner core and the other European countries. However, in all its versions the 'larger Europe' was anathema to the 'Europeans', since they felt that it threatened their own construction. Had the British negotiation for accession to the Community succeeded, it would have been difficult to quarrel with the 'European' view that acceptance by the United Kingdom (at least) of the Treaty of Rome and its implications was a surer way to unify Europe than the various British alternatives, since it would seem to be axiomatic that the higher the common denominator of agreement among the principal participants, the easier and more rapid the progress. But the way in which the United Kingdom was excluded from the Community and the reasons which apparently lay behind the French veto mean that for the present it must remain an open question whether the looser, more inclusive, less clear-cut, evolutionary process might, in the end, have resulted in as integrated a European system as the Six will achieve, and on a broader basis.

If in 1960–1 an early agreement on any of the kinds of 'bridges' between the Six and the Seven or of 'close association' with the Six that the United Kingdom had formally suggested or informally explored had appeared probable, it is very unlikely that the decision to join the Community would have been taken, despite the conviction of many of those in positions of responsibility that membership rather than association was in the British interest, particularly once it had become clear that any accommodation with the Six would have to take the form of a customs union rather than a free trade area. However, by early 1961 it was plain that the only effective choice before the British Government for the foreseeable future was between joining the Community as a full member and maintaining the same kind of relationships with the Six that the United States, Canada, and other third countries maintained in the context of organizations such as the OECD, the GATT, and the NATO. All middle positions which would have given the United Kingdom influence over the way 'Europe' developed on the one hand and, on the other, the economic and political advantages of participation in the emerging European Community had been ruled out by the combined opposition of the 'Europeans', the French, and the United States Administration. And much of the criticism in the United Kingdom of the Government's decision to seek to join the Community—which became more vociferous as the negotiations proceeded—stemmed from a wishful hankering after the unattainable and a stubborn and rather unrealistic unwillingness to accept the fact that the various kinds of arrangement, short of full membership, that the Government had tried for six years to negotiate were simply non-negotiable.

The shift in British policy and the application to join the Community were the product of many factors. But the controlling consideration was the belief that Britain would have more influence—in Europe, with the United States, and in the world generally—as a member of the European Community than it would alone. Although in the summer of 1962 both major political parties tended to turn the question of accession into a party issue, the decision to open negotiations was not taken on narrow political grounds but on broad, long-term considerations of national interest; Mr. Macmillan clearly believed that the shortest road to an effective Atlantic partnership and a more interdependent Western world lay through British membership in the Community and in the related political 'union' which then seemed to be foreshadowed by the Bonn declaration of the Six. Mr. Macmillan was slow to make plain to the country his reasons for seeking to join the Community, and he was particularly reticent about the full political implications of membership in the Community. With some justice he was criticized on both sides of the Channel (and of the Atlantic) for 'backing into Europe'. Given the divided state of opinion within the Government and in the country, 'backing in' presumably seemed to him to be the only way to get there, but precisely because the country was divided and uncertain a stronger lead might, in fact, have been tactically wiser domestically. However, any further underlining of the argument that it was necessary to lead the United Kingdom into Europe in order to open the way to a more durable relationship with the United States would scarcely have helped Mr. Macmillan's case across the Channel.

Despite the fact that opinion was sufficiently divided, so that the British Government would probably not have taken the decision to join the Community had the alternative of the larger, looser, more nebulous Europe existed, the shift in policy when it came was a genuine one. In the summer of 1961, when the British Government applied for membership in the Community, it fully recognized and accepted the fact that it was applying to join a Community which would—at the end of a transition period— act as a unit in its commercial relations and would possess many of the attributes of a full economic union. The British Government recognized as well that this held many implications for a possible evolution in the political field. Although it was far less ready than some of the 'Europeans' to talk in terms of eventual 'federation', it was fully aware of the unifying force of a common commercial policy and a common tariff and of the continental pressures for political unity.

The accession negotiations, like the earlier free trade area negotiations, caused the Six to formulate certain of their policies and to evolve a Community 'doctrine' about various aspects of their external relations more quickly than they would otherwise have been likely to do. And, as in the earlier negotiations, British views about the kind of 'Europe' they were ready to accept also developed considerably during the process of negotiation. Some of this forced growth of Community doctrines was necessary if the Six were to negotiate with the United Kingdom collectively as a Community, but the threat of British membership was also at times deliberately exploited—by some to push the Six farther along the road towards unity, by others to mould Community policy to meet the needs of the existing members before the British, with their rather different problems, acquired a voice in shaping policy. Similarly, some of the insistence placed by the Six during the negotiations on strict conformity with the Treaty of Rome, and the implementing decisions, stemmed from a genuine desire to ensure that there would be no watering down in the commitment to unity as a result of British entry, some from the hope that a steep initial commitment might be a higher price than the British could pay. However, regardless of motive, had it not been for General de Gaulle's veto and the crisis of confidence which it caused within the Community, not only the British but the Six themselves would have been more deeply committed to full economic union and closer to that objective at the end of the nego- tiations than they had been at the start. Moreover, the very length of the negotiations and the detail in which the problems posed by British entry had been discussed—although severely criticized at the time by 'Europeans' as well as by General de Gaulle—would have meant that an otherwise long process of assimilation would have been largely completed by the time of British entry.

During the accession negotiations the main arguments between the British and the Six were over the way the supplanting of national policies by Community policies was to be phased and over the character of the policies to be pursued by the enlarged Community, and not, as in the past, over the need for, and the scope of, Community policies. Although the failure of the negotiations was attributable, once again, to differences of view about the kind of European union that should be sought, General de Gaulle's particular vision of Europe was not shared by the rest of the Five. And when the break came it was clear that his main objection to British membership was that it threatened French leadership on the Continent and his own conception of a 'third force' Europe, not that the British had shown themselves unwilling to accept the kind of 'Europe' sketched out in the Treaty of Rome. Nevertheless, although the break itself had little to do with the differences of view between the British and those who were primarily concerned with building European unity on the Community model, differences of view—or at the least differences of priority and emphasis—about the kind of 'Europe' that was taking shape between the British on the one hand and those who were negotiating in good faith on behalf of the Six, coloured the negotiations. Moreover, recognition that these differences existed—as well as a considerable residue of mistrust of British intentions—clearly tempered the resistance of the Five, and particularly perhaps of the Commission, to the de Gaulle veto.

Perhaps the essential difference between the approach of the British and the approach of the Six derives from the fact that the Six are more convinced than are the British of the validity of the analogy between the building of 'Europe' and the formation of a single state. Most continental 'Europeans' think of the new 'Europe' as a new nation, a third 'super-state', and the forming of new allegiances and the breaking of old ones are a logical and necessary part of the construction. The kind of association that the EFTA neutrals wanted—and that the British Government would have favoured—that is, a form of partial participation, was obviously inconsistent with this concept, which logically excludes all middle positions. The emphasis the Six placed on the need for a 'choice' between Europe and the Commonwealth clearly owed something to their concept of Europe as a new state, although other considerations such as GATT commitments and American pressures were also important. Most British 'Europeans', as well as the British Government, shy away from the analogy with the formation of a single state and tend to see 'European unity' as a pooling of efforts and a merging of sovereignty for certain purposes. Although the British Government, when it decided to seek to join the Community, and British 'Europeans' recognized that the process, once begun, would be a cumulative one, and might well end in a new kind of European political system, they were clearly most attracted by that strand in 'Europeanism' which sees the building of 'Europe' as a part of the process of 'denationalization' and a step towards the progressive integration of the West.

From the start two logically distinct strands have, in fact, been intertwined in the European movement and in the concept of 'Europe' that has been elaborated by the two groups who have done most to give meaning to the 'making of Europe'—M. Monnet and his Action Committee for a United States of Europe and the Commission of the European Economic Community. Both groups, but M. Monnet's in particular, have frequently stressed that what they were seeking to do was to create a new 'method' of conducting affairs between states, a 'method' which by pooling sovereignty makes nationalism an anachronism. At the same time, both groups —the Commission recently rather more conspicuously but M. Monnet at times as well—have used the analogy between the building of 'Europe' and the formation of the United States of America. The seeming contradiction between stressing the analogy between the formation of a single state and insisting in the same breath that the European process or 'method' was a step away from nationalism has been avoided in various ways. M. Monnet has frequently indicated that he looks for an extension of the Community 'method' to the Atlantic area or to the whole Western world long before a new European nationalism has had a chance to develop and harden. The Commission and other leading 'Europeans' have argued—and argued very persuasively—that the route to more effective action on the international plane lies through the creation of a strong and unified Europe.

Nevertheless, although these two strands—the emphasis on 'method' and on 'denationalization' on the one hand and, on the other, the emphasis on the building of a new political entity—a new federal state—can be reconciled, there has always been a latent contradiction between them. And the drive for European unity has drawn its momentum partly from a wholly admirable desire to find a way round the dangers inherent in the national divisions of the past and partly from a less admirable and potentially corrosive concern with power. Both strands were also present in the British Government's decision to seek to join the Community, but it is fair to say that the British generally have always been more attracted by the first strand, the Continentals rather more by the second.

Unfortunately, much of the British comment about the dangers that were latent in too single-minded a pursuit of European unity and too complete a commitment to the single state analogy was frequently parochial, and simply camouflaged a basic unwillingness to accept restraints on their own freedom of action. This has obscured the force of their legitimate distrust of a concept which so clearly held the seeds of a new nationalism. The 'Europeans' have had one of the few compelling ideas of the post-war period and they have been fortunate in having highly intelligent, dedicated, and persuasive leaders who have not been afraid of taking enormous risks or of mixing vision with reality. Given the essentially negative character of so much of Britain's post-war policy towards Europe, the lack of imagination, the timidity, and the half-heartedness of the few British initiatives, it is scarcely surprising that the boldness of the 'Europeans' shone so brightly by contrast that, at times, it tended to be blinding. Thoughts tend to flow in accustomed patterns and the 'Europeans', in trying to overcome the limitations of the traditional pattern of intergovernmental action, have tended increasingly to accept another traditional pattern. It is a very open question whether in the second half of the twentieth century the analogy between the uniting of Europe and the forming of a federal state like the United States is not a dangerously facile one. In considering the future of Europe it might be wiser, although harder, to break away from all conventional patterns of thought about the relationships between states, as M. Monnet—although not with complete consistency—has tried to do.

The British application to join the Community inevitably gave a new urgency to the question of what the final stage of 'Europe' is to be. The addition of any large power would in itself have changed the character of the Community, and the prospect of the addition of the United Kingdom, with its rather spotty record of enthusiasm for European unity and its Commonwealth and EFTA ties, inevitably made the Six introspective and led them to try to define what it was in their own construction that was essential. In the United Kingdom the application to join the Six set off a much more profound and widespread discussion of Britain's role in the world and of what European unity was, and ought to be, than any that had previously taken place.[1] And in the United States the prospect of an enlarged Community added force to the argument that a uniting Europe not only made possible but made necessary a new relationship between the United States and Europe. By his veto on British membership, General de Gaulle sought to rule out certain kinds of 'Europe' and to create a situation in which it would be easier for him to impose his own form of Europe on the Six. His attempt to force the answer has not thus far succeeded, but one result of the attempt has been to give added point to the question. However, by exposing not only the uncertainties and contradictions in British policy but by bringing into the open the conflicts and contradictions that exist within the Six and in United States policy with respect to Europe, his action has not thus far produced clarity about the future of Europe, but, rather, confusion and immobility.

Today, six months after the veto, it is difficult to foresee the evolution either of the European Community or of British policy towards Europe. It seems probable that the drive for European unity is strongly enough rooted so that it can survive a period of immobility and that it will eventually again pick up momentum. General de Gaulle's veto, and particularly the manner in which it was imposed, has, for the present, destroyed the illusion harboured by many of the 'Europeans' that they could use the Gaullists, as well as the Gaullist illusion that they could use the 'Europeans', and has put an end to their uneasy, unhappy, and spasmodic alliance. There is, however, a risk that the 'Europeans' will grow impatient of *immobilisme* and will once again try compromising with the Gaullists. But there are also grounds for hoping that the re-examination of first principles and end objectives that was set in train by the British application and made inescapable by General de Gaulle's veto will yield enough agreement among the Five, the non-Gaullist French, Britain, and the

---

[1] One of the main weaknesses in the British negotiating position and perhaps, more basically, in the British method of policy formation was that the real debate in the United Kingdom came during the negotiations rather than before the decision to open negotiations had been taken.

United States, so that the excessive influence that General de Gaulle wields, when he and he alone sees clearly what he wants, will be cut down to size.

The durability of the British interest in Europe is even harder to assess. It is possible that British membership in the European Community was one of those developments which at a particular time appears to be the inevitable culmination of a series of events but which, if it is prevented from happening at the right moment, quickly loses its apparent inevitability. There clearly was a tide which, but for General de Gaulle's veto, would almost certainly have carried the British into the Community. That tide has now receded. But for the last ten years the United Kingdom has been moving continuously closer to Europe and, although the progression has now been broken, it is hard to believe that the trend will be reversed unless the process of European unification is stultified or corrupted by Gaullism. And, at the next stage in the search for the right relationship between Britain and the Continent, the errors as well as the progress made during the past decade may make it easier for the two countries that throughout have been the only real protagonists to find the way to overcome their rivalry and to pool their strengths. The French veto has obliterated with a larger, newer blot the earlier British mistakes in their relations with Europe. More important, there is now a rough parity of power between the United Kingdom and France which did not exist ten years ago. The British emerged from the war larger than life, the French far weaker than they knew themselves to be. The process of readjustment—both the building up and the contracting down to size—has inevitably affected national attitudes and has made agreement between the two countries peculiarly difficult. A kind of equilibrium has now been established which, unless the new nationalism of the Gaullists in the end prevails, should make it easier in the future for the French to accept the British in Europe and easier for the British to accept for themselves a role as 'Europeans'.

Appendix A

THE MESSINA RESOLUTION

Adopted by the Ministers of Foreign Affairs of the State Members of the E.C.S.C. at their meeting at Messina on 1 and 2 June 1955.[1]

THE Governments of the Federal Republic, Belgium, France, Italy, Luxembourg and the Netherlands believe that the time has come to make a fresh advance towards the building of Europe. They are of the opinion that this must be achieved, first of all, in the economic field.

They consider that it is necessary to work for the establishment of a united Europe by the development of common institutions, the progressive fusion of national economies, the creation of a common market and the progressive harmonisation of their social policies.

Such a policy seems to them indispensable if Europe is to maintain her position in the world, regain her influence and prestige and achieve a continuing increase in the standard of living of her population.

I

To these ends, the six Ministers have agreed on the following objectives:—

A. 1. The expansion of trade and the freedom of movement call for the joint development of the major channels of communication.

A joint study will accordingly be undertaken of development plans based on the establishment of a European network of canals, motor highways, electrified railways and on a standardisation of equipment, as well as a study of possible means of achieving a better co-ordination of air transport.

2. A fundamental condition of economic progress is that the European economies should have at their disposal cheaper and more plentiful supplies of power.

For this reason, all possible steps will have to be taken to develop exchanges of gas and electricity as necessary to increase the profitability of investment and to reduce the cost of supplies.

Study will be given to methods for co-ordinating a joint approach to questions affecting the future production and consumption of power, and for drawing up the general lines of an overall policy.

3. The development of atomic energy for peaceful purposes will in the near future open up the prospect of a new industrial revolution out

[1] White Paper (Cmd. 9525, July 1955, H.M.S.O.), pp. 7–9.

of all proportion to that which has taken place over the last hundred years. The six signatory States consider that it is necessary to study the creation of a common organisation to be entrusted with the responsibility and the means for ensuring the peaceful development of atomic energy, while taking into account the special arrangements made by certain Governments with third countries.

These means should comprise:

(a) The establishment of a common fund derived from contributions from each of the participating countries, from which provision could be made for financing the installations and research work already in progress or planned.

(b) Free and sufficient access to the raw materials, and the free exchange of expertise and technicians, by-products and specialised equipment.

(c) The pooling of the results obtained and the grant of financial assistance for their exploitation.

(d) Co-operation with non-member countries.

B. The six Governments recognise that the establishment of a European market, free from all customs duties and all quantitative restrictions, is the objective of their action in the field of economic policy.

They consider that this market must be achieved by stages and that its entry into force requires a study of the following questions:

(a) The appropriate procedure and pace for the progressive suppression of the obstacles to trade in the relations between the participating countries, as well as the appropriate measures for moving towards a progressive unification of their tariffs against third countries.

(b) The measures to be taken for harmonising the general policy of the participating countries in the financial, economic and social fields.

(c) The adoption of methods designed to make possible an adequate co-ordination of the monetary policies of the member countries so as to permit the creation and development of a common market.

(d) A system of escape clauses.

(e) The creation and operation of a readaptation fund.

(f) The gradual introduction of the free movement of manpower.

(g) The elaboration of rules which would ensure the play of competition within the common market so as to exclude, in particular, all discrimination on a national basis.

(h) The institutional arrangements appropriate for introducing and operating the common market.

C. The creation of a European Investment Fund will be studied. The object of this fund would be the joint development of European economic potentialities and in particular the development of the less developed regions of the participating states.

D. As regards the social field, the six Governments consider it essential to study the progressive harmonisation of the regulations in force in the different countries, notably those which concern working hours, overtime rates (night work, Sunday work and public holidays) and the length and rates of pay for holidays.

II

The six Governments have decided to adopt the following procedure:

(1) Conferences will be called to work out treaties or other arrangements concerning the questions under consideration.

(2) The preparatory work will be the responsibility of a Committee of Governmental representatives, assisted by experts, under the chairmanship of a political personality responsible for co-ordinating the work in the different fields.

(3) The Committee will invite the High Authority of the E.C.S.C. and the Secretariats of O.E.E.C., the Council of Europe and the European Conferences of Ministers of Transport, to give the necessary assistance.

(4) The report of the Committee, covering the whole field, will be submitted to the Ministers of Foreign Affairs by not later than the 1st of October, 1955.

(5) The Ministers for Foreign Affairs will meet before that date to take note of the interim reports prepared by the Committee and to give it the necessary directives.

(6) The Government of the United Kingdom, as a power which is a member of W.E.U. and is also associated with the E.C.S.C., will be invited to take part in this work.

(7) The Ministers for Foreign Affairs will decide in due course whether other States should subsequently be invited to take part in the conference or conferences referred to in paragraph (1) above.

Appendix B

THE BONN DECLARATION

Final communiqué of the meeting of the Six Heads of State or Government of the European Community held in Bonn on 18 July 1961.[1]

THE Heads of State or of Government of the Federal Republic of Germany, Belgium, France, Italy, and Luxembourg, as well as the Prime Minister and the Minister for Foreign Affairs of the Netherlands, desirous of affirming the spiritual values and political traditions which form their common heritage, united in the awareness of the great tasks which Europe is called upon to fulfil within the community of free peoples in order to safeguard liberty and peace in the world, anxious to strengthen the political, economic, social and cultural ties which exist between their peoples, especially in the framework of the European Communities, and to advance towards the union of Europe;

Convinced that only a united Europe, allied to the United States of America and to other free peoples, is in a position to face the dangers which menace the existence of Europe and of the whole free world, and that it is important to unite the energies, capabilities, and resources of all those for whom liberty is an inalienable possession; resolved to develop their political co-operation with a view to the union of Europe and to continue at the same time the work already undertaken in the European Communities;

Wishing for the adhesion to the European Communities of other European States ready to assume in all spheres the same responsibilities and the same obligations, have decided:

1. To give shape to the will for political union already implicit in the Treaties establishing the European Communities, and for this purpose to organise their co-operation, to provide for its development and to secure for it the regularity which will progressively create the conditions for a common policy and will ultimately make it possible to embody in institutions the work undertaken.

2. To hold, at regular intervals, meetings whose aim will be to compare their views, to concert their policies and to reach common positions in order to further the political union of Europe, thereby strengthening the Atlantic alliance. The necessary practical measures will be taken to prepare these meetings. In addition, the continuation of active co-operation among the Foreign Ministers will contribute

[1] From the text published by the Information Service of the European Communities.

to the continuity of the action undertaken in common. The co-operation of the six must go beyond the political field as such, and will in particular be extended to the sphere of education, of culture and of research, where it will be ensured by periodical meetings of the Ministers concerned.

3. To instruct their Committee to submit to them proposals on the means which will as soon as possible enable a statutory character to be given to the union of their peoples.

The Heads of State or of Government are convinced that by thus organising their co-operation they will thereby further the application of the Rome and Paris Treaties. They also believe that their co-operation will facilitate those reforms which might seem opportune in the interests of the Communities' greater efficiency.

To this end they have decided:

1. To have a study made of the various points of the Resolution of the European Parliament of 29 June 1961, on the subject of political co-operation among the member states of the European Communities;

2. To associate public opinion more closely with the efforts already undertaken, by inviting the European Parliament to extend the range of its debates to new fields, with the co-operation of the Governments.

Declaration on Cultural Co-operation

The Conference of Heads of State or of Government, meeting in Bonn on 18 July 1961, has taken note of the report drawn up by the Study Committee on the subject of co-operation in the field of higher education and research.

It has envisaged the establishment of a Council composed of the Ministers of National Education or the Ministers whose responsibilities include international cultural relations, assisted by a committee of experts, as well as the negotiation of one or several conventions on the following subjects:

co-operation and exchanges between universities of the Member Countries of the European Communities;

the 'European status' ('vocation européenne') which could be accorded to national university or research institutes;

the establishment by Italy of a European University in Florence, to the intellectual life and financing of which the six Governments will contribute;

the possible establishment of other European institutes devoted to university teaching or to scientific research.

The Study Committee has been given the mandate to work out as quickly as possible the draft of the conventions and acts which are to embody this plan for cultural co-operation.

Appendix C

EUROPEAN POLITICAL UNION

Text of a statement made by the Lord Privy Seal, the Rt. Hon. Edward Heath, M.B.E., M.P., to the Ministerial Council of Western European Union in London on 10 April 1962.[1]

I WOULD like to thank M. Couve de Murville for the statement he has just made. I fully appreciate the reasons why he is unable to provide us with more details today about your discussions. This means, I think, that the appropriate occasion has not yet arrived for a full discussion between us about future political relationships between our countries.

Nevertheless, I would like to take this very valuable opportunity of our being together in this forum, in which we have so often in the past discussed matters of common European interest, to tell my colleagues how Her Majesty's Government for their part are approaching these problems.

As you know we have been careful not to comment on the discussions which you have been holding among yourselves on a European Political Union. You have very kindly kept us informed of the progress of these discussions and we are very grateful for that; we are also grateful for the assurance which M. Couve de Murville has just given us, to the effect that there will be no difficulty in the next stage of the discussions about keeping us informed.

We are of course closely concerned with these matters: you yourselves have decided that those who want to join the Economic Communities as full members must also join the Political Union. I am sure that this was the right decision. If this European Union is going to achieve the great things which we confidently expect of it then, in our view, it must be political as well as economic. As members we should want to strengthen its political development.

But time is moving on. The Brussels talks are about to enter the stage of active and substantive negotiation: we are hoping, as you know, that within the next three or four months we shall be able to see the shape or the outline of a successful conclusion.

As these political matters are so closely linked with the economic, I thought the time had come when it would be helpful and even necessary for you to know where we stand. Or perhaps I should say where we *will* stand if we are able sucessfully to negotiate our entry into the European Economic Community.

[1] Cmnd. 1720, H.M.S.O., 10 April 1962.

I should like to begin by repeating what I said in Paris on October 10th.[2] I said then that 'we fully share the aims and objectives, political and otherwise, of those who drew up the Bonn Declaration and we shall be anxious, once we are members of the Community, to work with you in a positive spirit to reinforce the unity which you have already achieved'. Since then, we have watched not only with interest but with sympathy the efforts which you have been making to translate the Bonn Declaration into concrete terms.

We have all along recognised that the Treaties of Rome and Paris had a political as well as an economic objective. It therefore came as no surprise to us when the six Governments, having successfully established the foundations of their economic co-operation, began to consider how they could develop and define the conditions for closer political unity. Nor, if I may say so, did it come as any surprise to us to learn that this has proved rather a difficult task.

We ourselves have been thinking about this problem ever since we decided to seek negotiations for entry into the European Economic Community, and we, for our part, have not found it easy to see just how fast or how far it would be reasonable to try to go at the various stages.

Of course we have not been looking at the problem from exactly the same point as you yourselves. We have been thinking in terms of an enlarged community including not only the United Kingdom, but also other European States who will be joining the European Economic Community.

In other words, and this is the point I would like to make to you here, unlike you, we have had to take account of the problems of countries which would be called upon to accept the political and the economic implications of this experiment at one and the same time.

I might describe this as taking two hurdles together—whereas you have been able to separate them by several years. This is an important difference. It accounts for what you may sometimes feel to be a certain caution and hesitation in our approach to the question of future commitments in the political field. I shall come back to that later.

But broadly speaking the problems we have been examining are the same as those which you have been discussing together in your Commission during recent months.

Let me now describe our general approach to these particular questions.

In the first place I would say this:

In considering what might be the political structure for the enlarged European Community, we have always assumed that the existing European Communities would be the foundation on which Europe would be built.

[2] Miscellaneous No. 14 (1961), Cmnd. 1565.

These Communities, and especially of course the European Economic Community, are in themselves an achievement, for which you Six countries will always deserve the greatest admiration. I have had enough contact with those who direct the future of the Communities to appreciate what they have accomplished not only in resolving the difficult problems they face but in engendering the habit of working together and thinking as a community. This is undoubtedly something new in 20th century international life; it is one of the real inventions in our inventive age.

I can assure you that the entry of Britain will not be used by us to discourage this work or to obstruct in any way the development of the European idea. On the contrary, we shall join wholeheartedly in helping to build the new Europe.

At the same time it is evident that the existing Communities, though their objective is political as well as economic and technical, are not by themselves fully able to meet all the needs of Europe in the future, particularly on the political side.

For example, if we are to reconcile the vital interests of the member-States it is clear that there must be some machinery whereby those who carry the highest responsibilities in their respective States can play a part. This is not provided for in the existing Communities.

There is also clearly a need for more concentrated Ministerial machinery, especially of Ministers responsible for political questions. Periodic meetings of Heads of Government and of Foreign Ministers would promote and set their seal on the day to day consultation which already exists.

Secondly, if we accept the general formula that our purpose will be to harmonise, to co-ordinate and to unify the policies of member States, which seems to me a perfectly legitimate one, the question then arises what particular fields or subjects should be covered.

I do not want to be dogmatic about this this afternoon. The British Government has no fixed views on the subject. But I would like to give you some general indication of our thoughts on this point.

It is our desire to see the development of a strong political and economic community, composed of the countries who are full members, whose voice will be heard increasingly in world councils and whose influence will make itself felt more and more. Such a community will marshal the collective resources, energies and skills of the member-States. It will be in a position of leadership—an aggregate of power within the free world, standing shoulder to shoulder with the United States. Such a community is going to have opinions on many subjects—perhaps on most subjects.

We cannot tell how fast it will progress in this direction. But I should like to take one of the controversial subjects.

We quite accept that the European political union, if it is to be

effective, will have a common concern for defence problems and that
a European point of view on defence will emerge. What is essential,
however, is that any European point of view or policy on defence
should be directly related to the Atlantic Alliance. We must make it
clear beyond all doubt that the object of our common policy is to defend
and strengthen the liberties for which the Atlantic Alliance is the
indispensable shield.

But of course, as the European Community develops, the balance
within the Atlantic Alliance is going to change. In the course of time
there will be two great groupings in the West: North America and
Europe. The growth of this European point of view in the defence field
will not, we believe, be long in making itself felt. Already we have seen
the signs. We have the Western European Union itself, and we have the
beginnings of co-operation in joint defence projects.

There is no doubt in my mind that, with the closer integration of
our industries which will follow British accession to the European
Economic Community, we shall see great advances in European co-
operation over defence production, research and development.

These are some of the things to which we must look forward and for
which we must work.

Meanwhile, I should like to say two more things about the future
Europe as we see it, and about its relations with the rest of the world.

In the first place, we are working for a Europe with close and valuable
connections right across the globe—connections acquired through the
historical actions and achievements of individual European countries
and their peoples. These connections and friendships will be a vital possession for the whole community. We must take great care not to neglect
them or throw them away.

I am speaking just as much of the overseas influences and responsibilities of your countries as of the Commonwealth connections of
mine.

We shall, of course, retain our constitutional ties and the arrangements
for consultation with the Commonwealth, which we have worked out. In
my judgment these will be a source of strength to Europe. They will in
no way prevent us from participating fully in the growth of a new
Europe, and this in its turn will give fresh vitality to our Commonwealth
connections.

The Commonwealth is a grouping of countries with widely differing
views about the great questions which divide the world. In our opinion
it will be particularly important that Europe should continue to show a
sympathetic comprehension for these different attitudes towards world
affairs.

My second point is this: it is our view that the European Community
will form, as it were, a nucleus at the centre of the wider European
family.

We shall want to do nothing which might slow down the impetus towards the political unity of this central nucleus. At the same time we must ensure that other Western European countries which for various reasons cannot, or do not, join the central core remain nevertheless within the political and economic orbit of Western Europe and are not driven to seek support and comfort elsewhere.

I should like to mention in particular the position of the neutral members of EFTA—Austria, Sweden and Switzerland. All three are politically stable and staunchly anti-Communist. Historically they have played an important role in the life of the Continent. We believe it would be a serious political mistake to isolate them from the new Europe. I am convinced that their association with the community could be arranged in such a way as not to weaken the political and economic cohesion of the central nucleus of full members or impede their progress.

Now may I say something about another controversial question— how far should we try to lay down in advance the path of progress towards closer forms of European unity in the later stages?

My Government's view on this is that when we are drawing up texts we should make sure that they point the way to the future but that they do so without circumscribing our course of action. They should contain the principle of growth; they should allow the plant light and air, but without defining too meticulously how fast it should grow.

We do not think that at this stage it is wise to try to lay down the exact rhythm of future political developments. We are all politicians and we have to take account of present limitations as well as of future possibilities.

As you know, the British are much addicted to pragmatism, a word I hear more and more in Brussels circles. We think that the substance of political integration will grow most effectively out of the habit of working more and more closely together.

This does not mean that we are going to make difficulties about accepting written texts. We recognise that written texts are necessary, but we have a preference for those which leave open, as far as possible, the time-table for future development.

The element of caution in our present outlook might impose on us an attitude of reserve if we were asked to commit ourselves now to specific forms of political machinery, or to particular courses of action at a fixed moment in the future—whereas when we reach that moment we may well find that the course of action seems quite natural and perfectly obvious.

One example of this may well be the question of parliamentary control, to which we in this country attach a great deal of importance. As members of the Community we will, I am sure, want to see the European Parliament playing an important part. But it is not easy for us to commit ourselves, at this stage and before we have participated in the work of the Assembly, as to what that part should be or as to how it should be accomplished.

You have not invited me to comment on the texts which you have been discussing among yourselves and I have been careful not to do so. But as we shall be anxious to be able to join the political Union at the same time as we join the European Economic Community we shall naturally expect to have the opportunity of consulting with you and commenting on the draft Treaty before it is finally agreed and, of course, we already have your assurances to that effect.

But in view of the progress which we hope to make in the negotiations in Brussels in the next few months, I wonder whether it might now be helpful if we, as impending members of the European Economic Community, were to join with you now in your discussions about the future political framework of Europe.

Might this not be a great stimulus to our whole work together?

The two processes of discussion between us, both the economic and the political, might then go forward together, and we might find that they interacted favourably upon one another.

This is a thought that I would like to leave with you and on which no doubt you will want to consult together.

Perhaps I may be allowed to sum up our position in a few words.

We are looking forward to joining you as soon as possible in constructing a Europe united politically as well as economically.

We are thinking in terms of an enlarged Community whose members have accepted the same obligations and on whose shoulders will fall the main burden of the construction, while not forgetting other European countries who are unable to join us.

We see the existing Communities continuing and expanding their work but knit together with the new political structure in a coherent and effective whole.

This new Europe will be a great power, standing not alone but as an equal partner in the Atlantic Alliance, retaining its traditional ties overseas and fully conscious of its growing obligations towards the rest of the free world.

INDEX